Contemporary Europe in the Historical Imagination

George L. Mosse Series in the History of
European Culture, Sexuality, and Ideas

Series Editors
STEVEN E. ASCHHEIM, SKYE DONEY,
MARY LOUISE ROBERTS, AND DAVID J. SORKIN

Advisory Board
STEVEN E. ASCHHEIM,
Hebrew University of Jerusalem
OFER ASHKENAZI,
Hebrew University of Jerusalem
ANNETTE BECKER,
Université Paris-Nanterre
SKYE DONEY,
University of Wisconsin—Madison
DAGMAR HERZOG,
City University of New York
ETHAN KATZ,
University of California, Berkeley
RENATO MORO,
Università degli Studi Roma Tre
ANSON RABINBACH,
Princeton University
MARY LOUISE ROBERTS,
University of Wisconsin—Madison
JOAN WALLACH SCOTT,
Institute for Advanced Study
MOSHE SLUHOVSKY,
Hebrew University of Jerusalem
DAVID J. SORKIN,
Yale University
ANTHONY J. STEINHOFF,
Université du Québec à Montréal
JOHN TORTORICE,
University of Wisconsin—Madison
TILL VAN RAHDEN,
Université de Montréal

Contemporary Europe
in the Historical Imagination

Edited by Darcy Buerkle
and Skye Doney

THE UNIVERSITY OF WISCONSIN PRESS

Publication of this book has been made possible, in part,
through support from the George L. Mosse Program in History at the University of
Wisconsin–Madison and the Hebrew University of Jerusalem.

GEORGE L.
MOSSE
PROGRAM IN HISTORY

The University of Wisconsin Press
728 State Street, Suite 443
Madison, Wisconsin 53706
uwpress.wisc.edu

Gray's Inn House, 127 Clerkenwell Road
London EC1R 5DB, United Kingdom
eurospanbookstore.com

Copyright © 2023
The Board of Regents of the University of Wisconsin System
All rights reserved. Except in the case of brief quotations embedded in critical articles
and reviews, no part of this publication may be reproduced, stored in a retrieval system,
transmitted in any format or by any means—digital, electronic, mechanical, photocopying,
recording, or otherwise—or conveyed via the Internet or a website without written
permission of the University of Wisconsin Press. Rights inquiries should be directed to
rights@uwpress.wisc.edu.

Printed in the United States of America
This book may be available in a digital edition.

Library of Congress Cataloging-in-Publication Data

Names: Buerkle, Darcy C., editor. | Doney, Skye, editor.
Title: Contemporary Europe in the historical imagination / edited by Darcy Buerkle
and Skye Doney.
Other titles: George L. Mosse series in the history of European culture, sexuality, and ideas.
Description: Madison, Wisconsin : The University of Wisconsin Press, [2023] |
Series: George L. Mosse series in the history of European culture, sexuality, and ideas |
Includes bibliographical references and index.
Identifiers: LCCN 2022049571 | ISBN 9780299342401 (hardcover)
Subjects: LCSH: Mosse, George L. (George Lachmann), 1918–1999. |
Europe—Historiography. | Germany—Historiography. | Europe—History—20th century.
Classification: LCC D15.M668 C66 2023 | DDC 940.5072/2—dc23/eng/20221130
LC record available at https://lccn.loc.gov/2022049571

Past history is always contemporary.
—GEORGE L. MOSSE, *The Nationalization of the Masses*

CONTENTS

List of Illustrations — xi

Preface: Mosse's Berlins — xvii
    DARCY BUERKLE *and* SKYE DONEY

Acknowledgments — xxv

Introduction
    George L. Mosse: The Work, the Legacy, the Man — 3
    STEVEN E. ASCHHEIM

PART I. GEORGE L. MOSSE (1918–1999)

1 Civilizing the Nation: Can Mosse's Europe Be Saved? — 23
    ALEIDA ASSMANN

2 Past Subjunctive: George L. Mosse's Memoir — 40
    DARCY BUERKLE

PART II. NEW POLITICS OF EXCLUSION

3 Conceptualizing Fascism: The Legacy of George L. Mosse — 61
    ENZO TRAVERSO

4 Women, Gender, and the Radical Right: Then and Now — 79
    MARY NOLAN

5 Behemoth Rises Again: On Twenty-First-Century Fascism — 100
    ANDREAS HUYSSEN

PART III. GENDER, VIOLENCE, AND THE EVERYDAY

6 Sex and Violence: Race Defilement in Nazi Germany 117
   STEFANIE SCHÜLER-SPRINGORUM

7 People Working: Leisure, Love, and Violence in
   Nazi Concentration Camps 135
   ELISSA MAILÄNDER

PART IV. SOLDIERS

8 Morality, Nazi Ideology, and the Individual in the Third Reich:
   The Example of the Wehrmacht 157
   DAVID HARRISVILLE

9 Reading Mosse in Jerusalem: Fallen Soldiers and Israel's
   Culture of Commemoration 173
   ARIE DUBNOV

PART V. GERMAN JEWS BEYOND BERLIN

10 Religious Commitment and Leadership among German-Jewish
   Women in the Early Twentieth Century 201
   SARAH WOBICK-SEGEV

11 Who Owns the German Language? Zionism from Hochdeutsch
   to Kongressdeutsch 216
   MARC VOLOVICI

12 Photography between Empire and Nation: German-Jewish
   Displacement and the Global Camera 234
   REBEKKA GROSSMANN

13 Max Nordau between George L. Mosse and Benzion Netanyahu 253
   ADI ARMON

PART VI. MOSSE AND BERLIN, THEN AND TODAY

14 "There's Nothing Innocuous Left": The Everyday Transfigured 267
   ROBERT ZWARG

15 Absence/Presence: The Berlin Mosse Topography 285
   ELISABETH WAGNER

16 The Mosse Art Research Initiative (MARI) at
   Freie Universität Berlin 301
   MEIKE HOFFMANN

17 The Mosse Family in Berlin: Cultural Capital for
    Subsequent Generations   335
    FRANK MECKLENBURG

Afterword
    A Family Message: The Mosse Berlin Legacy   357
    ROGER STRAUCH

Bibliography   371

Contributors   403

Index   411

ILLUSTRATIONS

FIGURE P.1	Mosse's Berlin	15
FIGURE 7.1	Map of the Majdanek camp area	136
FIGURE 7.2	Map of the city of Lublin with German entertainment facilities	141
FIGURE 7.3	A birthday party at the "Deutsches Haus" in Lublin, March 1944	142
FIGURE 9.1	Nathan Rapoport's 1951 statue of Mordechai Anielewicz	188
FIGURE 9.2	The Israeli sabra (Arik Lavie) wrestles with an ex-SS officer who joined the Egyptian army (Azariah Rappaport) in the 1955 movie *Hill 24 Doesn't Answer*	189
FIGURE 12.1	Tim Gidal, Basra, Iraq, 1940	235
FIGURE 12.2	Tim Gidal, Gandhi, All India Congress Committee, 1940	240
FIGURE 12.3	Tim Gidal, All India Congress Committee, 1940	242
FIGURE 12.4	Tim Gidal, Bombay, India, 1940	243
FIGURE 12.5	Tim Gidal, family picture, 1940	244
FIGURE 12.6	Sonia Gidal and Tim Gidal, *My Village in India*, cover	246
FIGURE 12.7	Sonia Gidal and Tim Gidal, *My Village in India*, 32	247
FIGURE 14.1	Robert Zwarg illustration	270
FIGURE 14.2	Robert Zwarg illustration	271
FIGURE 14.3	Robert Zwarg illustration	272
FIGURE 14.4	Robert Zwarg illustration	273

FIGURE 14.5 Robert Zwarg illustration 281
FIGURE 14.6 Berlin memorial plaque (*Berliner gedenktafel*) 282
FIGURE 14.7 Lehrlings- u. Jugendwohnheim 282
FIGURE 15.1 George L. Mosse at the graveside of his ancestors, Berlin-Weißensee 286
FIGURE 15.2 The void at Potsdamer and Leipziger Platz in Wim Wenders's movie *Der Himmel über Berlin* 286
FIGURE 15.3 The lonely house, reconstruction of the Mosse Palais in 1997 287
FIGURE 15.4 The original Mosse Palais 288
FIGURE 15.5 Mosse Palais with honor court, Voßstraße 22, 1935 288
FIGURE 15.6 Maria Eichhorn's installation at the *documenta 14*, 2017 289
FIGURE 15.7 Soviet soldiers with August Gaul's sculpture *Reclining Lion* in the court of the former Mosse Palais, 1945 290
FIGURE 15.8 Reform Synagogue, Berlin: excavated foundation walls, 2016 291
FIGURE 15.9 The Reform Synagogue as it was in the 1920s from the outside 292
FIGURE 15.10 Bust of Rudolf Mosse in the devastated synagogue 293
FIGURE 15.11 The Schenkendorf estate as it was 294
FIGURE 15.12 The former Mosse Schenkendorf estate in 2016 294
FIGURE 15.13 Mosse Schenkendorf estate inside, today 295
FIGURE 15.14 Mosse-Stift, built 1893–95 296
FIGURE 15.15 The Mosse-Stift in Berlin-Wilmersdorf 2008 with the "Emilie und Rudolf" Café in the right wing 296
FIGURE 15.16 The original Mosse printing house 297
FIGURE 15.17 The *Berliner Tageblatt* printing house after reconstruction and modernization, 1921–23 298
FIGURE 15.18 The Mosse Center in Berlin, 2010 299
FIGURE 16.1 Mosse Art Research Initiative—MARI-Portal 301
FIGURE 16.2 Rudolf Mosse (1843–1920), ca. 1880 302
FIGURE 16.3 Zeitungskatalog Rudolf Mosse, 1908 305
FIGURE 16.4 Greetings from a reader of the *Berliner Morgenzeitung*, undated postcard 306

Illustrations   xiii

FIGURE 16.5 Mosse Publishing House's headquarters, Berlin   307
FIGURE 16.6 Mosse Publishing House's headquarters, Berlin   308
FIGURE 16.7 August Gaul, *Liegender Löwe* (*Reclining Lion*), 1904   309
FIGURE 16.8 Rudolf, Emilie, and Erna Felicia Mosse, ca. 1895   310
FIGURE 16.9 Mosse Palais, Berlin, front facing Leipziger Platz   311
FIGURE 16.10 Anton von Werner, *Das Gastmahl der Familie Mosse* (*The Mosse Family Banquet*), 1899   314
FIGURE 16.11 Kunstsammlung Rudolf Mosse Berlin, Rudolph Lepke's Kunst-Auctions-Haus, 29–30 May 1934   316
FIGURE 16.12 Verzeichnis der Rudolf Moss'schen Kunstsammlung, Berlin, 1900   320
FIGURE 16.13 Lieselotte Friedländer, *Modezeichnung*, "Die Teilnehmer des Weltwerbekongresses," 1929   322
FIGURE 16.14 Lieselotte Friedländer, *Modezeichnung*, "Mode und Reklame," 1929   322
FIGURE 16.15 Peter Paul Rubens, *Die Büssende Magdalena* (*The Repentant Magdalene*), ca. 1634–1640   325
FIGURE 16.16 Gari Melchers, *Skaters/Winter*, ca. 1880–1890   327
FIGURE 16.17 Hanns Fechner, *Theodor Fontane*, 1893   328
FIGURE 16.18 MARI-Portal, Database   330
FIGURE 16.19 View from the Courtyard of the Destroyed Mosse Palais with the *Reclining Lion* by August Gaul, 1945   331
FIGURE 17.1 Mosse brothers: Albert, Salomon, Paul, Emil, Theodor, Rudolf, Max Mosse   336
FIGURE 17.2 Mosse sisters: Margrete Bloch, Anna Wetzlar, Clara Alexander, Elise Hartog, Leonore Cohn, Therese Litthauer   336
FIGURE 17.3 Anton von Werner, *Das Gastmahl der Familie Mosse*, 1899   338
FIGURE 17.4 Emil Mosse   338
FIGURE 17.5 Letter from Professor H. Braus, director of the Anatomical Institute of the University of Heidelberg, to Emilie Mosse, 16 November 1920   342
FIGURE 17.6 Albert Mosse   344
FIGURE 17.7 Medal of the Imperial Japanese Order of the Rising Sun, awarded to Albert Mosse   345

FIGURE 17.8 Albert Mosse, seated, 1870 — 346
FIGURE 17.9 Rudolf Mosse — 348
FIGURE 17.10 Hans Lachmann-Mosse — 349
FIGURE 17.11 Statistics and narrative about the expansion of the Mosse company — 349
FIGURE 17.12 One of the Medici tapestries from Rudolf Mosse's art collection — 352
FIGURE 17.13 Studio portrait of Hilde Mosse, Marianne Ginsberg (Gilbert), and Rudolf Mosse — 353
FIGURE A.1 Mosse Palais, 1888 — 358
FIGURE A.2 Hans Strauch with redesigned Mosse Palais, 1998 — 358
FIGURE A.3 Mosse Palais, 2016 — 359
FIGURE A.4 Rudolf Mosse's grandchildren in the 1930s — 360
FIGURE A.5 George and his nanny, Miss Squire, driving an electric vehicle — 361
FIGURE A.6 Karl Strauch (1922–2000) — 362
FIGURE A.7 Hilde Mosse (1912–1982) — 363
FIGURE A.8 The Mosse Art Restitution Project — 365
FIGURE A.9 Adolph von Menzel, *Emilie in a Red Blouse*, 1850 — 366
FIGURE A.10 Karl Blechen, *View of Santa Scholastica at Subiaco*, 1832 — 367
FIGURE A.11 Roman child's sarcophagus — 367
FIGURE A.12 The Mosse Art Research Initiative (MARI) — 368
FIGURE A.13 George L. Mosse in Berlin, 1918 — 369

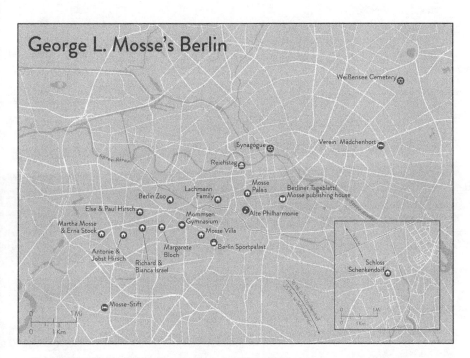

Figure P.1. Mosse's Berlin. (UW–Madison Cartography Lab, Aileen Clarke.)

PREFACE

Mosse's Berlins

DARCY BUERKLE AND SKYE DONEY

The occasion for this volume is to commemorate George L. Mosse's one hundredth birthday and to celebrate the twentieth anniversary of the programs he endowed at the University of Wisconsin–Madison and at the Hebrew University of Jerusalem. Historians from Germany, Israel, and the United States gathered in Mosse's childhood city of Berlin in June 2019 at the Deutsches Historisches Museum and Jüdisches Museum Berlin to discuss intertwined questions that continue to emerge from his pioneering research. What follows pays tribute to Mosse's work and the important interventions of three generations of his students and subsequent Mosse Fellows.[1] Barred from the life he was born into, Mosse went to college in the United States and professionalized the field of history that still defined its ranks narrowly; antisemitism and homophobia were standard. At the Berlin conference, we reflected on Mosse's origins and his field-defining contributions. We hope the essays in this volume enable continued capacious thinking about his writings and about his life.

We would be remiss if we did not acknowledge at the outset the consequential political circumstances at the time we gathered in Berlin in mid-2019 and its impact on the scholarship in this volume. The meeting has an added poignancy now; we could not have known that we stood only months before a world-altering pandemic that would postpone the publication of our work. In what follows, we celebrate Mosse by tending to questions his scholarship has enabled, many of them inflected by the urgency of the particular historical moment in which they were produced. Each contribution is linked to the next through both the details and expansiveness of Mosse's work. For example: What role do sexual and racial stereotypes play in European political culture before and after 1945? How are gender and Nazi violence bound together? And what does commemoration reveal about national values? Importantly, the participants pursued matters inspired by Mosse's work that he did not directly consider: what are the boundaries of terms like "German," "Jewish," or "German Jews"? And how did Nazi perpetrators construct a moral system that could accommodate genocide? Much like Mosse's own publications, the essays that follow inspire a host of new lines of inquiry about the history of European gender and sexuality, Jewish identity during the rise of the Third Reich, and the many reincarnations of fascist pageantry and mass politics.

In George L. Mosse's earliest memories of Berlin, he recalled being sheltered from the turbulent politics and culture of the Weimar Republic. "I witnessed those years as a spectator," he wrote, "cushioned from the real world."[2] He spent much of his youth in the Mosse home on Maaßenstraße and on the grounds in Schenkendorf. In trips back to Germany as an adult, he noted that those who interviewed him hoped to get a sense of Weimar through his experiences. Thinking that maybe Mosse would tell them about personal encounters with Bertolt Brecht or Thomas Mann, they frequently quizzed him about what it was like to live in the fledgling Republic. With characteristic humor, Mosse noted that in his experience such individuals "do not want to hear about German nationalism or boarding schools."[3]

German nationalism and Mosse's varied education are central topics of the first three essays by Steven Aschheim, Aleida Assmann, and Darcy Buerkle. This opening section pays tribute to Mosse as scholar and historical figure. Both Aschheim and Assmann consider Mosse's historiographic interventions in the history of nationalism. For Aschheim, Mosse understood "that nationalism satisfied both legitimate and deep longings of community and could not be wished away." Mosse hoped for a return to inclusive ideals of the nation, along the lines of friendship in the eighteenth century, before totalizing and biological definitions of "community" took root in Europe. Picking up on this discussion, Assmann asks a key question: "Can Mosse's Europe Be Saved?" Perhaps. Writing before the outbreak of a new land war in Europe, Assmann found reason to hope in new transnational forms of war commemoration, including the "Ring of Remembrance" near Arras in France. Here the fallen soldiers of the First World War in the region are listed alphabetically, regardless of national origin or rank.

These opening chapters all emphasize the "autobiographical impulse," to borrow Aschheim's phrase, that animated many of George L. Mosse's studies in European history. From his unique vantage point as a Jewish refugee from Nazi antisemitism, and as a closeted man in the United States academy, Mosse cut up standard periodizations, emphasized popular culture previously dismissed, and empathized with the varied experiences of historical actors. Mosse's "autobiographical impulse" is most visible in Buerkle's engaging chapter on the posthumous editorial decisions undertaken in Mosse's memoir *Confronting History*. Buerkle finds that what was left unsaid or what Mosse writes *might have been* in the final publication offers new insights into not only the text but to the way that historians remember him. Mosse encountered nationalism but also the narrow, bourgeois masculinity expected of young men after the First World War. Analyzing how Mosse deploys the "past subjunctive" in passages excised from his memoir, Buerkle convincingly reveals how Mosse understood the interconnections of his own life and historiographic innovations.

The rest of this volume takes up Mosse's historiographical legacy. Subsequent sections make significant interventions in historical fields that were central to Mosse's scholarship: the politics of exclusion, the parameters of stereotypes, gender and violence, German Jews, and the culture of commemoration. Enzo Traverso, Mary Nolan, and Andreas Huyssen analyze the cultures of fascisms from Il Duce to 8chan. Traverso argues that Mosse's anthropological approach to the rituals of fascism turned Nazism and Italian Fascism into cultural objects. This approach led Mosse to overlook important social and economic factors, including the role of "capitalism and the bourgeois classes" in fueling these political movements. Mosse's stress on Italy and Germany as the focal points of a European "fascist revolution" also meant he did not integrate the role of colonialism, notes Traverso. These are directions for further analysis, Traverso argues, while also acknowledging that Mosse's work "has been canonized." Traverso provokes present and future scholars to treat Mosse's methodologies with "empathetic criticism more than pure celebration." Not only would such an approach further the conversation, but the challenge would also have pleased Mosse. As Aschheim writes, "Quite untypical for the professoriate, George was remarkably open to such criticism and, at least in my case, was quite pleased with it and saw it as a testament to the seriousness with which I took his work."

Nolan and Huyssen move into our present political crises by examining the idealized futures constructed in contemporary fascistic rhetoric. Though both are critical of the "f-word," they find remarkable promises of utopia throughout the European and North American far right. Huyssen outlines significant continuities between the Third Reich and Trumpism, including fascism as cultural synthesis, *Ungleichzeitigkeit* (nonsynchronicity), the authoritarian personality, the role of the fascist agitator, the place of utopian vision, white nationalism and racism, fascism as racketeering, and fascist politics as totalitarian Leviathan or chaotic Behemoth. While Huyssen notes the difference in these historical moments, both Nazism and the new right offer(ed) vague promises to restore order, declare victory, and turn back time to a more prosperous era. Even as the 2020s are not the 1920s, Huyssen identifies parallel antisemitic fantasies while convincingly pointing to the current dangers of normalizing threats of violence and antidemocratic behavior.

Coupled with Huyssen's observations of continuities and disruptions are far right discourses of "insiderdom." Nolan shows that populist parties have found a new, old ideal type to target in calls for rapid political change: "the immoral." The precise parameters of this concept vary by geographic context, but the immoral always constitutes an internal enemy. These can include the advocates of "gender ideology" (a Populist Radical Right term), Muslim immigrants, feminists, or any member of the LGBTQ+ community. Like the inconsistent nature of Huyssen's fascist Leviathan, Nolan notes that populists have been "riddled with contradictions" on questions of immigration, racism, and sexuality. Taken together, the three essays in "New Politics of Exclusion" remind historians of the persistent adaptability of "fascism," both now and in the twentieth century.

The following essays in "Gender, Violence, and the Everyday" offer two new and unique answers to the question of why Nazi perpetrators participated in acts of violence. For Stefanie Schüler-Springorum there is no one underlying reason that can explain why Nazi youth would physically assault and humiliate septuagenarians in 1940s Dresden. But she finds an explanation can be found in the "interweaving of violence and sexuality" in fascist propaganda coupled with the Nazi desire to publicly demarcate Jews from Aryans. Publicly shaming and harming individuals accused of "racial crimes" let loose a torrent of emotions for both participants and bystanders, "aversion and attraction, but also of shame and desire," Schüler-Springorum argues in her provocative essay.

Elissa Mailänder's contribution focuses on twenty-eight female SS guards in the concentration camp Majdanek and ultimately puts David Harrisville's conclusion to the test. Mailänder argues that concentration camp work was appealing because the SS provided opportunities for professional advancement and increased social status. Looking at how the female SS guards explained their decision to volunteer for a camp posting, Mailänder identifies a generation of lower-class women frustrated with their job prospects who hoped to move into the middle class via the Nazi bureaucracy of war and genocide. By examining what work and leisure meant in Majdanek, Mailänder demonstrates that leisure in the everydayness of their Holocaust participation "banalized violence and ultimately brutalized the guards." Her conclusion parallels Schüler-Springorum's but emphasizes that a more generalizable "dependence and independence, of rule-abiding and self-willed action" shaped the "work life" of guards and "the living and dying conditions of the camp inmates."

Schüler-Springorum's and Mailänder's guiding question *why* is further explored by David Harrisville. Harrisville weighs how Wehrmacht soldiers explained their actions during brutal fighting on the Eastern Front. He charts a wide-ranging collage of moral systems and justifications in explanatory notes soldiers included in their letters home. Some Wehrmacht members claimed meaning in the Nazi project and parroted the Party line against so-called racial inferiors the army encountered in Eastern Europe. Other individuals expressed personal uncertainty about summary execution, theft, forced labor, and crimes against civilians. Offering a fascinating glimpse of the moral topography among soldiers, Harrisville argues that the "relative freedom to choose whichever justifications they preferred ultimately worked to the regime's advantage by making it easier for individuals of different backgrounds and creeds to come to terms with their involvement in activities that furthered Nazi goals, all while maintaining the conviction ... that their personal decency remained intact." Here the *why* of Nazi crimes proves troublingly heterogeneous. Private uncertainty did not change the outcome of violence perpetuated on behalf of a brutal state. Harrisville concludes that "a similar pattern repeated itself across other Third Reich institutions."

Arie Dubnov further examines legacies of conflict, albeit in a very different context: the culture of memorializing Israel's fallen soldiers. Dubnov's point of departure is Mosse's preface to the Hebrew edition of *Fallen Soldiers*. In his contribution, Dubnov considers the evidence Mosse used for this piece and how Israel's commemorative culture has changed since 1990. While Mosse stressed physical "sites of *sepulcrum*," Dubnov contends that the culture of memory is not solely based in monuments but can be found in "bereaved families' memory activism" and the integration of commemoration into the Israeli calendar. Dubnov convincingly demonstrates the diffuse nature of remembrance, from parents publishing their dead children's correspondence to portrayals of the 1948 War in popular culture.

The following four essays in "German Jews beyond Berlin" complicate enduring ideal types, including "German Judaism," "liberal," and even "German." In her analysis of Reform Judaism, including the involvement of the Mosse family in the Berlin community, Sarah Wobick-Segev persuasively argues that German Jews were not beyond Judaism as Mosse posited in the mid-1980s. Many German Jews, she demonstrates, participated in a "rich history of religious engagement." To better understand religious practices, Wobick-Segev investigates the intersection of gender and synagogue life and shows the central role of Jewish women in "public debates on rituals, religious values, and education as well as on the place of women in Judaism."

Concurrent with Wobick-Segev's greater Berlin debates about whether or not a Jewish woman could become a rabbi, Marc Volovici's study of the lingua franca of European Zionism puts the lie to any definitive statements about "Jews" and "Germans." For Volovici, "far from reflecting a mere medium of a Germanophone hegemony, German served as a contested and multifaceted political vehicle—used by native and non-native speakers of German—channeling several divisions within Zionism." Volovici urges historians to think not only of German-speaking Jews in Europe but also of German-reading Jews who lived elsewhere, "from Palestine, Europe, and the Americas." The Zionist Congress debates about language were spirited, at times threatening, and indicate how "German" was simultaneously specific and amorphous, depending on who approached the Congress podium in the early twentieth century.

Rebekka Grossmann and Adi Armon respond to Volovici's "German-reading" challenge. Their essays examine German Jews beyond Berlin and indeed beyond Germany. Grossmann invites the reader to travel with Tim Gidal and the British Army from Palestine to Iraq to India. By accompanying Gidal, we gain "angles on the histories of the Jewish presence in colonial contexts, the roots of modern Western perceptions of the Global South, and the role of Jewish political voices in the humanitarian discourses that coined the early Cold War years." Through Gidal's camera lens, Grossmann views fascinating images of 1940s India, scrutinizing Gidal's image of Gandhi speaking. On the basis of Gidal's experience, Grossmann argues that historians must take a wide angle when considering "the variety of postwar German-Jewish realities."

In his analysis of how two historians—Benzion Netanyahu and George L. Mosse—interpreted Max Nordau's *Degeneration*, Adi Armon highlights the different afterlives of Nordau's Zionist project. Netanyahu deployed Nordau to support his own politics in Israel and wed the famous text to his own view of the West as in a state of decline. Here Nordau's liberal vision was pushed to the side in favor of a militant Nordau who advocated conquest from the Mediterranean to the Transjordan. Conversely, in his own introduction to *Degeneration*, Mosse portrayed Nordau as an optimistic, if cautious, Zionist and "man of the Enlightenment and of the values of the French Revolution." In both cases, Nordau's work was bent to fit Netanyahu's neoconservative Zionism or Mosse's respectable, liberal, bourgeois version. Like the contributions from Wobick-Segev, Grossmann, and Volovici, Armon's examination of the Mosse-Netanyahu dialogue that could have been reminds scholars that categories like "Zionist," "liberal," and "German" require careful qualification.

The final four chapters in "Mosse and Berlin: Then and Today" as well as the afterword expand the discussion of the Mosses in Berlin temporally and geographically. Frank Mecklenburg considers the intersection of emigration and scholarship. Both George and Werner Mosse became historians in part to better understand the "long shadow" cast by their grandfather, Rudolf Mosse. As Mecklenburg discusses, these Mosse cousins were marked by the Third Reich and ultimately used their research to better understand their family. Both Elisabeth Wagner and Robert Zwarg engage the ambiguity of Mossean spaces in Berlin after Nazi expropriation. For Wagner, "the Mosse family's heritage in Berlin is broken physically, or missing completely." She deftly excavates Mosse sites throughout the city. Zwarg deploys Mosse's concept of "Nazi culture" to discern how the Third Reich profoundly altered everyday life. Zwarg's contribution works to recover the memory of Berlin spaces literally from the recycling bin. Thinking back to Rudolf Mosse's "long shadow," Meike Hoffmann and Roger Strauch discuss the continued legacy of Rudolf and Emilie Mosse's art collection. Hoffmann's analysis reveals how Nazi-looted objects continue to raise important discussions about ownership, restitution, and the deeply personal responses to postwar reconciliation. Taken together, the final five contributions reveal the possibilities and limits of German-Jewish emancipation, which is a central theme throughout the volume.

Frank Mecklenburg notes that when George L. Mosse was a teenager, Berlin "was then at the center of German history. Now, a century and a half later, the city of Berlin has become the place that tries to remember an era that seems so unimaginable to us now." Berlin as historical and imagined site links all the essays: from Rudolf Mosse arriving in 1867 to the event in the summer of 2019 that led to this publication.

Mosse himself had an ambiguous relationship to the city even after the Cold War and restitution of family properties in the former East. In 2010 during a lecture on Rudolf Mosse's stolen art collection, Jost Hermand reflected on joining Mosse in Berlin in 1995. Mosse was back in the city to attend the dedication of the newly remodeled "Mosse Zentrum," built on the site of Rudolf Mosse's publishing house headquarters on the corner of Schützenstraße and Jerusalemer Straße. At the dedication, Berlin mayor Eberhard Diepgen reflected on the history of Germany since unification. "That was one of the worst speeches I ever heard," Hermand reflected. "[Diepgen] said, there are only two important dates in German history, 1871 and 1989, the two years of the unification of Germany. And therefore, Otto von Bismarck and Helmut Kohl are the two most important German politicians of the last 150 years. ... He jumped from Otto von Bismarck to Helmut Kohl without mentioning the Mosse family, without mentioning that George was sitting there." Outraged at Diepgen's historical analysis, Hermand wanted to get up and make a scene on live television but stopped short at Mosse's insistence. "He [Mosse] was always more pragmatic in this aspect."[4] In such settings Mosse was always uncomfortable: "I wanted to be measured solely by my own accomplishments, which were the fruits of exile, and not by what my name might represent. I am still not comfortable when in Berlin I am presented to audiences as the grandson of Rudolf Mosse."[5] This book therefore fulfills Mosse's wish in two ways. First, the assembled in Berlin were introduced not as being affiliated with Rudolf Mosse but with the historian George L. Mosse. And second, twenty years after his passing, historians are still vigorously discussing Mosse's "fruits of exile."

Notes

1. This volume joins other works that have explored Mosse's pervasive influence in European history, including Seymour Drescher, David Sabean, and Allan Sharlin, eds., *Political Symbolism in Modern Europe: Essays in Honor of George L. Mosse* (New Brunswick, NJ: Transaction Books, 1982); Stanley Payne, David Sorkin, and John Tortorice, eds., *What History Tells: George L. Mosse and the Culture of Modern Europe* (Madison: University of Wisconsin Press, 2004); Emilio Gentile, *Il fascino del persecutore: George L. Mosse e la catastrofe dell'uomo moderno* (Rome: Carocci, 2007), translated as *Fascination with the Persecutor: George L. Mosse and the Catastrophe of Modern Man* (Madison: University of Wisconsin Press, 2021); Donatello Aramini, *George L. Mosse, l'Italia e gli storici* (Milan: FrancoAngeli, 2010); Lorenzo Benadusi and Giorgio Caravale, eds., *George L. Mosse's Italy: Interpretation, Reception, and Intellectual Heritage* (New York: Palgrave, 2014); Karel Plessini, *The Perils of Normalcy: George L. Mosse and the Remaking of Cultural History* (Madison: University of Wisconsin Press, 2014); Andreas W. Daum and Sherry L. Föhr, "George Lachmann Mosse," in *The Second Generation: Émigrés from Nazi Germany as Historians*, ed. Andreas W. Daum, Hartmut Lehmann, and James J. Sheehan (New York: Berghahn, 2016), 414–16; Elisabeth Wagner, ed., *Mosse Almanach 2017: Zum zwanzigjährigen Jubiläum der Mosse-Lectures an der Humboldt Universität* (Berlin: Vorwerk 8, 2017); Klaus Berghahn, ed., *The German-Jewish Dialogue Reconsidered: A Symposium in Honor of George L. Mosse* (New York: Peter Lang, 1996); "George L. Mosse Memorial Symposium," special issue, *German Politics and Society* 18, no. 4 (2000).

2. George L. Mosse, *Confronting History: A Memoir* (Madison: University of Wisconsin Press, 2000), 79.

3. Mosse, *Confronting History*, 74–75.

4. Jost Hermand, "Fall of an Empire: The Fate of Rudolf Mosse's Art Collection," 2 December 2010, YouTube, https://www.youtube.com/watch?v=hgTWG-TuHNU.

5. Mosse, *Confronting History*, 213.

ACKNOWLEDGMENTS

We would like to thank the contributors for their dedication to this book even in the face of unprecedented challenges since we started the project in the summer of 2019. Sunny Yudkoff was instrumental in conceptualizing, designing, and editing. We thank her for her essential contributions in initiating this publication. Thanks also to the anonymous readers who undertook a thorough review of each contribution even as we all experienced new pandemic pressures on our time and energy.

The contributors to this volume had a wide range of relationships to George L. Mosse, from family to doctoral students and on to a new generation of scholars who never met him. The personal nature of many of these connections is reflected and respected in several of the following chapters.

The editors extend profound thanks to Steven E. Aschheim, Ofer Ashkenazi, Atina Grossmann, Mary Louise Roberts, Anson Rabinbach, Moshe Sluhovsky, David Sorkin, and John Tortorice for imagining and realizing an event and this publication to commemorate George L. Mosse's one-hundredth birthday and the twentieth anniversary of the Program he established.

All Berlin 2019 participants and attendees helped shape the chapters in this book with their insightful comments and questions. Andreas Huyssen published a version of his chapter previously as "Behemoth Rises Again: Not an Analogy!," *n+1*, 14 November 2022, https://www.nplusonemag.com/online-only/online-only/behemoth-rises-again/. Michael P. Steinberg's revised lecture appeared as "The Narcissism of Major Differences: Richard Wagner and the Peculiarities of German Antisemitism," *Social Research* 89, no. 1 (Spring 2022): 21–46.

Thanks also to George L. Mosse Program in History Fellows Conrad Allen and Chad S. A. Gibbs, who helped tremendously with logistics, and to Matthew

M. Greene for compiling the bibliography and reviewing the manuscript for consistency.

Additional thanks to Raphael Gross, Jenny Jakubik, and Barbara Wolf of the Deutsches Historisches Museum; Dr. Thomas Suermann, Patricia Avendung, Sabine Berchem, Verena Gorny, and Sandra Müller of the Fritz Thyssen Stiftung für Wissenschaftsförderung; Hans and Roger Strauch of the Mosse Foundation in New York; Sharon Lew of the Roda Group; Jennifer Conn, Dennis Lloyd, Nathan MacBrien, Sheila McMahon, and Adam Mehring of the University of Wisconsin Press; Klaus Scherpe and Elisabeth Wagner of the Mosse-Lectures an der Humboldt-Universität; Léontine Meijer-van Mensch, Martin Michaelis, Signe Rossbach, Peter Schäfer, and Stefan von Zwoll of the Jüdisches Museum Berlin; Ben Miller, Peter Rehberg, and Daniel Sander of the Schwules Musem Berlin; Georgia Bauer and Daniel Wildmann of the Leo Baeck Institute London; Frank Mecklenburg and Michael Simonson of the Leo Baeck Institute New York; Torsten Flüh of *Night Out @ Berlin*; Mor Hagbi of the Franz Rosenzweig/Minerva Research Center for German-Jewish Literature and Cultural History; Andreas Beckmann of *Deutschlandfunk* for his report "Kongress zum 100. Geburtstag von George Mosse: Wie die Kulturwissenschaft europäischen Faschismus erklärt"; Jonathon Catlin and Lotte Houwink ten Cate for their conference report "George Mosse at One Hundred: A Child of His Century" in the *Journal of the History of Ideas Blog*; Terrence Peterson for his H-German 24 July 2019 conference report.

This book was completed with financial support from the George L. Mosse Program in History at the University of Wisconsin–Madison and at the Hebrew University of Jerusalem, the Mosse Foundation in New York, the Fritz Thyssen Stiftung für Wissenschaftsförderung, the Deutsches Historisches Museum, the Jüdisches Museum Berlin, the George L. Mosse/Laurence A. Weinstein Center for Jewish Studies at the University of Wisconsin–Madison, the Department of History at the University of Wisconsin–Madison, the Hebrew University of Jerusalem, the Franz Rosenzweig/Minerva Research Center for German-Jewish Literature and Cultural History, the Hebrew University of Jerusalem's Department of History, the Richard Koebner Minerva Center for German History at the Hebrew University of Jerusalem, the Zentrum für Antisemitismusforschung, the Technische Universität Berlin, the Leo Baeck Institute New York, and the Leo Baeck Institute London.

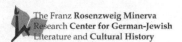

Contemporary Europe in the Historical Imagination

INTRODUCTION

George L. Mosse

The Work, the Legacy, the Man

STEVEN E. ASCHHEIM

George L. Mosse thought, spoke, and wrote prodigiously, pioneeringly, and almost always, provocatively. While not neglecting high culture, and indeed he incarnated the enlightened *Bildung* tradition he so often referenced, what stands out above all was his singular role in literally redefining the field of intellectual and cultural history. He consciously departed from the somewhat rarefied approach of traditional *Ideengeschichte*, with its inbuilt bias toward abstract ideas and a progressive Hegelian rationality, and turned to subjects like popular literature, myths and symbols, ideologies of "irrationalism," youth movements, muscle-building gymnastics, and nose-straightening surgery.[1] More than anything, he uncovered the crucial role of normative stereotypes and their excluding mechanisms.

Apart from these substantive and methodological contributions, his monographs and more specialized studies covered a wide range both of time periods and subject matter. His first works centered on the early modern period, on the struggle for sovereignty in England, on the Reformation and popular piety, and the problem of reason of state and Christian casuistry. Later, however, from the early 1960s on, he turned to topics that in one way or another had more obviously affected his own life. It was just prior to this turn that a colleague famously asked George: "Why is it that you are so interesting, and your books are so dull?" Though George himself did not agree with this verdict, claiming a certain continuity of thematic concern, there is no doubt that his impact has been mainly on the later period. Indeed, he admitted that as a new immigrant he first needed time to assimilate to his new environment. But after two decades in the United States, he wrote, "There was no more need to immerse myself in a respectable Anglo-Saxon subject in order to distance myself from my past as an outsider."[2]

A virtual flood of works ensued on völkisch ideology, fascism, Nazism, the Holocaust, German history, Jewish history, Zionism, and antisemitism; on monuments, secular religion, and mass politics; on liberalism and socialism and the role of intellectuals in politics; on war, shell shock, and processes of civic brutalization; on memory and modes of commemoration; on medicine, nervousness, and degenerative masturbation; on racism, aesthetics, and visual culture; on bourgeois respectability, masculinity, sexuality and nationalism. These are indeed varied topics. For all that, they possess a certain unity, linked, I would say, by George's driving critical concern with constricting processes of inclusion and exclusion, with ideal and anti-types, with straitjacketing definitions of "normalcy" and "abnormalcy," propelled by his Enlightenment belief in the autonomy of the individual, the expansion of humanizing experience, and his concern with its defeat by mass forces of homogenization. He brought to his work a commitment and passion that he said was decreasing among his colleagues who, he declared, "could just as well have been accountants!"[3]

As a German-Jewish émigré and, at first, an undeclared homosexual, who had experienced rejection and exclusion firsthand, there is little doubt that George's evolving work had both generational and above all autobiographical roots. It is telling that although he regarded his forced leaving of Germany in 1933 as a form of liberation, a rich man's son's opportunity to make his mark independently, he nevertheless ends his autobiography by ultimately defining himself "as a member of the Holocaust generation."[4] In all his works he went not into the mechanics of the Shoah, details that I think he would have dismissed as merely "technical" in nature, but rather into the multitude of deeper-lying cultural, ideological, and political building blocks that rendered it conceivable, a thinkable possibility that, under the correct contingent conditions, could be and was ultimately realized. His position on this was radical: "All my books," he declared, "in one way or another have dealt with the Jewish catastrophe of my time which I always regarded as no accident, structural fault or continuity of bureaucratic habits, but seemingly built into our society and toward life. Nothing in European history is a stranger to the Holocaust, and I have tried to delve ever more deeply into the nature of European society through analyzing its perceptions of and attitudes to the outsider."[5]

Typically, George insisted on "deghettoizing" Jewish history, rejecting a common ethnocentric bias that, by definition, it had to follow its own unique narrative and immanent laws. To some extent, certain critics argue, Mosse's view of Jewish history reflected his rarefied experience as a member of the highly acculturated wealthy, Berlin Jewish elite, removed from the more prosaic experience and attitudes of other coreligionists. After all, who else could write a paeon of praise titled *German Jews beyond Judaism* (1985)? (This may or may not have affected his scholarly writings but, in his personal life, as Walter Laqueur noted, one would never have known about this historical affluence. George probably never had more than two suits and lived more than modestly.[6]) At any rate, by linking Jewish fate inextricably to central currents of the European experience, he connected dimensions that too often remained compartmentalized.[7] Clearly *The Crisis of German Ideology* (1964, 2021) is the prime example of this approach. But over the years an even broader canvas, an evolution of thought and perspective, emerged. His work now became implicitly intertwined with an emerging acknowledgment of his own minority status on account of his sexuality. While Jewish victimization remained central (even unique), the scope of analysis became ever broader: Jews as victims formed part of a continuum and dynamic affecting other victims, their status and stereotype comprehensible only alongside other outsiders. (I will address this in greater detail a little later).

That broader canvas also hides other significant shifts. To understand these moves we need first to examine the "Crisis" book. (I write the "Crisis" book because George always used this shorthand to say he was working on his "Culture" or "War" or "Race" or "Masses" or "Sex" book!) This eye-opening work treated us to an erudite, richly detailed display of how völkisch ideology, that semi-mystic, organic *Weltanschauung*—with its metaphysic of eternal national rootedness, its symbolism of blood and soil, its antiliberal and antiurban bias—penetrated and informed German culture and politics and, by focusing on the Jewish stereotype of rootlessness and alienness, became the Nazi anti-Jewish revolution. Later critics, while appreciating this emphasis, have argued that George's neglect of its traditional religious Christian and medieval manifestations conceived of the antecedents and effectiveness of antisemitism too narrowly. Moreover, as original as it was, *The Crisis of German Ideology* nevertheless fitted the conventional *Sonderweg* paradigm of the time. German developments toward modernity, he held, were singular and differed fundamentally from the liberal, democratic West, its antimodernity repudiating the rational European Enlightenment and the social radicalism of the French Revolution.

But as he proceeded, George subtly softened the *Sonderweg*, Germano-centric explanation and moved increasingly to a wider European canvas. Thus his 1975 *Nationalization of the Masses* made it clear that ultimately fascism and Nazism were part of the broadest defining developments of political modernity, incomprehensible outside of the European-wide backdrop of the fusion of democracy and nationalism and the creation of a new, mobilizing liturgical politics, a visually oriented, participatory "counter" to liberal parliamentarism, rendering even the French Revolution as partly complicit. His 1978 *Toward the Final Solution*, to be sure, rendered Jews as its central victims, but it is also a wider history of European (not only German) racism. There, the world is divided into normative types and anti-types, and the major, subtle role of aesthetics (rather than science) as standards of racist judgments, rendered startlingly clear. Rooted in the ubiquitous ideal of Greek beauty, racists employed an aesthetic physiognomy predicated on making judgments not only about external appearance but—crucially—about inner moral qualities as well. These were European-wide stereotypes and clearly not limited to Jews. Just as no one could claim a Greek heritage for the stereotype of the ghetto Jew, this was equally true for the Black stereotype. If Jewish looks validated an inherent criminality and sly manipulativeness, Black deportment confirmed an essential inner violence and primitiveness. Concern for a widening perspective on European violence is equally apparent in Mosse's 1990 *Fallen Soldiers*. There it is World War I, with its well-nigh universal twentieth-century experience of mass death, that takes center stage. In that context, rather than an ongoing völkisch tradition or ingrained racism, it is the later militant, right-wing appropriation of the brutalized war experience, transposed into civil politics, that becomes paramount.

But George's most radical turn was not just the simple enlargement of his historical canvas that took in most of Europe and went beyond Germany. It concerns his portrait of the role of the middle classes in these deleterious developments. Although in *The Crisis of German Ideology* George did suggest that through antisemitism the bourgeoisie was integrated into the Nazi revolution, it was the antiurban, antimodern aspects that were emphasized, and the determinative role of the middle classes only minimally outlined. Yet their more pernicious role was already—if only embryonically—present. "Bourgeois respectability," he declared, was "successfully woven into the ideological fabric of the Nazis, who, upon assuming power, took to championing the völkisch concepts of rootedness, puritan morality, and bourgeois tastes, ethics, and values. . . . All things offensive to bourgeois ethics were rooted out of the party. . . . From both a völkisch and a radically National Socialist point of view, the Nazi Party had tailored the Germanic ideology to bourgeois standards."[8]

Nevertheless, in Mosse's 1985 *Nationalism and Sexuality* and 1996 *The Image of Man*, it is not simply that Nazis tailored their ideology to the middle class. Rather, the modern bourgeoisie, at least in some of its guises, has been transformed into a constitutive and essential expression of fascist and Nazi impulses. From the late eighteenth century on, Mosse argues, nationalism and middle-class morality entered into a powerful alliance, together defining modern standards of sexual behavior and other modes of respectable conduct in such a way that an ever-tightening distinction between normality and abnormality was developed and enforced. Manliness became part of normal and normative national and bourgeois self-definition. This alliance became increasingly totalized, insistent on assigning everyone a fixed place: the healthy and the degenerate; virile, self-controlled men and nervous, effeminate homosexuals; the sane and the insane; the energetically productive and the lazy; the settled native and the rootless foreigner. This rigid code, cloaked under the guise of respectability and *Sittlichkeit*, was invoked to control the reality that the alliance had itself created.

"Bourgeois society," George insisted, "needed its dialectical opposite in order to exist," and it is there that the critique of respectability becomes subversively and conceptually central. Nazism here is not about a peculiar German *Sonderweg* or a radical Nietzschean nihilism or the Noltean revolt *against* bourgeois transcendence but, rather, about corrupted and threatened middle-class men attempting to maintain the values of healthy manliness, orderliness, cleanliness, hard work, and family life against those outsider groups who, in their eyes, seemed morally, bodily, and aesthetically diseased and degenerate and who dangerously desecrated the basic tenets of bourgeois respectability. "The New Man of National Socialism," Mosse declared, "was the ideal bourgeois," and it was their anti-types—the sexual deviants, "Gypsies," Jews, permanently insane people— George declared in an interview in his special way of talking, whom "Hitler wanted to exterminate and whom he did exterminate. They all look alike. . . . They all look the opposite of the middle-class self-controlled idea of beauty, energy, all of this sort of thing."[9]

This, I would argue, was a typical, brilliant Mossean provocation. George surely was aware that Nazi perpetrators understood the highly transgressive, taboo-breaking—that is, highly un-bourgeois—nature of their acts. He would argue that Nazism combined both bourgeois and anti-bourgeois elements, and it was precisely in the combination of, and tension between, these elements, in the fusion of the conventional and the extraordinary, that Nazism radically transcended middle-class morality at the same time that it embodied it. At any rate, as George demonstrated especially in *The Image of Man*, middle-class respectability was and is by no means inevitably genocidal. Indeed, the force of his argument consists in delineating how it functioned in other far more conventional, obviously less lethal, contexts and the ways in which these controlling definitions of "the normal" and "the abnormal" operated and in many respects continue to do so. After all, in the last chapter of *Nationalism and*

Sexuality, George dubbed respectability's penetration into all classes of society as "Everyone's Morality."[10]

We have so far looked at some of Mosse's most pointed negative critiques. What about his more positive commitments, what he called his "points of redemption of the human spirit"?[11] He was clearly a liberal who believed deeply in the autonomy of the individual and personalizing relationships. More specifically, he constantly emphasized that these values were most clearly incarnated in the specific notion of *Bildung*, that untranslatable classical German idea of ethical and cultural development through self-cultivation. If, for Mosse, "respectability" represents the contraction of tolerance and human possibilities, *Bildung* embodied the ideal of openness, the expansion of human experience. Tolerance, cultured self-cultivation, and the autonomy of the individual were its trademarks. Implicitly, he applied these yardsticks as the moral measure in almost all his later works.

Yet once again, a clearly autobiographical impulse emerges, for he rendered the ethical history of *Bildung* virtually into a specific ethnic property. George's 1985 *German Jews beyond Judaism* is an analysis of the historical process whereby German Jewry slowly became essentially the sole carriers of that humanizing sensibility, witness to the gradual desertion by the non-Jewish German educated middle class of a doctrine they had originally shared with their emancipated Jewish co-citizens. Indeed, for George, the German-Jewish heritage *is* the heritage of *Bildung*, a kind of new Jewish tradition, a defining and constitutive ingredient of their postemancipation identity. For here was an ideal that seemed tailor-made for emancipatory integration because, as George put it, "it transcended all differences of nationality and religion through the unfolding of the individual personality."[12] This form of cultural humanism, George argued, became integrally interwoven into the very fabric of German-Jewish being. Certainly, it is these qualities that both as an historian and a human being George exemplified, a vision in which Jewishness became a metaphor for the critical yet always humanizing and autonomous mind. *German Jews beyond Judaism* is the work in which Mosse is clearly most identified, at home with his subject. It is, as he himself admitted, "certainly my most personal book, almost a confession of faith."[13]

But responsible historian that he was, George characteristically retained a certain critical perspective on his rendering of *Bildung*. Given their almost automatic belief in the primacy of culture over politics, *Bildung* Jews, he wrote, entirely misread their own situation and deluded themselves by projecting their own ethical ideals onto a Germany that possessed a quite different reality. Indeed, as he argued, while Jews were emancipated into the promises of *Bildung*, they were also taught to adjust to the norms and the mannered restrictions of respectability. Eventually they became caught in a vice: when *Bildung* became a nationalized—rather than an individual—value, it was very easy to stereotypically represent gesticulating, manipulating, nervous Jews as the antithesis of respectability.[14]

In all these ways, then, Mosse became perhaps the most important contemporary historian of the manifold strategies of inclusion and exclusion, of belonging and displacement, of disdained outsiders and normative insiders. Here was a conception of culture and cultural process determined by a dialectical relationship between center and periphery. The insider acquired identity and defined themselves in terms of the outsider they create. Moreover, these processes were always located within what George used to call "a fully furnished house." Despite his own liberalism, history for him comprised a totality: the political could not be separated from the religious, the scientific was informed by the aesthetic, the mythological never far from the rational.

Clearly then, George was interested not in history as a dry narrative but in the big questions and possible answers.[15] He was no positivist and certainly not a plodding antiquarian. Indeed, he could sometimes be quite cavalier with his quotes and stories. As his friend and coeditor Walter Laqueur (who, with George, was among the pioneers of what goes by the name of "contemporary history") correctly noted, George's spelling was uncertain in all languages "and he had the disdain of a grand seigneur vis-à-vis dates in history. In a memoir about his parents, he had written that his father had invited Edith Piaf to perform in Berlin in 1919. I pointed out that this seemed unlikely since Piaf was five years old at the time. Did he mean perhaps Yvette Guilbert or Mistinguett? Yes, of course, he said, but did it really matter?"[16] More seriously, it is also true that his work was never immune to criticism.

As just one instance, George's general portrait of *Bildung*, and his at times idealized portrait of German Jews, has received criticism from a variety of perspectives. Peter Jelavich has argued that for German Jews the *Bildung* paradigm is *itself* misleading. Jews, Jelavich proposes, were far more numerically and centrally invested in, and critically important to, the creation, dissemination, and consumption of *popular and mass culture* in Germany and not the heights of sensitive *Bildung*. Mosse's elitist bias, he argues, effaced this vital ingredient of German-Jewish identity and experience.[17] Shulamit Volkov, on the other hand, did not take issue with the *Bildung* paradigm itself but argued that German Jews were no more dedicated to its cultured precepts than other Germans and no less prone to embrace German nationalism, despite its affinity to racism and its inherent antisemitism.[18] I too have argued that, at least for the Weimar period, leading Jewish intellectuals radically rejected the *Bildung* paradigm of calm, gradual, and essentially progressive development and adopted a far more ecstatic, revolutionary, and immediate redemptive posture.[19]

But quite untypical for the professoriate, George was remarkably open to such criticism and, at least in my case, was quite pleased with it and saw it as a testament to the seriousness with which I took his work. As long as the argument was boldly stated and did not contain what he called "a wobble" it was acceptable. "Ever since I can remember," he noted, "I have disliked anything mushy, from personal attitudes to human bodies, to ripe fruit."[20] Still, however much he may have disliked wobbles, George was himself a complex figure who was aware of his many inner tensions and anxieties, which he creatively channeled into his work. It is precisely this complexity, if not outright conflicts and contradictions, that rendered his person so compelling and that endowed his writings with their dynamic energy and contemporary relevance. Who better to detail the dialectics between "nervousness" and "self-control" than George? His writing of history was so vital precisely because it was an encounter galvanized by his own autobiography. Let us illustrate this briefly with just two examples from his oeuvre.

The first and perhaps most obvious example is clearly apparent in *Nationalism and Sexuality* and *The Image of Man*. Existential roots and his own gayness, George candidly acknowledged, were behind this concern with bourgeois respectability and its construction of "normal" and "abnormal" categories of sexuality. As he put it, he had engaged with "the specific outsiderdoms of which I have been a member." Yet even though in the *Crisis* book George was the first to discuss male eros as part of völkisch thought, he only explicitly addressed homosexuality in the latter part of his life. Indeed, with extraordinary candor, he even claimed that perhaps these later works "failed to suppress sufficiently my anger over the fact that the strictures of respectability had made my own life so much more difficult."[21] Yet the critical historian in him never allowed his analyses to become embittered or simplistically partisan. Perhaps that is because, at the same time that he critiqued respectability, he not only personally internalized it but also understood its very necessity. If he advocated the expansion of boundaries and pressed for greater tolerance of minorities and sexual outsiders, he also fully understood the limits of such expansion. Perhaps one could permit greater latitude of sexual expression, a relaxation of overly repressive controls, he wrote, provided that it did not endanger respectability's power and dominance. This was so, simply because, as he put it, the normative manners and morals of respectability were essential for the creation of some kind of order, "for the cohesion and functioning of society itself."[22]

The second example of these tensions and inner contradictions concerns his analyses of, and personal relation to, nationalism in general and to Jewish nationalism in particular. How did that tension work? At the same time in which he unmasked and critiqued the deep dangers of nationalism, he also possessed a rather profound attraction to its blandishments. His school at Salem, he wrote, "gave me a first taste of nationalism, which at the time I found congenial; there was a danger that it might provide a belief system that I so badly lacked.... When as a historian much later I wrote about German nationalism, I did have an insight into its truly seductive nature."[23] Indeed, at the age of about fifteen he watched a Nazi demonstration in front of his home in Berlin. "The impression was so great," he later recalled, "that I ran away from home, it must have been in 1932, and went to a Hitler rally. I must admit, even today that it was an experience. I was swept away. First there were the masses of people; that was very captivating to be in the middle of it all. But it was also Hitler."[24] Nationalism as such, he understood, satisfied deep cravings for community. He systematized these insights about the power of this new mass politics, this secular religion with its "Holy Mountains," monuments, flags, myths, and symbols, in his *The Nationalization of the Masses*.[25] This same empathic duality also applied to Zionism and Israel.

No one better demonstrated how Zionism embodied precisely those categories that George had exposed. "This new [Zionist] Jew," he wrote, so different to the ghetto Jew—beautiful, muscular, filled with energy—actually "represented a normalization, an assimilation to general middle-class ideals and stereotypes."[26] Yet he identified with the very nationalist myths, symbols, and stereotypes he had done so much to demystify. As he candidly admitted, "I was far from consistent. My own engagement in Israel told of the need for a more concrete embodiment of my Jewish identity; my accelerated heartbeat when I witnessed the swearing-in of Israeli paratroopers on Masada—Israel's Holy Mountain— reveals the attraction of an emotional commitment even for one who prides himself on the use of his reason. Perhaps such a reaction is based upon the experience and the study of antisemitism and its constant denial of Jewish manhood—however, once again, ideal and reality differ even within my own person."[27] "I remember," he adds, "vividly my joy on my first visit when I saw sturdy, self-confident Jews, ... though this was, once again, a stereotype," and concluded that "I myself was far from immune to the irrational forces which as a historian I deplored and that especially when it came to that group which I regard as my own."[28]

Part of this affirmation may well have as one of its sources a largely unstated appreciation of the need for organized force and collective self-defense in a very imperfect, murderous world: a corrective, perhaps to the blind spot he identified among the *Bildung* intellectuals who habitually misdiagnosed the brutal political realities that confronted them. "There was," he reflected in his autobiography, "always a certain pull toward realism, to the feeling that if one did not belong to a strong nation one could slide back into the statelessness I had experienced."[29] But the commitment was even more primordial than that. Ultimately, this great unmasker, this champion of reason, would put his (historically conditioned) "special bond with his fellow Jews" quite simply in terms of "love."[30] Indeed, while initially agreeing with Hannah Arendt's statement that one could only love individuals, not whole peoples, Mosse—always ruthlessly self-honest—admitted that he had been "disingenuous, for I did feel a sense of belonging, close to love even as I taught the lasting importance of rationality and of the Enlightenment."[31] In the end, as he put it, "an emotional engagement always threatened that liberalism to which I tried to remain faithful."[32] Aware that Zionism embodied the normalizing nationalist and bourgeois ideals and stereotypes that, as he put it, he "otherwise ... professed to dislike," he "could not help myself; faced with this Zionist ideal my reason and historical knowledge were overcome."[33] Indeed, at one point he even went so far as to define his Zionism "as social redemption, as personal redemption."[34]

I want very briefly now to say something, not so much about George's legacy—his continuing extraordinary influence, especially in Italy, or the ways in which he has entered (or been ignored by) contemporary scholarship—but rather about the afterlife of his work, how it stands in relation to some current wider cultural and political developments. The first concerns his thinking on masculinity and sexuality. In his *The Image of Man*, George was certainly aware of significant positive developments, especially the continuing erosion of the traditional masculine stereotype. I have no doubt that he would have been positively delighted by many contemporary changes, the radical extent of which I do not think he foresaw, and which can be considered without exaggeration to be revolutionary. Within an almost unbelievably quick time, the constraints of sexual respectability have been remarkably relaxed. At least in many Western countries, gay marriage has become a legal fact of life. Seventy percent of the American public now supports the possibility of electing a gay president.[35] Older sexual notions and stereotypes that previously elicited distaste, even disgust, are dissolving before our eyes. Not too long ago the very idea of a grouping called LGBTQ+ would have been unrecognizable; today it has become a familiar, almost domesticated, collective noun. Toward the end of his life, George still felt it necessary to repeatedly warn: "Beware of normalcy." In this regard, one might argue that the tables have been triumphantly turned. One measure of this success is demonstrated by an Israeli Orthodox anti-LGBT, pro-heterosexual family organization called *Gevanim*, which recently posted huge billboards in Jerusalem encouraging people to "Have the courage to be normal"![36] (This is reminiscent of James Thurber's quip, "Must you be as non-conformist as everyone else.")

For all that, George never had simplistic illusions about sexuality and its cultural forms. Whatever positive changes there might be, it was difficult, he maintained, to envision either the downfall or even the radical challenge to respectability and a masculinity that provided the cement for order and social cohesion.[37] Indeed, he emphasized that middle-class masculinity, with its ideals of self-control, fair play, courage, and quiet strength, were of obvious value and often served to tame exaggerated displays of male power.[38] Regardless of their newly found confidence, George commented, many homosexuals continue to accept the ideal and "accent their own masculinity."[39] But most importantly, he foresaw that a clear reaction to these cited positive developments would set in. Quite apart from the persistence of traditional homophobic attitudes and legislation in large areas of the non-Western world, the inevitable countermovement in the West is underway. As both gayness and feminism gain the higher moral and political ground, what has broadly come to be called a major "crisis in masculinity" has set in. This is hardly the place to rehearse its numerous manifestations. The *Guardian* lately noted that one extreme symptom of the accompanying feeling of male inadequacy has been a mass demand for surgically enlarged penises.[40] Some high-profile politicians regularly preach the values of manly men, using themselves as examples. We have all seen pictures of Vladimir Putin's bare-chested muscular body astride a horse and heard Donald Trump trumping the prowess of his sexual organ. President Jair Bolsonaro of Brazil is a self-described homophobe (who is also concerned about the high number of penis amputations in his country). The party spokesman of the Spanish radical right movement VOX and a former judge, Francisco Serrano, claims that at present there "is a genocide against men, citing high suicide rates of men as proof."[41] Various intellectuals too are helping to articulate both the crisis and its possible remedies. They reach audiences of millions. Most prominent is the Canadian self-help writer Jordan B. Peterson—according to his book cover, dubbed by the *New York Times* as "the most influential public intellectual in the world right now"—who laments that the "west has lost faith in masculinity," hails the inherent value of patriarchy and denounces the "murderous equity doctrine" of women.[42]

Yet however the ultimate changes in the sexual arena work out, there remains George's lasting insight regarding society's insistence on clear definitional order, which, in some guise or another, necessitates outsiders. Indeed, the renegotiation of boundaries in our present reality is certainly not restricted to sexuality, although they are typically related: the most dominant among them, the central cry against immigration, is typically tied to antifeminist and antigay postures and legislation and increasingly also to racist and anti-Jewish (though often pro-Israel) attitudes. We are thus currently going through convulsions of identifying, labeling, and excluding any number of internal and external outsiders. All this brings us to the overriding question of nationalism, to which all these outsider issues are intrinsically related. Need one elaborate on the current nationalist populism, the coarsening of political discourse, the frightening threats to the very fabric of democracy, the neo-fascist atmosphere that is inflaming so many parts of the world? I do not want to intrude on Aleida Assmann's topic in the present book, "Can Mosse's Europe Be Saved?"; I just want to mention that some time ago I wrote that George's "Europe has always been peopled by strange and powerful forces threatening to engulf its precious but fragile humanist heritage. His cultural history is animated by a complex but unabashed commitment to that heritage; his work ... has also made clear its radical precariousness."[43] Of course, this is true. But in the afterlife of his work, I am less interested in discussing George's possible analysis of our present crises and dilemmas than in exploring his putative way of dealing with and solving the dilemmas of nationalism.

He understood, of course, that nationalism satisfied both legitimate and deep longings of community and could not be wished away. The idea, therefore, was not to abolish but rather humanize it, make it less aggressive, more inclusive. George even had in mind a model for that ideal, suggesting how that could be accomplished. He insisted on a principled distinction between "patriotic" and "integral" nationalism. Thus he argued that in eighteenth-century Germany, the idea of friendship, which symbolized the autonomy of personal relationships and the acceptance of individual differences, and the free exercise of citizenship coexisted with a sense of patriotism and national identification. Solidarity rather than domination prevailed. It was only in the nineteenth century that integral nationalism arose, with its controlling claims of totality that gave rise to a homogenized and ever-increasing brutalized conformity. As one example of a contemporary possibility of returning to the earlier promise of an eighteenth-century-like patriotic nationalism, he looked to those Central European Jewish intellectuals (like Hugo Bergmann, Hans Kohn, Robert Weltsch, and Gershom Scholem) who formed Brit Shalom in the interwar years and who preached a binational ethical solution to the Jewish-Arab problem. As outsiders and victims of integral nationalism, George argued, these Jews were more able to become "advocates of an alternative nationalism which might keep its earlier promise."[44] Indeed, as late as 1986 he continued to believe that this alternative remained a real possibility:

> That I have spent so much time investigating that nationalism which has made the Jews one of its principal victims does not mean that a nobler nationalism cannot exist—indeed, it has existed in the past ... based upon solidarity rather than aggression. Today, it seems almost forgotten that it was precisely the majority of Zionists in Eastern and Western Europe who for a long time continued into the twentieth century this noble but archaic nationalism. ... There would have been every reason for our own state [sic!] to have capitulated before this [exclusive, aggressive, and self-satisfied] modern nationalism, but it has not done so, the battle is still joined. ... We have a great opportunity based upon Jewish history and the history of Zionism to uphold the ideal of a nationalism whose essence is solidarity not exclusiveness.[45]

Ameliorating nationalism by reasserting the primacy of personal relationships and solidarity over domination and exclusion are surely admirable sentiments. As a great admirer of George, I certainly would identify with them. But, sadly, the present situation in Israel and in parts of Europe and the United States (not to mention a range of Middle Eastern and African countries) does not provide much hope of success for this vision. Indeed, the eighteenth-century patriotism of friendship and the free exercise of citizenship, of which George spoke, I fear, was really a very pale form of nationalism. Indeed, I rather think it was doomed from the beginning. George too, at certain moments, recognized that the combined ideals of this patriotism—liberation from foreign rule and self-determination—were incompatible. Even among its most progressive, early prophets, he wrote, "national liberation undermined ... democratic self-determination."[46] And in any case, in the context of nationalism, what is meant by "solidarity" and self-determination? Solidarity for and among whom? Potentially, the very notion of "self-determination" may negate the "self" of who is considered "other." At a different time, George himself expressed a certain skepticism. "What," he asked, "does self-determination mean? There are certain historical circumstances under which self-determination is impossible or self-determination leads to more conflicts than it solves."[47]

I wonder if today, however sadly, George would agree that under present circumstances his humanizing, expansive vision appears dim indeed. We cannot know. But what we do know is that in his own person he was the very incarnation of that vision.

And so, I want to conclude with a few comments about George simply as a person. As much as people are intertwined with, and revealed in, their work, this far from exhausts them. And with George it is his sheer, overflowing humanity—so refreshingly different from the usual, dry, run-of-the-mill academic—that so shone out. It was apparent in his charismatic teaching: passionate, direct, magnetically engaging, engendering thought through often outrageous but always illuminating assertions. His humanity was apparent in his insatiable curiosity, his personalizing of relationships, his friendships with people of all ages and persuasions. Anyone who has met him will tell you of the enormous and lasting impact he had on them. For those of us who were close to him, George entered into the core of our being (so much so that when I talk about him, I am compelled to do so in his accent and inimitable way of talking). This book may be a commemoration of his birth one hundred years ago, but for many of us, what is more significant is that twenty years after his death, he remains a constant, living presence.

The longevity of his posthumous presence is surely quite exceptional. What explains this? I suppose everyone has their own "George." As such, I can only speak personally of "my" George. It is only because of him that I became an academic and my life has taken the path it has (but that is a different story). Quite apart from all the other qualities enumerated in this introduction, "my George" was, above all, the hilarious, irreverent George, with the booming voice, the sometimes raised, bemused eyebrows, and the twinkle in his eyes. Who but George could worry about squirrels laying eggs in his attic or could sell the Mosse Schenkendorf estate to a Romanian prince called Count Dracula? We all have our George stories. One of my favorites occurred on the night I first met him. This was at the time of the 1968 student revolution when the University of Wisconsin–Madison was on political fire with rowdy demonstrations and disruptions. I asked him how he could possibly teach under such impossible circumstances. He looked at me and said, "Oh, Steve, no student revolution begins before two in the afternoon. I teach at ten in the morning!" I knew at that moment that he would be my mentor.

It is then his unique person as much as his scholarship that is George's real legacy. Of course, one cannot institutionalize humanity, especially George's special caring brand. But I have no doubt that attempting to emulate his passion for scholarship, his unending curiosity, his wonderful sense of the absurd, his instinctive personalizing of relationships, and his genius for friendship is to do that legacy proud.

Notes

1. George L. Mosse, *The Image of Man: The Creation of Modern Masculinity* (New York: Oxford University Press, 1996), 13.
2. George L. Mosse, *Confronting History: A Memoir* (Madison: University of Wisconsin Press, 2000), 142.
3. Mosse, *Confronting History*, 171.
4. Mosse, *Confronting History*, 219.
5. George L. Mosse, *George Mosse on the Occasion of His Retirement: 17.6.85* (Jerusalem: Hebrew University, 1986), xxviii.
6. Walter Laqueur, "Foreword," in Mosse, *Confronting History*, x.
7. See my "George Mosse and Jewish History," *German Politics and Society* 18, no. 4 (Winter 2000): 46–57.
8. George L. Mosse, *The Crisis of German Ideology: Intellectual Origins of the Third Reich* (Madison: University of Wisconsin Press, 2021), 310.
9. See Mosse interview with David Strassler in "Antisemitism," *Jerusalem Post*, 17 September 1991, 8.
10. George L. Mosse, *Nationalism and Sexuality: Middle-Class Morality and Sexual Norms in Modern Europe* (Madison: University of Wisconsin Press, 2020), 184–94.
11. Mosse, *Confronting History*, 182.
12. George L. Mosse, *German Jews beyond Judaism* (Cincinnati: Hebrew Union College Press, 1985) 3.
13. Mosse, *Confronting History*, 184.
14. George L. Mosse, "Jewish Emancipation: Between *Bildung* and Respectability," in Mosse's essay collection, *Confronting the Nation: Jewish and Western Nationalism* (Waltham, MA: Brandeis University Press, 1993), 131–45.
15. Mosse, *Confronting History*, 174.
16. Laqueur, "Foreword," in Mosse, *Confronting History*, xi.
17. Peter Jelavich, "Popular Entertainment and Mass Media: The Central Arenas of German-Jewish Cultural Engagement," in *The German Jewish Experience Revisited*, ed. Steven Aschheim and Vivian Liska (Berlin: De Gruyter, 2015), 103–16.
18. See her article "German Jewish History: Back to *Bildung* and Culture," in *What History Tells: George L. Mosse and the Culture of Modern Europe*, ed. Stanley G. Payne, David J. Sorkin, and John S. Tortorice (Madison: University of Wisconsin Press, 2004), 223–38.
19. Steven Aschheim, "German Jews beyond Bildung and Liberalism: The Radical Jewish Revival in the Weimar Republic," in *Culture and Catastrophe: German and Jewish Confrontations with National Socialism and Other Crises* (New York: New York University Press, 1996), 31–44.
20. Mosse, *Confronting History*, 207.
21. Mosse, *Confronting History*, 180.
22. Mosse, *Confronting History*, 180.
23. Mosse, *Confronting History*, 70.

24. Quoted in Emilio Gentile, "A Provisional Dwelling: The Origin and Development of the Concept of Fascism in Mosse's Historiography" in Payne, Sorkin, and Tortorice, *What History Tells*, 44.

25. George L. Mosse, *The Nationalization of the Masses: Political Symbolism and Mass Movements in Germany from the Napoleonic Wars through the Third Reich* (Madison: University of Wisconsin Press, 2023). See also Mosse interview with Michael Ledeen: George L. Mosse, *Nazism: A Historical and Comparative Analysis of National Socialism* (New Brunswick, NJ: Transaction Books, 1978).

26. Mosse, *Confronting History*, 190.

27. Mosse, *Confronting History*, 185.

28. Mosse, *Confronting History*, 190.

29. Mosse, *Confronting History*, 191.

30. Mosse, *Confronting History*, 172.

31. Mosse, *Confronting History*, 191.

32. Mosse, *Confronting History*, 191.

33. Mosse, *Confronting History*, 190.

34. See his "Response" in Mosse, *George Mosse on the Occasion of His Retirement*, xxix.

35. Carrie Dann, "Almost 70 Percent of Americans OK with Gay Presidential Candidate, Poll Finds," NBC News, 2 April 2019.

36. Shuki Sadeh, "Who's behind Anti-LGBT, Anti-Reform Signs in Cities?," *Ha'aretz*, 10 April 2019, 6.

37. Mosse, *The Image of Man*, 193.

38. Mosse, *The Image of Man*, 15. Similar observations are peppered throughout the book. Given this appreciation, it is interesting to speculate what George would have thought of Harvey G. Mansfield's modest defense of manliness, "that irrational manliness deserves to be endorsed by reason," and his conclusion that "women should be free to enter on careers but not compelled—yet they should also be expected to be women. And men should be expected, not merely free, to be manly. A free society cannot survive if we are so free that nothing is expected of us." Harvey G. Mansfield, *Manliness* (New Haven, CT: Yale University Press, 2006), ix, 244. Strangely, but perhaps also significantly, Mosse's work goes entirely unmentioned in this book.

39. Mosse, *The Image of Man*, 190.

40. Tom Usher, "Want a Larger Penis? Then Your Problems May Be Upstairs, not Downstairs," *Guardian*, 16 April 2019.

41. Elif Shafak, "From Spain to Turkey, the Rise of the Far Right Is a Clash of Cultures not Civilisations," *Guardian*, 6 May 2019.

42. Pankaj Mishra, "The Crisis in Modern Masculinity," *Guardian*, 17 March 2018: "The most lethal consequences of this mimic machismo unfolded in the first decades of the 20th century. 'Never before and never afterwards,' as historian George Mosse, the pioneering historian of masculinity, wrote, 'has masculinity been elevated to such heights as during fascism.'"

43. See my piece "George Mosse: Nationalism, Jewishness, Zionism and Israel," in "George L. Mosse, Nationalism, and the Crisis of Liberal Democracies," special issue, *Journal of Contemporary History* 56, no. 4 (October 2021): 854–63.

44. See his piece "Friendship and Nationhood: About the Promise and Failure of German Nationalism," *Journal of Contemporary History* 17, no. 2 (1982): 364.

45. "Response," in Mosse, *George Mosse on the Occasion of His Retirement*, xxx–xxxi.

46. George L. Mosse, *Can Nationalism Be Saved? About Zionism, Rightful and Unjust Nationalism* (Rehovot: Yad Chaim Weizmann, 1995), 163.

47. See "Mosse: Federation Is Best Hope," *Capital Times*, 27 August 1979, quoted in the booklet *Finally Home: The Legacy of George L. Mosse at UW–Madison*, 13.

Part I
GEORGE L. MOSSE (1918−1999)

1

Civilizing the Nation

Can Mosse's Europe be Saved?

ALEIDA ASSMANN

Around 1990 I had the good luck to come across the work of George L. Mosse. That was before I started my academic career in 1993 at the University of Konstanz, when I still referred to myself as a freelance housewife. I have to thank Ulrich Raulff for this contact, who at that time was the editor of the Campus Verlag. Raulff was publishing a German translation of Mosse's *German Jews beyond Judaism* and was looking for someone to write a preface to the book. To my great surprise he assigned me with this task, and I felt most honored and privileged. Mosse's book appeared with my preface in 1992 and, one year later, my own book *Shaping National Memory—A Short History of the German Idea of Bildung* came out in the same series. My work included many references to Mosse's book.

A little later I had a chance to meet George L. Mosse at a restaurant in Heidelberg. He was in very good spirits and full of amazing anecdotes about participating incognito at a meeting of right-wing nationalists at some German *Ritterburg* under the false name "Count something or other," in order to do undercover ethnography of these groups. When I told him that I had just started a job at the University of Konstanz, he informed me immediately that the Konstanz bridge used to have a medieval "Judensau" as part of its ornamentation. This sculpture must have disappeared immediately after the war and might lie on the bottom of the river Rhine. To this day, I have not found anyone in Konstanz to corroborate this piece of information; it is obviously still a strict taboo. A little later, I had the chance to listen to Mosse lecture in Jerusalem. He was filling in for the German historian Moshe Zimmermann that week. Mosse stepped in and taught a class on the symbols of nation building, referring to marching, flags, and hymns, performing all of them in a lively way, transforming the seminar room into a rapt audience. I am delighted that almost three decades later I was invited to participate in this book, which gave me the chance to rediscover further dimensions in Mosse's works.

The Perspective of the Outsider

George L. Mosse was a pioneer in many ways. He became a professor of modern history in the United States at a time when this field was still exclusively in the hands of—how shall I put it? "Native" doesn't sound right; let's say nonimmigrant U.S. scholars. As he explained later in an interview, in the 1960s, two fields in the humanities were still exclusively reserved for non-Jews: namely history and English. The first two Jewish professors in English at Yale University, Harold Bloom and Geoffrey Hartman, started as outsiders of the Anglo-Saxon tradition, turning their marginal status into an advantage by choosing topics that had been sidelined by the canonization of modernism, namely the Romantics. Bloom wrote about Percy Bysshe Shelley, Hartman about William Wordsworth. In doing so, both undermined the disciplinary canon by rediscovering the neglected Romantics and investigating their works. Mosse was not only among the first Jewish scholars in the prestigious field of modern history but also deviated from the course of mainstream historiography by discovering new topics in the 1960s like racism, body history, gender issues, and, not to forget, collective memory. He thus started a discourse that emerged in academia only in the 1980s and 1990s after a generational change when members of the 1968 generation created and established new subfields, such as oral history, women's history, and the history of sexuality, and adopted a cultural studies approach.

George L. Mosse's interests and projects as a scholar are tightly connected to his biography. He was born in Berlin in 1918 and became a refugee in 1933 when he was fifteen years old. This was a role that he had never considered for himself when he grew up. He had associated refugees with the Eastern European Jews who settled in the Scheunenviertel in Berlin. When at the age of fourteen Mosse became interested in Judaism and was attracted to Zionism or even wanted to become a rabbi, his father, Hans Lachmann-Mosse, put his son in his car and sent him with his driver to this district crowded with poor and orthodox families from Eastern Europe who were fleeing from pogroms and extreme poverty. This excursion was designed to give George an impression of Jewish immigrants as the exotic other. Until their unimaginable expulsion, the integration and assimilation of the Mosse family presented a totally different picture in the Weimar Republic, namely, that of the highly successful bourgeois family well connected in business relations and deeply anchored in German culture. The sudden uprooting and the violent closure of their Berlin existence was a deep shock that impacted Mosse's whole life.

A nation, he explained later, "is for me as good as its passport."[1] Although he acquired new passports, a "refugee mentality" remained with him throughout his life. He distinguished between his own biographical experience and the persecution and extermination of the Jews in general but also felt connected to and fully identified with their fate: "I cannot say that National Socialism wrecked my life, but it has perpetrated such horrors on Jews."[2] And he continued: "We [in German it is 'Man'] were always sitting in trains that left, and these are the years of exile. Therefore I remain an eternal emigrant."[3] Throughout his life, he retained a distinct aloofness and distance from his environment, which sharpened his perception and made him such an outstanding observer of the topics that he investigated. In Mosse's writings, this perspective of the outsider is part and parcel of the great project of Jewish intellectuals in Germany, which he defined in one of his books as "building a dam of scholarly and intellectual authority against the flood that is threatening to drown all rational and educated minds."[4]

Mosse was different from other historians because his "lived experience" was determined by various exclusions: in terms of Nazi racism he was the other as a Jew, in terms of nations and nationalism he remained an "eternal emigrant," and in terms of narrow bourgeois respectability he was the other because he was gay. As an outsider, Mosse remained highly conscious of social conventions that are unconsciously absorbed and internalized and was able to turn into objects of his study those national ideals and cultural norms that usually remain invisible because they are meant to be fully adapted and internalized. He referred to racism as the "secular religion" of the Nazi state and saw antisemitism not as a by-product but as the location of the obsession with racial selection and the gigantic project of extermination at the very center of National Socialism. Even after the war, Mosse still experienced forms of antisemitism in the United States. He was confronted with restricted access to hotels or received well-intended letters of recommendation that noted he had good manners despite his being a Jew.[5]

Mosse was relieved to see this rigid mental regime break up in the 1960s. Still, he had a very sober and realistic view of the continuity of racist mental habits. The common denominator between Mosse's two big topics, namely racism and repressive social norms, lies in notions about purity and a deep fear of anything that can contaminate a genuine core or substance. His great innovation was to lay bare the structure of bourgeois respectability as a repressive system that was also built on the exclusion of the other, this time not the racial but the social, cultural, and sexual outsider. Mosse had to hide his sexual orientation in the United States until the 1970s; it would have prevented him from making a career at a university. The repressive force of respectability was part of a strict ordering of family relations that clearly defined and sanctified the holy unit of the family, based on rigid gender roles and forms of sexuality. What was excluded on these grounds was stigmatized as unnatural, asocial, and deeply threatening to the persistence of the family and the state. Mosse's triple "excentric positionality"—to borrow a term from Helmuth Plessner—sharpened his sensibility and led him to insights that were far ahead of his time.[6]

German nationalism, for Mosse, went hand in hand with a code of bourgeois respectability. He saw this development in a long historical continuity. The "tightening of bourgeois manners and morals, and their eventual triumph, at first mainly affected those who came from the middle class."[7] But he observed that these precepts quickly spread up and down the social scale. He could show that the regime of bourgeois respectability coexisted with extremely different and even contrary political frames such as that of the Nazi state, postwar West Germany, and the German Democratic Republic (GDR). Mosse emphasized that the GDR was "a very bourgeois state, dominated by the norm of respectability.... Everything was so orderly, respectable, proper and bourgeois.... If you want to promote a "heile Welt, heil und gesund," then you have to generate prejudices." He pointed to the common ground of norms of behavior in vastly different political systems, commenting: "I don't see that the GDR has deviated from (this) norm when it came to bourgeois respectability."[8]

Mosse looked at societies from the point of view of what they exclude. "The enemy is always an outsider," he wrote.[9] For this reason he developed a new vantage point for the historian, namely, that of the outsider, taking them as a measure for the true moral standard of a society. His moral yardstick is the social position of the homosexual. He compares different countries and praises the Dutch as most progressive and open, because they respect homosexuality and assigned it a place in their society and academe at a time when Americans were only tolerating it. For Mosse, lived experience and research go hand in hand. In this case, he explicitly claimed for himself the status of a pioneer: "I was the first who has written about homosexuality!"[10] In his case research became an important tool for eroding the repressive silence of respectability and creating a public discourse that eventually led to a new sensibility and new social norms that created a new Europe. In this respect, Mosse was also an activist whose writings helped to transform a repressive code of behavior into one that respects diversity and includes the outsider in a new liberal framework. "What we are still missing," he wrote, "is a history of the outsider in bourgeois society, including emancipated women, lesbians, gays, Sinti and Roma, asocials. We must not exclude these things, we need to bring them together. The anti-type is as important as the ideal type itself. The one cannot exist without the other."[11]

The academic focus on the anti-type is so important because, for Mosse, he is the touchstone of the quality of civil society. To respect and integrate the outsider, civil society has to overcome not only the ideology of racism but also the ideologies of bourgeois respectability and uncontrolled capitalism.[12] Unlike so many of his colleagues, he did not believe in ordering the flow of time in clear-cut patterns of periodization. His focus on ideologies, mental maps, and habits taught him that cultural patterns can be tenacious and ready to return if the circumstances change. Mosse witnessed with great relief the loosening of the rules of bourgeois respectability and the growing respect for the rights of minorities and outsiders. "This is a great progress that strengthens the belief in human dignity."[13] But he remained cautious: "There are no radical ruptures in history when everything changes. There are long continuities. What vanishes in the West may turn up again in the East. Nothing disappears, some things are repressed, forbidden, and punished. I am in favor of anti-racist laws. This is the only thing that today can create a barrier against the growth of extreme nationalism."[14]

Mosse was a pioneer in many directions. In this chapter, I want to focus my attention on a field that I have hitherto mentioned only in passing, that is, memory studies. His emphasis on continuities across historical ruptures and the caesuras of periodization is already an important hint in this direction: "Nothing disappears," he writes, "some things are repressed, forbidden, and punished." He was obviously quite aware that there are other dynamics involved that are also worth the attention of the historian. This again sets him apart from other historians who read sources, register dates, and reconstruct events but hardly pay attention to the minds and emotions of those who are involved. Mosse is not primarily concerned with the making of history but, instead, looks at the way in which history is perceived, experienced, and remembered.

The Myth of the War Experience as Key to Understanding the History of the Twentieth Century

Let me introduce George L. Mosse as a pioneer in memory studies. His engagement with the consequences and iconography of war goes back to the 1970s and evolved during research stays in Australia in 1979 and in Israel in 1986. In his book *Fallen Soldiers: Reshaping the Memory of the World Wars* (1990), the word "memory" already appears prominently in the title, although at the time it had not yet become an analytic tool or a term of common reference. In the acknowledgments, Mosse mentions "Dr. J. M. Winter of Pembroke College, Cambridge University" with whom—no doubt as we can imagine today—the dialogue "has been especially rewarding over the years." He also mentions the work of German historian Reinhart Koselleck on war monuments. Mosse's central focus as a historian was the nation as an agent in history, including nation building, nationalism, and transformations of the nation. As a cultural historian he investigated these themes on a much broader basis than his colleagues, paying attention to the gendered body and social practices, to rites and symbols, and not to forget, to the role of emotions.

Instead of writing another history of the Great War, Mosse focused on the memory-making of this war and studied carefully the ways in which this conflict was prolonged and projected into the postwar years. Memory, he found, is a worthy object of study, because it is not irrelevant or innocent at all but, rather, an effective medium for shaping experience and politics. Depending on the shape that the memory of the First World War would be given, it could turn either toward grief and, thus, into a way of ending the war or toward the reinflammation of emotions and, thus, into a way of continuing it into the postwar period. Although the ceasefire on 11 November 1918 had been a huge relief, the war was not so easily terminated. Mosse's point of departure was that during and after the First World War, the concept of the nation itself underwent a deep transformation. Mechanical warfare, the daily encounter with mass death, and the loss of thirteen million soldiers had a tremendous impact on the entire population. It lingered in the hearts and minds of the people and demanded new responses. A huge gap had opened between the horror and the glory of war, and it was a great challenge for all the nations involved to fill that gap by creating symbols that helped to mask and transcend death in war. In this situation, all nations adopted "the memories of those veterans" as true and legitimate "who saw the war as containing positive elements, and not of those who rejected the war."[15] As the emphasis was on the glorification and not on the general tragedy of the war, the nations constructed "a myth which would draw the sting from death in war and emphasize the meaningfulness of heroic fighting and sacrifice."[16]

The result of this memory-making was what Mosse termed "the Myth of the War Experience" (MWE) that displaced the reality of war experience and refashioned it into a sacred experience, involving new "saints and martyrs, places of worship and a heritage to emulate."[17] This sacralization of war went hand in hand with the sacralization of the nation. Mosse did not use the term "myth" to expose and explode it as a lie. Deconstruction of the myth was the job of Erich Maria Remarque's *All Quiet on the Western Front* (1929) and the postwar generation and international anti-war movement. Mosse, on the contrary, was interested in the circumstances and ways in which it was constructed and how it shaped human behavior and the self-image of generations and nations. He wrote, "It was the accounts of the volunteers which were most apt to become part of the national canon" and conceded that this was only a small minority, "but as other volunteers remained silent, it was the minority's poetry and prose which attracted attention."[18]

The European nations developed different versions of the myth. While the victorious nations France and Britain transformed it into the dominant emotion of mourning, in German politics, the myth was saturated with resentment and eventually became the medium to prolong the Great War into peacetime and directly into the next war. Here, the memory of the Great War was kidnapped by the National Socialist state that raised its version of the MWE into its central ideology: National Socialism became "a manly faith steeled in war."[19] This furthered a new brutalization that invaded public life. The nascent democratic spirit in the Weimar Republic was up against a radical mode of constant political mobilization. The emphasis on heroic action, the normative ideal of male manliness and a vocabulary of "friend against foe" became more and more dominant, leaving little space for the normalization of postwar life and a civil spirit: "The vocabulary of political battle, the desire to utterly destroy the political enemy, and the way in which these adversaries were pictured, all seem to continue the First World War mostly against a set of different, internal foes."[20] Without ever mentioning Carl Schmitt, Mosse aptly characterized in this passage his "concept of the political" that has become so popular today and is generally invoked irrespective of the political climate from which this thinking emerged.

For Mosse, it was the business of the historian not to deconstruct and get easily rid of ideas but to analyze how ideas are constructed to serve the purposes of a society and to show how such constructs gain influence, hold sway over collectives and individuals, and become political weapons that influence the course of history. His use of the term myth was not that of Roland Barthes but closer to that of the anthropologist Bronisław Malinowski, who in the 1920s defined it as a founding narrative or story that backs up collective consciousness and identity. Myth in this sense stands for the stories we live by, stories that interpret and express our values and explain where we come from, who we are, or want to be. In exactly this sense, Mosse's "Myth of the War Experience" is a national narrative with religious overtones. Religious symbols were adopted and transformed not only to mask or justify the war experience but also to forge a cult of the dead that not only reinterpreted the past but was also to be transmitted from generation to generation, thus projecting its message and meaning into an indefinite future. "Remembering the dead" did not only mean honoring them retrospectively but also perpetuating forever the cult of their sacrifice and projecting it into an unlimited future. In this form, the memory of the Great War became the state ideology of the Third Reich.

One of the important effects of the MWE was that Germans perceived the Second World War in terms of the First World War—not as a war of ruthless aggression and expansion, but as a patriotic war of defense under ultimate threat. "How was it possible," asks Nicholas Stargardt, another historian of emotions and perception, in a recent book that "the Germans took a brutal war of conquest for a war of defense? How could they see themselves as endangered patriots and not as warriors for Hitler's manly race?"[21] I can offer a piece of evidence from a biographical interview that I conducted with a German who was drafted into the Second World War while still in school at the age of fifteen and, after 1945, spent a year as a prisoner of war in Siberia. His comments can show how different historical layers and irreconcilable positions and perspectives can coincide within one individual.[22]

My informant, Günther Thiele, was born in 1928. In his account of his formative experiences when growing up in Germany in the interwar years he testifies to the long shadow of the First World War that was maintained and reconstructed with considerable emphasis in intergenerational communication and public education: "I grew up in a time of exaggerated power rivalry among the nations. Germany was surrounded by enemies and thus particularly threatened in its central position in Europe. We had learnt from the old Romans: 'If you aspire to have peace, you better prepare for war!' Defending the Fatherland was a self-evident duty." At the age of fifteen, together with his schoolmates, he was drafted to serve at the air defense batteries and spent the final year in the war and another one as a prisoner of war in Siberia. After his return, Thiele became a history teacher and, together with a colleague, developed new principles for a democratic access to history for schoolteachers. He became a spirited educator who taught at a pedagogical institute with a pronounced mission to strengthen the individual and support the democratic institutions of postwar Germany. In his oral testimony, however, the ideological framing of his youth remains a fragment of the past side by side with Thiele's retrospective view of the Second World War as charged with today's hindsight: "Only after the raid on Poland did it become clear that Hitler used this strong patriotism for his geopolitical war in which he set the world on fire and committed unthinkable crimes." But why did the German population follow Hitler so dutifully on this murderous track? Thiele's comment is quite candid: "In my interpretation it was the hope for Germany's breakthrough to become a world power that also blinded the members of the former political elite."

To my mind, Mosse's work provides a coherent explanation for the false German perception of the Second World War: the MWE shaped the German perception and memory of the Second World War by "obliterating," which means literally "overwriting," it in the imagination of the people with the perception and memory of the First World War. Apparent still are the lingering effects and long-term consequences of this collective self-deceit, blocking German perception and emotions when it comes to the Polish and Russian victims of German aggression. It is only now, eighty years after the German assault on Poland, that there are plans to finally erect a monument in the center of Berlin for the Poles, Russians, and other victims of German aggression.[23]

How to Bring Wars to an End

At first, the MWE may sound rather far away from our contemporary problems. But it is not history, as I want to argue, it is still memory. History, wrote James Baldwin (and I am convinced that Mosse would have confirmed it), "is not merely something to be read. And it does not refer merely, or even principally, to the past. On the contrary, the great force of history comes from the fact that we carry it within us, are unconsciously controlled by it in many ways, and history is literally in the present in all that we do."[24] There is still emotional pressure in the unresolved issues that are part and parcel of the dynamics of forgetting and remembering and are thus a seminal part of an ongoing battle over emotions and values in Europe. The MWE is key to a better understanding of how wars are ended—or not ended. Mosse warned us: "There are no full-stops in history, when suddenly everything changes. There are long continuities in history."[25] With this wary and critical stance he alerted us to one of the most important questions that historians can ask, namely, how are wars ended? And what is the role that remembering and forgetting play in this process?

In Europe, the Myth of the War Experience was effectively ended after 1945 by forgetting it. Winston Churchill made this very clear in 1946 in a speech addressing young students at the university in Zurich on the future of Europe. In this speech, he explained the position of the Allies and argued that forgetting was the only way to a fresh start and a future for Europe: "We must all turn our backs upon the horrors of the past and look to the future. We cannot afford to drag forward across the years to come hatreds and revenges which have sprung from the injuries of the past. If Europe is to be saved from infinite misery, and indeed from final doom, there must be an act of faith in the European family and an act of oblivion against all the crimes and follies of the past."[26] This strategy of forgetting can be called a "Schlussstrich policy"; it draws a finishing line under the past and lets bygones be bygones. In Europe it laid the ground for transnational cooperation and was gladly accepted by the Germans. Such a policy of forgetting has worked many times in history after civil wars, when two parties were fighting in a more or less symmetrical power relationship.[27] When warfare, however, is accompanied by atrocities perpetrated against civilians and defenseless minorities, when, in other words, wars become genocidal, the policy of forgetting has a serious drawback, because it supports the perpetrators and harms the victims. The forgetting policy of the finishing line worked in Germany after 1945 for four decades, empowering the transnational union of a new Europe, but it did not bring the war to an end.

This Schlussstrich policy ended in the 1980s and 1990s. Because of a generational change and the fall of the wall, a new era started that saw an overwhelming return of repressed and excluded memories that had been held at bay by the social, cultural, and political frames constructed in the period of the Cold War. I know what I am talking about because I grew up in this period, so here my assessment of the situation contains the voice of a historical witness. There were many ways in which the silenced past returned to European nations, cities, and families in the 1980s and 1990s. Here is a short overview of the events affecting the two Germanys.

The 1980s saw two seminal events. The first of these was the famous 1985 speech of German president Richard Weizsäcker in the parliament in Bonn forty years after the end of the war. In this speech, which was experienced as a historical moment in itself and has become a canonical reference, Weizsäcker, who had been a soldier of the Wehrmacht throughout the war and had defended his father before the Nuremberg Trials, persuaded the Germans to adopt a new national narrative that conceived of the end of the war no longer in the vocabulary of defeat and catastrophe but in terms of liberation and commemoration. This event was followed in 1986 by the so-called historians' debate in which scholars discussed with great agitation the question of how to deal with the Holocaust professionally. Would it eventually recede back into the historical archive as all other events of the past do or would it retain some kind of presence as an exceptional status assuming a normative force in memory?

The decade of the 1990s was, in the words of Annette Wieviorka, "the era of the witness."[28] A new technology and public medium was created in 1994 by the Shoah Visual History Foundation. It was initiated by Steven Spielberg who started a worldwide collection of video testimonies of Holocaust survivors in the analog format of the VHS cassette. An important social event was the exhibition on the crimes of the Wehrmacht that opened in Hamburg in 1995 and toured many German and European cities. In the same years, a new public political ritual was created and repeatedly performed. This "international politics of regret" showcased in public media events in which high statesmen and representatives of institutions apologized for crimes perpetrated in their past and acknowledged the victims. Next to oral testimony, exhibitions, and political confessions, the 1990s also saw a boost of historical scholarship. After the fall of the Iron Curtain, the opening of Eastern European archives gave rise to a new wave of historical scholarship on the history of the Second World War and the Holocaust. This had an important effect on the public memory in different European states in which the national narratives, built on pride and honor, became more dialogic, inclusive, and self-critical.

The new millennium started with the Stockholm Declaration in January 2000 by the new International Holocaust Remembrance Alliance (IHRA). This alliance of states introduced a new annual commemoration day, 27 January 1945, the date of the liberation of Auschwitz by the Red Army. All European Union (EU) countries are member states of the IHRA. Five years later in 2005, the Central Holocaust monument by Peter Eisenman was dedicated in the center of Berlin, which in the meantime had turned into the political capital of the reunified Germany.

Mosse died just before the new millennium in 1999. But he lived to see the fall of the wall and the beginning of the post–Cold War era. He closely observed the social and political changes in Europe and interpreted them as a successful form of bringing the Second World War to an end. He welcomed in particular the peace-oriented mindset of the younger generation of Germans: "For me, this is the great achievement of the Second World War that the Germans just don't want to fight any more! . . . So they have learned something from the Second World War after all. I cannot tell you how happy I am about this. What more do you want? To put it short: For German history, this is perhaps a turning point."[29]

So the Second World War was brought to an end after half a century, but this time not through a conscious collective act of forgetting, but through a collective will to remember. But what about the First World War? It returned after a hundred years not as a repressed memory but in the conscious format of a centenary commemoration. Public anniversaries mark particular dates and offer the chance to bring an historic event back into the present, not necessarily only for the mere continuation of a memory, but also for its reinspection and reinterpretation. This happened on a large scale in the 2014–18 commemoration period that brought the First World War back to European nations, an event that had been celebrated annually in some countries such as France,

Belgium, and Britain, while in others such as Germany or Austria it had dropped completely from memory, school curricula, and public consciousness. While on every 11 November, the day of the truce, the French, Belgians, and British mourn and commemorate their war dead, the Germans start their Carnival season!

President François Hollande's contribution to the commemoration day in 2014 was an impressive gift called the "Ring of Remembrance" in the north of France near Arras. It is an outstanding monument, not only in terms of its large scale but also in its design. The five hundred brass plates of the huge cyclical structure list the names of more than half a million fallen soldiers in the region irrespective of their origin, regiments, or nations, in alphabetical order. With his interest in the symbolism of war memorials, George L. Mosse would certainly have been fascinated with this innovation. It is a huge shift in the use and meaning of war monuments as it deviates radically from the traditional pattern. I call it a truly European monument because it is dedicated to all the dead and a shared mourning and memory of the mutual slaughter. This monument abstains from the former rhetoric of honor and glory and clearly brings the war to an end. We can even call it a monument to the death of the Myth of the War Experience.[30]

While President Hollande opted out of a narrow national tradition of commemoration, David Cameron did the opposite. When he presented his plans for the commemoration year in the Imperial War Museum in 2012, he opted out of the European commemorative network and strongly reinforced the British version of the Myth of the War Experience. In his "truly national commemoration," he included the colonial troops of the "glorious" former empire. Cameron praised repeatedly "the service and sacrifice" of the fallen soldiers and promised to project their memory for another hundred years. "Lest we forget!"[31] This British exceptionalism is also clearly visible in the continuing annual rites of 11 November in the United Kingdom, a national commemoration day that is celebrated with growing ardor, judging from the size of its central symbol, the red poppy. What fell totally flat, however, in Cameron's commemoration plans was a reference to the former allies and partners of the EU. This emphatic affirmation of national sovereignty was already a clear signal for British isolationism four years before Brexit. While the national MWE was laid to rest in France to make place for a shared and more dialogical European memory, it continues fervently in the United Kingdom, where such a shared memory is not in sight.

In Europe we can observe today that there are other instances where the Second World War has not been ended in the hearts and minds of the people but continues to exert pressure on the EU. In Italy, for instance, 25 April is a national anniversary day commemorating the end of the Second World War. On this day in 1945, the Allies liberated Italy by putting an end to the Fascist regime. In 2019, however, the defeat of the Fascist forces by the Allies was no longer a date to remember for former Deputy Prime Minister and Minister of the Interior Matteo Salvini from the right-wing Lega Nord. He spent the day taking selfies with his voters in an election campaign in Sicily. Ostentatiously disrespecting the commemoration date, Salvini complied with a new, or rather old, trend in Italy that has rehabilitated Mussolini as a national hero and put him back on his pedestal in public space.[32] His colleague Luigi Di Maio of the Five Star Movement, however, objected to Salvini's provocation and confirmed that he stands behind those who liberated Italy, the resisters and partisans. This dissent among the leaders of the state is a visible sign that the Second World War has not ended in this country. The eruptions of dissent and protest show that a shared dialogic narrative that acknowledges the perspectives of both sides in a new national frame is still missing. The public consensus about the national narrative in Italy is not yet consolidated and was thus opened again for new rounds of public debates. It may be difficult to hold the nation together without some kind of consensus about seminal events in its history. Imagine for instance a Germany in which half of the population believes that erecting a wall in Berlin and Europe was a good thing.

We can point to other instances in the EU today where a war has not yet been mentally and emotionally ended. Spain is an obvious example of a nation where the unity of the nation is under double stress of political polarization and regional partition. These issues have their origin in twentieth-century history, reaching back to the Spanish Civil War. The pact of silence in 1977 had been a pragmatic decision and had enabled a successful and sustainable transition to democracy. But today there are also symptoms that the policy of forgetting is not a permanent solution and that the war is far from having been ended. An exhumation movement started after 2000 when many families recovered the bones of their republican ancestors from mass graves and relocated and reburied them privately. This was an obvious signal that this war had not yet ended and a shared memory of this seminal event in the nation's history had not yet been achieved. Franco's massive monument in the Valley of the Fallen had been an attempt to end the war symbolically by sealing it with his stamp, but it turned out that he had not laid the memory of the past to rest. Instead, he left future generations a huge scar and a historical wound. In October 2019, Franco himself became the object of reburial when he was transferred from his monumental resting place to a family grave.

Reimagining the Nation

Mosse's work is of abiding importance today. He died at the threshold of the millennium, and since then we have seen a new upsurge of nationalism in a new transnational European framework. Until recently, the EU was the framework for this reinvention and self-domestication of the nation, coexisting not only in an economic union but also, as I just argued in a recent book, in strengthening shared values such as peacekeeping, democratic principles, a self-critical memory culture, and human rights.[33] But since 2015, we also saw a rollback, when out of the EU arose another transnational framework in support of new nationalisms that are built on de-democratization, ethnic homogeneity, and a self-serving national memory built on pride and honor, while targeting the "other" in terms of minorities and migrants.

In such times, Mosse's warning words acquire a new actuality and resonance: "The political Right considered itself to be the inheritor of the war experience, not just in Germany but throughout Europe, and the process of brutalization was closely linked to the spread of the Right's influence among the population." He noted in the 1980s that "the myth as a whole seems to have passed into European history." But he also added: "The future is open.... If nationalism as a civic religion is once more in the ascendant, the myth will, once again, accompany it."[34] For Mosse, "war itself was the great brutalizer," so it followed for him that "some of what has been called the civilizing process was undone under such pressure."[35] Brutalizing and civilizing are different tracks along which nations may aspire. We must not forget that many Europeans joined the fight in the First World War, seeing it as a recipe for regeneration through violence. What was denounced as a degenerate and effeminate culture was to be replaced by a strong ideal of heroic manliness and a collective assertion of "megalo-thymia," as Fukuyama would call it.[36] In civil times these values quickly lose their grip and are banished from the scene. But for how long? When Norbert Elias wrote about this topic, he spoke of a "process of civilization." Civilization, however, is not a process but a project, and only humans themselves can drive this process according to their cultural values and programs of continuous education. It is worth rereading Mosse and giving due thought to his important questions: How can wars be ended mentally and emotionally? Treaties and contracts are obviously not enough. Are there other means to pacify and recivilize societies?

Mosse's other central concept was that of the outsider. In times of mass migration and a world of resentment, hate, and the violation of human rights, this topic has come back with full force in new guises. While the code of respectability that was produced vilified the excluded, deviant outsider, the code of civility stands for the very opposite and has become the "litmus test" of a truly democratic society: it humanizes, includes, and respects the other. The code of bourgeois respectability was the very opposite of the code of respect. Outsiders, noted a hopeful Mosse around 1990, "receive more rights, also in Germany. I see here a great progress that strengthens the belief in human dignity. Today the sensibility for minorities and discrimination is much more developed than twenty years ago, when such topics had hardly appeared on the social agenda."[37] The outsider, for Mosse, was not only the product of sexual, ethnic, cultural, or other identity stereotypes. Everybody can easily fall into this position through mere poverty.

I will end my reflections on this powerful intellectual by citing a comment that speaks directly to our time. In his youth, Mosse opted for communism, a political orientation that he later changed for the concept of the "welfare state."[38] He remained highly critical of what he called "uncontrolled capitalism" and pointed emphatically to its social and economic patterns of exclusion. "We are getting more and more accustomed to homeless people—as though this was quite a natural state of being.... The rough tone in dealing with those who have suffered social damage has not at all changed.... That people are no longer trying to alleviate these problems, that they are taking this for granted—that is a new development. This is a new phenomenon of the 1980s. The real outsiders are those who are damaged by this system. We are coaxed by a system that promises each individual a fair chance. But this is not true."[39]

Reimagining the nation, strengthening liberal democracy, and protecting the dignity of precarious humans is a task that has lost nothing of its urgency. Mosse's writings, concepts, and ideas are a great inspiration in dealing with these challenges.

Notes

1. Irene Runge and Uwe Stelbrink, *"Ich bleibe Emigrant": Gespräche mit George L. Mosse* (Berlin: Dietz Verlag, 1991), 36. Unless otherwise noted, all translations are my own.

2. Runge and Stelbrink, *"Ich bleibe Emigrant,"* 36.

3. Runge and Stelbrink, *"Ich bleibe Emigrant,"* 36.

4. George L. Mosse, *Jüdische Intellektuelle in Deutschland: Zwischen Religion und Nationalismus* (Frankfurt am Main: Campus Verlag, 1992), 72.

5. Similar remarks relating to citizens and politicians of African American descent were made until recently in public. In the 2008 presidential Democratic primary, Joe Biden recommended Barack Obama as "the first sort of mainstream African-American who is articulate and bright and clean and a nice-looking guy." Today, politicians have to apologize for such comments. See Edwin Battistella, "The Art of the Political Apology," *Politico*, 7 May 2014, https://www.politico.com/magazine/story/2014/05/the-art-of-the-political-apology-106458.

6. Helmuth Plessner, *Conditio Humana*, Gesammelte Schriften VIII., 1. Auflage (Frankfurt am Main: Suhrkamp Taschenbuch Wissenschaft, 2003).
7. George L. Mosse, *Fallen Soldiers: Reshaping the Memory of the World Wars* (New York: Oxford University Press, 1990), 26.
8. Runge and Stelbrink, "Ich bleibe Emigrant," 85.
9. Runge and Stelbrink, "Ich bleibe Emigrant," 85.
10. Runge and Stelbrink, "Ich bleibe Emigrant," 90.
11. Runge and Stelbrink, "Ich bleibe Emigrant," 91.
12. Runge and Stelbrink, "Ich bleibe Emigrant," 97.
13. Runge and Stelbrink, "Ich bleibe Emigrant," 96.
14. Runge and Stelbrink, "Ich bleibe Emigrant," 95.
15. Mosse, *Fallen Soldiers*, 6.
16. Mosse, *Fallen Soldiers*, 6–7.
17. Mosse, *Fallen Soldiers*, 7.
18. Mosse, *Fallen Soldiers*, 8.
19. Mosse, *Fallen Soldiers*, 28.
20. Mosse, *Fallen Soldiers*, 160.
21. Nicholas Stargardt, *Der deutsche Krieg: Zwischen Angst, Zweifel und Durchhaltewillen—wie die Menschen den Zweiten Weltkrieg erlebten, 1913–1945* (Frankfurt: Fischer, 2017), 32.
22. Aleida Assmann, "Das Zeitzeugengespräch als Quelle und Zugang zur Vergangenheit: Erinnerung, Geschichtsbewusstsein und Geschichtsvermittlung zwischen den Generationen," *heiEDUCATION Journal* 4 (2019): 29–49.
23. Stefan Troebst and Nicole Dittmer, "Verstoß für neues NS-Dokumentationszentrum," *Deutschlandfunk Kultur*, 22 May 2020, https://www.deutschlandfunkkultur.de/historiker-initiative-vorstoss-fuer-neues-ns.1008.de.html?dram:article_id=477208.
24. James Baldwin, "The White Man's Guilt," in *Collected Essays* (New York: Literary Classics, 1998), 722–23.
25. Runge and Stelbrink, "Ich bleibe Emigrant," 95.
26. Randolph S. Churchill, ed., *The Sinews of Peace: Post-war Speeches by Winston S. Churchill* (London: Riverside Press, 1949), 200.
27. Christian Meier, *Das Gebot zu Vergessen und die Unabweisbarkeit des Erinnerns: Vom öffentlichen Umgang mit schlimmer Vergangenheit* (Munich: Siedler Verlag, 2010).
28. Annette Wieviorka, *The Era of the Witness*, trans. Jared Stark (Ithaca, NY: Cornell University Press, 2006).
29. Runge and Stelbrink, "Ich bleibe Emigrant," 114–15.
30. Mosse directed this comment to the Vietnam War Memorial erected in 1982 and designed by Maya Ying Lin. *Fallen Soldiers*, 225.
31. David Cameron, "Speech at the Imperial War Museum on First World War Centenary Plans on 11 October 2012," https://www.gov.uk/government/speeches/speech-at-imperial-war-museum-on-first-world-war-centenary-plans.
32. As after the Great War, the growing brutalization of society is evident today in the use of militant and abusive language. An example is the use of the term "Gutmensch,"

the "do-gooder," as used by Matteo Salvini: "The European Dream Is Being Buried by the Bureaucrats, the *Buonistas*, and the Bankers Who Are Governing Europe for Too Much Time," *New York Times*, 15 April 2019.

33. Aleida Assmann, *Der Europäische Traum: Vier Lehren aus der Geschichte* (Munich: Beck Verlag, 2018).

34. Mosse, *Fallen Soldiers*, 224.

35. Mosse, *Fallen Soldiers*, 162.

36. Francis Fukuyama, *Identity: Contemporary Identity Politics and the Struggle for Recognition* (London: Profile Books, 2018).

37. Runge and Stelbrink, "Ich bleibe Emigrant," 96.

38. Runge and Stelbrink, "Ich bleibe Emigrant," 106.

39. Runge and Stelbrink, "Ich bleibe Emigrant," 97.

2

Past Subjunctive

George L. Mosse's Memoir

DARCY BUERKLE

When asked directly about his own life, George L. Mosse had the habit of deflecting by referring interlocutors to his bibliographic contributions in European history. His explication about that link was limited.[1] But in the end, Mosse did give an explanation.[2] In his posthumously published memoir, *Confronting History*, he connects his decades of historical writing to his life's story, referring provocatively, for example, to his 1985 *Nationalism and Sexuality* as his "coming out book."[3] In fact, Mosse had contributed to the history of sexuality from very early on. At least from 1961 in *The Crisis of German Ideology*, male bonding was a central site of his scholarship, in particular the historicizing of male desire. In his memoir, Mosse's own sexuality, while present, remains heavily circumscribed. This chapter highlights some of the details of that constraint in *Confronting History* in order to think again about the text's meaning and implications, not only for Mosse himself but also for the way the profession remembers and refers to him.[4]

As a German Jew, and later as an émigré historian in the United States who spent the first decades of his adult life living a closeted life as a gay man, Mosse grappled with the sustainability of his chosen professional identity. As a scholar and teacher, he faced the persistent threat of punishing homophobia in the academy. For many years, he necessarily invited from others professional and personal culpability in the evasions he cultivated. However, historicizing Mosse's contributions and memorializing his life without tending to the fact of his disciplining by the profession misses a persistent and vital matter about the disabling effects of homophobia and what it exacts from its subjects. Often remembered for his sweeping rhetoric and energy, his influence remains uncontestable. But the "secrets" he carried also remain inseparable from his work as an educator or as a historian.[5] Mosse's papers at the Leo Baeck Institute (LBI) alongside his published memoir allow the reader to read against evasion—Mosse's and that of the profession—and enter into a renewed understanding of his historical questions as well as his oft-referenced "restlessness." In tracing his rhetorical constraint, I have consulted multiple drafts of the memoir. Key editorial decisions made early on and recorded in these drafts document not only Mosse's rendering of his story but also the subsequent treatment of his manuscript and, therefore, of his legacy.[6]

The son of Hans Lachmann-Mosse and Felicia Lachmann-Mosse, George L. Mosse was born in 1918 into a well-known family and economic privilege on the precipice of the Weimar Republic. Exceptional archival holdings have thus enabled the work of biographers of the Mosse family. At the same time that George L. Mosse was writing his memoir, Elisabeth Kraus was finishing her nearly eight-hundred-page survey of the Mosse's family history.[7] Kraus consulted George L. Mosse, incorporating some of his insights, but a biography devoted to his life remains outstanding.[8] His memoir suggests that this absence may remain. Mosse subjected the verifiable facts of his life in *Confronting History* to a discernible rhetorical and narrotological treatment that has a recognizable choreography of its own. His repetitions and evasions make the case for the performativity of the text and more clearly profile aspects of his experience than he may have wished.

In introducing his beginnings, the Weimar Republic serves first as a statement of fact—a set of conditions—of politics and family life into which George L. Mosse arrived. As site of origin, Weimar was for Mosse a weighted invocation, but it was also, as he was careful to caution, almost entirely an invocation compounded in its inaccessibility not just by time but by youth as well. He notes repeatedly—including but not only in the memoir—that when asked to describe the experience of those years, he would demure, reminding the inquirer that he was only a child at the time; how much could he possibly remember? "It is ironic when today students ask me what it must have been like to experience the excitement of cultural life in the Weimar Republic. My experience was quite different from that of adults, and those who ask this question today do not want to hear about German nationalism or boarding schools."[9] Even so, in *Confronting History*, Mosse returns to Weimar repeatedly as the Freudian "unplumbable navel of the dream," dwelling precisely on the combination of not being able to remember and knowing exactly what happened.[10] Weimar's promise and, importantly, a category of the things he cannot remember, thus all take on connotative status in the memoir in both its unpublished and published iterations, making it the locus of both definite and elusive meaning, of the speculative.

Shaped not only by Weimar, the Mossean imaginary in *Confronting History* asserts a subjunctive past: if this had not happened, that could have happened, or that would not have happened. He writes in a calculus well known to the forced migrant, to the immigrant, conjuring the speculative as a past subjunctive, a grammatical feat as well as a psychological one. "My life," one of the chapters of the memoir begins, "*would* have been different had circumstances allowed me to remain in Germany."[11] His father, he tells us, expected to return to Berlin after the war and restart the family paper, a new *Berliner Tageblatt*. "It would not have worked," Mosse notes matter-of-factly, and speculatively too: "No one who came back from exile and reclaimed a pre-Nazi newspaper was destined to succeed."[12] The affective power of the statement for its clarity about a Weimar that is definitively lost stands, appearing as the site of a world he could refer to but not inhabit. Finally, in *Confronting History*, the subjunctive persists in the text in relationship to two especially repetitive and confounding matters, themselves linked to Weimar in his mind: first and primarily, his homosexuality; and second, the women in his family, his mother, Felicia, and sister, Hilde.

The specter of respectability on which Mosse's signal contributions hinge is the threat of humiliation, a factor and an outcome that he spent little time detailing. He seems to wave the prospect of public denigration away when rendering his own life, despite the labor of compartmentalization that was required to maintain his own public respectability. For Mosse, childhood and its pedagogies brought with it a lasting relationship to an "insistence on respectability which, for example, held the marriage of my parents together even [though] . . . the rows between my parents had become general knowledge."[13] He reports that such stringent demands on behavior were not extended to him—he often felt, he writes, that his parents had been too lenient with him.[14] Still, his compassion for his younger self remains limited at best. Describing himself as incorrigibly naughty as a child, "spoiled," he was, as he insists, "a child in protest, up to no good most of the time."[15] Similarly uncompromising in his evaluation of his own behavior as a young man and in early adulthood, Mosse rejects notions of his own victimization when he refers to his experiences of antisemitism and homophobia, minimizing his own suffering despite evidence to the contrary.

Mosse cites boarding school as the site of his first and most memorable experiences of antisemitism. It was here that he gained an awareness of his own masculinity and sexuality as an "outsider," even if he could not yet name the significance of the latter. His repeated references to his Weimar as "boarding school and nationalism" gain narrative context in the chapter devoted to his time at Kurt Hahn's boarding school at Schloss Salem's Hermannsberg. Having served as Prince Max of Baden's secretary and not so occasional ghostwriter, Hahn cofounded the school with the prince and Karl Reinhardt in the wake of their bitter disappointment with Germany's negotiations at the end of World War I. The goal was to "heal the diseased state" through an institution that would foster "moral courage."[16] In writing and oratory, Hahn referred to William James's idea of the "moral equivalent of war" and the related "longing to lose yourself in a common cause."[17] He set in place categories of behavior and thought that would accompany Mosse for the rest of his life, shaping his behavior. The school and its methods "left," Mosse claims, "a deeper mark than I realized at the time, ... gave me some backbone."[18] But the mark left by Salem was even more far-reaching than fortitude.

Entertaining the subjunctive as he introduces his education at the Hermannsberg at Schloss Salem, Mosse places his experience: "If I had been born in England, not Germany, and into the same social class, I would automatically have entered a boarding school at ten years of age, and I was indeed ten years of age when I entered Salem."[19] The school, as Mosse explains, educated "soldierly men and women who had internalized those qualities of character which Hahn thought essential." For example, Kurt Hahn would reconfigure his vaulted experiential learning (*Erlebnispädagogik*) in institutions internationally over decades—ultimately founding Outward Bound—but its foregrounding of a sacralized relation to country was a hallmark early on and influenced Mosse deeply. As he tells it, "We were impressed by Hahn's emphasis upon the grand passion a boy must possess in order to become a true man."[20] For Mosse, these passions included a lifelong love of the Swabian landscape near Salem, Romantic literature that "gave [the landscape] historical and emotional dimension," and the fact that "history was always present."[21] He was less interested or adept at the "fighting games" and daily running required. Still, he cites Salem as "his first real experience of community."[22]

In *The Crisis of German Ideology* in the middle of a paragraph, Hahn appears as an example of völkisch emphasis without, however, according to Mosse, "racist prejudice": "Kurt Hahn," Mosse asserts, "'emphasized giving oneself with all one's soul' to an effort and an idealism which would overcome the spiritual vacuum of postwar Germany."[23] Other themes in both Mosse's early and later work were arguably prefigured and first encountered at Schloss Salem through Hahn's pedagogies, with their emphasis on "moral courage" and the importance of balancing activity and intellectual engagement in each day. All of this gave Mosse the lived experience of one of his most significant and enduring insights, "the sacralization of politics."[24] In the Schloss Salem chapter, the reader witnesses contradiction and telling repetitions and, also, an emergent and lasting conjuncture between sexuality alongside many other of the most salient categories for Mosse's later historical writing.

Kurt Hahn was not only the cofounder along with Prince Max of Baden of the well-known boarding school; he was also Jewish and, like the Prince himself, gay.[25] Though Golo Mann, a student at Salem from 1923 to 1927, writes laudingly of Hahn, he remarks that Hahn had three "weaknesses." The "most serious" among them was that "he had practically no notion of sexuality or sexual education" and that he struggled with "moral compunctions about his own homoerotic inclinations, . . . stifl[ing] them in himself by an incredible effort of the will. As a result, he suspected and feared everywhere that which he had suppressed in himself and he employed truly inquisitorial methods against it. . . . This policy brought a tinge of dishonesty to the life of the school, whose fundamental principle was supposed to be honesty. Here, without realizing it, he forced us to be dishonest toward him as well as each other."[26] Self-overcoming was prized. Hahn's belief that the "sexual drive could break through at any moment and take complete possession of a boy's or girl's spiritual energy" was of particular consequence to Mosse's emergent adolescence.[27] In his own writings, Hahn argued that without the pedagogies he put in place, "out of one hundred boys only one will come through puberty intact."[28] As one of the most significant teachers at the school phrased it years later to Mann, the pressure to "skip puberty" only increased the guilt that boys felt when it could not be evaded.[29] Writing of the shame attached to masturbation as a capitulation in which the boys engaged, sometimes together, Mosse remembers that he was perpetually "plagued by guilt feelings."[30] In his historical work, Mosse explicated the power of maintaining appearances not only with the clarity that comes from his erudition and class background but also with the clarity that the familiarity of the threat of shaming brings. The memoir clarifies the source of that knowledge.

In this context, Mosse foreshadows his own sexual coming of age, writing that while at Salem he "felt no strong so-called perverse sexual drive as yet— that came with a vengeance in the quite different atmosphere of my English school."[31] Rhetorical linking of Hahn and his own sexuality occurs throughout, however; in this instance the sentence that follows turns directly to him: "Hahn himself was a lonely figure. . . . He was mainly interested in his male students. . . . However, we never gave his homoeroticism a thought."[32] Perhaps. But Mosse's depiction of himself in this chapter suggests a pronounced association between Hahn's influence, however distant, and Mosse's nascent sense of himself, particularly his masculinity and sexuality. Describing himself as decidedly unathletic in build and ambition, Mosse's version of his years at Salem conveys the precision with which he understood himself as other than the ideal that Hahn rewarded. Again refusing any notion of his own suffering for more than a sentence, Mosse nonetheless speaks twice of trauma in the Salem chapter. Retreating to the subjunctive, he suggests of the boys' elevation of Hahn that "this hero-worship could traumatize for life those who thought themselves ugly and who did not love sports but instead liked artistic or intellectual pursuits which most boys considered decidedly unmanly."[33] By this time in his story, Mosse has repeatedly clarified that the abstract boy described in his hypothetical was not hypothetical at all.[34]

A generation older, Hahn nonetheless came from Mosse's same German-Jewish Berlin world. He had attended Gymnasium with Mosse's father, and Hahn's mother, Charlotte (Landau) Hahn, entertained a sought-after salon in the family's Wannsee villa. Regular participants shaped Kurt Hahn's educational and political philosophies; some would reappear at Salem.[35] As in the Mosse household, the combination of politics and music in the Hahn salon was especially potent. Arthur Rubinstein, for example, played in the Mosse home, and also visited Hahn's salon as a young man.[36] Rubinstein records the experience, writing in his memoir of Charlotte Hahn that "she was a[n] enchanting lady of about thirty-five and a very fine pianist, well equipped for a brilliant career, if it hadn't been for her wealth, her husband, and children."[37] Mosse's father was a major supporter of the Berlin Philharmonic who, as he reports, bought the tuxedos for the orchestra and spent many New Year's Eves in the "company of the conductor, Wilhelm Furtwängler."[38] Berta Geissmar, Furtwängler's personal assistant, was a dinner guest Mosse describes as a "constant" at the family's dinner table, at which "conversations were all about music."[39]

The Hahn and Mosse households had much in common, both objectively discernible and recognizable in Hahn's 1910 fictionalized version of his mother's salon.[40] Years later in 1933 and 1934, George's sister Hilde recorded in her diary her mother's calls and conversations with an increasingly desperate Charlotte Hahn.[41] But Mosse notes none of this. Instead, he remains true to his stated intention to "analyze how I myself conceived of people and institutions, how they struck me as I lived among them." Therefore, of Charlotte Hahn's presence at Salem he observes that "Kurt Hahn's mother, who occupied an apartment at the Hermannsberg, was, in contrast to her son, a self-conscious Jew ... [who] kept the Jewish High Holidays and insisted that Jewish boys and girls attend them, much to our distress, for we did not want to be singled out in this manner."[42] The singling out that targeted him, though, and on which Mosse dwells, concerns his emergent sexuality and verbal humiliation by Kurt Hahn.

Observing the boys in required physical exercise because the school had "an emphasis on hardening the body," Mosse reports that Hahn stood at an upstairs window and yelled down to "various players and especially to me: '*Schlappschwanz*.'"[43] In his English memoir, Mosse uses this German word, a denigration on which he does not further comment—translating it without its crude sexualized etymology, leaving it at "weakling."[44] Notably, in an otherwise relatively short book, this is one of only two repetitions that I could find; he refers to the insult itself three times. Mosse commemorated this scene regularly in interviews as well. Emphasizing the intimidation he felt at Hahn's "idiocrasies" in this regard, Mosse linked them to his stringent objections at the prospect of being enrolled in Hahn's Scottish version of Salem founded in 1934 while in exile, Gordonstoun. But the effects of this scene—and doubtlessly others like it—were more lasting than the decision about what his new boarding school would be in 1934.

While the chapter on Salem was shaped by childhood memory, it also reads as protest. Mosse's faulty or partial memory of his own departure from Germany, for example, provides more testimony to his experience of the moment than he would have realized. He remembers that his "final departure from the school ... again illustrates how distant it was from the reality of the new Germany whose time had now come. ... Of course the main school had not yet been sealed off by the Nazis nor Hahn arrested, and the Nazis had not yet shown of what they were capable."[45] This is incorrect; by the time Mosse crossed Lake Constance to Switzerland on 31 March 1933, Hahn was under arrest. When he reports that he "remembers seeing swastikas burning as fiery symbols on the hills surrounding the Hermannsberg," he may well be thinking of 11 March 1933; on that day the SA and SS encircled the school, set fires, and removed Hahn. Notably, the consequential advocates for his release included Schloss Salem alumnus Claus von Stauffenberg.[46]

In other cases, the text registers more conscious repudiation of Hahn. Mosse draws attention to a letter he penned to the *New York Times* in 1950, one of the "few letters" he ever "wrote to a newspaper, ... when Kurt Hahn came to America ... to gather money for his school."[47] Though decades later in the memoir he allows that he was perhaps "unduly harsh," Mosse had advised in 1950 that "as an alumnus of that school as well as a member of a family that has in the past supported Salem financially, I feel that such a scheme is a dangerous one for the future of German democracy."[48] Notably, in significant contradiction to his version of events in the memoir in which he continues to at least imply critique, Mosse had written to the school in 1957 to apologize for the letter to the *Times*, deeming it "not only bad, but also relatively dumb. ... It was written at a time when many of the feelings of the war were still very much reverberating."[49] Reassured by the response he received, a few weeks later he replied to school administrators with gratitude: "I was especially happy that you have forgiven me for the dumb letter: the bitterness of the war is very difficult to overcome, especially when one is impacted by it oneself so directly. Then one is ashamed."[50] By 1957 he had been back to visit the school twice, and he continued to seek out the landscape, and sometimes the Schloss Salem itself, for the rest of his life.[51]

In his 1996 *The Image of Man*, Mosse explained that the construction of modern masculinity meant that "such outsiders, whether Jew or homosexual, could have no honor, which ... was regarded as an integral part of manhood."[52] He calls the era into which he was born the "climax of modern masculinity," and he devoted a chapter to describing "how the ideal was institutionalized."[53] In other words, Mosse turned directly from a book about masculinity, Jewishness, and sexuality in *The Image of Man* to a book about those same matters in his own life. Writing to Salem that same year to request a return visit, he noted that he had a first draft of his chapter for the memoir describing his time there. In the wake of his experiences at Salem in spring 1996, his letter of thanks to the school's director reads as conciliatory, the "dialogue with the students," he offered, was "truly open and substantive." Most compellingly, he deemed the visit "a very successful reconciliation."[54]

The uniformity of affect in the Salem chapter when it comes to Hahn conveys the significance of young Mosse's early understanding of leadership and nationalism coming apart. He condemns Hahn for not fully recognizing the dangers of National Socialism sooner than he did. But Mosse's rejection of Hahn also conveys effects of the memorable, closeted rage Hahn directed at him. When Mosse reports the "Schlappschwanz incident," he does so without lengthy commentary, writing that Hahn "was also said to be charming, ... a side I never saw."[55] But he wrote several books about precisely such moments and their related logics, their genesis and consequences. What he describes in the memoir reads today as intergenerational, queer trauma and the enduring cathexis to a painful but nonetheless beloved context of that trauma. It was not only that Hahn demeaned him but also that a Jewish and gay elder denied him; it is that the example of gayness he first perceived looked like repudiation. An abiding conflict thus produced may have enabled in Mosse the kind of understanding and generative contradiction for which he was prized as a historian and on which he insisted in the people he trained. Citing the letter to the *Times* without also citing the apology allows him to tell a different story that was perhaps more important in old age—to record and leave behind a protest and also report that

Hahn drafted an unsent and unsatisfactory response to that letter—a response, at last and at least, beyond humiliation.[56]

An unmitigated reference to his own homosexuality—rather than the oblique reference to himself as "a sexual outsider"—finally occurs halfway through the memoir when Mosse describes his late teenage years at a boarding school in England: "It was here, at Bootham, that I first experienced conscious attraction and temptation, and fell in love.... I was not able to give expression to two basic facts about my personality.... It was as if I were the carrier of unsavory secrets.... I came to joyful terms with my Jewishness, [but] more than two decades would pass before I could halfway acknowledge my homosexuality."[57] Mosse delivers his explanation for the silence he claims to have maintained in another invocation of the subjunctive: "Had I revealed it at this point not only would I have exposed myself to persecution, but I could never have aspired to a respectable position in society or in any profession—quite apart from the reaction of my family."[58] The reminders of possible humiliation persist throughout his telling of his life, but nowhere more so than in combination with sexuality.

The vaulted gregariousness and sharp wit of Mosse the teacher and scholar stand in contrast to the story he tells about his coming of age confounded by loneliness. He notes on multiple occasions that he "does not understand" why for so long he did not have "real friendships," nonetheless linking this fact rhetorically immediately to his homosexuality. Of his student days at Haverford College, for example, he writes that "I do not know why both here, and later at Harvard, few lasting and continuous friendships developed, or why I stayed in touch with hardly any of my friends from school."[59] This curiosity he follows with the observation that "[my] sexual orientation has not intruded much into this account up to now," only to be met again by a disavowal, "partly because I never experienced the trauma of despair which has driven other homosexual young people close to suicide because of the discrimination and the insults directed against them.... It was a little like the reason for the low rate of desertion of German soldiers on the Russian front during the Second World War: where were they going to desert to?" Thus he pointed clearly to his sense of entrapment in an incontrovertible identity, a forced lie, and the related compensation. He reports a lack of continuity in his friendships until he arrived at the University of Iowa; linking this observation again to sexuality, he notes that from that point forward, he was "continent in matters of sexuality for almost another thirty years."[60]

Mosse stipulates that his compensations were coterminous with his professionalization and the life he created for himself: his commitments to scholarship, teaching, and friendship sustained him. Of his first job at the University of Iowa, he continues: "I would have been kicked out; it was not possible.... I became convinced early on that any distinction I might achieve in my work depended upon a focusing of those energies in the classroom which I might have expended upon a sexual relationship. Today, this seems a rationalization, ... but at the time these were genuinely held beliefs." Turning once again to the subjunctive, he continues: "How matters would have turned out if the environment had been less hostile ... I cannot say."[61] The phrasing here reverberates throughout his story of homophobia: he "could not say."

As elsewhere, in *Confronting History*, Mosse cultivated his own shadow cabinet of gay thinkers and advisors whose significance is redoubled for their deployment in the memoir too—Theodor Mommsen, Klaus Mann, Johann Joachim Winckelmann, among others, through whom he was able to say something more about, among other things, the threat of humiliation on which respectability relies. They passed muster for their relevant contributions but bore repeating for him as a kind of incantation, perhaps also, both for their uniformly tragic endings and for the sustenance they provided. Robert Nye's writing mirrors Mosse's own rhetorical turn, and at least alludes to something similar, when he notes that Winkelmann represents the pivot of *The Image of Man*: "The chief trope animating this insightful book is pathos: the pathos of lost opportunities, crushed hopes, and self-betrayal, a narrative not unlike the tragic saga of liberalism that occupies Mosse in so much of his work. Johann Joachim Winkelmann is the pivot of this book, *in more ways than one can say*."[62]

In his final unedited draft of the memoir, Mosse had used the word "gay" to refer to himself, indicating a certain comfort with this part of his life and the historical moment in which he wrote. Multiple drafts show, however, that editors at the Press initially changed the word "gay" to the more clinical "homosexuality" in key passages, thus making not just a rhetorical choice but also altering what could otherwise have been read as politically declarative. In some instances, it appears, friends and students who read these excisions intervened and returned to Mosse's word choice. But despite his ultimate willingness to write about himself as gay, Mosse's acknowledgments and struggles remain layered between disavowals. The insidiousness of homophobia resides in the story he tells but also in the story implied and in the speculative exercise of what might have been, not only as potentiality, but as actuality. In the memoir, the life that George L. Mosse lived as a gay man, beyond sublimation, is almost entirely missing.

The text again performs a more clarifying testimony than some of Mosse's narrative content in the last pages of the memoir, when he asserts that the fact that he has "not mentioned it [his homosexuality] often up to this point corresponds to the necessary suppression of that part of my personality, or rather its sublimation into work and a fantasy life."[63] But in fact the thread of marginalized sexuality as a defining feature of his life persists throughout the memoir, even as it is constrained by rhetorical disavowals. To cite another example: he maintains that it was ultimately in Israel that he was first fully able to experience himself without shame not only as Jewish but also as a gay man. Still, that story, in the memoir, remains relegated to deferrals and summations. The reader learns little about "David," the Israeli man to whom Mosse refers only by his first name but with whom he traveled widely and had a nearly two-decade relationship. Though a photo of the two men is the final page in the book, Mosse's description of "a relationship" that everyone "came to accept" in Madison is a reference to John Tortorice, who goes otherwise wholly unnamed.[64] Speaking of the subjunctive, without John, there would not have been a memoir; he assisted George throughout its writing and it was his steadfastness that ultimately brought the book posthumously to publication.

The primary beneficiaries of George L. Mosse's decisions to sublimate were his students and, of course, the profession itself, since it meant he avoided expulsion from its ranks. His sublimation enabled not just the arguments he made but how he made them and also the conditions under which he labored. For all the things that Iowa and Wisconsin gave him, he performed that labor and lived that life with the hum of possible removal; he always heard it. However accustomed he was to that abiding threat, bracketing that kind of institutional power in historical writing about him elides something very consequential and insidious in which the profession remains both complicit and implicated. Mosse's decisions required a negotiation with an openly *and* implicitly hostile culture and profession, unreflective as the historical profession has long been about its own homosociality, however much Mosse's own historical arguments might have exemplified the relevance of that situation.

Mosse refers in the memoir to colleagues that he "knew were gay" but with whom he never spoke about such things, claiming of his Wisconsin colleague Harvey Goldberg, for example, that "we never mentioned such matters.... The taboo was too strong to be broken, not just on his side but on mine as well."[65] At least one graduate assistant from this period claims that this was absolutely not the case and that George tried to intervene in Harvey's self-destructive relational choices.[66] But what interests me is the degree to which Mosse was at pains to still engage in a performative decorum while, at the same time, making a more profound and historical point in this memoir, highlighting the significance of homophobia in the profession and, therefore, the residual subjunctive thus produced. Put differently: What is the status of claiming not to have spoken? How many other such conversations did he in fact not have? How many did he feel compelled to claim he had not had? There are others among his peers whom he treats with similar circumspection. For example, he describes the closeted Norbert Elias—who he knew for decades—not in terms of the source of their disagreement or the doubtlessly related matter that would have bound them, namely Elias's own struggle with homophobia, but as "difficult to get along with, touchy and opinionated."[67]

Even though their personalities clashed, groundbreaking Wisconsin women's historian Gerda Lerner celebrated their friendship in her eulogy for him.[68] Mosse was not and will not be remembered for an early interest in women's history, yet he nonetheless enabled it meaningfully. In this late life memoir, especially in its original and unpublished form, he demonstrates an interest and empathy for the lives of women in his family in a draft that was excised but that I would have wished to have been retained in the published text. Referring again to the constraints of the profession, he noted bracingly in his original draft that what he called "the formerly radical historians" would have rejected the field in which "Wisconsin was once again [to be] a pioneer:... women's history." His criticism of colleagues in that same paragraph whom he called "patriarchal at best" were deleted by editors as well.[69]

It also becomes clear from an earlier draft that the story of women in Mosse's family remains to be told. He provided some openings in his telling of their relation to him, making claims that are similar to the ones that he makes about his relationship to Weimar: he was there, present, only barely, but he reaches nonetheless. In *Confronting History*, gender and Weimar converge through his sister Hilde and mother Felicia: the cultural left in Weimar that students over decades asked Mosse about, he associates most strongly with his sister. The eldest of the three children, Mosse saw her early engagement as emancipatory and emblematic of her coming of age during the Weimar Republic.[70] Later an accomplished and activist psychiatrist in New York, Hilde, like her brother, acted with conviction without ruining her respectability, though she, like her brother, took risks in her personal life that could have made her vulnerable had they become public.[71]

Even as Mosse narrates his closeness to his sister, he marks the kind of persistent limits I have tried to suggest were significant and prohibitive: he claims that he never revealed his homosexuality to her, and he states unequivocally that Hilde thought homosexuality was "degenerate."[72] He truncates again, does not elaborate further; there is no explanation or telling of a conversation in which he learned this judgment; it remains a speculation to suggest whence he may have discerned Hilde's position. Perhaps it was her leftist politics and

Mosse's regularly referenced sentiment of the 1930s crystalized in a quotation from Klaus Mann that "homosexuals" were the "Jews of the antifascist Left."[73] Or perhaps it was Hilde's involvement in Fredric Wertham's crusade against comics, which did involve the observation—though, notably, no condemnation of—homosexuality in comics.[74] Mosse links his evaluation of his sister's possible response rhetorically to that of his beloved stepmother, Carola, who was "highly conventional in her attitudes and reactions."[75] He relegates to a parenthetical the fact that he "never discussed with her [his] feelings of outsiderdom." The speculative "what might have been" runs once more alongside a story about closeness constrained. Notably though, 1982 was the year that both Hilde Mosse and Carola Strauch Lachmann died; 1982 is also the year that George L. Mosse first self-identified as gay in a professional context. His perception of Hilde's position may be made even more significant by what it might suggest about their discussions regarding their mother, for whom Hilde cared in New York for decades. George described their mother in the memoir as volatile, difficult, in the 1920s often absent, and, in exile, isolated, taking to her bed. He also describes her as always having a female companion to assist her. Perhaps it was in relation to her that he had the conversation about homosexuality with Hilde that he did not have about himself.

As I have noted, since delivery of the manuscript came just weeks before Mosse's passing, decisions were made regarding edits and title without his input, some of them more challenging than others. Reading the drafts deposited at the Leo Baeck Institue, a further amplification of the choice to turn his gayness into "homosexuality" appears in surprising deletions of lesbianism in his own family. Paragraphs devoted to his mother's cousin, Martha Mosse, have been entirely deleted and therefore also his direct reference to her "female companion," Erna Stock, née Sprenger, and "lesbianism which," as he posited in his draft, "was largely ignored" rather than punished during National Socialism. His great-aunt, Bertha Mermann, "lived until her death with her long-time maid," with whom Carola corresponded until "well after the Second World War."[76] But the chasm left by the deletion of passages devoted to his mother proves perhaps most striking.

In the published version of the most telling passages about Felicia Mosse, there remains no trace of the significance that Mosse ascribed to his Aunt Lunia Lachmann, his mother's "closest friend—a life-long friend, ... a Russian woman of great beauty and charm, ... a woman of the world."[77] Most compellingly, however, the published version of one of the lengthier descriptions of a childhood memory with his mother reads, "The happiest I saw her was when surrounded by beautiful Russian women visiting Schenkendorf.... I am not sure if I should draw any conclusions from the presence of these beautiful young women surrounding my mother."[78] The full text as he submitted it to the press, however, was less ambiguous about what he thought about this recollection. The passage was edited down dramatically. What Mosse appears to have considered the final version reads:

> However, an additional burden must have imposed an almost insuperable stress upon her, and further encouraged her hysterical outbursts and the scenes with the mostly innocent servants. It was an older cousin who one day, as we were having lunch in New York, sometime in the mid-1970s, told me in casual conversation that *it was general knowledge in Berlin that my mother was a lesbian*. Much became clear at that moment: why my mother was often surrounded by beautiful mostly Russian women.... My mother was constantly on trips abroad—surely a sign of her unhappiness—always with a female companion. Through my own research I now know something about Lesbianism [sic] in Weimar Germany, but I cannot say if my mother joined any of their social circles or clubs. At any rate, given the primacy of respectability, the absolute necessity not to lose face, *her lot as both a lesbian and in all probability an illegitimate child must have been a [sic] very difficult to bear for a highly visible member of society* [emphasis mine].[79]

What reads as a mobilization of Mossean empathy to think about his mother's plight and, to my mind, to offer a kind of homage to her while acknowledging their distance and to the "what might have been" was expunged. While the precise interventions that resulted in these deletions remain opaque, the prospect of humiliation that Mosse knew well was certainly the reason.

Mosse did try several times in his text to make sense of his mother's "outbursts," which clearly impacted him significantly, and of the pressures on her as a Jewish woman in the circumstance in which she found herself. What ultimately becomes "the additional burden" had to do with the fact that Felicia Mosse was biologically Rudolf Mosse's daughter by another woman, "Frl. Marx."[80] She was legally adopted only in 1919 after she already had three children of her own, having learned of her status first from a civil servant on the day she was married. In what one imagines might be the youngest son's devotion to his mother's respectability, he was resolute here and in other interviews claiming not to know who his biological grandmother was, nor revealing the extent of his mother's mental instability, for which there is, however, substantial archival evidence. Moreover, he shows a sensitivity to her isolation, noting both in the memoir and incredulously elsewhere when asked about her, that what she did with her life was "nothing, she could not as a woman of her social class.

Nothing."[81] That she was a "known lesbian," however, was consigned to the archive despite his efforts. Even here, there remains a traceable incursion of the personal in his work: though it did not materialize, his solicitation of an article on "lesbianism in the 1920s" for the important 1982 special issue on the history of sexuality of the *Journal of Contemporary History* suggests another possible tribute to his mother in the subjunctive; to a conversation that they might have had and did not: "It would fit very well," he wrote in his solicitation of the essay, "because that is a subject that is neglected in the issue as it stands."[82]

Mosse not only allowed but also relied in his memoir on the grammar of not-knowing or even *maybe* knowing for important aspects of his story. The *Berliner Tageblatt* could not be restarted, but he wrote toward the Weimar he missed nonetheless, believing to have found its vestiges in Jerusalem. He resisted totalizing notions generally, and he also specifically separated himself from the often-pugnacious rhetoric of his peers by not writing totalizing history either. As in the first line of the memoir—"why write an autobiography?"—his inquiries were framed by the clarity of his questions. "Respectability," Mosse wrote in the concluding paragraph of *Nationalism and Sexuality*, "provided society with an essential cohesion that was as important in the perceptions of men and women as any economic or political interests.... Was the price," he asked, "exacted for this morality too high? That depends upon how the conflict between society's felt need for cohesion and tolerance of the outsider can be resolved."[83] Mosse paid a price, even if he disavowed it to the end, or claimed not to care or notice. The history of the life of a closeted man—even a celebrated and life-affirming historian like George L. Mosse—is certainly the history of irretrievable stories that cannot be told because the record is scant. But it is also a story about a history of what was not, what lay outside the realm of possibility as defined and enforced by the profession that sustained him. It was a vexed situation that demanded contradiction from the start.

Mosse argued that historical oblivion and self-delusion were dangerous and also, importantly, eminently *comprehensible*, the latter point being perhaps the most resolutely consistent and, in the historical moment in which we now live, politically crucial. His classic liberalism did not detract from the urgency of empathy that he communicated in his work, nor did it provide a way out of a radicalized notion of understanding. When it came to producing his memoir, this rhetorical and also ethical commitment to refuse a final answer stands. Still, the use of the subjunctive that undergirds his telling suggests that if not for the cruelty and strictures he historicizes that took their own shape in the story he tells, everything could indeed have been very different. When George L. Mosse imagined that "they would have kicked me out," he was quite right. The least we can do as readers and historians of his final work is to allow the speculative its full weight.

Notes

1. The link between Mosse's own life and the subjects he chose was evident at least from 1957 on with "The Image of the Jew in Popular Literature: Felix Dahn and Gustav Freytag," *Leo Baeck Institute Year Book* 2 (1957): 218–27. For more on the significance of 1957 as "hinge year," see David Warren Sabean, "George Mosse and *The Holy Pretence*," in *What History Tells: George L. Mosse and the Culture of Modern Europe*, ed. Stanley G. Payne, David Sorkin, and John S. Tortorice (Madison: University of Wisconsin Press, 2004), 15–24.

2. Around the time Mosse began the memoir, he sat for an oral history: United States Holocaust Memorial Museum Oral History Branch, Washington, DC, Joan Ringelheim, Oral History Interview with George L. Mosse, 13 March 1995.

3. George L. Mosse, *Confronting History: A Memoir* (Madison: University of Wisconsin Press, 2000), 180.

4. For example: Klaus Berghahn, ed., *The German-Jewish Dialogue Reconsidered: A Symposium in Honor of George L. Mosse* (New York: Peter Lang, 1996); special issue, George L. Mosse Memorial Symposium, *German Politics and Society* 18, no. 4 (2000); Payne, Sorkin, and Tortorice, *What History Tells*.

5. Mosse, *Confronting History*, 83.

6. George L. Mosse Collection (hereafter GLMC), Leo Baeck Institute (hereafter LBI), AR 25137, "Confronting History." Betty Steinberg was the senior editor at the University of Wisconsin Press and a close friend of Mosse's. The decisions that were made on his behalf are likely attributable to her affection for and protectiveness of George L. Mosse.

7. Elisabeth Kraus, *Die Familie Mosse* (Munich: C.H. Beck, 1999). George L. Mosse anonymously paid a hefty subvention for publication of this book on Kraus's request. Kraus, Elisabeth, 1991–1999, Box 36, Folder 80, GLMC, LBI AR 25137.

8. Elisabeth Kraus, 1991–1999, Box 36, Folder 80, GLMC, LBI AR 25137. With very special thanks to John Tortorice and the Mosse Estate for permission to read and cite these letters and to Michael Simonson of the Leo Baeck Institute and Smith College student Keelan Clifford, who made sure I was able to see them despite a closed archive during COVID-19.

9. Mosse, *Confronting History*, 5.

10. Sigmund Freud, *The Standard Edition of the Complete Psychological Works of Sigmund Freud*, vol. 4, *1900: The Interpretation of Dreams* (London: Hogarth Press, 1953), ix–627, 525.

11. Mosse, *Confronting History*, 212, emphasis mine.

12. Mosse, *Confronting History*, 212.

13. Mosse, *Confronting History*, 27.

14. Mosse, *Confronting History*, 47.

15. Mosse, *Confronting History*, 48.

16. Kurt Hahn, "An Experiment in Education," *The Listener*, 16 November 1950.

17. Kurt Hahn, "Address at the Founding Day Ceremony of the Athenian School," 21 November 1965. See also Lodewijk van Oord, "Kurt Hahn's Moral Equivalent of War," *Oxford Review of Education* 36, no. 3 (June 2010): 253–65, 257.

18. Mosse, *Confronting History*, 69.

19. Mosse, *Confronting History*, 48.

20. Mosse, *Confronting History*, 63.

21. Mosse, *Confronting History*, 54.

22. Mosse, *Confronting History*, 57.

23. George L. Mosse, *The Crisis of German Ideology* (Madison: University of Wisconsin Press, 2021), 171.

24. George L. Mosse, *The Nationalization of the Masses: Political Symbolism and Mass Movements in Germany from the Napoleonic Wars through the Third Reich* (Madison: University of Wisconsin Press, 2023).

25. Lothar Machtan, *Prinz Max von Baden: Eine Biographie* (Berlin: Suhrkamp, 2013).

26. Golo Mann, *Reminiscences and Reflections: A Youth in Germany*, trans. Krishna Windsont (New York: Norton, 1990), 89–90. See also Golo Mann, "Der Pädagoge als Politiker: Kurt Hahn (1965)," in *Zwölf Versuche* (Frankfurt: Suhrkamp, 1973), 61–104.

27. Mosse, *Confronting History*, 59.

28. Hahn qtd. in Heinz Stübig, "Kurt Hahn und seine Erlebnistherapie," in *Abenteuer, Erlebnisse und die Pädagogik*, ed. Peter Becker, Karl-Heinz Braun, and Jochem Schirp (Leverkusen: Barbara Budrich, 2007), 99–114, 101.

29. This formulation is a paraphrase from Golo Mann's description of a conversation he had with Hahn's longtime collaborator at Salem, Marina Ewald (Mann, *Reminiscences*, 90).

30. Mosse, *Confronting History*, 62.

31. Mosse, *Confronting History*, 63.

32. Mosse, *Confronting History*, 63.

33. Mosse, *Confronting History*, 63.

34. See, for example, Mosse, *Confronting History*, 55. Mosse also reports that his brother Rudolf had a conflicted relationship to Salem as well: "With his artistic sensibilities ... [he] felt crushed there." *Confronting History*, 56.

35. Alan Sica, ed., *The Anthem Companion to Max Weber* (London: Anthem, 2016), 148; Sabine Lepsius, *Ein Berliner Künstlerleben* (Munich: G. Müller, 1972), 209.

36. United States Holocaust Memorial Museum Oral History Branch, Washington, DC, Joan Ringelheim, Oral History Interview with George L. Mosse, 13 March 1995.

37. Arthur Rubinstein, *My Young Years* (New York: Knopf, 1999), 42.

38. Mosse, *Confronting History*, 35.

39. Mosse, *Confronting History*, 39; Berta Geissmar, *The Baton and the Jackboot* (London: Hamish Hamilton, 1944). Mosse describes his father's interest in and contributions to liturgical music in *Confronting History*, 36.

40. Kurt Hahn, *Frau Elses Verheißung* (Munich: Albert Langen, 1910).

41. Mosse Family Collection (hereafter MFC), Diaries and calendars, 1926–1934, Box 3, Folder 39, LBI AR 25184, writing of "Frau Hahn": "Trauig. Verzweifelt. Heimatlos." [Sad. Desperate. Homeless]. Charlotte Hahn died in Berlin on 2 June 1934.
42. Mosse, *Confronting History*, 64.
43. Mosse, *Confronting History*, 57.
44. Etymology dates to eighteenth century: "Man with a sleeping penis, an impotent man." *Herkunftswörterbuch: Etymologie der deutschen Sprache* (Mannheim: Duden Verlag, 2001).
45. Mosse, *Confronting History*, 68.
46. Banished from Baden even after his release, Hahn went to Berlin, still nurturing the kinds of illusions that had occupied him at the end of World War I, that reasoned appeals would be heard and heeded by Hitler's men. Instead, he was in Scotland by July 1933, returning to Salem only in 1954.
47. Mosse, *Confronting History*, 56; Mosse, "School for Germany Opposed," *New York Times*, 24 January 1950.
48. GLMC, LBI AR 25137, Schule Schloss Salem, 1933, 1945–1961, 1997–1998, Box 44, File 53.
49. GLMC, LBI AR 25137, Schule Schloss Salem, 1933, 1945–1961, 1997–1998, Box 44, File 53.
50. GLMC, LBI AR 25137, Schule Schloss Salem, 1933, 1945–1961, 1997–1998, Box 44, File 53.
51. For reference to another visit to Salem, see Anson Rabinbach, "George L. Mosse 1919–1999: An Appreciation," *Central European History* 32, no. 3 (1999): 331–36.
52. George L. Mosse, *The Image of Man: The Creation of Modern Masculinity* (New York: Oxford University Press, 1996), 63.
53. Mosse, *The Image of Man*, 133.
54. GLMC, LBI AR 25137, Schule Schloss Salem, 1933, 1945–1961, 1997–1998, Box 44, File 53.
55. Mosse, *Confronting History*, 57.
56. I have not been able to locate archival evidence of Hahn's drafted response.
57. Mosse, *Confronting History*, 83.
58. Mosse, *Confronting History*, 83.
59. Mosse, *Confronting History*, 118.
60. Mosse, *Confronting History*, 97.
61. Mosse, *Confronting History*, 97.
62. Payne, Sorkin, and Tortorice, *What History Tells*, 190.
63. Mosse, *Confronting History*, 197.
64. Notably, John and David are two of the three "random" names he uses to tell a story about Iowa earlier in the book, though he is not referring to either of the men in question. Mosse, *Confronting History*, 145.
65. Mosse, *Confronting History*, 161.
66. Personal communication, possession of the author, June 2019.
67. Mosse, *Confronting History*, 210.

68. Gerda Lerner, 1916–2013, MC 769, George Mosse, 1998–1999, Box 23, Folder 9, Schlesinger Library on the History of Women in America, Radcliffe Institute for Advanced Study, Cambridge, MA.

69. GLMC, LBI AR 25137 (iii) Edited Manuscript.

70. For example: Mosse, *Confronting History*, 50. Kraus points out that Hilde was not old enough to vote in 1928. *Die Familie Mosse*, 709.

71. I refer here to Hilde's own recording of her sexual adventures as a young woman and her decades-long relationship with Clesbie Daniels, an African American educator and psychologist with whom she also collaborated professionally.

72. Mosse, *Confronting History*, 85.

73. Klaus Mann, "Homosexualität und Faschismus (1934/35)," in *Heute und Morgen: Schriften zur Zeit* (Munich: Nymphenburger, 1969), 130–37. Mann's observation suggests more compassion than Mosse grants it here. "Man ist im Begriff, aus 'dem Homosexuellen' den Sündenbock zu machen—etwa, 'den Juden' der Antifaschisten," 137.

74. Frederic Wertham, *Seduction of the Innocent* (Port Washington, NY: Kennikat, 1953), 134.

75. Mosse, *Confronting History*, 84.

76. GLMC, LBI AR 25137 (iv) Final Version, Chapter II, 1998, Box 5, File 24.

77. Lunia (Gizella) Lachmann was married to George's father's Uncle Edmund (Lachmann). Mosse maintained contact with her after her arrival in the United States.

78. Mosse, *Confronting History*, 31. A later, only slightly less truncated iteration produced by editors also did not make it into print.

79. GLMC, LBI AR 25137.

80. Kraus, *Die Familie Mosse*, 307.

81. Wisconsin Historical Society Jewish Oral History Collection, Madison, Wisconsin, Peter Gordy Interview, 26 March 1975.

82. GLMC, LBI AR 25137, Editorial Correspondence, 1981–1985, Box 47, Folder 14 (13 July 1981).

83. George L. Mosse, *Nationalism and Sexuality: Middle-Class Morality and Sexual Norms in Modern Europe* (Madison: University of Wisconsin Press, 2020), 193.

Part II
NEW POLITICS OF EXCLUSION

3

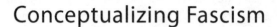

Conceptualizing Fascism

The Legacy of George L. Mosse

ENZO TRAVERSO

The historiographical turn related to George L. Mosse's interpretation of fascism does not need to be emphasized. In this piece, I will try to place it in its intellectual context by considering both its originality, its hermeneutic strength, and its limits, all of which are more easily recognizable twenty years after his death. The price of his powerful scholarly advance—notably a completely new anthropological and cultural approach—was his significant disregard for the social and economic bases of fascism, on which scholarship previously focused. This shift inevitably produced a quite problematic imbalance in his ambitious "general theory of fascism," wherein fascism became a purely cultural object. At the same time, his pathbreaking innovations did not abandon an essentially Eurocentric gaze—shared by most representatives of German-Jewish culture in exile—that disregarded the colonial dimension of fascist culture and violence. Mosse's historiographical turn was almost synchronous with the emergence of postcolonialism, but their paths did not cross. Even so, Mosse set the premises for a "meeting" that took place later.

A critical reassessment of George L. Mosse's theory of fascism could fruitfully start from its Italian reception in the 1970s and the early 1980s, when Mosse's writings were extensively translated and had a strong impact on contemporary historiography.[1] At that time, scholarship was so deeply entangled with the public use of the past that a historical interpretation of fascism disconnected from its political stigmatization was simply inconceivable. Renzo De Felice, the most important biographer of Mussolini who had pointed out the necessity of removing this moral and political burden, was criticized as a "revisionist" scholar. But methodologically, he was a very conventional historian and politically an ex-communist who had moved toward much more conservative positions.[2] Unlike De Felice, Mosse did not target antifascism; and his writings were much more easily accepted. As a German Jew exiled in the United States, he could not be suspected of any complicity or sympathy when he wrote that fascism had to be investigated from inside, taking seriously its discourse and self-representations, its symbols and ideology, and trying to penetrate the mental universe of its actors. This claim to "empathy"—depicted in his autobiography as "the chief quality of a historian," an operation that "means putting contemporary prejudice aside while looking at the past without fear or favor"— was quite unusual among historians of fascism.[3] Antifascism belonged to his existential—even more than political or ideological—background, but it certainly could not become a method of historical investigation. Defending his friend De Felice from charges of "revisionism"—and attributing to De Felice his own methodology—Mosse emphasized the importance of empathy as an irreplaceable tool for historical investigation. De Felice, he wrote, had tried "to proceed from inside" by "figuring out how Mussolini himself conceived of his own actions." This was a necessary step: "If we do not understand its self-representation and do not learn how its disciples looked at their own actions, we cannot recognize the terrible appeal of fascism."[4]

Mosse was deeply grateful to De Felice, who had introduced his work in Italy, and usually tended to underestimate or consciously hide their methodological discrepancies. The biographer of Mussolini had very quickly understood, as he pointed out in his preface to the Italian translation of *The Nationalization of the Masses*, the novelty of Mosse's interpretation of fascism as a culture and a general "attitude toward life," far beyond its usual depiction as a nationalist ideology and an authoritarian regime. But their investigations followed very different paths. A study on nationalism and sexuality by De Felice is almost unthinkable, as is a biography of Hitler by Mosse. The true Italian representative of Mosse's "historiographical revolution" was Emilio Gentile, a disciple of De Felice, who investigated fascism extensively as a political style and a culture made of symbols, emblems, and myths.[5] Thus, De Felice played the role of an intermediary who laid the bases for the reception of Mosse's work by a following generation. They deeply esteemed and mutually supported each other in their respective countries. This is one of the reasons that, in their relationship, they generally bracketed off some controversial issues. Mosse never accepted De Felice's paradigmatic distinction between Fascism and National Socialism as left and right forms of totalitarianism.

Empathy was so important for Mosse that he did not hesitate to correspond with Albert Speer, the minister of armaments and war of the Third Reich and one of Hitler's closest collaborators. Hitler admired Speer as an architect and had charged him to sketch the map of Berlin for the future. In the 1970s, Mosse and Speer met regularly and traveled together to Munich. In an interview, Mosse mentions his embarrassment when, in a restaurant, their conversations were interrupted by admirers who asked Speer for an autograph. After overcoming his initial suspicion, Speer became an essential interlocutor for Mosse, so important that he read *The Nationalization of the Masses* before publication. At the beginning, their exchange dealt with "technical questions" like lighting at the Nuremberg rally, since the historian told the witness that he was not interested in his moral assumptions or troubles: "That's between you and God." But their relationship deepened: "Then we went from technical to other things and it worked I think very well."[6] And he gave an example of what he meant by studying fascism from inside—or what Susan Sontag called "fascinating fascism"—by observing that Speer, despite his reappraisal of National Socialism, unconsciously unveiled how Hitler had subjugated him: "Whenever he talked about Hitler negatively, his eyes lit up. Hitler must have had a tremendous charisma because this man even, you know, denying everything, thinking everything was dreadful now, his eyes lit up when he talked about Hitler."[7]

Reminiscent of the historicist *Einfühlung* prescribed by Ranke—"placing oneself back into (a given) time, into the mind of the contemporary"—which implies a certain degree of comprehension, "empathy" is a controversial concept. Dominick LaCapra, who thought very highly of Mosse and established with him a fruitful relationship, prefers to speak of "empathetic unsettlement" or "hetero-pathetic identification," which clearly point out a critical distance.[8] Nonetheless, the liberating effects of Mosse's approach are uncontestable. A powerful epistemological obstacle was removed, and many previous debates on the lack of a fascist culture were suddenly eclipsed. Ideology and political strategies were not enough to understand fascism. Considering its powerful appeal—what Emilio Gentile, analyzing Mosse's method, defined as "the appeal of the persecutor"—was a necessary step, without which the other constitutive elements of fascism were not understandable.[9]

The conventional approach of postwar scholars consisted of denying the existence itself of a fascist culture. For Gordon A. Craig, the expression "Nazi culture" was a *contradictio in adjecto*.[10] For Norberto Bobbio, fascism "failed to produce a culture of its own."[11] He distinguished "Italian culture under fascism" from fascist anti-culture, which he presented as a set of simple negations: antidemocracy, antiliberalism, anticommunism, antihumanism, and anti-Enlightenment. From his seminal work *The Crisis of German Ideology* (1964, 2021) onward, Mosse radically broke with this mainstream approach that today is no longer defendable.[12] He considered fascism as a vision of humanity and history, a project of society and civilization, a cultural and political revolution. Fascism was a revolution because it aimed at rebuilding society as a whole; it was a worldvision, since it wished to create a "New Man" and depicted itself as a providential destiny for race and nation. For Mosse, fascist movements had a unique culture, since fascism proclaimed its will to transform collective imaginations and styles of life as well as to erase any difference between public and private life. In Mosse's words, fascism was a "third way" between Marxism and capitalism: "Fascism was itself a revolution, seizing power by using twentieth-century methods of mass mobilization and control, and replacing an old with a new elite."[13] It is true that, as Marxist scholars pertinently observed, it never put into question the foundations of capitalism and the power of the industrial and financial elites, but Mosse emphasized that "economic policy was subordinated to the political goals of fascism," whose ultimate ambition was "to create a new social order." Mosse continued: "The fascist revolution saw itself as a 'Third Force,' rejecting both 'materialist Marxism' and 'finance capitalism' in the capitalist and materialist present. This was the revolutionary tradition within which fascism worked."[14]

The components of fascist culture were diverse and heterogeneous. They included a romantic impulse and a national mysticism that idealized ancient traditions, often forging a mythical past. Fascist culture glorified values such as virility, race, youth, action, and struggle by translating them into rituals, emblems, and symbols that reshaped national identity. These emphases were further expressed in a certain idealized image of the body. Mosse depicted fascism as a product of the "nationalization of the masses," a process that had started with the French Revolution but was powerfully intensified and extended by the Great War. Unlike the nineteenth century liberal order, which had distrusted democracy and despised the masses, fascism mobilized the people by giving them the illusion of no longer being passive spectators and made them feel they were active participants of history. The nationalization of the masses meant an ensemble of collective rituals—nationalist rallies, the cult of martyrs, national festivals, monuments, flags, and songs—that created a fascist liturgy well expressed by the speeches of Mussolini and Hitler.

There is no doubt that fascism emerged as a consequence of the Great War, but its premises had been created during the nineteenth century by the transformation of the "plebs" into modern "peoples" as collective communities. Fascism was a product of "mass movements" and "mass democracy" that appeared in Europe much earlier than the collapse of the dynastic order in 1914. They coalesced a whole set of values, symbols, and myths that greatly transcended the institutional framework of democracy and that fascism was able to mobilize against this framework itself:

> It was precisely the myths and cults of the earlier mass movements that gave fascism a base from which to work and that enabled it to present an alternative to parliamentary democracy. Millions saw in the traditions of which Mussolini spoke an expression of political participation more vital and meaningful than the "bourgeois" idea of parliamentary democracy. This could happen only because of a long previous tradition, exemplified not only by nationalist mass movements but by the workers' mass movement as well.... Such mass movements demanded a new political style which would transform the crowd into a coherent political force, and nationalism in its use of the new politics provided the cult and liturgy which could accomplish this purpose. The rise of nationalism and of mass democracy, the two which stimulated the worship of the people as a secular religion, joined hands in Germany during the nineteenth century. Nationalism defined itself as a movement of the people, as it succeeded in obtaining a mass base. The mass which concerns us cannot be equated with a mob.[15]

Unlike nineteenth-century conservative thinkers such as the German Gottfried Gervinus or the French Arthur de Gobineau, who looked at mass movements both fearfully and contemptuously, fascism had understood that they embodied nationalism as a new secular religion. In *Triumph of the Will* (1935), her movie on the Nazi Party rally of Nuremberg, Leni Riefenstahl captured the liturgical character of fascism by making a popular spectacle. By transforming nationalism into a "secular religion" provided with a coherent cultural and political form, fascism invented a new kind of nationalist modernity. Since it was the French Revolution that, by sacralizing its secular institutions, had created nationalism as a collective belief and forged a new relationship between aesthetics and politics, Mosse considered fascism as "a direct descendant" of Jacobinism.[16] Reassessing the French Revolution through the prism of fascism, Mosse grasped a genetic link between them: "The French Revolution put its stamp on a novel view of the sacred: it created a full-blown civic religion that modern nationalism made its own, and fascism, whatever its variety was, above all, a nationalist movement. Moreover, some fascisms, almost in spite of themselves, did show some continuity of mind with the French Revolution."[17] It is known that this thesis provoked a clash with François Furet, for whom Jacobinism was exclusively the matrix of communism.

In his polemical essay *Interpreting the French Revolution* (1978), Furet had pointed out a genealogical link between 1793 and the Gulag, which was "leading to a rethinking of the Terror precisely because the two undertakings [were] identical." Furet concluded that "the two revolutions are connected." But he also considered that France had "invented democratic culture through the Revolution."[18] Whereas he recognized a filiation between Jacobinism and Bolshevism, he did not see any between Jacobinism and fascism. Therefore, in 1988 he refused to publish Mosse's "Fascism and the French Revolution" in a collected book he was editing for the bicentenary of 1789. A direct transition from Jacobinism to fascism, he stressed in a letter to the publisher, was "a rough anachronism."[19] Mosse published his text in the *Journal of Contemporary History* and finally included it in *The Fascist Revolution* (1999, 2021).[20]

The cult of the nation conceived of and practiced as a secular religion, the invention of new symbols, the ritualization of politics as an aesthetic liturgy, the myth of the New Man, and the mobilization of the masses "marked the beginning of a democratization of politics that climaxed in twentieth-century fascism."[21] This original interpretation points out significant elements of continuity between Jacobinism and fascism that the historiography had ignored for several decades, but it stresses them so unilaterally that, although seductive, it inevitably raises skepticism. The universal idea of humanity claimed by the French Revolution was antipodal to the fascist New Man—the embodiment of a racial community—and its democratization of politics channeled emancipatory values that did not find any equivalent in fascist nationalism. It is true that the legacy of Jacobinism was differently received by Mussolini—a political leader who came from the left—and Hitler, but both clearly rejected any filiation with the tradition of the Enlightenment. For the Nazis, the destruction of the USSR and the annihilation of Bolshevism was a way to eradicate this tradition. Mosse's tendency to split completely political style and ideology in both Jacobinism and fascism does not seem very convincing. Whereas aestheticizing politics and sacralizing the nation were inventions of the French Revolution that shaped the whole of our political modernity—what scholars call secularization, "politics as religion," or even modern political theology—fascisms explicitly saw anti-Enlightenment as their own ideological matrix.[22] From this point of view, Steven E. Aschheim's observation about Mosse's methodological Hegelianism— "a kind of updated Hegelian totality, a dialectic in which the political cannot be separated from the religious, the scientific from the aesthetic, the rational from the mythological"—has to be accepted with some reservations.[23] In many respects, Mosse's interpretation is neither more accurate nor more convincing than Karl Löwith's and György Lukács's idea of fascism as nihilism or as the "destruction of reason."[24] All of them are extremely unilateral in emphasizing either the political style or the ideological irrationalism of fascism. All of them stress the internal coherence of fascism, but Mosse viewed it as the extreme result of the "nationalization of the masses" invented by the French Revolution, whereas Löwith and Lukács reduced it to a radical form of counter-Enlightenment.

There are no doubts that, however controversial it was, Mosse's "empathic" approach opened new perspectives and inspired observations on fascism through a different lens. In Italy, its impact was both liberating and fruitful: it closed the postwar years and inaugurated a new historiographical era. After the war, antifascist historiography had been in many respects inevitable and even necessary, but thirty years later it had exhausted both its function and its potentialities. Coming from abroad, Mosse unsettled it and allowed its renewal. (From this point of view, his impact was similar to that of Robert O. Paxton's and Ze'ev Sternhell's works on Vichy France).[25] Of course, these observations are restrictive, insofar as Mosse transformed the entire historiography of fascism far beyond the Italian borders (a journal like *New German Critique* is an eloquent mirror of Mosse's scholarly "revolution"). The fact remains that the German academy proved to be more reluctant in accepting his new paradigms, and he did not try to change this situation. This relative distance explains the silence he kept during the *Historikerstreit* in the middle of the 1980s, a time in which he chose to participate in some Italian historical controversies (for instance by defending De Felice).[26]

Mosse's methodological change required an epistemic displacement that was quite exceptional for the intellectual generation that had experienced the years of fascism and the Second World War. Maybe one of the keys of his originality lies precisely in his relative indifference to historiographical debates. He followed his own path and never felt compelled to defend his innovations by criticizing canonical interpretations and dominant points of view. This allowed him to avoid scholarly inhibitions but also had some more-than-negligible consequences. If blazing the path for a new exploration of fascism as a political, cultural, and aesthetic revolution had incontestably fruitful results, his "general theory of fascism" was not without certain aporias. His attention to the anthropological features of fascism—myths, rituals, and emotional commitment[27]—came at the expense of neglecting other relevant elements. Mosse blamed Marxist scholars who had focused exclusively on the social and economic bases of fascism for underestimating its aesthetic and cultural dimensions, but they could have similarly replied that he simply ignored the complexity of its relationship with capitalism and the bourgeois classes, which was ultimately not reducible to respectability and sexual conformity.

Emphasizing the historical singularity of fascism as a coherent political phenomenon, Mosse frequently expressed his skepticism toward theories of totalitarianism that put fascism and communism together as twin enemies of classical liberalism. (He also criticized Jacob Talmon's interpretation of "totalitarian democracy," which grasped its roots in the Enlightenment and more particularly in Rousseau's thought.[28]) Since the concept of totalitarianism dominated political scholarship in both Western Europe and the United States in the 1950s, a new appraisal inevitably meant rejecting the ideological framework of the Cold War. Mosse did not engage in strong polemics against these mainstream historiographical views—at least his criticism was not comparable with the "revisionist" offensive launched by scholars such as Moshe Lewin, Sheila Fitzpatrick, or Arch Getty against the "totalitarian" school of Soviet studies in the 1960s—but he repeatedly admitted he felt uncomfortable with this category: "I am opposed to the word totalitarianism because it seems to me an untrue generalization." This consisted, he pointed out, in using "totalitarianism as a general catch phrase for anything that is antiliberal."[29] Fascism went far beyond a mere opposition to democracy as defined by liberalism—the rule of law and a set of constitutional rules warranting both the alternation of legitimate governments and the prerogatives of minorities—insofar as it established a deep emotional relationship with the masses. As he explained, "To millions this was the true democracy and the use of the pejorative term 'totalitarianism' merely serves to obscure this fact."[30]

According to Mosse, the core of Jacobinism did not lie in the Enlightenment but rather in the nationalization of the masses, the reinterpretation of nation as a "civic religion," and the invention of a new—liturgical—political style made of festivals and rituals. Therefore, the most authentic inheritor of Jacobinism was not the Marxist left; it was European nationalisms and, finally, fascism. Splitting Jacobinism from the Enlightenment, however, means recognizing that fascism was a Janus head with two faces: one modern (nationalism) and one conservative (anti-Enlightenment). Whereas its political style was modern, its rejection of the values of equality, democracy, liberty, and universalism inscribed it into the ideological and political realm of *reaction*. This simple statement introduces some nuances and problematizes the concept of a "fascist revolution." The entire trajectory of fascism was incapsulated in anticommunism: an aggressive and violent anticommunism that transformed its "political religion" into a crusade against Bolshevism and the Soviet Union. Viewed as a radical form of anticommunism, fascism loses its "revolutionary" dimension and appears as counterrevolution: not the inheritor of Jacobinism, rather a secularized version of legitimism. In the late 1930s and 1940s, Carl Schmitt depicted Donoso Cortés as a forerunner of National Socialism.

The self-representation of fascism as revolution—whose apogee was the celebration of the tenth anniversary of the March on Rome in 1932—cannot be separated from its irreducible antagonism with the communist revolution. Mosse stressed that, in contrast with Bolshevism, the fascist revolution did not have a social and economic content, but this was far from being their only difference. By historicizing fascism and Bolshevism, both the Spanish Civil War and the war on the Eastern Front between 1941 and 1945 appear as crucial moments in a confrontation between revolution and counterrevolution that deeply shaped the first half of the twentieth century. In other words, fascism was much more than "an anti-bourgeois revolution that the bourgeoisie could fully accept," or "a revolution that did not mean to and did not change the existing class or social structure"; it was a "revolution against the revolution," that is, an attempt at building a new order by destroying Bolshevism and its socialist revolution.[31] For fascism, outlining the features of a new civilization meant stressing a radical opposition to the values, ideas, symbols, and political forms of communism.

Whereas his first book on Nazism, *The Crisis of German Ideology* (1964, 2021), pointed out the origins of völkisch nationalism in a reactionary version of Romanticism and a radical criticism of the Enlightenment, in the 1970s Mosse discovered the link between fascism and Jacobinism and elaborated a conception of fascist revolution that privileged its aesthetic and cultural forms, thus emphasizing quite unilaterally its modern character. He never paid much attention to the definition of fascism as an inheritor of the conservative revolution or an extreme form of reactionary modernism, that is, as a hybrid and eclectic combination—Anson Rabinbach calls it a "cultural synthesis"—of conservatism and modernism, faith and science, reactionary values and futuristic myths, romantic ideals and biological racism, anti-Enlightenment and cult of technology.[32] Fascism certainly had abandoned the cultural despair of the old European conservatism, but its modernism radically rejected the legacy of humanism, universalism, and the rights of man. Joseph Goebbels, who in his famous speech on 1 May 1933 had announced the end of the era of the French Revolution, depicted National Socialism as a kind of "steel romanticism" (*stahlerte Romantik*).[33] As a form of reactionary modernism, fascism was more a result of the "dialectic of Enlightenment" than a "direct descendant of Jacobinism."

In fact, fascism aestheticized not only politics but also war and technique. In a deeply irrational way, Italian Futurism celebrated war as a triumph of velocity, as beauty, as invention of new forms and new landscapes created by rationalized violence. Acclaiming the Ethiopian War in 1935, Filippo Tommaso Marinetti emphasized the beauty of war because it established "man's dominion over the subjugated machinery by means of gas masks, terrifying megaphones, flame throwers, and small tanks." War is beautiful, he added, "because it initiates the dream of a steel human body" and "enriches a flowering meadow with the fiery orchids of machine guns."[34] Celebrating soldiers as mechanical bodies and landscapes disfigured by bombings is not exactly the way the Jacobins aestheticized politics. Before fascist futurism, Ernst Jünger had already glorified war as an "eruption of sensuality" and admitted his enjoyment of the "ecstasy of the combat." In his vision, war was a supreme moment of life. One year before the rise of Hitler to power, Jünger published *The Worker* (1932), an essay in which he claimed the advent of a New Man (*Arbeiter*) created by the trenches: the apotheosis of a producer completely mechanized and militarized, a kind of modern man-machine.[35] According to Herbert Marcuse, the Jüngerian "worker" was a fusion of mythology and technology, where fascist nationalism and the Nazi ideology of blood and soil were presented as "a gigantic company, totally mechanized and rationalized."[36] Political existentialism and irrationalism merged into fascism, but Mosse was not very interested in this original entanglement.

In contrast to most scholars of totalitarianism, including De Felice, Mosse defended a general theory of fascism that refused to separate its Italian and German components. Even so, he did not ignore their ideological discrepancies: the Italian regime was founded on the idea of the state and the Third Reich upon the concept of race. Whereas Italian Fascism aimed at building a totalitarian state, Nazi juridical thinkers rejected the notion of totalitarianism itself and reduced the state to a simple tool of racial rule. Nevertheless, these discordances did not exclude a progressive convergence, particularly after the Italian antisemitic turn of 1938 that led to the promulgation of racial laws. Despite their ideological and cultural differences—the Italian valorization of the aesthetic avant-garde did not fit the Nazi rejection of "degenerate art"—Italian Fascism and National Socialism belonged to the same political family. Mosse did not include Francoism in this heterogeneous category. As opposed to "revolutionary" fascism, Francoism was an extreme form of Catholic reaction. There is a contradiction nevertheless between the exclusion of Francoism from the concept of fascism and the emphasis placed in his autobiography on the Spanish Civil War as the crucial event that pushed him toward antifascism.[37] He never tried to historicize antifascism, which according to his own definition, he had experienced as a "political and emotional commitment" and which Anson Rabinbach has pertinently depicted as the ethos of his generation.[38] The fact is that the Spanish Civil War had affected him as a clash between fascism and antifascism, but Franco's clerical rituals left him quite indifferent. He was not as interested in the Christian crusade against the reds, republicans, and freemasons as he was in the "light cathedrals" of National Socialism and the "oceanic rallies" of fascism, the creativity of futurism, or the peculiar blend of moral conservatism, repressive authoritarianism, and transgressive imagination that powerfully attracted representatives of the aesthetic avant-garde such as Gottfried Benn, Pierre Drieu La Rochelle, and Robert Brasillach. Maybe this is also the reason why he did not pay attention to some of the historiographical debates that raged in the last two decades of his life, like those on the relationship of the Catholic thinkers Martin Heidegger and Carl Schmitt with Nazism. This statement, however, does not justify Mosse's expulsion of Francoism from his concept of fascism, which deserves further scrutiny.

Fascism was a peculiar synthesis of a whole set of values inherited from conservatism (authority, hierarchy, order, discipline, obedience, Romanticism, tradition, mythical past, etc.) and modernity (industrialism as national strength, militarism as powerful technology, nationalism as biological racism). It was a form of radical nationalism; it conceived of the nation as a homogeneous, monolithic, and ethnically closed community, embodied by a charismatic leader; its existential philosophy was a form of irrationalism and antihumanism; it opposed both liberalism and communism, perceiving the latter as a radical version of Enlightenment; its nationalism was militaristic and expansionist; it wished to "re-enchant" the world by means of a modern, "steel romanticism" diffused through radio, cinema, and mass meetings. From this point of view, the similarities between Fascist Italy and Nazi Germany were certainly larger than their differences. But the political spectrum of fascism was much larger than Mussolini's Italy and Hitler's Germany, and the fascist label is currently used as a singular collective that includes many national variations. Fascism was plural. In Spain the Falange, which was authentically fascist, was progressively absorbed by Francoism, which was a form of national Catholicism, much more conservative and traditionalist.[39] In Portugal, Salazarism was even more opposed to modernity. In Central Europe since 1918, several nationalist and military movements shared many features of fascism. Most of them, from Admiral Miklós Horthy's Hungary to Ion Antonescu's Romania, from the Croatian Ustasha to the Norwegian Vidkun Quisling, collaborated with Nazism during the Second World War. This plurality of fascisms explains the conflicts that sometimes occurred between them (think of the opposition between the "Austro-fascist" Engelbert Dollfuss and Nazism, the conflicts between Horthy and the nationalist dictatorships of Romania and Czechoslovakia, etc.). In France, the exact nature of the Vichy regime still nourishes a rich scholarly debate: whereas some historians deny its fascist character, Ze'ev Sternhell viewed French nationalism as the foundational experience of fascist revolution itself.[40]

Fascism was not a monolithic category; it was a *force field* in interwar Europe that polarized many nationalistic movements.[41] From the 1930s onward, fascism was exported outside of Europe, notably to Latin America.[42] After the Second World War, the military dictatorships of the 1970s in Brazil, Chile, Argentina, Uruguay, and Paraguay were often depicted as fascistic. It is significant that Mosse preferred to avoid any historiographical assessment about the notion of a "generic fascism," and he never proceeded to a systematic comparison between fascist regimes and ideologies. Instead of comparing Fascism and National Socialism, he drew from them the elements of his theory of "fascist revolution." But a comparison would have revealed the existence of multiple fascisms *without* revolution.[43] Mosse rejected the notion of totalitarianism, but his definition of fascism was narrowly limited to Italy and Germany, with some additional references to a few French intellectuals and ideologists. Whereas it certainly did not possess any "revolutionary" character, Francoism was a radical nationalism whose racism (*Casticismo*), anticommunism, antisemitism, eugenics, and endemic violence were closer to fascism and National Fascism than to any variant of political conservatism.[44]

Sometimes Mosse's comparisons were affected by his empathetic perspective. "The Duce showed more human dimensions than the Führer," he wrote in *The Fascist Revolution* in order to explain that "Mussolini had no Auschwitz."[45] Whereas National Socialism had arisen from völkisch ideology, Italian Fascism, he stressed, had its roots in the more humanistic tradition of the Risorgimento. Some passages from his memoirs give a key to clarifying this complacent view. In 1936, when Mosse was in Italy with his mother, Mussolini promised them his protection: he had not forgotten the financial help that George's father had given him when he left the Socialist Party at the outbreak of the First World War. This episode, Mosse concluded, "throws light on Mussolini's character, at least upon his sense of gratitude."[46] One could observe that, in the same year, 1936, the dictator's letters and telegrams approving gas bombings and fascist massacres in Ethiopia equally throw light on his personality, and it is highly improbable that an Ethiopian scholar could be touched by his "human dimension." Like many other tyrants, Mussolini proved to be both very generous and very cruel. Historians, however, should avoid drawing general assessments from unilateral sources, even more from their own personal experience.

This stimulates other critical remarks on Mosse's interpretation of fascism, notably its complete silence on colonialism. It is true that he elaborated his theory before the rise of postcolonial studies, but he did not change his perspective during the 1980s or the 1990s. His numerous essays on fascism do not include any substantial mention of the Ethiopian War or the Nazi campaign against the USSR as colonial wars for conquering the Italian and German "vital space" (*spazio vitale, Lebensraum*). His successful book *Toward the Final Solution* (1978, 2020), whose subtitle reads "A History of European Racism," almost completely ignores the history of colonial racism.[47] It even suggests that the concept of "sub-humanity" (*Untermenschentum*) was rarely used before 1914, skipping over its relevance during the Herero genocide in 1904 and also, in broader terms, its trivialization in the lexicon of European colonialism. The literature on the "lower races" could easily fill the shelves of entire libraries in several Western languages. This gap is all the more astonishing insofar as since 1935 colonialism had played a very important role in fascist culture and aesthetics, to the point of becoming an obsessive reference in propaganda exhibitions, posters, monuments, architecture, movies, popular songs, and newspaper and street advertisements. But Mosse was far from being an exception: a similar disregard for colonialism distinguishes the ensemble of German-Jewish culture in exile. Colonialism and imperialism are almost nonexistent entries in the collected works of Theodor Adorno, Max Horkheimer, Walter Benjamin, Siegfried Kracauer, Franz Neumann, Ernst Cassirer, Karl Löwith, et cetera. The exceptions were Herbert Marcuse, especially during the Vietnam War, and Hannah Arendt, for a very short moment, when she wrote *The Origins of Totalitarianism* (1951), a work that devotes an entire section to "imperialism." But she quickly joined her fellow emigrants a few years later, when she criticized Jean-Paul Sartre and Frantz Fanon and depicted colonial revolutions as "mad fury" and "nightmares."[48] For this intellectual generation, antisemitism was such a deep, devastating, and traumatic experience that it absorbed all their existential concerns and analytic efforts, thus eclipsing colonialism. It is significant that Mosse's book on racism and his pioneering essay on fascism chronologically correspond with Edward Said's *Orientalism* (1978), the work that reinterpreted Western culture and literature through their symbiotic and conflicting relationship with the colonial world.[49] This missed encounter was highly regrettable.

According to Mosse, fascism built a physical and spiritual ideal of the "New Man" that was rooted in a militaristic and aggressive vision of manliness, virility, and bodily strength. This ideal needed its "countertypes," which he identified primarily with the Jew and the homosexual. The Jew was the "anti-race," a foreign element that, having once penetrated the body of the national community, corrupted and destroyed it from the inside as a virus and a cancer; the homosexual emasculated the nation because of his femininity, his nervousness, his lack of virility, and his weakness of character. Thus, fascism simply radicalized many stereotypes of racial and gender conformity that defined the norms of bourgeois respectability:

> The new fascist or National Socialist man was not so new after all. Most of his basic traits were shared with normative masculinity, but he extended them, giving them an aggressive and uncompromising cast as an essential tool in the struggle for dominance. There is, surely, a world of difference between the clean-cut Englishman, the all-American boy, and the ideal member of the SS. Yet all shared essentially the same masculine stereotype with its virtues, strength, and aesthetic appeal.... Fascism, and especially National Socialism, demonstrated the awesome possibilities inherent in modern masculinity when it was stripped down to its warlike functions.[50]

The countertypes could also be the women who did not accept the role of domestic angels and racial breeders that nationalism assigned them, according to Hans Mayer's model of the "outsider" (*Außenseiter*).[51] But Mosse never mentioned colonized subjects, upon whose racial otherness was fixed a clear separation between rulers and ruled in terms of juridical and political status, aesthetic representation, and spatial location. Analogously to the Nuremberg Laws of 1935, Italy's Fascist laws of 1938 aimed at excluding the Jews from citizenship and the national community, but their purpose was also to establish rigorous racial boundaries in the Italian empire. From this point of view, fascism simply deepened the political anthropology of colonialism that had been one of the sources of European nationalism since the middle of the nineteenth century.

Some topics are subjacent in Mosse's works. On the last page of his memoirs, he writes that "the Holocaust was never very far from [his] mind," adding that he was "a member of the Holocaust generation" and that he had "constantly tried to understand an event too monstrous to contemplate." All his studies on racism, völkisch thought, and sexual otherness, even when they were not directly related to the Holocaust, converged toward the search for interpreting the extermination of the Jews. "Finding an explanation," he wrote, had been "vital not only for the understanding of modern history, but also for my own peace of mind. This is a question my generation had to face, and eventually I felt that I had come closer to an understanding of the Holocaust as a historical phenomenon. We have to live with an undertone of horror in spite of the sort of advance that made it so much easier for me to accept my own nature."[52] In fact, a book like *Fallen Soldiers* (1990) is a decisive contribution to the analysis of the historical premises of the Holocaust by devoting many chapters to the advent of industrial massacre, the trivialization of mass death, and the brutalization of politics engendered by the Great War.[53] In contrast to colonialism, which in 2020 appears to his readers as a major absence, the Holocaust was a hidden—and constantly present nonetheless—dimension of his work.

Mosse contributed greatly to the conceptualization of fascism by forging analytical categories such as "fascist revolution," the nationalization of the masses, the brutalization of politics, sexual conformity, and the contrast between *Bildung* and *Sittlichkeit*, which have become milestones of historical studies. Twenty years after his death, his work has been canonized and does not need to be discovered or exhumed from oblivion. His concepts, theses, and paradigms have inspired two generations of scholars that have analyzed Italian Fascist and Nazi culture in all its dimensions. This certainly does not mean that everything has been said on these topics, but the historiographical renewal of the most recent years has come back to some of the aspects of fascism that Mosse usually neglected, such as colonial violence and the economy. The magnitude of his intellectual innovation and his scholarly achievements is self-evident, and in his own spirit, his work deserves empathetic criticism more than pure celebration.

Notes

1. See Lorenzo Benadusi and Giorgio Caravale, eds., *George L. Mosse's Italy: Interpretation, Reception, and Intellectual Heritage* (New York: Palgrave Macmillan, 2014).

2. See Emilio Gentile, *Renzo De Felice: Lo storico e il personaggio* (Rome: Laterza, 2003). For an assessment of De Felice's historical "revisionism," see Gianpasquale Santomassimo, "Il ruolo di Renzo De Felice," in *Fascismo e antifascismo: Rimozioni, revisioni, negazioni*, ed. Enzo Collotti (Rome: Laterza, 2000), 415–29.

3. George L. Mosse, *Confronting History: A Memoir* (Madison: University of Wisconsin Press, 2000), 5.

4. George L. Mosse, "Renzo De Felice e il revisionismo storico," *Nuova Antologia* 133, no. 2206 (1998): 181, 185.

5. See Emilio Gentile, *Il fascino del persecutore: George L. Mosse e la catastrofe dell'uomo moderno* (Rome: Carocci, 2007), translated as *Fascination with the Persecutor: George L. Mosse and the Catastrophe of Modern Man*, trans. John and Anne C. Tedeschi (Madison: University of Wisconsin Press, 2021). The most "Mossean" contribution by Gentile is *The Sacralization of Politics in Fascist Italy* (Cambridge, MA: Harvard University Press, 1996). See also the introduction by Benadusi and Caravale to *George L. Mosse's Italy*.

6. Joan Ringelheim, "Interview with George Mosse" (1995), quoted in Karel Plessini, *The Perils of Normalcy: George L. Mosse and the Remaking of Cultural History* (Madison: University of Wisconsin Press, 2014), 89.

7. Plessini, *The Perils of Normalcy*, 89.

8. See Dominick LaCapra, *Writing History, Writing Trauma* (Baltimore: Johns Hopkins University Press, 2001), 40.
9. Gentile, *Il fascino del persecutore*.
10. Gordon A. Craig, *Germany 1866–1945* (Oxford: Clarendon Press, 1978), 469.
11. Norberto Bobbio, *Ideological Profile of Twentieth-Century Italy*, trans. Lydia Cochrane (Princeton, NJ: Princeton University Press, 1995), 133.
12. George L. Mosse, *The Crisis of German Ideology* (1964; repr., Madison: University of Wisconsin Press, 2021). A couple of years later, Mosse gathered and edited an ensemble of Nazi texts with the provocative title *Nazi Culture: Intellectual, Cultural, and Social Life in the Third Reich* (1966; repr., Madison: University of Wisconsin Press, 2003).
13. George L. Mosse, *The Fascist Revolution: Toward a General Theory of Fascism* (Madison: University of Wisconsin Press, 2021), 7.
14. Mosse, *The Fascist Revolution*, 7.
15. George L. Mosse, *The Nationalization of the Masses: Political Symbolism and Mass Movements in Germany from the Napoleonic Wars through the Third Reich* (Madison: University of Wisconsin Press, 2023), 4–5.
16. Mosse, *The Fascist Revolution*, 7.
17. Mosse, *The Fascist Revolution*, 57.
18. François Furet, *Interpreting the French Revolution* (New York: Cambridge University Press, 1981), 12, 24.
19. Gentile, *Fascination with the Persecutor*, 182–84, 231.
20. See Gentile, *Il fascino del persecutore*, 191–93; and Mosse, *The Fascist Revolution*, chap. 4, 57–76. Quite significantly, this episode is not even mentioned by Stéphane Audoin-Rouzeau in his assessment of the French reception of Mosse's work: "George L. Mosse: Réflections sur une méconnaissance française," *Annales: Histoire, Sciences sociales* 56, no. 1 (2001): 183–86.
21. Audoin-Rouzeau, "George L. Mosse," 87.
22. See, for instance, Emilio Gentile, *Politics as Religion* (Princeton, NJ: Princeton University Press, 2006).
23. Steven E. Aschheim, "George Mosse: The Man and the Work," in George L. Mosse, *George Mosse: On the Occasion of His Retirement: 17.6.85* (Jerusalem: Hebrew University, 1986), quoted in Plessini, *The Perils of Normalcy*, 90. See also George L. Mosse, interview with Michael Ledeen, in *Nazism: A Historical and Comparative Analysis of National Socialism* (New Brunswick, NJ: Transaction Books, 1978), 30.
24. See Karl Löwith, *From Hegel to Nietzsche: The Revolution in Nineteenth-Century Thought* (New York: Holt, 1964); Georg Lukács, *The Destruction of Reason* (Atlantic Highlands, NJ: Humanities Press, 1981).
25. See Robert Wohl, "French Fascism, Both Right and Left: Reflections on the Sternhell Controversy," *Journal of Modern History* 63, no. 1 (1991): 91–98, and the essays edited by Michel Dobry, *Le mythe de l'allergie française au fascism* (Paris: Albin Michel, 2003).
26. Mosse's silence during the *Historikerstreit* was probably the epilogue of an older misunderstanding with German historiography, which had almost ignored a pathbreaking work like *The Crisis of German Ideology* (1964, 2021), at the time of the so-called

Fischer Controversy. See Philipp Stelzel, *History after Hitler: A Transatlantic Enterprise* (Philadelphia: University of Philadelphia Press, 2019), 77–79.

27. See Roger Griffin, "Withstanding the Rush of Time: The Prescience of Mosse's Anthropological View of Fascism," in *What History Tells: George L. Mosse and the Culture of Modern Europe*, ed. Stanley G. Payne, David J. Sorkin, and John S. Tortorice (Madison: University of Wisconsin Press, 2004), 110–33.

28. Jacob L. Talmon, *The Origins of Totalitarian Democracy* (London: Secker & Warburg, 1952); George L. Mosse, "Political Style and Political Theory: Totalitarian Democracy Revisited" (1984), in *Confronting the Nation: Jewish and Western Nationalism* (Waltham, MA: Brandeis University Press, 1993), 60–69.

29. Mosse, *Nazism*, 77–78. See also Plessini, *The Perils of Normalcy*, 137–38. On the "revisionist" school in Soviet studies, see Sheila Fitzpatrick, "Revisionism in Retrospect: A Personal View," *Slavic Review* 67, no. 3 (2008): 682–704.

30. Mosse, "Political Style and Political Theory," 169.

31. George L. Mosse, "What Is Fascism?," Seminar on the Intellectual Foundations of National Socialism, quoted in Plessini, *The Perils of Normalcy*, 140.

32. See Jeffrey Herf, *Reactionary Modernism: Technology, Culture, and Politics in Weimar and the Third Reich* (Cambridge: Cambridge University Press, 1984); and Anson Rabinbach, "'The Abyss That Opened Before Us': Thinking about Auschwitz and Modernity," in *Catastrophe and Meaning: The Holocaust and the Twentieth Century*, ed. Moishe Postone and Eric Santner (Chicago: University of Chicago Press, 2003), 51–66 (on National Socialism as "cultural synthesis," 61).

33. Quoted by Herf, *Reactionary Modernism*, 195.

34. Quoted in Walter Benjamin, "The Work of Art in the Age of Mechanical Reproduction," in *Illuminations: Essays and Reflections*, ed. Hannah Arendt (New York: Schocken Books, 1968), 241–42.

35. See Ernst Jünger, *The Worker: Domination and Form*, ed. Laurence P. Hemming (Evanston, IL: Northwestern University Press, 2017).

36. Herbert Marcuse, "The New German Mentality" (1942), in *Technology, War and Fascism: Collected Papers of Herbert Marcuse*, ed. Douglas Kellner (London: Routledge, 1998), 153.

37. Mosse, *Confronting History*, 101–4. In the early 1960s, Mosse considered "clerical fascism" as a specific current of a broader fascist culture. See George L. Mosse, *The Culture of Western Europe: The Nineteenth and Twentieth Centuries* (Madison: University of Wisconsin Press, 2023), 386, 388. He abandoned this assessment in his following works, shaped by a more anthropological approach to the history of fascism. This shift is stressed by Stanley G. Payne, "George L. Mosse and Walter Laqueur on the History of Fascism," *Journal of Contemporary History* 50, no. 4 (2015): 750–67.

38. Anson Rabinbach, "George Mosse and the Culture of Antifascism," *German Politics and Society* 18, no. 4 (2000): 30–45.

39. It is interesting to observe Mosse's closeness with Stanley G. Payne, the historian of Francoism who played a "revisionist" role in Spanish historiography quite similar to that of De Felice in Italy or Ernst Nolte in Germany. But Payne's "revisionist" tendencies

clearly appeared only after Mosse's death. See Stanley G. Payne, *The Collapse of the Spanish Republic, 1933–1936: Origins of the Civil War* (New Haven, CT: Yale University Press, 2006). On "revisionist" tendencies in scholarship on fascism and Francoism, see Enzo Traverso, *The New Faces of Fascism* (New York: Verso, 2019), 138–41.

40. See Ze'ev Sternhell, *La Droite révolutionnaire: Les origines françaises du fascisme* (1978; repr. Paris: Gallimard, 1997); and Ze'ev Sternhell, *Neither Right Nor Left: The Fascist Ideology in France* (Berkeley: University of California Press, 1986)

41. See Philippe Burrin, "Le champ magnétique des fascismes," in *Fascisme, nazisme, autoritarisme* (Paris: Seuil, 2000), 211–46.

42. See Federico Finchelstein, *Transatlantic Fascism: Ideology, Violence, and the Sacred in Argentina and Italy, 1919–1945* (Durham, NC: Duke University Press, 2010).

43. See Philippe Burrin, "Le fascisme: La révolution sans révolutionnaires," *Le Débat* 38 (1986): 164–76, then republished as "L'imaginaire politique du fascisme," in Burrin, *Fascisme, nazisme, autoritarisme*, 49–72.

44. See Julián Casanova, *The Spanish Republic and Civil War* (New York: Cambridge University Press, 2010).

45. Mosse, *The Fascist Revolution*, 35.

46. Mosse, *Confronting History*, 109.

47. George L. Mosse, *Toward the Final Solution: A History of European Racism* (Madison: University of Wisconsin Press, 2020).

48. On Arendt's Eurocentrism, see Judith Butler, *Parting Ways: Jewishness and the Critique of Zionism* (New York: Columbia University Press, 2013), 139–41.

49. Edward Said, *Orientalism* (New York: Pantheon Books, 1978).

50. George L. Mosse, *The Image of Man: The Creation of Modern Masculinity* (New York: Oxford University Press, 1996), 180. This work expands and develops many ideas already sketched in Mosse's pioneering book *Nationalism and Sexuality: Middle-Class Morality and Sexual Norms in Modern Europe* (Madison: University of Wisconsin Press, 2020).

51. Hans Mayer, *Outsiders: A Study in Life and Letters* (Cambridge, MA: MIT Press, 1982).

52. Mosse, *Confronting History*, 185.

53. George L. Mosse, *Fallen Soldiers: Reshaping the Memory of the World Wars* (New York: Oxford University Press, 1990). See also Saul Friedländer, "Mosse's Influence on the Historiography of the Holocaust," in Payne, Sorkin, and Tortorice, *What History Tells*, 134–50.

4

Women, Gender, and the Radical Right

Then and Now

Mary Nolan

Is right radical populism a new fascism? Or is this label analytically misleading and politically counterproductive? Since the ascendance of such populist leaders as Viktor Orbán, Recep Tayyip Erdoğan, Donald Trump, Narendra Modi, and Jair Bolsonaro and the proliferation of right-wing populist parties across Europe, that question has troubled politicians and journalists, historians and social scientists, as well as progressive political activists. Some, such as Timothy Snyder and Jason Stanley, insist the category is apt, the parallels with interwar fascism numerous, and the danger great.[1] Others, like Federico Finchelstein and Udi Greenberg, argue that the contexts in which old and new right-wing movements emerged differ as radically as the forms of organization, the place of violence, and many elements of ideology.[2] Right radical populism, for example, is a response to a globalized, neoliberal, and multipolar political and economic order, the end of the Cold War, and mass migration and refugee crises. This context is very different than that of World War I and its aftermath of political instability, emergent communism, and economic crises. As Kim Schepple insists, right-wing movements will try to come to power—or in Hungary already have—not by classic fascist means but by creeping constitutional coups.[3] I am sympathetic to arguments about differences and worry that the f-word is used too readily to condemn rather than to analyze and strategize against these new forms of right radicalism.

Yet fascism is a good concept to think with. Classic fascism helps us understand the appeals of authoritarianism, nationalism, and charismatic leaders and the nature of antisemitism and racism. Classic fascism shows us that culture wars were pervasive in the interwar period and that gender politics were central to the appeal and practices of interwar movements. And many women were enthusiastic supporters of them. To be sure, in the first decades after World War II, scholarship on Nazism and other fascist movements paid little or no attention to issues of women, gender, sexuality, and family. That changed in the 1980s and 1990s when George L. Mosse and feminist historians in the United States and Germany did pioneering work on these issues. In *Nationalism and Sexuality* (1985, 2020) and *The Image of Man* (1996), Mosse explored the centrality of the dominant German conception of masculinity to the definition of nationalism throughout the nineteenth century and under National Socialism. He suggestively illustrated Nazism's preoccupation with promoting its understanding of proper manliness, with its not easily reconcilable commitments to male sacrifice to the nation and deep loyalty to other men, on the one hand, and to bourgeois family life and respectable sexuality on the other. Claudia Koonz and Carola Sachse reconstructed the multiple activities of Nazi women's organizations, while Gisela Bock dissected National Socialism's racist pronatalism and Marion Kaplan explored the gendered dimensions of growing antisemitism.[4] Dagmar Herzog produced major works on fascism and sexuality that took the pioneering work of Mosse in new directions.[5] Since then, scholarship on these themes has grown exponentially.

Yet current studies of right radical populism, most of them by men, have not attended to issues of women, gender, family, and sexuality: they focus instead, and at the expense of gender, on the illiberalism and authoritarianism of these movements, their varieties of nationalism, antisemitism, and racism, and their efforts to both build on and distance themselves from their interwar predecessors. They analyze class and race, "the people" versus elites, authoritarianism, nativism, and violence but ignore the gendered aspects of these discourses and practices.[6] It is unclear whether this is because scholars of right radical populism deem such issues as unimportant or because they have neglected even to ask about how gender structures society and politics as well as discourses of power or to consider why other scholars have paid so much attention to reproduction, LGBTQ+ rights, and gender construction. Women scholars across several disciplines have, however, done pioneering work on these issues.[7] This essay draws on that work as well as the work of scholars such as Mosse to suggest the contours of women's roles in right radical populist movements, the gendered character of their discourses and policies, and the centrality of family, sexuality, and reproduction to their appeals. This will help us understand both how these movements and ideologies are similar to and build on their interwar predecessors and how they have tried to reinvent themselves for the new world of the twenty-first century.

Since the 1990s, populist radical right (PRR) parties in the West have been trying to modernize. They accept the parliamentary rules of the game, even if they prefer authoritarian variants thereof, and avoid explicitly fascist language—mostly. They present themselves as legitimate coalition partners. The new gender politics of right radical populist movements reflect these efforts to shed the baggage of fascist forebears and to become "normal" parties. New approaches to gender are also a product of the growing role of women as populist voters and activists. PRR parties insist on women's equal value and simultaneously wage war on what they call "gender ideology." In support of their vision of women, family, and sexuality, they combine attacks on social policy and state intervention with advocacy of extensive pronatalist and pro-family welfare measures—but only for the ethnic majority of a country. In their appeals to the gendered fears and fantasies of potential supporters, right radical populists offer a heady mix of strident rhetoric and contradictory policies.

The European PRR parties are a diverse lot in terms of origins, size, influence, and stances on particular issues, but they all share ethnonationalism or nativism and a vision of society as divided between "the people," comprised of the virtuous, ethnic majority only, and the decadent, cosmopolitan elites, out of touch with the interests of ordinary citizens.[8] They have developed in response to their particular national contexts but recognize one another as kindred. Their vehement rejection of the social construction of gender, their nostalgia for the male breadwinner family (one always more imagined than real), their opposition to LGBTQ+ rights, and their sexualized attacks on Muslims are central unifying ideas. On a practical level, they cooperate online and in places like the European Parliament and have strong ties with politicians, churches, and right-wing institutes throughout Europe and across the Atlantic.

Women and the Radical Right

Interwar European fascist movements offered clear and traditional views of gender, family, and sexuality—many of which were actively endorsed by women.[9] Militarized masculinity and the patriarchal family were valorized. *Kinder, Küche, Kirche* designated the proper places and functions of women, who were excluded from the male-run party and state, deemed unsuitable to grapple with ideological questions, and relegated to special women's organizations dealing with maternity and charity. As the second sex of the master race, "Aryan" German women were, in theory, to leave paid work and have many children; in practice, working-class women remained employed throughout the Third Reich, as did many white-collar women in government, military, and party offices from the late 1930s on. In Germany and Italy, pronatalist social policies benefited only those deemed racially pure and politically acceptable, and abortion was prohibited. Yet none of this successfully raised the birth rate.[10] Male homosexuality remained outlawed, however much homosocial bonds were privileged, while lesbianism was passed over in silence. Nazi ideology and iconography depicted the Jew as a sexual predator who threatened the purity of the "Aryan" race, propagating deviant sexual practices including but not limited to homosexuality. Antisemitic laws prohibited sexual relations between "Aryans" and Jews.[11]

Traditional gender ideologies and biological racism persisted in small neo-Nazi and neofascist movements of the first postwar decades and their membership remained overwhelmingly male. Although the German Constitutional Court outlawed several of these parties, they were not a significant threat in the Federal Republic or elsewhere in Western Europe. Thereafter, radical right parties underwent a slow but significant change. During the 1980s the radical right gained new visibility in Western Europe—as a reaction to the sixties' protests and seventies' economic crises. PRR parties embraced the emerging neoliberal critique of Keynesianism, corporatism, the interventionist state, and expansive social policy. From the mid-1990s on, a growing number of Western and Northern European radical right parties embraced ethnonationalism, adopting new or intensified forms of anti-immigrant rhetoric combined with calls for stronger law and order policies.[12] In the early twenty-first century, they were joined by new populist parties in the formerly communist countries of Central and Eastern Europe.

Changes in the role of women and discourses on gender were integral to the reorientation of the radical right. Interwar fascist movements were male-dominated, even though they enjoyed extensive support from women, and after 1945 former fascist men were the mainstay of the successor neofascist parties. Since the 1990s, European PRR parties are no longer exclusively *Männerparteien*. Some have prominent women leaders, most of whom are not related to high-ranking male figures.[13] Pia Kjærsgaard founded and for thirteen years led the Danish People's Party (DF); Marine Le Pen, the divorced daughter of Front National founder Jean-Marie Le Pen, has led the Front National, now renamed the National Rally, to enormous electoral success. Siv Jensen runs the Norwegian Progress Party. Frauke Petry had a stormy tenure as head of the Alternative for Germany (AfD), as did Alice Weidel, a former Goldman Sachs banker and lesbian mother of two with a Swiss partner of Sri Lankan heritage. Women staff the parties and run for offices on lower levels as well, and they are active, at times prominent, in some of the social movements and subcultures that support right-wing populist parties.[14] This would have been unimaginable in interwar fascist movements.

As in mainstream parties, the desired attributes of a woman leader are unclear and the actual models offered vary. Like Margaret Thatcher, Angela Merkel, and Theresa May, leaders such as Kjærsgaard and Le Pen are shrewd politicians, tough, outspoken, and controlling. But even these PRR women leaders seem under pressure to be traditionally feminine. Le Pen presents herself now as a woman warrior in the mold of Joan of Arc, now a caring matriarch attuned to the needs of her national children. Her frequent displays of masculine virility are occasionally softened by a sexualization of her image.[15] Kjærsgaard depicts herself as both a determined party leader and an emotional motherly "private Pia."[16] In social movements, such as the Identitarians or Pegida (Patriotic Europeans Against the Islamization of the West), women sometimes demonstrate militantly in the streets alongside men and at other times claim to act alone in defense of women's interests, which they understand better than feminists.[17] There are no women leaders in Eastern European populist parties, whether because of entrenched patriarchy or the association of women politicians with the communist past or the Western feminist present.[18]

One of the key differences between the PRR now and interwar fascism is that no one talks of excluding women from politics. Radical right parties appeal to women in their propaganda, run women candidates, and promote women functionaries, even if these are often relegated to family and social issues. Every party platform includes policies on women and family, and LGBTQ+ and reproductive rights.

As attention to women has increased, so too has support from women. While a majority of populist voters are male, the percentage of women varies, from roughly 33 percent to 40 percent on average in Germany, Austria, and France to a high of 67 percent in Poland, and it has been growing.[19] The gender gap among PRR women office holders is similar to that of mainstream parties; only the left does substantially better in running women candidates and winning women's votes.[20] The existing literature on the gender gap attributes the predominance of male voters to continuity with older right-wing movements, the economic situation, or sociopsychological dispositions such as authoritarian personalities.[21] Male PRR voters are said to be the losers of modernization and individualization and marginal to politics and hegemonic masculinity.[22] Unemployment, stagnant or downward mobility, and weak economic and social infrastructure encourage men to support the populist radical right.[23] Yet male support for the PRR is by no means limited to precarious blue-collar workers. Opinion polls and electoral analyses seldom ask directly about reactions to gender issues and family policy—abortion and gay marriage being the exception—but journalists and populist propagandists frequently speak of a crisis of masculinity, of weakened traditional fatherhood, and the miseducation of boys by the state and feminists. Polish activists call for the restoration of formerly hegemonic masculinity.[24] Men in the former German Democratic Republic say they vote AfD because they lack not only jobs but also potential marriage partners. Women, they resentfully complain, have been the winners from reunification (even though women massively lost jobs and political positions in the 1990s).[25] In 2018 the AfD published an Advent calendar behind each of whose windows were famous men ranging from Martin Luther and Helmut Schmidt to Ronald Reagan and Thilo Sarrazin. The explicit aim was to combat the "public denigration of white men."[26]

Male-centered theories are even more inadequate for women.[27] Some female activists come from far-right milieus; this is especially true with the French Nationalists (FN) and the Freedom Party of Austria (FPÖ); but others are new to this kind of politics, having migrated from the center-right or occasionally from the left. Women who vote populist are less likely to feel themselves to be on the losing side of modern, postindustrial economies, as fewer have blue-collar jobs and many hold public sector positions. They may be less identified than men with their jobs or find alternative communities within the family or the church. Electoral analyses indicate that women support PRR parties because of their allegiance to nationalism and nativism and the appeals of authoritarianism. According to opinion polls, women are every bit as anti-immigrant and Islamophobic as men.[28] But are they anti-immigrant for the same reasons? The PRR argues obsessively about the ostensible economic and sexual dangers that immigrants present. Job competition is a much more immediate issue for men, especially in France and Italy, than for women, because immigrant women do not compete with native ones for the public sector or white-collar service jobs. Rather, immigrant women across Western Europe are doing the domestic and caring labor for the young, the sick, and the elderly that enable women of the ethnic majority to do paid work.[29] If the economic threat from migrants seems more external or distant to women, the sexual danger is imagined as internal and immediate.

Feminists argue that women dislike the gender policies of these parties. Cas Mudde, the most prolific writer on the European PRR, however, claims such assertions reflect a feminist bias and are not empirically grounded.[30] On the one hand, women are generally more concerned with issues of health and education, to which the PRR pays less attention.[31] Women who find the ethnonationalism and Islamophobia of the PRR appealing may dislike the physically violent and militaristic radical right subcultures and social movements that actively support these parties. They can find endorsement for their anti-immigrant policies and criticism of multiculturalism in center-right and even center-left parties across Europe and need not turn to the PRR. On the other hand, many women share the attitudes of the PRR parties on abortion, gay marriage, traditional family roles, and "gender ideology." Given how explicitly PRR parties lay out their gender politics, they assume these will attract women as well as men.

Family

PRR party programs and electoral propaganda speak extensively and passionately about family, women's labor force participation, sexuality, and immigration and Islam. So, too, does the literature produced by growing and internationally linked groups of far-right intellectuals and organizations.[32] These themes are linked by the PRR's obsession with "gender ideology" as the underlying threat to the normative family, sexuality, and women's roles. PRR views on gender and sexuality vary significantly from country to country and have changed over time, as these parties try to accommodate to the mainstream views of their national cultures. In general, Scandinavian PRR parties take more liberal stands, especially on gay and lesbian rights, while those in Austria, Spain, and Eastern Europe are most conservative. In France, Germany, and Italy, PRR parties unhappily accept many LGBTQ+ and reproductive rights in the short run, while hoping for their eventual abolition. There is much more commonality in the gendered discourses on Islam and immigration, and all abhor the idea of gender as socially constructed.

The heterosexual nuclear family, with women fulfilling their true calling of motherhood, occupies a central place in PRR discourse just as it did in interwar fascism. It is seen as the only healthy family form, a key bloc of society and the protector of national values. Populists describe this family as "natural," a term linking it both to natural law and more vaguely to the natural world and science.[33] Some populists deploy the language of human rights, arguing that this family is "entitled to protection by Society and the State" (Article 16/3 of the Universal Declaration of Human Rights).[34] While fascists sought to mobilize the family, as a whole and in its parts, into the fascist movement and state, the PRR seeks to protect the family from the state. The Spanish right-wing VOX Party, for example, states that "the family is a reality existing before the state"; the "natural family" must be defended legally and supported materially.[35] The FPÖ insists that the state should not interfere with parental rights and, along with the Swiss People's Party, opposes state-run childcare.[36] The Belgian Vlaams Blok, however, does endorse public childcare.[37] Many oppose UN or

EU conventions on domestic violence as an unjust interference in the private sphere of the heteronormative family.[38]

Although PRR parties prefer the traditional family of interwar fantasy, with a patriarchal husband, nonemployed wife, and many children, they recognize that this is for most neither economically possible nor politically enforceable. And many women leaders and functionaries of these movements don't live that model. Many PRR parties offer some variant of what sociologists call "modern traditionalism," urging the state to enable women to combine work and family either in different phases of their life or lifelong.[39] Some posit equal pay or flexible hours as a way to do this. Whereas her father had denounced "women's invasion" of the workplace, Marine Le Pen does not advocate pushing women out of the labor force—nor does she propose any positive policies to enable women to manage the double burden.[40] Others envision neotraditional arrangements. Hungarian Prime Minister Viktor Orbán insists that the state must support work, performance, and family equally; rather than gender mainstreaming there should be family mainstreaming, which ideally would enable women to stay at home with their children.[41] (Given acute labor shortages and high out-migration, that vision has not been realized.)

PRR discussions of family say surprisingly little about men. Interwar fascism wanted men to be muscular, militaristic, nationalistic, and antisemitic, willing to use violence and sacrifice oneself for the fatherland. Men should rule their families, even if their most intense emotional bonds were with right-wing comrades. Defeat discredited but did not entirely eliminate this model. It survives in some of the German male *Kameradschaften* and *Burschenschaften*, and violence and disdain for bourgeois norms pervades the skinhead culture. For the PRR parties, pursuing a modern image, the street fighter, student dueler, and tough blue-collar worker are less attractive models. PRR party leaders present themselves as competent, efficient, and knowledgeable politicians and respectable bourgeois functionaries. The National Democratic Party of Germany, for example, offered both a radicalized version of tough, risk-taking masculinity to potential young supporters and a model of the orderly, punctual, hard-working, productivity-oriented manager to potential middle-class ones.[42] Some AfD leaders parade their economic expertise in suits and ties; others engage in provocative racist polemics, while Pegida and elements of the subculture take to the streets.[43] Whatever their public personae, populist right radicals want men to be fathers in stable heterosexual marriages, a role, they claim, the state and feminists are eroding. In Austria, the 2001 coalition government in which the FPÖ participated established a division for men's affairs in the Ministry for Social Security and Generations.[44] The AfD electoral program promises to strengthen fathers' rights.

PRR parties want not only "natural" families but large ones, at least for the ethnic majority. Children are not only protectors of the national culture but also promoters of a desired ethnic homogeneity. For most right radical populists, increasing the birth rate is the necessary alternative to immigration in order to sustain an aging population and fulfill labor market needs. In the more extreme formulations of some French, Dutch, and German populists, unless their nationals have more children, Europe faces the danger of a "demographic holocaust" or a great "replacement" by Muslims.[45] This defensive and frightened pronationalism is a far cry from its interwar counterpart that linked large families to territorial expansion and national glory.

At first glance, right-wing populists are promoting the ideal of the neoliberal, self-reliant family, responsible for its own welfare, education, and socialization. Yet PRR parties also favor social policies that support this "natural" family. The FPÖ supports tax benefits and child allowances for families and flexible work schedules to enable women to combine work and motherhood.[46] The AfD wants to encourage more German births by ending discrimination against full-time mothers, implementing taxes and social policies for families with children, and outlawing abortion.[47] The Danish People's Party and the Dutch Party for Freedom endorse such measures and in addition want to limit benefits going to nonethnic Danes and Dutch, either by capping the number of eligible children at two or by prohibiting child support to the children of workers living abroad.[48] The FN favors maternal income equal to the minimum wage and pensions for stay-at-home mothers as well as subsidies and housing loans for families with several children.[49] Wages for housework, a radical demand of some second-wave feminists in the 1970s and 1980s, has now migrated to the radical right as part of a host of positive and negative pronatalist measures.

Attitudes toward social policies for women and families reflect the contradictions within the PRR around the market and the state. Although right-radical populists criticize globalization and the EU, they do not reject all neoliberal ideas or advocate autarky, as interwar fascists did. In varied combinations, PRR parties simultaneously advocate anti-neoliberal protectionism and neoliberal deregulation and privatization at home.[50] They want to shrink the state, balance budgets, and lower taxes on the one hand and offer subsidies and tax benefits to families on the other hand. They reject redistributive policies except for full-time mothers—of the ethnic majority only. PRR parties oppose state interference in family decisions regarding childcare, parental rights, and education yet urge the state to intervene in the labor market to encourage women to leave it and reproduce. Like neoliberals and classical liberals, the PRR's emphasis puts much more responsibility on families, and especially women. Populists urge families to raise self-reliant, disciplined, productive individuals who will provide, in gendered ways, the labor on which neoliberal capitalism depends, while asking little positive from the state. The goal, according to the AfD program is *"Weniger Staat, mehr Freiheit und Selbstverantwortung"* (less state, more freedom and responsibility for oneself).[51] Like interwar fascism, PRR parties want a gendered division of labor at home and in the workplace and social policies targeted by ethnicity and race. Unlike their predecessors, they do not want the family subsumed into the state and mobilized for expansion abroad. Rather, the family is to protect itself and be protected from forces at home and abroad deemed foreign and dangerous.

Right radical populism in the United States is an outlier here. Negative pronatalist measures abound such as restrictions on abortion and the defunding of Planned Parenthood. Since the 1980s, a joint neoliberal and neoconservative onslaught on the welfare state has drastically cut state aid to women and children, forcing individuals and families to take sole responsibility for the young as well as the ill and the elderly. Communities of color have been especially hard hit. No positive family measures of the sort European populists advocate are favored, even for whites.

Sexuality

Sexuality presents multiple challenges to the natural family of populist dreams. Reproductive rights; lesbian, gay, bisexual, trans, and queer movements; sex education in schools; and reproductive technologies are seen as both threats and as useful targets against which to mobilize support. They are also sources of division within the populist right. All agree that abortion is undesirable but disagree on its continued legality. Scandinavian and Dutch PRR parties accept abortion as a right. While Jean-Marie Le Pen regarded abortion as "an anti-French genocide," Marine Le Pen respects the legality of abortion because conditions that would enable women to choose not to have one are lacking.[52] The AfD insists that abortion is not a human right and urges state support for poor or single pregnant women to minimize abortions. The FPÖ, Law and Justice, and Fidesz oppose abortion, and the 2011 Hungarian Constitution defined life as beginning at conception.[53] Despite ongoing antiabortion campaigns, European PRR parties have been less successful than their American counterparts in restricting funding for abortions or implementing "conscience clauses" that permit medical professionals to refuse to perform abortions or provide information about them.[54] Party platforms are silent on the issue of contraception, but the extremist advocacy network Agenda Europe wants to outlaw all artificial contraception, viewing it as the "tip of the iceberg in the Culture War."[55]

LGBTQ+ rights are a major preoccupation of the populist radical right. The concern is less with outlawing homosexual acts, as was the case with fascist movements, than with banning gay marriage. Only the Dutch Party for Freedom supports gay marriage. AfD activists are divided on the issue, while the FN accepts gay civil unions but opposes marriage or gay adoptions and most PRR parties reject both.[56] PRR parties have won wide support by opposing gay marriage in Eastern Europe, where EU norms on gay rights are denounced as the imposition of foreign norms that violate Polish culture and deny Poles their human right to enforce their own values.[57] In France in 2012, the FN was part of the massive *Manif pour tous* that drew tens of thousands to Paris to protest the proposed Taubira law on Marriage for All. Protestors claimed gay marriage would "jeopardize the foundations of human identity" and lead to a "denatured society." They reject gay parenting, whether through adoption, surrogacy, or reproductive technologies.[58] The right-wing World Congress of Families goes farther and opposes surrogacy of any kind.[59] Other countries have held similar but smaller "demonstrations for all."[60] The populist right has been promoting referenda to put prohibitions against gay marriage in national constitutions. They succeeded in Croatia but failed in Slovakia and Romania because of insufficient turnout.[61]

Many radical right populists seek to provoke a moral panic about schools, secular governments, and the EU, which ostensibly endangers innocent children by exposing them to false ideas about the social construction of gender, the naturalness of homosexuality, and the variety of families.[62] This pernicious miseducation of children, along with threats to the "natural family" and the spread of LGBTQ+ rights is due to and is justified by something the right calls "gender ideology."

Anti-Genderism

The parties of the PRR, with the AfD, FPÖ, and the Polish Law and Justice Party in the lead, have joined the growing movement against what they label "gender ideology" or "gender theory." These capacious and amorphous terms demonize the ideas, policies, and behaviors that the PRR hates.[63] "Gender ideology" is "the symbolic glue" that holds together the seemingly disparate concerns of the PRR with the birth rate and gay adoption, sex education and employment quotas, IVF and abortion. Anti-genderism is a response to the multiplicity of family forms, sexual practices, and women's lives that emerged from the cultural revolution of the 1960s and 1970s in Western Europe; in East Central Europe, it is a reaction against communist efforts to emancipate women and repress religion. Critics of "gender ideology" insist that men and women are fundamentally different and that difference is rooted in nature; education and social policy must recognize this. While PRR parties assert women's equal rights and accord them political roles, they argue that equal worth does not mean sameness. They engage critically with new gender theories like Judith Butler's, which insist on the constructed character of gender and sexuality and the fluidity and multiplicity of sexual practices and family forms. These challenge the natural order and the social order built on it. The populists seek not only to combat particular practices and policies but also to refute their underlying justification, which is dismissed as mere theory or, worse yet, ideology, a term raising the specter of totalitarianism.[64]

A stark biological determinism pervades PRR discourses, a strong belief that to challenge immutable roles, norms, and practices is to risk the downfall of culture and society. This biological determinism is at odds with attempts to avoid the biological racism of fascism. PRR parties make cultural arguments about immigrants and Islam, claiming, at least rhetorically, that every culture has a right to exist and all are equally valuable. But they should not be mixed or homogenized, for there are ineradicable differences among ethnicities, races, and religions. Only by separating them can one preserve the nation and the families foundational to it. But on what grounds can they argue for the distinctiveness of women of the ethnic majority? Here a biological determinism akin to racism creeps back in, disguised as defense of the "natural order."

While Catholics are hardly the only opponents of equal rights for women and theories about the social construction of gender, Vatican activism has played a major role in developing discourses attacking gender ideology or the theory of gender as it is also called.[65] Since the 1994 UN Cairo Conference on Population and Development and the 1995 UN Beijing Women's Conference, popes Paul VI, John Paul II, and Benedict XVI have deployed the language of personalism and Christian human rights to combat "gender feminism." They argue that men and women have "equal dignity as persons" but "equal dignity is premised on and manifest in essential and complementary differences, physical, psychological and ontological."[66] Some conservative clergy and laity engage seriously with gender theory and try to develop an alternative humanism that stresses social connections over the individualism associated with neoliberalism and feminism.[67] Others, such as the widely translated German Gabriele Kuby, argue in lurid tones that "gender ideology" means "the destruction of freedom in the name of freedom." It is a totalitarian endeavor that wages war on Christianity.[68]

Numerous authors assert that "gender ideology" promotes a "culture of death." Pope Francis, the Guinean Cardinal Robert Sarah, and Polish populists see gender ideology as a form of "ideological colonization" promoted by secular states, international organizations, feminists, and gays.[69] According to Sarah Bracke and David Paternotte, religion, family, and the natural order are threatened by "on the one hand the idolatry of Western freedom; on the other, Islamic fundamentalism: atheistic secularism versus religious fanaticism.... We find ourselves between 'gender ideology and ISIS.'"[70]

The assault on "gender ideology" has spread far beyond the Vatican through a dense transnational network spanning Europe, North and South America, the Middle East, and Africa.[71] It is central to the platform of the World Congress of Families, which held its twelfth large convention in Budapest in 2017 with support from Orbán and its thirteenth in Verona with the blessing of Deputy Prime Minister Matteo Salvini.[72] It permeates Agenda Europe, a Euro-American organization that opposes sexual and reproductive rights in the name of enforcing natural law and warding off the impending destruction of Western civilization. Agenda Europe has an information sharing blog, regular summits, and a manifesto titled "Restoring the Natural Order." Activists in these circles, many of whom hold positions in PRR parties and EU institutions, share ideas and strategies via social media, as members of the European parliament, and with financial support from the Vatican as well as from the Christian right in the United States through organizations like the Howard Center for Family, Religion & Society.[73] When it comes to gender, right-wing populist internationalism functions much more effectively than did fascist internationalism in the interwar years.

PRR parties speak the language of anti-genderism. The FPÖ endorses the "equal worth" of women and men but opposes "equality," understood as sameness, which it dismisses as "unnatural."[74] The 2017 AfD electoral program claims gender ideology will "destroy the classical family as a model for life and roles" and is thus "unconstitutional [*verfassungsfeindlich*]." Participants in the 2014 *Manif pour tous* in Paris carried signs reading "No to the theory of gender," "We want sex not gender," and "Don't touch our gender stereotypes."[75] More recently, "gender ideology" has moved into the political mainstream; the 2016 party program of the Christian Democratic Party (CDU) proclaimed its opposition to "gender ideology and early sexualization."[76]

PRR parties oppose any gender mainstreaming, whether or not it directly impacts family and sexuality. They reject all affirmative action laws, quotas, and gender sensitive language as socially disruptive and indicative of state overreach. Many dismiss gender studies as quasi-totalitarian indoctrination. The AfD insists it is not a legitimate scholarly discipline and has no place in the university. The Orbán government closed the single gender studies program in Hungary.[77] Populists want to purge the school curriculum of sex education and gender studies, for these ostensibly contribute to the early sexualization of children and undermine heteronormativity.

Gender has proven a more useful target than feminism, the preferred enemy of interwar fascism. PRR parties are, to be sure, antifeminist, but feminism is too narrow a target for their multiple concerns; gender is more encompassing and modern. By singling out "gender ideology," populists deploy their enemies' key concept against them. The attack on "gender ideology" brings together those committed to essentialism versus constructionism, those concerned about abortion with those most strongly opposed to LGBTQ+ rights, whether they be religious or secular, from the far right or the conservative mainstream. It links gender and sexuality to concerns about education, deploying discourses of the endangered child most effectively. It builds on a growing discomfort with multiculturalism that is simultaneously religious, racial and ethnic, and sexual and familial. Anti-genderism provides a common pan-European language that papers over differences between Eastern and Western European populists on many particular issues concerning gender as well as economics and politics. Finally, gender is a term that is seldom if ever translated from the English to indicate its foreign and subversive character; it can be dismissed as a dangerous import, coming either from the United States, the EU, or the UN. Anti-genderism thus appeals to nationalist populists, eager to protect national cultures, Christianity, or Europe and the West.[78]

Islam and Immigration

Right radical populism's preoccupation with gender, family, and sexuality permeates its view of those it defines as the enemy threatening the purity of the nation. Unlike interwar fascism, it is the Muslim and the immigrant/refugee, often conflated, who is demonized, more than the Jew. Their early marriages and large families are said to erode cultural homogeneity, overload the welfare state, and threaten the numerical superiority of Christian Europeans, according to populist politicians and publications. Veiling is considered anti-European and anti-Christian and should be outlawed. Male immigrants and refugees are seen not only as economic competitors for working-class jobs but also as oppressors of their own women and sexual predators on those of the dominant ethnicity. Populists relish in telling tales—real and imagined—of sexual harassment, rape, pimping, and drug dealing.

As in colonial discourse, populists depict immigrant women as victims of a patriarchal religion and oppressive cultures and claim their treatment marks all

Muslims as inferior. Populists demand Muslim assimilation to dominant family and sexual norms but simultaneously consider that impossible, for culture is immutable. Separation by means of exclusion from Europe is the preferred remedy. Once again, the biological determinism that populists have sought to shed creeps back in. The line between cultural and racial arguments regarding Muslim immigrants and refugees is porous in PRR parties and nonexistent in radical right subcultures. Francesca Scrinzi has aptly called this "the racialization of sexism."[79]

Populist discourses on Muslims, migrants, and sexuality are riddled with contradictions. Most populists condemn individual sexual choice when women and LGBTQ+ people practice it and national, EU, and UN laws legitimize it, yet some, especially in Scandinavia and the Netherlands, condemn Muslims for opposing homosexuality, gay marriage, and abortion. In criticizing Islam's treatment of women, populists resort to defending a liberal, secular view of gender and family in which they at best only partially believe. The FN papers over tensions by simultaneously condemning Islam in the name of French Republican *laïcité* and in the name of traditional Christianity as the foundation of European culture.[80] Elsewhere in Europe, defense of the "natural family" coexists with a condemnation of its Muslim counterpart. Yet many Muslims share the PRR's advocacy of more traditional, hierarchical families and sexual propriety, its condemnation of abortion and homosexuality, and its opposition to gender ideology.[81] Rather than viewing them as potential allies on issues of family and sexuality, however, populists see them as an even more dangerous enemy than "gender ideology," for immigrants and refugees are obstacles to populist economic protectionism, opposition to multiculturalism, and a stripped-down neoliberal welfare state. Instead, as Sarah Farris pointed out, there is a de facto coalition of populists, feminists, and neoliberals who jointly attack veiling and portray Muslim men as sexual predators. All lament the oppression of Muslim women, yet neither PRR parties nor their mainstream counterparts offer proposals to improve their situation.[82]

In Eastern Europe, populist governments and parties are as anti-immigrant as those in Western Europe, but Islam is not singled out as the principle threat to desired forms of gender, sexuality, and family. Countries like Poland and Hungary, which have few immigrants, focus their discriminatory practices on the Roma, but they are nonetheless vehemently opposed to taking refugees and insist Islam is a threat to European civilization. They blame the EU, international NGOs, and the UN, and in Poland, Germany as well, for imposing a foreign "gender ideology," be it women's rights, abortion, gay rights, or the Istanbul convention on domestic violence.[83]

Conclusion

PRR parties have shaped mainstream policies toward women, gender, sexuality, and family. In some cases, they embed prevalent center-right views, like opposition to abortion or gay marriage, in broader discourses of ethnonationalism, opposition to immigration, and Islamophobia.[84] Populists have made welfare chauvinism a legitimate topic of discussion and policy by championing popular positive pro-family social policies for the ethnic majority only. They have made abortion, LGBTQ+ rights, and gay marriage hot-button issues. In ways that seem modern, they incorporate women, acknowledging their political rights while emphasizing their vocation as mothers. They defend the traditional family in a new language of human rights. Their insistence on gender essentialism and complementarity appeals to those seeking stability and security in a world whose macro and micro contours are precarious and shifting. Populists now lead the chorus of those claiming that gays, feminists, and Muslims endanger culture and usher in moral decline. The attacks on "gender ideology" draw support from the PRR and the conservative center, contributing to the normalization of the far right.[85]

Most PRR parties have not come to power or become acceptable coalition partners, yet they have unsettled the long-standing dominance of conservative and social democratic parties in Western Europe and replaced more liberal ones in Eastern Europe. They have gained legitimacy, occupying a position within the legal party spectrum, rather than outside, by masking racism behind the discourse of cultural difference, softening antidemocratic tendencies with calls for law and order, and rallying support behind the defense of nation, Europe (but not the EU), the West, and Christianity. The PRR is closer to the center than one likes to think, for the center is moving right in every country in Europe.

Notes

1. Timothy Snyder, *The Road to Unfreedom: Russia, Europe and America* (New York: Tim Duggan Books, 2018); Jason Stanley, *How Fascism Works: The Politics of Us and Them* (New York: Random House, 2018).

2. Federico Finchelstein, *From Fascism to Populism in History* (Berkeley: University of California Press, 2017); Udi Greenberg, "The Myth of a New Nazism," *Spiked*, 10 August 2018, https://www.spiked-online.com/2018/08/10/the-myth-of-a-new-nazism/.

3. Kim Schepple "Worst Practices and the Transnational Legal Order (or How to Build a Constitutional 'Democratorship' in Plain Sight)," http://lawsdocbox.com/Politics/780 00703-Worst-practices-and-the-transnational-legal-order-or-how-to-build-a-constitu tional-democratorship-in-plain-sight-kim-lane-scheppele.html.

4. Claudia Koonz, *Women, Family and Nazi Politics* (New York: St. Martin's, 1988); Carola Sachse, *Siemens, der Nationalsozialismus und die moderne Familie: Eine Untersuchung*

zur sozialen Rationalisierung in Deutschland im 20. Jahrhundert (Bremen: Rasch und Röhring, 1990); Gisela Bock, *Zwangssterilisation im Nationalsozialismus: Studien zur Rassenpolitik und Frauenpolitik* (Opladen: Westdeutscher Verlag, 1986); Marion Kaplan, *Between Dignity and Despair: Jewish Life in Nazi Germany* (Oxford: Oxford University Press, 1999).

5. Dagmar Herzog, *Sex after Fascism: Memory and Morality in Twentieth-Century Germany* (Princeton, NJ: Princeton University Press, 2007).

6. John B. Judis, *The Populist Explosion: How the Great Recession Transformed American and European Politics* (New York: Columbia Global Reports, 2016); Jan-Werner Müller, *What Is Populism?* (Philadelphia: University of Pennsylvania Press, 2016).

7. New works exploring women and gender include: Helga Amesberger and Brigitte Halbmayr, *Rechtsextreme Parteien-eine mögliche Heimat für Frauen?* (Wiesbaden: Leske and Budrich Verlag, 2002); Robert Claus, Esther Lehnert, and Yves Müller, eds., *"Was ein rechter Mann ist . . .": Männlichkeiten im Rechtsextremismus* (Berlin: Karl Dietz, 2010); Michaela Köttig, Renate Bitzan, and Andrea Pető, eds., *Gender and Far Right Politics in Europe* (London: Palgrave Macmillan, 2017); "Gender and Populist Right Radical Politics," special issue, *Patterns of Prejudice* 49, nos. 1/2 (2015); Heinrich Böll Stiftung, *Anti-Gender Movements on the Rise? Strategising for Gender Equality in Central and Eastern Europe*, (Berlin: Heinrich Böll Stiftung, 2015), https://www.boell.de/en/2015/04/21/anti-gender-movements-rise.

8. Elisabeth Carter, "Party Ideology," in *The Populist Radical Right: A Reader*, ed. Cas Mudde (London: Routledge, 2017), 29–58; Cas Mudde, "Introduction," in *The Populist Radical Right*.

9. Victoria de Grazia, *How Fascism Ruled Women: Italy, 1922–1945* (Berkeley: University of California Press, 1993); Koonz, *Women, Family, and Nazi Politics*; Dörte Winkler, *Frauenarbeit im "Dritten Reich"* (Hamburg: Hoffmann und Campe, 1975).

10. Timothy Mason, "Women in Nazi Germany," *History Workshop* 1 (Spring 1976): 74–113, and 2 (Autumn 1976): 5–32.

11. Barbara Loomis and William N. Bonds, eds., "Sexuality and German Fascism," special issue, *Journal of the History of Sexuality* 11, nos. 1/2 (January–April 2002).

12. Cas Mudde, *Populist Radical Right Parties in Europe* (Cambridge: Cambridge University Press, 2007), 3–4.

13. Mudde exaggerates the extent of familial connections and nepotism. *Populist Radical Right Parties*, 98–100.

14. José Pedro Zúquete, *The Identitarians: The Movement Against Globalism and Islam in Europe* (Notre Dame: University of Notre Dame Press, 2018), 57–91.

15. Dorit Geva, "Daughter, Mother, Captain: Marine Le Pen, Gender, and Populism in the French National Front," *Social Politics* 27, no. 1 (2020): 11–17.

16. Susi Meret, "Charismatic Female Leadership and Gender: Pia Kjærsgaard and the Danish People's Party," *Patterns of Prejudice* 49, nos. 1–2 (2015): 92–94.

17. Johannes Finke and Christian Unger, "Jung, weiblich, rechts," *Berliner Morgenpost*, 5 April 2018, https://www.morgenpost.de/politik/article213924617/Jung-weiblich-rechts.html.

18. For a view of gender confusion in the Polish radical right, see the *Guardian* documentary "Pretty Radical," https://www.theguardian.com/world/video/2015/jan/19/pretty-radical-young-woman-oikabd-far-right-video.
19. Terri E. Givens, "The Radical Right Gender Gap," in Mudde, *The Populist Radical Right*, 291; Mudde, *Populist Radical Right Parties*, 112.
20. Mudde, *Populist Radical Right Parties*, 106, 117.
21. Niels Spierings, Andrej Zaslove, Liza M. Mügge, and Sarah L. de Lange, "Gender and Populist Radical-Right Parties: An Introduction," *Patterns of Prejudice* 49, nos. 1–2 (2015): 3–15.
22. Johannes Hillje, *Return to the Politically Abandoned: Conversations in Right-Wing Populist Strongholds in Germany and France* (Berlin: Progressives Zentrum, 2018).
23. Hillje, *Return to the Politically Abandoned*, 2018; Richard Hilmer, Bettina Kohlrausch, Rits Müller-Hilmer, and Jérmie Gagné, "Einstellung und soziale Lebenslage: Eine Spurensuche nach Gründen für rechtspopulistische Orientierung, auch unter Gewerkschaftsmitgliedern," *Working Paper Forschungsförderung* 44 (Düsseldorf: Hans Böckler Stiftung, August 2017).
24. Elżbieta Korolczuk and Agnieszka Graff, "Gender as 'Ebola from Brussels': The Anticolonial Frame and the Rise of Illiberal Populism," *Signs, Journal of Women in Culture and Society* 43, no. 4 (2018): 797–821, 803; Pankaj Mishra, "The Crisis in Modern Masculinity," *Guardian*, 17 March 2018.
25. Katrin Bennhold, "One Legacy of Merkel? Angry East German Men Fueling the Far Right," *New York Times*, 5 November 2018; Barbara Einhorn, *Cinderella Goes to Market: Citizenship, Gender and Women's Movements in East Central Europe* (London: Verso, 1993).
26. Markus Wehner, "AfD-Adventskalender: Luther, Brecht und andere weiße Männer," *Frankfurter Allgemeine*, 6 December 2018, https://www.faz.net/aktuell/politik/inland/afd-adventskalender-hinter-jeden-tuerchen-ein-weisser-mann-15928357.html.
27. Kai Arzheimer, "Electoral Sociology—Who Votes for the Extreme Right and Why—and When?," in Mudde, *The Populist Radical Right*, 277–89.
28. Niels Spierings and Andrej Zaslove, "Gendering the Vote for Populist Radical Right Parties," *Patterns of Prejudice* 49, nos. 1–2 (2015): 135–38.
29. Givens, "The Radical Right Gender Gap," 295–97; Sara R. Farris, "Femonationalism and the 'Regular' Army of Labor Called Migrant Women," *History of the Present* 2, no. 2 (Fall 2012): 193.
30. Mudde, *Populist Radical Right Parties*, 91.
31. Eelco Harteveld, Wouter van der Brug, Stefan Dahlberg, and Andrej Kokkonen, "The Gender Gap in Populist Radical-Right Voting: Examining the Demand Side in Western and Eastern Europe," *Patterns of Prejudice* 49, nos. 1–2 (2015): 103–30, 112.
32. These include the Nouvelle Droite, Casa Pound Italia, and some in the Identitarian movement as well as religious groups such as the World Congress of Families and Agenda Europe. Volker Weiss, *Die autoritäre Revolte: Die neue Rechte und der Untergang des Abendlandes* (Stuttgart: Klett-Cotta, 2017); Zúquete, *The Identitarians*.
33. Éric Fassin, "Gender and the Problem of Universals: Catholic Mobilizations and Sexual Democracy in France," *Religion and Gender* 6, no. 2 (2016): 173–86, 181.

34. Verona Declaration, XIII World Congress of Families, 31 March 1919, https://pro fam.org/verona-declaration-adopted-at-wcf-xiii-on-31-march-2019/.
35. VOX, *Asuntos sociales*, Capítulo 2 y 3, Familia, Democracia y Natalidad, https://www.voxespana.es/wp-content/uploads/2015/05/2.3.FAMILIA-150518-1.pdf.
36. Amesberger and Halbmayr, "Österreich," 278, in Party program of the Freedom Party of Austria, https://www.fpoe.at/themen/parteiprogramm/parteiprogramm-englisch/.
37. Tjitske Akkerman, "Gender and the Radical Right in Western Europe: A Comparative Analysis of Policy Agendas," *Patterns of Prejudice* 49, nos. 1–2 (2015): 37–60, 47.
38. This is especially true in Eastern Europe. See Heinrich Böll Stiftung, *Anti-Gender Movements on the Rise?*, for related essays.
39. Mudde, *Populist Radical Right Parties*, 93.
40. Nonna Mayer and Mariette Sineau, "France: The Front National," in *Rechtsextreme Parteien*, ed. Helga Amesberger and Brigitte Halbmayr (Leverkusen: Leske & Budrich, 2002), 85; Francesca Scrinzi, "Gender and Women in the Front National Discourse and Policy: From 'Mothers of the Nation' to 'Working Mothers'?," *New Formations* 91 (2017): 87–101, 93, 96.
41. Anikó Félix, "Hungary," in *Gender as Symbolic Glue: The Position and Role of Conservative and Far Right Parties in the Anti-Gender Movement in Europe*, ed. Eszter Kováts and Maari Põim (Brussels: Foundation for European Progressive Studies, 2015), 62–82, 64.
42. Claus, Lehnert, and Müller, *"Was ein Rechter Mann ist . . . ,"* 58–59.
43. Hajo Funke, Von Wutbürgern und Brandstiftern: AfD-Pegida-Gewaltnetze (Berlin: vbb, 2016), 73–120.
44. AfD Wahlprogramm, https://www.afd.de/grundsatzprogramm/; Amesberger and Halbmayr, "Österreich," 279.
45. Renaud Camus, *You Will Not Replace Us!* (Plieux: Chez l'auteur, 2018).
46. Amesberger and Halbmayr, "Österreich," 278.
47. AfD 2017 electoral program, https://www.afd.de/grundsatzprogramm/; Andreas Kemper, *Keimzelle der Nation? Familien- und geschlechterpolitische Positionen der AfD—eine Expertise*, Friedrich Ebert Stiftung, 2014, http://library.fes.de/pdf-files/dialog/10641-20140414.pdf.
48. Cas Mudde and Cristóbal Rovira Kaltwasser, "*Vox populi* or *vox masculini*? Populism and Gender in Northern Europe and South America," *Patterns of Prejudice*, 49 nos. 1–2 (2015): 16–36, 27.
49. Mayer and Sineau, "France: The Front National," 96–97.
50. Quinn Slobodian, "Neoliberalism's Populist Bastards: A New Political Divide between National Economies," *Public Seminar*, 15 February 2018, http://www.publicseminar.org/2018/02/neoliberalisms-populist-bastards/.
51. AfD 2017 electoral program, www.afd.de/wahlprogramm, quote p. 30, Kurzprogramm.
52. Angelique Chrisafis, "'We Feel Very Close to Her': Can 'Fake Feminist' Marine Le Pen Win the Female Vote?," *Guardian*, 18 March 2017; Francesca Scrinzi, "A 'New'

National Front? Gender, Religion, Secularism and the French Populist Radical Right," in Köttig, Bitzan, and Petö, *Gender and Far Right Politics in Europe*, 127–39.

53. Amesberger and Halbmayr, "Österreich," 278; AfD 2017 electoral program; Kemper, *Keimzelle der Nation?*

54. Niel Datta, *Restoring the Natural Order: The Religious Extremists' Vision to Mobilize European Societies against Human Rights on Sexuality and Reproduction* (Brussels: European Forum on Population and Development, 2018), 29.

55. Datta, *Restoring the Natural Order*, 12.

56. AfD 2017 electoral program; Kemper, *Keimzelle der Nation?*; Akkerman, "Gender and the Radical Right in Western Europe," 45.

57. See Heinrich Böll Stiftung, *Anti-Gender Movements on the Rise?*

58. Camille Robcis, "Catholics, the 'Theory of Gender,' and the Turn to the Human in France: A New Dreyfus Affair?," *Journal of Modern History* 87 (December 2015): 892–923, 893.

59. World Congress of Families, Verona Declaration.

60. Sarah Bracke and David Paternotte, "Unpacking the Sin of Gender," *Religion & Politics* 6, no. 2 (2016): 143–54, 145.

61. Datta, *Restoring the Natural Order*, 28.

62. Imke Schmincke, "Das Kind als Chiffre politischer Auseinandersetzung am Beispiel neuer konservativer Protestbewegungen in Frankreich und Deutschland," in *Anti-Genderismus: Sexualität und Geschlecht als Schauplätze aktueller politischer Auseinandersetzungen*, ed. Sabine Hark and Paula-Irene Villa (Bielefeld: Transcript Verlag, 2015), 93–107.

63. PRR parties benefit from criticism of gender ideology, but while some, like Law and Justice, use it extensively, Fidesz and Jobbik deploy it less, and the FN avoids it. Eszter Kováts and Maari Põim, eds., *Gender as Symbolic Glue: The Position and Role of Conservative and Far Right Parties in the Anti-Gender Movement in Europe* (Brussels: Foundation for European Progressive Studies, 2015).

64. Fassin, "Gender and the Problem of Universals," 177; Bracke and Paternotte, "Unpacking the Sin of Gender," 144; Robcis, "Catholics, the 'Theory of Gender,' and the Turn to the Human in France," 915–16.

65. Bracke and Paternotte, "Unpacking the Sin of Gender," 145; Robcis, "Catholics, the 'Theory of Gender,' and the Turn to the Human in France," 899.

66. Mary-Ann Case, "The Role of the Popes in the Invention of Complementarity and the Vatican's Anathematization of Gender," *Religion & Gender* 6, no. 2 (2016): 155–72, 156.

67. Robcis, "Catholics, the 'Theory of Gender,' and the Turn to the Human in France," 905–13.

68. Gabriele Kuby, *The Global Sexual Revolution: Destruction of Freedom in the Name of Freedom* (Kettering, OH: Angelico Press 2015).

69. Bracke and Paternotte, "Unpacking the Sin of Gender"; Korolczuk and Graff, "Gender as 'Ebola from Brussels,'" 807.

70. Bracke and Paternotte, "Unpacking the Sin of Gender," 147.

71. Korolczuk and Graff, "Gender as 'Ebola from Brussels,'" 799–804. Clifford Bob has labeled this the Baptist-Burka network. *The Global Right Wing and the Clash of World Politics* (Cambridge: Cambridge University Press, 2012).
72. World Congress of Families, Verona Declaration.
73. See Datta, *Restoring the Natural Order*.
74. Amesberger and Halbmayr, "Österreich," 278.
75. Robcis, "Catholics, the 'Theory of Gender,' and the Turn to the Human in France."
76. "Julbrot backen ist nicht mehr attraktiv," interview with Juliane Lang, https://www.akweb.de/ak_s/ak637/38.htm.
77. Elizabeth Redden, "Hungary Officially Ends Gender Studies Programs, *Inside Higher Ed*, 17 October 2018, https://www.insidehighered.com/quicktakes/2018/10/17/hungary-officially-ends-gender-studies-programs.
78. Sabina Hark and Paula-Irene Villa, eds., *Anti-Genderismus: Sexualität und Geschlecht als Schauplätze aktueller politischer Auseinandersetzungen* (Bielefeld: Transcript Verlag, 2015); Fassin, "Gender and the Problem of Universals," 2016.
79. Scrinzi, "A 'New' National Front?," 132.
80. See Funke, *Von Wutbürgern und Brandstiftern*, for elaboration.
81. Sarah Carol and Nadja Milewski, "Attitudes toward Abortion among the Muslim Minority and Non-Muslim Majority in Cross-National Perspective: Can Religiosity Explain the Differences?," *Sociology of Religion* 78, no. 4 (Winter 2017): 456–91; Antje Röder "Immigrants' Attitudes toward Homosexuality: Socialization, Religion, and Acculturation in European Host Societies," *International Migration Review* 49, no. 4 (2015): 1042–70; Antje Röder, "Religious Differences in Immigrants' Gender Role Attitudes: The Changing Impact of Origin Country and Individual Religiosity," *Ethnic and Racial Studies* 37, no. 14 (2014): 2615–35.
82. Farris, "Femonationalism and the 'Regular' Army of Labor Called Migrant Women," 184–199, and Farris, *In the Name of Women's Rights: The Rise of Femonationalism* (Durham, NC: Duke University Press, 2017). The Dutch Party for Freedom (PVV) and the Belgian Flemish Interest (VB) advocate equality for immigrant women, but the FN and the Swiss People's Party do not discuss this. Tjitske Akkerman, "Gender and the Radical Right in Western Europe."
83. Félix, "Hungary," 68–70; Weronika Grzebalska, "Poland," in Kováts and Põim, *Gender as Symbolic Glue*, 89–92; Borbála Juhász, "Forwards or Backwards? Strategies to Overcome Gender Backlash in Hungary," in *Anti-Gender Movements on the Rise? Strategising for Gender Equality in Central and Eastern Europe* (Berlin: Heinrich Böll Stiftung, 2015), 28–32, 29.
84. Udi Greenberg, "Christianity, Democracy, and Populism," *Boston Review*, 22 October 2019.
85. Maik Fielitz and Laura Lotte Laloire, "Introductory Remarks," in *Trouble on the Far Right: Contemporary Right-Wing Strategies and Practices in Europe*, ed. Maik Fielitz and Laura Lotte Laloire (Bielefeld: Transcript Verlag, 2016), 13–26.

5

Behemoth Rises Again

On Twenty-First-Century Fascism

Andreas Huyssen

When George L. Mosse reoriented fascism research in the 1960s and 1970s, fascism was history. Or so it seemed. As we now experience the resurgence of fascist motifs, images, and tropes in our polity and their proliferation on social media in the United States, fascism is fast becoming a serious threat to American democracy. When Andrew Breitbart famously argued that politics is downstream from culture, it was as if the American "alt-right" had taken a lesson from Mosse. Mosse's work was the first that focused on the deep cultural dimensions of fascism as they manifested themselves in perceptions of reality, attitudes, popular culture, mentalities, symbols, and myths about better pasts. The task of historical analysis now is to disentangle the various long-term cultural and historical threads by which fascist modes of thought and behavior have survived and how and under what conditions they have been reinvigorated in the age of Donald Trump.

In a variation on what Theodor Adorno once said about nationalism, I would suggest that today fascism is both obsolete and up to date.[1] Rather than embracing facile analogies of interwar fascism and the present, I want to examine some of the categories used by the Frankfurt School and its orbit to describe interwar fascism and National Socialism and explore their continuing relevance and simultaneous obsolescence in today's context. These categories are fascism as cultural synthesis, *Ungleichzeitigkeit* (nonsynchronicity), the authoritarian personality, the role of the fascist agitator, the place of utopian vision, white nationalism and racism, fascism as racketeering, and fascist politics as totalitarian Leviathan or chaotic Behemoth. Focusing on the Frankfurt School is pertinent in light of the fact that its work has become the basis for the right's virulent attack on cultural Marxism, which has recently moved from the lunatic fringe into the mainstream.

There is no question that radical right-wing fringe phenomena have been normalized under Donald Trump, most spectacularly when he claimed that there were good people on both sides in the 2017 Charlottesville riots. What used to be called the lunatic fringe in American politics has been made respectable by such pronouncements as well as by the euphemism of "alt-right" itself, a term innocuous enough to disguise its white supremacist ideology. Adorno also warned that the afterlife of fascist tendencies *within* democracy is more menacing than the survival of fascist tendencies *against* democracy.[2] Today we face a situation where Adorno's distinction has been cashed in. Tendencies from within, brilliantly analyzed by Wendy Brown in her 2015 book *Undoing the Demos: Neoliberalism's Stealth Revolution*, are merging in the United States with outright tendencies against democracy.[3] The Trump regime participated in both. A torch-carrying, Nazi-slogan-shouting mob marched at the Unite the Right rally in Charlottesville, and the Republican Party stood by. Indeed, the right seemed united at the time, and Trump was the bond between the mob and the Tea Party elite. Even after he lost the 2020 election, Trump's chokehold on the Republican Party has remained intact. The "big lie" of a stolen election is widely supported by Republicans who are cynically using it to create new laws limiting voting rights in the red states and threatening the very process of a fair and correct vote count by installing followers of Trump in key supervisory positions at the state and local levels. Ever more, Trumpism is a cross-class movement, which directs its fury at liberal economic and cultural elites as much as it shuns traditional conservatism. It aims to attack and dismantle American governmental institutions, a practice that is fully in sync with Steve Bannon's demand to "deconstruct the administrative state" and with Breitbart's call to attack the "Democrat media complex" online. All of it is clearly revolutionary in its aims. It is only a small step from Mark Zuckerberg's Silicon Valley motto to "move fast and break things" to the seditious insurrection on 6 January 2021 in Washington, DC. Throughout the Trump presidency and since, the false "fake news" mantra, coupled with occult conspiracy theories à la QAnon, have been used to gaslight the electorate and to normalize an alternative reality. In the meantime, much of the real deconstruction of governmental institutions regarding the law and the constitution, healthcare, the environment, housing, foreign policy, and climate change has rarely caught the headlines in any sustained fashion. While neofascist parties have also gained ground in the European Union, with few exceptions (Hungary and Poland), they are not (yet) the mainstream. In the United States, the Trump Republicans *are* mainstream and further to the right than either the Alternative für Deutschland in Germany or the latest incarnation of the National Rally in France. The outlook for the next U.S. elections remains dark.

It was Charlottesville and the zombie fascism of a long-festering white supremacist right that made talk about fascism today unavoidable. The role of the Oath Keepers and the Proud Boys in the January 6 insurrection only added urgency to do more than talk. At the same time, it is clear that comparing Trump to Hitler or Mussolini amounts to nothing so much as a helpless antifascism, a mirror image of what it opposes. The careless use of the analogy may also suggest to many Americans that fascism is an import from Europe, rather than being indigenous to American politics. Hitler, after all, considered New York lawyer Madison Grant's *The Passing of the Great Race* (1916) his bible.[4] And the 1935 German race laws took American race legislation as their model. Fascism was always already transnational, just as it is today. We forget this at our peril.

Cultural Synthesis and Nonsynchronism

In his book *Heritage of Our Time* (1934), the German philosopher Ernst Bloch analyzed fascism as a mass movement, based on a cultural synthesis of major social contradictions. He argued that fascist ideology was riven by two opposing tendencies: technological modernization and reactionary modernism on the one hand versus mythic beliefs in the soul and essence of the German nation and its supreme calling being realized in a Third Reich on the other. Such mythic beliefs, fatally ignored by the Marxist Left of the Third International, were captured by Bloch's concept of *Ungleichzeitigkeit* (nonsynchronism).[5] The concept usefully pointed to a rift between temporal perception and lived reality, between modern and premodern ways of life in the daily experience of segments of Germany's population. Bloch emphasized the force of "irrational" or "mythic" imaginaries, which could be mobilized among peasants or the lower middle classes whose life experiences had not caught up with the pace of metropolitan modernity and technological cultural change. He focused on divergent temporalities of experience pervading these social strata, which were susceptible to slogans of Führer charisma, *Blut und Boden*, hostility to urban modernity, racial superiority, and völkisch ideology—slogans that were all thoroughly modern rather than archaic.

It seems evident that cultural synthesis—not as homogenization but as a bundling of contradictory dimensions—is at stake with the various layers of the Trump movement and its diverse electorate in the United States today. What once was the culture war, waged by the "neocons" in the 1980s, has morphed into an ever more radical cultural self-understanding of the alt-right in the United States today, for whom the neocons are merely "cuckservatives" (cuckold conservatives). Not content to attack the influence of postmodernism in the academy, the alt-right has constructed another bogeyman called cultural Marxism, held to be responsible for the betrayal of American values and equated with political correctness. Cultural Marxism now occupies the discursive space Bolshevism once held as dominant enemy image in Nazi ideology. It is neither the primacy of politics (as in Nazism), nor the primacy of economics (as in traditional Marxism) that holds sway today. The alt-right mobilizes the primacy of culture. The notion that politics is downstream from culture is very much in sync with the Republican attacks on Black Lives Matter and critical race theory, on feminism and sexual identity debates, and on leftist "woke" culture in general. It also shows in their embrace of COVID-19 denial and the refusal of vaccination in the name of liberty, all supported not just by right-wing television, radio, and Internet platforms but by a party that no longer has any substantive political program. It is like Marcuse's "great refusal" on the right.

The core, however, is racist. It is instructive to listen in on the alt-right's self-description. The back cover of a recent volume of essays, *A Fair Hearing: The Alt-Right in the Words of Its Members and Leaders* (2018), describes the alt-right as "foremost an intellectual movement" whose main goal is to "offer meaningful resistance to and finally rout the left." In his introduction, the editor George T. Shaw makes no bones about the movement's targets: "Diversity and multiculturalism ... tend to make white societies poorer, more dangerous, and finally unlivable for whites." And: "White genocide is on the way" because "cultural manipulations such as state, academic, and media promotion of feminism, diversity, promiscuity, and homo- and transsexuality heavily suppress white birthrates."[6] Clearly, this is the contemporary version of a cultural synthesis, but is it based on some objective nonsynchronism in Bloch's sense? A mark of difference between then and the United States today may be that such objective *Ungleichzeitigkeit* may not even exist any longer in twenty-first-century America. Different real-life temporal experiences have long since been ground down by the homogenization of life worlds achieved by the mass media and the force of capital. In the age of the Internet and social media, the present rules supreme.

There is of course a political gap between red and blue states, between rural areas and urban centers. But such very real economic and social differences present in American life, similar to those in the Europe of the interwar period, have been culturally recoded to create a kind of artificial, largely subjective *Ungleichzeitigkeit* between a corrupt present dominated by liberal urban elites and an allegedly more authentic past. This world view, captured in Trump's promise to drain the Washington swamp and to make America great again, is nourished 24/7 with propaganda by Fox News, Sinclair Broadcast Group, Talk Radio, and the Murdoch newspapers. But the main outlets for the revival of tropes and images of interwar fascism, which has itself become *(un)gleichzeitig* in a new way, are of course platforms like Twitter, Facebook, YouTube, Reddit, Discord, 8chan, and others. Real *Ungleichzeitigkeit* in Bloch's sense has been undermined by the Internet, which sucks all available pasts into its eternal present. In his last, posthumously published book, *The Fascist Revolution* (1999, 2021), Mosse had this to say about the rise of nationalisms in the 1990s: "The fragments of our Western cultural and ideological past which fascism used for its own purposes still lie ready to be formed into a new synthesis, even if in a different way."[7]

Utopian Visions

Many other differences with interwar European fascism are just too obvious. There is no lost war to feed *ressentiment* in the populace as a whole. There are no centrally organized paramilitary forces to speak of. Government institutions and the rule of law, one must hope, are still stronger than they were in the Weimar Republic. More importantly and contrary to Hitler or Mussolini, Trump does not have a future-oriented utopian vision for all of the United States. He is not the great charismatic leader unifying the nation. Trump speaks only to his base rather than to the nation as a whole. He plays the strong man at his rallies, whipping up the crowds, but simultaneously he claims to be a victim of the deep state, just as the alt-right claims to be victimized by liberal censorship of free speech. Of course, the Nazis also played the victim card (Versailles, *Dolchstoßlegende*), but this was counterbalanced by an ideologically seductive vision for a nationalist German future. "MAGA" (Make America Great Again) is at best a *Schwundstufe*, a vestige of such a vision. That's the difference between the grandiose Nazi spectacles and a baseball cap. Much has been made of the real purchase of this deliberately amorphous appeal to another America, which encompasses a vast array of memories, fantasies, and dreams: not just the good times of post–World War II high wages and full employment but also the Confederacy and the nostalgia for a pre-civil-rights South; not just the victory over fascism in World War II but also the romanticizing of indigenous forms of American fascism, which never gained power. Past glory and seamy dreams of white supremacy are the two sides of the explosive mix that fires up Trump's followers at his rallies. After four years of the Trump presidency and in the midst of the COVID-19 debacle, it is difficult to imagine anybody believing that MAGA is possible. And yet, Trump's bubble of false promises and outright lies still enjoys major public support. As a simulacrum of desire after loss, the

MAGA slogan has not lost its irrational appeal. The less it seems able to command reality, the more it needs an image of an insidious enemy that prevents America from being made great again. The alleged illegitimacy of the Biden presidency and the January 6 congressional investigation are primary targets; but it is the proliferation of conspiracy theories that, unhinged as they are, serve to normalize an alternative reality.

Cultural Marxism

Which brings me back to the alt-right's bogeyman of cultural Marxism. Several years ago, after the election of Trump and with Steve Bannon in the White House, I stumbled upon the role of the Frankfurt School as *bête noire* in American white nationalist discourse. The idea did not originate with Breitbart, but he was its great amplifier on the Internet and in social media. Here is Breitbart himself in his book *Righteous Indignation* (2011): "Critical Theory was exactly the material we were taught at Tulane. It was quite literally, a theory of criticizing everyone and everything everywhere. It was an attempt to tear down the social fabric by using all the social sciences...; it was an infinite and unending criticism of the status quo, adolescent rebellion against all established rules and norms.... The real idea behind all of this was to make society totally unworkable by making everything basically meaningless."[8]

The term "adolescent rebellion" is odd here. None of the Critical Theorists were adolescents when they developed their work on the culture industry and the dark side of enlightenment. Their American reception, however, is fundamentally linked to the youth rebellions of the 1960s, an obsession of Breitbart and especially of Bannon, who blamed the sixties generation for the decline of America in his 2010 docufiction film *Generation Zero: The Untold Story about the Financial Meltdown*. In that film, the sixties generation is held responsible both for cultural Marxism in the academy and for the banking crisis of 2008, a variant of another zombie-like pattern from earlier times: Bolsheviks and bankers. Underlying Bannon's *Generation Zero* is the absurd rise-and-decline theory of eighty-year cycles of American history, popularized by amateur historians William Strauss and Neil Howe in their 1997 book *The Fourth Turning: An American Prophecy*. Theirs is a generational theory of cyclical history, divided into roughly twenty-year "highs," "awakenings," "unravelings," and "crises": upon the crisis of the Great Depression there followed the high of victory in war and the affluent 1950s and early 1960s, the awakening of the rebellion of the 1960s and the tax revolts of the early 1980s, the unraveling of self-centered boom decades and the culture wars, until a new cycle started with another crisis of destruction. Bannon has celebrated the moment after 2008 as the coming destruction of the administrative state from the remains of which, after a period of chaos, the phoenix of a new old America would rise again in the 2020s. Twelve years after *Generation Zero*, we have deepening threats to democracy but not much of a sign of a phoenix rising from the ashes.

Bannon's obsession with the baby boomers points back to the Clinton years, when another right-wing author, William S. Lind, gave an influential speech about "The Origins of Political Correctness" (2000) at a meeting of Accuracy in Academia, an organization that always linked communism with liberalism in order to better attack the latter. To Lind political correctness is "Marxism translated from economic into cultural terms."[9] The superficial and distorted focus of his many speeches and articles targeted György Lukács, Antonio Gramsci, Herbert Marcuse, and the Frankfurt School, the latter being especially dangerous because it was allegedly successful in disguising its Marxism as it migrated to the United States, fleeing the Nazis, and was given a home at Columbia University. The generalized attack on the baby boomers has been a conservative cliché for many years, but its outright weaponization is meant to play well with subsequent generations, especially millennials and Generation X, prime targets of alt-right proselytizing.

I have written elsewhere about this strange right-wing obsession with the Frankfurt School and cultural Marxism.[10] Of course the Frankfurt School was a welcome code name on the right for Jewish influence at a time when open antisemitism was still mostly shunned.[11] But there is also an elective affinity to a popular and perverted understanding of Critical Theory as gravedigger of American democracy. Looking into the mirror of Critical Theory and its analysis of race hatred and media domination, Lind, Breitbart, Bannon, and their likes could recognize themselves and their history. Their over-the-top attack on the Frankfurt School points to the fact that they themselves were doing what they falsely accused their opponents of doing: subverting American politics and culture. For what is the difference between making society unworkable and destroying the administrative state? Between making everything meaningless and creating alternative facts through fake news grounded in conspiracy theories? Adorno and Max Horkheimer analyzed such processes of mimesis, projection, and inversion in their *Dialectic of Enlightenment*. Leo Löwenthal and Norbert Guterman put it quite succinctly in their 1949 book about fascist tendencies in the United States titled *Prophets of Deceit*: The follower of right-wing ideology "is nothing but the inverted reflection of the enemy."[12] In the same way, the alt-right has adapted strategies of left-wing critique and turned them against the left: antiracism as proof that the left is racist toward whites and so on. The alleged insurgency of cultural Marxism must thus be confronted by a counterinsurgency from the right.[13] This hall of mirrors is what Schmittian friend/foe thinking produces in the real world.

The Fascist Agitator and the Authoritarian Personality

In 2016 it was quite tempting to see Trump as a reembodiment of Löwenthal and Guterman's description of the fascist agitator: "The agitator's statements are often ambiguous and unserious. It is difficult to pin him down to anything and he gives the impression that he is deliberately playacting. He seems to be trying to give himself a margin of uncertainty, a possibility of retreat in case any of his improvisations fall flat. He does not commit himself for he is willing, temporarily at least, to juggle his notions and test his powers. Moving in a twilight zone between the respectable and the forbidden, he is ready to use any device, from jokes to doubletalk to wild extravagances."[14] Once in office, Trump certainly confirmed this analysis. His rhetorical strategies seemed to appeal to what Adorno might have described as the fascist unconscious of the authoritarian personality. Clearly several of the variables of the famous F-scale in the 1950 study of *The Authoritarian Personality*, such as aggression, stereotypy, and projectivity, still characterize many of Trump's followers today.[15] But Adorno's notion of the authoritarian personality as a social type, whose unconscious is the fertile ground for the fascist agitator's antics and appeals, seems less persuasive as an explanation of Trumpism.

Peter Gordon has recently pointed to some of the conceptual limits of Adorno's attempt to develop a correlation between socioeconomic conditions and psychoanalysis by positing the authoritarian personality as a type. More importantly, Gordon has shown by immanent critique of Adorno's thought "how Trump at once instantiates the category of the 'authoritarian personality' *but also challenges its meaning.*"[16] Historical and sociological differences, too, make the notion problematic for today. Sure, there will always be the Archie Bunkers of the world, many of whom belong to Trump's male base, but even if this psychological type was once predominant in society, it no longer is. Conventional middle-class values no longer enjoy unquestioned legitimacy, nor do sexual repression and authoritarian submission count among privileged society-wide forms of behavior. More importantly, we must recognize the antiauthoritarianism and anticonformism of the radical right, which targets democracy itself and goes together perfectly with admiration for the great leader as authoritarian strongman and disruptive force. Just as the Frankfurt School has taught us to analyze the dialectic of enlightenment, we should ask about the potential dialectic of the current counterenlightenment as a way out of the deadlocked situation we find ourselves in.[17] Clearly, the authoritarian personality today is simultaneously antiauthoritarian. Directed against the elites and experts of all kinds, with its suspicion of a deep state and the embrace of a post-fact and post-truth ideology, this antiauthoritarian streak of Trumpism echoes the antiauthoritarian protests of the 1960s, confirming a long history of right-wing extremism getting its tools of protest from the left. To be sure, the alt-right is not a generational rebellion, and its antiauthoritarianism is fundamentally authoritarian in its manifestations on social media, where misogyny, racism, xenophobia, scapegoating, and all kinds of conspiracy theories are writ large.

In line with the above, the mode of operation of the fascist agitator has also changed. Fundamental differences have emerged regarding the relationship to authority and to our agitator former president. While certain analogies between now and the interwar period cannot be denied, the whole structure of agitation and the narcissistic identification with the Führer as ego ideal, as Adorno had it, has changed, as have educational practices that used to be key to instilling authoritarian personality features in the first place. Whereas adherence to authority was part of a social compact in the past, blind submission to authority is clearly not in tune with the neoliberal focus on creativity and self-investment. And when the agitator in chief used Twitter, not to articulate a coherent vision of the future but rather to present himself as victim of a deep state cabal and America as victim of global economic wrongdoing and exploitation by other nations, he played on his followers' very real sense of being disenfranchised and betrayed. But the followers themselves are no longer just passive consumers of radio speeches. They have also become agents on social media platforms. The older one-way, top-down communication between leader and the masses has been replaced by multidirectional communication and agency in the anonymity of chat networks. Anonymity in digital public space, a key ingredient of Facebook's business model, is one of the main reasons for the alt-right's success in normalizing and spreading hate speech. The antiauthoritarianism of today's authoritarians is given full play in the social media. Thus the talk about the authoritarian personality 2.0.[18]

Racketeering in the Age of Social Media

The new role of agency changes the relationship between chief agitator and followers in yet another way. The chief agitator can limit himself to racist and misogynist dog whistles—until recently immediately disavowed or "walked back"—that his followers would then amplify on digital platforms. Dog whistles point to an efficient practice of maintaining control and inciting action without accountability: that of not giving explicit orders, but of insinuating what should be done, a practice we know was prevalent among mobsters. The congressional hearings of Trump's former lawyer Michael Cohen first gave new life to another, formerly discredited characterization of fascism in action, which Adorno and Horkheimer had fragmentarily developed, that of racketeering.[19] In 1941 Horkheimer described the criminal racket with its demand of loyalty for protection as "the archetype of domination," different from universal moral norms and the rule of law.[20] Classical racketeering practices such as intimidation of witnesses, retaliation for revealing testimony, public vilification of critics, and protection of loyalists are writ large in Trump world. The difference is that all this racketeering is not happening in secret but in plain sight of the public. Of course, protection can never be total when publicly displayed and reported by the media. The multiple indictments and sentencing of people in Trump's closest circle show that political and economic racketeering have merged under the Trump regime, and they are intimately linked to a persistent attack on the law, something no mobster can get away with but a president evidently can when helped by his attorney general: "A gangster White House," as David Frum had it in *The Atlantic*.[21] Prime examples of racketeering on the international stage were the quid pro quo in the Ukraine affair that led to Trump's impeachment and to the demand that NATO pay for American protection. It is no surprise that racketeering is one of the charges in the Georgia grand jury investigation of Trump's blatant attempt to falsify the state's election results.

Discursive racketeering also describes the link between Trump's use of media and his base, including the alt-right. The same digital platforms that have helped spread radical right-wing ideas have been dominant in the mobilization for events like the Charlottesville rally and the January 6 insurrection. The technological development from mere websites to interactive platforms in recent years has vastly increased the reach of alt-right ideology into the mainstream. There are large differences in the rhetoric of such platforms: some are dedicated to recruiting followers with seemingly mainstream discussions; some make use of the privileged status of memory in our culture and call for the protection of the Southern heritage, inciting a debate about monuments to the Confederacy; others focus on the alleged violation of free speech by the Left. Calls for violence, on the other hand, take place in private groups on Discord or Facebook. And there are a lot of them.

The normalization of imaginary violence is writ large in many products of the online gaming industry, and sometimes even in fiction, as in the novel *Victoria: A Novel of 4th Generation War* (2014) by the aforementioned William S. Lind, about the wholesale killing of leftist faculty at Lind's alma mater, Dartmouth College, by Christian militia warriors at a time when the U.S. government has collapsed. Lind's fictional fantasy of anti-left violence finds its resonance in

George Shaw's *A Fair Hearing*, in a piece by Augustus Invictus, publisher of the website theconservativerevolutionary.com, when he muses: "The meme of physically removing leftists has gained so much traction because the idea is instinctively both logical and appealing. The means of physically removing leftists, however, is not as simple. While throwing commies from helicopters à la Pinochet has become the alt-right's favorite policy proposal, this is clearly an inefficient solution."[22] And so on, and on. It would be a mistake simply to dismiss such ravings. They are part of a climate that has led to some of the mass shootings in Norway, Australia, and the United States with their perpetrator manifestoes.

Tara McPherson, a media researcher from the University of Southern California, has argued that the interactive platforms where this growing right-wing public sphere is emerging produce a new era of racial formation, an emergent structure of feeling (Raymond Williams's phrase) she calls "immersive racism."[23] The very immersive design of platforms helps the alt-right by encouraging anonymous comments on postings, trolling, and the proliferation of fake news. Hate speech is not a bug in the platform but a generative feature of the business model. What Habermas and others once described as the decline of the public sphere that went hand in hand with the refeudalization of society has now reached a dangerous stage of disintegration into multiple online publics that threaten to impede any coherent discourse about society and any consensus on the public good. The spreading rule of the white nationalist racket has become a major threat to democratic societies.

Trump's practice of racketeering was not just discursive and ego-related, nor did it stay within the confines of Twitter and television. During the COVID-19 crisis in spring 2020, it reached the very structure of government in the United States. Not only had Trump, for some time already, systematically occupied key positions in federal institutions with often unqualified lackeys, retracted environmental laws to protect the fossil fuel industry and other polluters, or simply bled federal institutions such as the Center for Disease Control dry, he also shamelessly showered federal help on loyalist governors and demanded gratitude or punished those governors, mainly of democratic statehouses, who dared criticize him for continuing to exacerbate the health crisis by denial. At the same time, he denied any responsibility for the lack of preparedness of the country, blaming others instead for the pandemic: Obama, the Chinese, the World Health Organization, and the state governors who demanded a more proactive role of the federal government. One day he claimed "total authority," in violation of the Constitution. The next day he rejected the notion that he had any responsibility. So far, this cocktail of "total authority" with "no responsibility" has not damaged his movement's belief that he is the One who will make America great again after Biden's "illegitimate" presidency will have ended.

Behemoth

Let me conclude with another quote from a Frankfurt School source: "Trumpism has no political or social theory. It has no philosophy and no concern for the truth. In a given situation it will accept any theory that might prove useful; and it will abandon that theory as soon as the situation changes. Trumpism is both capitalistic and anticapitalistic. It is authoritarian and antiauthoritarian. It will cooperate with any group ... that is amenable to Trumpist propaganda but it will not hesitate to flatter anti-authoritarian movements when that is more expedient.... Trumpism is for agrarian reform and against it, for private property and against it, for idealism and against it. Such versatility is unattainable in a democracy." The quote is from Franz Neumann's 1944 book *Behemoth: The Structure and Practice of National Socialism, 1933–1944*, an economic analysis of National Socialism that comes perhaps closest to a racket theory of society.[24] Of course, I have substituted "Trumpism" for the original "National Socialism." The irony is that this quote may capture Trump's rule by chaos better than it explains National Socialism. The Nazis, after all, did have a defined political ideology, a point George L. Mosse never tired of emphasizing. With Trump, however, there just is an ever-shifting void of floating lies, contradictions, self-promoting narratives, and personal attacks on perceived enemies.

In *Behemoth*, Neumann analyzed the Nazi regime's unprecedented assault on the law and on the state, thus opposing Friedrich Pollock's alternative Frankfurt School analysis of fascism as state capitalism, a view more in tune with later theories of totalitarian command economies. Neumann wrote: "Nothing remains but profit, power, prestige, and above all fear. Devoid of any loyalty, and concerned solely with the preservation of their own interests, the ruling groups will break apart as soon as the miracle-producing leader meets a worthy opponent."[25] Clearly, we are not yet at that stage. Adam Tooze, historian of the Third Reich's economy and of the 2008 crash, has argued that Neumann's insights are quite germane today, "noting that there is no natural harmony between developed capitalism and legal, political, and social order; that modern capitalism is a fundamentally disruptive force that constantly challenges the rule of law as such."[26] Read this together with the warning by David Frum, conservative political commentator and author of *Trumpocracy: The Corruption of the American Republic* (2018): "If conservatives become convinced that they cannot win democratically, they will not abandon conservatism. They will reject democracy."[27] With or without Trump, the Republican Party today is forging ahead on that road.

Notes

This is an expanded and updated version of the 2019 conference presentation, which appeared in condensed form in July 2019 in *n+1 online* (https://nplusonemag.com/on line-only/online-only/behemoth-rises-again/).

1. Theodor W. Adorno, "The Meaning of Working through the Past," in *Critical Models: Interventions and Catchwords* (New York: Columbia University Press, 2005), 97.
2. Adorno, "The Meaning of Working through the Past," 90.
3. Wendy Brown, *Undoing the Demos: Neoliberalism's Stealth Revolution* (New York: Zone Books, 2015).
4. Adam Serwer, "White Nationalism's Deep American Roots," *The Atlantic*, April 2019.
5. Ernst Bloch, *Heritage of Our Times* (Berkeley: University of California Press, 1990), especially the chapter on nonsynchronism and dialectics. See also Anson Rabinbach, "Ernst Bloch's *Heritage of Our Times* and the Theory of Fascism," *New German Critique* 11 (Spring 1977): 5–21.
6. George T. Shaw, ed., *A Fair Hearing: The Alt-Right in the Words of Its Members and Leaders* (Middletown, DE: Arktos Media, 2018), xi and xii.
7. George L. Mosse, *The Fascist Revolution: Toward a General Theory of Fascism* (Madison: University of Wisconsin Press, 2021), 37.
8. Andrew Breitbart, *Righteous Indignation: Excuse Me While I Save the World* (New York: Grand Central Publishing, 2011), 113.
9. William S. Lind, "The Origins of Political Correctness," *Accuracy in Academia*, 5 February 2000, https://www.academia.org/the-origins-of-political-correctness/.
10. Andreas Huyssen, "Breitbart News und die Frankfurter Schule," *Merkur*, 71. Jahrgang, July 2017, 85–90. In English: http://www.publicseminar.org/2017/09/breitbart-ban non-trump-and-the-frankfurt-school/.
11. See Martin Jay, "Dialectic of Counter-Enlightenment: The Frankfurt School as Scapegoat of the Lunatic Fringe," *Salmagundi* 168/69 (Fall 2010/Winter 2011): 30–40. Also available at http://canisa.org/blog/dialectic-of-counter-enlightenment-the-frank furt-school-as-scapegoat-of-the-lunatic-fringe. Updated and expanded version in *Splinters in Your Eye* (New York: Verso, 2020), 151–72.
12. Norbert Guterman and Leo Löwenthal, *Prophets of Deceit: A Study of the Techniques of the American Agitator* (New York: Harper and Brothers, 1949), 117.
13. See Bernard E. Harcourt, *The Counterrevolution: How Our Government Went to War against Its Own Citizens* (New York: Basic Books, 2018).
14. Guterman and Löwenthal, *Prophets*, 5.
15. Theodor Adorno et al., *The Authoritarian Personality*, new edition introduced by Peter Gordon (New York: Verso, 2019).
16. Peter Gordon, "The Authoritarian Personality Revisited: Reading Adorno in the Age of Trump," in *boundary 2*, 15 June 2016, https://www.boundary2.org/2016/06/peter -gordon-the-authoritarian-personality-revisited-reading-adorno-in-the-age-of-trump/.
17. See Jay, "Dialectic of Counter-Enlightenment."

18. Moira Weigel, "The Authoritarian Personality 2.0," *Polity* 54, no. 1 (2022): 146–80.

19. See the superb piece by Martin Jay, "Trump, Scorcese, and the Frankfurt School's Theory of Racket Society," *Los Angeles Review of Books*, 5 April 2020, https://lareviewofbooks.org/article/trump-scorsese-and-the-frankfurt-schools-theory-of-racket-society/.

20. Max Horkheimer, "The End of Reason," in *The Essential Frankfurt School Reader*, ed. Andrew Arato and Eike Gebhardt (New York: Urizen Books, 1978).

21. David Frum, "A Gangster in the White House," *The Atlantic*, 28 December 2019.

22. Augustus Invictus, "Physical Removal: More Than a Meme," in Shaw, *A Fair Hearing*, 210.

23. Tara McPherson, "Platforming Hate: The Right in the Digital Age," lecture delivered in fall 2018 at the 50th Anniversary celebration of the Center for Twenty-First Century Studies at the University of Wisconsin–Milwaukee.

24. Franz Neumann, *Behemoth: The Structure and Practice of National Socialism, 1933–1944* (New York: Harper & Row, 1966), 437–38.

25. Neumann, *Behemoth*, 397.

26. Adam Tooze, "Framing Crashed (10): 'A New Bretton Woods' and the Problem of 'Economic Order'—Also a Reply to Adler and Varoufakis," 9 February 2019, https://adamtooze.com/2019/02/09/framing-crashed-10-a-new-bretton-woods-and-the-problem-of-economic-order-also-a-reply-to-adler-and-varoufakis/.

27. David Frum, *Trumpocracy: The Corruption of the American Republic* (New York: HarperCollins, 2018), 206.

Part III
GENDER, VIOLENCE, AND THE EVERYDAY

6

Sex and Violence

Race Defilement in Nazi Germany

STEFANIE SCHÜLER-SPRINGORUM

In the diaries of Victor Klemperer, we find repeated descriptions from the early 1940s of police officers conducting raids in old people's homes and, later, in the "Jews house" that Klemperer and his wife were forced to live in. In these raids, the elderly residents, most of them female, were humiliated, harassed, beaten, and kicked. Let me quote from his entry dated 11 May 1942, one among many: "The tyranny grows worse with every day.... House search in the Güntzstraße old people's home. Women between 70 and 85 years of age spat on, placed face to the wall, cold water poured over them from behind, their food ... taken from them, the filthiest words of abuse."[1] What I find especially unsettling in these descriptions is the double and even triple breach of a taboo: the repeated outbreaks of excessive violence, always accompanied by "filthy words of abuse" targeting the elderly, inflicted on women—and all this occurring right in the center of middle-class Dresden, Germany.

In the last decades, Holocaust research has provided us with a whole array of sometimes contradictory, sometimes complementary attempts to explain the acts of extreme violence that comprise the Holocaust. They have come to agree basically on one point: the "limited scope of monocausal interpretations," to put it in the words of Jürgen Matthäus, head of the research department of the United States Holocaust Memorial Museum (USHMM).[2] And none of the customary models works for what Klemperer again and again describes: the perpetrators were not young men socialized by Nazism, stoked up ideologically to action. Nor were they representatives of the "Uncompromising Generation" (*Generation des Unbedingten*), who regarded the mass murder as a task that had to be carried out calmly for obvious, rational reasons. Instead, they were older, experienced Dresden police officers, men who perhaps, as in the case of the famous Police Battalion 101, had earlier voted for the Social Democratic Party. And this was by no means an "orders are orders" situation (*Befehlsnotstand*); nor was this a group of men who had been welded together by the imperatives of comradeship, alcohol consumption, and murder. And all this did not happen at the war front, far away in the East. Dresden had not yet been bombed, the Wehrmacht had chalked up victories everywhere across Europe and reached the very height of its expansion. So it was not some kind of rearguard action, no fear of the approaching Red Army, no act of revenge or anything like that. And the victims were not suspected of being communists, nor were they subhuman Slavic *Untermenschen* or partisans—rather, they were drawn from the ranks of the older German middle class, or to put it very simply, these victims most probably looked and lived (or had lived) like the parents of the perpetrators.

For the past two decades, I have been pondering the question: what were the reasons for this form of violence perpetrated at home, in one's own environment—in short, why this violence for violence's sake? Furthermore, these incidents, as research in recent years has substantiated, were by no means exceptional cases or regionally limited to Saxony—rather they were reported from all over Germany, cities, large and small, rural and urban. In this context, Jürgen Matthäus has issued a forcefully worded warning against succumbing to the illusion of simple explanations. Rather, he poses the question differently, asking "what utility do concepts and abstractions have for explaining violent phenomena, whose quality only can become evident from the aggregated analysis of individual cases?" In his view, it is precisely in dealing with organized mass murder where historical writing—as an effort to infuse what is meaningless with meaning—becomes obviously absurd, because of "the tension ... between the enormous radicality of the events and the limited range of the attempts to explain it—even, indeed specifically on the level of individual events." Instead, he modestly argues for a critical descriptive history that has the potential, precisely by means of an astutely selected comparison coupled with careful contextualization, to shift the "boundaries of what is explainable into the realm of what to date has been the Unknown."[3]

I too wish to step away from resorting to that all-encompassing phenomenon that stands to a certain extent at the beginning and end of any reflection about how to explain the genocidal violence of German society: namely antisemitism.[4] However, that explanation only makes sense, and in this I follow Matthäus, if you "investigate its *concrete* role ... for each stage in the process of persecution and annihilation for each individual case separately" and then correspondingly contextualize that.[5] In the case of the anti-Jewish incident in Dresden described above, this would mean, for example, that I am less interested in the role of antisemitic ideology than in the role of the related *emotions* that appear to underlie and stand behind these excessive eruptions of violence.

Now as before, to what extent the concept of emotion can be properly operationalized for historiography remains controversial, and doubtless one has to concur with Alon Confino that we cannot simply readjust our "explanatory toolbox," transposed from "society" to "memory"—and thus shifted to concepts stemming from psychology like "emotions" or "empathy"—without critically confronting and dealing with the associated theories and methods that lie behind such concepts.[6] How such a critical encounter dealing with the relation between antisemitism and emotions might look is something Uffa Jensen and I have already sketched some time ago, and in other work I in turn have dealt critically with questions pertaining to the relation between gender and antisemitism.[7] Here I would like to suggest a direction of thought that reads antisemitism, emotion, and gender together, pinpointing the historical moments where the aversive feelings toward Jews and the ambivalent ones concerning "women" (or the gender order in general) were able to coalesce and thus account for unleashed violence within one's own neighborhood, even within one's own group. At the same time, the dynamic character of this relationship points to the ways in which these emotions can become interlaced with other forms of negative sentiment, such as homophobia, anti-Bolshevism, and racism, without implying a hierarchy or a causational nexus between them.

Antisemitism and Gender

Christina von Braun's longstanding insight into the links between a foundational binary in Christianity and classical antiquity before it that ascribes the carnal and material to the female gender and the Jew while ideality, intellect, and spirituality are ascribed to the male gender remains fundamental.[8] Her work has recently received an important confirmation through Delphine Horvilleur's gendered reading of traditional Jewish texts dealing with Gentile hostility.[9] What is interesting for our case is that the Enlightenment, arguing along lines of natural law, was hardly any different from this mode of thought when it sought arguments for the continuing exclusion of women and Jews from the free and equal civil society. Throughout the entire nineteenth century, the arguments in support of this inequality were repeatedly interlinked anew and ultimately rendered "scientific"—this goes for Jew hatred as well as for the so-called gender characteristics conceived as a kind of natural polarity—and we should be aware here that "gender polarity" is in fact a friendly wording for misogyny.

Middle-class normality and deviance were ultimately defined, toward the end of the nineteenth century, in medical and psychological terms. The result was unambiguous: the norm was male, heterosexual, and Christian; while female, homosexual, and Jewish were spliced together as deviance.

The Jew, the female, and the homosexual were utilized, as George L. Mosse so brilliantly analyzed decades ago, as different forms of representation of the other in modernity—and one should not forget in this context that the working class was always at risk of being classified as part of the deviant "Other" as well. All this has been amply shown by analyses of gender-political and antisemitic texts and imagery from different contexts of high and popular culture. At the same time, these gender-loaded images served to consolidate internally the supposed healthy, strongly heterosexual, male-dominant nation. Thus, around 1900 antisemitism, homophobia, and misogyny evolved into very closely intertwined expressions of the antimodern version of a clearly demarcated and hierarchically structured class society.[10] Or to put it differently: the constructs of masculinity and femininity do not happen in some separate sphere—rather they are all tightly interwoven with antisemitism and racism. Accordingly, antisemitic body images are not just to be understood as the expression of a certain ideology—rather they are an inherent component of that ideology itself, a building block in its construction, both in theory and practice.

Antisemitism and Sexuality

And while this level of gender imagery and theory seems to me to be quite adequately illuminated, it is precisely the level of practice that will be my focus today. And such practice means first and foremost, sexuality. Every form of racism, including antisemitism, is, as Sander Gilman has noted in his study *The Jew's Body*, preoccupied and obsessed with conceptions of sexuality—sexuality of the correct and incorrect kind, permitted and forbidden, good and bad.[11] The primary function of this perennial thematization should be obvious, since after all, what must be prevented is the feared prospect of racial miscegenation.

The significance of this defensive struggle to maintain racial purity can be traced down through the centuries: its spectrum extends from the legislation on blood purity first codified in 1449 in Toledo by the authorities of Catholic Spain to the racial-völkisch phantasmagorias à la Artur Dinter and his bestselling novel *The Sin Against the Blood* from 1917 and to the "one-drop rule" in U.S. legislation, which after all was still confirmed in 1983 by a court in Louisiana. Considering the fact that in these U.S. court cases, what was at stake was 1/32 or 1/20 of "impure" blood, the Nuremberg Laws appear in an alarming way rather pragmatic in nature. The huge campaign against "race defilement"

(*Rassenschande*) grounded on concepts of anti-miscegenation that accompanied those laws in 1935 must have likely also had another motive. As exemplified in the case of slavery in the United States, Abdul JanMohamed has pointed out that over and beyond "boundaries of race," sex always also implies the recognition of the essential humanness of the other—and that in racism, and I would add, even more in Nazi antisemitism, ultimately this was the real issue: the negation of this humanity.[12] Sexuality that per se transgressed a boundary claimed by the most vicious propaganda had to be prevented at all costs. To that extent, "the sin against the blood" can also be interpreted as the prelude to a movement that desired to render antisemitism plausible via sexuality: this worked so well because the sexual demonization of Jews was already a common feature of Weimar antisemitism.

Posters, films, and books, including *Mein Kampf*, conjured up in all colors and configurations what American historian Dagmar Herzog has called the "threat posed by a rapacious bestial Jewish male to innocent German femininity."[13] Especially prominent in spreading this notion was Julius Streicher's periodical *Der Stürmer*, whose singular proclivity for pornographic antisemitism is deeply etched in the memory at least of those whom it impacted. After 1933 these campaigns condensed and intensified, and as Dagmar Herzog puts it, "Weimar was reduced to sex." From then on in Nazi propaganda, the Weimar Republic was painted as the veritable hothouse of the "most vulgar stimulation of steamy, debauched eroticism."[14] In her path-breaking study, Herzog advanced the thesis that the proactive demarcation and dissociation from the sexually loaded "Jews Republic" (*Judenrepublik*) initially served the National Socialists as a means to win over the ecclesiastical and conservative circles to their völkisch-nationalist project. Although in the further course of their rule it fulfilled a totally different role: as Herzog notes, the constant reference to the supposed shamelessness and indecency of "Jewish" sexuality served at the same time as a strategy of denial, designed to divert attention from the numerous inducements abounding for extramarital and premarital sexuality that the Nazi regime was continuously proffering to the non-Jewish and heterosexual majority of the German population.[15] However, Herzog's actual impressive evidence for National Socialism as an Aryan sexual paradise interests us less here than the fact that the Nazi versions of sexually emancipatory ideas were always formulated by means of antisemitic counterimages. Despite the purported "Jewish" sexual reform, which was vehemently opposed by National Socialists and conservatives of all stripes, Jews were deemed far removed from "advocating a natural sexuality."[16] On the contrary, it was alleged that Jews exhibited a "disgusting lechery," animalistic sexuality, lascivious carnal sensuality, and perversity.

Central to my argument here is, on the one hand, Herzog's finding that there was perpetual talk in National Socialist Germany about sex, and on the other, that this discourse remained ambivalent in nature. At least in the regime's early years, it fluctuated between sexual outrages and pleasure, between sadism and temptation, or—depending on one's taste—both at the same time. That becomes especially clear in the race defilement trials, proceedings that were initiated after passage of the Nuremberg Laws and which the German press had a field day reporting. The female partners of the men charged were sometimes questioned in the dock about their sexual preferences, where special weight was accorded to admission of so-called abnormal practices—in most instances, this involved oral sex. This was then described in precise detail in the press. These court proceedings rendered possible, as Alexandra Przyrembel has noted, the public "breaching of established rules on what was permitted to be said, which possibly was a stimulus to curiosity, and sometimes also generated a certain fascination vis-à-vis the forbidden sexual relationship."[17] However, "possibly" and "sometimes" seem to me somewhat too cautious a formulation, because it was not without reason that *Der Stürmer* developed in the 1930s into the favorite magazine for German teenagers. Its popularity with adolescents repeatedly attracted the alarmed attention of concerned parents and church representatives.

Herzog attributes the "enormous allure" of *Der Stürmer* and its various scenarios to the "multiplicity of possibilities for libidinal identification": the "sexually successful Jewish man, the violated or seduced non-Jewish woman, the outraged non-Jewish male or female voyeur," an appeal with a broad spectrum.[18] The sexuality displayed each week anew was at the same time also segregated again and again along racial lines—both rhetorically and in lived experience of violence— and it is this close conjunction of desire, fear, disgust, and violence that seems to me to typify antisemitic propaganda in Nazi Germany—and, intriguingly, not just there alone. To cite but one example, Kristoff Kerl has recently published an impressive analysis of the case of Leo Frank in the United States that explores the 1915 lynching of a Jewish factory owner accused of having raped and murdered one of his young female employees. Kerl shows the importance of Frank's purported sexual practices for the trial, how the news media reported on it, and concludes that it was precisely this interlinking of sex and the print media boom at the time that made Frank's case the catalyst for a new and violent antisemitism in the United States, which led in the 1920s to the founding of the Second Ku Klux Klan.[19]

A further international example of this very effective conjuncture of sex, press, and antisemitism are the media reports on the Spanish Civil War. Here the focus was almost always and exclusively on sexual violence, even between the lines there is nothing suggesting any pleasure involved. During the first months of the war in summer and fall 1936, in numerous publications, not only in Germany but also in the international press, there were repeated descriptions of sexually loaded sadistic incidents, which were in part at the same time sacralized: the victims are almost always female, for the most part young girls and/or female clericals, and their ordeal most frequently took place in churches or monasteries. In all these descriptions, it is the female body that is violated in all imaginable ways with a lust for graphic detail that would be impossible to publish in today's press. If one seeks to decipher these sexually saturated descriptions (which by the way can be found almost identical in accounts from all sides on the Eastern Front), then it is necessary to also include the level of reception and the readership of such accounts. It appears that only through the close interweaving of violence *and* sexuality did the recurrent tales of outrage and atrocity become attractive for the readership, making a far stronger and lasting impression on the audience than normal wartime combat reportage; this was obvious to many, since it can be deduced from innumerable contemporary sources, not least of which include observers like Arthur Koestler, who already in 1936 spoke of sado-pornographic propaganda.[20]

But these repetitive propagandizing tropes were hardly just a specifically German matter, as evidenced in the memoirs of the American poet and novelist Gamel Woolsey, who had been living with her British husband, Gerald Brenan, in a small village near Málaga since 1933. As an eyewitness, she had initially dismissed the evident absurdity of these stories. But her dismissal soon turned into a pronounced sense of disgust, as Woolsey repeatedly observed the furtive sense of excitement of those narrating tales of outrage and atrocity: "I was struck by what I can only call a look of dreamy blood-lust upon their faces as they told such stories. I realized then, what I realized even more clearly later at Gibraltar, listening to the English talk of atrocities, what atrocity stories really are: they are the pornography of violence. The dreamy lustful look that accompanies them, the full enjoyment of horror (especially noticeable in respectable elderly Englishwomen speaking of the rape or torture of *naked* nuns: it is significant that they are always naked in such stories), shows only too plainly their erotic source."[21]

For our context this has a double significance: first, that even at first glance, stories that above all provoke a sense of disgust and anxiety can serve to speak to hidden or subconscious erotic needs or can stimulate those needs. And second, that they appear to have indeed fulfilled their underlying purpose in the mid-1930s, designed to direct as much attention as possible toward the looming image of the archenemy "Bolshevism." These trends were occurring in Germany simultaneous with the massive intensification of the propaganda of race defilement. Thus, it can be asserted with some plausibility that the construction of the "Jew" in Nazi propaganda that obviously aimed at generating negative feelings toward Jews was primarily built on a subcutaneous foundation of mixed emotions of anxiety or even terror on the one hand and lust and pleasure on the other. At the same time, this mixture was capable of expansion in its diverse variants: disgust and loathing for the effeminate male, constructing the homosexual— or anxiety and panic faced with the prospect of the Jewish Bolshevik, and even worse, his counterpart, the female partisan.

The Practice: Antisemitism, Racism, and Misogyny

The interstices on the level of imagery established, what was particular to Germany in the 1930s was the *implementation* in concrete practice of these convergences, everywhere, and over a number of years. In a large-scale study, Michael Wildt has described in detail the beginnings of the *Volk* community by means of anti-Jewish violence inflicted in rural Germany, analyzing this as a ritual of public humiliation. In view of the sexualized propaganda before 1933, it is hardly surprising that soon after the Nazis took power, there were already public processions in many localities, outdoor events in which persons alleged to have committed race defilement, mainly Jewish males, were forcibly paraded through the streets of their home town, to the great excitement and highly emotional involvement of their fellow citizens.[22] Here, perhaps, something else may have played a role: namely, that unlike in the case of conspiracy theories or other antisemitic fantasies, what was involved were concrete acts of people, "deeds" that in the petty bourgeois, small-town context were even largely familiar, that is, these were "offenses" that generally seemed to be plausible.

Such events of public shaming increased during the summer of 1935, accompanied by a corresponding reportage in the periodical *Der Stürmer*, growing into a genuine wave of so-called pillory processions. These were consciously reminiscent of medieval rituals of dishonoring, and the city of Breslau, for example, made new use of the old pillory (*Staupsäule*) on the market square for public denunciations. But it did not stop at humiliation, and the Sunday processions, if we can lend credence to the Gestapo reports, appear to have become ever more violent over the course of the summer, in this way in turn legitimizing the arrest (in the form of "protective custody") of the men and women involved as offenders.[23]

By means of the impressive photographic material of National Socialist terror in the German provinces that Klaus Hesse and Philipp Springer have put together, it is possible to gain a picture of the differential way in which the men and women endured public humiliation, sometimes with head lowered, at times with spine bent over, staring with a rigid fixed gaze ahead.[24] Only very few of these victims in the first years of Nazi rule sought to fight back by going to court. One of them, a wine merchant from Würzburg who stated after his arrest in August 1933: "I myself was until now a respected citizen of Würzburg, and my reputation has suffered great harm by having to be paraded through the streets of the city carrying a placard, and it also was very damaging to my business."[25] Two years later, protests by the Jews in which, for example, they returned medals awarded for service in World War I—received no such hearing and resulted instead in immediate arrest.[26]

It is certain that in numerous localities the processions did not end with simple humiliation; rather, public amusement at the pillory morphed into brutal violence. However, we have only a fragmentary picture of the extent of this violence through the small number of those who survived and who, after the war, gave testimony. One of those few witnesses is Christine Neemann, who in July 1935 together with her Jewish friend was pummeled and forcibly paraded through the streets of her hometown, Norden. She spoke about her experience in court after liberation: "We were forced to march together through the streets, each one with a placard hung around his or her neck: on it the words 'race defiler.' I was beaten up out in the open on the street, they yanked my hair out and then dragged me to the jail." The ordeal, which afterward was extended to include additional couples, was photographed by the town druggist, and subsequently was turned into a public photo exhibition. However, the extent of the violence is not visible in these photos. Christine Neemann was placed in the Moringen concentration camp, she was fired from her job, and was repeatedly harassed until the end of the Nazi regime. Her Jewish friend managed to escape to the United States.[27]

Even if the bystanders lining the street did not always appear to have obvious reasons for their presence, the race defilement campaign proved a great success. Already in the summer of 1935 the Gestapo was speaking in many localities about a "kind of race defilement psychosis," the effect of which was that "people began to smell race defilement everywhere, and in some cases demanded that the state police take action against such a crime in dealing with events, some of which lay many years in the past."[28] With passage of the Nuremberg Laws in September 1935, as Michael Wildt noted, "for the first time in Germany, the racist obsession to forbid sexual contact with Jews was made a state law. . . . This served to heighten enormously the already existing sexualization of race defilement behavior."[29] And it legalized the brutal punishment of an intimate act between two individuals—an act that almost always had to be reported to the authorities via a complaint stemming from the immediate private sphere of an individual.

According to Robert Gellately, more than half the race defilement legal proceedings from 1935 on were based on denunciation by an informant, and this high level remained operative until the end of 1938—one might say until the orchestrated violence of Kristallnacht in November 1938.[30] That powerful, emotion-laden motives, desirous of achieving a harsh penalty, were principally what was driving these denunciations is proven by the fact that even the Gestapo responded with skepticism to a significant proportion of such accusations.[31] Nonetheless, between 1935 and 1943 a total of 2,211 men were found guilty in race defilement trials. There were significantly more preliminary investigations, which meant condemnation and ostracization for the men and women so denounced. As far as we know, between 1941 and 1943, judges imposed the death penalty (for which actually there was no provision in such cases) a total of six times against German Jews; they did this by combining the offense of race defilement with other crimes (ban on collusion, suppression of evidence).[32] The number of those men who as the result of their incarceration were unable to emigrate, and who after release from prison were deported and murdered, remains unknown.[33]

In this way, the segregation of Jewish from non-Jewish Germans embedded in the rituals of racial defilement was ultimately taken to its consequential ultimate extreme at the beginning of the 1940s. At the same time, from the perspective of the German government, with the outbreak of war a new and numerically far greater danger of "miscegenation, mixture of the races" now flooded into the country: hundreds of thousands, later millions, of prisoners of war (POWs) and forced conscript laborers. Ulrich Herbert has described how those officials in responsible positions on various levels of the Nazi Party and the German state began to ponder only a few weeks after the outbreak of the war about how to prevent close contact between Germans and Polish POWs who were dispersed to work in the German countryside. Among the factors influencing this concern—along with the ideologically imbued racist fantasies—was a very concrete experience: namely, that especially in the rural countryside and within the Catholic population, a relatively friendly attitude toward the Poles prevailed, whether based on custom (Poles were long familiar as seasonal agricultural workers) or owing to religious ties as Roman Catholics.[34] Although neither one of such bonding elements necessarily had to eventuate sexual relations, officials obsessed about this fear of racial mixing, as noted in a memo of the Office for Racial Policy in 1940: "We cannot and must not stand idly by when persons from an alien national stock, who a short time ago were our most bitter enemies and who in their hearts still are, penetrate into the fabric of our most deeply characteristic folk life, making pregnant German-blooded women and ruining our offspring."[35] These "German-blooded women," who apparently were deemed to be highly "unsafe factors," were at the very center of all these reflections driven by an impressive fixation on sexuality, since after all, as Herbert put it, they had "not only offended German honor more generally by engaging in intimate relations with Poles, but the honor of German males in particular."[36]

Already a few days after the war's outbreak, on 10 September, Himmler had asked Hitler how to proceed with such cases of "illicit" sex: "The Führer has ordered that all POWs, who have had intimate relations with a German woman or girl should be shot, and the woman or girl should be publicly disgraced in some way, by shaving her head or confinement in a concentration camp. The Party should become as closely involved as possible in the intended educational impact of such measures."[37] In the "Polish Decrees" (*Polen-Erlasse*) issued in March 1940—which formulated a comprehensive special body of laws initially for Polish and later for additional Eastern conscript laborers—this instruction was rendered concrete; at the same time the image of the Slavic *Untermensch* was radicalized and placed in a clear relation to the already demonized Jews.[38] Thus, the compulsory wearing of an identifying badge for Poles was introduced eighteen months before the "Jewish Star" in Germany, and in a leaflet from spring 1940 with the heading "How to behave toward the Poles," it was explicitly stated: "Just as it is considered the greatest disgrace to become involved with a Jew, any German engaging in intimate relations with a Polish male or female is guilty of sinful behavior. Despise the bestial urges of this race! Be racially conscious and protect your children. Otherwise you will forfeit your greatest asset: your honor."[39]

Thus, if in the 1930s the "sexual-racist anxieties" of the regime had targeted mainly German-Jewish males, the rage of propaganda now turned against German women and involved more draconian penalties, perhaps because of the now-erupted war. The practice in force already since 1940 at the level of local initiatives was now energetically expanded, comprehensively, nationwide: a woman accused of having committed an "SR crime" (a sexual relations crime, so-called *GV-Verbrechen*) with a forced conscript laborer was usually forced to wear a placard hanging from her neck and then paraded through the streets of her hometown. Then, on a raised platform in the market square, her hair was shorn, and after that, in a pillory procession she was taken to the prison. Here, too, extant photos document the extreme brutality of the event.[40] What followed was imprisonment for several years, with loss of honor, and from 1941 on, standard internment in a concentration camp, which often ended in the inmate's death. Those who survived, like their fellow sufferers in the 1930s, had to endure various forms of discrimination right into the postwar period. The Polish and later Soviet POWs involved, in contrast with the Western POWs, were without exception sentenced to death, initially executed publicly and, later, at least strung up and hanged in the presence of other POWs or forced foreign laborers. The precise figure of women and men condemned, charged with this form of race defilement, remains unknown, but numbers in the thousands.[41]

Demarcation of Boundaries

If one looks at the photographic legacy of these modern public stigmatizations as a penalty for illicit sexual behavior because of transgression of newly established "racial laws," what strikes one repeatedly in the photos are the onlookers standing there, the so-called bystanders. Their faces lit up with joy or evident scorn, in any case approving—or so it seems, for one must take into account that almost all photos were taken on the explicit orders of the Nazi Party. In addition, the pillory rituals took place for the most part in small and medium-sized towns, later also in villages. On the one hand, this increased the humiliation of the victims, but on the other, it also heightened the pressure on the spectators to conform. In any case, one fact can be substantiated: they did not stay at home. By their mere presence they were an integral part of the public staging.[42] The few written sources that provide information about the mood among the bystanders are contradictory and remain difficult to interpret. Taken as a whole, the small number of accounts by the victims—and also those accounts prepared by the various perpetrator agencies (Gestapo, Security Service, local press)—permit only one conclusion, as was cautiously formulated by Alexandra Przyrembel: "There existed already before Kristallnacht a potential readiness for violent attacks against Jews in German society."[43] However, this "pleasure in violence"—and this is the core point—was fueled by conceptions regarding permitted and illicit sexuality, and it impacted in the same brutal manner likewise on the non-Jewish partners, and later on the conscripted Eastern European forced laborers. In the case mentioned from the town of Norden in East Frisia, the bands of perpetrators marched not once but twice with their victims through the town, which, as Michael Wildt noted, points "to the emotions that were in play, the passion not yet satisfied, and which demanded a continuation of the public humiliation."[44]

However, one can also suspect the presence here and there of dissenting voices between the lines, and perhaps it is no accident that they come specifically from the city of Breslau. Breslau was the only large city from which pillory procession in a grand style was reported, and which at the same time was home to a large, self-confident Jewish community. To what extent Jewish onlookers actually commented on the processions in the summer of 1935 with "cheeky, insolent remarks," as the Gestapo reported, we do not know. However, it cannot be totally ruled out that Jewish and non-Jewish citizens of Breslau expressed their dislike of this form of "blatant medievalism" likewise in public. The head of the Breslau administration, for example, described the reaction of the onlookers as being "concurring in part, in part rejecting."[45]

Interestingly, little changed in this ambivalence when the boundaries of racist violence against the female, non-Jewish population in Germany were tightened ever more a few years later, given the presence of millions of Polish, Ukrainian, and Western European men in Germany as conscript laborers. Although the Security Service initially reported that there was a "positive view" and acceptance in the population of the need for a strict public response toward the women accused, dissatisfaction about how the manner in which those intimate "SR crimes" were being handled appears to have increased over the course of 1940–41.[46] Some regarded the differential treatment of POWs from the west and the east unfair, others were critical of the illegal acts involved when young Poles were strung up from trees "in a manner reminiscent of the Wild West" (*in Wildwestmanier*).[47]

While the Nazi sources repeatedly quote voices from the population demanding an even more severe punishment for the women involved, the few available sources on the local scene yield a different picture. Thus, in her study on conscript labor in Friedrichshafen, Christa Tholander concluded that most of the cases of race defilement involved women and girls from the surrounding rural villages, and that the rituals of public humiliation there "left a deep impression in the form of a sense of revulsion": "People then also felt sympathy for the German farmer's daughter from the local community, and also for the Polish man."[48] On the occasion of a case that transpired in Ulm, which is impressively documented in photos done by a professional photographer, the local press even felt the necessity of publicly criticizing the "sloppy sentimentalities" of a portion of the population, which appear to have been emotional responses principally by women.[49] One can only speculate about the underlying reasons behind this presumably largely female empathy: in some cases in Oldenburg, Birthe Kundrus has noted a generally heightened feeling of female self-confidence, which also included a greater sense of sexual independence—and which could have been a direct result of the Nazi sexual politics described by Herzog. Thus, for example, the much more severe punishment of women was perceived as unfair since for the same offense German men usually were let off with a three-month sentence behind bars if their intimate relationships were indeed penalized at all.[50]

Presumably—and the photographic documentation suggests this—the ritual of public shearing of the hair constituted such a traumatic bodily intrusion that female onlookers in particular could scarcely elude its powerful effect. Although during the anti-Jewish campaign of the 1930s such a measure against women had still not been applied, this act of shaving of the head as punishment became in the 1940s *the* very symbol of race defilement.[51] In any case, the "unrest in the population" appears to have become so perceptible that directives were issued at the end of 1941 to cease the rituals of humiliation on the streets. However, the death sentences against Eastern European males and draconian penalties against women were maintained.

Despite this measure, the "terror on the spot, in the everyday life of the cities and villages ... in one's own sphere of life and experience," as Reinhard Rürup had noted some years ago, certainly left palpable traces in German memory.[52] This is substantiated not only by the interview statements from the local studies cited above or the fact that an impressive novel on the topic of a love affair between a lonely married German woman and a Russian conscript farmhand was published already in the 1950s, Brigitte Reimann's *The Woman on the Pillory*.[53] Rather, and above all, there were continuities under the skin: the fury about the "unfaithful German woman," which let off steam in the public rituals of race defilement, appears to have crossed over seamlessly into postwar outrage and indignation over the "sweetheart of the Yankee soldier" (*das Amiliebchen*)[54]— and even in the case of the victims of rape at the end of the war, the male official representatives of agencies often insinuated that in reality the women had "voluntarily consented."[55]

This *longue durée* may point to just how much potency is involved when racist norms about the body and sexuality are anchored in the heads (and perhaps souls?) of men and women by means of constant sensual thematization and violent visual rituals. Michael Wildt has rightly pointed out that what was involved in the Nazi practices was not like practices in the jurisdiction of honor in the Middle Ages and Early Modern era, entailing a restoration of the Old Order. Rather, it was the implementation of a New Order that was based on racist demarcation of boundaries.[56] However, as Ute Frevert has argued, resorting to these "traditional practices of shaming" was so extremely successful for one reason: it made it possible to "exaggerate it as a radical innovation *and* at the same time to embed it in society."[57]

To what extent then can the scenes such as the one described by Klemperer at the start of this essay help describe this convergence and assist in decoding the powerful but highly ambivalent emotions produced in this manner? Did the "mass murder," as Philipp Springer writes, really have its "point of departure in the villages and towns?"[58] In any case, there are certainly hints and references in the sources pointing to the fact that the sexually grounded rage discharged in these villages and towns was rapidly transformed into fantasies of murder. Thus, a journalist at the *Schlesische Tageszeitung*, in response to critical commentary voiced abroad, summed up the pillory processions in Breslau in the summer of 1935 as follows: "We did *not* murder those individuals, persons who had literally wrecked the lives of many a German man and German woman. We let them live and only sent them to a place that they deserved."[59] A few years later, in July 1941, Nazi officials were far less merciful toward non-Jewish German women because, as detailed in a document sent to Joseph Goebbels's Ministry of Propaganda, "cutting off their hair in public has had virtually no success." The officials called for the death penalty for women who had become intimately involved with foreigners. They justified this by stating that these women were committing "the greatest crime imaginable in National Socialist Germany."[60]

Such wishes for eradication, even of female members of one's "own" group, prove once more the destructive power that antisemitism, racism, and misogyny can unleash—if they are solidly anchored in the body via images of gender and concepts of sexuality and then are interwoven with emotions of fear and desire, excitation and loathing, attraction and repulsion. And perhaps it is precisely the ambivalence of the emotions bound up in the way described—the simultaneity of aversion and attraction but also of shame and desire—that produces a legacy of untrammeled aggression.

Going back to the mistreated women of the Güntzstrasse in Dresden, one might speculate that in this doubly tabooed case—torturing *old* women—it was a mixture of shame and aversion that might explain the specifically monstrous behavior of the policemen, or to put it differently: they "somehow" knew that what they did was wrong, which means that remnants of the pre-Nazi moral system were still working, albeit buried under heaps of anti-Jewish resentment. This stands in stark contrast to the men of the Uncompromising Generation, described by Michael Wildt and others, who were able to style themselves as unemotional perpetrators driven by the supposedly rational realization of "what had to be done," based on their profound antisemitic worldview.[61] Thus, the pathway sketched out here seems promising, both in its relevance for understanding the dynamics of antisemitism and also of other attitudes of hostility and resentment. Certainly, the emotion-driven nexus between violence, sexuality, and exclusion is still entirely functional and very much with us today.

Notes

A German version of this chapter ("Geschlecht und Gewalt: Zur Emotionsgeschichte des Antisemitismus") appeared in *Emotionen und Antisemitismus: Geschichte—Literatur—Theorie*, ed. Stefanie Schüler-Springorum and Jan Süselbeck (Göttingen: Wallstein, 2021), 212–32.

1. Victor Klemperer, *I Shall Bear Witness: The Diaries, 1942–1945* (London: Weidenfeld & Nicolson, 1999), 50.
2. Jürgen Matthäus, "Holocaust als angewandter Antisemitismus? Potential und Grenzen eines Erklärungsfaktors," in *Der Holocaust: Ergebnisse und neue Fragen der Forschung*, ed. Frank Bajohr and Andrea Löw (Frankfurt am Main: Fischer, 2015), 102–23, 102.
3. Matthäus, "Holocaust als angewandter Antisemitismus?," 117.
4. I consciously use the term "Antisemitism" in this text because I am referring first and foremost to Germany in the late nineteenth and twentieth century. For a more general understanding of the pitfalls and shortcomings of this term, see Jonathan Judaken, "Introduction," *American Historical Review* 123, no. 4 (2018): 1122–38.
5. Matthäus, "Holocaust als angewandter Antisemitismus?," 102.
6. Alon Confino, "From Psychohistory to Memory Studies: Or, How Some Germans Became Jews and Some Jews Nazis," in *History Flows through Us*, ed. Roger Frie (New York: Routledge, 2018), 17–30, 21.
7. See Uffa Jensen and Stefanie Schüler-Springorum, "Einführung: Gefühle gegen Juden: Die Emotionsgeschichte des modernen Antisemitismus," *Geschichte und Gesellschaft* 39, no. 4 (2013): 413–42; Stefanie Schüler-Springorum, "Gender and the Politics of Anti-Semitism," *American Historical Review* 123, no. 4 (2018): 1210–22.
8. Christina von Braun, "Zur Bedeutung der Sexualbilder im rassistischen Antisemitismus," *Feministische Studien* 33, no. 2 (2015): 293–307, 295.
9. Delphine Horvilleur, *Réflexions sur la question antisémite* (Paris: Grasset, 2019).
10. George L. Mosse, *Nationalism and Sexuality: Middle-Class Morality and Sexual Norms in Modern Europe* (Madison: University of Wisconsin Press, 2020).
11. Sander Gilman, *The Jew's Body* (New York: Routledge, 1991).
12. Abdul R. JanMohamed, "Sexuality on/of the Racial Border: Foucault, Wright, and the Articulation of 'Racialized Sexuality,'" in *Discourses of Sexuality: From Aristotle to AIDS*, ed. Donna C. Stanton (Ann Arbor: University of Michigan Press, 1992), 94–116, 98.
13. Dagmar Herzog, *Sex after Fascism: Memory and Morality in Twentieth-Century Germany* (Princeton, NJ: Princeton University Press, 2007), 19.
14. Herzog, *Sex after Fascism*, 21.
15. Herzog, *Sex after Fascism*, 26–36.
16. Herzog, *Sex after Fascism*, 36–53.
17. Alexandra Przyrembel, "Ambivalente Gefühle: Sexualität und Antisemitismus während des Nationalsozialismus," *Geschichte und Gesellschaft* 39, no. 4 (2013): 527–54, 551.
18. Herzog, *Sex after Fascism*, 40.
19. Kristoff Kerl, *Männlichkeit und moderner Antisemitismus: Eine Genealogie des Leo-Frank-Case, 1860er bis 1920er Jahre* (Cologne: Böhlau, 2017).

20. See Stefanie Schüler-Springorum, "Gewalt gegen Tote: Zur Ikonographie des Spanischen Bürgerkriegs," in *Bilder kollektiver Gewalt—Kollektive Gewalt im Bild: Annäherungen an eine Ikonographie der Gewalt*, ed. Michael Kohlstruck, Stefanie Schüler-Springorum, and Ulrich Wyrwa (Berlin: Metropol, 2015), 137–45.

21. Gamel Woolsey, *Death's Other Kingdom* (London: Longman, 1939), 126.

22. Michael Wildt, *Volksgemeinschaft als Selbstermächtigung: Gewalt gegen Juden in der deutschen Provinz 1919 bis 1939* (Hamburg: Hamburger Edition, 2007).

23. See Alexandra Przyrembel, *"Rassenschande": Reinheitsmythos und Vernichtungslegitimation im Nationalsozialismus* (Göttingen: Vandenhoeck & Ruprecht, 2003), 73–75.

24. See Klaus Hesse and Philipp Springer, eds., *Vor aller Augen: Fotodokumente des nationalsozialistischen Terrors in der Provinz* (Essen: Klartext, 2002).

25. Quoted in Przyrembel, *"Rassenschande,"* 83.

26. Przyrembel, *"Rassenschande,"* 76.

27. See Wildt, *Volksgemeinschaft*, 234–39.

28. Quoted in Przyrembel, "Ambivalente Gefühle," 540–41.

29. Wildt, *Volksgemeinschaft*, 264.

30. Robert Gellately, *Hingeschaut und Weggesehen: Hitler und sein Volk* (Stuttgart and Munich: Deutsche Verlags-Anstalt, 2002), 188–93.

31. See Wildt, *Volksgemeinschaft*, 240.

32. Przyrembel, *"Rassenschande,"* 499, 505.

33. See for example the case of the Königsberg merchant Max Rawraway in Stefanie Schüler-Springorum, *Die jüdische Minderheit in Königsberg, 1871–1945* (Göttingen: Vandenhoeck & Ruprecht, 1996), 306.

34. See Ulrich Herbert, *Hitler's Foreign Workers: Enforced Foreign Labor in Germany under the Third Reich* (New York: Cambridge University Press, 1997), 69–75.

35. Quoted in Birthe Kundrus, "'Verbotener Umgang.' Liebesbeziehungen zwischen Ausländern und Deutschen 1939–1945," in *Nationalsozialismus und Zwangsarbeit in der Region Oldenburg*, ed. Katharina Hoffmann and Andreas Lambeck (Oldenburg: Universität Oldenburg, 1999), 149–70, 150.

36. Herbert, *Hitler's Foreign Workers*, 77.

37. Herbert, *Hitler's Foreign Workers*, 75.

38. Herbert, *Hitler's Foreign Workers*, 141.

39. Quoted in Kundrus, "Verbotener Umgang," 153.

40. See Hesse and Springer, *Vor aller Augen*.

41. See Herbert, *Hitler's Foreign Workers*, 79–81, 122–29.

42. This contradicts the otherwise very convincing analysis of Thomas Kohut, *A German Generation: An Experiential History of the Twentieth Century* (New Haven, CT: Yale University Press, 2012), 137.

43. Przyrembel, *"Rassenschande,"* 71.

44. Wildt, *Volksgemeinschaft*, 238.

45. Przyrembel, *"Rassenschande,"* 73–75.

46. Quoted in Herbert, *Hitler's Foreign Workers*, 64.

47. Herbert, *Hitler's Foreign Workers*, 135.

48. See Christa Tholander, *Fremdarbeiter 1939 bis 1945: Ausländische Arbeitskräfte in der Zeppelin-Stadt Friedrichshafen* (Essen: Klartext, 2001), 59–66, quote 63.

49. See Martin König, "Die 'deutsche Frau und Mutter': Ideologie und Wirklichkeit," in *Ulm im Zweiten Weltkrieg*, ed. Hans Eugen Specker (Stuttgart: Kohlhammer, 1996), 99–127, 116.

50. See Kundrus, *Verbotener Umgang*.

51. See Przyrembel, *"Rassenschande,"* 83–84, for the only known case where a woman's hair was shorn in 1933, not in public, however.

52. See Reinhard Rürup, "Vorwort," in Hesse and Springer, *Vor aller Augen*, 7–9, 8.

53. See Brigitte Reimann, *Die Frau am Pranger* (Berlin: Neues Leben, 1956).

54. See Susanne zur Nieden, "'Erotic Fraternization.' The Legend of German Women's Quick Surrender," in *Home/Front: The Military, War and Gender in Twentieth Century Germany*, ed. Karen Hagemann and Stefanie Schüler-Springorum (Oxford: Berg, 2002), 297–310.

55. Quoted in Miriam Gebhardt, *Als die Soldaten kamen: Die Vergewaltigung deutscher Frauen am Ende des Zweiten Weltkriegs* (Munich: DVA, 2015), 240.

56. See Wildt, *Volksgemeinschaft*, 257.

57. Ute Frevert, *Die Politik der Demütigung: Schauplätze von Macht und Ohnmacht* (Frankfurt am Main: Fischer, 2017), 65.

58. Philipp Springer, "Auf Straßen und Plätzen: Zur Fotogeschichte des nationalsozialistischen Deutschland," in Hesse and Springer, *Vor aller Augen*, 11–33, 18.

59. Quoted in Przyrembel, *"Rassenschande,"* 79.

60. Quoted in Herbert, *Hitler's Foreign Workers*, 129.

61. Michael Wildt, *An Uncompromising Generation: The Nazi Leadership of the Reich Security Main Office* (Madison: University of Wisconsin Press, 2009).

7

People Working

Leisure, Love, and Violence in Nazi Concentration Camps

ELISSA MAILÄNDER

On the night of 29 January 1943, after a 560-mile (900-km) train ride from Fürstenberg an der Havel, a small spa town 50 miles (80 km) from Berlin, to the city of Lublin on the southeastern border of Nazi-occupied Poland, five exhausted female SS guards (*Aufseherinnen*) reported for duty at Majdanek.[1] No welcoming committee greeted the newcomers. Just a few SS men quickly showed them to their accommodation before inviting the women for drinks in their own quarters. Rosa Reischl was tired and wanted to leave but did not know where to go, so she followed her colleagues. When she stepped outside the SS men's compound to get some fresh air, an SS officer suddenly approached, warning her to be careful: "Beware, they want to get you."[2] By this point, Rosa was very worried. She rushed back into the barracks and grabbed her friend Herta Ehlert. Relieved at having escaped the men, Rosa and Herta wandered around the camp in the dark looking for their own quarters.

Spotting a light, they knocked on the door of a little house. A sixteen- or seventeen-year-old Jewish boy with a dog opened it: "What are you doing?" he said. "You're not allowed in here." Confused, the two women nevertheless entered the room, where they saw three SS men lying on their beds: "There was a radio in the room," Rosa remembered, and "there was a skull on it." One of these uniformed SS men immediately grabbed Herta while at the same time trying to pull Rosa toward him. The other two SS men invited the women to sit down on their beds. Herta and Rosa, frightened, grasped chairs and sat down. "We both started trembling and held onto each other," Rosa Reischl told the public prosecutors in a hearing in 1973. "Herta said we should get out of there. So I ran to a door, thinking it was the exit, but instead ended up inside a large

ELISSA MAILÄNDER

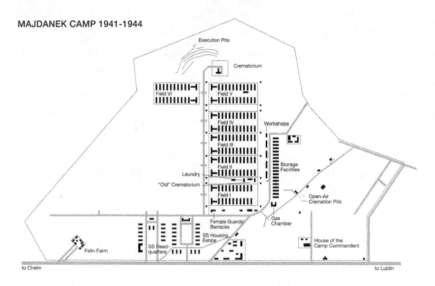

Figure 7.1. Map of the Majdanek camp area. (Photograph by Ralph Gabriel.)

room. In the light from the door, I could see a big oven. Oil was dripping from it. An SS man ran after me. I was faster, and he didn't catch me. There was a door at the other end of the room, and in my fear I ran toward it. The room was pitch dark. When I ran in, I fell straight onto a pile of corpses. I screamed but at that point I must have fainted."[3] Nearly thirty years after the event, Rosa Reischl remembered her arrival at the Majdanek concentration and extermination camp in vivid terms. Although it sounds like a 1970s Nazisploitation movie,[4] it is indeed quite plausible that, in her confusion, she accidentally stumbled into the crematorium, which happened to be near the camp's entry gates as well as the female guards' accommodations.

Reading through Reischl's statement, we share her sense of horror and might even feel some empathy with the twenty-three-year-old and her thirty-eight-year-old colleague. The young woman's distress seems genuine and her despair plausible, and yet, we also know that she was part of the SS staff, first of a concentration camp (Ravensbrück) and later of an extermination camp (Majdanek). Commonly we imagine people like Rosa Reischl, one of twenty-eight female SS guards who served alongside almost one thousand SS men at Majdanek, to be fundamentally alien from mainstream society—and from us. By looking at the workaday lives of these women and men, however, we realize that their work of surveying and killing occasionally caused them distress, which they countered by developing individual strategies to adjust to the concentration camp work environment, such as collective routines and horseplay, closely linked with and inspired by contemporary culture, music, fashion, movies, and advertisements.[5] Taken together, these tactics and strategies helped make their job more "comfortable" and, as I will demonstrate, more efficient. This chapter steps back from a strictly positivistic analysis of the concentration camps, based on so-called hard facts in the files, instead emphasizing the guards' social practices and material culture. This approach will allow me to probe violence within the specific political, institutional, and sociocultural contexts of the concentration and extermination camp Majdanek. After Reischl's and Ehlert's horrified reaction to the extermination camp on arrival, how did they get accustomed to Majdanek and to the omnipresence of murder and death? And how did ordinary female guards contribute legitimacy to the mass killing in the camps? The notion of everyday life, or *Alltag*, is a key lens that allows us to look at the transformation of seemingly—if I may—banal women into Nazi perpetrators.

Building on Alf Lüdtke's and George L. Mosse's work on German fascism, the premise here is to draw on everyday life and popular culture in the camps in order to answer the deceptively simple question: How did the guards "*do it*"?[6] How did ordinary German and Austrian men and women adapt to camp life and handle the work in Nazi camps day by day, for up to twelve years?

Working in the Camps

From the establishment of the very first SS concentration camp in Dachau, work was carried out around the clock. Tasked with ensuring the smoothest possible camp functioning, male, and from 1939, also female, guards oversaw the surveillance of the prisoners, whereas the Death's Head Units (*Totenkopf Wachstrumbann*) policed the entire campsite.[7] But it was the detainees who built the camps, cultivated the fields, cooked, and cleaned. The SS not only used their workforce for maintenance purposes; from the beginning of World War II, they also exploited the inmates economically by forcing them to work under extreme pressure and inhumane conditions in SS-owned companies or by leasing them cheaply to third-party companies.[8] Most importantly, the SS managed the murder: the SS doctors who provided medical care for the staff carried out lethal "research" projects on the prisoners, while the SS battalions took charge of the mass killings and SS officers operated the gas chambers. It might come as little surprise that the actual "dirty work" was done by the inmates: prisoner commandos emptied and cleaned the gas chambers; they unloaded the shooting pits and buried or burned the corpses after the killings.

In our common understanding, work has an overall positive connotation. It is therefore rather discomfiting to frame a genocide and mass killing as "work."

Yet murder on such a mass scale was only possible because the SS camp staff drew on industrial work processes and perfected them in a step-by-step manner with the purpose of annihilating human life. If allusions to work (division of labor, regularity of repetitious actions, professionalism, and so forth) allowed German Wehrmacht soldiers to normalize their actions and behavior, as Alf Lüdtke has demonstrated, this was also the case for the camp guards.[9] It is precisely the workaday habits of the historical agents in all their complexity and presumed normalcy, and the social dynamics within these habits, that deserve our attention.

While in his study *The Order of Terror*, sociologist Wolfgang Sofsky paid attention to work as a form of organized economic and physical exploitation of the inmates, little is said about the SS staff's workaday habits. Sofsky's groundbreaking typology recognizes the social foundations of violence and murder, yet his prime focus on institutionalized and habituated terror obscures the microsocial dynamics of power, reducing the Nazi concentration camp to an "institutional model" and the camp staff to "machines" and thereby underestimating the impact of individual as well as cultural practices.[10] Mass violence and genocide do not suspend the everyday; looking closely at daily work routines in the Nazi camps reveals, on the contrary, how intimately work, leisure, and extermination were bound together and how the SS guards primarily experienced the camps as a workplace and as "nothing but work."

According to the Nazis' own statistics for January 1945, 3,508 female camp guards and 37,674 SS men kept 750,000 inmates (202,674 women and 511,537 men) under surveillance in fifteen main concentration (*Stammlager*) and five hundred satellite camps distributed all over Europe.[11] Since the beginning of World War II and the European expansion of the SS archipelago, the camps were chronically understaffed, with the prisoners largely outnumbering the SS.[12] Of course, the total number of SS staff for the entire period of the camps' existence (1933–45) is much higher than these figures for January 1945, but the inventory nevertheless illuminates the gender ratio and careers of the people who became experts in death and killing.

Physical violence was certainly not the primary motivation for signing up for a concentration camp guard job, although the recruits quickly developed a taste for it. Rather, the male SS officer staff at Majdanek perceived an opportunity for career advancement. In a 1981 interview, for example, former first camp compound leader (*Schutzhaftlagerführer*) Hermann Hackmann admitted that it was ambition that led him to seek a career in the SS, while former SS corporal (*Rottenführer*) Heinz Villain saw his voluntary service with the Armed SS as part of a broader plan to join the civil service and work for the police. Hackmann, born in Osnabrück in 1913, hoped to become an architect and completed an apprenticeship as a bricklayer from 1930 to 1933, but he abandoned that plan owing to economic difficulties and instead joined the SS.[13] Heinz Villain, who was born in 1921 in Reichsberg (Brandenburg), trained as a blacksmith after primary school. After his journeyman's examination, he joined the SS Death's Head Unit Brandenburg in Oranienburg in 1938, with a plan to enter the police force after twelve years of camp service. "Honestly, what stinks to me the most," Villain vented in frustration during the 1981 Majdanek trial, "is that at the time we volunteered to have a future—after all; you did not know then how long that goes with Hitler's dictatorship."[14] Hackmann's and Villain's deliberate choices to join the SS force can be considered political, since as early members of the SS, they undoubtedly had an idea of the nature of their work, yet what seemed to motivate them most was a clear career perspective.

The picture of female guards is slightly different. In contrast to their male colleagues, the female guards had no long-term military career plans. The Berliner Herta Ehlert, born in 1905, was a trained saleswoman running the branch of a shop. Although she claimed during the Majdanek trial to have been forcibly appointed as an SS guard by the employment office (*Arbeitsamt*) in November 1939, it is very likely that Ehlert applied voluntarily, like the majority of the women recruited during the first year after Ravensbrück opened.[15] Rosa Reischl, on the other hand, joined the female SS force much later. Born in 1920 in the Bavarian countryside, she was originally trained as an infant care nurse at a nursery run by the National Socialist People's Welfare Organization (Nationalsozialistische Volkswohlfahrt, NSV), before the employment office (*Arbeitsamt*) tried to send her to work at a sawmill in summer 1942. Reischl firmly refused and, instead, was appointed as a camp guard and sent to Ravensbrück in fall 1942.[16]

When Ravensbrück, the first female concentration camp, opened in 1939, the SS was looking for women aged between twenty-one and forty-five, preferably single, explicitly demanding "*no professional skills*" of prospective guards.[17] In the beginning, former housemaids and factory workers applied on their own initiative, but from 1940 the employment office (*Arbeitsamt*) helped increase the female workforce by referring unemployed women. In addition, the SS used recruitment drives and promotion tours to appeal to factory workers. Like their peers, Herta Ehlert and Rosa Reischl perfectly fit the age and social profile of women targeted by the SS: single, preferably young women from a modest social background, and with no higher education. Reischl, a trained but unemployed infant care nurse, was an exception in this regard. Most female recruits were, indeed, unskilled factory workers or domestic maids trying to escape from difficult working conditions and low wages, but it seems that the job also had some financial advantages to offer a trained saleswoman and a nurse.

Recent studies have shown that only 4.1 percent of sixteen hundred female guards working in Ravensbrück, the central concentration camp for women, were members of the Nazi Party.[18] For working and middle-class women in their twenties and thirties, the job of guarding detainees was a golden opportunity to acquire a better and, above all, stable livelihood.[19] In a postwar cross-examination, Herta Ehlert did not mince words: "Well, I want to be quite honest," she told the British interrogators in 1945, "I never had such a good life as in the beginning at Ravensbrück when I arrived."[20] Applying for work as a camp guard did not necessarily imply a strong political commitment or ideological motivation; rather, it indicated working- or lower-middle-class women's desires for higher social status, economic independence, and a degree of comfort.

Living in the Camps

Life in the camps offered these women a heretofore unknown standard of "luxury," with a room of their own and a decent salary that left them money to send home to their families or to spend on clothing and entertainment. Hence camp life was not solely about higher wages, or new, comfortable accommodations; it was also about regular leisure time and fun.

For sure, the female guards who had previously served in Ravensbrück found life at Majdanek in occupied Poland far more modest and difficult to handle. Former camp compound leader Hackmann recalled in 1973 in court that the camp's mess hall did not meet the standards of the SS officers, who felt it was "too primitive."[21] For the female guards, too, their quarters were too spartan for their tastes.[22] The camp's mismanagement and poor maintenance made the sanitation arrangements life threatening for the inmates, but the problems with the sewage system also affected the SS staff. The *Aufseherinnen* slept in simple wooden barracks, which, lacking indoor plumbing, were simply outfitted with latrines.[23]

At first glance, this concentration and extermination camp located in the far East did not look like a promotion. Being on the eastern periphery of the Nazi empire came with financial incentives, however, as the SS received bonus pay and extra rations of alcohol, cigarettes, and food, which were precious goods during the war, especially for trade.[24] Another "advantage" of Majdanek was that since it was a killing site, the *Aufseherinnen* and SS men could secretly "supply" themselves with clothing, shoes, and all kinds of other commodities from the camp's well-stocked storerooms.[25] Finally, the remote location allowed the rules to be more easily skirted, offering more latitude and greater margins of maneuver for the Majdanek SS staff.

After a full day of work, Hildegard Lächert went horseback riding on the camp's Arabian thoroughbreds, a rather luxurious pastime given her social background.[26] But Majdanek offered additional entertainment outside the camp's perimeters, notably in the city of Lublin, where the German occupiers could spend their free time in public baths, an outdoor swimming pool, two libraries, a bookshop, and in a variety of coffeehouses and restaurants. A theater and cinema (the *Deutsche Lichtspiele*) offered entertainment during the evenings.[27] The German House (*Deutsches Haus*) included a casino as well as a concert and dance hall, which the former *Aufseherinnen* remembered fondly during their interrogations.

In Eberhard Fechner's documentary, former guard Luzie Halata enthusiastically recalled the casino as her favorite spot (*Stammlokal*) to hang out. When she entered, the band immediately greeted her with her favorite song, "Alte Kameraden," after which she threw a round: "Once, the husband of my cousin was visiting and he was astonished that they played my song and that the band raised their glasses to us. And I said, 'yes, that is my favorite song and my favorite place.'"[28] The self-assured appearance of this thirty-three-year-old single woman must surely have made a great impression on her cousin visiting from the Reich. In her research on women who served in the Nazi East as settlement instructors and teachers, Elizabeth Harvey has explained this attitude as an Aryan arrogance and "instilling colonial entitlement" (*Herrenbewußtsein*).[29]

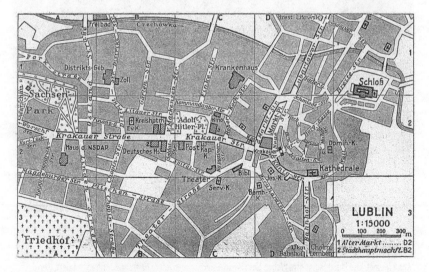

Figure 7.2. Map of the city of Lublin with German entertainment facilities. Reprinted from von Karl Baedeker, *Das Generalgouvernement: Reisehandbuch* (Leipzig, 1943).

The same applied to the female guards in Majdanek—no wonder that despite the hardships, the *Aufseherinnen* settled into Majdanek quite quickly. Clearly, once in service, the female guards enjoyed their powerful positions and multiple privileges, which added another motivator beyond the attempt to advance their careers. Enjoying a new social standing might also explain why so few tried to leave the camps and look for another job.

Yet Majdanek offered one other "bonus" that occasionally caused trouble: in contrast to Ravensbrück, the staff in Majdanek was not only mixed but the SS men also greatly outnumbered the female guards. The SS men could be quite predatory, as we have seen, and it was not always easy for the *Aufseherinnen* to adjust to this male-dominated, paramilitary work environment.[30] At the same time, their presence offered the opportunity to become romantically or sexually involved, to find a husband, and to marry. Four female guards, born between 1918 and 1922, married members of the SS Death's Head Unit while on duty.[31] At least two of them were five months pregnant when their fiancés filed for

Figure 7.3. A birthday party at the "Deutsches Haus" in Lublin. Private photograph presumably taken in March 1944 on the occasion of a birthday party for chief guard Else Ehrich. A print was given by former SS guard Elisabeth Haselof to the public prosecutor Dieter Ambach of the Majdanek Trial in 1975. The image represents almost the complete *Aufseherinnen* staff of that time. *Front row, left to right*: Hermine Brückner, Luzie Halata, Anna Meinel, Else Ehrich, Charlotte Weber, Rosa Reischl. *Second row, left to right*: pres. Anna Scharbert, Herta Bieneck, Elfriede Zimmermann, Emilie Macha, Herta Ehlert, Luise Danz, Charlotte Wöllert, Alice Orlowksi, Gertrud Heise, Anna David, Erna Bodem. (Reprint from the private archive of prosecutor Dieter Ambach.)

permission to marry with the SS Race and Settlement Head Office (RuSHA).[32] Postwar interrogations of former camp staff and testimonies of survivors further suggest that a number of female guards had affairs with married SS men.[33] It appears, for instance, that Hermine Braunsteiner and Charlotte Wöllert were involved with married SS officers until their respective wives joined them in Lublin.[34]

A German Kapo even told the investigation authorities of the Central Office of the Land Judicial Authorities for the Investigation of National Socialist Crimes in 1963 that the SS medic in charge of the gas chamber, *SS Oberscharführer* Hans Perschon, had a crush on *Aufseherin* Anni David, and that "one day he was so broken-hearted that he even wanted to take his own life in the gas chamber."[35] This incongruous image of frivolous romantic desire coexisting with the gas chamber points to the fact that—like in any other workplace—romantic relations and pre- or extramarital sexual encounters functioned as a popular pastime for SS staff.[36] Specific to the camps was the attempt to distract oneself from the deadly atmosphere; it suggests a shocking banality of genocide within what we could frame as the SS camp society.[37]

Killing in the Camps

Scholars of concentration camps tend to emphasize the institutional and political elements: the very structure and organization of the camps was to incarcerate, exploit, and kill.[38] But a closer look at the Majdanek guards' workaday violence complicates the picture. It shows that individual violent behavior of the male and certain female guards far exceeded the guidelines defined in Berlin or by their superiors. At Majdanek, both female and male guards dealt with inmates from Eastern Europe who, whether Jewish or "Slavic," functioned in Nazi ideology as racial and political enemies of the Reich. Nevertheless, it is difficult to explain their behavioral radicalization from a solely ideological viewpoint. Violence against Jews, Poles, and Russians should instead be understood as a social practice that had its own situational dynamics and emotional economies.

Female guards performed the same supervisory duties as their male colleagues, with one notable exception: women did not participate in gassings or mass shootings. But female guards held roll calls, supervised women inmates in the barracks and at work, selected female inmates for gassing, and guarded prisoners outside the gas chambers. Hence, the female guards exercised direct power over, and perpetrated physical violence on, the prisoners. In contrast to her colleagues, the former inmates recognized camp guard Luzie Halata as "nice" and rather "mild." Born in Breslau in 1910, she was trained at the Ravensbrück concentration camp in November 1942, only to be transferred to Majdanek in

March 1943.[39] At the Majdanek trial that took place in Düsseldorf between 1975 and 1981, Luzie Halata was the only one among the former female Majdanek guards willing to testify about their participation in selections of Jewish women and children.

Even though the female guards did not directly participate in the systematic killing, some of Halata's statements nevertheless demonstrate how deeply the daily work of mass murder penetrated her off-duty existence. After work, Luzie Halata sometimes paid a visit to an SS man whom she had befriended at his workplace: "I had an acquaintance there, a dentist. When he did his work up there. Well, I don't know where that was, but when he came back, he knocked on my door. And the first time—I didn't know what he'd been doing—I said to him, 'Aren't you going to shake my hand?' And he replied, 'Luzie, we'll talk about that later. But I can't shake your hand right now.'"[40] This episode is another striking example of how some female guards tried to shut out the environment in which they were working and living by trying to lead a "normal" life. But the befriended dentist confronted Halata with the true nature of their work: having spent all day extracting gold teeth from murdered Jewish bodies, he did not want to shake her hand without washing it first. Despite efforts on the part of the concentration camp staff to keep their work lives separate from their personal lives, the killing work necessarily encroached on the private sphere, and a certain level of unease remained with the constant presence of death.

Herta Ehlert, whom Ravensbrück survivor Margarete Buber-Neumann described as a "big blonde Valkyrie who enjoyed laughing loudly, eating well and amply," also counted as a rather kind guard. "Horrified by the idea that others had to starve," as Buber-Neumann put it, "she often gave food to the prisoners."[41] When Ehlert came to Majdanek in January 1943, she was appointed to the laundry service where she supervised a group of twenty to forty Polish and Jewish inmates. It was a rather "pleasant" job, as she put it in an interrogation in 1972, "one of the quietest and nicest detachments. The others envied me because of it. In our detachment, there were no beatings, nor were other cruelties meted out."[42] From this "quiet" and "protected" place, Ehlert could see and hear little of what was going on elsewhere in the camp. Clearly, her motto was to "look away"—the less she saw and knew, the better.

Yet as it turns out, the laundry at Majdanek was located near the old crematorium and across from the gas chambers, where laundry was taken for delousing.[43] Although the crematorium, because of technical problems, was not used on a regular basis, it remained one of the most shunned places in the entire camp. Luzie Halata once went there to get some eggs, when Muhsfeldt came toward her and said, "Don't look." To get her eggs from his room, she had to pass the vestibule, a spacious area with nooses up top where inmates were hanged. Halata recalled that the bodies had been taken down already: "They were all lying on the floor."[44]

It comes with little surprise that the former female guards vividly recalled the head of the crematory's gallows humor.[45] Erich "Mussfeld [sic], knew that I found the place repulsive," Herta Ehlert stated in a 1970 interrogation. "That's why he often called out 'crematorium' to me when I walked by, or waved a dead body part at me."[46] Seen from an everyday historical perspective, this gruesome gesture—as derisory as it may seem—is a revealing source, because it allows us to grasp the atmosphere in which people were working and living.

First, I see in this macabre joke an attempt by Muhsfeldt to assert himself as a man vis-à-vis a scared female guard. Just as in Auschwitz, the "removal" of corpses in Majdanek demanded special skills and was an extremely important task in the extermination process: it was a measure of hygiene in order to prevent epidemics but also a highly political job of removing evidence of mass murder.[47] As the chief of the crematorium, Muhsfeldt, together with his assistant Robert Seitz, led a team of Jewish and Soviet prisoners who were, in turn, regularly killed and replaced.

Although Muhsfeldt enjoyed undisputed authority among his own team and the camp commanders, the interrogations also revealed a lonely man who lived by himself.[48] It is not surprising that most of the Majdanek SS men, and even more so the supervisors, avoided the crematorium and Muhsfeldt's team. SS personnel and prisoners who had observed the team agreed that there was a particularly sinister atmosphere. Beyond the purview of the rest of the camp, the Muhsfeldt team worked daily with half-decomposed dead bodies; the alcohol supplied by the camp leaders flowed, and the jokes were brutal. This was precisely the place into which the four newly arrived guards from Ravensbrück, quoted at the beginning of this chapter, stumbled upon their arrival—*in medias res*, because Majdanek was a concentration and extermination camp.

Ultimately, his attempted teasing of Herta Ehlert underscores Muhsfeldt's own marginalization inside the SS camp. In constant contact with corpses, Muhsfeldt carried "the smell of death," which led to his colleagues' avoidance. Ehlert and others, for instance, refused to shake his hand, and it was said that he always ate alone in the SS canteen. It is interesting that neither the SS men, who regularly killed prisoners with injections of gasoline or phenol, nor those of the SS execution platoons, were stigmatized in such a way. Although modern hygiene codes differ from premodern rituals, anthropologist Mary Douglas has shown that even modern behavior borrows from the symbolic system of defilement.[49] His "vital" work preserving public health thus did not protect Muhsfeldt from the

SS staff's fear and disgust of corpses, which remained deeply rooted in what German culture and society ascribed as profane or impure. His colleagues reacted in much the same way as the German civilians forced by the Allies at the end of the war to visit the camps and *look at* the crimes perpetrated there.[50] There is indeed a correlation between the concept of defilement and social order, as Douglas argued. Muhsfeldt's work might have been decorated by the commanders and appreciated by his superiors, but for his colleagues it remained a "dirty job"—stinky, exhausting, and socially damning—a real "defilement."

Second, we have to ask ourselves why this joke affected Herta Ehlert in such a way. With his morbid humor, Muhsfeldt regularly reminded Ehlert that she was working in a concentration and extermination camp. His horseplay made it momentarily impossible for her to separate her "honorable job" of supervising the inmates at the laundry from his "dirty work" of mass killing and genocide.[51] Not only did Muhsfeldt confront Ehlert with the raw reality of his work of destruction, but he also reminded her of her own role in what she desperately tried to ignore. This allows us, perhaps, to better understand why Ehlert told the British interrogators in 1945 at the Belsen trial that she experienced Majdanek as a "punishment." Although she got some "extras" above her pay in occupied Poland, in comparison to Ravensbrück, she "did not feel very well in such a camp."[52]

The example of the chief of the Majdanek crematory, on the other hand, shows how one gets accustomed to genocide as "work." Born in Brandenburg in 1913, Muhsfeldt was a trained baker. He had joined the SA in 1933, switching to the SS in 1940. After a short training in Sachsenhausen, he was transferred to Auschwitz and in November 1941 to Majdanek, where he was appointed to the so-called funeral squad. At first, he took up this job reluctantly, only to develop a very specific "talent" in cremation and a pride in a job "well done."[53] As he proudly stated during the 1947 Krakow trial, he and his team allegedly burned more than thirty-three thousand bodies between November 1941 and May 1944. People like Muhsfeldt were gaining a new social standing and wanted to commit crimes in the most "professional" way possible. Even as the main task of genocide continued, there was still respectability at stake, as George L. Mosse argued.[54] Or to frame it in Alf Lüdtke's words, mass killing on such a large scale entailed an increasingly professional work "ethic" that featured characteristics of "German quality work."[55]

Conclusion: Beyond Motives—Toward a Patchwork History of Experiences

Heinrich Himmler targeted a generation without prospects (1913–20) from the impoverished middle or working class, who were struggling with social and economic insecurity as a result of the economic crisis of the 1930s. For many men and women, the basic decision to volunteer for a job in the camps was based on dissatisfaction with their current work situation (as a servant, industrial worker, or craftsman) and the desire to change, indeed, to improve one's life. By adopting gender and race as categories of analysis to study women under National Socialism in Germany, Gisela Bock rightly pointed toward the presence and interconnectedness of sexism and racism in Nazi state policy.[56] Applying this to camp guards, one can argue that racist sexism and classism constantly intertwined and reinforced one another as a means of dominating women under Nazi rule, highlighting a huge class disparity and social racism toward lower-class women considered socially inferior by their educated, middle-class peers. However, this does not make the camp guards solely victims. On the contrary: an intersectional reading clearly shows that within the camp universe as well as in German society, these women were considered full members of the Nazi People's Community (Volksgemeinschaft), equipped with power and a meaningful uniform.

As virtually no written evidence has survived to document the mass killings carried out at the Majdanek concentration and extermination camp, and we have found, so far, no personal documents such as letters or diaries, other than occasional photographs, we rely heavily on witness testimonies. This chapter has drawn on postwar perpetrator interrogations carried out in a legal context: the Krakow Auschwitz Trial (1946–47), where several members of the Majdanek camp staff were tried, including the chief of the crematorium, who was sentenced to death and executed. Female guard Hertha Ehlert was charged in the first Bergen-Belsen trial, which took place from 17 September 1945 to 17 November 1945 in Lüneburg at the British military tribunal. Sentenced to fifteen years in prison, Ehlert was granted early release on 7 May 1953 and continued to live in freedom until her death in 1997. Luzie Halata was never charged but instead offered rather eloquent and collaborative testimony at the Majdanek trial, which took place between 26 November 1975 and 30 June 1981 at the Regional Court (*Landesgericht*) in Düsseldorf. Charges were brought against a group of six former guards and eleven SS men.[57] Alongside the defendants, an additional 340 witnesses testified, among them 215 Majdanek survivors. Though undoubtedly extraordinary sources, these trial records have been rather overlooked by historians.

As historical sources, courtroom and legal records and especially perpetrator accounts pose inherent problems, as the former camp staff, for obvious reasons, attempted to deny participation in violent and criminal acts and to present themselves in the best possible light. Nonetheless, as we have seen, there are instances of surprisingly frank testimony, especially when they spoke about more trivial camp experiences, such as work conditions, leisure activities, uniforms, and so forth. It is astonishing to see how the mental geographies of the former SS guards do not lie. Instead, their testimony, some of which is extremely detailed, speaks to a desire, even a compulsion, to tell their stories and to remember and "normalize" their work. New research on private photographs has shown how important leisure time was for those who executed the killing "work"—in close vicinity of mass killing and genocide, guards were having snowball fights and romantic gatherings or cheerful boozy country outings.[58]

Drawing on Karl Marx, Alf Lüdtke developed the concept of "appropriation" (*Aneignung*) to describe a diverse, formative, and "sensual" interpretation of the lived reality—discourses, practices, and compulsions—by the historical actors. From this perspective, social norms are not implicit but something that individuals must first reify and then enact in ways that are not always consistent. Hence, the ambiguous social practices of ordinary citizens, rather than their political motivations, explain broad support for, or assimilation within, a dictatorial regime. This microhistorical approach to the everyday necessitates not only a reduction in scale to the level of the individual but also a highly nuanced understanding of people's everyday lives and agency.

Everyday life is, however, not a given. According to anthropologist Gerald Sider, it is "a domain of social life that takes on its importance because it belongs to the people who 'have it'—it is their time, their space, what makes their moments and their interactions, their space and place."[59] In contrast, refugees on the run, or people detained in extermination camps or on death marches, do not have much of an everyday life. Following Sider, this is not because they are constantly on the move—traveling salespeople are too—but because their lives have no coherence, no predictability.[60] If having an everyday life requires "a reasonable grounded expectation of a livable tomorrow"[61]—that is, money to pay for rent and food, health, and a decently positive projection into the future—the female camp guards had it all: health insurance, pension, some vacations, sick days, and a new, professional career path.

The case studies of Luzie Halata, Herta Ehlert, and Erich Muhsfeldt reveal the ways in which the structure of the camp and the social and gendered interactions among the male and female staff contributed to making these more mild-mannered women into direct perpetrators, or at least accomplices, of genocide—be it in the front or second row. Not all female camp guards were keen on violence; some, like Halata and Ehlert, tried to stay out of it as much as they could while still doing their jobs, adopting a head-in-the-sand policy about the excessive violence with which they were surrounded. Precisely by averting their eyes, these female guards accommodated themselves to the camp. And even though they did everything they could to block out the environment in which they worked and lived, death and killing reentered their lives in the most banal situations.

Although Halata and Ehlert did not recognize their responsibility, these female guards enabled and supported the killing. People do not always act according to their convictions or beliefs, as Alf Lüdtke has so often pointed out in his work; people actually "meander from and between seemingly contradictory stances."[62] Hence, it is not solely about individual guards orienting their behavior to maximize calculated personal benefits. Seen from up close, their actions are much messier and more contradictory, with some trying to do their jobs (read: commit crimes) in the most professional way possible and others turning a blind eye and ignoring the odor of death that literally covered the camp area, including the SS barracks. It is the dynamic of simultaneous dependence and independence, of rule-abiding and self-willed action, that led people to become compliant and active accomplices.[63]

Paying attention to what guards actually *did* during their workaday and leisure time allows us to explore how their interactions and encounters produced, reproduced, and transformed "the historical 'concrete'"[64] of the camps. It is not about scrutinizing the motivations of the historical agents but, rather, about investigating the multiple and shifting meanings of their social and cultural practices. Films and music, entertainment culture, and leisure time certainly normalized life in the camps, yet following George L. Mosse's analysis, one can also argue that they banalized violence and ultimately brutalized the guards.[65] Incontestably, the guards' tastes, choices, and playful self-reliance (*Eigensinn*) had a performative dimension and thus a highly political impact: they shaped not only their living environment (*Lebenswelt*) but also the living and dying conditions of the camp inmates, something for which the overwhelming majority of the guards refused to take responsibility until the end of their lives.

Notes

I wish to sincerely thank Darcy Buerkle, Skye Doney, Rachel Johnston-White, and the anonymous reviewers for their challenging questions and thoughtful comments that helped sharpen my focus and thoughts.

1. Telegram of KGL Lublin to the WVHA on 29 January 1943, Hauptstaatsarchiv (HStA) Düsseldorf, Gerichte Republik (Ger. Rep.) 432 No. 429, 15.

2. Statement by Rosa Süss (born Reischl) on 29 August 1973 in Düsseldorf, HStA Düsseldorf, Ger. Rep. 432 No. 252, 72–74.

3. Statement by Rosa Süss (born Reischl) on 29 August 1973 in Düsseldorf, HStA Düsseldorf, Ger. Rep. 432 No. 252, 72–74.

4. Elissa Mailänder, "Meshes of Power: The Concentration Camp as Pulp or Art House in Liliana Cavani's *The Night Porter*," in *Nazisploitation! The Nazi Image in Low-Brow Cinema and Culture*, ed. Daniel H. Magilow, Elizabeth Bridges, and Kristin T. Vander Lugt (New York: Continuum, 2012), 175–95.

5. Elissa Mailänder, *Female SS Guards and Workaday Violence: The Majdanek Concentration Camp, 1942–1944*, trans. Patricia Szobar (Lansing: Michigan State University Press, 2015); Elissa Mailänder Koslov, "'Going East': Colonial Experiences and Practices of Violence of the Female and Male Camp Guards in Majdanek (1941–1944)," *Journal of Genocide Research* 10, no. 4 (2008): 563–82.

6. George L. Mosse, *Nazi Culture: Intellectual, Cultural, and Social Life in the Third Reich* (Madison: University of Wisconsin Press, 2003); Alf Lüdtke, "Working the Passage: East German Border Checkpoints, 1961–90. The Case of *GÜSt Bahnhof Friedrichstrasse*, Berlin," *Journal of Contemporary History* 50, no. 3 (2015): 600–705; Alf Lüdtke, "People Working: Everyday Life and German Fascism," *History Workshop Journal* 50, no. 1 (2000): 74–92.

7. Christopher Dillon, *Dachau and the SS: A Schooling in Violence* (Oxford: Oxford University Press, 2015).

8. Marc Buggeln, *Arbeit & Gewalt: Das Außenlagersystem des KZ Neuegamme* (Göttingen: Wallstein, 2009).

9. Alf Lüdtke, "War as Work: Aspects of Soldiering in the Twentieth-Century Wars," in *No Man's Land of Violence: Extreme Wars in the 20th Century*, ed. Alf Lüdtke, Bernd Weisbrod (Göttingen: Wallstein, 2006), 127–51, 151.

10. Wolfgang Sofsky, *The Order of Terror: The Concentration Camp* (Princeton, NJ: Princeton University Press, 1999). Sofsky deals with a paradigmatic camp that, historically speaking, never actually existed.

11. SS Statistik vom 1. und 15. Januar 1945, Bundesarchiv Berlin Lichterfelde (hereafter BA) NS/3/439.

12. Stefan Hördler, *Ordnung und Inferno: Das KZ-System im letzten Kriegsjahr* (Göttingen: Wallstein, 2013); Nikolaus Wachsmann, *KL: A History of the Nazi Concentration Camps* (New York: Farrar, Straus and Giroux, 2015).

13. Statement by Hermann Hackmann on 27 November 1967 in Göttingen, HStA Düsseldorf, Ger. Rep. 432 No. 247, 568; Hermann Hackmann, in Eberhard Fechner, *Der Prozess: Eine Darstellung des Majdanek-Verfahrens in Düsseldorf*, 3 parts (video cassettes) (Norddeutscher Rundfunk, 1984), 270 min., part 1.

14. Heinz Villain, in Fechner, *Der Prozess*, part 1.

15. Statement by Hertha Nauman formerly Ehlert, 9 July 1975 in Bad Homburg, HStA Düsseldorf, Ger. Rep. 432 no. 252, 142.

16. Statement by Rosa Süss (born Reischl) on 29 August 1973 in Düsseldorf, HStA Düsseldorf, Ger. Rep. 432 No. 252, 68.

17. Ravensbrück recruitment form, undated, BA NS/4/Ra 1.

18. Lavern Wolfram, "KZ-Aufseherinnen—Parteigängerinnen der NSDAP?," in *Im Gefolge der SS: Aufseherinnen des Frauen-KZ Ravensbrück. Begleitband zur Ausstellung*, ed. Simone Erpel (Berlin: Metropol, 2007), 39–47, 46; see also Johannes Schwartz, "Weibliche

Angelegenheiten": Handlungsräume von KZ-Aufseherinnen in Ravensbrück und Neubrandenburg (Hamburg: Hamburger Edition, 2018), 66–109.

19. Mailänder, *Female SS Guards and Workaday Violence*, 45–70.

20. Herta Ehlert, cross-examination by Colonel Backhouse, 15 October 1945, PRO WO (Public Record Office, War Office) 235/15, 84.

21. Statement by Hermann Hackmann on 26 September 1973 in Düsseldorf, HStA Düsseldorf, Ger. Rep. 432 No. 248, 729.

22. Statement by Charlotte Mayer (born Wöllert) on 31 March 1976, HStA Düsseldorf, Ger. Rep. 432 No. 288, 66; see also transcript, interview Eberhard Fechner with Erna Wallisch, 15 June 1980, manuscript, 41 pages (private collection of the author), 15.

23. Mailänder, *Female SS Guards and Workaday Violence*, 107–40.

24. Hildegard Lächert, in Fechner, *Der Prozess*, part 2; see also Otto Z., in Fechner, *Der Prozess*, part 2.

25. Statement by Georg W. on 13 January 1965 in Vienna, Dokumentationsarchiv des österreichischen Widerstandes (hereafter DÖW), Vienna, Austria, LG Graz 13/Vr 3329/63, vol. 1, 457; see also Mailänder, *Female SS Guards and Workaday Violence*, chaps. 6, 7, and 9.

26. Hildegard Lächert, in Fechner, *Der Prozess*, part 2. See also statement by Herta B. on 30 October 1974 in Waldshut, HStA Düsseldorf, Ger. Rep. 432 No. 203, 28; statement by Rosa Süss (born Reischl) on 29 August 1973 in Düsseldorf, HStA Düsseldorf, Ger. Rep. 432 No. 252, 82; statement by Charlotte Mayer (born Wöllert) on 27 June 1979, main hearing, HStA Düsseldorf, Ger. Rep. 432 No. 285, 4; statement by Charlotte Mayer (born Wöllert) on 31 March 1976, main hearing, HStA Düsseldorf, Ger. Rep. 432 No. 288 (no page number).

27. Karl Baedeker, *Das Generalgouvernement: Reisehandbuch von Karl Baedeker* (Leipzig: Baedeker, 1943), 126–27.

28. Luzie H., in Fechner, *Der Prozess*, part 2, author's translation. See also Mailänder Koslov, "'Going East,'" 559–78.

29. Elizabeth Harvey, *Women in the Nazi East: Agents and Witnesses of Germanization* (New Haven, CT: Yale University Press, 2003), 145–90, 167; cf. Lora Wildenthal, *German Women for Empire, 1884–1945* (Durham, NC: Duke University Press, 2001).

30. Statement by Rosa Süss (born Reischl) on 29 August 1973 in Düsseldorf, HStA Düsseldorf, Ger. Rep. 432 No. 252, 72–74; see Mailänder, *Female SS Guards and Workaday Violence*, 150–58.

31. Elisabeth E. (born 1919) and Ferdinand K. (born 1916), Charlotte Wöllert (born 1918) and Robert M. (born 1917), Erna Pfannstiel (born 1922) and Georg Wallisch (born 1922), Ruth E. (born 1922) and Anton W. (born 1901). See Mailänder, *Female SS Guards and Workaday Violence*, 130–39.

32. The marriage office then investigated the physical and mental fitness of the applicants and eventually attested the applicants' "health and hereditary biology," issuing a permission to marry or what in Nazi jargon was known as the "Certificate of Unobjectionability to Marry" (*Eheunbedenklichkeitsbescheinigung*).

33. See statement by Rosa Süss (born Reischl) on 9 May 1974 in Neureichenau, HStA Düsseldorf, Ger. Rep. 432 No. 252, 120; statement by Elisabeth H. on 27 August 1975 in Cologne, HStA Düsseldorf, Ger. Rep. 432 No. 252, 133 R/134V.

34. Jan M. and his wife had married in 1938 and had three children between 1938 and 1940; statement by Charlotte W. on 7 August 1972 in Düsseldorf, HStA Düsseldorf, Ger. Rep. 432 No. 235, 78 f; statement by Jan Ude M. on 27 September 1972 in Düsseldorf, HStA Düsseldorf, Ger. Rep. 432 No. 228, 150/151; see also statement by Rosa Süss (born Reischl) on 26 June 1979, main hearing, HStA Düsseldorf, Ger. Rep. 432 No. 286, 6.

35. Statement by Georg Gröner on 28 November 1963 in Ansbach, HStA Düsseldorf, Ger. Rep. 432 No. 240, 223.

36. Irith Dublon Knebel, "'Erinnern kann ich mich nur an eine Frau Danz...' die Aufseherin Luise Danz in der Erinnerung ihrer Opfer," in *Genozid und Geschlecht: Jüdische Frauen im nationalsozialistischen Lagersystem*, ed. Gisela Bock (Frankfurt am Main: Campus, 2005), 66–84.

37. See Birthe Kundrus, "'Die Unmoral deutscher Soldatenfrauen': Diskurs, Alltagsverhalten und Ahndungspraxis 1939–1945," in *Zwischen Karriere und Verfolgung. Handlungsräume von Frauen im nationalsozialistischen Deutschland*, ed. Kirsten Heinsohn, Barbara Vogel and Ulrike Weckel (Frankfurt am Main: Campus, 1997), 96–110; Cornelie Usborne, "Female Sexual Desire and Male Honor: German Women's Illicit Love Affairs with Prisoners of War during the Second World War," *Journal of the History of Sexuality* 26, no. 3 (2017): 454–88.

38. Jane Caplan and Nikolaus Wachsmann, *Concentration Camps in Nazi Germany: The New Histories* (London: Routledge, 2010); Ulrich Herbert, Karin Orth, and Christoph Dieckmann, *Die nationalsozialistische Konzentrationslager: Entwicklung und Struktur* (Frankfurt am Main: Fischer Taschenbuch, 1998); Wolfgang Sofsky, *Traktat über die Gewalt* (Frankfurt am Main and Vienna: Büchergilde Gutenberg, 1997).

39. Roll call by name of civilian employees on 29 September 1943 to the Senior SS and Police Leaders in the Generalgouvernement, Krakow, DÖW, LG Graz 13/Vr 3329/63, vol. 4, 129.

40. Luzie H., in Fechner, *Der Prozess*, part 2.

41. Margarete Buber-Neumann, *Als Gefangene bei Stalin und Hitler: Eine Welt im Dunkel* (1949; repr., Berlin: Ullstein, 1997), 305.

42. "It was quiet there; I didn't see or hear anything," Ehlert said. "It was pleasant there, to the extent that anything can be pleasant in a concentration camp." Statement by Hertha Nauman (divorced name: Ehlert) on 18 April 1972 in Bad Homburg, HStA Düsseldorf, Ger. Rep. 432 No. 296, 7467.

43. Statement by Hertha Nauman (divorced name: Ehlert) on 9 June 1976, main hearing, HStA Düsseldorf, Ger. Rep. 432 No. 285, 186 f.

44. Luzie H., in Fechner, *Der Prozess*, part 2.

45. Statement by Anna M. on 2 August 1961 in Stuttgart, HStA Düsseldorf, Ger. Rep. 432 No. 234, 20 f.

46. Statement by Hertha Nauman (divorced name: Ehlert) on 9 June 1970 in Bad Homburg, HStA Düsseldorf, Ger. Rep. 432 No. 292, 43.

47. Elissa Mailänder, "A Specialist: The Daily Work of Erich Muhsfeldt, Chief of the Crematorium at Majdanek Concentration and Extermination Camp, 1942–44," in *Destruction and Human Remains. Disposal and Concealment in Genocide and Mass Violence*, ed. Elisabeth Anstett and Jean-Marc Dreyfus (Manchester: Manchester University Press, 2014), 46–68.

48. Mailänder, *Female SS Guards and Workaday Violence*, 115 and 322, n. 32.

49. Mary Douglas, *Purity and Danger: An Analysis of Concepts of Pollution and Taboo* (1966; repr., London: Routledge, 2002).

50. Barbie Zelizer, "Covering Atrocity in Image," in *Remembering to Forget: Holocaust Memory through the Camera's Eye* (Chicago: Chicago University Press, 1998), 86–140.

51. Everett Hughes, "Good People and Dirty Work," *Social Problems* 10, no. 1 (1962): 3–11.

52. Statement by Herta Ehlert on 15 October 1945 in Lüneburg, Transcript of the Official Shorthand Notes, Trial against Josef Kramer and 44 Others, PRO WO 235/15, 99/100.

53. Statement by Herta Ehlert on 15 October 1945 in Lüneburg, Transcript of the Official Shorthand Notes, Trial against Josef Kramer and 44 Others, PRO WO 235/15, 99/100.

54. George L. Mosse, *Nationalism and Sexuality: Middle-Class Morality and Sexual Norms in Modern Europe* (Madison: University of Wisconsin Press, 2020), 184–93.

55. Alf Lüdtke, "Soldiering and Working: Almost the Same? Reviewing Practices in Industry and the Military in Twentieth-Century Contexts," in *Work in a Modern Society: The German Historical Experience in Comparative Perspective*, ed. Jürgen Kocka (New York: Berghahn Books, 2010), 109–30.

56. Gisela Bock, "Racism and Sexism in Nazi Germany: Motherhood, Compulsory Sterilization, and the State," *Signs: Journal of Women in Culture and Society* 8, no. 3 (1983): 400–421.

57. The six guards: Hermine Böttcher, Hildegard Lächert, Charlotte Mayer née Wöllert, Alice Orlowski, Hermine Ryan Braunsteiner, and Rosa Süss née Reischl. The eleven SS men: Thomas Ellwanger, Heinrich Groffmann, Hermann Hackmann, Günther Konietzny, Emil Laurich, Fritz Petrick, August Wilhelm Reinartz, Ernst Schmidt, Robert Seitz, Arnold Strippel, and Heinz Villain.

58. Stephan Matyus, "Auszeit vom KZ Alltag: Das Bretstein-Album," in *Täter: Österreichische Akteure im Nationalsozialismus* ed. Dokumentationsarchiv des österreichischen Widerstandes (Vienna: Jahrbuch, 2014), 107–33; Tal Bruttmann, Stefan Hördler, and Christoph Kreutzmüller, *Die fotografische Inszenierung des Verbrechens: Ein Album aus Auschwitz* (Darmstadt: WBG, 2019).

59. Gerald Sider, "Anthropology, History, and the Problem of Everyday Life," in *Alltag, Erfahrung, Eigensinn. Historisch-anthropologische Erkundungen*, ed. Belinda Davis, Thomas Lindenberger, and Michael Wildt (Frankfurt am Main: Campus, 2008), 121–32, 128.

60. Sider, "Anthropology, History, and the Problem of Everyday Life," 132.

61. Sider, "Anthropology, History, and the Problem of Everyday Life," 130.

62. Lüdtke, "People Working," 80.
63. Lüdtke, "People Working," 90.
64. Lüdtke, "People Working," 75.
65. George L. Mosse, "From Culture as the Faith in an Ideal Reich to Its Diffusion among the Masses," in *Nazi Culture: Intellectual, Cultural, and Social Life in the Third Reich* (Madison: University of Wisconsin Press, 2003), 5–10.

Part IV
SOLDIERS

8

Morality, Nazi Ideology, and the Individual in the Third Reich

The Example of the Wehrmacht

DAVID HARRISVILLE

In the summer of 1941, Harald Hoffman found himself advancing deep into the Soviet Union. A private in the 23rd Infantry Division, he numbered among the more than three million members of the Wehrmacht—the German military— who took part in Hitler's grand scheme to secure *Lebensraum* for Nazi Germany.[1] In his letters home, Hoffman openly discussed the atrocities he and his fellow soldiers committed against civilians and prisoners of war, including summary executions, rampant theft, the use of forced labor, and the destruction of entire villages. His side's brutal conduct caused him deep misgivings. "The enormous destruction," he wrote in one letter, "the way in which our troops ... behave toward the civilian population and use them for slave labor, the views and opinions that one hears, all this makes me sick from sorrow and misery."[2] On one occasion, Hoffman described how he and fellow soldiers forced a woman to cook the last of her potatoes for them as her crying children looked on. He and his comrades knew they had just condemned the family to death by starvation in the deepening winter. He expressed his dismay at his participation in the theft but explained in a letter to his parents and sister that his actions were necessary because his unit was running low on supplies: "We also had to eat, had to at least have potatoes with the three teaspoons of dark sauce with two pieces of meat that we received as goulash from the [field] kitchen."[3] Until his death in December 1941, Hoffman spent more time grappling with the pangs of conscience than the average German soldier. As the quotation above illustrates, however, he managed to consistently justify his conduct and preserve his sense of personal integrity even as he played an active part in a war that historians have come to recognize as a *Vernichtungskrieg*, an ideologically inspired war of extermination aimed at killing or enslaving "subhuman" Eastern Europeans. Blatantly disregarding established rules of war, the Wehrmacht committed atrocities on an unprecedented scale.[4] By the campaign's end, roughly 70,000 villages and 1,710 towns and cities would be reduced to rubble and some 27 million Soviet citizens lay dead, including 3 million prisoners of war (POWs) and 2.4 million Jews.[5]

Harald Hoffman's description of atrocities adds to the growing discussion surrounding a topic that previously received little attention from historians—the moral landscape of Nazi Germany. Some now argue that the Nazis were not "amoral" or self-consciously evil, as they have habitually been portrayed. Instead, they constructed their own self-contained ethical system that diverged sharply from older norms.[6] "Nazi morality," as Claudia Koonz has termed it, was grounded in a combination of völkisch and Social Darwinist principles that depicted all life as a struggle among distinct races as well as the Jewish "anti-race." Since the biological essence of the Aryan race was superior to that of its counterparts, everything that helped the Aryans in their struggle for existence was redefined as good, while anything that hindered them was now defined as evil.

To date, the scholarship on morality in the Third Reich has typically involved one of two approaches. Some scholars, most notably Claudia Koonz, have worked to demonstrate how the Nazis disseminated their new ethic to the population through propaganda, youth programs, the education system, and other means—in her view, with great success.[7] Another interpretation, put forward by Raphael Gross, highlights the ways in which the Nazis redefined, modified, and appropriated existing value systems as they sought to persuade Germans to support their goals.[8] In many ways, this second interpretation reflects a central observation made decades before by George L. Mosse. In his classic work *Toward the Final Solution*, Mosse characterized European racism as a "scavenger ideology," whose purveyors proved willing to draw on any sources of moral and intellectual legitimacy they could find—from nationalism to middle-class conceptions of respectability—to advance their views.[9] Falling between these two poles, Wolfgang Bialas acknowledges both the newness of the Nazi biological ethic and its partial reliance on older values. Although individual perspectives have differed, most studies of morality in the Third Reich—including those mentioned above—have taken a similar approach by focusing attention on the top-down process by which the regime imposed its ideas of right and wrong on the populace.[10]

Contributing to these discussions, this chapter engages with the question of how individuals navigated the moral world of the Third Reich and to what extent German society had transitioned from a more traditional pre-1933 value system grounded in Jewish and Christian theological traditions, Enlightenment humanism, and German law, and stressing the dignity of all life, to that of Nazi morality with its sharp racial distinctions.[11] It makes two chief claims. First, the moral discourse of the regime—and the institutions that served it—remained rife with ambiguities and contradictions throughout its time in power. As Claudia Koonz has pointed out, Nazi leaders were determined not to rest until every man, woman, and child had adopted what Goebbels referred to as "the radical revaluation of all values." The regime expended considerable resources to this end.[12] But Raphael Gross is equally correct to point out that the Nazi state frequently injected more traditional moral reasoning into its arguments as well. Both approaches, this chapter will demonstrate, were in fact employed side by side. The end result was a jumble of mixed messaging: regime officials and their surrogates encouraged the public to embrace the principles of Nazi morality but at the same time also continued to rely on more traditional moral discourse to secure popular support, evidently in the pragmatic recognition that not all Germans would instantly accept the transition to the new value system. As a result, Germans were presented with a diverse and often contradictory array of moral options by which they were encouraged to judge their actions and those of the regime.

Second, to achieve a more complete understanding of the Third Reich's moral world, scholars must move beyond an exclusive focus on the regime's efforts to impose its values on the populace by also taking into account how individual Germans of all walks of life navigated the difficult ethical terrain on which they found themselves.[13] Ideas about right and wrong are indeed entwined with the public sphere and the rhetoric of national leaders; however, morality is also a deeply personal aspect of life that can differ greatly from individual to individual. How did ordinary Germans react to the moral climate of the Third Reich, including the many atrocities committed in Hitler's name? Did they quickly adopt the tenets of Nazi morality, or, like Hoffman, did they seek out other ways to come to terms with the choices they made?

Members of the German public, this chapter will argue, frequently responded to the state's ambiguous moral discourse by mixing and matching whatever values or moral arguments they believed best helped them to preserve their own personal sense of integrity and decency. To borrow the phrase from Mosse noted above, they acted as moral "scavengers," sometimes embracing the Nazi ethic and at other times falling back on more traditional values to justify their words and deeds—including participation in Nazi-inspired crimes against humanity. Partly because of the opaque moral rhetoric issuing from Germany's new leaders, individuals enjoyed wide latitude to choose whichever justifications were most salient to them, without fear of censure. This situation may not have been ideal from the point of view of Hitler and his closest subordinates, who would have preferred all Germans to fully adopt the Nazi worldview. However, it ultimately worked to the regime's advantage by making it easier for individuals of different backgrounds and creeds to come to terms with their involvement in activities that furthered Nazi goals, all while maintaining the conviction—like Hoffman—that their personal decency remained intact. The road to complicity was paved not only with speeches by Party bosses but with a thousand small rationalizations made by ordinary people.

The primary example here will be the Wehrmacht, an institution comprising millions of ordinary German men who were thoroughly exposed to the regime's efforts at indoctrination and who—particularly on the Eastern Front—took part in many of the worst atrocities of the Nazi era. As they fought, they came face to face with numerous questions regarding the morality of their own personal conduct while being exposed to the rhetoric of national and military leaders. The chapter opens with an examination of the army's top-down moral discourse before zooming in to investigate how several individuals developed their personal moral self-understanding within this context.[14]

What was the nature of moral discourse in the Wehrmacht, as disseminated from above through propaganda, orders, and other means? As was the case with most institutions in the Third Reich, the army did not fail to transmit the tenets of Nazi morality to the men in its ranks. Following Hitler's purge of its SA rival in 1934, the Wehrmacht voluntarily adopted the infamous oath of loyalty, through which soldiers effectively abrogated moral responsibility for their actions to the Führer. Training manuals and instruction booklets were soon modified to accommodate the worldview of its new masters, part of a sweeping indoctrination program that encompassed officers as well as the rank and file.[15] As the army defined them, the "duties of the German soldier" now centered on protecting "the German Reich and Fatherland, the people united in National Socialism, and their living space."[16] The infamous Criminal Orders, issued at the start of the campaign in the Soviet Union, framed the invasion as an existential racial conflict in which the dictates of ordinary morality and military custom would no longer hold. Troops would not be prosecuted for crimes against civilians. Commissars (Soviet functionaries) were to be shot on the spot and prisoners treated as expendable.[17] The 1942 code of conduct, issued by the Army High Command

(Oberkommando des Heeres—OKH), encouraged the German soldier to see himself as "lord in the East" by virtue of his racial superiority.[18]

Once the campaign got underway in late June 1941, commanders at lower levels of the Wehrmacht hierarchy issued draconian regulations that prescribed the death penalty for even the smallest civilian infraction, denied food supplies to starving POWs, encouraged soldiers not to feel sympathy for the plight of Soviet noncombatants, and cast Jews as special targets for violence. Numerous units ordered the execution of all members of the Red Army found behind the front lines, along with any civilians accused of suspicious activity—particularly Jews or members of the Communist Party.[19] Propaganda outlets such as *Mitteilungen für die Truppe* (Messages for the Troops), issued by the Oberkommando der Wehrmacht (Supreme Command of the Wehrmacht, or OKW), spoke of "exterminating" Bolshevism and defending Europe from the "red flood breaking out of the Asiatic steppe" and incited brutality toward Jews, communists, and any who resisted German rule.[20] Such pronouncements encouraged soldiers to embrace the principles of Nazi morality and justify their participation in the conflict by defining themselves as members of a superior race taking what belonged to it by the right of the stronger.

Even as it sought to produce ideologically hardened racial warriors, however, the Wehrmacht simultaneously continued to rely on traditional moral principles to motivate its men. According to the army's 1940 training manual, soldiers were to remain "upright," "modest," "God-fearing," and "incorruptible," while safeguarding their honor through "unimpeachable conduct."[21] The same manual encouraged soldiers to obey international laws of war, refrain from killing prisoners, and respect the life and property of enemy noncombatants. Prisoners were to be "treated humanely," the noncombatant status of medics was to be respected, and soldiers were instructed that "war is not waged against the peaceful civilian population."[22] Thus, at the same time as they were expected to play the role of merciless racial warriors, Wehrmacht servicemen were told to think of themselves as paragons of chivalry and virtue along more traditional lines.

Further complicating the matter, messaging at the start of Operation Barbarossa incorporated not only ideological arguments about the need to destroy the country's "racial enemies" but a host of attempts at moral persuasion that could appeal even to men who rejected Nazi values. For one, the army—and the regime it served—insisted that the attack on the Soviet Union constituted a defensive measure, a preemptive strike designed to forestall a devious plot by a communist state intent on invading the European continent. As one newspaper for soldiers put it, "The plague of Bolshevism had swollen to a massive boil and was just about to break over Western Europe—then we came just in time to prevent our women and children and all of Europe from meeting an unimaginable end in rape and blood with [the arrival of] this new storm from the East."[23] This claim was accompanied by manufactured evidence purporting to reveal the details of the USSR's dastardly plot.[24] Here, military officials relied on the long-standing concept of the "just war," a conflict waged to protect the innocent. In so doing, they cast the aggressive assault as nothing less than an effort to rescue European civilization, a campaign any right-minded German could get behind.

Religious appeals also figured prominently in the Wehrmacht's propaganda. Troops were told that they were battling a hellish atheist system and that their actions would help restore Christian worship and Christian values to a population that had suffered two decades of religious persecution. Franz Justus Rarkowski, who headed the Catholic chaplaincy, proclaimed that the operation constituted a "European crusade" against a "demonic regime of barbarism," a stance repeated in various Wehrmacht publications.[25] Similarly, the army sometimes attempted to depict the war of extermination as a noble act of liberation aimed at freeing Eastern Europeans from the clutches of an oppressive government whose mismanagement had driven the country to the brink of economic ruin. In typical fashion, one Wehrmacht newspaper informed soldiers that "we are waging this war in the east not against the peoples of the Soviet Union; the fight only applies to the eternal disturber of the peace and world enemy: Bolshevism," and emphasized the population's gratitude at being rid of their former rulers.[26] Although appeals like these were based on traditional moral concepts such as justice, human dignity, and religious values rather than the language of the biological ethic, military leaders appear to have viewed them as a useful tool for convincing their men of the conflict's moral necessity.

To bolster the notion that the campaign was fully justified, Wehrmacht propagandists worked to publicize evidence that the invaders were displaying generosity toward conquered peoples and improving living conditions in the Soviet Union. German medics, army news outlets informed their men, not only helped their own wounded but "saw it as their doctorly duty to also care for the civilian sick who were brought to them. Exactly like for the civilian infirm, captured supplies from the plentiful Soviet stores will be used for the prisoners who fell into our hands."[27] Army engineers, it was reported, put out fires and repaired damage to civilian homes while local commanders worked to quickly rebuild the economy, ensuring that no one went hungry.[28] Meanwhile, propagandists highlighted the Wehrmacht's commitment to religious freedom by pointing out that the army allowed Soviet civilians to worship once again and even went out of its way to reopen churches the Soviet regime had shuttered.[29] In doing so, they portrayed the army as a force for good and its personnel as honorable saviors by any traditional moral standard, even as they continued to call for the annihilation of "Jewish Bolshevism" and the total exploitation of the newly conquered lands.

Wehrmacht commanders followed a similar pattern, mixing injunctions to mercilessly suppress all opposition with orders to treat the mass of the Soviet population with dignity and respect. The commander of Panzer Group 3, for instance, insisted on "strict execution of the measures that have been ordered, merciless hardness in every case of oppositional attitude and even the most limited attempt at resistance, and in addition correct behavior, yes even care for the good-willing people who cooperate so far as is possible and justice in the administration of the land!"[30] In its 1942 guidelines on the treatment of the Soviet population, OKH called on its men to behave "strictly but justly. The German soldier protects the property of the working and peaceful citizenry, he respects the honor of Russian women and girls, [and] he promotes reconstruction in the rearward areas," it insisted. He would have to adopt a ruthless posture toward any resisters but refrain from harming the innocent. "Through strict but correct treatment of the population, the German soldier must be the best propagandist for the German Reich," it concluded.[31] The 46th Infantry Division went even further, telling its men to consider Ukraine "the *Lebensraum* of a friendly people" and to act accordingly.[32]

Much of this messaging was more strategic than humanitarian, designed to ensure soldiers did not turn the local population against the army as they brought conquered regions under control. Indeed, OKH's 1942 regulations explicitly cited the "domination of the occupied areas and the exploitation of the land" as the ultimate goal of its policies. At the same time, however, by simultaneously promoting both the language of existential racial conflict associated with Nazi morality and more traditional moral tropes, the Wehrmacht offered its men a wide variety of justifications and self-understandings from which they could choose. As a result, soldiers of all backgrounds and ethical orientations—including those who had still not fully adopted the Nazi value system—would find it easier to live with their actions and continue functioning as effective fighters.

For some combatants the tenets of Nazi morality by themselves constituted sufficient motivation. Among these was Lance Corporal Heinz Sartorio, a former insurance salesman turned military engineer who largely rationalized German brutality toward Eastern Europeans and Jews on the grounds of their racial inferiority. An avid supporter of Hitler and a regular reader of Goebbels's newspaper *Das Reich*, Sartorio agreed with the propaganda minister that the Russians "sometimes really seem like animals."[33] Elsewhere, he referred to them as "unintelligent" and "unpleasant," reserving his greatest contempt for the partisans, whom he termed a "group of vermin."[34] Confiding to his sister in the spring of 1942, he approvingly described the mass murder of thousands of Jews and Russians by the SS in his sector. "At first one is certainly shocked by this, but when one thinks about the big idea, then one must say to oneself that it was necessary."[35] Noncommissioned officer Walter Neuser, who handled supplies for an artillery regiment, expressed similar views. Neuser was a member of the Nationalsozialistische Deutsche Arbeiterpartei (NSDAP, National Socialist German Workers' Party) and, like Sartorio, an avid consumer of the regime's propaganda. His view of the Soviet population was sometimes more nuanced, but this did not stop him from insisting to his mother that his Red Army counterparts "deserv[ed] a hanging" and describing Soviet soldiers and POWs as a repellent racial mixture including many "Mongolian types."[36] For men like Sartorio and Neuser, it appears that Nazi morality provided ample justification for compliance or complicity. These were individuals who had made considerable strides toward shedding their pre-1933 notions of right and wrong and comfortably adapting to Nazi morality.

On the opposite end of the spectrum were those who rarely made recourse to Nazi ideology as they sought to explain their actions to themselves or their relatives. For his part, Heinz Rahe, a Protestant pastor and lieutenant with the 13th Panzer Division, favored religious justifications for the Wehrmacht's campaign in the USSR. A month after the invasion began, he described a conversation with his comrades over the meaning of the war. One cited the need to end the rule of the "mostly Jewish commissars" and establish a "new order," but Rahe questioned whether it was "worth it to sacrifice German blood" for such a cause. Another opined that Ukraine would supply the Reich with precious resources, an explanation Rahe found somewhat plausible. He himself, however, settled on a different reason: "As we then were walking by [a] former church, the hope grew again in me that in a free Ukraine perhaps also Christian preaching would be possible again. This wish is also a goal for me, for which it is worth fighting."[37] Coupled with this notion that the Wehrmacht was restoring Christianity to communist lands, Rahe also hoped that Ukraine in particular would become a free territory ruled over by a "just order," even going so far as to write a poem on the subject.[38]

Whenever he discussed the brutality of his own side, Rahe proffered a variety of arguments, most of them based not on racial concerns but more traditional moral tropes. To explain why the Germans executed commissars (Soviet political functionaries) as they advanced, Rahe told his wife that the commissars had "killed [*umgebracht*] many Ukrainians" during their retreat.[39] In other words, the Wehrmacht's response was nothing less than simple justice being meted out to its murderous opponents. In general, Rahe personally shied away from helping himself to civilian property and expressed sympathy for the victims, but he rarely intervened when his men took advantage of their position of power. On one occasion during a retreat in 1943 when his men went on a particularly wild search for spoils, he explained that "in general one says to oneself that the war has its own justice." It pained him to see civilians suffer, he wrote, but in the end he rationalized that his first duty as an officer was to take care of his men and make sure they could still "live as well as possible" during difficult times.[40]

Indeed, when they discussed their own criminal actions, which they did with surprising frequency and candor, many soldiers typically turned to run-of-the-mill moral arguments rather than the Nazi racial ethic to explain their actions to themselves and their correspondents in the homeland. One common tactic was to emphasize the alleged misdeeds of civilians, POWs, and other targets of the Wehrmacht's brutality. Fritz F., on the road to Smolensk with the 7th Panzer Division, revealed to his wife that he and his comrades shot every political functionary they captured. By way of explanation, he expressed his disgust that Soviet officials lived well while their population suffered and added that they frequently attacked German troops after pretending to surrender.[41] In other cases, soldiers cited their own lack of food and equipment as justification for ransacking civilian property. They further invoked the principle of "military necessity" to explain why they participated in scorched-earth campaigns.[42] Perhaps these soldiers had not fully embraced Nazi ideology, or perhaps they sensed that traditional arguments would be more comprehensible to the loved ones at home who would read their letters. Either way, they seem to have taken advantage of the flexibility within the Wehrmacht's own messaging to settle for whatever justifications they found most compelling.

A third group of soldiers responded to the range of moral justifications presented in the Wehrmacht by selectively adopting elements of Nazi morality and combining these with more traditional lines of moral argumentation. Private Wilhelm Moldenhauser was such a man. A father of two who owned a retail store for colonial imports in a village near Hanover, he had joined the SA in 1937, partly to enhance his business opportunities. But in 1940, he was conscripted into the Wehrmacht and trained in radio communications. One year later, he found himself working as a mobile radio operator with the 60th Infantry Division as it surged into Ukraine.[43]

Moldenhauser readily accepted many of the tenets of Nazi morality, including the belief that Jews constituted a grave threat and that the invasion of the

Soviet Union had been necessary to combat "Bolshevism and Jewry."[44] He was also enamored with the fantasy that ethnic Germans would one day colonize the vast regions of the East, ruling over the inferior locals with an iron hand: "If we want to become a great people, with the requisite colonial possessions, ... then we still must learn a great deal from the English. This people [the Russians] does better when it is handled firmly as a matter of routine," he wrote his wife.[45] Like other soldiers, he expressed astonishment that the "mixed-race" Red Army put up such a stout defense.[46]

Despite his apparent agreement with much of the Nazi program and its attendant "revaluation of values," Moldenhauser simultaneously relied on a host of other rationalizations for his or his comrades' actions. One was his persistent belief that the German Army had "liberated" Ukrainians and other Soviet peoples from the oppression of their Bolshevik and Jewish leaders and that the Germans were bringing with them a better future for conquered peoples.[47] Although he admitted to occasionally partaking in the theft of civilian property and exploiting civilian labor, Moldenhauser habitually insisted that he personally treated the local population very well, perhaps even too well. He stressed that he paid whenever he could for any items he acquired from civilians, shared food and tobacco, and described how his unit's doctor treated civilians.[48] On another occasion, he expressed his deepest admiration for the "tough" Russian children who began working at a young age and excelled at sports. He even encouraged his own young son, Peter, to emulate them.[49] By emphasizing his own small acts of sympathy and relatively good relations with the population, Moldenhauser salved his own conscience and transmuted a brutal campaign into a mission for good and himself into a noble warrior. Of the Ukrainians he met early in the campaign, he wrote, "They feel only affection and sympathy toward us Germans," he told his wife, Erika. "And now the Germans are here and the people can always see for themselves that the Germans are decent, nice guys."[50] Throughout the war, Moldenhauser cycled through a wide range of rationalizations—some based on the concept of racial superiority and others on older concepts of decency and justice—to make sense of his participation in the conflict and explain it to his family back home. He may have relied on Nazi morality to explain to himself why the enemy needed to be destroyed, but in the end he still treasured his moral self-image as a "nice guy" as much as he did his identity as an enforcer of racial hierarchies.

Another soldier who interspersed the tenets of Nazi ethics with more traditional values as he attempted to make sense of his role in the *Vernichtungskrieg* was Franz Siebeler, a twenty-two-year-old private first class in the 14th Panzer Division. Formerly employed in a bank, he now served as a motorcycle courier relaying messages to and from his unit's headquarters in Ukraine. Although he frequently stated that war was a terrible thing, Siebeler cited a wide variety of reasons why he believed the Germans were justified in bringing such destruction to the Soviet lands. A committed Catholic, he found some solace in religious arguments, writing to his relatives the day before the invasion, "I would not like to wage war against anyone, but these murderers and God-deniers must receive their punishment." Like so many others, he also subscribed to the myth that the USSR had been secretly planning to assault Western Europe. "With the Russians there would have been no long-term friendship. They would only have waited for the most favorable opportunity to pounce on us," he opined.[51] The justification to which he most consistently returned, however, was his belief that Bolshevism was an evil system that had to be destroyed at all costs. Soviet leaders had oppressed their people and turned the country into a nightmarish world of poverty and injustice. "One thing is always the same: miserable huts and indescribable poverty," he penned. "One word repeatedly comes into my mind: Workers' Paradise.... Let all of our previous wars be as they may, just or unjust, let them be the machinations of diplomats, one thing however is certain[:] this war against the criminal work of Bolshevism is the battle for a righteous cause."[52]

Like Moldenhauser, Siebeler incorporated elements of the Nazis' racial ethic into his worldview. He referred to Red Army soldiers as "Asiatic hordes" intent on overrunning the German homeland and parroted the Nazi line that Jews were at the helm of the Soviet state, slowly driving the country into the ground.[53] He expressed his faith in the Führer, who would lead Germany to the *Endsieg* (final victory).[54] He displayed contempt for the locals he encountered: "The Russian is ... a lazy guy," he remarked in one letter. "He is content with the bare necessities of life. A typical Slav! They still need to learn order."[55] Even so, Siebeler focused most of his hatred on the communist regime, rather than on the common people. He openly recognized, like Moldenhauser, that the vast majority were not convinced Bolsheviks, and he was impressed by the fact that they had held on to their religious traditions despite state persecution.[56]

When he mentioned atrocities committed by the German side, Siebeler tended to cast these as acts of justice or as necessary measures to ensure survival, rather than resorting to ideological arguments regarding the racial inferiority of the victims. In one early letter, he described how his unit executed twenty civilians because they had taken up arms to resist the invaders. "That is ... more than just," he wrote, "since there is scarcely anything so vile."[57] His unit stopped taking prisoners, he explained in another letter, because the Soviets slaughtered any Germans who fell into their hands, a practice he claimed to have witnessed firsthand.[58] When he described how he and his comrades habitually took food from Soviet residents, he rationalized their actions on the grounds that their unit was chronically short on supplies.[59] Ultimately, Siebeler, like Moldenhauser, tended to fall back on whatever moral arguments struck him as most compelling as he weighed the rationale for his and his comrades' actions.

In moral terms, the Third Reich was a society in transition, making its way from older values to the new ones prescribed by the Nazi regime. By examining the sources left behind by individual Germans—not just those issuing from the country's leadership—we can better understand how this process unfolded. What emerges is a complex and uneven picture. Within the Wehrmacht, which has been the example here, some individuals, like Heinz Sartorio, quickly embraced Nazi morality. Others, like Heinz Rahe, lingered, resorting to pre-Nazi conceptions of right and wrong to justify their actions. Still others preferred a combination of the two. Within the Wehrmacht, and throughout German society as a whole, they were constantly bombarded by messaging from leaders who encouraged them to adopt the Nazi ethic while also promoting a diverse and sometimes contradictory selection of values and moral arguments aimed at appealing to as many citizens as possible. In the face of such ambiguity, it appears individual Germans enjoyed a degree of freedom to decide for themselves how best to justify their compliance, without necessarily feeling the need to immediately adopt a new value system that some were not yet ready to accept. Regardless of where they derived their ideas about right and wrong, the result was often the same: soldiers were able to maintain the belief that they were honorable men fighting for a worthy cause.

This situation may not have fully satisfied Nazi leaders who were anxious to see every German citizen shed their existing beliefs and embrace the biological ethic quickly and wholeheartedly. In the end, however, the complex and varied nature of the Third Reich's moral landscape often worked to the regime's benefit. Within such an ambiguous discursive environment, even those individuals who were unwilling or unable to take the last step by undergoing a "revaluation of all values" still found it possible to work toward the regime's goals and sleep soundly at night, secure in the illusion that they had retained their personal integrity.

Although the army has been the primary focus of this chapter, a similar pattern may have repeated itself across other Third Reich institutions. To take just one example—the medical establishment—the regime employed arguments rooted in Nazi morality, such as the claim that racial purity had to be maintained and inferior forms of life eliminated, to encourage German doctors and nurses to comply with its euthanasia laws. At the same time, however, the Nazi state also stressed that the victims and their families would be spared from further suffering, an argument more likely to resonate with medical personnel still attached to a pre-1933 value system. In this context, individual doctors and nurses were able to decide for themselves which rationales to emphasize.[60] Further research examining other sectors of society, taking into account both the regime's rhetoric and individual experiences, will provide a more nuanced picture of the moral history of the Third Reich.

Notes

1. Some names in this chapter have been changed to comply with archival regulations.

2. Harald Hoffman to parents and Marion, 21.10.1941, Museumsstiftung Post und Telekommunikation (hereafter MSPT) 3.2002.0382.

3. Harald Hoffman to parents and Marion, 15.11.1941, MSPT 3.2002.0382.

4. Key works of scholarship on the war in the East and the crimes of the Wehrmacht include Omer Bartov, *Hitler's Army: Soldiers, Nazis, and War in the Third Reich* (New York: Oxford University Press, 1991); Hannes Heer and Klaus Naumann, eds., *War of Extermination: The German Military in World War II, 1941–1944*, trans. Roy Shelton (New York: Berghahn Books, 2000); Waitman Beorn, *Marching into Darkness: The Wehrmacht and the Holocaust in Belarus* (Cambridge, MA: Harvard University Press, 2014); Alex J. Kay, Jeff Rutherford, and David Stahel, eds., *Nazi Policy on the Eastern Front, 1941: Total War, Genocide, and Radicalization* (Rochester, NY: University of Rochester Press, 2012); Jeff Rutherford, *Combat and Genocide on the Eastern Front: The German Infantry's War, 1941–1944* (Cambridge: Cambridge University Press, 2014).

5. Statistics from Christian Hartmann, *Wehrmacht im Ostkrieg: Front und militärisches Hinterland 1941/42* (Munich: R. Oldenbourg Verlag, 2009), 789.

6. See Claudia Koonz, *The Nazi Conscience* (Cambridge, MA: Harvard University Press, 2003); Wolfgang Bialas, *Moralische Ordnungen des Nationalsozialismus* (Göttingen: Vandenhoeck & Ruprecht, 2014); Richard Weikart, *Hitler's Ethic: The Nazi Pursuit of Evolutionary Progress* (New York: Palgrave Macmillan, 2009); Raphael Gross, *Anständig geblieben: Nationalsozialistische Moral* (Frankfurt am Main: S. Fischer, 2010); Peter Haas, *Morality after Auschwitz: The Radical Challenge of the Nazi Ethic* (Philadelphia: Fortress Press, 1988); Raphael Gross and Werner Konitzer, eds., *Moralität des Bösen: Ethik und nationalsozialistische Verbrechen* (Frankfurt am Main: Campus-Verlag, 2009).

7. Koonz, *Nazi Conscience*, 2003.

8. See Wolfgang Bialas, "Nationalsozialistische Ethik und Moral: Konzepte, Probleme, offene Fragen," in *Ideologie und Moral im Nationalsozialismus*, ed. Wolfgang Bialas and Lothar Fritze (Göttingen: Vandenhoeck & Ruprecht, 2014), 23–63.

9. George L. Mosse, *Toward the Final Solution: A History of European Racism* (Madison: University of Wisconsin Press, 2020).

10. See, for example, Haas, *Morality after Auschwitz*; Weikart, *Hitler's Ethic*; André Mineau, *Operation Barbarossa: Ideology and Ethics against Human Dignity* (Amsterdam: Rodopi, 2004).

11. See Mineau, *Operation Barbarossa*, 8–10; Bialas, "Nationalsozialistische Ethik," 32.

12. Quoted in Jonathan Glover, *Humanity: A Moral History of the Twentieth Century* (New Haven, CT: Yale University Press, 2012), 356.

13. Examples illustrating the fruitfulness of this line of inquiry can be found in Wolfgang Bialas and Lothar Fritze, eds., *Ideologie und Moral im Nationalsozialismus* (Göttingen: Vandenhoeck & Ruprecht, 2014); Timothy L. Schroer, "Civilization, Barbarism, and the Ethos of Self-Control among the Perpetrators," *German Studies Review* 35, no. 1 (February 2012): 33–54.

14. The men studied here hail from a sample of thirty Wehrmacht servicemen who have been investigated by the author. More information about their stories can be found in David A. Harrisville, *The Virtuous Wehrmacht: Crafting the Myth of the German Soldier on the Eastern Front, 1941–1944* (Ithaca, NY: Cornell University Press, 2021).

15. For a classic and a more recent work on this subject of indoctrination within the Wehrmacht, see Manfred Messerschmidt, *Die Wehrmacht im NS-Staat: Zeit der Indoktrination* (Hamburg: R.v. Deckers Verlag, 1969); Bryce Sait, *The Indoctrination of the Wehrmacht: Nazi Ideology and the War Crimes of the German Military* (New York: Berghahn Books, 2019).

16. W. Reibert, *Der Dienstunterricht im Heer: Ausgabe für den Kanonier der bespannten Batterie* (Berlin: E.S. Mittler & Sohn, 1940), 31.

17. For copies of the Criminal Orders and related instructions, see Gerd R. Ueberschär and Wolfram Wette, eds., *"Unternehmen Barbarossa": Der deutsche Überfall auf die Sowjetunion 1941* (Paderborn: Schöningh, 1984), 302–14.

18. OKH, Nr II 3033/42 geh, Richtlinien für die Behandlung der einheimischen Bevölkerung im Osten, 10.5.1942, Bundesarchiv-Militärarchiv Freiburg (hereafter BA-MA) RH 26–285/44.

19. For example, see 102nd Infantry Division, Anlage to Ic Activity Report for 1.8.1941–3.9.1941, 13.8.1941, BA-MA RH 26–102/61.

20. "Welche besonderen Pflichten erwachsen jetzt den im Osten nicht eingesetzten Soldaten?," *Mitteilungen für die Truppe*, no. 116, July 1941, BA-MA RW 4/357.

21. Reibert, *Der Dienstunterricht im Heer*, 31 and 33.

22. Reibert, *Der Dienstunterricht im Heer*, 48–49.

23. Quotation from "Vom Sogenannten Europäischen Russland," 17.12.1941, *Das Neuste für den Soldaten*, BA-MA RHD 69/14.

24. See for instance "Sowjetrussischer Aufmarsch gegen Deutschland," 26.6.1941, *Feldzeitung von der Maas bis an die Memel*, BA-MA RHD 69/15.

25. Franz Justus Rarkowski, "Hirtenwort an die katholischen Wehrmachtsangehörigen zu dem großen Entscheidungskampf im Osten," 29 July 1941, in Heinrich Missalla, *Wie der Krieg zur Schule Gottes wurde. Hitlers Feldbischof Rarkowski. Eine notwendige Erinnerung* (Oberursel: Publik-Forum, 1997), 57–58. See also Dr. Sven Hedin, "Kreuzzug gegen den Kommunismus," *Der Durchbruch*, 16.11.1941, BA-MA RHD 69/19.

26. "Die Gefangenen von Minsk. Tag und Nacht marschieren die geschlagenen Divisionen," *Ost-Front*, 12.7.1941, BA-MA RHD 53/20.

Morality, Nazi Ideology, and the Individual in the Third Reich   171

27. "Vor den Deutschen haben wir keine Angst," *Der Durchbruch*, 6.10.1941, BA-MA RHD 69/19.
28. See, for example, "Kiew: Ein Sonderbericht. Aufnahmen: Kriegsberichter Mittelstädt," BA-MA RW 4/1175; "Wiederaufbau im eroberten Gebiet. Beim Ortskommandanten von Opotschka—Die russische Bevölkerung macht mit," 16.9.1941, *Feldzeitung von der Maas bis an die Memel*, BA-MA RHD 69/76.
29. For example, see *Der Deutsche Kamerad*, 20.7.1941, BA-MA RHD 69/30; "Nach 23 Jahren öffnet sich die Tür ... Soldaten erleben die Öffnung einer russischen Kirche," *Feldzeitung von der Maas bis an die Memel*, 31.8.1941, BA-MA RHD 69/76.
30. PzAOK3, Oberbefehlshaber, O.Qu./Qu.2/Ic/AO Nr 522/43 geh, Behandlung der einheimischen Bevölkerung, 1.2.1943, BA-MA RH 21-3/470.
31. 6th Inf. Div., Abt. Ic, Nr 130/42 geh, Richtlinien für die Behandlung der einheimischen Bevölkerung im Osten, 22.5.1942, BA-MA RH 26-6/67.
32. 46th Inf. Div., Abt. Ic., Betr: Verhalten der Truppe gegenüber der ukrainischen Bevölkerung, 18.7.1941, BA-MA RH 26-46/49.
33. Heinz Sartorio to Elly (sister), 4.8.1942, MSPT 3.2002.0827.
34. Heinz Sartorio to Elly and Fred, 28.3.1942, MSPT 3.2002.0827.
35. Heinz Sartorio to Elly, 20.5.1942, MSPT 3.2002.0827.
36. Quotations from Walter Neuser to Leni (sister), 9.7.1941, and to mother, 4.7.1941, MSPT 3.2002.0947.
37. Heinz Rahe to Ursula (wife), 18–20.7.1941, MSPT 3.2002.0985.
38. Heinz Rahe to Ursula, 23.11.1941 (quotation) and 18–20.7.1941, MSPT 3.2002.0985.
39. Heinz Rahe to Ursula, 29.6.1941, MSPT 3.2002.0985.
40. Heinz Rahe to Ursula, 29.1.1943, MSPT 3.2002.0985.
41. Fritz F. to wife, 19 July 1941, BA-MA MSG 2/4048.
42. For example, see Harald Hoffman to parents and Marion (sister), 5.9.1941, MSPT 3.2002.0382.
43. See Wilhelm Moldenhauser, *Im Funkwagen der Wehrmacht durch Europa: Balkan, Ukraine, Stalingrad: Feldpostbriefe des Gefreiten Wilhelm Moldenhauser 1940–1943*, ed. Jens Ebert (Berlin: Trafo, 2008).
44. Wilhelm Moldenhauser to Erika (wife), 6.9.1941, in Moldenhauser, *Im Funkwagen der Wehrmacht*. Also see letter of 11.4.1941.
45. Wilhelm Moldenhauser to Erika, 20.3.1942, in Moldenhauser, *Im Funkwagen der Wehrmacht*.
46. Wilhelm Moldenhauser to Erika, 20.9.1941, in Moldenhauser, *Im Funkwagen der Wehrmacht*.
47. Wilhelm Moldenhauser to Erika, 6.9.1941, in Moldenhauser, *Im Funkwagen der Wehrmacht*.
48. See, for example, Wilhelm Moldenhauser to parents, 24.8.1941 and to Erika, 31.1.1942, in Moldenhauser, *Im Funkwagen der Wehrmacht*.
49. Wilhelm Moldenhauser to Erika, 18.6.1942, in Moldenhauser, *Im Funkwagen der Wehrmacht*.

50. Wilhelm Moldenhauser to Erika (wife), 17.9.1941, in Moldenhauser, *Im Funkwagen der Wehrmacht*.
51. Wilhelm Moldenhauser to Erika (wife), 17.9.1941, in Moldenhauser, *Im Funkwagen der Wehrmacht*.
52. Franz Siebeler to parents and siblings, 23.11.1941, MSPT 3.2002.1285.
53. Franz Siebeler to parents and siblings, 23.11.1941, 15.7.1941, and 24.7.1941, MSPT 3.2002.1285.
54. See Franz Siebeler to parents and siblings, 2.9.1941, MSPT 3.2002.1285.
55. Franz Siebeler to parents and siblings, 19.9.1941, MSPT 3.2002.1285.
56. See especially Franz Siebeler to parents and siblings, 15.7.1941, MSPT 3.2002.1285.
57. Franz Siebeler to parents and siblings, 24.6.1941, MSPT 3.2002.1285.
58. Franz Siebeler to parents and siblings, 5.7.1941, MSPT 3.2002.1285.
59. Franz Siebeler to parents and siblings, 10.11.1941, MSPT 3.2002.1285.
60. See Robert Jay Lifton, *The Nazi Doctors: Medical Killing and the Psychology of Genocide* (New York: Basic Books, 1986); William Lafleur and Susumu Shimazono, eds., *Dark Medicine: Rationalizing Unethical Medical Research* (Bloomington: Indiana University Press, 2008); Claudia Koonz, "Eugenics, Gender, and Ethics in Nazi Germany: The Debate about Involuntary Sterilization, 1933–1936," in *Reevaluating the Third Reich*, ed. Thomas Childers and Jane Caplan (New York: Homes & Meier, 1992), 66–85.

9

Reading Mosse in Jerusalem

Fallen Soldiers and Israel's Culture of Commemoration

ARIE DUBNOV

The temptation of art, a temptation to which every work of art yields except the greatest ones, is to console.

—IRIS MURDOCH, "Against Dryness"

Israeli Exceptionalism?

Alongside Paul Fussell, Pierre Nora, and Jay Winter, George L. Mosse's *Fallen Soldiers* helped inaugurate a new subfield of cultural history: the study of commemoration, "remembrance culture," and its connection to nationalist ideology and politics.[1] Recognizing World War I and its aftermath as a watershed in European history, Mosse came to the conclusion that the commemoration of the dead became an essential element of a "new style of mass politics," a heroic melodrama and a secular religion, with its own symbolism, rituals, public festivals, and mythologies. Can these insights be applied to Israeli society and its culture of commemoration? Mosse's carefully written preface to the 1990 Hebrew translation of *Fallen Soldiers* provides more than a hint as to the way he might have answered this question:

> European traditions ... are known for having an important influence on the formation of Israel as a state. Moreover, Israel seems to have more war monuments than many European countries. To these, we must add the numerous military cemeteries and so many memorial ceremonies.... But to the best of my knowledge, there are only a few war memorials in Israel that can be defined as aggressive, and hardly a single monument can be found with a patriotic oration, as was common in interwar Europe. Mourning here, in Israel, even when it is public,

seems more personal: take, for example, the mention of nicknames alongside the official names of the fallen [soldiers], which is customary in many monuments in Israel; in Europe that would have been considered to be detrimental to the sacred character of the monument.... What is this difference about the development of national consciousness in Israel? Is Israeli nationalism careful to maintain a liberal nucleus that refuses to imitate the civil religion of [European] nationalism?[2]

According to this hypothesis, if commemorative practices are to be used as the main parameter for comparison between Israeli and European histories, they would surely reveal more divergences and differences than similarities. Unlike Yosef Hayim Yerushalmi and his disciples who sought to isolate Jewish mnemonic practices, Mosse refused to explain the relative scarcity of monumental sites in Israel only as derivative of an adherence to traditional Judaism. Yerushalmi explained these tendencies as a preference for textual remembrance over the later Christian and magisterial cult of "Fama"—a celebration of glory and great deeds performed by heroic forebears—which justified the erection of grand physical memorials.[3] Indeed, Mosse, who was a frequent visitor to Israel, refused to divorce it from European history, commenting in his memoir that he considered the country to be a living laboratory for any scholar of nationalism.[4] Nonetheless, he argued that he found in Israel what he took as a more private and intimate ("liberal") national commemoration, free of Christian tropes of martyrdom and sacrifice that were used and abused in interwar Europe.

Mosse's book was well received in Israel, a happy convergence of both his scholarly brilliance and the fortuitous timing of its appearance. The book met Israeli culture at a moment in the 1980s and 1990s when wider swathes of the local intelligentsia began casting a critical eye at earlier performances of jingoism and militarist nationalism. The controversies surrounding the first Lebanon War (1982) played a central role in this drama: the catchphrase *milkhemet breira*, war of choice, that is, a war of aggression and conquest, as opposed to *milkhemet ein breira*, a war of self-defense, entered circulation during the first weeks of the Lebanon War and was recurrently applied to condemn the government and military elite.[5] Significantly, among those who distanced themselves from hegemonic models of state-orchestrated commemoration were also bereaved parents, including the poet Ra'yah Harnik (née Witkowski), who publicly criticized the government after her son Goni was killed in the Battle of the Beaufort (June 1982). Harnik also tried to develop a grassroots form of personal commemoration that would emancipate the dead from nationalistic pathos.[6] In her rave review of Mosse's book, Israeli novelist Batya Gur could not resist speculating:

"One wonders how such a book would have been received here [in Israel] before the Lebanon War."[7] It was a clear hint and perhaps wishful thinking: Was the Israeli public for whom the translation was intended more suspicious than before, no longer willing to swallow warmongering grandiloquences? The feeling was that a widening gap emerged between "official" and "vernacular" forms of commemoration and that Mosse's book could speak to that new sensibility, providing numerous examples of hypernationalist manipulation of private pain.

No less significant was the impact of the First Intifada (1987–92), which broke out three years before the Hebrew translation appeared and before the controversies surrounding the work of the so-called New Historians. The popular uprising forced Israelis to come to terms with a different kind of military confrontation: no longer conventional warfare with Arab armies but an asymmetrical skirmish in an attempt to crush a rebelling civilian Palestinian population. It provided an intense backdrop to the controversies surrounding the revisionist works of historians such as Benny Morris, Tom Segev, and Avi Shalim, who relied on newly declassified archival materials related to the 1948 War to discard traditional accounts of causes, motivations, and scales of the expulsions of Palestinians in 1948.[8] Old David-versus-Goliath narratives were inspected with a more critical eye, at times even reversed, and the use of force by "our troops" no longer escaped public scrutiny.

To a large degree, Mosse's preface to the Hebrew edition of his own book can be regarded as his humble contribution to the nouvelle mode of Israeli historiography. It was written after Tom Segev, one of the New Historians, took Mosse on a private tour of Israeli war heritage monuments in early spring 1990.[9] During the trip, the two historians visited numerous monuments scattered around the country, yet notably, many of these were erected after 1967 by local communities or by military veterans rather than by the Israeli Ministry of Defense.[10] Interestingly enough, even after visiting Mount Herzl, Israel's equivalent of Arlington National Cemetery or Britain's Brookwood Military Cemetery, Mosse still contended that Israeli national commemoration was quintessentially different from its European predecessors:

> The message that Mt. Herzl radiates is that of a nation that was resurrected from the abysses of the Holocaust—whose memory is reflected on one side of the hill—while on the other side is the National Military Cemetery.... We shall reiterate that the difference in attitude toward death and revival that are customary national subjects in Israel is due in large measure to the difference and contrast between Christianity and Judaism. Yet, nevertheless, it teaches us something about Israeli national consciousness. Despite the use of traditional national symbols, in most

cases, individuality is preserved as the very bone of the way the nation presents itself.[11]

Was George L. Mosse correct in advocating for Israeli exceptionalism in the realms of commemoration of fallen soldiers? Taking Mosse's prefatory comments from 1990 as my point of departure, I shall attempt, modestly, to follow his footsteps and answer this question. I shall do so, however, while departing from Mosse's terminology and by looking at a different set of primary sources. One of the difficulties in accepting Mosse's brief portrayal of Israel's commemoration culture has to do with the specific evidence on which he relied. Mosse, after all, did not study the nascent Israeli society during the immediate aftermath of the 1948 War but based his evaluation, as we have seen, on brief encounters he had with a very different society decades later. Moreover, Mosse (and several Israeli geographers who followed him) focused almost exclusively on "sites of *sepulcrum*," which are merely one component among many constituting a culture of commemoration.[12]

The following pages will provide a corrective in the form of a crude outline of the beginnings of the Israeli culture of commemoration by employing four categories: *Necrography*, the production and dissemination of physical artifacts (plastic art, the statue or the monument, the photograph, postcard, and painting) in memory of the dead; *Necrogeography*, the making of the physical place of the dead into a site of commemoration, which is by no means confined to the battlefield or cemetery; *Necropoesis*, which pertains to the literary language of commemoration; and *Necrochronology*, commemoration through the national calendar.[13] These four modes of action often culminate in the *institutionalization of memory*.

The present chapter suggests that the Israeli commemoration culture, which emerged during the immediate aftermath of the 1948 War, was the result of an interplay between these four different modes of commemoration. Mosse's short analysis of Israel, which put much emphasis on monumental and necrographic artifacts, failed to capture that dynamic. I argue that Israel's commemoration institutions were not instigated by the state in a top-down manner alone but originated with bereaved families' memory activism and, in particular, through the efforts of bereaved fathers. Second, while Mosse's analysis put much emphasis on monumental and necrographic artifacts, it paid little to no attention to Israeli necropoesis (partly also owing to the lack of necessary linguistic skills) and necrochronology, the creation of a national calendar that echoes the Jewish religious year cycle yet includes new special days of commemoration for fallen soldiers alongside Holocaust victims as an additional layer of meaning.

Conditions of Necropoesis: Fallen Sons, as Written by Bereaved Fathers

It would be difficult to overstate the impact the 1948 War had on Israeli culture in general and Israel's commemoration in particular.[14] Though Zionist notions of masculinity and virility are as old as the movement itself, originating with Max Nordau's degeneration anxieties (deciphered brilliantly by Mosse), the "rhetoric of conflict," as literary scholar Shai Ginsburg called it, together with the Hebrew tropes of male bonding and devotion and a new local style and slang, was crystallized in Palmach tents and produced for the most part by local authors—both native-born "sabras" and second-generation immigrants who spent their youth in pre-statehood Palestine—who reached the prime of their youth in the late 1940s and fought in the 1948 War.[15] No wonder, then, that the literary texts produced by this group commonly referred to as the "1948 generation" in studies of Hebrew literature—Palmach veterans who became poets and novelists such as Haim Gouri, S. Yizhar (Yizhar Smilansky), Amir Gilboa (né Berl Feldmann), Aharon Megged, Hanoch Bartov, and others—are often regarded as the urtexts of the Israeli culture of commemoration.[16]

And yet, privileging the voice of the warrior-poets and identifying Israeli necropoesis with the veterans' voices can give a false impression. At a closer look, we cannot but appreciate the significant active involvement of parents, and in particular fathers of fallen soldiers during the immediate aftermath of the 1948 War, who played a crucial role in constructing the first institutions of commemoration. This parental voice and gaze took the fallen soldiers to be collective sons (banim), and this family-like language was and remains to this day a vital feature of Israeli commemoration culture. As the state negotiated with and co-opted the biological progenitors' commemoration efforts, they created new conditions of necropoesis.

State legislation played a role in creating these conditions. Indeed, one of the defining characteristics of the Israeli context is the speedy appropriation of the various modes of commemoration by the new state organs, accompanied by legislation. Two 1950 bills—the Families of Soldiers Who Perished in Campaigns (Remuneration and Rehabilitation) Law and the Military Cemetery Law—defined the rights to aids and benefits of bereaved parents, widows, and orphans as well as the proper, standard, and identical shape in which graves, cemeteries, and state-owned commemoration would be designed. This legislation was passed less than a year after the 1949 Armistice Agreements were signed and at the same time as the far more famous Law of Return. The law created not only the state institutions in charge of commemoration to this day but also a new social unit, namely the *mishpachat ha-shkhol* (the bereaved family). It put the Israeli Ministry of Defense—not the Ministry of Interior or the Ministry of Labor, Social Affairs, and Social Services—in charge of the welfare of families of fallen soldiers.[17] This state legislation created new legal norms and a new sociological reality. Unlike the United States, for instance, where we see a considerable chronological gap between the creation of a new republic (1776) and the commemoration of fallen soldiers (1863, primarily after the Battle of Gettysburg), or the European states' commemoration surrounding the Great War, the simultaneity of commemoration and the moment of the "birth of a nation" in Israel created a different social and cultural dynamic, making the work of the dead far more central in the national ethos.

Yet when it comes to the nexus of necrography and necrogeography, state intervention was surprisingly negligible and often followed grassroots initiatives. There were numerous cases of "spontaneous monumentalizing," in which leftover material objects not removed from battlefields acquired new meanings as veterans and family members of fallen soldiers turned them into sites of commemoration. The debris of the burned armored vehicles ambushed on the road to Jerusalem is the most iconic example of this dynamic: the nonbodily relics, lifeless lumps of machines that lost their ability to function and were left as reminders of a brutal battle in a picturesque landscape, turned into necrographic objects, acquiring a commemorative aura. Their particular location—a major highway and the site of a battlefield—added another significant layer of meaning, constituting today part of symbolic Israeli geography.[18]

The origin story of the Yad Labanim (literally, A Memorial to the Sons) museums scattered around the country follows a similar pattern. They originated in the activities of bereaved parents who set up the organization as early as 1949, which sought to combine welfare and aid to widows and orphans of war with commemoration.[19] State bureaucrats were seldom involved directly in crafting the language, literary tropes, and modes of representation but, rather, recognized preexisting or grassroots practices of commemoration, negotiating with the families, and appropriating them.

The stories of three bereaved fathers—Reuven Mass, Reuven Avinoam (né Grossman), and Judah Even-Shmuel (né Kaufman)—demonstrate the extent to which well-educated, middle-class parents, rather than the veterans who became poets and novelists, set the stage for the creation of Israeli necropoesis. Born in Lithuania and raised in Germany, Rubin Mass (1894–1979) was a middle-class publisher and bookseller who emigrated to Palestine after working in the Hebrew publishing industry. He settled in Jerusalem in 1933 and was appointed the *Mukhtar* (head of the village) of the Arab neighborhood of Talbiyah. His son Danny Mass (1923–48) was killed in action during the early stages of the war: he served as a platoon commander who led a convoy of Haganah fighters. They tried to reach the blockaded Gush Etzion but were ambushed and killed by Arab irregulars and local villagers before reaching their destination. In addition to serving as chairman of the Yad Labanim organization, Rubin Mass began publishing a series of popular science books under the title "Danny Library for Popular Science," thus making each book a memorial of his son and blurring the lines separating "private" commemoration from public activities as a chairman of an organization that became an official arm of the state.

More than any other text, however, it was the poem "Hineh mutalot gufoteinu" ("Here Lie Our Bodies"), written by Haim Gouri in memory of Danny Mass and his platoon, the "convoy of 35," that contributed to the "immortalization" (*hantzacha*) of this battle. Historian Anita Shapira points out that Gouri's poem helped transform a catastrophically failed battle into one of the founding myths of the 1948 War and, ultimately, into one of the treasures of the Israeli culture of commemoration.[20] The poem's rhetorical power—using the collective first-person plural ("Here lie our bodies, a long, long line.... And we do not breathe ... See, we did not betray!"), the way it speaks on behalf of the dead, affirming the ideal of individual sacrifice for the collective good—also explains why it was included in numerous *yizkor* booklet anthologies and recited in commemoration ceremonies.[21] Here text meets with context, and poetic style meets sociology, which creates the conditions of necropoetics. In addition to Haim Gouri's personal acquaintance with Danny Mass, the platoon commander, it would be safe to assume that Rubin Mass's key role at Yad Labanim and an early commemoration industry also contributed to the poem's instant canonization. The fact that Gouri was a member of the Palmach should not detract from attention to the fact that his aesthetics and style echo that of Natan Alterman (1910–70) and that Gouri's poem visibly echoed one of the characteristic motifs of Alterman's poetry—the ghostly image of the "living dead."[22]

The veteran-turned-poet, in other words, borrowed his literary instruments from the poet laureate of the previous generation and rose to eminence because his lamentation of a collective sacrifice fit the needs of the bereaved fathers more than that of his peers, who often found his pathos alien and imposing. Thanks to recitations in numerous ceremonies and its inclusion in numerous anthologies, the poem became, to a large degree, a Hebrew equivalent of Wilfred Owen's "Dulce et Decorum est." Besides substituting expressionist Hebrew for Horace's Latin, Owen died in the trenches, while Gouri survived, and Gouri never hinted that the idea to die for one's country is sweet was, ultimately, an "old lie." The story of the "convoy of 35" gained a second life after the 1967 War when Gush Etzion (located between Jerusalem and Hebron) fell again under Israeli control. As Amia Lieblich has shown, the story of the failed 1948 attempt to reach the besieged area played a central role in the subsequent ideology developed by Gush Emunim, the nationalist religious group that spearheaded the settlement movement.[23] Haim Gouri's willingness to lend his support to the Greater Israel Movement provided an additional push.

Reuven Avinoam (1905–74) was a Jewish American author and teacher and one of Mass's partners in Yad Labanim. He was born as Reuven Grossman in Chicago and studied in New York before emigrating to Palestine (1929), where he worked as an English language and literature teacher at the Herzliya Gymnasium in Tel Aviv. His son Noam Grossman (1927–48) joined the Haganah in late 1947, also served as a company commander, and was killed in early March 1948 in an ambush north of Jerusalem. Grossman began using the penname "Reuven Avi-Noam" (literally "Noam's father") prior to his son's death. In 1949 he made this his legal surname, thus carving the name of the dead son into a new persona. Soon after, he approached Prime Minister David Ben-Gurion with a proposal to collect and publish excerpts from writings of the fallen soldiers and began working with Mass at Yad Labanim.

The first anthology edited by Avinoam, titled *Gevilei Esh* (literally, parchments of fire), was published three years later.[24] The book inaugurated what became a distinctively Israeli literary subgenre: anthologies of unpublished writings of fallen soldiers. The state was soon called in and took over Avinoam's project, and today it is part of the duty of the Ministry of Defense's Commemoration Unit to continue collecting, editing, and publishing the stories of the lives of the fallen in yizkor books (and now also the Yizkor website) and new editions of *Gevilei Esh*.[25] Commonly referred to as "yizkor books," the volumes include stories, letters, photographs, drawings, diary entries, poetry, and other documents meant to preserve a fallen soldier's personality rather than solely their name.

Grossman/Avinoam's anthologizing project emerged at the point of convergence between private and public commemoration. Not less significant, they resulted in producing cultural artifacts that functioned (to use Jan Assmann's terminology) as "ritual texts" which brought together collective and cultural memories.[26] Significantly, the term "yizkor" (literally "remember" in the imperative) used for these commemoration booklets predates Israel's War for Independence by more than six centuries: in Central and Eastern Europe, they were used to record the history of their communities, including major rabbis, prayers, persecutions, and lists of martyrs, which were consistently updated and recited. In the context of the 1940s, and particularly in post-Holocaust Poland, as Gabriel Finder explains, yizkor books had a funerary function, memorializing thousands of Jews who were murdered in undisclosed locations or without proper burial and grave, texts that were symbolic substitutes to a tombstone.[27] In Israel, however, these were booklets dedicated to the individual soldier. Yizkor books, in that respect, offer a quintessentially Israeli genre of soldier commemoration (necropoesis), while hinting at earlier, pre-state, Jewish communal forms of commemoration.

Unlike Mass and Avinoam, Judah Even-Shmuel (Kaufman, 1886–1976) was not a founding member of Yad Labanim but a philologist, lexicographer, and scholar of Jewish theology. He immigrated to Palestine in 1926 after studying in yeshivas in Kishinev and Odessa, followed by academic studies at the Sorbonne and McGill University. He compiled the first major English-Hebrew dictionary (1929) and published the first modern scholarly edition of Shmuel ibn-Tibbon's Hebrew translation of Maimonides's *Guide for the Perplexed* (1935–38, 1959), after which he was appointed a member of the Hebrew Language Committee (Va'ad ha-lashon ha-'Ivrit, precursor of the Academy of the Hebrew Language) and an editor of the *Encyclopedia Hebraica*.[28] His son, Shmuel Asher Kaufman (1927–47), was a Palmach fighter who died as a result of a training accident in spring 1947, before the outbreak of the war. Like Avinoam, this father adopted the last name Even-Shmuel. To commemorate his son, he dedicated the next decade to publishing a series of books that included a biography and carefully edited selections of his son's writings.[29]

While excavating his son's juvenilia and unpublished papers, Even-Shmuel stumbled on his letters to his fiancée, Zohara Levyatov (1927–48). A few months after Even-Shmuel's son's death, Zohara was among the first women to join the Israeli Air Force after completing a hurried pilot training course. She was appointed deputy commander of a transport squadron based at the Tel Aviv airport and became romantically involved with another pilot, Amnon Berman (1926–48). Berman died after his plane was shot down over Lydia on 7 July 1948. Less than a month later, Zohara was killed shortly after takeoff when a technical malfunction resulted in her aircraft crashing against the wall of the Monastery of the Cross in Jerusalem. After discovering the love letters between Zohara and his late son, Even-Shmuel approached Zohara's family and was granted permission to memorialize their daughter as well. In 1952 he published a book that included the love letters between the two.[30] Although in his sociological profile, Even-Shmuel, an Orthodox Jew, was not a prototypical secular labor Zionist, he identified the melodramatic potential of the tragic love story. Subsequently, Shmulik and Zohara's tale became a national epic, and thanks to Even-Shumel's literary commemoration work, the story of the 1948 War's Romeo and Juliet was kept alive. These carefully curated works provided the raw materials for Devorah 'Omer, a highly popular novelist who returned to the story in 1980, producing a best-selling young adult novel, which gave the couple's story a second life and prompted a "rediscovery" wave of commemoration that led to a republication of the letters and the biography alongside the production of a theatrical play.[31] 'Omer, who grew up in a kibbutz, dimmed the religious Zionist origin of the story and situated it firmly in the well-established repository of images associated with the prototypical labor Zionist Palmach culture she was familiar with. Even Shmuel himself kept memory alive in his own way by dedicating his Hebrew translation of the Kuzari, one the most important works of Jewish theology, which he completed in 1973, in memory of his son.[32]

In all three cases, then, the fathers' generation, and not the veterans themselves, produced and disseminated the necropoetic texts, creating the institutions as well as the idioms of collective memory. Before they were hailed as fallen soldiers or comrades, these were fallen sons. Similarly, it is not a coincidence that the catchphrase "The Silver Platter"—also popularized by a poem by Alterman describing the dead warriors presenting a platter on which the Jewish state was offered—was the brainchild of a poet who was a generation older than the "1948 Generation" in Hebrew literature. Notwithstanding his combat service in the 1948 War, the young Yehuda Amichai (né Ludwig Pfeuffer, 1924–2000) struggled to liberate himself from the exceedingly nationalistic, collectivist, and pathos-filled language of early Israeli poetry and thus distance himself not only from Gouri and other writers of his generation who began their career in the Palmach but also from the older, fathers' generation.

Paternal narratives were canonized almost instantly because they fitted with the hegemonic ideology of Mapai, David Ben-Gurion's ruling party, and because the fathers themselves were central actors in setting up the very institutions of memory. It sidelined the members of the right-wing Etzel (Irgun) as well as the Lehi (a.k.a. "the Stern gang"), two paramilitary organizations that did not take orders from Ben-Gurion. This division created a deep-seated bitterness and animosity that would haunt Israeli politics in years to come. Waging a political campaign against exclusion from the national pantheon was a known leitmotif in the political rhetoric of Menachem Begin, the Irgun's ex-commander, and accusations that state-sponsored commemorations were part of a deliberate strategy combining historical erasure with political delegitimization haunts Israeli public discourse to this day.[33]

Bereaved mothers played a limited role in these early institutionalization efforts, and their names rarely make it into the historical record. The only notable exception is that of Rivka Guber (née Bumaghina, 1902–81), who lost her two sons, Ephraim (1927–48) and Zvi (1931–48), during the 1948 War.[34] Guber turned to literature to commemorate her sons, publishing *Im ha-Banim* (With my sons), which established her literary reputation. Departing from the path cut by Mass and Avinoam, she alluded to the story of Hannah and her seven sons (2 Maccabees) to express her grief and sacrifice as a mother. Subsequently, Guber came to be known as "Em ha-Banim" (mother of the sons) and was commemorated herself.

Necrogeography accompanied these literary efforts, as a new *moshav* (cooperative settlement) named Kfar Ahim (literally, Village of the Brothers) was established in 1949 near the town of Kiryat Malakhi. Critically, while the name of the moshav commemorated the 1948 warriors, it was named after Efraim and Zvi Guber, the two brothers who fell during the war—Kfar Ahim was built as a community of Holocaust survivors from Hungary and Romania, thus tying the memory of the war in Palestine with the European catastrophe. David Ben-Gurion considered Rivka Guber a role model and a symbol of volunteerism and devotion. She was awarded the Israel Prize in 1967 for her life's work in education and immigrant absorption. The following year she moved to Kfar Ahim, where she gathered testimonies from moshav members who were Holocaust survivors.[35] In 1979 Prime Minister Begin invited Guber to join the Israeli delegation that traveled to Washington, DC, for the signing of the peace treaty with Egypt. In sum, in most of these cases, parent-driven memory activism blended naturally with the hegemonic ideology and seldom challenged it.

Necrogeography and Reburial: Competing Sites of Commemoration

Unlike grassroots initiatives by war veterans or bereaved parents, the decision to turn Mount Herzl in Jerusalem into the national Mount of Remembrance was a product of a top-down configuration. The resolution to rename the mountain after Theodor Herzl and to transfer his remains from Vienna to the newly founded Jewish state was made in December 1948, before the end of the 1948 War. The plan to build a military cemetery on the eastern slopes of the mountain was made soon thereafter, along with the planting of the nearby Forest of the Martyrs (Ya'ar HaKdoshim), a Jewish National Fund memorial to the Jews massacred by the Nazis. The 1953 legislation resulting in the construction of Yad Vashem—Israel's official memorial to the victims of the Holocaust—on the western slope of the same mountain completed the ambitious memorial project. Taken together, these decisions were made with the explicit intention of engraving the narrative of "mi-shoa le'tkuma" (from the ashes of the Holocaust to national rebirth) on the landscape. Inspired by Mosse's work, the Israeli geographer Maoz Azaryahu described the resulting socially organized and culturally regulated encounter between the fallen soldiers and the "founding father" as a "reinterpretation of the sacred."[36] As Ron Zweig has shown, around the same time, Israeli authorities discussed but quickly rejected a proposal to grant "commemorative citizenship" of the State of Israel to Holocaust victims.[37]

But why was that site chosen? Here again, the motivation behind these imposing projects had less to do with a master plan than we might suspect today. Part of the decision to open a new burial site on Jerusalem's western side had to do with the fact that the Mount of Olives, the oldest and the most notable final resting place for observant Jews, as well as some distinguished Zionist figures (e.g., Eliezer Ben-Yehuda and Rabbi Abraham Isaac Kook), was cut off during the war and remained under Jordanian control until 1967. Moreover, the new state choreography also contained much that was not new, as the reburial of Zionist leaders who passed away in the diaspora was a familiar pre-statehood Zionist practice (notable examples of reburial include Leon Pinsker and Max Nordau).[38] The creation of a central site of burial—a national pantheon—had to compete with local cemeteries, using the dead to display centralized sovereignty and a new statist order radiating from Jerusalem. Next to Herzl's remains, a decision was also made to rebury David Wolffsohn, the uncharismatic and almost forgotten second president of the Zionist Congress who died in Bad Homburg in 1914. However, this standardization and centralization effort flopped, first and foremost, because the great majority of Israel's founding fathers preferred burial in places of personal significance. For example, Chaim Weizmann, Israel's first president, was buried in Rehovot, on the premises of the scientific research institute he established; David Ben-Gurion, the first prime minister, insisted on being buried in Kibbutz Sde Boker, on the edge of an imposing cliff overlooking the vast plains of the Negev desert; and Yitzhak Ben-Zvi, the second and longest-serving president of Israel, insisted that he would be brought to final rest near his parents, in a family plot in Har HaMenuchot in Jerusalem. Similarly, Mount Herzl failed to compete with preexisting local cemeteries such as the Trumpeldor Cemetery in Tel Aviv (opened 1902) or the Kinneret Cemetery (opened 1911), where numerous notable members of the Zionist intelligentsia were buried in earlier years. To a large extent, the erection of a central National Cemetery in Jerusalem did not render these local cemeteries inapt or obsolete as much as it elevated their status and turned them into secondary pantheons. For local patriots, these sites were far more attractive. Thus, numerous poets, artists, and members of Tel Aviv's bohemian circles were buried next to the remains of Ahad Ha'am, Max Nordau, Meir Dizengoff, and Haim Arlosoroff at the Trumpeldor Cemetery, which is now considered an urban pantheon, while the pioneer settlers of the Galilee were paid final tribute in the rural Kinneret Cemetery, the rural and picturesque site of the burial of the founders of the Labor movement such as Berl Katznelson and Dov Ber Borochov. Expectedly, these prestigious sites opened disputes concerning dynamics of social inclusion and exclusion in life as well as in death.[39]

Israeli necrogeography, together with the continual practice of reburial of notable Zionist figures, made the internal variances and tensions between different Zionist factions visible. Thus, the posthumous reclaiming of Moses Hess by the Labor Zionists, who considered him their spiritual father, can explain why in 1961, the remains of the famous Jewish socialist were moved from Cologne to picturesque Kinneret Cemetery. In parallel, Revisionist Zionists headed by Joseph Klausner launched a campaign to bring to final rest in Israel the remains of Naphtali Herz Imber, the composer of "Hatikva" (who died in 1909 in New York) and Peretz (Piotr) Smolenskin, the Russian Jewish author and journalist (who died 1885 in Meran), both of whom were eventually reburied in a special plot in Givat Shaul in 1953 and 1952, respectively.

These projects exposed the limits of the state's ability to impose harmony on the intra-Zionist ideological cacophony. Furthermore, reburial campaigns became sites of political contestation. The prolonged debates surrounding the reburial of Vladimir (Ze'ev) Jabotinsky in Israel is perhaps the most notable example of that ideological animosity. It took the members of the Herut movement no less than thirteen years—from 1951 until July 1964—to bring their leader to final rest in Jerusalem. "The country needs living Jews, not bones," David Ben-Gurion declared in one of the endless cabinet meetings debating the proposal. For over a decade, his sole opinion, objecting to the proposal, was the determining factor, and it was only under Levi Eshkol's government that Jabotinsky's remains were reburied in Mount Herzl as part of an homage of national reconciliation. This protracted campaign exposed how politically fraught the attempt to construct a new national pantheon was.[40]

Fallen soldiers were supposed to be immune from such intra-Zionist ideological tensions. And yet they resurfaced owing to the decision to also grant the status of a fallen soldier retroactively to members of Jewish paramilitary groups operating in preindependence Palestine. For Mapai, the ruling party until 1977, there was nothing controversial about commemorating members of early self-defense groups such as Hashomer (est. 1909), the Haganah (1921), and the Palmach. Yet it would not be until 1979, two years after Menachem Begin's rise to power, that the Ministry of Defense would hand out medals to veterans of the Etzel and the Lehi as well. Begin also tried, albeit unsuccessfully, to alter the necrochronological order established by his Labor Zionist predecessors by proposing to commemorate the heroism of the partisans and the Warsaw Ghetto uprising separately from the general Holocaust Memorial Day. According to his proposal, the Ghetto uprising would be marked on Independence Day, while Tisha B'Av would be preserved for the Holocaust Memorial Day, an attempt to distinguish resistance from those who "went like sheep to the slaughter" and adding the Holocaust to the destructions of the ancient Jewish temples and the series of catastrophes in the history of the Jews that are traditionally associated with the day of Tisha B'Av. The fact that these proposals were put forward by Begin as early as August 1977, only a few months after he was elected prime minister, attests to their importance in his mind.[41]

Mosse was correct, therefore, in recognizing that Israeli culture tied Holocaust remembrance together with the 1948 War commemoration, yet this had more to do with the development of a national calendar (necrochronology) than the creation of monuments (necrogeography), with Mount Herzl's imposing planning being the great exception to the rule. A powerful "civil religious" instrument, Israeli necrochronology derived its power from the fact that it came to be regarded as a natural add-on, a supplementary layer organically connected to the Jewish religious calendar, which is known for its numerous historical festivals and days of commemoration that provide "'islands of time' ... of a completely different temporality suspended from time."[42] The creation of such a national calendar is perhaps the most effective tool for routinization, guaranteeing not only that the commemorative ceremony would be regular and repeated but also planting the commemoration of the modern dead in a preexisting agricultural and religious calendar. It thus makes the commemorative performances part of a natural seasonal cycle, akin to earlier, prenational commemorative and often religiously significant dates. It inscribed the work of the dead not only into the landscape—a crucial element in the context of Zionism and the contested geography of Israel/Palestine—but also into the seasonal cycle.

This necrochronology was codified into law in April 1959 with the enactment of Yom Ha-Shoah (officially the Holocaust Martyrs' and Heroes' Remembrance Day Act). The law banned the opening of cafes and entertainment businesses on that day, stated that radio broadcasts "would express the uniqueness of the day," and stipulated that special memorial ceremonies and public services would be held on that day in all military bases and schools. A classic case of successful memory activism, representatives of the Organization of Partisans Underground Fighters and Ghetto Rebels in Israel (established 1950) were invited to join the meetings of the special Knesset Commission appointed to advance the legislation and had a strong bearing on the final result. More than anyone else, it was the Holocaust survivor Dr. Marc (Meir) Dworzecki, speaking on behalf of the organization, who stressed the importance of making "yom hashoa" qualitatively different and emphasized "the need for a section in the law that would stipulate the cessation of performances in theaters and cinemas that night," so that there would be "no difference in the mental state between people who attend [memorial] assemblies and rallies on that day and the common folk who continue to consume daily entertainment." It was also Dworzecki who highlighted the importance of introducing ceremonies into the military bases to tie the memory of the Jewish resistance during the Holocaust with the edification of "the Jewish fighter in free and liberated Israel."[43]

Moreover, grandiose state enterprises coexisted side by side with local initiatives. Kibbutz Yad Mordechai provides a good example: The decision to establish a kibbutz named after Mordechai Anielewicz, the leader of the Warsaw ghetto uprising, was made before statehood, in 1946, by the socialist Zionist movement Hashomer Hatza'ir. During the 1948 War, the kibbutz withstood several attacks by the Egyptian army. The heavy artillery shelling left their mark on the kibbutz and, as in nearby Kibbutz Negba, a decision was made not to demolish the water tower, heavily damaged in the fighting, leaving it standing as a testament, an accidental monument, that served as a physical *aide-mémoire* of the heroism of 1948. Shortly thereafter, the iconic statue of Anielewicz, prepared by the Polish Jewish sculptor Nathan Rapoport, was placed nearby, with the bullet-filled water tower serving as its immediate background (fig. 9.1). The local museum was curated accordingly, highlighting armed resistance that tied Anielewicz in Poland in 1943 to defenders of the kibbutz in 1948 and the role of the Hashomer Hatza'ir youth movement in the organization of the ghetto uprising.

The story of the kibbutz and its iconic monuments illustrates the contingent process by which the binding of Holocaust resistance and the 1948 War was manufactured. Commissioning Rapoport to prepare the statue was not coincidental. He was most known at the time thanks to his 1948 monument commemorating the Warsaw Ghetto Uprising, echoing Eugène Delacroix's "La Liberté guidant le peuple" and the nineteenth-century aesthetics of Romanticism and emancipatory revolt. Rapoport's Polish monument was unveiled in the center of the old Jewish ghetto in Warsaw on the fifth anniversary of the uprising (April 1948), one month before Israel declared independence and several weeks before the deadly clashes with the Egyptian army in the northern Negev. It would be only in later years that a revised replica of the Polish monument, now located in Yad Vashem's main plaza, would be reproduced in Jerusalem. Contra Walter Benjamin, in this case, the reproducibility of the artwork did not damage but added to the aura. Rapoport's romanticist aesthetics, with its masculine bodily images, proved a useful medium to transmit a postwar Polish national self-image of heroism and resistance to the German occupier to young Israel. Rapoport himself affirmed the affinity of European images of manhood

Figure 9.1. Nathan Rapoport's 1951 statue of Mordechai Anielewicz, leader of the Warsaw Ghetto fighters, situated near the Kibbutz Yad Mordechai's water tower that was damaged during the 1948 War. (Photograph by Benny Shilo.)

to Zionist ideals of masculinity when choosing a kibbutznik living in Paris as the model for Anielewicz.[44] This implicit connection, together with the setting of Rapoport's statue against the dramatic Negev scenery, produced a powerful necrographic artifact.

Poignantly, *visualizing* an imagined link between the brave struggle against the Nazis and the 1948 War in the Negev found its way also to *Hill 24 Doesn't Answer* (1955), the first feature movie to be released in Israel. Providing a fictionalized account of the war, one of the most dramatic scenes is a life-or-death battle between an Israeli sabra Palmachnik (performed by Arik Lavie) and an ex-SS officer (played by Azaria Rappaport) who became a mercenary and joined the Egyptian army (fig. 9.2). The scene ends, climactically, after the Nazi mercenary

Figure 9.2. The Israeli sabra (performed by Arik Lavie) wrestles with an ex-SS officer who joined the Egyptian army (Azariah Rappaport) in the 1955 movie *Hill 24 Doesn't Answer* (directed by Thorold Dickinson, story and screenplay by Zvi Kolitz). (Image courtesy of Ergo Media Inc.)

imagines, in the twilight of his injury, the image of the sabra as an exilic Jewish figure dressed in black and raises his hand in a Hitler salute.[45]

This obscure scene becomes more intelligible when read in context: the movie's story and screenplay were written by Zvi Kolitz, a former Revisionist Zionist activist, journalist, and author. During the 1930s, Kolitz was an outspoken supporter of Italian Fascism and among the first to demand that Vladimir Jabotinsky declare himself Il Duce. His 1936 biography of Benito Mussolini remains the only Hebrew biography of the Fascist leader.[46] In 1946 he published *Yosl Rakover Talks to God* (originally, "Yosel Rakover vending tsu Got"), an instant Holocaust literature classic. Written in Yiddish in the form of the last confessions of a Hassidic Jew writing his final words before dying in the Warsaw Ghetto Uprising, the fictional story was mistaken for an authentic document. Rakover, the fictionalized Hassid, is not dying the death of passive martyrdom but has an epiphany that the essence of God, ultimately, is vengeance: "Foolish humanists may say what they will; revenge and the longing for retribution have always fueled resistance of the oppressed to the very last, and will always do so. Nothing else brings such solace to their souls. Until now I had never really understood the passage in the Talmud that says, 'Vengeance is holy, for it is mentioned between two names of God, as it is written: *A God of vengeance is the Lord!*' Now I understand it."[47] The moral of Kulitz's 1946 short story serves as the subtext of the 1955 movie. Yet the movie also demonstrates the difficulty of early Israeli society in assigning agency to Holocaust survivors, despite the fact many of them fought in the 1948 War. Not by coincidence, in *Hill 24 Doesn't Answer*, the task of exacting revenge from the Nazi officer was assigned to Lavie, cast as a prototypical sabra in the movie, not an overseas recruit, volunteer, or a recent newcomer. It seems that by 1955 the commemorative code, marking Holocaust refugees as inferior, traumatized, lost souls, incapable of heroic resistance, had been established. Though overseas recruits from North Africa and Europe constituted about a quarter of the Israeli army in 1948–49 (roughly twenty thousand soldiers), and although numerous Holocaust survivors were recruited into the army, this commemorative necrography suggested that the prototypical fallen soldier was a native-born, Ashkenazi, and preferably Labor Zionist fighter. It would be only in 2003 that a monument memorializing Holocaust survivors who fell during the 1948 War was erected on Mount Herzl.[48]

Tropes of Commemoration, Language of Dissent

Was the history of Europe's fallen soldiers a cautionary tale that could warn Israelis, as Mosse seems to have hoped? Mosse's major assumptions about the nature of Israel's culture of commemoration—that it is focused on the intimate, single individual, is less militaristic, and that masculine versus feminine stereotypes played out differently—were not flatly wrong, and yet they were, to a large degree, divorced from meaning-generating texts and sociology alike. Mosse's introduction emphasized necrography and the institutionalization of memory but did not take into consideration necrogeography and necrochronology. Similarly, he ignored the unique process of making "a family of bereavement" that was one of the defining features of Israeli commemoration culture, and his conclusions were derived from evidence that had little to do with the 1948 War and more to do with later attempts to foster a different language of grief. What I have called necropoesis was not accessible to Mosse, who lacked the linguistic skills needed to study this aspect of Israeli culture. Hebrew literature could provide one of the best media to think beyond the statist language, yet such an examination is beyond the scope of the present chapter.

Israeli literature was at once associated with the new state's commemoration efforts, as in the case of Gouri and many of the authors of the 1948 generation, but also reacted to its institutionalization and routinization. Indeed, the Israeli society Mosse encountered in the early 1990s, when preparing his translation, was not only the Israel of the New Historians but also of *Har ha-To'im* (The mountain of losses), to borrow the name of Yehudit Hendel's lyrical novella.⁴⁹ Hendel's book, published in 1991, has no real plot. It centers around a coincidental, mundane meeting of bereaved parents in Kiryat Shaul's military cemetery, a setting that serves for some critical reflections on the state-organized ceremonies in military cemeteries. It describes the futile efforts of the parents to communicate with the dead "from the wrong side of the earth." It contains detailed and plastic descriptions of the silent, identical tombstones of the "dead sons," the parents' cultivation work, as they add a personal touch to the silent stone, and the way this displacement is a substitute for human and living contact. But above all, it was a book about language itself, a plea for a genuine and heartfelt private mourning ritual freed from the state's imposing language. Israeli literary critic and translator Rina Litvin accurately portrayed the book as one "in which the language of literature functions as a language for itself," creating the hidden texts which conceal the true meaning that lies behind what is said in the open.⁵⁰

A year after Hendel published her novella, the question of private commemoration was brought to the public eye by way of the supreme court's intervention in the Shula Melet affair. Melet, an observant woman from Yokne'am, a northern and peripheral town, lost her son Amir on 21 July 1992, in what appeared to be an accident on the Hatzerim Air Force Base. The bereaved mother, who did not come from a privileged background, soon came to learn that her son had died in a "net roulette game," an initiation ritual for new soldiers, involving the net at the end of an aircraft runway. The attempt to cover up the negligence of her son's commanding officers (one of whom was a daughter of a former commander of the Israeli Air Force) led to a prolonged legal dispute with the Israel Defense Forces authorities. In addition, Melet fought the Ministry of Defense, which demanded the removal of her controversial inscription on her son's tombstone, reading: "My son, pure and innocent, was led like sheep to the slaughter after he was critically injured by the net to block planes." A few months later, she took her own life after inscribing on the tombstone, "murdered by his commanders."⁵¹

By the early 2000s, it became clear that literary tropes could work both ways, as modes of falling in line with national commemoration and as pleas for the emancipation of personal grief from the collectivist grip. The fallen soldiers of the 1948 War reappeared, now in the memoirs of their surviving siblings, who in the meantime had grown old and alienated from the post-1967 Israeli state. Ariel Hirschfeld, a prominent Israeli literary critic, wrote in a 2006 memoir about the enormous burden the old photograph of his handsome older brother, who died in 1948, five years before his birth, put on his shoulders. In adolescence, it made him realize that he came to the world as a substitute, that his "own life was not real life," and that for his parents, he was the "'great consolation' that had to be well guarded." His epiphany came as a literature student, realizing that he was the embodiment of the living dead, Alterman's poetry signature figure.[52]

The memoir, published two years earlier by the translator and author Shimon Sandbank, provides another example:

> My brother Uri, who was older than me, had already left the house a few years earlier and went to the Palmach. And all that was left to me was that heavy silence of a laden coexistence, full of unspoken emotion, with my mother, who was always mourning, a constant reminder of guilt.... The burned armored vehicles on the way to Jerusalem were a reminder of the fear [I felt as a young boy] that something bad would happen to my heroic brother. And then [the song] 'Mi She'khalam,' recited during the days of national remembrance. All these served for many years as our blood-soul, producing tears almost automatically. Now, these were replaced by rejection. The joy of mourning, the famed celebrations of grief, the photogenic ecstasy of bereavement only conceals the guilt that has been obliterated so rudely. No nation has so enthusiastically developed, with such feelings of guilt, the art of embroidering on *Tachrichim* [the traditional white burial furnishings].[53]

It is no coincidence that Sandbank was one of the first Israeli literary critics to read T.S. Eliot and identify in the domestic poetry of the early 1950s the rise of a new individualistic, purposely nonpompous and antiheroic poetic voice, resisting the epic and the virtuosic style of Natan Alterman and the prestate poetry.[54] Did the voices of the 1990s and 2000s, which George L. Mosse must have heard during his frequent visits to Jerusalem, signify the beginning of the end of the Israeli collectivist mode of bereavement and commemoration? Perhaps. In the meantime, it appears that the reports of its death are greatly exaggerated.

Notes

I would like to thank Benny Shilo, Eric Goldman, and Meir Russo (Israel Film Archive at the Jerusalem Cinematheque) for the images included in this chapter. Immense gratitude goes to the editors of the volume, alongside Ella Ayalon, Kathryn Brackney, Rivka Brot, Raz Chen-Morris, Stefanos Geroulanos, Shai Ginsburg, Doris Bergen, Lee Rotbrad, David Sorkin, Noga Wolff, Sarah Wagner, Orian Zakai, and Sunny Yudkoff, for their invaluable comments and suggestions on earlier versions of this chapter.

I would like to dedicate this chapter to Chayuta Dubnov, who chose life.

1. Paul Fussell, *The Great War and Modern Memory* (1975; repr., Oxford: Oxford University Press, 2014); Pierre Nora, *Rethinking France: Les Lieux de mémoire*, 4 vols., trans. Richard C. Holbrook et al. (1985; repr., Chicago: University of Chicago Press, 2001); J. M. Winter, *Sites of Memory, Sites of Mourning: The Great War in European Cultural History* (Cambridge: Cambridge University Press, 1995); J. M. Winter and Emmanuel Sivan, eds., *War and Remembrance in the Twentieth Century* (Cambridge: Cambridge University Press, 1999); J. M. Winter, *War Beyond Words: Languages of Remembrance from the Great War to the Present* (Cambridge: Cambridge University Press, 2017).

2. George L. Mosse, *Hanoflim Bakrav* [Hebrew edition of *Fallen Soldiers*] (Tel-Aviv: 'Am 'Oved, 1990), 12–13 (my translation).

3. Yosef Hayim Yerushalmi, *Zakhor: Jewish History and Jewish Memory*, ed. Harold Bloom (Seattle: University of Washington Press, 1996). On Fama (a Latin word meaning "rumor," "report," and "tradition"), see Philip R. Hardie, *Rumour and Renown: Representations of Fama in Western Literature* (Cambridge: Cambridge University Press, 2012); Karl Galinsky, ed., *Memoria Romana: Memory in Rome and Rome in Memory* (Ann Arbor: University of Michigan Press, 2014).

4. George L. Mosse, *Confronting History: A Memoir* (Madison: University of Wisconsin Press, 2000), chap. 11.

5. Paradoxically, it was a boastful article by Prime Minister Menachem Begin, which was intended to justify the government's decision to launch a military operation in Lebanon, that contributed probably more than any other text to the popularization of the concept "melhemet breira" (war of choice): Menachem Begin, "Milhama Belit Breira—O Milhama 'Im Breira [War of No Choice—or War of Choice]," *Ma'ariv*, 20 August 1982, 20.

6. See in particular Ra'yah Harnik, *Shirim Le-Guni* [Poems for Guni] (Tel Aviv: Hakibbutz Hameuchad, 1983). For discussion, see Yagil Levy, *Israel's Death Hierarchy: Casualty Aversion in a Militarized Democracy* (New York: New York University Press, 2016), chap. 2; Dana Olmert, *Ke-Homah 'Amodnah: Imahot Le-Lohamim Ba-Sifrut Ha-'Ivrit* ["A barricade of mothers": Mothers of soldiers in Israeli Zionist culture and literature] (Bene Brak: Hakibbutz Hameuchad, 2018), 182–90.

7. Batya Gur, "Hachaver shenafal bakrav" [The comrade who died in battle], *Ha'aretz, Tarbut v'sifrut* [Ha'aretz literary supplement], 3 December 1993, 1.

8. The first appearance of the term was in Benny Morris, "The New Historiography: Israel Confronts Its Past," *Tikkun* 3, no. 6 (1988): 19–23, 99–102.

9. Tom Segev, "Ma 'Osot Ha-Andarteot Baleylot: Dokh Mas'a" [What do the monuments do at night: Report from a journey], *Ha'aretz*, 27 April 1990, 1. I would like to thank Tom Segev for sending me a copy of his article. According to Segev, there were close to one thousand monuments in memory of fallen soldiers in Israel at the time. In his calculations, this number equals roughly one monument per every sixteen dead, thereby making Israel the most commemorative country in the world. Notably, 1998 state legislation redefined the National Memorial Day (Yom Ha-zikaron), which was renamed Yom ha-zikaron Lehalalei Ma'arakhot Yisrael ul'nifge'ei pe'ulot ha-eivah (Memorial Day for the Fallen Soldiers of Israel and Victims of Terrorism), thereby adding to it the civilian casualties of conflict to the death toll. This renders the earlier statistic no longer relevant.

10. Segev's article reports the Jordan Valley monument (designed by Igael Tumarkin, 1972), the Ammunition Hill (Givat Hatachmoshet) memorial in Jerusalem (inaugurated 1975 and recognized as a state museum only in 1990), Nathan Rapoport's statue in memory of Captain Gad ("Gadi") Manela in kibbutz Tel Yitzhak (made in memory of a kibbutz member who was killed in action in July 1968, during the War of Attrition), the Almagor Monument (inaugurated in September 1967, in memory of seven noncombatants—residents of Moshav Almagor and Jewish National Fund workers—who were killed by Syrian troops between 1963 and 1966), the Golani Brigade Museum (established in 1982 on the basis of a more modest monument from 1949), the monument to the fallen of the 68th Battalion near Jerusalem (designed by Arik Ophir, 1975, in memory of the soldiers who fell at the Bar-Lev Line during the Yom Kippur War in October 1973), and an unrecognized monument near Gamla in the Golan Heights. There is little in common in this list of monuments when it comes to both aesthetic style and the source of funding and original motivation to create them. Crucially, there are far fewer monuments created to commemorate the 1948 fallen soldiers compared to monuments created to commemorate later conflicts, including the Yom Kippur War (1973). This also has an impact on the geographic distribution of the monuments: the number and density of monuments created after the 1973 War in the Golan Heights surpass any other area in Israel. See Na'ama Riba, "165 Monuments: How the Golan Heights Became the Most Commemorated Place." *Ha'aretz*, 20 September 2015, https://www.haaretz.co.il/gallery/architecture/1.2735063. This chapter will focus only on the 1948 War commemoration.

11. Mosse, *Hanoflim Bakrav*, 13 (my translation).

12. A Latin word derived from the verb "to bury," but in Indo-European languages, the root also means "to render honor." See Robert Pogue Harrison, *The Dominion of the Dead* (Chicago: University of Chicago Press, 2003), 28.

13. I borrow this term from Laqueur's magnum opus: Thomas Walter Laqueur, *The Work of the Dead: A Cultural History of Mortal Remains* (Princeton, NJ: Princeton University Press, 2015). To clarify, I distinguish the term "culture of commemoration" and the different modes described henceforth from the term "necropolitics." The latter is often understood as referring to the use of politics to dictate how some people may live and how some must die, with "biopolitics" being the other side of the same Foucauldian coin.

14. Emmanuel Sivan, *Dor Tashach: Mitos, Deyokan Ve-Zikaron* [The 1948 Generation: Myth, portrait, memory] (Tel Aviv: Ma'archot, 1991).

15. George L. Mosse, "Max Nordau, Liberalism and the New Jew," *Journal of Contemporary History* 27, no. 4 (1992): 565–81; Shai Ginsburg, *Rhetoric and Nation: The Formation of Hebrew National Culture, 1880–1990* (Syracuse, NY: Syracuse University Press, 2014).

16. See also Dan Miron, *Mul Ha'ah Hashoteq, 'Iyyunim Beshirat Milhemet Ha'atsma'ut* [Facing the silent brother: Essays on the poetry of the War of Independence] (Tel Aviv: Keter, 1992); Danny Kaplan, *The Men We Loved: Male Friendship and Nationalism in Israeli Culture* (New York: Berghahn Books, 2006); Nurit Govrin, "'Yalkut Hare'im': Metziut Shel Hemsheck Umitos Shel Hatchala" ["Yalkut Hare'im"—Continuity or myth of a new beginning?], in *Keri'at Ha-Dorot: Sifrut 'Ivrit Be-Ma'aglehah* [Reading the generations: Contextual studies in Hebrew literature] (Tel Aviv: Gevanim, 2015), 101–31; Uri S. Cohen,

Ha'nosach Ha'bitchoni Ve'tarbut Hamilchama Ha'ivrit [Security style and the Hebrew culture of war] (Jerusalem: The Bialik Institute, 2017); Philip Hollander, *From Schlemiel to Sabra: Zionist Masculinity and Palestinian Hebrew Literature* (Bloomington: Indiana University Press, 2019).

17. The official name is Families and Commemoration Division of the Israeli Ministry of Defense, an IDF unit in charge of burial and commemoration of fallen soldiers operated as soon as January 1949.

18. The contrast between the non-urban, picturesque scenery and the vehicles themselves echoes similar dynamics Mosse recognized in his studies of British commemoration of fallen soldiers in parks and gardens, reaffirming the nation's preindustrial image. See George L. Mosse, "Two World Wars and the Myth of the War Experience," *Journal of Contemporary History* 21, no. 4 (1986): 491–513. Years later, a similar dynamic would shape the landscape of the Golan Heights, where numerous wrecked tanks from October 1973 were scattered, now functioning as the official sites of commemoration of specific IDF units. In both the 1948 and 1973 cases, leaving the debris served as a reminder that Israel's war fronts are not some foreign field but next door.

19. The official history of the Yad Labanim organization begins in late 1948 with petitions sent by three bereaved mothers who suggested establishing orphanages that also would include a modest hall dedicated to fallen soldiers where their "photos, obituaries, stories of their activities and work during their short lives" could be exhibited. Those houses, the three women further suggested, "should be built near a kibbutz, which requires outside labor, and it will be able to service the house, and perhaps also provide free land, and the education in a village atmosphere will root the children in the homeland." See Miriam Shapira, Slava Danziger-Caspi, and Yehudit Chernaki, "Yad Labanim," *Davar*, 28 December 1948, 2. A recent dissertation by Ella Ayalon suggests that welfare and aid efforts were often sidelined as commemoration took a central place in the organization: Ella Ayalon, "Who Is an Orphan? Orphan Care as a Touchstone for Changes in the Jewish Community in Mandatory Palestine and Israel, 1920–1960" (PhD diss. [in Hebrew], Tel Aviv University, 2021). I would like to thank the author for sharing her work with me.

20. Anita Shapira, "Kola Shel 'Mahleket Ha-Har Ha-Ilemet'" [The Voice of the "Mute Mountain Company"], *Ha'aretz*, 10 May 2011, https://www.haaretz.co.il/1.1173528.

21. Goerry [Haim Gouri], "Hineh Mutalot Gufoteinu," *'Itim: hadashot be-sifrut uve-amnut*, 19 March 1946, 1 (my translation). Soon afterward, the poem was first included in Gouri's debut poetry book: Haim Gouri, *Pirḥe-Esh: Shirim* [Flowers of fire: Poems] (Merhavia: Sifriyat Po'alim, 1949). As he would later recall, the poet Haim Gouri was in Hungary at the time, as part of a delegation of members of the Palmach and Haganah in Europe, and learned about the catastrophic battle in Budapest from reading an English newspaper sent for the American troops. Haim Gouri, *'Ad 'Alot Ha-Shahar* [Until the breaking of day] (Tel-Aviv: ha-Kibuts ha-meuhad, 2000), 35–36. See also Sivan, *Dor Tashach*, 121.

22. Miron, *Mul Ha'ah Hashoteq*, 197–234; Hannan Hever, *Suddenly, the Sight of War: Violence and Nationalism in Hebrew Poetry in the 1940s* (Stanford, CA: Stanford University Press, 2016): 175–77; Reuven Shoham, "From the Naive to the Nostalgic in the Poetry

of Haim Gouri," *Prooftexts* 18, no. 1 (1998): 19–43; Ortsion Bartana, "The Image of the 'Living-Dead' in Nathan Alterman's Poetry: From Archetype to National Symbol," *Israel Affairs* 20, no. 2 (2014): 182–94.

23. Amia Lieblich, *Yalde Kefar 'etsyon* [Children of Kfar Etzion] (Jerusalem: Keter, 2007).

24. An abbreviated English translation appeared under a slightly different title: Reuven Avinoam, ed., *Such Were Our Fighters: Anthology of Writings by Soldiers Who Died for Israel* (New York: Herzl Press, 1965)

25. See the Yizkor website, http://www.izkor.gov.il.

26. Jan Assmann, "Collective Memory and Cultural Identity," *New German Critique* 65 (1995): 125–33; Jan Assmann, *Religion and Cultural Memory: Ten Studies*, trans. Rodney Livingstone (Stanford, CA: Stanford University Press, 2006).

27. Gabriel N. Finder, "Final Chapter: Portraying the Exhumation and Reburial of Polish Jewish Holocaust Victims in the Pages of Yizkor Books," in *Human Remains and Identification: Mass Violence, Genocide and the "Forensic Turn,"* ed. Jean-Marc Dreyfus and Élisabeth Gessat-Anstett (Manchester: Manchester University Press, 2015), 34–58.

28. A short biographical sketch is provided by Ira Robinson, "A Life to Remember: Yehuda Even Shmuel's Memorialization of His Son, Shmuel Asher Kaufman and the Crisis of His Zionist Vision," *Contemporary Review of the Middle East* 6, nos. 3–4 (2019): 280–92.

29. In order of publication: Shmuel Kaufman, *Mivḥar Ketavim Huv'u Le-Defus Be-Yede Aviv* [Selected writings brought to press by his father], ed. Judah Even Shmuel (Jerusalem: Defus Hashiloach, 1949); Judah Even Shmuel, *Zikkaron Le-Shmuel* [Memorial for Shmuel] (Jerusalem: n.p., 1950 [expanded ed. 1959]); Shmuel Kaufman, *Imrot Ve-Hagigim* [Sayings and meditations] (Jerusalem: n.p., 1956); Kaufman, *Mivhar Ketavim* [Selected writings], expanded ed. (Jerusalem: Defus Ronald, 1959).

30. Judah Even Shmuel, ed. *Zohara Levyatov: Ketavim Nivharim* [Zohara Levyatov: Selected writings] (Jerusalem: n.p., 1952), republished.

31. Devorah 'Omer, *Le-ehov 'ad Mavet* [Until death do us part] (Tel Aviv: Y. Sreberk, 1980). 'Omer's novel went through numerous editions, prompting the family's republication of Zohara's biography (ed. Yehuda Levyatov, 1981), which inspired a popular play that premiered in Tel Aviv's children's theater in 1981, and a republication of the famous correspondence. See Zohara Levyatov and Shmuel Even Shemu'el [Kaufman], *Ule-Hatḥil Mi-Bereshit: Mikhtavim* [To begin, once again: Letters], ed. Meir Edelstein (Jerusalem: Y. Marḳus, 1982). For additional details, see Nir Mann, "Zohara Levyatov: Giboret Mofet O Mitos? [Zohara Levyatov: Perfect Heroine or Myth?]," *Cathedra: For the History of Eretz Israel and Its Yishuv* 118 (2006): 145–76.

32. Judah Halevy, *Sefer Ha-Kozari* [Kuzari], trans. Yehuda (Judah) Even-Shemuel (Tel Aviv: Devir, 1973).

33. Udi Lebel, *Ha-Derekh El Ha-Panten: Etsel, Lehi U-Gevulot Ha-Zikaron Ha-Israeli* [The road to the Pantheon: Etzel, Lehi, and the limits of Israeli memory] (Jerusalem: Sapir, 2007). The main arguments of the book are summarized in Udi Lebel, "'Beyond

the Pantheon': Bereavement, Memory and the Strategy of Delegitimization against Herut," *Israel Studies* 10, no. 3 (2005): 104–26.

34. Olmert, *Ke-Homah 'Amodnah*, 16–17, 87–100.

35. Compiled and edited by Guber, these testimonies were published in 1974 in a book titled *Eleh Toldot Kefar Ahim* [These are the generations of the village of the brothers] (Tel Aviv: Hotsa'at Melo, 1974).

36. Maoz Azaryahu, "Mount Herzl: The Creation of Israel's National Cemetery," *Israel Studies* 1, no. 2 (1996): 46–74.

37. Ronald W. Zweig, *German Reparations and the Jewish World: A History of the Claims Conference* (Hoboken, NJ: Taylor and Francis, 2014), chap. 7.

38. Doron Barr, *Ide'ologyah Ve-Nof Simli: Ḳevuratam Ba-Shenit Shel Anshe Shem Be-Admat Erets Yiśra'el 1904–1967* [Ideology and landscape: Reinternment of renowned Jews in the land of Israel, 1904–1967] (Jerusalem: Magnes Press, 2015).

39. On the Trumpeldor Cemetery, see Barbara Mann, *A Place in History: Modernism, Tel Aviv, and the Creation of Jewish Urban Space* (Stanford, CA: Stanford University Press, 2005), chap. 2. On Kinneret, see Muky Tsur, *Le-Hofe Yarden Ve-Kineret: Be-'Ikvot Shire Rahel, Bet Ha-Kevarot Shel Kineret* [To the shores of the Jordan River and the Sea of Galilee: Following Rachel's poems, the Kinneret Cemetery] (Jerusalem: Ariel, 1998). As the late historian Yehuda Nini revealed, members of the nearby Kinneret moshava refused to allow the small local Yemenite Jewish community to bury its dead in the cemetery. Only after a while were the Yemenites assigned a separate plot. Yehuda Nini, *He-Hayit O Halamti Halom: Teimanei Kinneret, Parashat Hityashvutam Ve'akiiratam, 5672–5690* [Have you been or have you dreamed a dream: The Yemenites of Kinneret, the story of their settlement and displacement, 1912–1930] (Tel Aviv: 'Am 'Oved, 1996).

40. Yechiam Weitz and Ofira Gravis-Kowalski, "The Reburial of Ze'ev Jabotinsky in the Discussions of Israel's Cabinet" [in Hebrew], *Cathedra* 155 (2014): 161–94.

41. For discussion, see Tom Segev, *The Seventh Million: The Israelis and the Holocaust*, trans. Haim Watzman (New York: Hill and Wang, 1993); Hanna Yablonka, "Holocaust Consciousness as an Identity-Shaping Factor," in *He-'Asor Ha-Sheni: 718–728* [The second decade: 1958–68], ed. Tsevi Tsameret and Hanna Yablonka (Jerusalem: Yad Yitshak Ben-Tsevi, 2000), 363–78; Moshe Zuckermann, *Haroshet Ha-Yisreeliyut: Mitosim Ve-Ideologyah Be-Hevrah Mesukhsekhet* [On the fabrication of Israelism: Myths and ideologies in a conflictual society] (Tel Aviv: Resling, 2001); Jackie Feldman, *Above the Death Pits, Beneath the Flag: Youth Voyages to Poland and the Performance of Israeli National Identity* (New York: Berghahn Books, 2010).

42. Assmann, "Collective Memory," 129.

43. Minutes No. 32/D of the Knesset Committee Session March 23, 1959: Holocaust and Heroism Remembrance Day Law, 1959, 2 (my translation).

44. This argument appears in James E. Young, "The Biography of a Memorial Icon: Nathan Rapoport's Warsaw Ghetto Monument," *Representations* 26 (1989): 69–106. See also Batia Donner, *Natan Rapoport: Oman Yehudi* [Nathan Rapoport: A Jewish artist] (Jerusalem: Yad Yitsḥaḳ Ben-Tsevi; Yad ya'ari, 2014).

45. Thorold Dickinson (director), *Hill 24 Doesn't Answer* (Tel-Aviv, 1955, 101 mins). For discussion, see Nitzan S. Ben-Shaul, "Israeli Persecution Films," in *Traditions in World Cinema*, ed. Linda Badley, R. Barton Palmer, and Steven Jay Schneider (Edinburgh: Edinburgh University Press, 2006), 160–76; Ariel Feldestein, "Filming War: The 1948 War in 'Hill 24 Doesn't Answer' and 'Kedma'" [in Hebrew], *Zmanim: A Historical Quarterly* 113 (2011): 58–67.

46. Zvi Kolitz, *Mussolini: Ishiyuto Ve'torato* [Mussolini: His personality and teachings] (Tel Aviv: Tevel, 1936). For discussion, see Dan Tamir, *Hebrew Fascism in Palestine, 1922–1942* (New York: Palgrave Macmillan, 2018); Matteo Quadrifoglio, "Statism and Italophilia: Risorgimento and the Italian State in the Zionist-Revisionist Imagination, 1922–1940" (MA thesis, University of Haifa, 2018).

47. Zvi Kolitz, *Yosl Rakover Talks to God*, trans. and ed. Carol Brown Janeway (New York: Pantheon Books, 1999), 11. The story was first published in 1946 in a Yiddish magazine published in Buenos Aires. The misreading was a result of later reprints of the text without the author's name.

48. Hanna Yablonka, *Survivors of the Holocaust: Israel after the War*, trans. Ora Cummings (New York: New York University Press, 1999), esp. chap. 8; Derek J. Penslar, *Jews and the Military: A History* (Princeton, NJ: Princeton University Press, 2013), chap. 7. Drafting about 20,000 overseas soldiers, *Gahal* (Hebrew acronym for *giyus hutz la-aretz*, overseas recruitment) recruits constituted about a quarter of the Israeli army in 1948–49. Holocaust survivors were not necessarily part of *Gahal*. If they immigrated before the outbreak of the war, they were recruited alongside native-born Jewish "sabras" into the regular units. As Yablonka shows, of the Jewish soldiers who fell during the 1948 War, 1,462 were listed as recent immigrants (1,170 of them immigrated between 1940 and 1947; 292 immigrated during 1948), while 1,239 were native-born "sabras."

49. Yehudit Hendel, *Har Ha-Toim* [The mountain of losses] (Tel Aviv: Hakibbutz Hameuchad, 1991).

50. Rina Litvin, "Hatekst hasamui shel hakhayim hashakulim" [The hidden text of bereaved life], *'Iton 77: Journal of Literature and Culture* 144–45 (1992): 44–45.

51. For additional details, see Rubik Rozental, *Ha-Im Ha-Shekhol Met?* [Is bereavement dead?] (Jerusalem: Keter, 2001), 117–25; Galit Bronstein, "Kulam Hayu Baneino? Siach Shakulim Ve-Shikulei Ha-Shkhol" [Were they all our sons? Bereaved discourse and bereavement considerations], *Hamishpat* 13 (2002): 54–65; Olmert, *Ke-Homah 'Amodnah*, 14, n. 2. Batya Gur authored a fictional novel based on the case, which was not well received by the family: Batya Gur, *Even Tahat Even* [Stone for a stone] (Jerusalem: Keter, 1998).

52. Ariel Hirschfeld, *Rishumim Shel Hitgalut* [Notes on Epiphany] (Tel Aviv: 'Am 'Oved, 2006), 13–15 (my translation).

53. Shimon Sandbank, *Avot Ve-Bahim: Memuar* [Fathers and brothers: A memoir] (Tel Aviv: Hostaat ha-kibuts ha-meuhad, 2004), 16, 24 (my translation). "Mi She'khalam" (Of those who dreamed) is a 1967 song by Didi Menusi (lyrics) and Yohana Zarai (music), performed by the Armored Corps Military Band.

54. Shimon Sandbank, *Ha-Shir Ha-Nachon* [The true poem] (Tel Aviv: Sifriat Po'alim, 1982).

Part V
GERMAN JEWS BEYOND BERLIN

10

Religious Commitment and Leadership among German-Jewish Women in the Early Twentieth Century

SARAH WOBICK-SEGEV

In his short but influential work *German Jews beyond Judaism* (published in 1985), George L. Mosse paints a very particular picture of the cultural emancipation of German Jews and their efforts to integrate into wider German society. With an eye firmly fixed on the rise of Nazism and the Holocaust, Mosse uses the first chapter to chart out the development of a new Jewish identity that arose as a response to emancipation and assimilation. Relying on the writings of an "articulate minority," Mosse suggests that German Jews sought to "transcend the gulf between their own history and the German tradition" and, with their "liberal outlook," aimed to achieve "self-cultivation."[1] Their search for a new, personal identity went "beyond religion and nationality" and instead was centered on *Bildung*—an "inward process of development through which the inherent abilities of the individual were developed and realized."[2] Critically, Mosse's German Jews were secular, male intellectuals who were "aware of their Jewish *origins*," but in their present-time activities appeared to have made little space for Jewishness.[3] Instead, transcending Judaism, and simultaneously rejecting conversion to Christianity, the spokesmen of the community voiced their dedication to humanity and cosmopolitan humanism. In this way, and with these values, they hoped to integrate effectively into German society, not noticing, however, again according to Mosse, that these ideals were less and less *en vogue* among the masses (if they had ever been popular among them to begin with). While Mosse's central contention in the opening chapter of his book rests on the assertion that Jewish identity was based on a "noble illusion," and as a consequence, that Jewish integration into German society was ultimately chimerical, his thesis gives voice to what are now common historiographical assertions about the secular nature of German-Jewish identity—namely, that modern German Jews were "beyond religion."[4]

The image of German-Jewish identity as anchored in a *Bildung* that espoused secularism and Enlightenment values has influenced the field profoundly. Scholars have since variously nuanced or revised Mosse's thesis.[5] Yet the overall image of German Jews having been *beyond* Judaism has been hard to shake. For instance, Jay Howard Geller's recent book on the Scholem brothers presents the options for Jewish self-identification in secular (read, areligious), political, and cultural terms. Geller argues that religious practice "had ceased to be a primary marker of Jewishness for most German Jews" even as they nevertheless affiliated socially, culturally, and professionally with Jewish organizations. Cultural identity, he asserts, stood in for a religious one.[6] To be sure, the cultural identity that Geller and others depict is no longer merely *Bildung* as a uniform cultural code but, in the revised historical understanding, comes in a variety of autonomous, internally driven movements, albeit largely secular (again, areligious) formulations.

Mosse's working definition of secularization, along with that of many scholars both before and after, links the term firmly to a process of decline in religious practice and belief. On this point, it would seem, at least initially, hard to argue with him. If we consider *halakhically* based religious observance, we must concede that the religious practices of the majority of German Jews most distinctly changed over the course of the nineteenth century and that most German Jews abandoned a thorough-going dedication to the *halakhah* (or Jewish law). According to historian Adam Ferziger, in the first decade of the twentieth century, most German Jews—an impressive 80 percent—did not observe Shabbat according to the *halakhah*.[7] Robin Judd similarly points out that "by 1871, most German-Jewish communities supported Reform Judaism (at the time referred to as Liberal Judaism). Jews who continued to adhere to Jewish law and prescription now comprised a minority of only approximately 20 percent."[8] Yet, as Judd and Marion Kaplan have underscored, German Jews nonetheless continued to practice many Jewish rituals in significant numbers. Circumcision, for example, remained both symbolically and in numerical terms a very widespread practice; bar mitzvah ceremonies were occasions not to be missed; and German Jews continued to celebrate Jewish holidays, albeit no longer always according to Jewish custom.[9] Instead of presenting a narrative of straightforward religious decline, Kaplan has pointed to the "rich variety of Judaisms" that coexisted in Imperial Germany, even if she also notes the growing importance of *Bildung* for Jewish self-definition.[10] From this perspective, we do not have to see secularization as an act of replacement or "an inevitable or a deliberate loss of an autonomous religious culture." Rather, as Andreas Gotzmann has suggested, secularization can (and perhaps should) "be characterized as an increasingly ambivalent interactive process, in which its [that is, German-Jewish culture's] own heritage was redefined."[11] Critically, this was a process that was both private and based on personal choice.[12] Despite this process of personalization and privatization of religious belief and practice, Judaism remained important for a broad swath of the population, albeit in new and different ways.[13]

Are we then to conclude that Mosse was simply wrong? Did he miss an opportunity to identify and understand the numerous changing forms of Judaism and also to take them seriously as modern expressions of an evolving Judaism? First, we must acknowledge that Mosse had a very different agenda in penning his short volume. Arguably, Mosse wrote *German Jews beyond Judaism* to explain, and perhaps rescue, a universal humanist message that he believed German Jews had epitomized and as émigrés and refugees took with them abroad. This worldview, encapsulated in all that the term *Bildung* stood for, encouraged autonomous individuals to seek self-improvement through rational and mutually guaranteed tolerance and solidarity.[14] This humanism was not necessarily defunct or discredited but could perhaps serve as a model for others in distant contexts. It was thus a message worth repeating and exploring in greater detail. A study of the religious life of German Jews, strictly speaking, was thus not his goal.

Mosse's different agenda notwithstanding, however, his narrative has had lasting impact and has diverted scholars' attention away from an important facet of modern German-Jewish life: namely, a rich history of religious engagement relevant to a significant number of German Jews, including members of his own family. To understand the ways in which Judaism remained an important aspect of the lives of German Jews as well as how German Judaism changed over the nineteenth and into the twentieth century, we are well served by turning to gender, a topic addressed in Mosse's later scholarly work. In the remainder of this short essay, I will explore how the changing place of the synagogue in Jewish life and the evolving role of the rabbi over the nineteenth century and into the twentieth reveal the continued importance of Judaism for many German Jews during the interwar years. As German Jewish religiosity transformed, women began to take on greater roles in the synagogue and in one significant case, included ordination of a woman rabbi.

The Berlin *Reformgemeinde* and the Mosse Family

In his memoirs, Mosse notes that "both sides" of his family, despite their differences, were "conscious and proud Jews."[15] Although he illustrates this statement by stressing the role of familial pride in this act of self-identification, in the subsequent pages Mosse recounts the ways in which his family actively maintained strong and regular connections to Judaism, in general, and to the synagogue, in particular. To be sure, Mosse presents a secularist narrative about his family's relationship to Judaism, depicting his family's story as a tale of its progressive enlightenment (one that dovetailed with the family's migration from Posen to Berlin). Accordingly, the first Berlin generation, that of his grandfather, Rudolf Mosse, would "discard" a religion seemingly from the Middle Ages and choose to affiliate with a faith that mirrored "the spirit of the times." Yet to suggest that this path would lead them beyond Judaism would be a mistake. Rudolf Mosse would instead become a prominent and active member of the Berlin *Reformgemeinde*, a radical Reform community founded in 1845 that included, like Rudolf Mosse himself, many of the leading members of Berlin's Jewish community.[16] George L. Mosse's parents counted among the leading figures of this *Gemeinde* until they fled Germany in the early 1930s.[17]

George L. Mosse's father, Hans Lachmann-Mosse, for example, was far from being a passive member of the *Gemeinde*. He became the "chairman" and "driving force" of the Commission on Liturgy, mixing his dedication to the community with his deep love for music and further continuing the *Gemeinde*'s "tradition" of continuously revising its liturgy. From 1928 to 1930, Lachmann-Mosse financed and oversaw the selection, arrangement, performance, and recording of liturgy that was used not just locally by the *Gemeinde* in Berlin but by Reform communities elsewhere as well.[18] Lachmann-Mosse also played a noticeable role in the World Congress of the World Union for Progressive Judaism that took place in August 1928, an event to which we will return below. The family maintained very close ties to the preacher of the *Reformgemeinde*, the "charismatic" Rabbi Joseph Lehmann. As Mosse noted both in his memoirs and in other texts, Rabbi Lehmann acted as a "valued counselor" for the family and served as a kind of "father-confessor" to his older sister, Hilde.[19] In reading Hilde's diaries from this time period, it becomes clear that Rabbi Lehmann was more than an emotional counselor. The diaries reveal Hilde's general preoccupation with religious and theological matters (along with pedagogical and political ones). Her conversations with Rabbi Lehmann offered her fruitful opportunities to deliberate upon heady questions regarding God's intentions for humanity (including thoughts on the subject of interiority and contemplation).[20] Additionally, Hilde was active in the synagogue's youth society (the Jugendgemeinschaft der jüdischen Reformgemeinde) and participated in events at the synagogue.[21] She celebrated her confirmation along with over fifty other youths at the synagogue in April 1926; not incidentally, Lehmann's sermon given at the important life cycle event was published by Rudolf Mosse's publishing house.[22] Again, the family's ties to the Reform community were multiple and diverse in nature. Rabbi Lehmann was even charged with the task of teaching the young George L. Mosse about the facts of life. This did not go as his parents planned, however. Mosse recounts in his memoirs how he took the opportunity to regale poor Rabbi Lehmann with tales of his sexual adventures, and was thus expelled from religious school (much to Mosse's clear delight).[23] Nevertheless, as much as recalling this episode brought palpable satisfaction to Mosse, even many years after the fact, we must acknowledge that despite his own personal attempts to narrativize his distance from the religious community in his memoirs, his family had remained deeply involved in Reform Judaism throughout his own childhood and youth.[24]

The Modern Synagogue and the New Rabbi

Mosse's description of Rabbi Lehmann's place in the family's life further emphasizes a critical transformation in the position of the rabbi, especially as it concerned the specific tasks rabbis were expected to carry out. Already in the early nineteenth century, as a result of both internal and external pressures, the various duties expected of a rabbi were altered. Making *halakhic* rulings and giving advice about religious legal matters would be joined, and sometimes entirely replaced, by the expectation that rabbis give morally uplifting and educational sermons as well as provide emotional counsel and pastoral care to their congregants.[25] This was particularly true in Reform congregations, where religious services were intended to bring "about the spiritual elevation of the participants," and wherein women just as much as men were targets of moralistic lessons.[26] Even in neo-Orthodox circles, rabbis spoke a (newer) language of spirituality and religiosity to their communities.[27] The leading nineteenth-century Orthodox rabbi, Samson Raphael Hirsch, gave German-language sermons, and in his writings would appeal to his audience not only on *halakhic* but also on emotional grounds.[28] Across the religious spectrum, Judaism was to be a meaningful religion of the heart.

As both the goals of religious services and the associated tasks assigned to rabbis tended more toward spiritual, emotional, and moral edification, religious practice was increasingly gendered female.[29] Thus, even though the position of the rabbi had been exclusively and categorically understood as a male role, the new tasks assigned to him and the language used to discuss religion and religiosity from the early nineteenth century onward catered to female audiences. By the early twentieth century, the gendering of religion in general and Judaism in particular would be used as a justification for the greater participation of women in positions of religious authority (parallel discussions were taking place in Protestant circles as well). Moreover, debates over leadership roles of women in religious institutions occurred in tandem with the broader struggles and notable successes of the German and the German-Jewish women's movement to obtain voting rights for women on communal, municipal, and national levels.[30] In this broader context of religious and political change, a series of discussions emerged, at the heart of which stood the issue of the nature and extent of women's participation within the synagogue. In religious circles, individuals deliberated over the extent to which women could or should enjoy complete equality within houses of worship. They asked: could women preach, and could they serve as religious leaders?[31] In the liberal Jewish world, leading voices in the community debated the controversial question: could a woman serve as a rabbi?

For a number of historians, the answer to this question has revolved neatly and perhaps at times also, too centrally around the figure of Regina Jonas who, in 1935, became the first woman to receive rabbinic ordination (*smicha*).[32] Jonas's story is often presented in isolation; even her biographers tend to give the impression that she was *sui generis*. Elisa Klapheck, for instance, suggests that in the 1920s few would have imagined that one day a woman would become a rabbi (even in ideologically committed liberal circles).[33] This statement is a bit misleading; a number of individuals in the 1920s not only imagined the possibility but debated it, laying the ideological groundwork for Regina Jonas, and ultimately others, to seek rabbinical ordination. The broader discussion on the roles women could play in public Jewish life remind us that as much as Jonas's 1935 ordination was groundbreaking and her own story unique, she was not alone in her quest to realize her religious calling.

Let us consider two important milestones that took place during the 1920s— one rhetorical and theoretical and another practical. First, on the rhetorical-theoretical level, in November 1926 the Berlin-based *Jüdisch-liberale Zeitung* published a series of responses by lay and religious leaders of the time on the theme "Die Frau im Gotteshaus" (The Woman in the House of God).[34] The responses highlighted points of consensus and disagreement within liberal Judaism about the various roles women could play within the synagogue, touching on themes such as mixed-gender seating, whether women could sing solos or in choirs in the synagogue, their participation on communal boards (*Gemeindevorstände*), and the possibility of women serving as preachers and/or rabbis.

Rabbi Dr. Hermann Vogelstein—a prominent liberal rabbi who served in Breslau at the time—proclaimed with great pride and certainty that "the question of the participation [*Beteiligung*] of the Jewish woman in religious services has long since practically been resolved." Citing the existence of women's choirs and the fact that women were allowed to sing solos (overturning the *halakhic* ruling against *kol isha*, the prohibition against hearing a woman sing, which has also at times been extended to hearing a women speak publicly) as well as the lack of *meḥitzot* (barriers between the men's and women's sections) in numerous liberal synagogues, Rabbi Vogelstein stressed that women were now both visible and audible participants in prayer services. Blaming developments in Judaism since the Talmudic era and especially in the Middle Ages for devaluing the importance of education among Jewish girls, he further stressed how the Liberal movement now placed great importance on educating Jewish girls and on encouraging their participation in Confirmation ceremonies. Yet Rabbi Vogelstein was no advocate of what others defined as full gender equality. For him, Judaism was a family religion—not just a religion of the synagogue—and the main role of women was to be played out in the home. In his short response, he essentially drew a line in the sand by outright ignoring the more provocative question addressed in several of the subsequent responses—namely, whether a woman could be a rabbi.[35]

Indeed, of the total ten responses printed in the *Jüdisch-liberale Zeitung*, six raised the topic of female rabbis (and also female preachers), with four writing in favor of women serving as rabbis.[36] It is important to note that even among respondents who suggested that women would only gain full equality within the community by becoming rabbis, the justifications these same commentators made were frequently based on traditional gender roles.

Else Dormitzer—children's book author and the first woman to serve on the executive committee (*Hauptvorstand*) of the Centralverein deutscher Staatsbürger jüdischen Glaubens—began by highlighting the recent advances made by women in the political realm of various local *Gemeinden* as they gained voting rights and the right to sit on local religious communal boards in certain towns and cities. She also lauded the introduction of family seating, suggesting that it ensured better manners in the synagogue. These changes were not enough for her, however, and she questioned whether the time had not come for women to read from the Torah, and even more importantly whether they could serve as rabbis. Some of her reasoning was based on false information and erroneous conclusions. For instance, she mistakenly concluded that "if women were allowed in early times to bring their own sacrifices to the Temple [in Jerusalem], they must thus have had access to the Holy of Holies [*Allerheiligsten*]."[37] Being expected to bring a sacrifice to the Temple was, however, in no way identical to having access to an area deemed so holy that only the High Priest could enter it once a year on Yom Kippur. Beyond being a slightly curious grounds on which to argue for women to receive the honor of being called to the Torah, it is still worth pointing out that even in Reform circles, attempts were often made to ground ritual innovations on the basis of (even exceptional) historical precedents. Addressing the question of whether women could become rabbis, she also turned to the non-Jewish world where similar discussions about the possibility of Protestant women serving as preachers and clergy were being held.

Answering her own rhetorical questions, Dormitzer maintained that women could certainly fulfill these roles. Moreover, for her, full equality for Jewish women would only come when women, too, could serve as rabbis. Dormitzer further argued that women were in fact ideally suited to the task: women's "gentle and personable" nature made them excellent at "comforting those in mourning" and "supporting the fallen." There were, as she told the readers, educated Jewish women who could read Hebrew and were learned in the Talmud and Torah. In short, she suggested that there was nothing stopping women from taking on the various tasks associated with the rabbinical calling. She even declared that there was nothing innovative about women becoming rabbis. Jewish women in the Middle Ages, like Rebekka Tiktiner—who served as a preacher and teacher to other women and wrote the homiletic *Meineket Rivkah*—had played the role of preachers.[38] A female rabbi, Dormitzer intoned, would be "nothing new under the sun."

A further commentator, Hedwig Rietz, concurred with the idea that women could play the role of "*Rabbinerin*" and echoed several of Dormitzer's contentions. In contrast to Rabbi Vogelstein, who urged women to return to the family home to find their calling, Rietz argued that precisely because women had come to play such important pedagogic and spiritual roles in the family home—showing "their children the way to Judaism"—they had proved their capacity and importance as Jewish educators. Rietz added that women were also naturally gifted in precisely the tasks that were so critical to the contemporary rabbi. Why shouldn't an educated, qualified, and capable woman be called to the Torah, she asked, and what stopped a woman from preaching? Given women's talents at giving spiritual counsel (an argument made by Dormitzer and by Martha Coblenz, another supporter of female rabbis in the series), were women not ideally suited for the pastoral roles that were, in her opinion, so lacking in most congregations?[39]

Not all, of course, agreed with these commentators, and not all wrote directly on the question of whether women could serve as rabbis. Furthermore, the debate was not split neatly with women, on the one hand, supporting the innovation of ordaining female rabbis, and men, on the other, opposing it. Minna Schwarz—philanthropist and founder of a women's chapter of the B'nai B'rith lodge in Berlin—firmly and in very gendered language argued against female ordination or, for that matter, being called to the Torah. Emil Blumenau—the chairman (*Vorstandsvorsitzender*) of the Jewish community of Cologne—wrote that he did not think that most people (women and men) *wanted* a female rabbi. Yet he admitted that this was a matter of feeling and not based on a study of religious rulings.[40]

While the debate in the pages of the *Jüdisch-liberale Zeitung* was essentially hypothetical at the time, practical advances were already in the making. In post–World War I England, Jewish women were allowed to recite liturgy and give sermons in liberal congregations. A significant trailblazer behind many of these changes was Lily H. Montagu, born into the Orthodox household of the wealthy banker and liberal member of Parliament Samuel Montagu. She would argue for women's inclusion in leadership positions and would also take to the pulpit herself, giving the first of many sermons at London's Liberal Synagogue in 1918.[41] One and a half months prior to the printing of the ten responses about women's place in the synagogue, Montagu made waves by giving a sermon titled "Man's Answer to God's Call" on Yom Kippur in London's Liberal synagogue. Two short years later, on 19 August 1928, she would preach again, but this time in German in the Reform synagogue on Johannisstraße in Berlin, the very congregation to which Mosse's family belonged. Montagu's sermon was the first given by a woman in a synagogue in Germany.[42]

Montagu's appearance from the pulpit was part of a larger event that she was quite instrumental in calling into being: the first official conference of the World Union for Progressive Judaism held in Berlin on 18–21 August 1928. The Congress included two special religious services, one on Saturday morning and another on Sunday morning, which featured the sermon by Montagu; a conference in which leading Reform rabbis, including Rabbis Leo Baeck and David Philipson, gave lectures; and a special evening hosted by Hans Lachmann-Mosse and Felicia Mosse at the Mosse-Haus on Leipziger Platz.[43] Lachmann-Mosse's participation in the Congress provided material and logistical support. The Rudolf Mosse Publishing House, which by that point was under Lachmann-Mosse's direction, also published reports about the Congress along with excerpts of conference discussions in the Reform community's own newspaper, the *Mitteilungen der Jüdischen Reformgemeinde zu Berlin*. The articles and material reprinted in the *Mitteilungen* included a copy of Montagu's sermon and a note from Montagu and Claude Montefiore (the first president of the World Union for Progressive Judaism) thanking Hans and Felicia Lachmann-Mosse for the particularly cheerful "party" they had hosted and the opportunities for conversation that it had provided.[44]

Montagu's sermon as reprinted in the *Mitteilungen der Jüdischen Reformgemeinde zu Berlin* explored the topic of men's and women's relationship to God through two interrelated but separate vantage points: communal religion and personal religion. Montagu argued forcefully for the spiritual possibilities that Judaism offered and insisted that communal religion (*"Gemeinschaftsreligion"*) as expressed in participation in communal services and prayer were vital for individuals to breathe life into religion. Being a good person, she insisted, was not sufficient for individuals to live a religious or Jewish life. Instead, one needed to connect with the community. Participation in services on "days of rest" and on holidays provided the occasion for people to experience the "feeling of sanctification" (*"das Gefühl der Heiligung"*), to be inspired to pray, and to be reminded of their social duties and responsibilities. Yet the relationship between personal religion and communal religion was, in her opinion, symbiotic and mutually beneficial. Personal religion—expressed in the individual's need for "love, truth and beauty"—was the inner motivation that propelled forth thought, prayer, and study, especially the study of teachings passed down through the generations.[45]

Montagu's spirituality and religion of the heart was not a unique vision of liberal Judaism. Her insistence on speaking to the individual, but also pulling him or her back to the community, reflected the challenges that Judaism (both in its Reform and in its Neo-Orthodox variations) faced over the course of the nineteenth and twentieth centuries in inspiring followers and maintaining communal cohesion. Yet beyond her own message and its resonance with Judaism at the time, her transgression of gendered boundaries by preaching to mixed audiences on pulpits both in England and in Germany was significant for widening the roles Jewish women could play in religious life. We can also point to other pathbreaking women, like the numerous female students at the Hochschule für die Wissenschaft des Judentums, including Ellen Littmann, who would later teach Bible at the Leo Baeck College in the United Kingdom, for expanding adjacent aspects of women's religious leadership such as studying religious texts and teaching.[46]

Regina Jonas's private ordination in late December 1935 thus followed a public debate over the place of women in the synagogue and the pioneering actions of other women who advocated for greater participation in the public religious sphere. At the same time, despite her ordination, Jonas was not immediately accepted as a full-fledged rabbi even by the Liberal and Reform establishments. Jonas would in fact spend most of her short career as a rabbi focusing on pastoral care and preaching, tasks that were less controversial and, as the debate in the *Jüdisch-liberale Zeitung* suggested, were deemed particularly well suited to women.[47] To be sure, from the mid-1930s until the early 1940s, Jonas would be given more and more rabbinical duties: she preached at the synagogue at the retirement home on Iranische Straße and was given pastoral responsibilities for the sick in the local hospitals as well as for female inmates. She was eventually allowed to lead services in the retirement home and in hospitals, but not in the major synagogues—indeed, there was open reticence to allowing her to preach on the main pulpit of the Oranienburger Straße synagogue—and she did not sit on *batei din* (rabbinical courts) or officiate marriages.[48] There were clear limits to the tasks she was allowed to carry out as a female rabbi.

Conclusion

George L. Mosse's *German Jews beyond Judaism* remains a fascinating meditation on the humanist values that a vocal group of elite Jewish men firmly believed in and espoused, values that Mosse believed were worth promoting. Yet in focusing on the secular values of German Jews in the modern era, his narrative obscures the continued importance of religion in the daily lives of German Jews well into the twentieth century, including in the lives of his own immediate family members. German Jews were in many ways far from being removed from Judaism, and religious belief and practice were not simply relics from a bygone ("traditional") era.

Moreover, German-Jewish women were noticeably involved in creating religious culture: they engaged in public debates on rituals, religious values, and education as well as on the place of women in Judaism; they wrote historical and educational texts, seeking to provide a set of old-new heroes for Jewish girls and women; they translated religious texts (especially *siddurim* [prayer books]) into the modern vernacular and penned their own; and they took on new public leadership roles.[49] The participation of Jewish women in creating religious culture was a significant phenomenon during the early twentieth century and especially during the interwar years, and these activities could span denominational lines, as they actively reassessed and reconfigured Judaisms in the synagogue, in associations, on communal boards, and in print.

Notes

I would like to take this opportunity to thank the volume editors, Darcy Buerkle and Skye Doney, for their thoughtful and careful reading of this chapter, and Sunny Yudkoff for her comments on an earlier draft. Research for this chapter was made possible by the generosity of the Minerva Stiftung. Since completing the first draft, I have had the pleasure of continuing my research at the Maimonides Centre for Advanced Studies at the Universität Hamburg. I owe a debt of gratitude to Professor Giuseppe Veltri, Dr. Yoav Meyrav, and the entire team at MCAS. A final word of profound thanks goes to the

George L. Mosse Program, John Tortorice, Professor David Sorkin, Skye Doney, and the many friends and scholars I have had the pleasure of meeting over the years and who have made the Mosse Program what it is.

1. George L. Mosse, *German Jews beyond Judaism* (Cincinnati: Hebrew Union College Press, 1985), 1.
2. Mosse, *German Jews*, 2, 3.
3. Mosse, *German Jews*, 3 (emphasis my own).
4. Mosse, *German Jews*, 12.
5. For but a few examples: Shulamit Volkov explores the inherent tensions and complications in the very conceptualizations and components of *Bildung* in Volkov, "The Ambivalence of *Bildung*," in *Germans, Jews, and Antisemites: Trials in Emancipation* (Cambridge: Cambridge University Press, 2006), 248–55. Leora Batnitzky explores how Judaism was transformed in the nineteenth century in *How Judaism Became a Religion: An Introduction to Modern Jewish Thought* (Princeton, NJ: Princeton University Press, 2011). Consider also the works on German Judaism by Benjamin M. Baader, *Gender, Judaism, and Bourgeois Culture in Germany, 1800–1870* (Bloomington: Indiana University Press, 2006); and Michael A. Meyer, "'How Awesome Is This Place!' The Reconceptualization of the Synagogue in Nineteenth-Century Germany," *Leo Baeck Institute Year Book* 41 (1996): 51–63; and Michael A. Meyer, *Response to Modernity: A History of the Reform Movement in Judaism* (New York: Oxford University Press, 1988).
6. Jay Howard Geller, *The Scholems: A Story of the German-Jewish Bourgeoisie from Emancipation to Destruction* (Ithaca, NY: Cornell University Press, 2019), 106.
7. Adam S. Ferziger, "Ashes to Outcasts: Cremation, Jewish Law, and Identity in Early Twentieth-Century Germany," *AJS Review* 36, no. 1 (2012): 71–102, 80.
8. Robin Judd, *Contested Rituals: Circumcision, Kosher Butchering, and Jewish Political Life in Germany, 1843–1933* (Ithaca, NY: Cornell University Press, 2011), 59.
9. Judd, *Contested Rituals*, 10 (on radical reform positions on circumcision, see 48–49); Marion A. Kaplan, "Religious Practices, Mentalities, and Community," in *Jewish Daily Life in Germany, 1618–1945*, ed. Marion A. Kaplan (Oxford: Oxford University Press, 2005), 235–51, 239; Marion A. Kaplan, "Redefining Judaism in Imperial Germany: Practices, Mentalities, and Communities," *Jewish Social Studies* 9, no. 1 (2002): 1–33, 7–8, 10.
10. Kaplan, "Redefining Judaism," 1, 11.
11. Andreas Gotzmann, "Reconsidering Judaism as a Religion—The Religious Emancipation Period," *Jewish Studies Quarterly* 7, no. 4 (2000): 352–66, 353.
12. See Batnitzky, *How Judaism Became a Religion*; Kaplan, "Redefining Judaism," 2.
13. Kaplan, "Redefining Judaism." Consider also the example of the liberal Stern family: Sarah Wobick-Segev, "'The Religion We Plant in Their Hearts': A Critical Exploration of the Religiosity of a German-Jewish Family at the Beginning of the Twentieth Century," *Jewish History* 28, no. 2 (2014): 159–85. Saskia Coenen Snyder's work on synagogue construction provides another prism for understanding the importance of Judaism in modern Jewish communities: *Building a Public Judaism: Synagogues and Jewish Identity in Nineteenth-Century Europe* (Cambridge, MA: Harvard University Press, 2013).

14. Volkov, "The Ambivalence of *Bildung*," 248.
15. George L. Mosse, *Confronting History: A Memoir* (Madison: University of Wisconsin Press, 2000), 26.
16. Michael A. Meyer, "Liberal Judaism in Nazi Germany," in *On Germans and Jews under the Nazi Regime: Essays by Three Generations of Historians*, ed. Moshe Zimmermann (Jerusalem: Magnes, 2006), 282; Michael A. Meyer, "Women in the Thought and Practice of the European Jewish Reform Movement," in *Gender and Jewish History*, ed. Marion A. Kaplan and Deborah Dash Moore (Bloomington: Indiana University Press, 2010), 141; Elisabeth Kraus, *Die Familie Mosse: Deutsch-jüdisches Bürgertum im 19. und 20. Jahrhundert* (Munich: C.H. Beck, 1999), 357, 365–68.
17. Mosse, *Confronting History*, 26–27.
18. Remarkably, copies of this compilation are still available today through the Beit Hatfutsot: Museum of the Jewish People in Tel Aviv, https://www.bh.org.il/shop/music/product/the-musical-tradition-of-the-jewish-reform-congregation-in-berlin/. See Mosse, *Confronting History*, 35–37; Mosse, "Preface to the Liturgy of the Reform Jewish Community," Leo Baeck Institute Archives, New York (hereafter LBI), George L. Mosse Collection, AR 25137, Box 9, Folder 22, 1.
19. Mosse, *Confronting History*, 36–37. Mosse notes the importance of Rabbi Lehmann for both his family in general and his sister, noting that he was a "father figure" of a sort for his sister. Mosse uses the term "father-confessor" in his "Preface to the Liturgy," 2.
20. In her first diary, for example, Hilde reflects about life after death and the differences between Protestant and Jewish perspectives on it in her entry from 14 June 1928. LBI Memoir Collection ME1211, Diary 1, her entry from 14 June 1928. She reports on her discussion with Rabbi Lehmann on interiority and contemplation in Diary 2, entry from 11 January 1929.
21. LBI, Memoir Collection ME1211, Diary 3, entry from 13 February 1929.
22. Dr. J. Lehmann, "Predigt zur Einsegnungsfeier gehalten im Gotteshause der Jüdischen Reformgemeinde zu Berlin am 4. April 1926" (printed by Rudolf Mosse, Berlin). LBI, Joseph Lehmann Collection AR1596, Box 1, Folder 2.
23. Mosse, *Confronting History*, 37.
24. We can also add that much of Mosse's own *Weltanschauung* as well as the central themes of his book *German Jews beyond Judaism* actually reflected the fundamental tenets of radical reform Judaism as espoused by the *Reformgemeinde*, notably its dedication to universalism and ethical humanism. Meyer, "Liberal Judaism in Nazi Germany," 282, 284.
25. Meyer, "How Awesome Is This Place!," 51–63; Meyer, *Response to Modernity*, 34–36, 100–103.
26. Meyer, "Women in the Thought and Practice of the European Jewish Reform Movement," 140.
27. Baader, *Gender, Judaism, and Bourgeois Culture*, 12.
28. For but one example, in his essay "Religion Allied to Progress," Hirsch appealed to the emotional pain individuals felt in the absence of religion. Rabbi Samson Raphael Hirsch, "Religion Allied to Progress," in *Judaism Eternal: Selected Essays from the Writings*

of *Rabbi Samson Raphael Hirsch*, vol. 2, trans. and annotated by Dr. I. Grunfeld (London: Soncino Press, 1956), 224–44.

29. Baader, *Gender, Judaism, and Bourgeois Culture*; Simone Lässig, *Jüdische Wege ins Bürgertum: Kulturelles Kapital und sozialer Aufstieg im 19. Jahrhundert* (Göttingen: Vandenhoeck & Ruprecht, 2004), 326–61.

30. Donald L. Niewyk, *The Jews in Weimar Germany* (New Brunswick, NJ: Transaction Books, 2001), 121–22.

31. Among German Protestants, the question of female ordination also was raised within the context of religious resistance to Nazism. In 1943 Annemarie Grosch and five other women were ordained in Berlin as the first female ministers of the Confessing Church—the ordination was illegal at the time. Victoria Barnett, *For the Soul of the People: Protestant Protest against Hitler* (Oxford: Oxford University Press, 1992), 169–70.

32. She was ordained by Rabbi Max Dienemann. Meyer, "Women in the Thought and Practice of the European Jewish Reform Movement," 152.

33. Elisa Klapheck, *Fräulein Rabbiner Jonas: Kann die Frau das rabbinische Amt bekleiden?* (Teetz: Hentrich & Hentrich, 1999), 30.

34. Michael A. Meyer sees the writings in the *Jüdisch-liberale Zeitung* as a response to the growing dissatisfaction with "the status quo" as it related to the roles available to, and the participation of, Jewish women in the synagogue. Michael A. Meyer, "*Gemeinschaft* within *Gemeinde*: Religious Ferment in Weimar Liberal Judaism," in *In Search of Jewish Community: Jewish Identities in Germany and Austria, 1918–1933*, ed. Michael Brenner and Derek J. Penslar (Bloomington: Indiana University Press, 1998), 21. See also Meyer, "Women in the Thought and Practice of the European Jewish Reform Movement," 151–52.

35. Rabbi Dr. Hermann Vogelstein, "Die Frau im Gotteshaus," in *Jüdisch-liberale Zeitung*, 5 November 1926, 1. In the same series, Paula Ollendorf also does not engage the question of whether women could become rabbis and instead focuses on the importance of attending synagogue, and how this can help raise good Jewish children and vitalize the community (her response is found on page 3 of the same issue of the *Jüdische-liberale Zeitung*).

36. Preachers, who sometimes were also trained and ordained rabbis themselves (like Rabbi Lehmann), were hired specifically with the task of giving sermons. Their role was thus homiletical and did not involve making *halakhic* rulings, which was left to rabbis. For more on this, see Meyer, *Response to Modernity*, 55. The four respondents in favor of women rabbis were Else Dormitzer, Hedwig Rietz, Henriette May, and Martha Coblenz. Coblenz cites Ismar Elbogen's "Der jüdische Gottesdienst in seiner geschichtlichen Entwicklung," which was also cited by Bianka Hamburger, who was largely positive to women's involvement in the synagogue but stopped shy of discussing the question of whether women could serve as rabbis.

37. Else Dormitzer, "Die Frau im Gotteshaus," *Jüdisch-liberale Zeitung*, 5 November 1926, 1.

38. Yet Rebekka bat Meir Tiktiner appears to be an example of what Ada Rapoport-Albert has identified as the very exceptional category of well-connected women who

enjoyed access to power and leadership roles because of their relationship to key men in their lives since it appears that both her father and husband had rabbinic training. Ada Rapoport-Albert, "From Woman as Hasid to Woman as 'Tsadik' in the Teachings of the Last Two Lubavitcher Rebbes," *Jewish History* 27, nos. 2/4 (2013): 435–73.

39. Hedwig Rietz, "Die Frau im Gotteshaus," *Jüdisch-liberale Zeitung*, 5 November 1926, 1–2.

40. Minna Schwarz, "Die Frau im Gotteshaus," *Jüdisch-liberale Zeitung*, 5 November 1926, 2–3; Emil Blumenau, "Die Frau im Gotteshaus," in *Jüdisch-liberale Zeitung*, 5 November 1926, 3.

41. Ellen M. Umansky, "The Origins of Liberal Judaism in England: The Contribution of Lily H. Montagu," *Hebrew Union College Annual* 55 (1984): 320–21.

42. The sermon was described as a "sensation" in "Die Konferenz-Beratungen des Sonntags," *Jüdisch-Liberale Zeitung* 8 (24 August 1928): n.p. See also Hartmut Bomhoff, "'The Woman in the House of God' (1926) Revisited," in *Gender and Religious Leadership: Women Rabbis, Pastors, and Ministers*, ed. Hartmut Bomhoff et al. (Lanham: Lexington Books, 2019), 71–88, 75.

43. LBI, Weltverband für religiös-liberales Judentum Collection AR 3499, "Programm der Tagung in Berlin, 18.–21. August 1928"; and written invitation to the evening at the Mosse-Haus.

44. Reprinted note by Lily Montagu and Claude Montefiore, LBI, Weltverband für religiös-liberales Judentum Collection, LBI AR 3499, dated 7 September 1928, 33, *Mitteilungen der Jüdischen Reformgemeinde zu Berlin*, 1 October 1928, 63; see also Kraus, *Die Familie Mosse*, 369–70.

45. LBI AR 3499, "Predigt beim Festgottesdienst aus Anlaß des Weltkongresses am Sonntag, den 19. August," *Mitteilungen der Jüdischen Reformgemeinde zu Berlin*, 1 October 1928, 67–69.

46. Esther Seidel, "Women Students at the Berlin Hochschule für die Wissenschaft des Judentums," in Bomhoff et al., *Gender and Religious Leadership*, 53–70.

47. Regina Jonas perished in Auschwitz in late 1944. Prior to this, she had been interned in Theresienstadt, where she continued to serve as a rabbi.

48. Klapheck, *Fräulein Rabbiner Jonas*, 57.

49. Consider the examples of Fanny Neuda, author of the popular German-language prayer book *Stunden der Andacht*; Else Dormitzer, author of *Berühmte jüdische Frauen in Vergangenheit und Gegenwart*; and Bertha Pappenheim, who translated the women's Bible *Ze'enah Ure'enah* into German.

11

Who Owns the German Language?

Zionism from Hochdeutsch to Kongressdeutsch

Marc Volovici

The *Zionist A-B-C Book*, a lexicon published in 1908 by the Zionist Federation of Germany, included an entry on "Zionism and German Politics." It explained the compatibility between Germany's economic interests in the Middle East and the Zionist goal of obtaining national autonomy in Palestine. Beyond the geopolitical affinity, the entry emphasized that "Judaism is tied up with German culture.... Eight million Jews speak German or the German-Jewish dialect.... German has always been the official language of communication of Zionism and the spoken language of the Zionist Congress."[1] It was no exaggeration that the Zionist movement was largely a German-speaking movement: until the First World War, its headquarters were located in German and Austrian cities, and German was the language of the movement's chief periodicals, debates, and publications. The programmatic texts of early Zionism—above all Theodor Herzl's *Altneuland* and *Der Judenstaat*—were written in German as well. The Zionist conceptual apparatus emerging in the 1890s—including the very term *Zionismus*—was largely conceived in German.[2] Far more controversial, however, was the implicit claim that the linguistic predicament of speakers of Yiddish, "the German-Jewish dialect," could be seen as part of a potentially productive affinity between Zionism and German politics. This depiction reflected a key tension of early Zionism, deriving from the fact that the movement associated itself with German culture and politics, whereas its mass of supporters—and source of legitimacy—resided in Eastern Europe, chiefly in Russia and Romania.

The historiography of Zionism has emphasized different facets of the "Germanness" of Zionism, mostly the influence of German philosophy and culture on the movement.[3] The German language has been treated in this context chiefly as a carrier of concepts and ideas, but not in its more concrete, mundane quality as a language of communication. In this capacity, the history of German within Zionism extended beyond the boundaries of German-speaking lands. For the majority of Eastern European Jewry, German was not a household language, though it was not a mere foreign tongue either. This was because of the linguistic relationship between Yiddish and German as well as the centrality of German among strands of the Eastern European Jewish Enlightenment (Haskalah).[4] The engagement of Eastern European Zionists with language questions, and specifically with the status of German, was an ambivalent one, shaped at once by proximity to and distance from the ideological and cultural ideas propagated by the leadership of the movement. The *Zionist A-B-C Book*'s attempt to integrate Yiddish speakers into a German-oriented whole was part of an ongoing effort to present a rather unitary image of European Jewry. In doing so, it brought to the surface the fraught relationship between German and Yiddish, and their respective speakers.

In this chapter, I situate the "Germanness" of early Zionism within the longer Jewish history of the German language. I argue that far from reflecting a mere medium of a Germanophone hegemony, German served as a contested and multifaceted political vehicle—used by native and non-native speakers of German—channeling several divisions within Zionism, for example, around the place of Hebrew culture in the Zionist agenda and the movement's efforts to appeal to the high echelons of European diplomacy. Ideological divisions, as we shall see, surfaced not only in debates *on* language but also *in* language—most tellingly in Kongressdeutsch, a linguistic variety that was used in the Zionist Congress, emerging in response to the limited ability of High German to serve as a lingua franca. The different meanings and functions of German—many of which have been forgotten after the Holocaust—illustrate how steeped Zionism was in older and deeper tensions in Jewish history.

Jews and German: An International Affair

For European Jews, German was more than a language. Since the late eighteenth century, it had come to be associated with several promises and perils: Jewish emancipation, religious reform, cultural progress, antisemitism, and mass political agitation. A key factor underlying these associations was the relationship between Yiddish and German.

For centuries, Jews' use of Yiddish and other Jewish languages served as a marker of social differentiation in the eyes of Jews and non-Jews alike. In German-speaking lands, the Germanic features of Yiddish made the language prone to designations as "corrupted" or "distorted" German.[5] With the emergence of Enlightenment thought, statesmen, writers, as well as Jewish proponents of the Enlightenment in German principalities considered linguistic transformation to be a vital first step for the "civic improvement" of Jews. This approach did not apply to Jews only. In the same decades, German rulers and writers promoted the status of High German (Hochdeutsch) in an effort to render it a standardized, cultural language, a major aspect of the rising German national consciousness. Jews' acquisition of German was thus part of a broader process of linguistic unification.[6]

Jewish acquisition of High German in the first decades of the nineteenth century was met with considerable unease among German nationalists. Jewish intellectuals and writers—who constituted a small minority among German Jewry but were more visible than the rest—were occasionally scorned for their putatively pretentious or suspiciously elegant German.[7] Some writers depicted the German spoken by Jews as stained by their ineradicable alienness. Richard Wagner remarked in his 1850 essay that "the Jew speaks the language of the nation in which he lives from generation to generation, but he always speaks it as a foreigner."[8] Wagner identified language as a trait that gives away Jews' foreign essence, notwithstanding processes of emancipation. At a time when visual markers distinguishing German Jews from non-Jews were nearly absent, constructing linguistic difference—whether taken literally or metaphorically— remained an effective means to designate Jews' otherness.

German-Jewish emancipation generated then a powerful link between Jews and High German, a link that Jews often invoked when articulating their relationship to German culture. Gabriel Riesser, the foremost advocate of Jewish emancipation, wrote in 1830: "The thundering sounds of the German language, the songs of the German poets, are those that inflamed and fed us with the holy fire of freedom."[9] Over the next decades, cultural and intellectual output of German Jews, such as the work of German-Jewish scholars of Jewish studies (*Wissenschaft des Judentums*), mirrored the rootedness of Jewish writers in German language and culture. A number of Reform rabbis introduced German into prayer books, stirring heated debates in religious circles on whether this signaled a withdrawal from Hebrew as the language of Jewish religious practice. German Orthodox Jews were critical of these reformist tendencies, but they too found in German an integral part of their being. Orthodox rabbi Samson Raphael Hirsch published in 1836 a book in German that presented the fundamentals of Orthodox Jewry, deeming it a suitable language to communicate these matters to his readership.[10] By the end of the nineteenth century, the German language had turned into a key aspect of German Jews' self-understanding. As

Jakob Wassermann wrote in 1921, German "shaped my features, illuminated my eye, guided my hand, taught my heart to feel and my brain to think."[11]

The tendency to highlight the profound link between German Jews and the German language, however, runs the risk of overlooking the far wider presence of German in European Jewish life in the modern period.[12] Indeed, the very emphasis on the category of German-*speaking* Jews fails to consider that German had a steady presence in Jewish society and culture well beyond German-speaking lands. It would be useful to consider the category of German-*reading* Jews—a broad, transnational collective of Jews spanning from Palestine to Europe and the Americas who exercised various degrees of fluency in German, read German literature and science, engaged with it critically, and recognized the value of German for the advancement of Jewish society and culture.

Consider the Habsburg lands. Emperor Joseph II introduced in the 1780s reforms that forbade Jews from using Hebrew and Yiddish in domains that are not strictly religious.[13] In Galicia, Bukovina, Hungary, and other territories where German was not the dominant language, Jews were motivated to acquire the language, which provided access to imperial administrative, scientific, and cultural domains, and was deemed a catalyst of upward mobility. Toward the end of the nineteenth century, Hungarian Jews were the largest German-speaking Jewish community in Europe, though for most it was a second language.[14]

The history of German encompassed Russia too. After centuries of intense cultural and economic exchange facilitated by similar linguistic and social practices, German Jews' gradual adoption of German created a linguistic rift between Jews in Russia and German-speaking lands, part of an emerging tension between "Western" and "Eastern" Ashkenazi Jews. Some Russian proponents of Jewish Enlightenment (Maskilim) found in the German-Jewish Enlightenment a source of inspiration.[15] Isaac-Bär Levinsohn, for instance, wrote in 1828 that as part of a process of advancing Jews' social condition, Jews should learn either Russian, the language of the state, or "the pure German language," internalizing the idea that Yiddish was an improper German dialect.[16] For segments of Russian Jewry, particularly those drawn to ideas of the Enlightenment, learning German was a valuable means for pursuing universal knowledge. The relative proximity of Yiddish to German made the latter more accessible than other major languages. The label "Berliner" was attached to Russian Maskilim, a derogatory term that some Maskilim reclaimed with pride. During Tsar Nicholas II's reign, some Russian officials presumed that learning German could have a positive impact on the Jewish population and established modern Jewish schools in which German was taught. A German rabbi, Max Lilienthal, was invited in 1841 to advise the government on educational and other reforms. This generated controversy in Jewish communities, deriving from existing tensions over the influence of German-Jewish ideas on Jewish life in Eastern Europe as well as from mistrust toward the Russian state.[17] In nineteenth-century Yiddish and Hebrew literature, characters speaking German or a Yiddish with a heavy presence of German words were often represented as transmitters of Western ideas. Starting in the 1880s, with the waning of Haskalah ideas of self-reform, representations of Germanness carried a more negative connotation, emphasizing assimilatory proclivities and a withdrawal from Jewish self-understanding.[18]

During these decades, German acquired additional functions in Jewish political life, serving as a medium of political activism across Central and Eastern Europe. Jewish political writers, in particular nationalists, socialists, and anarchists, frequently relied on the conceptual apparatus of German political writing, and often tilted their Yiddish toward German, using "*daytshmerish*," a style of writing that incorporated modern German words. *Daytshmerish* was the subject of heated debates in the Yiddish political and literary spheres since the late nineteenth century. For some commentators, the close contact between strands of modern Yiddish writing and the German language testified to the vitality of Yiddish. For others, the ubiquity of *daytshmerish* was an alarming phenomenon insofar as it reflected a submissive, even assimilatory, attitude of Yiddish writers toward the German language.[19]

Eastern European Jews' access to German allowed various Jewish writers and activists to engage with German-language literature. Major Hebrew periodicals of the 1870s and 1880s, such as *Ha-Shahar*, *Ha-Magid*, and *Ha-Asif*, regularly reviewed works written by German-Jewish writers. Popular writers Perets Smolenskin and Nahum Sokolow, while not native German speakers, were up to date with the intellectual and political debates taking place in German and German-Jewish periodicals, translated texts from German into Hebrew, and engaged critically with literature in German. By the 1880s, German had already represented both progress and assimilation, Jewish religiosity and secularity, Jewish self-assertion, and antisemitism. It could not be seen merely as the property of the Germans. It had become part of Jewish life across Europe and beyond.

A Germanophone Jewish Nationalism

German language and culture left an imprint on Jewish nationalist ideas too. The thought of Johann Gottfried Herder and Johann Gottlieb Fichte, key German romanticist thinkers, was tremendously influential in Central and Eastern European nationalist movements. Its impact on Jewish nationalist thought derived in particular from its emphasis on language and culture, rather than territorial unity, as pillars of a nation's historical chain. Hebrew essayist Asher Ginzberg (Ahad Ha-Am), growing up near Kiev, found much interest in Herder when reading him as an adolescent.[20] He would later introduce the idea of "national spirit"— a term coined by Herder as *Volksgeist*—into the Hebrew intellectual realm.

Beyond their affinity to German language and thought, in the 1880s Russian Jewish nationalists began using German as a language of political agitation across borders, most famously with Leon Pinsker's 1882 *Autoemancipation! A Call to His Brethren from a Russian Jew*.[21] Pinsker, a Russian Jewish doctor from Odessa, had been active in Jewish political organizations during the 1860s and 1870s, promoting educational reforms and acquisition of Russian, while defending Jews' rights as a nationality within the Russian Empire. He was taught German and Russian from an early age, went to a modern Jewish school, and spent lengthy periods in Germany and Austria. While proficient in German, it was only in 1882 that he decided to make use of it to tackle Jewish political concerns. The pamphlet, published anonymously in Berlin, came in the wake of a wave of anti-Jewish pogroms in the Russian Pale of Settlement and an ensuing immigration crisis. Pinsker proclaimed that the only way to address this predicament would be by acquiring an autonomous territory in which impoverished Jews could find a haven and regain their dignity. Transforming their age-old status as merely a religious minority, the plan to obtain a territory would be predicated on a self-proclaimed—and internationally affirmed—recognition of Jews as a national group. This, he believed, would offer a remedy not only to Jews living in miserable conditions in Eastern Europe, but would also be beneficial to assimilated, better-off Jews facing antisemitism in Western Europe.[22]

Pinsker's decision to write in German resulted from his realization that the idea he advocated could not be advanced without the aid of Jewish elites in the West and without the approval of major European powers. In the same years, Otto von Bismarck's Germany had been Europe's main diplomatic power and was willing, in the 1878 Berlin Congress to address the plight of Jews in Balkan states. A highly esteemed international language of politics, German appeared to Pinsker as an effective vehicle to make the call for Jewish national self-determination audible. His pamphlet drew on German scientific and nationalist idioms, for instance, when describing Jewish nationality as an "organism dangerously ill" seeking to reinvigorate its dormant strength, rooted in its ancient history.[23] The fact that such a call was published in German, on German soil, in the midst of an antisemitic campaign against Jewish emancipation in Germany, made the text particularly provocative. Responses in German-Jewish periodicals were mostly negative, expressing concern over the pamphlet's proclamation of Jewish nationhood and its affirmation of Jewish foreignness in non-Jewish society.[24] For Russian Jewish nationalists, the fact that the pamphlet was published in German was one of its main virtues. Perets Smolenskin wrote that the pamphlet had no novel ideas, and yet its main achievement was that it "proclaimed in the German language [sefat ashkenaz] the idea that we are a people and that we must pay heed to our existence by guaranteeing ourselves an asylum. And for this we praise the writer and express our gratitude."[25]

In the following year, Pinsker was appointed president of Hovevei Zion, an umbrella organization coordinating the work of Jewish nationalist circles advancing the settlement of Jews in Palestine. Under his term as president, protocols and pamphlets were routinely published in German. In Vienna, a group of Jewish students, chief among them Nathan Birnbaum, sought to disseminate Jewish national ideas in German, establishing the Jewish newspaper *Selbst-Emancipation* (named after Pinsker's pamphlet), and frequently translated texts from the Hebrew press. In the 1880s, then, German had begun serving as a transnational language of Jewish political activism, imbuing ideas of Jewish emancipation with a stark nationalist tone.

And yet it was only with the entry of Theodor Herzl and Max Nordau into Jewish politics that Zionism turned into a Germanophone movement. The two knew barely any Yiddish or Hebrew and paid little attention to the language question in Jewish nationalism. In his 1896 pamphlet *Der Judenstaat*, Herzl envisioned the future land of the Jews as a multilingual federation in which Jews would maintain their previous languages. Similar to the German-Jewish Enlightenment's linguistic ideology, Herzl hoped that Yiddish and other Jewish vernaculars—"miserable stunted jargons"—would no longer be heard.[26] In an 1895 diary entry, he noted that German would likely be an official language in the Jews' future land.[27] This dismissive approach to Yiddish was in tune with Herzl's and Nordau's wish to grant Zionism an aura of respectability, aligning it with the diplomatic mores of the period and strengthening its appeal in the eyes of the German Empire and other European powers.[28]

Before the First World War, Zionism gained only limited success among German Jewry. The movement's momentum drew to a large degree from its growing popularity in Eastern Europe. It was there that Zionist activists, speakers, and writers agitated—in every necessary language—in search of popular legitimacy and support. The Zionist movement was thus pursuing in its early decades two somewhat opposing goals. On the one hand, it sought to create a public image of an advanced, respectable movement that follows the norms of European diplomacy. On the other hand, it was seeking to energize the Jewish masses in Eastern Europe, invoking messianic ideas and conveying a more radical, even revolutionary, promise for self-emancipation in the Holy Land.

Reflecting this dual ambition of Zionism, ideological divisions were part and parcel of the movement's activity, with German often serving as an object through which these disagreements were tackled. To be sure, there was no easy alternative—most Western Jews could not speak Yiddish and did not consider it commensurate with the movement's cultural ideology. Hebrew was only beginning to be used as a vernacular in Palestine and in several circles in the diaspora but remained entirely foreign to most Jews who lacked traditional religious background. Other languages, such as French, Russian, English, Arabic, and Ladino, formed part of the multilingual setting of Zionism, but none was adequately widespread to serve as a lingua franca. Using German was thus a pragmatic compromise justified by practical considerations but tempered by its ideological implications. The movement's first years witnessed a continuous debate over the *Kulturfrage*, namely, over the place of Jewish culture, particularly Hebrew culture and language, on the Zionist agenda. For critics of Herzl and Nordau, the Zionist leadership's insufficient attention to these matters, coupled with its unapologetic "Germanness," hampered the movement's efforts to garner wide support from different Jewish communities in the diaspora.

Seen from this angle, it should come as no surprise that the largest campaign in Jewish language politics before the Holocaust revolved around the German language. It followed the 1913 decision of the board of trustees of the Technical University of Haifa (which was being built with the financial backing of the German, non-Zionist philanthropic organization Hilfsverein der deutschen Juden) to set German as a language of instruction of scientific subjects. According to the stated decision, German would "connect the students to the scientific development of the modern period through one of the greatest cultural languages."[29] Some Zionist leaders in Palestine claimed the argument was but a cover for the organization's wish to advance German imperial interests in Palestine at the expense of the Hebrew language. Ahad Ha-Am, who was a member of the university's board of trustees, did not deny that German was better equipped to transmit scientific material to students. In private correspondence, he described Zionist demands to teach solely in Hebrew as "radical" and hardly realizable. He nonetheless joined the protests and resigned from the board, seeing the campaign as an opportunity to stir national sentiments in the Jewish population of Palestine.[30] In a 1914 essay—published, notably, in German—Ahad Ha-Am argued that accepting the Hilfsverein's demands would strengthen the common allegation that Zionism was a vehicle of German imperial interests in the Middle East.[31]

The campaign to set Hebrew as the language of scientific instruction was thus part of an effort to enhance the status of Hebrew in Palestine, but it drew on political and historical sensitivities around the link between Jews and German. The German language symbolized in this context Jewish dependence on European powers, politically and spiritually. Herein is the dual nature of German in Zionism: the establishment of a technical university, with German serving a pedagogic role within it, was meant to bolster the goal of building a modern, Western-oriented society. Yet German simultaneously represented for many a historical threat to Jewish nationhood and to its historical language, Hebrew. German stood both for the promise and the limits of the Zionist political aspirations.

The Rise and Fall of Kongressdeutsch

In the most important venue of Zionist politics—the Zionist Congress, assembling annually or biennially in different European cities from 1897—the tensions around German obtained a concrete dimension.[32] The participants were free to use any language they chose, but the dominance of German was evident. It was manifested in the fact that, until 1935, the protocols appeared exclusively in German. The transcribers were German speakers and were unable to record other languages. Speeches were translated simultaneously by other delegates. Before the First World War, those who spoke in languages that the stenographers did not understand, appeared in the protocols only through the words of those who translated them—often paraphrased and abbreviated. In 1898 Bernard Lazare appealed to the participants to guarantee that the Congress's protocols and publications are made accessible to those Jews, mostly of Sephardi descent, who did not understand German or Yiddish. Lazare himself spoke in French, and his participation in the discussion appeared only through Nordau's German translation.[33] Another delegate apologized for his poor German and admitted he would rather speak in Russian, "but certain misunderstandings emerge in the translations."[34]

Unlike the speeches, the discussions were only occasionally translated simultaneously, and the transcription reflected this linguistic hierarchy. The protocols from the Congress's first decade record various cases in which the comments made by non-German speakers do not appear in the protocol. In such cases, the protocols state, for instance: "Delegate Seph: (speaks in Jargon),"[35] or: "Delegate Ettigen: (speaks Russian)."[36] The 1898 protocol refers at one point to a French delegate who "speaks in a manner that is unintelligible to the stenographers."[37] It was thus also in the printed version of the discussions that the linguistic order could marginalize participants who did not speak German.[38] In the congress hall one could hear German, Yiddish, Russian, and other languages, building up, as one participant called it, "a Babel tower of languages," in which "many of our brethren cannot understand each other."[39] The Germanophone atmosphere ascribed to the Zionist Congress thus often concealed a more contentious multilingual reality.

The discomfort resulting from the need to translate the speeches held in various languages also touched on cultural divisions within the Jewish world. Russian Zionist Menahem Ussishkin declined Herzl's request at the congress of 1899 to speak in German, replying: "I speak mainly to those who understand me and who wish to understand me.... I want to speak only in a manner that will allow my position to be properly understood, and this I can achieve only in Russian."[40] A different approach was put forward by Aaron Marcus, a Hasidic, Zionist rabbi from Krakow and of German descent, who wrote in 1900 in his (German-language) newspaper about the "Babel-like confusion" of the congress. The root of the confusion, according to Marcus, lay in the "modern, assimilatory education" and the damage that it had inflicted on the "rightly famous Jewish linguistic genius." He wondered bitterly why a "Levantine Talmudic Jew" could speak five or six languages, whereas a Russian Jewish student "does not understand a word of any other world language."[41] Marcus's reproach of Jewish assimilatory currents was directed against Russian Jews, although the currents had been prevalent within the German-speaking realm as well. Yet because of German's status as a world language and its role in the Jewish world, it was not, in Marcus's eyes, part of the Zionist language problem.

German's centrality also played a role in quarrels between the proponents of a diplomatic approach and a grassroots approach to Zionist matters. In the Jewish political discourse of the period, the term "Congress-Zionism" denoted Western European Zionists' clinging to diplomatic channels and philanthropy. It was also used derogatorily to highlight the ceremonialism of the congress and its remoteness from the experience of the Jewish masses.[42] In the 1903 Congress, Russian Zionist and future leader of the Revisionist party, Vladimir Jabotinsky, gave a provocative speech in "highly eloquent Russian," as he put it, and exceeded the fifteen-minute limit. In his autobiography, Jabotinsky quoted the words with which Herzl and his assistants requested him to get off the podium ("Herzl told me: Ihre Zeit ist um [your time is up]. One of his assistants, Herr Friedman, told me in his native Prussian way: gehen Sie herunter, sonst werden Sie heruntergeschleppt [come down, or you will be dragged down]."[43]

According to the historian Michael Stanislawski, Herzl was not present in the hall, and "Herr Friedman" was actually Max Bodenheimer. The veracity of the incident is therefore questionable.[44] Be that as it may, Jabotinsky's decision to speak in Russian seems to have been aimed at disrupting the German-centric atmosphere of the congress—or at least this is how he hoped this incident would go down in history. In this manner, Jabotinsky sharpened the divide between the ideological world of the "Prussian" Zionists and its Russian counterparts.

German's dominance in the congress was also an inevitable but symbolically serious disruption of Zionism's Hebraist agenda. In the 1907 Congress, Nahum Sokolow, the movement's general secretary, issued a proposal to declare Hebrew the official language of the movement and the congress. This included an instruction that the opening speech would be held in Hebrew, while allowing other languages to be used later for pragmatic purposes. The proposal received negative responses. Byelorussian delegate Shimshon Rosenbaum argued that Sokolow was in essence expecting Zionist leader Max Nordau "to learn Hebrew within two years so well that he would be able to give his speech in Hebrew." In other words, "we will not hear this speech."[45] Another delegate, a Lithuanian rabbi, objected on theological grounds. He argued that as long as Judaism's diasporic condition persisted, Hebrew should not be the language of the congress: "The exile congress must have an exile language, so that we keep awake our longing for Hebrew. Out of love for the Hebrew language, please decline Sokolow's proposal."[46] According to this argument, using a foreign language such as German was not merely a communicative convenience but indeed a spiritual necessity.

David Wolffsohn, Herzl's successor as president of the Zionist Organization, stated that in its present form, Sokolow's suggestion "might make the congress a laughingstock."[47] Sokolow then proposed an amended version, in which Hebrew's official status would be of symbolic importance only. This version was approved, despite protests from several attendees. Wolffsohn proceeded to the next subject on the agenda, as Max Bodenheimer, a German Zionist with no knowledge of Hebrew, interjected—"In Hebrew, please!"[48]

The next congresses continued to be held predominantly in German. At the 1911 Congress, a Russian delegate began his speech by reproaching in Hebrew the Zionist delegates for the fact that the official endorsement of Hebrew remained "on paper only." He then added, "Since I already see angry faces in the hall, I must now defy the rule as well and turn to German."[49] In another discussion in the same congress, German delegate Sammy Gronemann proclaimed unapologetically that for the sake of proper debate that would be reflected fairly in the protocols, participants should speak in German rather in Hebrew: "The congress is not merely a demonstration, it deals with serious matters." His request was followed by both applause and protest.[50] In the following congress, delegate Shlomo Bendersky started his speech with festive words in Hebrew but added that he would continue his speech in German as it concerns a "pan-Jewish" matter, which he would like all participants to understand.[51]

In the aftermath of World War I and the Balfour Declaration, Zionist politics evinced a structural shift, as London became its imperial center of gravity. Moreover, the consolidation of the principle of national self-determination in European politics—predicated on shared ethnicity, territory, and language—strengthened Zionists' resolve to mobilize it. Against this backdrop, not knowing Hebrew, from the point of view of Zionists in Eastern Europe and Palestine, had detrimental implications, as it impeded Jews' ability to demonstrate their national cohesiveness. The Zionist Congress witnessed in these years more vocal resentment over the language problem. In a speech given in German in the 1921 congress, Jabotinsky asserted that he had intended not to say "a single word" in any language other than Hebrew, adding: "We will pay a heavy price for the fact that this congress is linguistically foreign and hence acquires foreign characteristics." He explained that it was only because he sought to "attack" certain participants who do not speak Hebrew that he turned to German. He added that he was hoping that "this would be the last time."[52] Jabotinsky's hope, however, had yet to materialize. A Hebrew periodical reported during the 1927 Congress that despite the fact that Hebrew, Yiddish, and English were accepted languages of speech, German remained "the true 'owner' of the congress."[53]

At this point, however, we should ask what kind of German was heard in the congress. The answer is not straightforward. A Yiddish writer who participated in the 1902 Congress noted that the congress was "its own little world" with its own congress language ("*kongres-loshen*"). It is "brief and sharp.... It is neither holy nor mundane. It isn't German, or French, or English, or Russian. It's ... kongres-loshen," comprising a limited number of matter-of-fact words necessary to get by in the congress hall.[54] Other participants and reporters frequently referred to the language of the congress as Kongressdeutsch—a form of Yiddishized German, or perhaps Germanized Yiddish, which served as a surrogate language in the multilingual setting of the congress. German Zionist Heinrich Loewe asserted that Kongressdeutsch "was extremely close to Hochdeutsch."[55] On the other hand, some historians asserted that Kongressdeutsch was essentially Yiddish,[56] or "a highly Germanized form of Yiddish" invented by Eastern European delegates.[57] According to Yiddish scholar Nathan Süsskind, Kongressdeutsch was nothing but the recent manifestation of a longer phenomenon of Yiddish speakers attempting to speak in German while in fact speaking Yiddish.[58] By the same token, Yiddish linguist Yudl Mark placed Kongressdeutsch within a historical tradition of attempts to "refine" Yiddish and bring it closer to "proper" German.[59]

A Russian delegate recalled how his compatriots could not participate in discussions in the first congress because of the language barrier. Only in the following years, after acquiring Kongressdeutsch, could they engage in the discussions.[60] From this remark, it seems that Kongressdeutsch was indeed closer to German. Chaim Weizman wrote that "every Jew thought he knew German very well, but Herzl's German was not Kongressdeutsch," hence strengthening the view that Kongressdeutsch meant simple, unembellished German.[61] According to a perceptive definition of an American Jewish journalist, a self-proclaimed speaker of Kongressdeutsch, it was "neither German nor Yiddish but a rather interesting conflict between the two."[62]

The different views indicate how, depending on the point of view of the speaker, Kongressdeutsch could mean German, Yiddish, both, or neither. It could serve as a means of communication and of miscommunication. For Yiddish speakers, Kongressdeutsch embodied the extent to which Yiddish could be modified to maximally approximate German. For German speakers, Kongressdeutsch embodied the extent to which German could be simplified to be comprehensible to Yiddish speakers. Kongressdeutsch was not a clear linguistic entity but a discursive site of interaction between the speakers of these languages. The fact that Kongressdeutsch could not be easily defined was one of its main sources of practicality, allowing participants to transcend some of the political sensitivities involved in making a language choice, while maintaining the impression of German and the respectability it presumed.

It was the rise of the Third Reich that diminished German's eroding centrality in the congress. In his opening speech in August 1933, Sokolow started by speaking in Hebrew, then announcing that his next words would be in "the preferred international language of politics," French.[63] As German was heard less and less in the congress, it was not only Hebrew but also Yiddish that gained legitimacy as an alternative to German. An American Yiddish periodical reporting from the congress declared: "Kongressdeutsch is no more. [Only] Hebrew and Yiddish are spoken," adding that even those who had previously spoken Kongressdeutsch were now speaking in Yiddish.[64] That said, such reports should be taken with a pinch of salt, not least because the question of how to describe the linguistic practice of the congress was, more often than not, a matter of perspective.

Conclusion

After the establishment of the State of Israel, the pre-Holocaust quarrels within the Zionist movement over language questions were often misrepresented, or simply forgotten. Rather expectedly, German figured prominently in postwar political and cultural debates as the language of the Nazi murderers.[65] While the "Germanness" of early Zionism was never concealed, it tended to be framed as part of the "Western-centric" phase of Zionism.

Yet as I have argued here, the Jewish history of the German language was never confined to German-speaking lands, and German was not merely the linguistic and spiritual possession of German Jews. It served as an important vehicle for political agitation across borders, a marker of Jewish affinity with imperial interests, a language of mass political action, a vessel of Jewish emancipation and enlightenment, and, above all, a language of profound import in Ashkenazi culture owing to its relation to Yiddish. It was the latter factor that also facilitated a constant—if often contentious—interaction between Jews in different parts of the diaspora. As a cultural marker, German was mobilized to delineate the boundaries of respectable conduct, to demonstrate the cohesiveness of the Jewish world, or to prove its fragmentation. When discussing the history of German Jewry, it is worth bearing in mind that the meaning of "German" in Jewish societies was shaped not only by those born and educated into German culture but also by broader circles of Jews from Eastern Europe for whom German was part and parcel of their political and intellectual horizon.

On the surface, the linguistic tensions in Zionism were an inevitable outcome of the Jewish multilingual condition. Yet these tensions and their manifestations cannot be properly deciphered without paying heed to broader historical processes underlying the transformations of European Jewry and German nationhood since the Enlightenment. Paradoxically, German was a crucial vehicle in the formation of a political movement that sought to challenge the historical legacies of German in Jewish life. In this respect, the case of German epitomized the difficulties involved in creating an autonomous Jewish sphere. By speaking or not speaking German, Zionists were engaging in a debate on the proper way to express Jewish nationhood. At the same time, they were inadvertently weighing in on a perennial question that had its fraught meanings in Jewish history: *Was ist deutsch*?

Notes

I am grateful to David Feldman, Yaniv Feller, Skye Doney, and Sunny Yudkoff for their comments on previous drafts of this chapter.

    1. Zionistische Vereinigung für Deutschland, *Zionistisches A-B-C Buch* (Berlin: Zionistisches Zentralbureau, 1908), 276.

    2. Joachim Doron, "Social Concepts Prevalent in German Zionism: 1883–1914," *Studies in Zionism* 5 (April 1982): 1–31.

    3. For instance: Stefan Vogt, *Subalterne Positionierungen: Der deutsche Zionismus im Feld des Nationalismus in Deutschland, 1890–1933* (Göttingen: Wallstein Verlag, 2016); Michael Berkowitz, *Zionist Culture and West European Jewry before the First World War* (New York: Cambridge University Press, 1993); Steven E. Aschheim, *At the Edges of Liberalism: Junctions of European, German, and Jewish History* (New York: Palgrave Macmillan,

2012), 39–55; Yfaat Weiss, "Central European Ethnonationalism and Zionist Binationalism," *Jewish Social Studies* 11, no. 1 (Fall 2004): 93–117; Mark H. Gelber, *Melancholy Pride: Nation, Race, and Gender in the German Literature of Cultural Zionism* (Tübingen: Niemeyer Verlag, 2000); George L. Mosse, *German Jews beyond Judaism* (Cincinnati: Hebrew Union College Press, 1985).

4. For a detailed account of the history of German in Central and Eastern Europe and its impact on Jewish nationalism, see Marc Volovici, *German as a Jewish Problem: The Language Politics of Jewish Nationalism* (Stanford, CA: Stanford University Press, 2020).

5. Jeffrey A. Grossman, *The Discourse on Yiddish in Germany: From the Enlightenment to the Second Empire* (Rochester, NY: Camden House, 2000); Aya Elyada, *A Goy Who Speaks Yiddish: Christians and the Jewish Language in Early Modern Germany* (Stanford, CA: Stanford University Press, 2012); Sander Gilman, *Jewish Self-Hatred: Anti-Semitism and the Hidden Language of the Jews* (Baltimore: Johns Hopkins University Press, 1986).

6. Peter Freimark, "Language Behaviour and Assimilation: The Situation of the Jews in Northern Germany in the First Half of the Nineteenth Century," *Leo Baeck Institute Year Book* 24, no. 1 (January 1979): 157–78.

7. Jacob Toury, "Die Sprache als Problem der jüdischen Einordnung im deutschen Kulturraum," *Jahrbuch des Instituts für deutsche Geschichte* 4 (1982): 75–96; Dietz Bering, "Jews and the German Language: The Concept of Kulturnation and Anti-Semitic Propaganda," in *Identity and Intolerance: Nationalism, Racism, and Xenophobia in Germany and the United States*, ed. Norbert Finzsch and Dietmar Schirmer (Cambridge: Cambridge University Press, 1998), 251–91; Shulamit Volkov, "Sprache als Ort der Auseinandersetzung mit Juden und Judentum in Deutschland, 1780–1933," in *Jüdische Intellektuelle und die Philologen in Deutschland, 1871–1933*, ed. Wilfried Barner and Christoph König (Göttingen: Wallstein, 2001), 223–38.

8. Richard Wagner, "Judaism in Music," in *Richard Wagner: Stories and Essays*, ed. Charles Osborne (London: Peter Owen, 1973), 27.

9. Gabriel Riesser, *Gesammelte Schriften* (1867; repr., Hildesheim: Georg Olms, 2001), 2:183.

10. Mordechai Breuer, "1873: Samson Raphael Hirsch Oversees the Secession of Jewish Orthodoxy in Nineteenth-Century Germany," in *Yale Companion to Jewish Writing and Thought in German Culture, 1096–1996*, ed. Sander L. Gilman and Jack Zipes (New Haven, CT: Yale University Press, 1997), 205–11.

11. Jakob Wassermann, *Mein Weg als Deutscher und Jude* (Berlin: S. Fischer, 1921), 48. Translation from Bering, "Jews and the German," 251.

12. Volovici, *German as a Jewish Problem*; Tobias Brinkmann, *Migration und Transnationalität* (Paderborn: Verlag Ferdinand Schöningh, 2012); Jay Howard Geller and Leslie Morris, eds., *Three-Way Street: Jews, Germans, and the Transnational* (Ann Arbor: University of Michigan Press, 2016).

13. Michael K. Silber, "Josephinian Reforms," in *The YIVO Encyclopedia of Jews in Eastern Europe*, ed. Gershon David Hundert (New Haven, CT: Yale University Press, 2008), 1:831–34.

14. Michael K. Silber, "The Historical Experience of German Jewry and Its Impact on Haskalah and Reform in Hungary," in *Toward Modernity: The European Jewish Model*, ed. Jacob Katz (New Brunswick, NJ: Transaction Books, 1987), 107–57, 127.

15. Khone Shmeruk, *Yiddish Literature: Aspects of Its History* [in Hebrew] (Tel Aviv: Mif'alim universita'iyim le'hotsa'ah le'or, 1978), 261–93.

16. Isaac-Bär Levinsohn, *Teuda Be-Israel* (1828; Vilnius, 1855), 38–39.

17. Tobias Grill, *Der Westen im Osten: Deutsches Judentum und jüdische Bildungsreform in Osteuropa (1783–1939)* (Göttingen: Vandenhoeck & Ruprecht, 2013), 62–153.

18. Israel Bartal, "The Image of Germany and German Jewry in East European Jewish Society during the 19th Century," in *Danzig, between East and West: Aspects of Modern Jewish History*, ed. Isadore Twersky (Cambridge, MA: Harvard University Press, 1985), 3–17.

19. Steffen Krogh, "'Dos iz eyne vahre geshikhte...': On the Germanization of Eastern Yiddish in the Nineteenth Century," in *Jews and Germans in Eastern Europe*, ed. Tobias Grill (Berlin: De Gruyter, 2018), 88–114; Volovici, *German as a Jewish Problem*, 190–97; Rakmiel Peltz, "The Undoing of Language Planning from the Vantage of Cultural History: Two Twentieth Century Examples," *Undoing and Redoing Corpus Planning*, ed. Michael Clyne (Berlin: De Gruyter, 1997), 327–56.

20. Ahad Ha-Am, "Pirkei zikhronot," in *Kol kitve ahad ha-am* (Jerusalem: Dvir, 1964), 466–67, 495.

21. Leon Pinsker, *Autoemancipation! Mahnruf an seine Stammesgenossen von einem russischen Juden* (Berlin: Commissions-Verlag von W. Issleib, 1882).

22. Dmitry Shumsky, *Beyond the Nation-State: The Zionist Political Imagination from Pinsker to Ben-Gurion* (New Haven, CT: Yale University Press, 2018), 24–49.

23. Marc Volovici, "Leon Pinsker's *Autoemancipation!* and the Emergence of German as a Language of Jewish Nationalism," *Central European History* 50, no. 1 (March 2017): 34–58.

24. Volovici, "Leon Pinsker's *Autoemancipation!*," 43–44.

25. [Perets Smolenskin], "Yedi'at sfarim," *Ha-Shahar* 3 (1883): 185.

26. Theodor Herzl, *Der Judenstaat: Versuch einer modernen Lösung der Judenfrage* (Leipzig; Vienna: M. Breitenstein, 1896), 75. Translation from Theodor Herzl, *The Jewish State: An Attempt at a Modern Solution of the Jewish Question*, trans. Sylvie d'Avigdor and Israel Cohen (New York: Scopus, 1943), 100.

27. Theodor Herzl, *Zionistisches Tagebuch 1895–1899*, ed. Johannes Wachten and Chaya Harel (Berlin: Ullstein, 1983), 2:90.

28. Berkowitz, *Zionist Culture*, 8–39; George L. Mosse, "Max Nordau, Liberalism and the New Jew," *Journal of Contemporary History* 27, no. 4 (1992).

29. Paul Nathan, *Palästina und palästinensischer Zionismus* (Berlin: H. S. Hermann, 1914), 4.

30. Ahad Ha-Am to Osip Zeitlin, 24 August 1913, in *Ahad Ha-Am: mikhtavim be'inyanei erets yisrael (1891–1926)*, ed. Shulamit Laskov (Jerusalem: Yad Ben Zvi, 2000), 444–45.

31. Achad Ha-am, "Zur Sprachenfrage an den jüdischen Schulen Palästinas," *Ost und West* 1 (January 1914): 19–26, 26.

32. This section is partially based on Volovici, *German as a Jewish Problem*, 93–96, 117–18, 146, 197–99.

33. *Stenographisches Protokoll der Verhandlungen des II. Zionisten-Congresses gehalten zu Basel vom 28. bis 31. August 1898* (Vienna: Verlag des Vereines "Erez Israel," 1898), 72–73.

34. *Stenographisches Protokoll 1898*, 94.

35. At the time, "jargon" was commonly used to refer to Yiddish. *Stenographisches Protokoll 1898*, 181.

36. *Stenographisches Protokoll 1898*, 172.

37. *Stenographisches Protokoll 1898*, 133.

38. Ivonne Meybohm, *David Wolffsohn: Aufsteiger, Grenzgänger, Mediator* (Göttingen: Vandenhoeck & Ruprecht, 2013), 28–29, 119.

39. Leib Jaffe, *Bishelihut am: mikhtavim uteudot* (Jerusalem: Ha-sifria ha-tsiyonit, 1968), 263.

40. *Stenographisches Protokoll der Verhandlungen des V. Zionisten-Congresses in Basel, 26., 27., 28., 29. und 30. December 1901* (Vienna: Verlag des Vereins "Eretz Israel," 1901), 354–55.

41. "Der vierte Zionistencongress," *Krakauer jüdische Zeitung* 1, no. 23 (July 1900): 5.

42. Yosef Luria, "Be'shulei ma'halakho shel ha-kongres," *Sefer ha-kongres*, 161.

43. Ze'ev Jabotinsky, *Avtobiografia* (Jerusalem: Eri Jabotinsky, 1946), 48–49.

44. Michael Stanislawski, *Zionism and the Fin de Siècle: Cosmopolitanism and Nationalism from Nordau to Jabotinsky* (Berkeley: University of California Press, 2001), 161–62.

45. *Stenographisches Protokoll der Verhandlungen des VII. Zionisten-Kongresses in Haag vom 14. bis inklusive 21. August 1907* (Cologne: Juedischer Verlag, 1907), 336.

46. *Stenographisches Protokoll 1907*, 337.

47. *Stenographisches Protokoll 1907*, 339.

48. *Stenographisches Protokoll 1907*, 339.

49. *Stenographisches Protokoll der Verhandlungen des X. Zionisten-Kongresses in Basel vom 9. bis inklusive 15. August 1911* (Berlin, Leipzig: Kommission beim Juedischen Verlag, 1911), 265.

50. *Stenographisches Protokoll 1911*, 210–11.

51. *Stenographisches Protokoll der Verhandlungen des XI. Zionisten-Kongresses in Basel vom 2. bis 9. September 1913* (Berlin, Leipzig: Kommission beim Juedischen Verlag, 1914), 317.

52. *Stenographisches Protokoll der Verhandlungen des XII. Zionisten-Kongresses in Karlsbad vom 1. bis 14. September 1921* (Berlin: Jüdischer Verlag, 1922), 174–75.

53. M. Ungerfeld, "Ha-kongres ha-hamisha asar, mikhtavim me'ha-kongres," *Ha-Tsfira*, 6 September 1927, 2.

54. E. L. Lewinsky, "A bisele kongres-loshen," *Der Yud*, 16 January 1902.

55. Heinrich Loewe, *Die Sprachen der Juden* (Cologne: Jüdischer Verlag, 1911), 60.

56. Eli Lederhendler, *Jewish Responses to Modernity: New Voices in America and Eastern Europe* (New York: New York University Press, 1994), 15; Raphael Patai, *Tents of Jacob: The Diaspora, Yesterday and Today* (Englewood Cliffs, NJ: Prentice-Hall, 1971), 128.

57. Stanislawski, *Zionism and the Fin de Siècle*, 161.
58. Natan Süsskind, "Printsipn baym forshn yidishe leshoynes," *Yidishe shprakh* 25, no. 1 (June 1965): 1–17, 3.
59. Yudl Mark, "Problemen baym normiren di yidishe klal-shprakh," *Yidishe shprakh* 18, no. 2 (September 1958): 33–50, 38.
60. Gershon Swet, "Russian Jews in Zionism and the Building of Palestine," in *Russian Jewry*, ed. Jacob Frumkin, Gregor Aronson, and Alexis Goldenweiser (New York: Thomas Yoseloff, 1966), 1:172–208, 191.
61. Chaim Weizman, "Fifty Years of Zionism," in *The Jubilee of the First Zionist Congress, 1897–1947* (Jerusalem: The Executive of the Zionist Organization, 1947), 9–24, 11.
62. Meyer Wolfe Weisgal, *Meyer Weisgal... So Far: An Autobiography* (New York: Random House, 1972), 94.
63. *Stenographisches Protokoll der Verhandlungen des XVIII. Zionistenkongresses und der dritten Tagung des Council der Jewish Agency für Palästina, Prag, 21. August bis 4. September 1933* (Vienna: Fiba Verlag, 1934), 27.
64. Yehuda Piltsch, "Der goldener tseylem," *Daily Jewish Courier*, 7 September 1933.
65. Liora R. Halperin, *Babel in Zion: Jews, Nationalism, and Language Diversity in Palestine, 1920–1948* (New Haven, CT: Yale University Press, 2014), 222–30; Volovici, *German as a Jewish Problem*, 200–228.

12

Photography between Empire and Nation

German-Jewish Displacement and the Global Camera

Rebekka Grossmann

A group of Iraqi women stands close together. Their veils cover their heads and bodies; the dark color of their clothes contrasts with the bright background. Their silhouettes can hardly be distinguished and their proximity to one another makes them appear like a single statue. Nevertheless, they engage with the photographer, each one in her own way (fig. 12.1). The faces of the women in the front even shine through their face covers, revealing that they are not only aware of the camera but interested in meeting its gaze. The woman on the right places her arm on her hips; the figure at the front makes an opposite pose, by crossing her arms. A different version of the same photograph discloses the high-heel shoes worn under their gowns.

The picture was taken by the German-Jewish photographer Tim Gidal in Basra, Iraq, in 1940—a stop on his travels between India and Palestine. While Gidal's career as a photographer had begun in the close circles of late 1920s Berlin and Munich, his photography in the following decade would be characterized by displacement and travel. With the political situation deteriorating, he left Germany in the early 1930s on a series of trips that brought him to Palestine and Eastern Europe, Switzerland, and back to Palestine, before reaching Britain in 1938. In 1940 he traveled to India on a chartered British ship that sent a contingent of civil servants and marines to Asia.[1] This chapter follows Gidal along parts of his journey to Central and South Asia. It explores how this Weimar German photographer perceived the regions through which he traveled and argues that the way Gidal captured his surroundings was shaped by both

Photography between Empire and Nation 235

Figure 12.1. Tim Gidal, Basra, Iraq, 1940. (Image courtesy of the Israel Museum, Jerusalem.)

his training as a photojournalist and his personal story of racialized exclusion from German society. His multiple displacements turned his journeys into temporary homes and shaped his gaze and his work. Gidal's photography of both colonial and anticolonial contexts, accordingly, reflected the nature of his artistic aspirations and his interactions as a stateless traveler. Ultimately, his photography would shape postwar Western conceptions of what came to be dubbed the Global South, contributing to Western narratives of global connectivity.

Inspired by the lessons learned from Mosse's scholarship, this chapter supports and corroborates the suggestions made by Aleida Assmann in her keynote lecture during the 2019 Mosse's Europe conference to follow Mosse's advice and "reimagine" the nation.[2] It does so by leaving Europe's past in order to later return to it with the aim of showing that German-Jewish history and culture is, in fact, a long series of intercultural and interreligious encounters both within and beyond Germany's borders. It is a history that engages with the modern striving for national sovereignty while also engaging in its pitfalls and alternatives. The women in Basra, veiled but intrigued by the camera, reflect the mutual interests that ignited Gidal's photographic reconsiderations of the nation and the layers of knowledge acquired and unraveled by this kind of stateless travel.

At the same time, the Basra photograph and the travels that brought Gidal to Central Asia and India challenge simple, harmonious narratives of the humanitarian photographic encounter at the peripheries of World War II. This kind of tension will surface throughout the examples that follow. Such tension is symptomatic for the process of seeing and unseeing through the camera in the wartime Middle East and South Asia and anticipates ways this camera would shape Western perceptions of the Global South for years to come. The travels of the photographer Gidal, who was a friend of George L. Mosse's, demonstrate that extending the geographical angle of German-Jewish experience reveals new insights about the histories of the Jewish presence in colonial contexts, the roots of modern Western perceptions of the Global South, and the role of Jewish political voices in the humanitarian discourses that characterized the early Cold War years.

Cameras Astray

The kind of photography that had shaped Gidal's early career acquired its political voice through its close connection with journalism. Initially, a persistent skepticism prevailed among the avant-garde over whether photography could be anything more than a commodity. The Bauhaus artists and designers were initially disinterested in identifying with the mass medium they believed photography had become.[3] To its founders, photography was a product of the "age of mechanical reproduction" and, as such, corrupted by the lures of modern life, placed in the direct service of mass consumption.[4] Slowly, however, a new photographic formalism, suggested, for example, by László Moholy-Nagy, made its way into the school's artistic production. Moholy-Nagy demanded radical shifts of perspectives, aimed at directing the spectator's senses to what had hitherto been ignored and thereby reached a new level of authenticity.[5] Searching for ways to challenge social narratives, journalism welcomed such new forms of seeing and offered a platform for merging photographic formalism and the kind of documentary seeing that turned photography into a sociopolitical voice. This combination worked at bringing local political struggles into the public debate, illustrated, for example, by the photomontages of John Heartfield or the emerging "photographers' guild" of the large liberal illustrated papers. Many of the members of this "guild" ultimately bridged the gap between the Bauhaus and the street, moving back and forth between the two.[6]

The focus of these photographers was primarily on domestic political and social issues. Yet photography's increasing mobility, enabled through technical advancements, allowed for the growth of an international exchange of ideas and techniques as well as the importation of global topics. One of the pioneers of such new international travel photography was the Swiss photographer Walter Bosshard. In 1930 Bosshard traveled to India on assignment for the *Munich Illustrated Press* to document Mahatma Gandhi's growing struggle for Indian independence. Accompanying Gandhi on his "March to the Salt" and portraying him and his followers in five consecutive weekly photo essays, Bosshard familiarized German audiences with India's political debates.[7] Even earlier, in 1928 and 1929, the German-Jewish photographer Lotte Errell had undertaken a trip through Africa; in 1931, she published the photobook *Kleine Reise zu schwarzen Menschen*. While the title of the book is racially charged, Errell's photographic encounters sought to suggest a new, more egalitarian angle to the photographed subjects by expanding the photographic vocabulary of travel photography through low angles, close-ups, or other rather unconventional photographic approaches.[8] Both photographers were preceded by the Austrian-Jewish traveler Alice Schalek, whose cameratic lens, while guided by the traditional gaze of the explorer-traveler in the beginning of the century, turned increasingly toward local social and political issues during the 1920s.[9] Photographers like Schalek, Errell, and Bosshard reimagined travel photography by actively seeking contact with the inhabitants and the political topics of places that had formerly been pursued primarily for their exotic allure. In their photographs, they worked to diminish the sense of distance between the photographer and the landscape or peoples being observed, thereby rejecting earlier attempts to assert the presumed superiority of the "Western" photographer over and against the colonial subject.[10]

These first attempts to extend photographic studies beyond the immediate *Arbeitermilieu* instilled within the photographer's guild of the late 1920s the understanding that photography could challenge global stereotypes. Tim Gidal, joining the photojournalistic guild in 1929, would later attest that he was influenced by this kind of new, ostensibly more political kind of travel photography. In a later portrait of these first years of German photojournalism, he would grant photographers like Bosshard the status of a trailblazer who engaged in entirely new ways with foreign contexts.[11]

Many of the styles promoted in this new kind of documentary photography were fostered by international artists' exchanges; the 1929 Stuttgart exhibition *Film und Foto*, for example, featured many international guests.[12] The ambition for international exchange coincided with new international frameworks of global governance—such as first and foremost the League of Nations—which were closely followed by photojournalists across the globe.[13] The twilight years of the Weimar Republic and the political upheavals of 1933 saw a forceful acceleration of these artists' liberal internationalism. Many of the photographers who had actively contributed to the liberal press were driven out of Germany and found themselves abroad, where they shifted their focus to new local affairs. Tim Gidal was one of them. After travels in Europe and Palestine, he departed for Central and South Asia in 1940 alongside British officials. In Bombay, Gidal met Mahatma Gandhi and Pandit Nehru and was invited to join them at their All India Congress Committee meeting.[14] Reports about his trip are scarce. His photographs, however, demonstrate just how much he was influenced by the kind of reportage his colleagues had introduced. At the same time, his travels through Asia reflect the many layers that colored his stateless travel as a German Jew and a passenger arriving on the coattails of British Imperial functionaries.

Exchanging Viewpoints

Gidal was not simply a stowaway with the Royal Navy and British diplomats. Some of his impressions of early 1930s Palestine suggest a favorable view of the British presence in the Middle East; in the late 1930s, he spent extended periods of time in London, and after his trip to India he would work for some time as an army reporter in Cairo.[15] Yet from the start, Gidal's photographs signify the liminal status of his works as objects straddling experiences of displacement, migration, and photographic exploration. While his photographs of India must be scrutinized for photographic orientalism, shaped by a Western gaze, they also mirror the ambition to acquire a distinct knowledge about the places and people he saw. His "homelessness" seemed to fuel the need to "adopt" new places with his gaze and to enter the respective environments as fully as possible, thereby acquiring a new kind of knowledge and translating it into visuals.[16]

The appearance of German-Jewish refugees in India was no rarity. Since 1933 large numbers of German Jews had entered India as escapees from German rule, Gidal among them.[17] However, he did not arrive in India with the intention of finding temporary refuge. The historical record and his short report of the trip do not indicate that he was in contact with any of the local *landsmanschaftn* or local representatives of Zionist organizations, which were in frequent contact with the Keren Hayesod and the Keren Kayemet in Jerusalem.[18] Instead, Gidal's travels were shaped by the way photographers experienced and handled exile: by forming ties through an ongoing flow of their images received by journalists and editors who, though interested in the peripheries of World War II, were not able to see these places for themselves. While local connections might indeed have helped facilitate his contact with Gandhi, a prime catalyst for the relationship was his camera.[19]

Beginning with Walter Bosshard's reports in 1930, photographers had become welcome visitors to Gandhi's India; photography had served Gandhi's movement well. His closest advisors themselves turned to photography to document their struggle. Mahatma Gandhi's nephew Kanu Gandhi, for example, portrayed his uncle extensively throughout the final and most decisive decade of his life.[20] Such close interest in photography among India's leaders demonstrates that for travelers like Gidal the camera was not only an object of documentation but also a kind of cultural barter that could facilitate the movement's entrance into global consciousness and thus grant him access to contexts that would otherwise have been difficult to enter. A portrait of Gandhi taken during the All India Congress Committee meeting of 1940 reflects this mutual interest of political leader and photographer (fig. 12.2).

Gidal witnessed the speech from the raised dais accessible only to Gandhi's closest followers. Yet the photographer did not capture the leader at eye level. Rather, he portrayed Gandhi from a slightly low angle, which causes him to appear taller and, consequently, more authoritative. This perspective is only enhanced by inclusion of the audience members in the frame. Male and female congress participants are seated in rows on a lower level, listening to Gandhi's words. Once again, the emphasis of the photograph appears to make Gandhi stand tall, above the crowd. Gandhi's elevated index finger points up in the air in front of him, inviting his audience, no less than Gidal's viewer, to continue to raise their gaze.

The hall is decorated with flags of the Indian National Congress and with garlands hanging from the ceiling and wrapped around the columns. While their presence is notable, they are not in focus. Rather, Gidal renders them blurry, avoiding anything that would detract from the crisp appearance of Gandhi, simply clothed and concomitantly concise in his goals and speech. The combination of the simplicity of the speaker and the framing of the portrait showing him above a silently listening crowd extends the speaker's authority. By elevating the leader visually, he invigorates his cause, writing his own fascination with the leader into the photograph and offering himself to be a mouthpiece to Indian anticolonial resistance.

Aware that he was one of very few Western photojournalists roaming South Asia during the war, Gidal seemed eager to introduce the world to Indian national emancipation and invite audiences to empathize with India's disenfranchised. One of his receptive contacts in the West was Herbert L. Matthews, a foreign correspondent for the *New York Times*. Matthews had spent the Civil War in

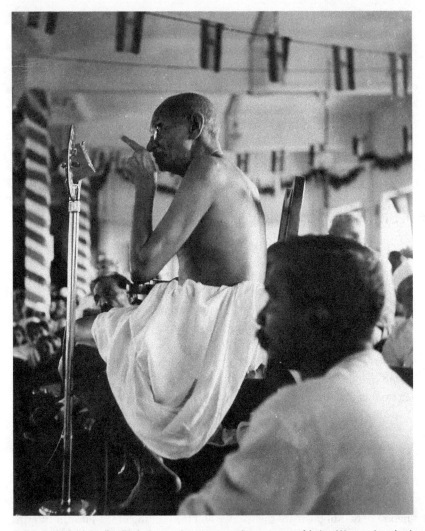

Figure 12.2. Tim Gidal, Gandhi, All India Congress Committee, 1940. (Image courtesy of the Israel Museum, Jerusalem.)

Spain, where he might have made contact with photographers who would put him in touch with Gidal.[21]

"Saint or Charlatan?" Gandhi's India as a Comment

Matthews introduced his March 1943 article on Gandhi with the question whether the leader of the movement was a "Saint" or a "Charlatan," a question that suggests limited knowledge about the Indian national movement among American readers at the time.[22] Portraying Gandhi as a national and religious leader, controversial in India and Britain but ultimately too powerful in his claims and following to be ignored, the journalist put a strong emphasis on Gandhi's abilities to draw his political power from his religious practices.[23] The text was accompanied by two photographs of Gandhi taken by Gidal. The first shows him as a larger-than-life figure; the dark print emphasizes his bright but simple wear. The photograph fills as much space as the text, supporting the impression that he and his movement could not further be ignored by the West. The garland diagonally cutting the background on the first page suggests that the photograph was part of Gidal's series of photographs of the Congress Committee meeting. The second photograph complements this view by showing Gandhi as part of a large crowd at a railway station, conveying the sense not only that he was a national leader but also that he was well connected, mobile, and that his voice was being heard across the country. In this photograph, too, the focus is on Gandhi's simplicity traveling in trains and merging with groups of people like him. Gandhi, while lacking the usual visual signifiers of a celebrity, is elevated by Gidal to the status of a leader. During his 1940 visit, the photographer rendered a similar service to one of Gandhi's fellows at the Congress Committee meeting, however, this time in a way that suggests a note of commentary on the responsibility that comes with power (fig. 12.3).

The speaker, Abul Kalam Azad, an Islamic theologian and the leader of the Indian National Congress in the early 1940s, appears in this photograph from an angle lower than that used to capture Gandhi. The angle and the garlands cut the scene diagonally in the background; the leader's lifted arms, closed eyes, and open mouth render the photograph dynamic and dramatic in nature. The round microphone with the letters "Chicago Radio" alludes to a direct medial connection between India and the Western world, adding to the grandiose appearance of the speaker and the implied reach of his speech. However, the camera comes a bit too close and is a bit too low to not imply a certain feeling of trepidation. Taking into account the backdrop of the photographer's experience with racialized exclusion in Europe, the photograph's strong emphasis on charismatic authority conveys unease rather than unrestrained admiration.

Not only do his photojournalistic views of Gandhi and his movement substantiate the impression that Gidal sought to actively engage with the local struggle for self-determination and offer his own commentaries through his camera, but his images of the street and of the people he met also reflect his impressions of the relationship between the Indian national movement and the British colonizers. One street scene, in its photographic framing, carries traits of a swan song on imperialist power while also offering comments on the risks

Figure 12.3. Tim Gidal, All India Congress Committee, 1940. (Image courtesy of the Israel Museum, Jerusalem.)

of new power imbalances and ill-considered substitutes to the imperial regime (fig. 12.4).

The picture shows a couple in a rickshaw drawn by a young boy with a turban. The man and woman seem to be locals or of East Asian descent. A car drives next to the rickshaw; lines on the ground and cables spanned above the street let the spectator know that the street is also used by streetcars, adding to the mélange of temporalities shaping the street scene. A policeman, ordered to manage Bombay's traffic, stands on a round pedestal. He wears what looks like an imperial uniform and his arm points in the direction of traffic, but the pedestal shows signs of rust and the man's authority is ignored by the different

Figure 12.4. Tim Gidal, Bombay, India, 1940. (Image courtesy of the Israel Museum, Jerusalem.)

drivers, an impression that the photographer corroborates by placing him at the margin of the frame. The wide road is flanked by large imperial buildings, an advertisement decorates the street scene from the background. White, centered letters read "Brooke Bond Tea," promoting Britain's largest tea company, which, while it had its origins in nineteenth-century London, had come to dominate the Indian colonial market too, selling Indian products at British prices. A few men mingle underneath the poster, unconcerned by the British grandeur it pretends to represent. The photograph seems to suggest that everything that reflects the British presence is driven by the need to be elevated or oversized or come with grand gestures of the kind the policeman tries to make to be acknowledged. At the same time the photograph provides evidence of an unequal distribution of wealth and the persistence of imbalances of power prominently signified by the rickshaw, its frail driver, and its placid passengers. The street scene mirrors the ambition that drove European street photography of the late 1920s to catch a moment and convey an atmosphere. While Gidal's other images offer a reflection of his fascination with Gandhi's cause, this snapshot points to the decay of imperial power and the continuities of colonial exploitation.

A third perspective on India in 1940 is offered by Gidal through close meetings with India's population, reflecting the photographer's ambition to "participate," which he claimed was one of the most important incentives of his work as a photojournalist.[24] His portraits of India's people confirm this aspiration. While during some such encounters Gidal's own stance as a Western visitor to the East shines through, reflecting the camera's limitations to act as a mediating device, it would be these photographs that would be characterized by a particularly long afterlife, shaping Western views long after Gidal's visit.

In one image, two men the photographer met in a private or semiprivate setting actively engage with Gidal, while a boy stares into the empty space behind the photographer (fig. 12.5). Everyone, including the photographer, sits on the floor; some more men mingle in the background. The two men looking at Gidal seem comfortable with the camera. While their clothes and demeanor appear simple, even poor, their eyes are radiant. Their posture and smile reflect their confidence. The little boy's stare likewise conveys security in a place where he seems to feel at home. Gidal's camera is situated between him and his interlocutors; it does not have to be tilted or lifted to create a distinct angle. The gaze is direct and straight, seeking to create an encounter; the photographer seems to suggest using the camera as a tool for translation, not distinction. The camera

Figure 12.5. Tim Gidal, family picture, 1940. (Image courtesy of the Israel Museum, Jerusalem.)

claims to create a *mise-en-scène* of the colonial context, not in the tradition of orientalist and colonialist photography from a distance but by offering insights of the nearest sense, thereby endowing the men with the agency of claiming a presence.

Some of the visual tropes Gidal employs remain rooted in an orientalist optics. With their smile reflecting lightheartedness, the scantily clad men corroborate the cynical Western habit of seeing a certain romantic beauty in poverty. Moreover, while the men are active participants in the encounter, they cannot decide about the photograph's use, its dissemination, or its reception. Gidal cannot call himself devoid of a certain imperial bias either, embracing the British presence in the Middle East and his life in London. He does not acknowledge—or does not engage with—the fact that the very reason he finds himself in India is also the reason for the local striving for power. At the same time, the mere fact that he travels through South Asia is a result of his marginalization and exclusion, which apparently makes him open to seeing and documenting the marginalization of others. His seeing turns both his own subjectivity and that of his colonial counterparts from victim-others into active shapers of their situation. While Gidal's German-Jewish story of refuge and the reason why he is in India is not immediately transmitted in the photographs, the connection between the desire to see the country through the eyes of its inhabitants—rather than its colonizers—and his individual experience becomes difficult to ignore. At the same time, his camera offers a tool of mediation that protects him from reproaches of partisanship. He can support local struggles for nationalism in spite of his loyalties to the British because his camera ostensibly merely translates to Western readers "What India wants from England," as one of the articles he supplied with photographs claimed to explain.[25]

The New "South"

Gidal's backstreet sights of the Indian population found a new platform more than ten years later in the 1956 photo book *My Village in India*. The book, which Gidal published together with his wife Sonia, appeared with the New York–based Pantheon Books and was subsequently translated into different languages and circulated widely. *My Village in India* was the first of a series of books on different "villages" in Korea, Brazil, Morocco, and Ghana, in addition to several countries in Europe such as Portugal, Norway, and Greece, published by Sonia and Tim Gidal during the 1950s and 1960s and directed primarily at young readers. The books were written as first-person accounts of children whose homes were portrayed in a series of photographs. They were curated as virtual trips around the world, inviting the young reader to identify with their peers. *My*

Figure 12.6. Sonia Gidal and Tim Gidal, *My Village in India*, cover. (New York: Pantheon Books, 1956.)

Figure 12.7. Sonia Gidal and Tim Gidal, *My Village in India*, 32. (New York: Pantheon Books, 1956.)

Village in India introduces children to the figure of the village's young inhabitant Dhan and follows him on a fictitious trip through his village (figs. 12.6, 12.7).

The inside of the binding features a map enabling readers to follow the journey through the village. The book then offers a variety of insights into Dhan's everyday life. Fellows to Gidal's travels recognize faces of his trip made in 1940 who now appear as the boy's "family members." One of them is presented as the boy's grandfather who is busy sowing rice. His face carries a daring look, confident and whimsical. The photograph promotes the feeling of a distinct skillfulness grounded in tradition, again celebrating the simplicity of preindustrial life in a paternalist fashion.

The book, while promoting knowledge and encounter, perpetuates the naive gaze of the Western tourist. The people represented continue to play the role of "protagonists" of "typical" village scenes. Books such as this were part of a larger discourse promoted by the different channels of cultural diplomacy eager to render those faces familiar that had now become part of a "Global South." One year prior to the publication of the Gidals' India book, the Museum of Modern Art had opened its exhibition *Family of Man*, which, compiled by photographer and photo curator Edward Steichen, promoted a similarly humanitarian agenda to the one Tim and Sonia Gidal offered with their photo books. Steichen's *Family* was meant as a mediating device between the world's different blocs, yet it was widely criticized for constructing a universal harmony that existed as such only in the Western mind.[26] The appearance of such celebrations of global solidarity was no haphazard embracing of universal values. It reflected larger political transformations, particularly the general attraction of new global humanitarian frameworks, accelerated in particular by the foundation of the United Nations in 1945 and the 1948 Declaration of Human Rights.[27] Images like Gidal's, who had entered his career when a similar internationalism had promoted the first transformation of travel photography in the late 1920s, show that the Weimar ambition for egalitarian views was carried into the Global South by displaced photographers. They also reveal that the exoticism that intrigued 1920s audiences continued to be an integral part of photography in colonial and postcolonial contexts. This ambivalence of a fascination for the rootedness represented by the villagers and the simultaneous promotion of bringing photographed objects and seeing audiences closer together in an effort to advocate global connections can be found to be a characteristic of Jewish exiles and migrant travelers of the kind Gidal represented. On the one hand, they shared voices advocating for individual determination, and on the other, they recognized the benefits of a distance to national causes. While his Jewish background and fascination for Zionism tied Gidal to the attraction of ethnic and individual self-determination, his profession put some of the securities that came with its convictions back into question, not however without making use of the same stereotypes that were in the way of such universal sights. Gidal's book, then, stands in continuity with his earlier images, but the purpose of the images has shifted. Instead of a connection between the fates of the disenfranchised, the photographs now propagated global connectivity across borders. The memories of exclusion and travel without a home turned into the demand for connectivity among nations and an ongoing Western engagement with the history of post-imperial contexts at a time when thinkers such as Hannah Arendt and Aimé Césaire began to suggest reading the histories of imperial and European anti-Jewish violence in conversation.[28] By the 1950s, Gidal's multidirectional encounters of 1940 read as early suggestions for a "multidirectional memory."

Conclusion

Tim Gidal was not the only or even the first European Jewish traveler in India. The Yiddish writer Perets Hirshbeyn, for example, had traveled in India more than a decade before, and he, too, oscillated in his perceptions and comments between a desire to grant importance to the Indian national cause and reiteration of an orientalist view.[29] At times, Gidal's insights seem to reflect such earlier attempts of Jewish travelers to position themselves between East and West. Yet while the indexical character of the photographs might have been a result of a photographic semiotics of power exerted by means of the apparatus, the encounters he captured must be seen in a larger context, namely, as the product both of a number of unplanned processes of displacement leveling and sharing experiences of powerlessness as well as of Gidal's sense of vocation and dedication as a photojournalist. This combination accounts for Gidal's double provincialization of the photographic and colonialist master narrative: on the one hand, by force—by the exclusion of the liberal photographic grammar that had been shaped by a distinct group of photojournalists and that shaped their seeing in return—and on the other hand, voluntary—by directing the photographic lens toward the Indian anticolonial struggle. This provincialization did not rid Gidal's gaze of the subject position of the Western visitor. The encounters between Gidal and the people he met often remained superficial. While some, like the men in India, met him eagerly, others, like the women in Basra, remained reserved. And yet the camera succeeded in engaging them in an interaction. Gidal's own openness, rooted in the necessity of travel, helped him modify his marginalization and that of his interlocutors by complicating it with the simultaneous attraction to both ethnic particularism and the modern universalist language he expected his camera to speak. His works can thus be said to have compromised both ghosts that Allan Sekula has claimed haunted much of twentieth-century photography: "the voice of a reifying technocratic objectivism and the redemptive voice of a liberal subjectivism."[30]

While some of the photographs rely on photographic liberalism and its limitations, born out of the dawn of the Weimar years and brought into foreign contexts, they remain documents of a distinct kind of "migrant knowledge." The new scenes and peoples Gidal encountered and whose portraits he transferred westward via the channels of journalistic circulation challenged a worldview.[31] His way of seeing was fueled by the aspiration to make the world as familiar a place as possible in times of exclusion and to challenge claims of a home necessarily bound to a particular territory or a nationalist creed. This kind of seeing was not limited to his wartime reflections; such vision would shape Western perceptions of countries in the Global South long thereafter. Gidal's images are part of the story of the trauma of Jewish exclusion, and they thus belong to the history and dynamics of German Jews beyond Germany. Such insights demonstrate that extending the scope of the modern German-Jewish experience enables an understanding of the variety of wartime German-Jewish realities and their influences on postwar perceptions of modern belonging. Navigating this discourse between inside and outside, foreign and common, is not only a matter of the past; it will also be one of the litmus tests for the future of Mosse's Europe.

Notes

1. Nachum Tim Gidal, "Photography Is My Passion," *Nachum Tim Gidal: Photographs, 1929–1991*, ed. The Open Museum (Migdal Tefen: Open Museum—Tefen Industrial Park, 1992), n.p.

2. Aleida Assmann, "Civilizing the Nation: Can Mosse's Europe Be Saved?" (keynote lecture, Mosse's Europe: New Perspectives in the History of German Judaism, Fascism, and Sexuality, Jüdisches Museum Berlin, 9 June 2019).

3. Andreas Haus, "Photography at the Bauhaus: Discovery of a Medium," in *Photography at the Bauhaus*, ed. Jeannine Fiedler (Cambridge, MA: MIT Press, 1990), 126–83, 127.

4. George L. Mosse, *German Jews beyond Judaism* (Cincinnati: Hebrew Union College Press, 1985), 59; Walter Benjamin, *Das Kunstwerk im Zeitalter seiner technischen Reproduzierbarkeit*, 4th ed. (Berlin: Suhrkamp Verlag, 2010).

5. See, for example, László Moholy-Nagy, "Production-Reproduction," in *Photography in the Modern Era: European Documents and Critical Writings, 1913–1940*, ed. Christopher Phillips (New York: Metropolitan Museum of Art/Aperture, 1989), 79–82.

6. For this development, see Daniel Magilow, *The Photography of Crisis: The Photo Essays of Weimar Germany* (University Park: Pennsylvania State University Press, 2012); Andrés Mario Zervigón, *John Heartfield and the Agitated Image: Photography, Persuasion, and the Rise of Avant-Garde Photomontage* (Chicago: University of Chicago Press, 2012).

7. Tim Gidal, *Deutschland: Beginn des modernen Photojournalismus* (Luzern: Bucher, 1972), 22–23. On new trends in the photography of travel in Weimar Germany, see also Gabriele Saure, "Eine neue Künstlergilde? Serielle Bildformen in der illustrierten Presse 1925 bis 1944," in *Photo-Sequenzen: Reportage, Bildgeschichten, Serien aus dem Ullstein Bilderdienst von 1925 bis 1944*, ed. Gabriele Saure (Berlin: Haus am Waldsee, 1993), 19–38.

8. Errell would later work for Ullstein, Associated Press, and *Life* magazine; the Africa photos were especially constitutive for her career. Britta Schilling, "Crossing Boundaries: German Women in Africa, 1919–33," in *German Colonialism and National Identity*, ed. Michael Perraudin and Juergen Zimmerer (New York: Routledge, 2010), 150–69.

9. Katharina Manojlovic, "Strolling through India: The Austrian Photographer and Journalist Alice Schalek," *Austrian Studies* 20 (2012): 193–205, 198.

10. An example is the photo book series *Orbis Terrarum*, which instructed its traveling photographers to omit everything that had been added to the landscape only recently. Roland Jaeger, "Die Länder der Erde im Bild: Die Reihe Orbis Terrarum im Verlag Ernst Wasmuth, Berlin, und im Atlantis-Verlag, Berlin/Zürich," in *Autopsie: Deutschsprachige Fotobücher 1918 bis 1945*, ed. Manfred Heiting and Roland Jaeger (Göttingen: Steidl, 2012), 98–131, 101.

11. Gidal, *Deutschland*, 22–23.

12. Karl Steinorth, ed., *Internationale Ausstellung des Deutschen Werkbundes, Film und Foto: Stuttgart, 1929* (Stuttgart: Deutsche Verlags-Anstalt GmbH, 1979), 13–14.

13. The prolific celebrity photographer Erich Salomon, for example, was a frequent guest to the League of Nations conventions in Geneva.

14. Tim Gidal, "A Photo Reporter in Israel," *Ariel* 57 (1984): 106–22, 120.

15. Gidal, "A Photo Reporter in Israel." Publishing favorable articles on the British presence in Palestine on the basis of Gidal's photographs was Stefan Lorant, who served as a photo editor to a variety of Gidal's contributions. Rebekka Grossmann, "Image Transfer and Visual Friction: Stating Palestine in the National Socialist Spectacle," *Leo Baeck Institute Year Book* 64 (2019): 19–45.

16. Simone Lässig and Swen Steinberg, "Knowledge on the Move: New Approaches toward a History of Migrant Knowledge," *Geschichte und Gesellschaft* 43, no. 3 (2017): 313–46, 325.

17. Joan G. Roland, *The Jewish Communities of India: Identity in a Colonial Era* (New Brunswick, NJ: Transaction Books, 1998), 177. They would be joined by a large stream of refugees from all over Europe, the Mediterranean, and the Middle East escaping persecution and war. Yasmin Khan, *India at War: The Subcontinent and the Second World War* (Oxford: Oxford University Press, 2015), 122–23.

18. On Zionist activities in India, see Roland, *The Jewish Communities of India*, 151, 233.

19. Gidal, "Photography Is My Passion," n.p.

20. See Peter Rühe, *Gandhi: A Photo Biography* (New York: Phaidon Press, 2001).

21. Anthony DePalma, "Myths of the Enemy: Castro, Cuba and Herbert L. Matthews of the *New York Times*," Kellogg Institute for International Studies Working Papers, July 2004, https://kellogg.nd.edu/sites/default/files/old_files/documents/313_0.pdf. Later, Matthews

would cover Castro's Cuba during the 1950s and would interview Che Guevara, contacts that would lead him to be accused of harboring communist sympathies but that also rendered him one of the foremost American documenters of decolonization movements across the globe. For photographers' and journalists' networks during the 1930s and 1940s, see Annette Vowinckel, "German (Jewish) Photojournalists in Exile: A Story of Networks and Success," *German History* 31, no. 4 (2013): 473–96.

22. Apparently, some strata of the American population, especially GIs stationed in India, were deliberately kept in ignorance about Indian domestic politics. Khan, *India at War*, 146.

23. Herbert L. Matthews, "Saint or Charlatan?," *New York Times*, 28 March 1943.

24. Gidal, "A Photo Reporter in Israel," 122.

25. Photograph of the article, Tim Gidal Collection, Israel Museum, publication unknown.

26. See Roland Barthes, "La grande famille des hommes," in *Mythologies* (Paris: Éditions du Seuil, 1957), 173–76; Allan Sekula, "The Traffic in Photographs," *Art Journal* 41, no. 1 (Spring 1981): 15–25; Fred Turner, "The Family of Man and the Politics of Attention in Cold War America," *Public Culture* 24, no. 1 (66) (2012): 55–84.

27. On international public policy models and the impact on civic engagement including the role of Jews in these discourses, see James Loeffler, *Rooted Cosmopolitans. Jews and Human Rights in the Twentieth Century* (New Haven, CT: Yale University Press, 2018). On the impact of the declaration of human rights in particular, see Loeffler, *Rooted Cosmopolitans*, 87.

28. Michael Rothberg discusses both works in support of his concept of "multidirectional memory" in *Multidirectional Memory: Remembering the Holocaust in the Age of Decolonization* (Stanford, CA: Stanford University Press, 2009), chaps. 2 and 3.

29. See Marusz Kałczewiak, "Anticolonial Orientalism: Perets Hirshbeyn's Indian Travelogue," *In Geveb: A Journal of Yiddish Studies* (July 2019): 1–20.

30. Allan Sekula, *Photography against the Grain: Essays and Photo Works, 1973–1983* (London: Mack, 2016), 93.

31. Lässig and Steinberg, "Knowledge on the Move," 337–38.

13

Max Nordau between George L. Mosse and Benzion Netanyahu

ADI ARMON

Nordau at the Margins

Max Nordau (né Simon Simcha Sudfeld [1849–1923]), the prominent Zionist thinker, novelist, journalist, physician, and culture and literary critic, author of *The Conventional Lies of Our Civilization* (1883), *Paradoxes* (1885), and *Degeneration* (1892), died in 1923 at the age of seventy-four. For many years, he was considered one of the most prominent Jewish intellectuals in the Zionist movement; indeed, he was second to, if no less famous than, the playwright, journalist, and founding figure of political Zionism, Theodor Herzl (1860–1904). However, in the final years of Nordau's life and in the decade following his death, he was nearly completely forgotten, and his ideas—about political Zionism, nineteenth-century bourgeois liberalism, positivism, and psychology—were abandoned and rejected, especially by mainstream Zionist circles.

Cultural Zionists instead had other sources of inspiration, including Ahad Ha'am (1856–1927). At the beginning of the century, Ahad Ha'am had engaged in an important, ideological debate with Nordau over Herzl's *Altneuland* (1902).[1] Yet by Nordau's death and even in his last years, the controversy had become muted. Socialist Zionists and the growing labor movement on the other side also had their own sources of inspiration, such as A. D. Gordon (1856–1922), who wrote about redemption through manual labor and cultivation of the soil. Other Marxist and socialist thinkers who wrote about the proletarian and class struggle were very far from Nordau's worldview and his Western European *fin de siècle* world. This world lay just too far from the emerging reality in the blistering Middle East, where Arabs and Jews found themselves on opposing sides, with growing violence and tension that would become the new focal point of political discourse.

Nordau was not the only Zionist thinker relegated to the margins of history. This lot was shared by Herzl too, as well as Leon Pinsker (1821–91), the author of *Auto-Emancipation*, or Israel Zangwill (1864–1926), the prime thinker behind the territorial movement. All or most of these Zionist thinkers were viewed by many young Zionists in Palestine as too European, bourgeois, clean, straitlaced, exilic, and anachronistic—in short, irrelevant to the spirit of the age after the First World War. The conflict between the Arabs and the Jews turned out to be more and more violent, making optimistic and utopian visions such as Herzl's *Altneuland* dismissible as pipe dreams unsuited to Zionism after the events of 1920, 1921, and 1929. Nordau's early writings and his critique of art, literature, and culture were perceived as outdated and foreign and not as something that could be of any value to the new challenges of the Jews in the Near East.

This, however, would change. Two Jewish historians, ideologically different in almost every aspect, embraced the forgotten Nordau and made him a key figure in their writings. George L. Mosse singled out Nordau, and especially his *Degeneration*, as a symbol of the nineteenth century's waning sense of respectability. Benzion Netanyahu (1910–2012) saw himself as one of Nordau's followers and understood Nordau as one of the true founding fathers of Zionism. While Mosse was more ambivalent toward Nordau, he was critical and fascinated by him at the same time; Netanyahu admired Nordau and tried to revive and propagate his worldview. While Netanyahu and the Revisionists instrumentalized Nordau's thought to justify their nationalism, Mosse, in his liberal reading of Nordau, thought they were deracinating him, stripping his work of nuance, and reading his understanding of the New Jew as primarily an excuse for militarism. Thus, this chapter will compare their two approaches in the hope of shedding new light on the multifaceted history of Nordau's reception.

The Revival of Nordau: Netanyahu and the Revisionist Zionists

Herzl, Nordau, and the so-called political Zionists were enthusiastically adopted by a growing minority: the Revisionist Zionists and the Far Right in Palestine. Ze'ev Vladimir Jabotinsky (1880–1940), the leader of the Revisionist movement, was the self-proclaimed successor of Herzl and Nordau and was seen as such by his followers.[2] He emphasized the importance of the political in Zionism, the establishment of a Jewish state, and the importance of sovereignty, power, rule, and authority. Some of Jabotinsky's ideas, such as the "evacuation plan" to move millions of Jews from Eastern Europe and bring them to Palestine (which at the time would have seemed feasible, given the Greece-Turkey population exchange starting in 1923), were compared with similar plans suggested by Herzl or by

Nordau, who decades earlier had suggested a mass transfer of Jews from Europe. Moreover, the bourgeois respectability of some of the political Zionists, flatly rejected by Socialist Zionism, became a source of inspiration for the Revisionists. Jabotinsky and his followers called it in Hebrew "Hadar," which can be translated as honor or majesty, and was meant to be an anti-Marxist, antisocialist urban alternative to the conduct and morality of the left.

Jabotinsky described Nordau as one of the most revolutionary thinkers of the *fin de siècle* generation. Yehusha Yeivin (1891–1970), one of the leaders of the Far Right movement in Palestine called "Brit Habirionim" ("the strongmen alliance" or "the alliance of thugs"), along with the political poet Uri Zvi Greenberg (1896–1981) and journalist Abba Ahimeir (1897–1962), wrote that "Nordau foresaw the upcoming of the great catastrophe in Europe and the complete moral bankruptcy of assimilation and exile.... He noticed with his eye, his eagle eye, that instead of true Zionism, the [practical] Zionists in Palestine are creating a Zionist substitute, completely destroying the messianic hope ... and our great political rights.... That was the moment which led to his complete destruction."[3] These are but two examples indicating how Nordau, a nineteenth-century liberal, was adopted by Zionist right-wing activists in the twentieth century.[4] However, no one in the Revisionist movement or within Zionism embraced Nordau like a certain young graduate student and journalist who would later become a historian—Benzion Netanyahu.

Already in February 1931, at the age of twenty-one, Netanyahu published a short piece in the newspaper *Doar Ha-Yom* (*Palestine Daily Mail*) titled "Lezichro shel Nordoy" (In remembrance of Nordau), expressing regret that the Zionist thinker had been forgotten, especially when

> the major content of his work is still relevant today, and the flaws that he discovered or emphasized, their existence in the various parts of the human organism were verified even more in the period of destruction and war and in the years that followed.... What set Nordau's ideas apart from the ideas of other moral warriors was the scientific value that he attached to morality. To him, morality was a form of "mental health" that science emphatically demanded. He fought for morality in the name of science, in the name of objective truth only. It was a prophetic burst of fire in the cold fields of positivist science.[5]

Netanyahu's Nordau was endowed with prophetic virtues and recruited to the battle against socialism at a time when "the spread of revolutionary socialism, the emergence of which Nordau battled, and the tendency towards irrational elements currently taking over the science of the mind, may ... provide a partial explanation for the disappearance from memory of Nordau, whom Cesare Lombroso held to be 'The Genius' with capital letters."[6] Mentioning the physician and criminologist Cesare Lombroso, who wrote a book titled *The Man of Genius* in 1889, was, of course, not accidental. In contrast to all the writers whom Lombroso accused of moral degeneration, Nordau believed in contemporary science and morality, in progress, in willpower, in discipline, in hard work, order, and duty, and especially in psychology that was based on Social Darwinism and on the doctrine of Lombroso, to whom he dedicated *Degeneration*, his most important and controversial work.[7]

According to Lombroso, there are anatomical differences between criminals and noncriminals. Criminals exhibit various kinds of physical abnormality whose origins lie in processes of degeneration and atavism—that is to say, in pathological deterioration, a remnant of wild and primitive times. Lombroso examined criminals in several prisons in Italy and, after studying the skull of one prisoner, concluded that this criminal and others had "enormous jaws, high cheek bones, prominent supraciliary arches, solitary lines in the palms, extreme size of the orbits, ... insensibility to pain, extremely acute sight, tattooing, excessive idleness, love of orgies and the irresistible craving for evil for its own sake, the desire not only to extinguish life in the victim, but to mutilate the corpse, tear its flesh, and drink its blood."[8] Nordau adopted Lombroso's early concept of criminology and translated it into discussions of art, literature, and culture. Netanyahu accepted these as absolute truths and wished to spread the word to as many people as possible in Palestine.

In that spirit, a few years later, between 1936 and 1938, a series of six books appeared, published by a new independent publishing house in Palestine called Hozaa Medinit (Political Publishing). The series, which over the following two decades came out in several editions, included the Zionist writings of Nordau (in two volumes), Herzl (in two volumes), British territorialist Israel Zangwill, and historian Joseph Klausner (1874–1958)—Netanyahu's mentor and spiritual father, and the only living thinker of the four.

Yehushua Yeivin translated most of the books from German and English into Hebrew, and Netanyahu, the young publisher, edited them and wrote short prefaces to most of them. Reading the prefaces offers a glimpse of Benzion Netanyahu's Zionist ideology: the ideas he embraced or attributed to the Zionist right, the ones he ignored, and the kinds of ideas he rejected. It also indicates how Netanyahu read these thinkers through a Revisionist lens and tried to revive their thought in the 1930s. While exhuming them, Netanyahu threw away what amounted to, in his interpretation, any surplus liberal baggage, thereby reshaping them in his own image.

In the prefaces to Nordau's writings, for instance, Netanyahu portrayed the author of *Degeneration* as an ardent fighter for the establishment of a Jewish army and for Eretz Israel Ha-Shlema (the Greater Israel), which included Transjordan as well as mandatory Palestine. For example, Netanyahu emphasized the importance of self-defense and power in Nordau's writings:

> Nordau was no unrealistic pacifist. That is why he called for the establishment of "a Jewish militia that will be ready and waiting for any summons that may come to defend the land."... He aspired to a nation that would raise the banner of "revival and independence" and understand that revival can only be possible where there is independence, and that independence can only be possible where there is military defense. He hoped for a nation that would learn, not from the decayed present but from its glorious past, and create its future out of a sense of mastery over the land.... Instead of relinquishing Transjordan, he called for an insistent, uncompromising position that would preserve the historical borders of the land; instead of a class struggle, he called for class cooperation.... Instead of fake pacifism and reliance upon Britain's military forces, he called for the establishment of a Jewish defense army.[9]

Indeed, Nordau did call for the creation of a Jewish military force. He claimed the Arabs were uncivilized and spoke about the role of Zionism: "To do in the Near East what the English did in India—I mean the cultural work, not the governing and ruling. We mean to come to Palestine as the emissaries of civilization and expand the moral borders of Europe to the Euphrates."[10] Yet his attitude to Palestine, to the use of force, and to the Arabs was much more complex and ambivalent. He warned against the use of power by the state or the army and was more moderate than the militaristic character painted by Netanyahu. For example, in an article titled "The Arabs and Us," Nordau wrote:

> Palestine is not a wasteland.... It is inhabited ... whether we like it or not—this is a fact we must take into account.... Let the Arabs fear not! ... We abhor violence. We suffered it for eighteen hundred years and were its victims. We will not hurt a soul.... We are certain from the outset that we will reach a successful agreement with our Arab neighbors.... We cannot protest or wonder if, at first sight, the Arabs will not be pleased with our settlement of the land that for generations they have considered their own.... With our honesty and the righteousness of our leadership, we will manage to extinguish in them the moment of basic distrust towards us, we will form more or less polite relations with them, and these will soon become—I hope—cordial ties.... The most pressing need in Palestine

is to have Zionists who are well versed in Arabic, in Arab literature and law, in Muslim history, in the mentality and habits of the Arabs—people who can enter into civilized and amiable negotiations with them.... If we consistently follow this line that I have laid out, we can hope to resolve the Arab question to the satisfaction of our neighbors and ourselves. An unsuccessful approach may result in very grave danger to our immediate future.[11]

Thus, Netanyahu revived Nordau, but in this process of resuscitation, a thinner, less liberal version of Nordau survived. Herzl, Pinsker, and Zangwill met with the same fate. In the 1930s, just before the Second World War and the Holocaust began, Netanyahu described the three as the founding fathers of Zionism and saw them as his most important sources of inspiration. In the following decades, he did not change his worldview. On the contrary, he kept writing about his Zionist heroes, blending his reading of them with his new studies: a dissertation on fifteenth-century Jewish philosopher and statesman Don Isaac Abarbanel and research on Jewish history during the Spanish Inquisition. In 1943 Netanyahu wrote an introduction to the English translation of Nordau's Zionist writings, and in 1954, an introduction to a new Hebrew edition, this time published after the State of Israel was established.

The Revival of Nordau: George L. Mosse

At least in Hebrew, it seems that Nordau was revived only because of his Zionist writing. However, in 1968 the publication of a new English edition of *Degeneration* restored him as an important symbol of nineteenth-century cultural and intellectual history. The historian who played the key role in placing Nordau at the eye of the *fin de siècle* storm and liberating him from the shackles of his Zionist writings was George L. Mosse, who wrote an important introduction to the translation in 1966.

During the 1960s, some German-Jewish-American historians revisited the nineteenth century in an attempt to trace the origins of the traditions and ideas that led to the destruction of Europe in the twentieth century. In 1961, for example, Fritz Stern (1926–2016) published *The Politics of Cultural Despair*, focusing on the worldviews of Paul de Lagarde (1827–91), Julius Langbehn (1851–1907), and Arthur Moeller van den Bruck (1876–1925)—all harbingers of the conservative revolution in German thought. In 1964 Mosse published *The Crisis of German Ideology*, exploring nineteenth-century racism, antisemitism, Romanticism, nationalism, youth movements, mysticism, and utopianism. Both books were attempts to decipher the circumstances that enabled the rise of Nazism and uncover the emotional, intellectual, cultural, and literary undercurrents that spread beyond small circles of antisemitic thought into a mass movement. Stern focused on his protagonists' attack on modernity and liberalism, which crystallized into a Germanic ideology and combined cultural despair with mystical nationalism. Mosse focused on the growth of völkisch ideology and of other ideas, which were "a direct product of the romantic movement of nineteenth-century Europe" and "showed a distinct tendency toward the irrational and emotional, and were focused primarily on man and the world."[12]

Mosse's introduction to *Degeneration* is, in a sense, a direct continuation of this historiographical trend: searching for ideas in the present or the near past with origins or expression already apparent in the nineteenth century. Nordau was a nineteenth-century liberal. He was an optimist and a rationalist who opposed any expression of mysticism or irrationality. He was a positivist and relied on contemporary science. However, reliance on science was a central element in racist thinking of his time, and the discourse of degeneration—even if Nordau played a minor role in it—guided Nazi ideology in labeling enemies, moral sickness, and abnormality.

For Mosse, Nordau was an important link in the chain, connecting his interest in the crisis of German ideology with his interest in nationalism and sexuality, or the image of man as it was created in the eighteenth and nineteenth centuries. In Mosse's introduction, Nordau becomes a distinct representative of the ways in which the bourgeoisie drew the lines of respectability, determining who is morally healthy and who is diseased, who is an insider and who is an outsider, who is ugly and who is beautiful, who is clean and who is dirty, who is a real man and who behaves in an unmanly fashion, who is normal and who is abnormal. *Degeneration* and other writings embodied an archetype of manhood or masculinity founded on self-discipline, a sense of duty and honor, reflecting Nordau's psychology and attaching the physical with the spiritual and moral, emphasizing sport, or more exactly athletics or gymnastics. *Degeneration* internalized Jewish stereotypes and called for the emergence of a New Jew, a new Jewishness, and muscular Judaism.[13]

Zionism plays an important role here because it sheds light on Mosse's ambivalence toward Nordau. Twenty-five years after the republication of *Degeneration*, Mosse wrote another article on Nordau titled "Nordau, Liberalism and the New Jew." If in the introduction to *Degeneration* Mosse proved mostly critical of Nordau's bourgeois worldviews, in the new article he defended Nordau's liberal Zionism, especially against the way he was received and embraced by Revisionist Zionism and its successors:

To be sure, Nordau's New Jew was a fighting Jew, but his achievement lay not on the field of battle but in his physical development and in putting down roots, thus recapturing his dignity. Jabotinsky's and the Revisionists' New Jew was similar to Max Nordau's in appearance and comportment, except for his glorification of military values. But this distinction was important, for the revisionists [sic] were apt to raise physical force almost to a value in and of itself. Jabotinsky thought liberalism irrelevant in a world ruled by the struggle for survival. Nordau's liberalism mitigated any aggressiveness on the part of the New Jew who was, after all, also a man of action. Here, liberalism meant regard for the individual, even though this individual voluntarily identified himself with a group.[14]

Mosse thought that the Revisionists stripped Nordau of all ambiguity and inner contradictions. They took away his controversial nineteenth-century liberalism, leaving only a narrow, aggressive rendering that they used to promote their own militaristic sentiments and aspirations.

A version of Mosse's article was first presented at an International Colloquium on Max Nordau that took place in Paris in July 1992, a few weeks after the Israeli elections that Yitzhak Rabin (1922–95) won and the Likud party, the successor of Revisionist Zionism, lost. We can assume that Mosse's paper had been written beforehand, during more than a decade of Israeli right-wing rule. The period was yet another tumultuous one in the region, with Israel's moral code challenged and shaken following the First Lebanon War and the First Intifada. Several Israeli historians, younger than Mosse, criticized the policy of the Israeli government by turning their scholarly attention to the Zionist idea. Anita Shapira published *Land and Power*, which was conceptualized during the Lebanon War and focused on Zionism and violence or the use of force. Shlomo Avineri published *The Making of Modern Zionism*, which harshly criticized Jabotinsky and presented his worldview as close to fascism.[15] In this regard, Mosse was no different. He wished to defend Nordau's Zionism as liberal Zionism and the enabling of the Zionist idea itself by distinguishing it from his understanding of Revisionist Zionism and its theory as well as from Likud policy and practice.

According to Mosse, Nordau may have called for the creation of a New Jew, but this Jew was supposed to be a good bourgeois, not a nationalist or militarist. Muscular Judaism and Nordau's concept of manhood were supposed to dwell in a liberal world that rejected any call for organic or völkisch development of a nation and opposed romanticizing nationalism. Mosse's Nordau is a man of the Enlightenment and the values of the French Revolution, a protector of individualism who, in contrast to Jabotinsky, distanced himself from any expression of aggression and militarism: "Nordau's nationalism rose above the conventional nationalism of his time. Nationalism was part of a process which led from barbarism to altruism—that is, to a love of all humanity—it struck a balance between individual rights as against the state on the one hand, and national solidarity on the other. While Nordau's version of the New Man observed the conventions of bourgeois life, he lacked most of the historical sense of exclusiveness required of nationalists, as well as the inborn hostility towards other countries and peoples inherent in modern nationalism."[16] For Mosse, Nordau was a thinker crucial to understanding *fin de siècle* Europe. He epitomized the merits and many faults of that time—the blind faith in accepted scientific methods and assumptions and the unconscious, surprising support for social and cultural conventions even by people, such as Nordau himself, who pretended to expose the lies of European societies. However, Mosse rejected the new glorification of Nordau's thought in Revisionist interpretation, which adopted him as a central source for their nationalism.

Nordau between Mosse and Netanyahu

In the 1992 article, Mosse refers to Nordau's Zionist writings based on the 1909 German edition, rather than the 1943 English translation or Netanyahu's introduction. Both Mosse and Netanyahu shared an interest in Nordau, but a direct intellectual confrontation or debate never took place between them. Instead, they wrote two contrasting monologues that, in retrospect, represent the contemporary struggle between right and left. Mosse, a concerned liberal Zionist, found his home outside of Israel and shaped the field of modern European history. Netanyahu, a far-right Zionist, came back to Israel after many years in America following the death of his elder son, Yoni, in Operation Entebbe (1976), and eventually shaped Israeli thought by proxy through his second son, Benjamin, in the twenty-first century.

Mosse wanted to show that Zionism in general and Nordau's vision in particular are essentially optimistic. In contrast, Netanyahu understood *Degeneration* as an inseparable part of the pessimistic decline of the West. Mosse wished to sever the bond between Nordau and the Revisionist Zionists while Netanyahu claimed a natural connection between Nordau's vision, militarism, and the Revisionist ideal of Greater Israel. Mosse claimed that Nordau disappeared because his alleged rational world was no longer relevant amid the chaos that reigned after the First World War. Netanyahu revived Nordau and thought that his views symbolized the Zionist ideal, a nineteenth-century concept of rationality in a chaotic twentieth-century world, a moral and political cure in times of catastrophe.

Both historians needed Nordau. For Mosse, Nordau was the embodiment of the *fin de siècle* heterosexual bourgeois world. Nordau was the glue between *The Crisis of German Ideology* and *The Image of Man*, as one of the builders of the wall separating insiders from outsiders. Mosse would have been an outsider in Nordau's world, but, as in so many cases, sometimes the outsider uses this wall for self-definition. Mosse, who was both a Jew and a homosexual, dedicated his life to the study of racism and antisemitism as well as homophobia and masculinity, tracing the images and ideas that had direct consequences for history and for the course of his own life.

Netanyahu was an outsider, too, but his exclusion was shaped in a different context. He spent most of his life on the margins of Zionist politics and the academic world, full of resentment toward the mainstream Zionist establishment, liberalism, and the left. Nordau, a nineteenth-century liberal, was to him a source of inspiration for adapting a neoconservative stand in the twentieth century.

In the introduction to *Degeneration*, Mosse wrote that "Nordau had been typical of his age, and when that age died, he died with it." However, Mosse's and Netanyahu's writings prove that Nordau, or at least the history of his reception, remains very much alive. Nordau indeed died and was forgotten, but he was also resurrected in several metamorphoses. In Netanyahu's interpretation, he became one of the ideological fathers of the right wing in the Land of Israel. In Mosse's interpretation, he became one of the founding fathers of respectability. Mosse may have depicted Nordau more accurately, paying attention to contradictions, complexities, nuances, and context. However, politically, Netanyahu's Zionism, which is based on his understanding of Nordau, changed the way Nordau was received and was also ultimately more influential, at least in Israel— especially more than Mosse's distant, seemingly blurred version of Zionism.

Mosse had many students who broadened and shaped European cultural and intellectual history. Netanyahu had only a few, though one of them, Norman Roth, taught for many years at the University of Wisconsin–Madison, Mosse's university and home for many years. However, Netanyahu did have one student: his son, who, in the name of the father, is (alas) influencing our present and future history more than all Mosse's (academic) children and grandchildren.

Notes

1. While Ahad Ha'am claimed that Herzl's vision lacked any Jewish content or sentiment and was detached from reality, Nordau stood by the founder of political Zionism, asserting that Herzl did not see any contradiction between Jewishness and European culture. See Ahad Ha'am, "Altneuland," *Hashiloach* 8, no. 60 (December 1902); Max Nordau,

"Ahad Ha'am über Altneuland," *Die Welt*, 13 March 1903. See also Jacques Kornberg, ed., *At the Crossroads: Essays on Ahad Ha'am* (Albany: State University of New York Press, 1983); Steven J. Zipperstein, *Elusive Prophet: Ahad Ha'am and the Origins of Zionism* (Berkeley: University of California Press, 1993).

2. On Jabotinsky's life and thought, see Joseph B. Schechtman, *The Life and Times of Vladimir Jabotinsky: Rebel and Statesman* (Silver Spring, MD: Eshel Books, 1986); Ya'aḳov Shaviṭ, *Jabotinsky and the Revisionist Movement, 1925–1948* (London: F. Cass, 1988); Hillel Halkin, *Jabotinsky: A Life* (New Haven, CT: Yale University Press, 2014). On Jabotinsky's followers, see Daniel Kupfert Heller, *Jabotinsky's Children: Polish Jews and the Rise of Right-Wing Zionism* (Princeton, NJ: Princeton University Press, 2017).

3. See Ze'ev Vladimir Jabotinsky, "Max Nordau," *Memories of a Son of My Generation* (Tel Aviv: Amichai Publishing, 1957), 227–35; Yehushua Yeivin, "Max Nordau," *Beitar* 2 (1933): 179–84.

4. Various right-wing conservative Revisionists tended to adopt the vocabulary of corruption and decadence. Reviving Nordau's *Degeneration* is but one example. However, Nordau was not the only thinker who captivated their minds. Ahimeir, for example, did not write extensively about Nordau or degeneration but was preoccupied with a very different kind of decline: he wrote his 1924 dissertation on Oswald Spengler's *Decline of the West*.

5. Benzion Netanyahu, "In Remembrance of Nordau," *Doar Ha-Yom*, 3 February 1931.

6. Netanyahu, "In Remembrance," 1931.

7. On Nordau's *Degeneration*, see Steven E. Aschheim, "Max Nordau, Friedrich Nietzsche and Degeneration," *Journal of Contemporary History* 28, no. 4 (October 1993): 643–57. See also P. M. Baldwin, "Liberalism, Nationalism, and Degeneration: The Case of Max Nordau," *Central European History* 13, no. 2 (June 1980): 99–120; Linda L. Maik, "Nordau's Degeneration: The American Controversy," *Journal of the History of Ideas* 50, no. 4 (Oct.–Dec. 1989): 607–23; Richard Dellamora, "Productive Decadence: 'The Queer Comradeship of Outlawed Thought': Vernon Lee, Max Nordau, and Oscar Wilde," *New Literary History* 35, no. 4 (Autumn 2004): 529–46; Richard D. Walter, "What Became of the Degenerate? A Brief History of a Concept," *Journal of the History of Medicine and Allied Sciences* 11, no. 4 (October 1956): 422–29. See also Anna and Maxa Nordau, *Max Nordau: A Biography* (New York: Nordau Committee, 1943).

8. Cesare Lombroso, "Introduction," in *Criminal Man—According to the Classification of Cesare Lombroso* (New York: Knickerbocker Press, 1911), 15.

9. Benzion Netanyahu, "Max Nordau" [in Hebrew], in *Max Nordau to His People* (Tel Aviv: Hozaa Medinit, 1936), 18–19. See also Max Simon Nordau, *Max Nordau to His People: A Summons and a Challenge* (New York: Scopus, 1941).

10. Max Nordau, "Speech at the Eighth Zionist Congress (1907)," in *Zionist Writings* (Jerusalem: Zionist Library, 1954), 3:44.

11. Max Nordau, "The Arabs and Us (1918)" [in Hebrew], in *Zionist Writings* (Jerusalem: Zionist Library, 1954), 4:49. On Nordau's Zionism, see also Michael Stanislawski, *Zionism and the Fin de Siècle: Cosmopolitanism and Nationalism from Nordau to Jabotinsky*

(Berkeley: University of California Press, 2001); and Gideon Shimoni, *The Zionist Ideology* (Waltham, MA: Brandeis University Press, 1995).

12. George L. Mosse, *The Crisis of German Ideology* (Madison: University of Wisconsin Press, 2021), 15.

13. See also Todd Samuel Presner, *Muscular Judaism: The Jewish Body and the Politics of Regeneration* (London: Routledge, 2010).

14. George L. Mosse, "Max Nordau, Liberalism and the New Jew," *Journal of Contemporary History* 27, no. 4 (1992): 575–76.

15. Anita Shapira, *Land and Power: The Zionist Resort to Force, 1881–1948* (New York: Oxford University Press, 1992); Shlomo Avineri, *The Making of Modern Zionism: Intellectual Origins of the Jewish State* (New York: Basic Books, 1981).

16. Mosse, "Max Nordau, Liberalism and the New Jew," 578–79.

Part VI
MOSSE AND BERLIN, THEN AND TODAY

14

"There's Nothing Innocuous Left"

The Everyday Transfigured

ROBERT ZWARG

Some preliminary remarks are warranted in order to contextualize this text. The talk that I presented at the "Mosse's Europe" conference in June 2019 in Berlin was not a traditional, academic paper, nor is this essay (which is an essay in the strict sense, an attempt or rather an experiment). At the conference, I tried to combine or narratively associate two things: first, the task given to us by the organizers to present something from our current research, and second, a personal anecdote or coincidence that was far too intriguing and fitting to not use for the occasion of the conference. In other words, I wanted to tell a story that I felt was related to my research—*which is on the notion of the everyday*—as well as connected to the title of the panel I was originally scheduled to talk at, "Mosse's Berlin." Combining these two things, however, required a certain degree of associativeness and narrative structure that translated well—I hope—into a talk, but works differently in a written text, which allows the reader to skip ahead and move back and forth. However, since I am still fascinated by the utter peculiarity of the coincidence, which was at the center of the talk, I have decided to present it here in its original structure, with some additions, cuts, and elaborations, which, alas, still does not make for a traditional, academic essay; rather, it keeps the dramatic development of the original talk, which relied on a certain moment of (mis)direction and surprise. However, I do hope that even in written form, the text does convey some of my astonishment about the intriguing intertwinement of moments that characterized the coincidence that animated the following reflection. Most importantly, with the gratitude of a lifetime, I want to dedicate the essay to Sabrina Walter, who plays a crucial part in this story. Without her, the pictures would have never found their way to me and many things would not have happened.

I

There is a peculiar resonance of translation between the following English, French, and German words that all appear to bear the same meaning: "chance," "by accident," "coincidence," the French *hasard*, and the German *Zufall*. Let's begin with the latter: *Zufall* reminds one of "falling," either of something actually falling into your hands or the act of falling into something. Similarly, the idea of the loss of control or even of danger is noticeable in the English formulation "by accident" as well as the French *hasard* (the stress on danger and risk still echoes in the English noun "hazard"), while "chance" seems to be the word that is usually chosen to translate *Zufall*, as for instance in the title of Jacques Monod's seminal *Chance and Necessity* (*Le hasard et la nécessité: Essai sur la philosophie naturelle de la biologie moderne*). Coincidence, however, stands out for highlighting the convergence of different factors or moments, and in fact, Monod himself uses the concept of "absolute coincidences," saying that they "result from the intersection of two totally independent chain of events."[1] Such a coincidence is at the beginning of this story, combined with a frustratingly unreliable memory.

One day, sometime at the beginning of 2019, I came upon a couple of photographs. Or put differently, the photographs came to me. On this day that I can't quite pin down, my partner and I were spending time in a room of her apartment that we normally don't use together: her study and guest room. I was reading and she was rearranging some things, when she rediscovered several loosely collected, small-format pictures, tucked between letters, postcards, invoices, and flyers, all assembled in an antique-looking paper holder that I had given her as a present four or five years ago. The paper holder functioned as something of a mnemonic device, an object to structure memory. It keeps certain paper-made memorabilia—both sentimental and rather profane and bureaucratic—for about a year, after which it gets cleaned out. Invoices are put into boxes, payroll information sheets move into folders, flyers of parties are either thrown away or collected somewhere else. Only these pictures, which she had never shown me before, had stayed in the paper holder, year after year. It is not quite correct to say that my partner had forgotten about them. She knew they were in her possession, but it was only about once a year—usually when the cleaning-out of the paper holder was due—that she looked at them. She never knew what to do with them, which is why they just stayed there. This time, with me being in the same room and maybe to spark my historical interest, she handed them to me: all in all, thirty-three black-and-white photographs, rather small and with jagged edges, the largest about 2.3 × 3.5 inches, the smallest 2.3 × 2.3 inches.

II

The origins of the pictures were murky, to say the least. It was a mystery to my partner how they exactly ended up in her possession. Everything about them—the size, the coloring, and most of all, what they showed—made them belong to the past. She was certain, however, that they didn't belong to her or her family. To the best of her memory, she had found the pictures in the collective trash at her grandmother's multilevel apartment building in Berlin Tiergarten near Schloss Bellevue, just a stone's throw away from that park, which, according to Walter Benjamin, "unlike every other, seemed open to children," and only about two miles north of the Mosse family's Maaßenstrasse mansion (formerly Karl-Heinrich-Ulrichs-Strasse).[2] Speaking in terms of the twentieth century, the apartment used to be in West Berlin, but my partner's grandmother hadn't always lived there—nor was she, in the biological sense, her grandmother. She was born in the late 1920s and had for many years lived in East Berlin, in Mitte's oldest street, Chausseestrasse, not far from one of the checkpoints. At the end of the 1970s, a young man moved into the house, who, as an electrical engineer, was able to provide a special and much sought-after service: illegally connecting the televisions of the house to the programming in West Germany. He befriended the woman (she was about twenty years older than him, and the arrangement consisted in her cooking meals and him being the handyman) and soon trusted her with his two children, one of them being my partner. This form of neighborly solidarity was not uncommon in the German Democratic Republic and is, not surprisingly, heavily romanticized today, even though it seems to be the mere reverse of—or at least connected to—neighbors spying on each other.[3] In any case, nobody knows when the kids started to call the woman "Oma" (nana), but that is who she was. Owing to parts of her family living in West Berlin, she was eventually allowed to move to the other part of the divided city, which in turn provided sufficient reasons for her social grandchildren to visit her every once in a while, see West Berlin, and make use of the infinitely more exciting libraries. As far as my partner can remember—but nowhere close to being certain—it was there, at the apartment building near Bellevue, in the patio where the garbage bins for the whole building are located, orderly separated into paper, waste, and plastic, that she one day found the pictures in the paper bin, which she then took home and kept in the aforementioned paper holder.

III

Taking a first look at the pictures (fig. 14.1), approaching them, as it were, on the level on what Roland Barthes called the *studium*, we see snapshots taken in what seems to be a medical setting, likely a children's hospital or an orphanage.[4] And like Barthes looking at his mother's pictures, it was clear to me and my partner that it is history that "separates" us "from them," that we can read our "nonexistence"[5] in the clothes, the furniture, and the surroundings. Many decades have certainly passed since the moments these pictures were first recorded; but time shall be of a later concern. By all accounts, these are scenes of the ordinary, moments of everyday life. There are doctors and nurses holding children and toddlers and young kids in their rooms and cots. Some photographs seem to be taken on special occasions, yet they do not shed their appearance of belonging to everyday life; the occasions seem to be a holiday, some sort of celebration, or simply a Sunday. The frame, distances, and motives are varying, some are taken from up close, with the photographer likely cowering as if to adopt the perspective of the children, others are taken standing; one gets the impression that there might be several photographers responsible for the pictures. A woman reappears in a couple of them, prompting the idea that she might have taken the

Figure 14.1. Illustration by Robert Zwarg.

others. What seems certain though, because of the naturalness of the reaction of the people who are being photographed, is that whoever took the pictures worked in the place where they were taken. He or she was one of them.

Almost certainly, these pictures were not intended as art but, rather, as a means of personal memory. Yet despite not being intended as art, they still inhabit an aesthetic quality. One picture (fig. 14.2), for instance, has a nurse located on the left side of the picture, taken in a room that the photographer was likely in as well. There is no indication regarding the nature of the room, but because of the nurse, the whole picture raises a couple of questions: is it a patient's room, a common room for other hospital workers, or a personal apartment? Has someone died? It is unclear whether the nurse is moving or standing; this uncertainty coupled with the fact that she seems occupied or absorbed, not reacting to the photographer, is part of a gloomy atmosphere that the picture emits. In addition, the interior is rather dark, with the gleaming light from outside shining through the window, which has the effect that the outside, which is likely pretty close, has vanished. Both the subject of the photograph, the photographer, and the viewer are part of the same obscure interior. Another picture (fig. 14.3) exhibits a certain aesthetic quality through the row of children's beds as well as the almost prearranged children themselves who seem to flee into the back-right corner of the picture, again dominated by the light that falls into the

Figure 14.2. Illustration by Robert Zwarg.

Figure 14.3. Illustration by Robert Zwarg.

room but now with a much colder atmosphere. The row of children suggests a certain seriality, hinting at the fact that many children before those in the picture have slept in these beds, as will many after.

All in all, however, there is nothing threatening or eerie about the pictures of children, doctors, and nurses; they are, by all accounts, innocuous snapshots from everyday life, appearing innocent, happy, and relaxed. One picture, though, contains a constellation of details that "prick" my interest, coalescing in a difficult-to-describe atmosphere and a much different composition than the other interests.[6] The photograph (fig. 14.4) shows a little pathway leading into the back of the picture, crossed by a street, creating something of a symmetry, underscored by the two trees on either side. A woman's figure is curiously standing in the center, as if she had stopped to think, is waiting, or is looking at something,

Figure 14.4. Illustration by Robert Zwarg.

with another woman walking away from the spectator, raising the question whether there is any relation between the two. There is snow, the weather seems to be uncomfortable, with the leafless trees blocking the view of the surrounding buildings, which we therefore cannot quite discern. Also, the perspective of the photographer is not on the same level as the women on the street but a couple of meters higher, suggesting that the picture was taken from a window in the first or second floor of a building nearby. However, for us as well as the photographer, the trees are blocking the view.

IV

If we had to guess when these pictures were taken, we'd most likely point to the first half of the twentieth century, to a time when photography must have been available and somewhat affordable, but not yet in color. The suggestive black-and-white, gray, and sepia tones, the clothing, the interior, the few buildings, and the lack of military imagery and other historical or political indicators might make us think of the 1950s. In fact, a couple of notes on some of the pictures' backs mention the years 1950, 1951, and 1953. And maybe, this is the moment when some of the suggested innocuousness begins to waver.

In one of these mentioned years, a book was published that can be described as a working-through of the experience when all innocuousness and innocence vanish: Theodor W. Adorno's 1951 *Minima Moralia*, written largely during the philosopher's exile in the United States. At its core is the conviction that it would be "idiotic" to assume that after the war, "life will continue 'normally' or even that culture might be 'rebuilt'—as if the rebuilding of culture were not already its negation."[7] Aside from its many philosophical and aesthetic reflections, *Minima Moralia* consists most of all in a careful, almost tactile search for the "rifts and crevices" in the fabric of everyday life.[8] But given the intransigence with which this search is undertaken as well as the radicality of its judgment, it is peculiar that the elegantly written, densely composed aphorisms became a huge success in the country of the perpetrators. Because, to a large degree, its readers were still the old subjects living under new conditions that only a couple of years earlier they had not wanted. No less than thirty reviews appeared in the first six months after its publication. To its author, this success was facilitated by an intellectual and political "vacuum" in which the "unhomely" book (*unhäusliche*) could "make itself a home" (*sich häuslich einrichten*).[9] The curious phrase highlights the underlying theme of the book, the becoming questionable of everyday life, since the home and the house has long been a stand-in metaphor for that special social dimension of the everyday.

There is one aphorism in particular that deals with the question of how to continue living after the catastrophe that was National Socialism and its core ideological element, the destruction of the European Jews, a regime that had—as George L. Mosse put it in his seminal 1966 reader *Nazi Culture*—"like the spider in its web, controlled all the lifelines of the nation."[10] Just as Mosse hints at the infusion of everyday by National Socialist ideology, the aphorism registers the lasting influence that the Holocaust had on everyday interactions. By noticing the absence of innocuousness, the aphorism does not just speak negatively, as it were, about the notion of everyday life; it does so by placing at its center an object that was highlighted in the photographs above and can also serve as a metaphor for the innocence whose loss is registered by Adorno, namely, the tree. The aphorism bears a title that certainly resounded with readers in the 1950s and would have most certainly sounded familiar to Mosse and his family. The fifth aphorism of *Minima Moralia* is titled "Herr Doktor, das ist schön von Euch" (How nice of you, Doctor), a quote taken from the second scene of Johann Wolfgang von Goethe's *Faust*—which Mosse, whose father reportedly had many first editions by Goethe and Gotthold Ephraim Lessing, the "patron saints of German Jewry," would certainly have recognized.[11] The reference is not to a medical doctor but to Faust, the academic—which is why many English versions translate "Doktor" as "professor." In the scene outside the city gate ("Vor dem Tor"), Faust and his disciple Wagner embark on an Easter walk and talk about religion. During the stroll, they come across an old peasant who utters the following words: "Herr Doktor, das ist schön von Euch, / Daß Ihr uns heute nicht verschmäht, / Und unter dieses Volksgedräng, / Als ein so Hochgelehrter geht." The English translation by Stuart Atkins puts it the following way: "Professor, it is good of you / to deign to be with us today / and, learned doctor though you are, / to mingle with us ordinary folk."[12] What Adorno is interested in here is the juxtaposition of the "learned doctor" and the common "folk," taken as a symbol for the relationship of the intellectual to the masses. The benevolent gesture, indicating praise for the learned man who has come down to the everyman, is the inversion of how Adorno considers the intellectual attitude to be, for whom "isolation is now the only way of showing some measure of solidarity. All collaboration, all the human worth of social mixing and participation, merely masks a tacit acceptance of inhumanity."[13]

Leaving aside the question of how Adorno understands both criticism and the role of the intellectual in these reflections, I want to focus on another aspect of the passage. We can understand the reference to "social mixing and participation" as an extension of that which is called "innocuous" in the first sentence of the aphorism, something which, at the same time, is deemed to have disappeared: "There is nothing innocuous left." The once innocuous, we learn, are the harmless, innocent, almost unconscious gestures and actions that make up a big part of everyday life. As Adorno says in the follow-up sentence: "The little pleasures, expressions of life that seemed exempt from the responsibility of thought, not only have an element of defiant silliness, of callous refusal to see, but directly serve their diametrical opposite." What Adorno is describing here can be understood as the loss of a certain innocence as well as the (involuntary) reversal of something good into something bad. In the following passages we find examples of these "little pleasures." There's the visit to the cinema, which, as Adorno famously says about himself, "leaves him stupider and worse." Earlier, there is the famous line about the "chance conversation on the train," where the concession of certain statements in order to avoid dispute ultimately "implicate[s] murder." But it's most of all a series of nouns that give us the best idea of what this special stratum of everyday life characterizes: "sociability" (*Umgänglichkeit*), "uninhibitedness" (*Unbefangenheit*, which the English version of *Minima Moralia* unfortunately translates as "spontaneity"), "ease" (*Behagen*), being "leger" (*Legeren*, wrongly translated as "impetuosity"), "letting oneself go" (*Sich gehen lassen*), or "affability" (*Leutseligkeit*). What connects these characteristics is a certain informality and looseness, each is oriented against force or duty. However, the punchline of Adorno's train of thought is, of course, that these interactions have become increasingly problematic, shallow, and even wrong. There is one famous phrase in which this idea is condensed: "Even the blossoming tree lies the moment its bloom is seen without the shadow of terror; even the innocent 'How lovely!' becomes an excuse for an existence outrageously unlovely, and there is no longer beauty or consolation except in the gaze falling on horror, withstanding it, and in unalleviated consciousness of negativity holding fast to the possibility of what is better."[14] On the one hand, this is another take on how Adorno demands the critical perspective to be—the decisive and strict deployment of a "consciousness of negativity." On the other hand, there's the curiously placed tree at the beginning of the sentence that establishes the loss of innocence and innocuousness which, as Adorno seems to imply and I have implied likewise, characterizes much of what we call the everyday. In taking this a little further, that is, following the trail that the metaphor of the tree has laid out, we can begin to better understand the process of innocuousness vanishing and what this could mean historically, before eventually returning to the pictures in which the trees are blocking the view.

V

In the aphorism from *Minima Moralia*, the tree seems to be an anomaly. All other references are from the social sphere, while the tree is an object from nature that simultaneously takes on a person-like status, in that it becomes capable of lying. In the overall context of Adorno's work, however, it is less surprising that we should come across a reference to nature. As is well known, nature plays an important role in Adorno's thought, maybe most fundamentally in the conception of a *Dialectic of Enlightenment*, which he elaborated together with Max Horkheimer in the book by the same title. In fact, it is with reference to a tree that Adorno and Horkheimer illustrate one of the core ideas, namely, that "myth is already enlightenment":[15] "If the tree is addressed no longer as simply a tree but as evidence of something else, a location of *mana*, language expresses the contradiction that it is at the same time itself and something other than itself, identical and not identical."[16] In another instance, an indication of the regressive reversal of the tree's innocence, society is described as a "forest of cliques and institutions."[17]

These are not the only references to a tree (or its multiplication in a forest) in the work of Adorno, who was certainly aware of the enormous symbolism of the tree, given that it is no less than a "literary universal" as well as an almost mythological notion in German history, materialized, for instance, as George L. Mosse reminds us of in *The Nationalization of the Masses*, the symbol of the German oak, or in the groves honoring fallen soldiers (*Ehrenhain* or *Heldenhain*).[18] Even in Adorno's final great work, the posthumously published *Aesthetic Theory*, we come across the tree in two crucial moments. One gives us a better picture of the systematic relevance of its appearance; the other gives us an insight into what might have inspired the use of the symbol. As to the first, I will only briefly note that the tree leads us to Adorno's understanding of the Kantian idea of natural beauty, which in effect works as an important aesthetic ideal in the narrative on modern art that *Aesthetic Theory* elaborates. Natural beauty functions as the reminder (and the sublimated remnant) of repressed nature, which Adorno illustrates in one moment with a reference to Friedrich Hölderlin's poem *Winkel von Hahrdt*: "In this poem, a stand of trees becomes perceived as beautiful, as more beautiful than the others, because it bears, however vaguely, the mark of a past event."[19] In other words, natural beauty is infused with history, or as Adorno says, "natural and historical elements interact in a musical and kaleidoscopically changing fashion."[20]

If we take the tree deemed beautiful in *Minima Moralia* as an instance of natural beauty, then it seems that natural beauty is itself subject to historical change, that it can become a lie, as the aphorism says. In fact, this is what the second mention of a tree in *Aesthetic Theory* suggests, which also offers us a clue as to the origins of the tree metaphor (a suspicion no doubt held already by the knowledgeable reader). In the chapter "Situation," Adorno speaks about the necessity of artworks to "equate themselves with that reality" in order not to sell out; they have, as he goes on, to adhere to the "ideal of blackness," one of "the deepest impulses of abstraction."[21] To illustrate the deliberate asceticism of art and the conscious refusal to naively indulge in color and traditional notions of the beautiful, Adorno quotes a famous poem by Bertolt Brecht, which may account for the prominent use of the tree metaphor in *Minima Moralia* as well: "Perhaps art will one day be able to abolish this axiom [the ideal of blackness] without self-betrayal, which is what Brecht may have sensed when he wrote: 'What times are these, when / to speak of trees is almost a crime / because it passes in silence over such infamy!'"[22] In other words, it is not a transhistorical condition but rather an imposition by the cruelty of history that to speak about trees is almost a crime.

Bertolt Brecht's *To Those Born Later* (*An die Nachgeborenen*) was written between 1934 and 1938 and published in 1939, when Germany attacked Poland

and Brecht was in exile in Denmark. Compared with Brecht's usual style, it is uncommonly personal, indicated by the first person singular, which keeps reappearing in the famous line: "Truly I live in dark times."[23] However, it is probably most famous for precisely the passage that is quoted by Adorno. Not unlike Adorno's aphorism, the poem unpacks the scandal that it is alluding to by setting up a counterimage of normalcy, again evoking fragments of everyday life, but they are already put into brackets so to speak: "It is true I still earn my keep / But, believe me, that is only an accident." Addressing three temporal planes—the present in exile, the past as the "time of disorder," and the future readers who are addressed at the end—the poem contains a curious self-reference. Looking back at wilder times, the narrator says he had "little patience for nature's beauty." And yet, it is nature's beauty—a talk about trees—that is mentioned in order to highlight that which has been either destroyed by National Socialism or, as following the First World War, had been transformed into a mythological nationalist symbol, as the *Ehrenhain* or *Heldenhain*. As is well known, Brecht's understanding of political and artistic commitment could not be further from a Kantian notion of natural beauty, which makes the reference to the tree even more curious. It turns out to be something of an inverted foreshadowing of how Adorno will use the idea of natural beauty to contrast with the horrors of National Socialism. For Adorno, the innocence that the remark "How lovely" about a tree conveys, is lost with the advent of the Nazis, but for Brecht this idea had always been fraught; only now, in exile, the pleasures and beauty of nature attain for Brecht a somewhat changed quality, as something that can only be appreciated when the times are the darkest.

Brecht's line from *To Those Born Later* has since taken on a life of its own and one could mention many more examples. Think of Paul Celan's 1968 response *A leaf, treeless* (*EIN BLATT, baumlos*), which is dedicated to Bertolt Brecht, where the tree has vanished and the force of the poem is concentrated on the language itself: "What times are these / when a conversation / is almost a crime / because it includes / so much made explicit?"[24] We could also look to Erich Fried's 1967 *Talk about Trees* (*Gespräch über Bäume*), in which seemingly random notes about the garden, the kids, and the house of the narrator are interrupted by the single-line insertion of statements about Vietnam.[25] Or we could point to a more subtle reference that emerges in the opening chapter of Jorge Semprún's novel *Quel beau dimanche!* (*What a Beautiful Sunday*). Here the narrative voice of the chapter titled "Zero" describes how the protagonist sluggishly walks through the "snowy eternity" after having heard a noise somewhere, when he suddenly sees a tree (a leafless tree, not incidentally, was also on the cover of the English edition of the book).[26] He stops, fascinated by the beauty of the tree and nothing else. In the reflection of the protagonist, the snow-covered tree turns into something of an opening in the fabric of time, relativizing in its momentary grandeur the lifetime of the individual: "He laughed at the sun," the novel goes on, "at the tree, at the landscape, at the idea of his own probable, pitiful absence."[27] The reason why a tree could suddenly attain such an aesthetic significance, is, of course, revealed only moments later, when the protagonist, still nameless, is interrupted by an SS soldier who holds him at gunpoint. The protagonist points at the tree and says, "The tree ... a beautiful tree."[28] For a couple of moments they stand in front of the tree together, and what the protagonist is actually imagining during those minutes is what foreclosed in Adorno and Brecht: a talk about a tree. But it remains just an imagination; the moment passes, and innocence is nothing but a faint possibility. After all, we are on the outskirts of the Buchenwald concentration camp, the protagonist is inmate "Nr. 44904," and the smoke, referenced in passing just moments before, turns out to be the smoke of the crematorium.

VI

In Adorno's *Minima Moralia*, judging a tree as beautiful becomes a lie after the horror that has unfolded under National Socialism; for Brecht (who appears, despite the ambivalent relationship with Adorno in the latter's *Aesthetic Theory*), to talk about trees means to not talk about the historical infamy that characterizes these "dark times"; in Semprún, the joyful experience of a tree's beauty is the phantasmatic backdrop against which the grim realities of the concentration camp are set. In each of the examples, the tree seems to be a metaphorical stand-in for something lost, a sphere of innocuous pleasures and interactions that up until now have been characterized—rather unsystematically—as pertaining to the everyday (a sphere of life that we have seen represented in the found photographs). In other words, each of the mentioned instances registers a disappearance of everyday life or at least a certain stratum of the everyday in the face of the horrors of National Socialism.

This is not the place to elaborate a full-fledged notion of the everyday (if that is possible at all) but, rather, to close in on an idea to which we are led not the least by Mosse's work itself. When the aforementioned seminal source book *Nazi Culture* was published in Germany—something defamiliarizing to begin with, since it was almost exclusively German sources but had appeared in English first—it appeared with a slightly different title: *Der nationalsozialistische Alltag: So lebte man unter Hitler* (National Socialist Everyday Life: Life under Hitler).

This translator's choice deserves a closer look. The term "Nazi culture" was obviously used to highlight what was, at the time, the oft-neglected aspects of National Socialism, society under and beyond Hitler's declarations and the hard-boiled political decisions—in other words, the sphere of everyday life, namely, matters of arts, science, sports, education. Given the historical and geographical distance, especially among young students, the book allowed them to approach National Socialism via references to a sphere that everyone knew. Moreover, it was highlighted that the Third Reich had been much more than a ruling clique exercising power from above through traditional political means. Instead, it was a habitual form of life, carried both by a ruling class and the general population. In a way, we can understand the notion of "everyday life" as an attempt to broaden the perspective—something that up until today adds to a notorious vagueness of the concept of everyday life. However, in his introduction, Mosse characterizes the regime of National Socialism precisely by the abolishment of a certain idea of everyday life, that is, a sphere situated in a relative distance from politics, a sphere we might describe as "innocuous." Mosse writes: "This society [National Socialism] would not allow for the differentiation between politics and daily life which many of us naturally make. Today, in most of the non-communist Western world, politics is regarded as merely one compartment of life; it does not have to penetrate our very thought and being. But Hitler's aim was to construct an organic society in which every aspect of life would be integrated with its basic purpose."[29] Through countless original documents, Mosse's source book illustrates that National Socialism operated by infusing everyday life with politics, eventually breaking down the barriers between public, political, and private. Family life, sexual politics, music, literature, it all was subjugated to National Socialist ideology; even minor details of everyday life, like the five o'clock tea—to mention just one of the examples in Mosse's anthology—turned into a political question on which the fate of the German race depended.[30]

The concentration camp, we could continue this thought, would then be the most extreme form of abolishing everyday life by creating a barbaric and perverted simulation of its key features. Put differently, for the prisoner, life is broken down to a set of routines and tasks that follow a repetitive chronological structure, even retaining, cruelly and cynically, some of the elements of ordinary life, like the division between labor and leisure. However, not only can every moment and every action, banal as it may be, become the occasion for punishment and death, but the whole institution and thus every act that constitutes it, is oriented toward the brutal realization of the National Socialists' ideological mission. This is the background for Adorno's formulation, which would have no doubt been understood by Mosse, that there is "nothing innocuous left."

VII

The pictures with which I began my talk—doctors, nurses, kids, and trees—seemed to show the innocence and innocuousness that for Adorno had been lost. How do we look at them now? Are we still convinced by their innocuous everydayness? Do the photographs of doctors and nurses, well in the age of having lived in Hitler's Germany, retain the innocence that they might have evoked at the beginning? Do we see the women passing each other by on that avenue between the trees differently than we have before? Do we think about the history of the children in their cots, do we maybe wonder about the history of the place at all and whether the trees in the picture are—metaphorically speaking—blocking more than light and view? These are, as any reader certainly suspects, rather leading questions. A couple of notes on the backs of the pictures did reveal where most of the photographs were taken, a place that embodies the loss of innocuousness that Adorno mentioned. It is a place in Berlin, located between Schmargendorf and Wilmersdorf, built when both were still villages, between 1893 and 1895. When it was opened in 1895 as an orphanage for ninety-one children, it also got a proper name: Mossesche Erziehungsanstalt für Knaben und Mädchen—or, as the shorthand goes—"Mosse-Stift" (figure 14.5).[31]

According to the mission statement of the foundation that Emilie Mosse created in 1908, the orphanage was specifically intended to help children from the

Figure 14.5. Illustration by Robert Zwarg.

Figure 14.6. Berlin memorial plaque (*Berliner gedenktafel*).

Figure 14.7. Lehrlings- u. Jugendwohnheim.

"learned classes"—in other words, the increasingly suffering middle class—no matter their religious background. In 1922, under the pressure of inflation, the family could not finance the orphanage anymore and donated it to the city of Berlin, under the condition that the name of the founder was kept and that the mission was not changed, to which the city complied. In the late 1920s, the building was reconstructed and turned into a hostel for apprentices and children (*Lehrlings- und Säuglingsheim*), but it didn't remain the Mosse-Stift for long. The Nazis erased the name of the Mosse family—even though, as the note on the back of the pictures indicates, personal memory lasted much longer. Starting in 1936, the Nazis used the building as a children's hospital, which it essentially remained until the 1970s, after which it underwent more reconstruction, housing multiple operations. Two plaques (figs. 14.6 and 14.7), one of which was put there in 1989, commemorate the Mosse family who created the building, which still exists today. In the tradition of its founders, the building is now home to a youth center as well as a café for parents that offers counseling; the name of the café is honoring those who made the building possible: "Emilie und Rudolf" Café.

Notes

1. Jacques Monod, *Chance and Necessity: An Essay on the Natural Philosophy of Modern Biology* (New York: Alfred A. Knopf, 1971), 114.

2. Walter Benjamin, *Berlin Childhood around 1900* (Cambridge, MA: Belknap Press of Harvard University Press, 2006), 55.

3. On the memory of the German Democratic Republic in today's Germany, with a heavy reliance on everyday, material culture, see Jonathan Bach, *What Remains: Everyday Encounters with the Socialist Past* (New York: Columbia University Press, 2017).

4. See Roland Barthes, *Camera Lucida* (New York: Hill & Wang, 1981), 25–26.

5. Barthes, *Camera Lucida*, 64.

6. Barthes, *Camera Lucida*, 47.

7. Theodor W. Adorno, *Minima Moralia: Reflections from Damaged Life* (New York: Verso, 2005), 55.

8. Adorno, *Minima Moralia*, 247.

9. Letter from Theodor W. Adorno to Siegfried Kracauer, 19 July 1951, in Theodor W. Adorno and Siegfried Kracauer, *Briefwechsel 1923–1966* (Frankfurt am Main: Suhrkamp, 2008), 459.

10. George L. Mosse, *Nazi Culture: Intellectual, Cultural, and Social Life in the Third Reich* (1966; repr., Madison: University of Wisconsin Press, 2003), xx.

11. Adorno, *Minima Moralia*, 25; George L. Mosse, *Confronting History: A Memoir* (Madison: University of Wisconsin Press, 2000), 23.

12. Wolfgang von Goethe, *Faust I & II*, trans. Stuart Atkins (Princeton, NJ: Princeton University Press, 1994), 27.

13. Adorno, *Minima Moralia*, 26.
14. Adorno, *Minima Moralia*, 25.
15. Theodor W. Adorno and Max Horkheimer, *Dialectic of Enlightenment* (Stanford, CA: Stanford University Press, 2002), xviii.
16. Adorno and Horkheimer, *Dialectic*, 11.
17. Adorno and Horkheimer, *Dialectic*, 30 (the English translation renders the formulation as "tangled mass of cliques and institutions").
18. On the "literary universal," see Burkhard Moennighoff, "Baum," in *Metzler Lexikon literarischer Symbole*, ed. Günter Butzer and Joachim Jacob (Stuttgart: Metzler, 2008), 36–37; George L. Mosse, *The Nationalization of the Masses: Political Symbolism and Mass Movements in Germany from the Napoleonic Wars Through the Third Reich* (Madison: University of Wisconsin Press, 2023), 36.
19. Theodor W. Adorno, *Aesthetic Theory* (New York: Continuum, 1997), 71.
20. Adorno, *Aesthetic Theory*, 71.
21. Adorno, *Aesthetic Theory*, 39–40.
22. Adorno, *Aesthetic Theory*, 40.
23. Bertolt Brecht, *Poems, 1913–1956*, ed. John Willet and Ralph Manheim (London: Eyre Methuen, 1976), 318–20.
24. Paul Celan, *Selected Poems* (Middlesex: Penguin, 1972), 108.
25. See Erich Fried, *Anfechtungen: Fünfzig Gedichte* (Berlin: Wagenbach, 1967), 60.
26. Jorge Semprún, *What a Beautiful Sunday* (London: Abacus, 1982), 4.
27. Semprún, *What a Beautiful Sunday*, 6.
28. Semprún, *What a Beautiful Sunday*, 7.
29. George L. Mosse, *Nazi Culture*, xx. In the German version, the translator uses "Alltagsleben" for "daily life." See George L. Mosse, "Einführung," in *Der nationalsozialistische Alltag: So lebte man unter Hitler* (Königstein, Ts.: Athenäum, 1979), 1.
30. See Mosse, *Der nationalsozialistische Alltag*, 73.
31. See especially Elisabeth Kraus, *Die Familie Mosse: Deutsch-jüdisches Bürgertum im 19. und 20. Jahrhundert* (Munich: C.H. Beck, 1999), 413.

15

Absence/Presence

The Berlin Mosse Topography

ELISABETH WAGNER

The Mosse family's heritage in Berlin is broken physically or missing completely. The places where they lived and worked and the sights of their distinction and concern, including the Mosse Palais at Leipziger Platz, the villa of the Lachmann-Mosse family in Maaßenstraße, which was completely destroyed in the Second World War, the Mosse Publishing House at the corner of Schützenstraße and Jerusalemer Straße, the manor house in Schenkendorf, where George spent many days of his childhood, the reform synagogue in Johannisstraße, where his father was especially engaged in the composition of a new liturgy—these places are now completely changed from the pre-Nazi Berlin that the Mosse family enjoyed. "East Berlin, it was the heart of a cosmopolitan Berlin that 160,000 Jews called home," the journalist Nina Bernstein wrote in *Newsweek* on 30 September 1990 when she accompanied George L. Mosse to view the family's former possessions in the German Democratic Republic. The properties were now eligible for restitution claims. During their journey, George visited the Jewish Cemetery in Berlin Weißensee, where he saw the tombs of his ancestors, including those of his grandfather Rudolf Mosse, the founder of one of the press empires in Berlin, and his grandmother Emilie, the eminent benefactor and philanthropist who was honored in 1909 with the imperial Wilhelm-Orden. The honor was exceptional for a Jewish woman at that time.

"The road of annihilation runs through the contemporary culture of Berlin," wrote Daniel Libeskind, the architect of the Berlin Jewish Museum and one of the first speakers in the series of the Mosse Lectures, founded by Klaus Scherpe and George L. Mosse in 1997 at the Humboldt University.[1] Before following the traces of Jewish life in Berlin, before viewing the remnants and ruins, before

Figure 15.1. George L. Mosse at the graveside of his ancestors, Berlin-Weißensee. (George L. Mosse at the Tombs of Ulrike Mosse [née Wolff], Rudolf Mosse, and Wolfgang Mosse, F81044. George L. Mosse Collection AR 25137. Image courtesy of Leo Baeck Institute, New York / Photographer unknown.)

Figure 15.2. The void at Potsdamer and Leipziger Platz in Wim Wenders's movie *Der Himmel über Berlin*. (Wenders, Wim, dir. *Der Himmel über Berlin* [*Wings of Desire*]. Paris: Argos Films, 1988.)

discussing renovation and restitution matters, we must first acknowledge this terrible absence of the former Jewish presence, represented by the void built into the Jewish Museum: as Libeskind describes it, "Very little remains of the Jewish presence in Berlin—small things, documents, archive materials, evocative of an absence rather than a presence."[2]

How then can we come to feel what has been lost? Before and after the fall of the wall at Potsdamer Platz and Leipziger Platz there was this haunting empty space that we see in Wim Wenders's movie *Der Himmel über Berlin* (*Wings of Desire*). For a short moment of history, in 1990, there was a movement to preserve symbolically this void at the center of the city.

The first building restored in this emptiness, on the site of the prestigious Mosse Palais, Leipziger Platz 15, was an office center, built by the American architect and step-nephew of George L. Mosse, Hans Strauch. Strauch designed the new building with allusions to the former architecture and included the inscription "Mosse Palais" on the façade. As a sign of respect and reconciliation, the new owner, Hans Röder, gave a floor free of rent to the American Jewish Committee. The lonely house at the empty space of Leipziger Platz, the new Mosse Palais, was soon to be surrounded and constricted by hotels and a shopping mall.

Figure 15.3. The lonely house, reconstruction of the Mosse Palais in 1997. Major construction site Potsdamer Platz—Construction of the Mosse Palais at Leipziger Platz, Berlin, 15 April 1997. (Image courtesy of imago images / Gueffroy / Photographer unknown.)

Figure 15.4. The original Mosse Palais: Mosse Palais from the Southside, Leipziger Platz 15, between 1895 and 1920. (Reprinted from the archive of Dr. Franz Stoedtner, fm1007258. Image courtesy of Bildarchiv Foto Marburg / Photographer unknown.)

Figure 15.5. Mosse Palais with honor court, Voßstraße 22, 1935. (Image courtesy of bpk / Photograph by Atelier Bieber / Nather.)

Look at the front view of the Mosse Palais (fig. 15.5), the original chateau-esque city residence, decorated with an inscription "Die Erhebung des deutschen Geistes" (The Rise of the German Genius). Built in the early 1880s and destroyed in an air raid in February 1945, the Palais testified to the wealth of Rudolf Mosse, the economic ennoblement of the Jewish press baron. After Rudolf Mosse died in 1920, the Palais stood as a representation of the integration of the family into the very center of German political and cultural life.

Figure 15.6. Maria Eichhorn's installation at the *documenta 14*, 2017. Under the name of the Rose Valland Institute, Maria Eichhorn presented this tower of nonrestituted books and other documents at the Documenta exhibition in Kassel in 2017, an ongoing project, which she presented again in the Berlin Mosse Lectures on 9 May 2019. (Image courtesy of Maria Eichhorn / Photograph by Mathias Völzke.)

The Palais was the home of the famous Mosse Art Collection, now the object of the Mosse Art Research Initiative (MARI). And there was also a library, the famous book collection of Erich Schmidt, the former rector of the Friedrich-Wilhelms-Universität, which Rudolf Mosse purchased from the family of the celebrated professor of literature after his death in 1913. It is worth noting that not only works of art but also rare manuscripts and collections of books in Jewish possession were looted by the Nazis and are still missing in the stacks of public libraries: "presently absent," as shown in figure 15.6 in the restitution project of the artist Maria Eichhorn.

In 1935 the Nazis moved August Gaul's *Reclining Lion* out of the Palais and into the front courtyard. Gaul's sculpture replaced Walter Schott's Nymph Fountain that originally greeted visitors. Before visiting Gaul's restituted art object at the Staatliche Museen Berlin, take a look at a documentary photo of May 1945, showing the lion as a kind of hunting trophy of the Red Army (fig. 15.7).

The Mosses were prominent supporters and members of the Jewish Reform Congregation. The Reform Congregation built a new synagogue in downtown Berlin between Oranienburger and Johannisstraße between 1852 and 1853. The Jewish Reform Congregation dedicated the building in 1854. The Reform services did not segregate participants by gender, did not require a head covering, included

Figure 15.7. Soviet soldiers with August Gaul's sculpture *Reclining Lion* in the court of the former Mosse Palais, 1945. (Image courtesy of bpk / Photograph by Friedrich Seidenstücker.)

an organ accompaniment, and increased the use of the German language. Hans Lachmann-Mosse commissioned contemporary music for the synagogue. One photo shows the fallow ground between Oranienburger and Johannisstraße, where in 2016 archaeologists excavated the foundation walls of the synagogue (fig. 15.8).

The synagogue was damaged on Kristallnacht (called "Reichskristallnacht" by the Nazis) on 9 November 1938 and was only partly restored. It was used as a substitute for the nearby New Synagogue from 1941 until the middle of 1942. Destroyed during the war, its ruins were later removed entirely.

Jewish orthodoxy left behind, German Jews like the Mosses adjusted to "the spirit of the time," as George wrote in his memoir, not religious but concerned with Jewish life within German culture. Rabbi Joseph Lehmann of the Reform Congregation played an important role for the family, notably in the children's education. George's father, Hans Lachmann-Mosse, as mentioned before, took an active part in the new composition of the liturgy, which was recorded and then used in many Reform Congregations, including in Jerusalem and in Madison, Wisconsin.

What remained after the annihilation of Jewish life in the community of Johannisstraße? One photograph was taken in the ruins of the synagogue

Figure 15.8. Reform Synagogue, Berlin: excavated foundation walls, 2016. (Photograph by Dirk Jericho.)

(fig. 15.10). It shows the bust of Rudolf Mosse, the great benefactor of the Congregation, thrown to the floor. What remains? In a moving passage of his memoir, George writes: "The liturgy was perhaps the only real bond with my youth left to me—much to my amazement, I heard parts of it when I attended a synagogue in Madison, Wisconsin, some twenty-five years after I had left Germany."[3]

With students of our Mosse project at the Humboldt University I made an excursion to Schenkendorf. Together we climbed across the broken fences of

Figure 15.9. The Reform Synagogue as it was in the 1920s from the outside. (Image courtesy of bpk / Photograph by Abraham Pisarek.)

Absence/Presence 293

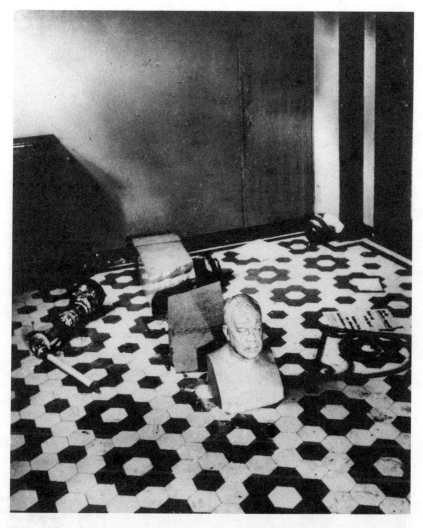

Figure 15.10. Bust of Rudolf Mosse in the devastated synagogue. (View of the destroyed interior and the bust of Rudolf Mosse. Image courtesy of Stiftung Neue Synagoge Berlin—Centrum Judaicum / Photographer unknown.)

the surrounding park und managed to get into the building through a broken window. We found only the despairing remains of former splendor.

When George visited Schenkendorf several times with the journalist Nina Bernstein in the early 1990s, he pointed out in his typical manner of sovereign coolness and a flash of emotional remembrance that the only item in the village meaningful to him was the church bell his father donated to the

Figure 15.11. The Schenkendorf estate as it was. (Mosse Residence Schenkendorf, F27726. Reprinted from George L. Mosse Collection AR 25137. Image courtesy of Leo Baeck Institute, New York / Photographer unknown.)

Figure 15.12. The former Mosse Schenkendorf estate in 2016. (Photograph by Daniel Bastmeyer.)

village. The bell includes an engraving of his given name: Gerhard Lachmann Mosse.

As George L. Mosse recalled, the extensive philanthropic projects of the Mosses reflected the status and self-confirmation of the economically successful Jewish entrepreneur. Through generations, the Mosse women were especially dedicated to charity, education, and healthcare for the disadvantaged. This charitable spirit was pioneered by Emilie Mosse, who made her own mark by establishing a *Mädchenhort* (girls' shelter) in 1895. There disadvantaged girls and mothers of all classes and religious affiliation could find shelter and food. During the Weimar Republic, George's mother Felicia continued these activities. Felicia's daughter Hilde, George's elder sister, the doctor and psychiatrist, furthered this commitment in her American exile by founding the Lafargue Clinic in Harlem with Frederic Wertham.

The stately and palace-like building of the Rudolf and Emilie Mosse Foundation, built between 1893 and 1895 in Berlin Schmargendorf, was home to various educational projects. Under the Nazis, the Mosse-Stift was used as a children's hospital, and Emilie and Rudolf Mosse's names were removed from the building. More recently, the building was renovated and is still used as a center of rehabilitation and youth work. When you pass the building now you will come

Figure 15.13. Mosse Schenkendorf estate inside, today. (Photograph by Elisabeth Wagner.)

across the Mosse memorial tablet and discover inside the "Emilie und Rudolf" Café, a meeting place for children, parents, and educators (fig. 15.15).

The most recognizable Mosse building in Berlin, an icon of architectural history in the emerging metropolis, was the Rudolf Mosse Publishing House. The *Berliner Tageblatt*—famous as the German *New York Times*—headquarters operated as the center of the press empire. The Press House, with more than

Figure 15.14. Mosse-Stift, built 1893–95. (Reprinted from picture postcard with the building of Rudolf Mosse's educational home, Schmargendorf, around 1920, Inv.-Nr. 2010/141/4, offset print, cardboard, 8.9 × 13.9 cm. Image courtesy of Jüdisches Museum Berlin.)

Figure 15.15. The Mosse-Stift in Berlin-Wilmersdorf 2008 with the "Emilie und Rudolf" Café in the right wing. (Photograph by Elisabeth Wagner.)

four thousand employees at times, was built between 1900 and 1903, covered six thousand square meters, and included an impressive Art Deco façade. During the Spartacus Revolt of January 1919, the building was damaged as insurgents set up their headquarters in the editorial offices. The massive building complex was reconstructed and modernized from 1921 to 1923 by the architect Erich Mendelsohn, a friend of the family. Mendelsohn's Bauhaus remodel was largely destroyed in the Second World War. Afterward, in East Berlin, at the edge of the wall, the building was used again as a printing house. The latest iteration, the Mosse Zentrum, was opened in 1995 and housed Humboldt University's German Department.

With George's prestige and support, we convinced the Mosse Zentrum investor and new owner, Hans Röder, to engage in some sort of symbolic capital, funding the Berlin Mosse Lectures, a project to commemorate the history of the

Figure 15.16. The original Mosse printing house. (Reprinted from the archive of Dr. Franz Stoedtner; fm1081367. Image courtesy of Bildarchiv Foto Marburg / Photographer unknown.)

Figure 15.17. The printing house after reconstruction and modernization, 1921–23, by Erich Mendelsohn. (House of the *Berliner Tageblatt* after Reconstruction by Erich Mendelsohn. Image courtesy of VG Bild-Kunst, Bonn 2020 / Photograph by Arthur Köster.)

Mosse family and the Publishing House and to advance the Mosse family's dedication to liberalism and democracy. Up to the present day, up to two hundred events have taken place with prominent speakers, scholars, politicians, artists, and writers from around the world, generously supported by the Mosse Foundation and its chairman, Roger Strauch.

On 14 May 1997, George himself gave the first Berlin Mosse Lecture in the atrium of the new Mosse Business Center, the former Publishing House: "The Liberal Legacy and the Public of National Socialism." George left his typescript with the Mosse Lectures, and we reproduced it on the occasion of the twentieth anniversary of our project in the *Mosse Almanach* of 2017. In his inaugural address, he recalled the liberal "spirit of the house." The written draft, composed in his native tongue, contains a few errors and corrections. More significant is what is missing: the German umlauts, absent on his American typewriter. In

Figure 15.18. The Mosse Center in Berlin 2010, corner: Jerusalemer Straße and Schützenstraße. (Photograph by Torsten Flüh.)

this lecture again, George insisted that, historically, *Bildung* and the ideals of Enlightenment were meant to provide a sense of identity and security for the German Jews, who fatally ignored the power of antisemitism and the destructive energies of Hitler's *Volksgemeinschaft*.

There is this absence, a missing "spirit of the house," or a physical and material loss which, as George wrote, separated him from his past, the void in the architectural shape of Libeskind's Jewish Museum that cannot be filled, restored, or restituted. George's German writing on the American typewriter somehow made us feel that, before reconstructing and claiming this heritage, we have to face this absence, this loss, which the Mosse family must have experienced in exile. In 1997, at the end of his lecture, we heard his sorrows and warning that the liberal democracy we have achieved since then could easily become endangered again: "Although the völkisch voices are now only fringe groups, as they did before, they can propel themselves into the political [realm] when the time is ripe and political, economic, and social crises converge."[4]

Notes

1. Daniel Libeskind in his Mosse Lecture at Humboldt University, Berlin, 6 June 1997.
2. Daniel Libeskind, "Between the Lines," in *Extension of the Berlin Museum with Jewish Museum Department*, ed. Kristin Feireiss (Berlin: Ernst & Sohn 1992).
3. George L. Mosse, *Confronting History: A Memoir* (Madison: University of Wisconsin Press, 2000), 36. On German television there is a series "Verlorene Orte" (Lost Places). The Mosse estate in the countryside is one of those, grandiosely named a "Rittergut" by its owners (a "knight's castle"), though it was built in the 1890s in classicistic style. Today it is a rundown and ruined shell of the former property. Schenkendorf, 15 kilometers away from Berlin, was a wonderful playground for the Mosse children and a splendid, convivial place where the Mosses hosted the cultural, social, and political elite of Berlin. After the Nazis sold the property in 1935, the grounds were again expropriated by the German Democratic Republic, and Schloß Schenkendorf became a service place for state and military facilities.
4. George L. Mosse, "Im Geist des Hauses," in *Mosse Almanach 2017*, ed. Elisabeth Wagner (Berlin: Vorwerk 8 Verlag, 2017), 40, "obgleich die volkischen [Völkischen] nur kleine Randgruppen stellen, [können] sie auch wie damals in das politische Zentrum vorstossen, wenn die Zeit reif ist und sich wie damals politische, e[ö]konomische und soziale Krisen u[ü]berschlagen."

16

The Mosse Art Research Initiative (MARI) at Freie Universität Berlin

MEIKE HOFFMANN

On 1 March 2017, Rudolf Mosse's heirs, together with the Freie Universität Berlin, founded the Mosse Art Research Initiative (MARI). This opened a new chapter in the research of cultural objects confiscated or otherwise lost due to persecution during the Nazi regime. For the first time, descendants of the victims of racial persecution agreed to cooperate with German institutions. The initiative was pioneered in particular by two individuals, Isabel Pfeiffer-Poensgen, then still general secretary of the Kulturstiftung der Länder and as of July 2020 Minister

Figure 16.1. Mosse Art Research Initiative—MARI-Portal. (Logo by Stan Hema, Berlin; Web design by Jan Lindenberg, Berlin.)

for Culture and Science, North Rhine Westphalia, and Hermann Parzinger, President of the Stiftung Preußischer Kulturbesitz.

The concept behind MARI is innovative in a number of ways and has great relevance in terms of creating a new model for cultural policy and cooperation. The descendants making the claims and the institutions they confront—two positions that are usually diametrically opposed—here work together in a highly transparent network that is vital to shaping the culture of memory and memorialization in Germany. The parties involved in MARI are accordingly creating important initiatives that will articulate and preserve knowledge concerning the Nazi regime's confiscation of art objects.

MARI's primary focus concerns the former art collection of Rudolf Mosse (1843–1920). At issue is the formation of the collection, its significance at the time, and the whereabouts of individual works following the liquidation of the collection by the Nazi regime. The project also seeks to investigate the political strategies known as "*Gleichschaltung*" (coordinated Aryanization). The *Gleichschaltung* began right after the Nazis came to power in 1933. MARI's work not

Figure 16.2. Rudolf Mosse (1843–1920), ca. 1880. (Image courtesy of Leo Baeck Institute New York / Berlin / Photograph by Debenham and Company, West Cowes, I.W.)

only adds to the history of this period but also helps narrate the persecution that the Mosse family experienced while also tracing individual members' paths of emigration. Using these findings, the full extent of the family's fate continues to reveal itself alongside the consequences for the family until today.

Who Was Rudolf Mosse?

As one of the most influential figures of the economic elite in the late nineteenth century, the name of the Jewish German publisher Rudolf Mosse is closely linked to the history of Berlin, the former capital of the German Empire. But beyond that popular legacy, a great deal about Rudolf Mosse and his wonderful achievements has been forgotten.

In 1861 Rudolf Mosse moved to Berlin from his hometown of Grätz in the Prussian province of Posen at the age of eighteen. He later founded the company Annoncen-Expedition Rudolf Mosse. The name of the firm referred to his idea of leasing pages in newspapers to place advertisements and thus allowing manufacturers to directly communicate with customers. Before Mosse, advertising one's goods was frowned upon. However, Mosse allayed advertisers' concerns by introducing a sophisticated aesthetic design element to the advertising pages. In a short time, Mosse rose to become the most important advertiser in Germany. In just five years, Mosse's company boasted over 250 branch offices around Germany and abroad.[1]

The next step in his career took Rudolf Mosse from the realm of advertising to publishing. In 1903 he moved into a new building situated in the heart of the fast-developing newspaper district in Berlin. Mosse's publishing house was outfitted with the latest technology and offered a modern, worker-friendly environment, as was proudly announced in postcards. Mosse-Verlag published daily newspapers, popular magazines, and nearly 130 specialty journals, along with exhibition catalogs, art publications, and much more. Among the most famous publications was the *Berliner Tageblatt*. In publication in 1871, it became the journalistic pride of the company and the leading Berlin newspaper.[2]

As editor in chief, Theodor Wolff, Rudolf Mosse's cousin, made a key contribution during the heyday of the paper in the 1910s and 1920s.[3] Wolff positioned the paper as both bourgeois and liberal, advocating for a pan-European international understanding and democratic reforms. He succeeded in inviting the elite of German journalism to write for the paper, alongside prominent authors and scholars, including the German-born physicist Albert Einstein, the German-Jewish journalist Kurt Tucholsky, the journalist Egon Erwin Kisch from Czechoslovakia, the German author Erich Kästner, and the publisher Peter

AGENTUREN
der
Annoncen-Expedition Rudolf Mosse

Aachen	J.A.Mayer'sche Buchhdlg. (G.Schwiening)	**Erfurt**	Bruno Neumann, in Firma Keyserache Hofbuchhandlung, Anger 11
Aalen	Eugen Pahl, Kommissionsgeschäft	**Eschwege**	L. J. Cahn
Aarau	A. Wyder-Brust, am Rain	**Essen a. d. Ruhr**	Jul.Deiter'sche Buchhdlg. (Inh.V.Wornzer)
Altenburg (S.-A.)	Gebr. Behrens, Zigarrenhandlung	**Esslingen a. N.**	Ernst Kirn, Glashandlung
Amberg	Andreas Winter	**Forst i. L.**	Rich. Goldmann, i. Fa. Otto Ganze Nachf.
Ansbach	Max Eichinger, Hofbuchhandlung	**Frankenberg i. S.**	Rob. Hass, Buchhändler
Apolda	W. Erbich, j. F. Friedrich Lauth Buchhdlg.	**Frankfurt a. O.**	Georg Pinnow, i.F. Rud. Kaiser, Wilhelms-
Aschaffenburg	Hans Börner, Wilhelmer Strasse 2		platz 14
Aschersleben	Bernhard Hooijer, Zigarrenhandlung	**Freiberg i. Sachs.**	M. Duncker, Wasserturmstr. 3
Auerbach i.Vogtl.	Gebr. Röber, Speditionsgeschäft	**Freiburg i. Baden**	E. Riednatter, Münsterplatz 28
Augsburg	Ferd. Doempke, Maximilianstrasse D 1	**Füssen**	Magnus Richter's Buchhandlung
Backnang	K. Kreutzmann, vorm. J. Rauh's Buchhdlg.	**Furtwangen**	Andr. Uttenweiler (Furtwang.Nachricht.)
Baden-Baden	Fr. Trapp, Spediteur, Langestrasse 34a	**St. Gallen**	E. Diem-Saxer, St. Leonhardstrasse 6
Bad Reichenhall	L. Braechter, Effekten- u. Wechselgeschäft	**Gera (Reuss)**	Hugo Rauschenbach
Balingen	Herm. Bossert, Konditor	**Giessen**	Brühl'sche Univers.-Druckerei, R. Lange,
Bamberg	A. Boxleidner		Schulstrasse 7. Fernsprecher 51
Barmen	Heidsieck & Gottwald, Neuerweg 45	**Glarus**	Casp. Beglinger-Jenny
Basel	Schmidt & Staehelin, Freie-Strasse 42	**Glauchau**	Arno Peschke, Buchhandlung (Otto Streit)
Bautzen	F. A. Reichel, Buchhandlung	**Gleiwitz**	J. Bund jr., Ring 25
Bayreuth	Heinrich Heuschmann jun.	**Glogau**	E. Zimmermann, Buchhandlung
Berchtesgaden	L. Vonderhann & Sohn	**Gmünd, Schwäb.**	Fr. Häcker, am Markt
Bergedorf	Wilhelm Meyer Wwe.	**Godesberg**	Gebr. Hesseler
Bern	C. Tenger, Amtsnotar, Schwanengasse 1	**Gotha**	Eduard Grigat, Marktstrasse 24
Bernburg	Emil Lösche, Markt 5	**Göppingen**	Erwin Herwig, Buchhandlung
Berneck	F. W. Münch	**Görlitz**	Carl Scherzer jun., Postplatz 11
Biberach	R. Retsch (Dorn'sche Buchhandlung)	**Göttingen**	Louis Hofer (Göttinger Zeitung)
Biel (Schweiz)	Rob. v. Bergen,Versich.-Bur., Zentralstr. 18	**Greiz**	Carl Pfroepffer
Bingen a. Rh.	H. Seligmann, Rathausstrasse 17	**Grossenhain**	R. Berndt (vormals Hugo Hofmann)
Blankenburg i. Th.	August Meyer (Schwarzatal-Zeitung)	**Grosschönau**	C. G. Wenzel (J, G. Müller)
Bochum	C. Mönigkreit, Hochstrasse 9	**Grünberg i. Schl.**	Emil Fowe, Neben der Post
Bonn a. Rh.	J. Bieck, Hoflieferant	**Guben**	L. Otterburg, Buchhandlung
Brandenburg a.H.	Otto Jork, Kurstrasse 7	**Güstrow**	Emil Opitz, in Firma Opitz & Co.
Braunschweig	B. Loeb, Poststrasse 6	**Gunzenhausen**	Georg Bücheler
Bremen	Clussen & Rosenkranz, Gueren 6	**Hainichen**	G. A. Bachmann, Kaufmann
Bromberg	Carl Beck, Töpferstrasse 1	**Halberstadt**	Carl Böge, j. F. Franz'sche Buchhandlg.
Bruchsal	D. Weber, Buchdruckerei (Bruchsal. Ztg.)	**Hall (Württ.)**	Ernst Richter, Buchhandlung
Burgstädt i. S.	Emil Albrecht, Buchhandlung	**Halle a. S.**	Louis Heise, Brüderstrasse 4
Cannstatt	Rudolf Kraut (Cannstatter Zeitung)	**Hameln**	Th. Buendeling
Cassel	Aug. Pachmann, Kölnische Strasse	**Hamm i. Westf.**	C. Dietrich'sche Buchhdlg., Gr. Weststr. 38
Celle	F. Scheunemann	**Hanau**	Paul Lauser (A. Priors Nachf.)
Chemnitz	Robert Melachner, Plan 7	**Hannover**	H. Degener, i Fa. C. Kuhlmann, Thielenpl. 5
Chur	E.Hornauer, Buchdruck (Bündner Tagbl.)	**Harzburg**	H. Woldag, Buchhandlung
Coblenz	Gebr. Friedrich, Buchhandlung	**Heidelberg**	L. Meder Nachf. (P. Hönicke), Hauptstr. 83
Coethen i. Anh.	Eugen Thormeyer	**Heidenheim a. B.**	Carl Rumpus, Kaufmann
Colmar i. Els.	Bauer & Meid, Geschäftsagentur	**Heilbronn a. N.**	Theodor Cramer, i. Fa. A. Scheurlen'sche
Crimmitschau	Barkhardt'sche Buchhandlung		Sort.-Buchhandlung
Danzig	Rud. Loewenstein, Hansaplatz 2	**Hersfeld**	Heinrich Sauer
Darmstadt	Christ. Kullmann, Obere Elisabethenstr. 14	**Hildburghausen**	Expedition der Dorf-Zeitung
Dessau	Carl Bobbe, Johannisstrasse 7	**Hildesheim**	Herm. Holinke, Schulstrasse 4
Detmold	Fr. Preuss	**Hirschberg i.Schl.**	Paul Robbe (Kuh'sche Buchhandlung, früher G. Schwaab)
Dieburg	Carl Eeh, Kaufmann	**Hof a. S.**	H. Hörmann (Hofer Anzeiger)
Dillenburg	Gebr. Richter, Buch- u. Musikalienhandlg.	**Hohensalza**	Max Bibro
Dillingen a. D.	Max Keller, Schreibwarenhandlung	**Homburg v. d. H.**	Louis Staudt, Buchhandlung
Dinkelsbühl	Carl Zehender	**Jena**	Franz Kleeberg
Döbeln i. S.	Emil Steixner	**Ilmenau**	Paul Schulze, Buchhandlung, Poststr. 8
Dortmund	Köppen'sche Buchhandlg., Hans Hornung	**Ingolstadt**	L.Stadelmeier, Verl. des Ingolst. Tagblatt.
Dürkheim a. d. H.	Ludwig Strauss	**Isny**	Julius Muna, Kassierer d. Gewerbebank
Duisburg	Friedr. Krieger, Buchhandlg., Königstr. 58	**Itzehoe**	Th. Brodersen's Buchhandlg. (Oluf Kragh)
Eberswalde	Hans Langewiesche (Ernst Rust's Nachf.)	**Kaiserslautern**	Otto Choedy, Alleestrasse 4
Ebingen	August Matthes	**Karlsruhe i. B.**	R. Graebner, Kaiserstr. 190a, Eing. Waldstr.
Eisenach	Aug. Nestler, in Firma Fritz Nestler	**Kattowitz**	Julius Herlitz, Buch- u. Kunstdruckerei,
Eisleben	Hans Gräfenhan, in Firma Kuhat'sche Buchhandlung (E. Gräfenhan)		Bahnhofstrasse (vis-à-vis Zentralbahnh.)
Elberfeld	Fr. Dümmeler, Morianstrasse 38/40	**Kaufbeuren**	Fr. Jüngling
Elbing	Walter Grunau, i. Fa. George Grunau		

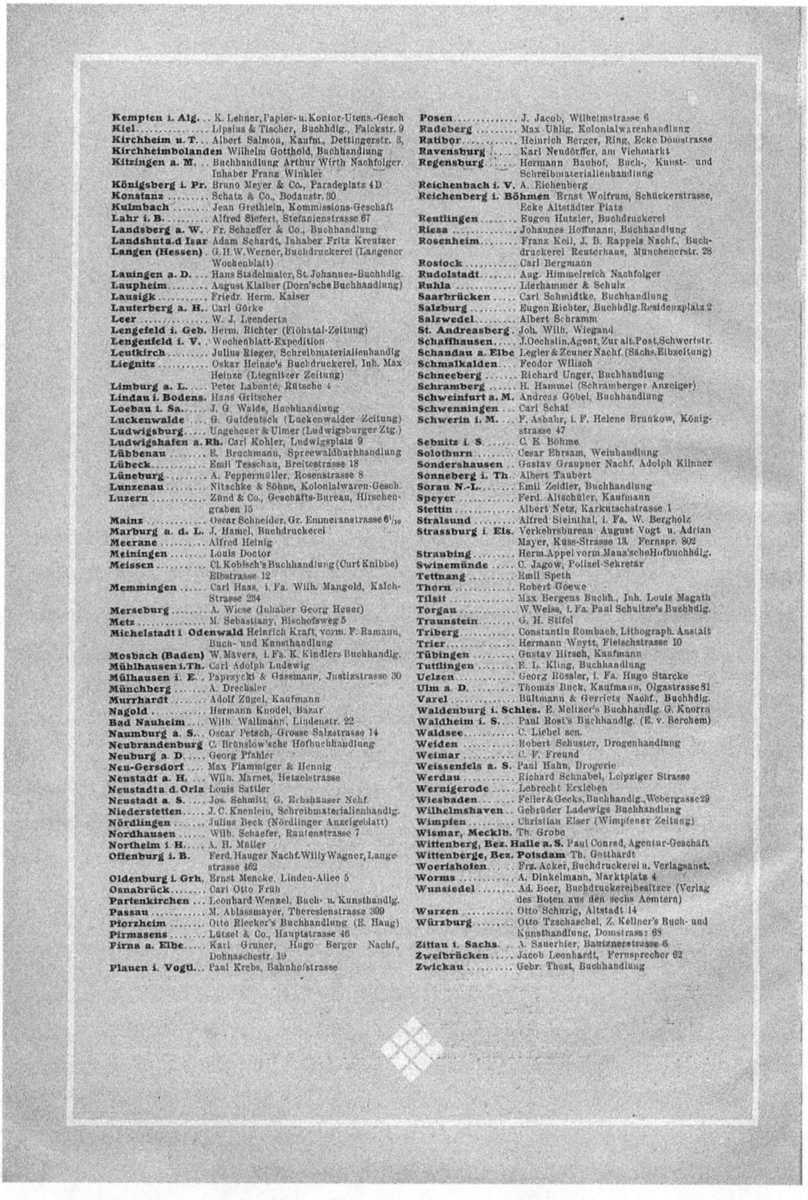

Kempten i. Alg. ... K. Lehner, Papier- u. Kontor-Utens.-Gesch
Kiel ... Lipsius & Tischer, Buchhdlg., Falckstr. 9
Kirchheim u. T. ... Albert Salmon, Kaufm., Dettingerstr. 3,
Kirchheimbolanden Wilhelm Gotthold, Buchhandlung
Kitzingen a. M. ... Buchhandlung Arthur Wirth Nachfolger. Inhaber Franz Winkler
Königsberg i. Pr. Bruno Meyer & Co., Paradeplatz 4D
Konstanz ... Schatz & Co., Bodanstr. 30
Kulmbach ... Jean Grethlein, Kommissions-Geschäft
Lahr i. B. ... Alfred Siefert, Stefanienstrasse 67
Landsberg a. W. .. Fr. Schaeffer & Co., Buchhandlung
Landshut a. d Isar Adam Schardt, Inhaber Fritz Kreutzer
Langen (Hessen) . G. H. W. Werner, Buchdruckerei (Langener Wochenblatt)
Lauingen a. D. ... Hans Stadelmaier, St. Johannes-Buchhdlg.
Laupheim ... August Klaiber (Dorn'sche Buchhandlung)
Lausigk ... Friedr. Herm. Kaiser
Lauterberg a. H. .. Carl Görke
Leer ... W. J. Leendertz
Lengefeld i. Geb. Herm. Richter (Flöhatal-Zeitung)
Lengenfeld i. V. . Wochenblatt-Expedition
Leutkirch ... Julius Rieger, Schreibmaterialienhandlg
Liegnitz ... Oskar Heinze's Buchdruckerei, Inh. Max Heinze (Liegnitzer Zeitung)
Limburg a. L. ... Peter Labonté, Rütsche 4
Lindau i. Bodens. Hans Gritscher
Loebau i. Sa. ... J. G. Walde, Buchhandlung
Luckenwalde ... G. Gutdeutsch (Luckenwalder Zeitung)
Ludwigsburg ... Ungeheuer & Ulmer (Ludwigsburger Ztg.)
Ludwigshafen a. Rh. Carl Kohler, Ludwigsplatz 9
Lübbenau ... E. Bruchmann, Spreewaldbuchhandlung
Lübeck ... Emil Tesschau, Breitestrasse 18
Lüneburg ... A. Peppermüller, Rosenstrasse 8
Lunzenau ... Nitschke & Söhne, Kolonialwaren-Gesch.
Luzern ... Zünd & Co., Geschäfts-Bureau, Hirschengraben 15
Mainz ... Oscar Schneider, Gr. Emmeranstrasse $6^{1}/_{10}$
Marburg a. d. L. J. Hamel, Buchdruckerei
Meerane ... Alfred Heinig
Meiningen ... Louis Doctor
Meissen ... Cl. Kobisch's Buchhandlung (Curt Knibbe) Elbstrasse 12
Memmingen ... Carl Haas, i. Fa. Wilh. Mangold, Kalchstrasse 234
Merseburg ... A. Wiese (Inhaber Georg Heuer)
Metz ... M. Sebastiany, Bischofsweg 5
Michelstadt i Odenwald Heinrich Kraft, vorm. F. Ramann, Buch- und Kunsthandlung
Mosbach (Baden) W. Mävers, i. Fa. K. Kindlers Buchhandlg.
Mühlhausen i. Th. Carl Adolph Ludewig
Mülhausen i. E. . Paprzycki & Gassmann, Justizstrasse 30
Münchberg ... A. Drechsler
Murrhardt ... Adolf Zügel, Kaufmann
Nagold ... Hermann Knodel, Bazar
Bad Nauheim ... Wilh. Wallmann, Lindenstr. 22
Naumburg a. S. .. Oscar Petsch, Grosse Salzstrasse 14
Neubrandenburg C. Brünslow'sche Hofbuchhandlung
Neuburg a. D. ... Georg Pfahler
Neu-Gersdorf ... Max Flammiger & Hennig
Neustadt a. H. ... Wilh. Marnet, Hetzelstrasse
Neustadt a. d. Orla Louis Sattler
Neustadt a. S. ... Jos. Schmitt, G. Erbshäuser Nchf.
Niederstetten ... J. C. Knenlein, Schreibmaterialienhandlg.
Nördlingen ... Julius Beck (Nördlinger Anzeigeblatt)
Nordhausen ... Wilh. Schaefer, Rautenstrasse 7
Northeim i. H. ... A. H. Müller
Offenburg i. B. Ferd. Hauger Nachf. Willy Wagner, Langestrasse 462
Oldenburg i. Grh. Ernst Mencke, Linden-Allee 5
Osnabrück ... Carl Otto Früh
Partenkirchen ... Leonhard Wenzel, Buch- u. Kunsthandlg.
Passau ... M. Ablassmayer, Theresienstrasse 399
Pforzheim ... Otto Riecker's Buchhandlung (E. Haug)
Pirmasens ... Lützel & Co., Hauptstrasse 46
Pirna a. Elbe ... Karl Gruner, Hugo Berger Nachf., Dohnaschestr. 19
Plauen i. Vogtl. .. Paul Krebs, Bahnhofstrasse

Posen ... J. Jacob, Wilhelmstrasse 6
Radeberg ... Max Uhlig, Kolonialwarenhandlung
Ratibor ... Heinrich Berger, Ring, Ecke Domstrasse
Ravensburg ... Karl Neudörffer, am Viehmarkt
Regensburg ... Hermann Bauhof, Buch-, Kunst- und Schreibmaterialienhandlung
Reichenbach i. V. A. Eichenberg
Reichenberg i. Böhmen Ernst Wolfrum, Schückerstrasse, Ecke Altstädter Platz
Reutlingen ... Eugen Hutzler, Buchdruckerei
Riesa ... Johannes Hoffmann, Buchhandlung
Rosenheim ... Franz Keil, J. B. Rappels Nachf., Buchdruckerei Reuterhaus, Münchenerstr. 28
Rostock ... Carl Bergmann
Rudolstadt ... Aug. Himmelreich Nachfolger
Ruhla ... Lierhammer & Schulz
Saarbrücken ... Carl Schmidtke, Buchhandlung
Salzburg ... Eugen Richter, Buchhdlg. Residenzplatz 2
Salzwedel ... Albert Schramm
St. Andreasberg . Joh. Wilh. Wiegand
Schaffhausen ... J. Oechslin, Agent, Zur alt. Post, Schwertstr.
Schandau a. Elbe Legler & Zeuner Nachf. (Sächs. Elbzeitung)
Schmalkalden ... Feodor Wilisch
Schneeberg ... Richard Unger, Buchhandlung
Schramberg ... H. Hammel (Schramberger Anzeiger)
Schweinfurt a. M. Andreas Göbel, Buchhandlung
Schwenningen ... Carl Schäl
Schwerin i. M. ... F. Asbahr, i. F. Helene Brunkow, Königstrasse 47
Sebnitz i. S. ... C. E. Böhme
Solothurn ... Cesar Ehrsam, Weinhandlung
Sondershausen .. Gustav Graupner Nachf. Adolph Klinner
Sonneberg i. Th. .. Albert Taubert
Sorau N.-L. ... Emil Zeidler, Buchhandlung
Speyer ... Ferd. Altschüler, Kaufmann
Stettin ... Albert Netz, Karkutschstrasse 1
Stralsund ... Alfred Steinthal, i. Fa. W. Bergholz
Strassburg i. Els. Verkehrsbureau August Vogt u. Adrian Mayer, Küss-Strasse 13. Fernspr. 802
Straubing ... Herm. Appel vorm. Manz'sche Hofbuchhdlg.
Swinemünde ... C. Jagow, Polizei-Sekretär
Tettnang ... Emil Speth
Thorn ... Robert Goewe
Tilsit ... Max Bergens Buchh., Inh. Louis Magath
Torgau ... W. Weiss, i. Fa. Paul Schultze's Buchhdlg.
Traunstein ... G. H. Stifel
Triberg ... Constantin Rombach, Lithograph. Anstalt
Trier ... Hermann Woytt, Fleischstrasse 10
Tübingen ... Gustav Hirsch, Kaufmann
Tuttlingen ... E. L. Kling, Buchhandlung
Uelzen ... Georg Rössler, i. Fa. Hugo Starcke
Ulm a. D. ... Thomas Buck, Kaufmann, Olgastrasse 81
Varel ... Bültmann & Gerriets Nachf., Buchhdlg.
Waldenburg i. Schles. E. Meltzer's Buchhandlg. G. Knorrn
Waldheim i. S. ... Paul Rost's Buchhandlg. (E. v. Berchem)
Waldsee ... C. Liebel sen.
Weiden ... Robert Schuster, Drogenhandlung
Weimar ... C. F. Freund
Weissenfels a. S. Paul Hahn, Drogerie
Werdau ... Richard Schnabel, Leipziger Strasse
Wernigerode ... Lebrecht Erxleben
Wiesbaden ... Feller & Gecks, Buchhandlg., Webergasse 29
Wilhelmshaven .. Gebrüder Ladewigs Buchhandlung
Wimpfen ... Christian Elser (Wimpfener Zeitung)
Wismar, Mecklb. Th. Grobe
Wittenberg, Bez. Halle a. S. Paul Conrad, Agentur-Geschäft
Wittenberge, Bez. Potsdam Th. Gotthardt
Woerishofen ... Frz. Acker, Buchdruckerei u. Verlagsanst.
Worms ... A. Dinkelmann, Marktplatz 4
Wunsiedel ... Ad. Beer, Buchdruckereibesitzer (Verlag des Boten aus den sechs Aemtern)
Wurzen ... Otto Schurig, Altstadt 14
Würzburg ... Otto Tzschaschel, Z. Kellner's Buch- und Kunsthandlung, Domstrasse 68
Zittau i. Sachs. .. A. Sauerbier, Bautznerstrasse 6
Zweibrücken ... Jacob Leonhardt, Fernsprecher 62
Zwickau ... Gebr. Thost, Buchhandlung

Figure 16.3. Zeitungskatalog Rudolf Mosse, 1908. (Image courtesy of private archive.)

Figure 16.4. "Greetings from a reader of the *Berliner Morgenzeitung*," n.d. Postcard. (Courtesy of private archive.)

Suhrkamp. In this way, the *Berliner Tageblatt* became the voice of an entire era, and sometimes was even called the "German Times."[4]

The design of the publishing house's headquarters was an art nouveau style, with the front corner of the building dominated by a huge relief with a female nude. Rudolf Mosse explained the depiction as an allegory of truth, since—as he put it—nothing but the naked truth gets reported in his newspapers. In her left hand, the female figure holds an owl, in her right a mirror, which along with the allegory of truth can be read as an expansive symbol for the reflection of wisdom.

Mosse's era ended with the fall of the German Empire. After Germany's defeat in the First World War and the establishment of the Republic on 9 November 1918, the left-wing extremists radicalized. In the early days of 1919, they initiated the Spartacist Uprising. The revolutionaries occupied the printing presses of the social democratic newspapers, and conditions approaching civil war took hold. Mosse's publishing house was also occupied by the rebels. The building, especially the corner decoration, was seriously damaged by gunfire.[5] On 11 January 1919, the provisional Council of the People's Deputies crushed the uprising. Just a few months later, the Weimar Constitution took effect, and the monarchy was replaced with a parliamentary democracy.

Although some of Rudolf Mosse's political goals were achieved, he did not feel up to the challenges posed by the new governmental system and withdrew

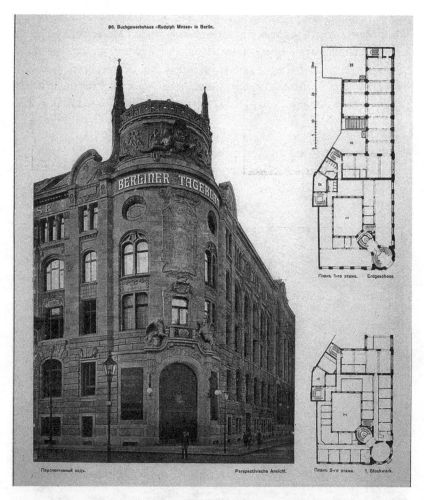

Figure 16.5. Mosse Publishing House's headquarters, Berlin. Architects: Cremer & Wolffenstein (1900–1903). (Gavriil V. Baranovskij, 2003. *Architekturnaja ènciklopedija vtoroj poloviny XIX veka: Detali; izbrannye tablicy*. Vol. 2 [Moscow: Strojizdat, 1902], 216.)

from the business in 1919 at the age of seventy-five. A short while later, in September 1920, he died of heart failure at his country estate, Rittergut Schenkendorf.[6] From then on, Mosse's son-in-law Hans Lachmann-Mosse took over the business. Between 1921 and 1923, the new head of the publishing house had the headquarters completely redesigned by the architect Erich Mendelsohn. His design was a paradigmatic example for the so-called streamlined modernism that can be considered a symbol for the progressive, dynamic Berlin of the 1920s.

The building, reconstructed in Berlin after being destroyed in the Second World War, attests to the legacy of the publisher Rudolf Mosse. And yet hardly anyone is familiar with Mosse as an art collector, a patron, a promoter of cultural projects, and a friend of numerous artists. A public acknowledgment of his work as a philanthropist in the cultural realm took place for the first time in 2017 at the exhibition *Mosse im Museum* (Mosse at the Museum) at Berlin's

Figure 16.6. Mosse Publishing House's headquarters, Berlin. Architect: Erich Mendelsohn (1921–23). (Image courtesy of Leo Baeck Institute New York / Berlin.)

Figure 16.7. August Gaul, *Liegender Löwe* (*Reclining Lion*), 1904. Installation at James Simon Gallery. (Photograph by Meike Hoffmann, 6 June 2019.)

Ägyptisches Museum.[7] And since the summer of 2019, a prominent work from the former collection of Rudolf Mosse, the *Reclining Lion* by August Gaul, has been on exhibit at the new James Simon Gallery, a reception building for visitors to Museum Island in the center of Berlin. James Simon was a contemporary of Rudolf Mosse, and just like him, an art collector and philanthropist.[8] Mosse's lion sculpture in combination with Simon's name is intended to honor the tradition of Berlin patronage, which was so important for the blossoming of the capital's cultural life.

What Art Did Rudolf Mosse Collect and What Can We Learn about Him from His Collection?

Having already become an affluent man, in 1874 Rudolf Mosse married Emilie Loewenstein, the daughter of a merchant family. Erna Felicia, Rudolf Mosse's child from a different relationship, was adopted by Emilie.[9] For himself and his family, Mosse had a neo-Baroque, majestic, three-story city residence built in the early 1880s. The palais, designed by the highly esteemed Berlin architects Gustav Ebe and Julius Benda, included a sculpture hall and a gallery for an art collection.[10] The home's location attested to Mosse's self-confidence. Mosse Palais, facing Leipziger Platz, was situated next to the glamorous department store Wertheim and was part of cosmopolitan city life. The court side on Voßstraße was also directly in the middle of the government district of the empire. As a representative of the business elite, Mosse saw himself as holding a position of responsibility in society and politics.

To symbolize his worldview, in 1883 Rudolf Mosse commissioned the Berlin sculptor Max Klein to create a monumental frieze, visible from afar, for the facade facing Leipziger Platz. The two-meter-high frieze with the title "Die Erhebung des deutschen Genius" (The Rise of German Genius), shows the development of the German Empire in several stages. In the final scene, the German eagle triumphs over the Gallic rooster.[11] Mosse obviously wanted to set a monument to the victory of the German states in the Franco-Prussian War of 1870–71 and, thus, to the long-awaited foundation of the German Empire. The frieze is interrupted by a figurative segmental pediment over the balcony niche on the top floor. The scrollwork cartouche, placed at the center, is emblazoned with the initials of Rudolf Mosse, RM. In this way, the owner of the residence inscribed himself right into the middle of German history.

Figure 16.8. Rudolf, Emilie, and Erna Felicia Mosse, ca. 1895. (Image courtesy of Leo Baeck Institute New York / Berlin.)

Figure 16.9. Mosse Palais, Berlin, front facing Leipziger Platz. Architects: Ebe & Benda (1882–85). (*Architektonische Studien-Blätter*, Series 1, No. 53, 1889 / Photograph by Hermann Rückwardt.)

Rudolf Mosse's childhood was shaped by the March Revolution in 1848, when liberal bourgeois, democratic circles called for the unification of the individual states of the German Confederation and the independence of the German nation as central goals. The struggle against restorative forces of the allied ruling houses also inspired the emancipation movement in the Jewish population, which identified with the German nation despite the antisemitism dominant in the country.[12] Mosse's pride about the triumph of the German nation over France and the newly achieved independence of a state, which seemed to fulfil the demands of the 1848 Revolution, defined not just this frieze but also the scope of his art collection.

With the completion of the Mosse Palais, he began to acquire his first works in the early 1880s. Besides acknowledged masters, such as Adolph von Menzel, Wilhelm Leibl, Franz von Lenbach, Anselm Feuerbach, and Reinhold Begas, Mosse also collected works by artists who were less well known, including Paul Meyerheim, Max Clarenbach, Eduard von Gebhardt, Gustav Eberlein, Walter Schott, and Hugo Lederer.[13] Important for him was not the individual masterpiece, but its inclusion within the current German cultural world. The art collection's emphasis was thus placed on German realism from the second half of the nineteenth century. In addition, Mosse assembled a library with nearly ten thousand volumes of German literature.

The nationalist orientation of his tastes helps explain why the collection included no French artists at all, despite the fact that they were considered world leaders on the art market at the time. Nevertheless, Mosse did acquire individual works by contemporary Swedish, Dutch, Italian, Spanish, and Swiss artists.[14] However, they were collected with a comparative purpose; they served as referential points to the development of art in neighboring countries and provided for the German art in Mosse's collection the sense of a pan-European international understanding. The contemporary national focus of his collection was only modified after Mosse began to listen to the advice of the culture journalist of the *Berliner Tageblatt* Fritz Stahl (pseudonym of Siegfried Lilienthal) and to his son-in-law Hans Lachmann-Mosse. This explains how Dutch, Italian, and English masters from the sixteenth, seventeenth, and eighteenth centuries became part of the collection, as well as bronzes from Benin and art objects from East Asia, giving the collection a broader historical value.[15] Still, the emphasis of the collection remained focused on German art from the nineteenth century, and all French art was still excluded.

Besides the national and temporal emphases, the preferred motifs of the works reveal more about Rudolf Mosse the collector. The paintings, drawings, and watercolors are dominated by popular genre scenes, portraits of famous figures from the period, and landscapes from the region, as was generally typical for realism. The artists of this current thus refused the academic art world of history painting, arcadian landscapes, allegories, and mythological scenes, opening art up to individual values. Behind this was the desire to create an art that could be understood by everyone and, hence, accessible not only to the educated elites.[16] German realism thus went down in history as an essentially democratic art. All the same, it should be noted that realism, in contrast to the naturalism of that time, did not depict negative aspects of life, excluding them in favor of a higher ideal. Indeed, realism was a romanticization of reality, and in collecting works of realism, Mosse paid homage to the period that allowed him his financial and social ascent.

As a donor and philanthropist, Rudolf Mosse also found himself in the company of several like-minded individuals. If collecting, promoting, and exhibiting art was reserved for the princes and noble houses in German states until the end of the eighteenth century, the bourgeois patron emerged in parallel with the social transformations of the nineteenth century and peaked with the rise of a financially powerful commercial bourgeoisie class. This was especially true in Berlin, where an extensive culture of art patronage emerged during the era of the German Empire and which found expression in a large number of important collections and newly founded museums.[17]

In the process, the promotion of art and culture was not a purpose in and of itself but was linked to concrete goals of social reform. It was further embedded in an overarching liberal concept of the social order. The practice of bourgeois patronage questioned the social limits of court etiquette and created an entirely new set of values, which served as the foundation for a contemporary society. To that extent, patronage and philanthropy linked the commercial bourgeoisie to the cultural bourgeoisie and thus strengthened the inner cohesion of the population against the politics of restoration under Emperor Wilhelm II.

A relatively large portion of Berlin's art patrons consisted of individuals of Jewish origin. Despite their legal and administrative restrictions, they felt a commitment to charitable work through their own financial rise. In the spirit of the Jewish religious obligation of *tzedakah*, roughly translated as charity, the promotion of science, art, and culture was also complemented by social projects as well. The Mosses had wide-ranging interests and were very active in charity work.[18] They supported health and social welfare programs. They donated scholarships and funded various associations, insured the social security of their employees, and financed the erection of hospitals and orphanages. On 1 April 1895, the "Mossesche Erziehungsanstalt für Knaben und Mädchen" was founded in Berlin-Wilmersdorf, a nondenominational orphanage free of charge, where children—predominantly from the impoverished middle classes—were cared for.[19] Emilie Mosse was later awarded a medal by the Emperor for her work at the orphanage, and Rudolf Mosse, besides many other honors, was granted an honorary doctorate by the University of Heidelberg.[20]

Accordingly, Mosse was a typical representative of Berlin art patronage and philanthropy, like the cotton dealer James Simon. Another prominent figure in these circles was Eduard Arnhold, who made his fortune in coal. Like Mosse and Simon, he was also active in social charity work. The personal artistic tastes of the three patrons, however, differed strikingly from one another. In purely financial terms, it would have been easy for Mosse to establish a collection of masterpieces of high value like those of Arnhold or Simon. At the time, he was considered Berlin's third-richest man.[21] But Mosse's taste was thoroughly down to earth.

Rudolf Mosse also seemed to have consciously avoided imperial circles. When the emperor offered him an aristocratic title, he declined the offer.[22] James Simon and Eduard Arnhold, in contrast, were among the "Emperor's Jews."[23] Although both Berlin patrons belonged to the bourgeois liberal movement, they became close confidants of the Emperor, who in turn supported them.

A quintessential aspect of Mosse's motivations for his collection and his political viewpoints can be seen in the wall painting *Das Gastmahl der Familie Mosse* (*The Mosse Family Banquet*) from 1899. The publisher commissioned Anton von Werner with the mural for the dining hall at his residence on Leipziger Platz. The painting shows the family members with friends seated at a richly set table against a landscape in the backdrop. Many of the figures in this scene are family members; Rudolf Mosse had six brothers and five sisters, most of whom lived in Berlin. But the focus of the painting is decidedly placed on the friends of Rudolf Mosse portrayed in the mural. In the painting, the hosts sit modestly in the background and on the sidelines. Because of the picture's compositional arrangement, the attention of the beholder is initially drawn to the upright male figure near the center with the raised chalice in his right hand. The person in question was the Privy Councillor of Justice and writer Albert Träger, who at the time sat in the German Reichstag for the Deutsche Freisinnige Partei (DFP). Additional figures in the painting were also members of that political

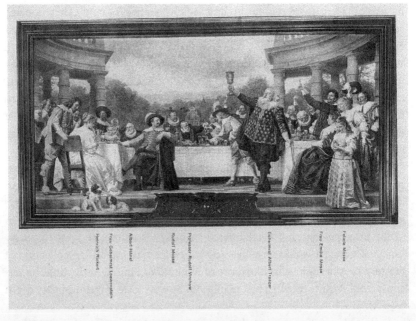

Figure 16.10. Anton von Werner, *Das Gastmahl der Familie Mosse* (*The Mosse Family Banquet*), 1899. Mural, dining hall, Mosse Palais (destroyed during the Second World War). (Haus der Sammlungen Rudolf Mosse [Rudolf Mosse Gallery], Berlin: Mosse, 1929.)

party, for example, the important Berlin pathologist Rudolf Virchow, with whom Mosse was close friends, as well as the lawyer Albert Haenel and the journalist and philosopher Heinrich Rickert: they all held important positions in the DFP and they had all published regularly in Mosse's *Berliner Tageblatt*.[24] Mosse, as host of this gathering, identifies with the political viewpoints of his guests. The DFP had a liberal-left program: it promoted increasing the role of parliament in the constitutional monarchy, securing press freedom, and establishing equality among all religions, including Judaism.

The painting shows Mosse and his friends in a form of representation otherwise reserved for the aristocracy, thereby questioning the primacy of the reactionary power elite of the German Empire. In addition, the banquet scene is placed in the Dutch seventeenth century, a heyday of art and scholarship, an era of religious freedom, and bourgeois prosperity. It seems that Mosse had the mural painted as a rejection of the Emperor. Emperor Wilhelm II, who began his rule in 1888, proved to be an increasingly stubborn enemy of liberalism in all its aspects. It must have been a provocation of a special kind when Mosse had the mural painted by none other than Anton von Werner, the so-called court painter of Wilhelm II. The mural was destroyed during the Second World War. It only exists now as an oil sketch that ended up, decades after the liquidation of the Mosse collection, in Berlin's Jüdisches Museum via the art trade and was restituted to the Mosse heirs in 2016.[25]

From the very beginning, Mosse had intended to make his art collection accessible to the public to communicate the message behind it and thereby fulfill its actual purpose. As of 1909, the Mosse Palais could be viewed after prior registration or in the framework of charity events for a fee of between two and five marks. The proceeds in turn went to charitable causes.[26] The collection enjoyed great popularity among expert circles and the general public alike and was even referred to as the Mosse Gallery or the "Mosseum."[27]

What Happened to the Art Collection after Rudolf Mosse's Death?

By the start of the First World War, Rudolf Mosse had essentially completed his collecting. Mosse died in 1920 and his wife Emilie passed away four years later. In 1924 Mosse's adopted daughter Felicia inherited his entire estate. With her husband Hans Lachmann-Mosse, they kept the Mosse Palais on Leipziger Platz and its art collection open to the interested public; large receptions continued to be held here. Meanwhile, the Lachmann-Mosse couple remained with their three children, Rudolf, Hilde, and George, in their own villa on Maaßenstraße in Berlin-Tiergarten and also resided at Mosse's country estate Rittergut Schenkendorf, southeast of Berlin.[28]

Figure 16.11. Kunstsammlung Rudolf Mosse Berlin, Rudolph Lepke's Kunst-Auctions-Haus, 29–30 May 1934. (Auction catalog, cover.)

Just after 1933, the Nazis confiscated Mosse's publishing company and drove the Lachmann-Mosse family into exile. Hans and Felicia left some of their possessions in storage with the old Berlin moving company Georg Silberstein & Co, which was soon afterward "Aryanized." The holdings in their warehouse became government property and were auctioned off. The possessions left in Berlin by the Mosses, their real estate as well as Mosse's art collection, were declared "ownerless" and placed under a trusteeship tasked with liquidating the Mosses' property. In May 1934 the collection objects and furnishings at the Mosse Palais were sold by the auction house Rudolph Lepke in Berlin. A week later, an additional auction of artworks and furnishings was held by the Berlin auction house Union at Felicia and Hans Lachmann-Mosse's villa on Maaßenstraße.[29]

After the end of the Second World War, Felicia Lachmann-Mosse made claims under the auspices of the reparation and compensation laws for her lost estate. At the end of 1954, the Berlin court confirmed her loss of control over her private estate as of April 1933. But she was forced to withdraw her claims for compensation for the collections auctioned in 1934. Although this court decision acknowledged the seizure of her art collection, Felicia would have had to submit a so-called *Verbringungsnachweis* (proof of transfer) for the purposes of compensation, which should have stated that the individual works had remained in Germany—in other words, in the area where the compensation laws applied—after the auction.[30] Of course, she was not able to comply with this requirement. The compensation case also did not account for the real estate owned by the Mosse family. Most of those properties were located in the newly founded GDR and thus outside the jurisdiction of the new West German laws. These included not only Mosse Palais on Leipziger Platz but also Rittergut Schenkendorf. In the early 1990s, after Germany's reunification, the heirs of Felicia and Hans Lachmann-Mosse received their real estate back on the basis of the newly released Act on the Settlement of Open Property Issues under Recognition of Losses Related to Nazi Persecution. Two decades later, the Mosse Foundation began the search for art works from the former Rudolf Mosse collection and established the Mosse Art Restitution Project (MARP) together with the American and German legal representatives of the heirs.[31]

What Are the Challenges of the Mosse Art Research Initiative?

This is the point of departure for the Berlin-based Mosse Art Research Initiative. MARI is faced with several challenges: unlike provenance research undertaken at museums to examine their own collections, the artworks of the Mosse collection are not present but absent. This means the team members have no access to the rear sides of the artworks with the stickers, stamps, notes, and numberings that are so important for provenance research. Before we can begin with the actual work, the collection must be reconstructed and all the associated artworks identified. Only then can the distribution paths of the confiscated objects, the exact circumstances of their confiscation, and their current location be investigated. Indeed, in addition to provenance research, MARI's project is also one of reconstruction, authentication, and localization, which requires methodological clarification. Further, the wide variety and extent of the former Mosse collection increases the difficulty of the research project; besides the works of German artists from the nineteenth century and the East Asian art and Benin bronzes already mentioned, applied art, tapestries, antiquities, and smaller excavation finds from Egypt completed the collection, not to mention the library with its ten thousand volumes. To that extent, a wide-ranging knowledge of art and cultural history and experience in source-based sorting of material of original and reproducible works define the wide parameters of the project.

Compounding these difficulties, the confiscation of the Mosse collection also occurred during the early phase of the Nazi regime. At the time, the looting of art was carried out in uncoordinated and nonuniform manner. It was only with the enactment of the Nuremberg Race Laws in September 1935 that the systematic seizure of assets began, which was then documented in detail. In this respect, the research of the MARI team extends beyond its importance for the Mosse family, specifically, and instead offers German and art historians unique insights into Aryanization and the seizure contexts of other cases between 1933 and 1935.

The complexity of the range of objects confiscated and dispersed has required the inclusion of partners with expertise on very different levels. For this reason, MARI was planned as a "cooperative research project." In addition to close collaboration with the heirs of Rudolf Mosse, the team of researchers works with colleagues from numerous other institutions, museums, and archives; some have already dealt with the Mosse case, others have been confronted with claims, and still others possess archival materials and documentation relevant to the Mosse family.

In this way, MARI researchers can bring together work that has already been conducted but might not have been shared between different individuals and institutions. MARI relies on an interdisciplinary, decentralized, academically coordinated network rather than the one-scholar provenance research that is primarily funded in Germany. In MARI, information does not flow as a kind of end product, from one direction to another, as in assigning tasks, but freely and openly among the circle of experts, where it is subject to friction and filter coefficients. The project is not hierarchically organized, and none of the partners is in charge of the final interpretation of the findings. Berlin's Freie Universität (FU Berlin) as an unbiased institution, unaffected by claims of restitution, is an ideal location for a project like MARI. In addition, research on Berlin's art patronage has a long tradition here, beginning in the late 1990s with the research of art historian Thomas W. Gaethgens, later director of the Getty Research Institute in Los Angeles, and of historian Bernd Sösemann, who has written on the *Berliner Tageblatt* and its editor in chief Theodor Wolff.[32] Furthermore, the possibility of involving students in the project is a great advantage in mastering the immense amount of research. In the framework of regularly offered seminars on the reconstruction of the Mosse Collection in the university's art department, the students undertake basic research in which they systematically evaluate source material before the MARI team takes on the in-depth research on the individual works in question.

Restitution negotiations are explicitly not part of the project. MARI is a research initiative, not a restitution initiative. Suggestions are not actively transmitted; instead, the facts are passively placed on a joint work platform to which all cooperation partners have access. Only in this way can the project maintain neutrality; this is essential for our concern, which promotes communication among the various parties involved. As long as priority is placed on fact-finding, all partners share the same interest orientation. Here, the project goes far beyond the frame of its actual research area. The joint work of claimants, current holders of the works in question, and independent scholars provides insights into various approaches and differing standpoints. In doing so, it works toward the goal announced by the Washington Principles to find just and fair solutions for all parties in a consensus manner. With its open policy of mutual understanding as a conceptual and, at the same time, praxis-driving strategy, MARI is able to prepare the foundation of a joint, and not only German, memorial culture.

What Results Has MARI Achieved?

At present, MARI has made a number of key findings concerning the profile and extent of Rudolf Mosse's collection. While an overall inventory is still not known, five additional collection catalogs from 1900, 1912, 1913, 1915, and 1921 have been located, expanding our knowledge already garnered from known catalogs from 1908 and 1932.[33] The catalogs, however, do not register all the works in the Mosse collection but, rather, only those works exhibited at Mosse Palais. These catalogs are unique because the artworks are cataloged according to display room rather than alphabetical by artist. In this way, we can precisely reconstruct how Mosse hung and then rehung or exchanged the works.[34] Furthermore, from their placement in the respective rooms, their identification can be undertaken

Verzeichniss
der
Rudolf Mosse'schen
Kunst-Sammlung

Parterre.
Skulpturenhalle.
Bronze-Gruppe — Ein Philosoph.

Erste Etage.
Saal I.

Oesterley	Waldlandschaft.
Gussow	Damenportrait.
Ruß	Meran.
Lappini	Ora et labora, Marmorgruppe.
Lappini	Volere è potere, Marmorgruppe.
Zerter	Kinderkopf, Marmorbüste.
Bermann	Centaur, Bronze.
Moser	Psyche, Bronze.
Wolff	Kaiser Wilhelm I., Bronze

Figure 16.12. Verzeichnis der Rudolf Moss'schen Kunstsammlung, Berlin: Mosse, 1900. Collection catalog, cover/first page. (Courtesy of Gutenberg-Museum Mainz, Bibliothek.)

in comparison with written testimony from visitors to the Mosse Palais or photographs of the interior, which are, however, very rare. Rudolf Mosse seems to have disliked photographs being taken of the interior of his home. While he often commissioned photographs of his family members and the publishing house, and of the interiors and offices there as well, we know of no photographs from his lifetime that show his collection in the Mosse Palais. This taboo was only broken by Mosse's heirs. In 1932 Hans Lachmann-Mosse invited the participants of the World Economic Conference being held in Berlin to a reception at Mosse Palais and, for this reason, allowed photographers. The Mosse Family Estate at New York's Leo Baeck Institute includes photographs taken by the journalist couple Wally and Walter Israel during that event. They show participants from the conference against the walls on which segments of paintings and tapestries or sculptures are visible. In combination with the catalogs, the rooms can be precisely mapped out with the works exhibited.

Already three years before, a similar event had taken place. In August 1929, the World Advertising Convention was held in Berlin. With over five thousand guests from all over the world, it remained for years the largest international conference in Germany. To complement the official events and banquets, Hans Lachmann-Mosse invited select participants to an afternoon tea reception at Mosse Palais. For this purpose, he had a German/English catalog printed that was illustrated with photographic reproductions of sixteen masterpieces from the Mosse Collection. In 1932 this catalog was once again published for the World Economic Conference. Until now, the MARI team has not been able to find historical photographs of the event in 1929, but we learned that the guest list included the artist Liselotte Friedländer. For the fashion section of the *Berliner Tageblatt*, she drew individual scenes of the tea reception, bearing great documentary value for our research. Several of her sketches and drawings show the lion by August Gaul in its place of display. Another drawing includes a bust that can clearly be identified as a portrait of Ludwig van Beethoven by the sculptor Gustav Landgrebe.

As a whole, the catalogs include 206 works. Besides the presentation at the Palais on Leipziger Platz, Mosse also acquired works for his other residences, especially Rittergut Schenkendorf, where the family spent the summer months. Here his art collection was ultimately incorporated into that of his daughter and son-in-law. By including the art objects kept there, together with the works not exhibited and the prints, works of applied art, antiquities, and East Asian art, the collection was much larger than the Mosse Palais catalogs suggest.

Likewise, the MARI team has gained important insights into the acquisition strategies of Rudolf Mosse. For example, Mosse rarely purchased works from

Figure 16.13. Lieselotte Friedländer, *Modezeichnung*: "Die Teilnehmer des Weltwerbekongresses als Gäste des Herrn Hans Lachmann-Mosse zum Tee im *Haus der Sammlungen Rudolf Mosse*" (Drawings from the Interior of the Mosse Palais for a Fashion Magazine, Berlin), 1929. Pencil, brush in ink, wash, opaque white on paper, 29.50 cm × 24.40 cm. (Courtesy of Stiftung Stadtmuseum Berlin.)

Figure 16.14. Lieselotte Friedländer, *Modezeichnung*: "Mode und Reklame" (Drawings from the interior of the Mosse Palais for a fashion magazine, Berlin), 1929. Pen and brush in ink on glassine, 25.50 cm × 17.60 cm. (Courtesy of Stiftung Stadtmuseum Berlin.)

the art trade. Instead, he attended the annual exhibitions at the art academies and the *Kunstvereine* (art associations) in Berlin, Munich, Dresden, and Düsseldorf; his publishing house produced the catalogs for these exhibitions, and he therefore had prior knowledge of the works to be shown and offered. He also used his business contacts, his wide-ranging social network, and his many personal contacts with artists to facilitate the purchase of art. Rudolf and Emilie enjoyed studio visits and were happy to commission artists with special requests, not least for the sake of artist welfare.

To reconstruct his social and business networks, MARI has also drawn on Rudolf Mosse's vast correspondence, available at Berlin's Landesarchiv.[35] As an entirely new source, the MARI team recently found a file at Berlin's Staatsbibliothek with more than two hundred photograph cards, kept under the title "Album Amicorum," previously unidentified.[36] The cardboard cards in a DIN A3 format were completed by artists, friends, and business partners of Rudolf Mosse and sent to him for his seventieth birthday in 1913. They each contain a photograph of the individual and a written dedication, sometimes also featuring drawings, prints, or watercolors. In cooperation with colleagues from the Staatsbibliothek Berlin, MARI could trace the path of this album as part of the liquidation of the Mosse library by the Nazis as well as the later location and acquisition of the cards in 1953 by the Wissenschaftliche Bibliothek in East Berlin, whose holdings became part of the collection at today's Staatsbibliothek. In the meantime, the album has been restituted to the Mosse heirs together with the publications from Mosse's library.

What Have Been the Results of More In-Depth Research into the Individual Artworks from the Mosse Collection?

Over the past three years, the MARI team has been able to clearly assign 828 works of art to the Mosse collection and conduct research on all the works. For 212 of the pieces, MARI has conducted more in-depth research, aided by its cooperation partners and the students involved in the project. These 212 pieces have been clearly identified and, for twenty-nine of them we were able to trace the individual steps of their whereabouts to their current location during the first two funding periods (2017–20).

In twenty-seven cases, the MARI team has been able to locate the art works, even if there are still gaps in their chain of provenance. For example, *Repentant Magdalene* has been identified and located; since 1947 the painting has been included as part of the art collection of the city of Düsseldorf. The painting is a partial copy of a painting from Berlin's Kaiser-Friedrich-Museum, destroyed during the Second World War. Rudolf Mosse purchased the *Magdalene* as a

Figure 16.15. Peter Paul Rubens (Werkstatt, Studio), *Die Büssende Magdalena* (*The Repentant Magdalene*), ca. 1634–1640. Oil on canvas, 115 × 170 cm. (Haus der Sammlungen Rudolf Mosse [Rudolf Mosse Gallery], Berlin: Mosse, 1929.)

painting by Rubens in 1912; today it is attributed to the Rubens studio. Until 1936, it was held by auction house Lepke, then the trail disappeared. Sometime before 1943, it was acquired by Moritz Julius Binder, former director of Berlin's Zeughaus and then an art dealer and advisor to Hermann Göring. After Binder's death, the painting came to Düsseldorf as a bequest. The gap in provenance between 1936 and 1943 could mean that there was a second aggrieved party, as shown in the case of another work from the Mosse Collection. In these cases, the Mosse heirs are always open to negotiations to achieve a consensus solution, although the fixed guidelines stipulate that the first party alone should be restituted. In this spirit—and without concrete reference to another purchaser during the remaining gap—the culture committee of the city of Düsseldorf in 2018 decided unanimously to restitute the work to the heirs of Felicia Lachmann-Mosse.[37]

For eleven works, all questions have been clarified and research concluded. This includes a self-portrait by the Berlin-based Swiss artist Karl Staufer-Bern in 1883.[38] In general, it remains difficult to identify drawings and to research their whereabouts, since they are only rarely clearly documented. In this case as well, no historical photos were available. The drawing could only be clearly identified on the basis of its inscription. A Swiss student from the FU Berlin discovered it at Kunstmuseum Winterthur, in her home country. The Berlin entrepreneur and collector Julius Freund purchased the work in 1934 for 320 RM at the Lepke auction; shortly thereafter, it was handed over to Kunstmuseum Winterthur in Switzerland for safekeeping along with the rest of his collection. After the death of Julius Freund in 1941, who had only left for Great Britain in 1939, it became part of the museum collection. This example points to the contentious nature of *Fluchtgut*, or "flight assets," that is specific to Switzerland and currently being discussed in a heated debate in the context of confiscations related to Nazi persecution.[39]

Another painting from this group, *Peasant Girl at the Window* by the Swedish painter Anders Zorn, was acquired by Mosse in 1907 at the latest.[40] At the 1934 Lepke auction, it was purchased by the Berlin art dealer Karl Haberstock, who was himself one of the auction's organizers. Haberstock purchased it in commission for the auction house Bukowski in Stockholm. There it was acquired in 1936 by a Swede as a marriage gift for his wife, who never lent it or exhibited it publicly. Only by chance did the MARI team learn that the painting is still held by the family. In 2013 it was stolen, but then it resurfaced briefly thereafter. Upon its return to the holders, the Stockholm tabloid *Aftonbladet* reported on the painting and illustrated the article with a photo of the painting's hitherto unknown color scheme. Via the director of Zorn Museum in Mora, Sweden, the MARI team tried to establish contact with the family, but there does not seem to be any interest in further clarification of the matter. Since the Washington Principles do not apply to private individuals, the lawyers of the Mosse heirs could do nothing further.

In total, eleven works have also been restituted on the basis of MARI provenance research, or consensual solutions have been found between the current holder and the heirs; the rest remain in negotiation. Considering the dimension of the number of restitutions in comparative projects, where one restitution a year takes place, MARI's methodology has more than proven its effectiveness.[41] MARI has also set a few precedents. In the United States, a case concerning the painting *Skater* by the American artist Gari Melchers was heard in court at the end of 2019.[42] The painting from the former Mosse Collection was discovered by another FU student in 2017 at Bartlett Arkell Museum in Canajoharie, New York. The museum posted a photograph of the painting to announce its closing for the winter season on Facebook. The MARI team then engaged in subsequent

Figure 16.16. Gari Melchers, *Skaters/Winter* (ca. 1880–1890), from the former Rudolf Mosse Collection, 2016/17.

in-depth research in close cooperation with the director of the museum, Suzan Friedländer, who provided us with the documentation available at the museum. According to our research, the work made its way to the Macbeth Gallery in New York just several months after the 1934 Lepke auction. From the Macbeth Gallery it was purchased by Bartlett Arkell and immediately donated to the Arkell Museum. So, in this case, there is a clearly established chain of provenance without gaps. But the Bartlett Arkell Museum, due to its private status, is not bound to comply with the Washington Principles, and frequently the bylaws of private foundations have clauses that make it difficult to restitute the works. For this reason, the U.S. Attorney General invoked the In-Rem process, whereby stolen goods imported to the United States—not just works looted from the Nazis, but all stolen goods—can be confiscated.

Among the latest discoveries in a private collection is Hanns Fechner's portrait of the famous writer Theodor Fontane, a key work in Mosse's collection.[43] He purchased it as one of his very first works since Theodor Fontane was one of the most important representatives of German realism in literature. The MARI

Figure 16.17. Hanns Fechner, *Theodor Fontane*, 1893. Oil on canvas, 120 × 87 cm. (Kunstsammlung Rudolf Mosse Berlin, Rudolph Lepke's Kunst-Auctions-Haus, 29–30 May 1934.)

team has found out that the portrait was sold at the Lepke auction to the Nazi Reichsbank president Hjalmar Schacht for 680 RM. By taking up contact with the heirs of Hjalmar Schacht, we learned that the painting was still in the possession of the family in southern Germany. The owner, herself a retired lawyer, refuses to acknowledge that the painting was confiscated as a result of racial persecution.

What Were the Results of the Contextual Research?

Parallel to research on individual works and closely linked to these investigations, the team also carries out contextual research. The most important finding to date regards Hans Lachmann-Mosse's formerly presumed declaration of the company's bankruptcy on 13 September 1932. As the MARI team was able to demonstrate, there is no evidence of this, although it would have had to be mentioned in several places since corporate bankruptcy already required public notice at the time.[44] Rather, the claim seems based on a numerical mistake in a publication from 1959, then accepted in the years to follow, further falsified to the point of saying that "Aryanization of the Mosse company in the usual sense" did not take place.[45] In fact, exactly a year later than claimed, on 13 September 1933, the Nazis opened settlement proceedings, which in the case of an existing formal bankruptcy would not even have been possible. The Mosse-Verlag is only one of many companies whose debt, due to inflation and the Great Depression, was used as leverage to push Jewish owners out of business.[46] The patterns of explanation used for this were continued in the postwar years in an undifferentiated way and continue until today, as the Mosse case shows.

Why Is MARI Portal an Essential Component of the Project?

On 2 May 2018, already a year after the start of the research, the MARI portal, a project website with a database, went online in German and in English.[47] At this point, the vastly beneficial cooperation with the heirs of Rudolf Mosse, who financed the IT part of the project, is to be pointed out once again. While provenance research in Germany is now supported all over the country by the federal and state governments, the lack of digital strategies is increasingly devastating. Online databases, until now primarily used in a unidimensional fashion, as a place of storing information, do not use the technical possibilities available to the fullest for networked and collaborative research. In addition, the researched data is subject to an individual process of selection and evaluation. Researched data that is considered wrong for the object in question or not relevant falls by the wayside. The results thus represent the tip of the iceberg and can be understood as fact-based interpretations depending on the researcher in question, which have no objective and consistent quality.

With this awareness in mind, the MARI team at the FU developed an open and flexible research instrument. Here, foundational information on Rudolf Mosse and his family, on the significance of his art collection and its loss are published, as well as current information, contributions from cooperation partners, and central sources, for example, the collection catalogs in PDF format.[48] The heart of the website is a database in which all works from the Mosse Collection—828 in all—that we have been able to research are listed. Since our project is about the reconstruction of a destroyed collection, the (so to say virtual) object is not the focus but, rather, the sources and the knowledge generated from them. All relevant information is transcribed, fragmented, and transferred to structured data, making it readable by computer to prepare for a future in the semantic web. The interlinked content is available on various levels for different users. Results can be critically questioned using metadata and rapidly updated with the link system, without losing any information. This establishes the most important foundations to make the research achieved effective and accessible over the long term. And as a special new feature, we now offer users a visualization of the hanging of the works at Mosse Palais. By clicking on

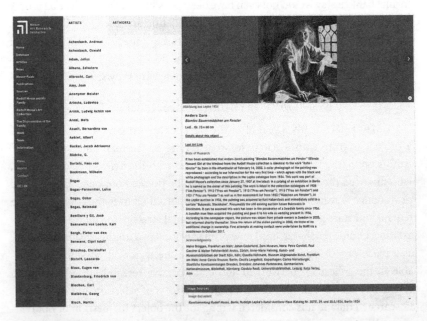

Figure 16.18. MARI-Portal, Database. (Conception by Michael Mueller.)

Figure 16.19. View from the Courtyard of the Destroyed Mosse Palais with the *Reclining Lion* by August Gaul, 1945. (Image courtesy of bpk Kunstbibliothek SMB / Photograph by Willy Römer.)

the different floors and the individual rooms, the reader encounters information about the works formerly shown there.[49]

A photo concludes this project report. It shows the *Reclining Lion* by August Gaul that is mentioned briefly several times in this chapter. This photograph with the sculpture in the courtyard of Mosse Palais was taken in May 1945 after the capitulation of Germany. To the left of the lion is the grave of a German soldier, and the Palais around it has been destroyed down to its foundations. Hitler's Neue Reichskanzlei, toward which the lion seems to be looking, is also in ruins. As if by way of a miracle, the lion—which unlike the Lachmann-Mosse family, who fled in 1933, and the artworks, auctioned off in 1934—was a witness of events at Mosse Palais and, ultimately, was spared the fate of catastrophic destruction under the Nazi regime. With its current installation in the James Simon Gallery, the sculpture is therefore not only a symbol of Rudolf Mosse's patronage, but also an authentic witness of the family's fate, a warning reminder of the Nazi regime, and at the same time a beacon of hope for overcoming the politics of racism and exclusion.

Notes

1. Richard Hamburger, *Zeitungsverlag und Annoncen-Expedition Rudolf Mosse Berlin* (Berlin: Organisation Verlagsgesellschaft (Hirzel), 1928).
2. Andreas Halen and Uwe Greve, *Vom Mosse-Verlag zum Mosse-Zentrum* (Berlin: DBM-Media-Verlag, 1995); Fritz Härtsch, *Rudolf Mosse—ein Verleger revolutioniert das Werbegeschäft* (Zürich: Mosse, 1996).
3. Bernd Sösemann, *Theodor Wolff: Ein Leben mit der Zeitung* (Stuttgart: Franz Steiner Verlag, 2013).
4. Elisabeth Kraus, *Die Familie Mosse: Deutsch-jüdisches Bürgertum im 19. und 20. Jahrhundert* (München: C.H. Beck), 495–96.
5. A. Gross, "Berlin im Zeichen des Terrors," *Weltspiegel*, Berlin, 19 January 1919.
6. Rudolf Mosse is buried in the Weißensee Cemetery, Berlin. Albert Katz, "Nachruf auf Rudolf Mosse," *Allgemeine Zeitung des Judentums* 84, no. 32 (17 September 1920).
7. Jana Helmbold-Doyé and Thomas Gertzen, "Mosse and Museum: The Support of Berlin Publisher Rudolf Mosse (1843–1920) for the Egyptian Museum Berlin, 2017," MARI-Portal, 14 July 2020, https://www.mari-portal.de/posts.
8. Olaf Matthes, *James Simon: Die Kunst des sinnvollen Gebens* (Berlin: Bostelmann & Siebenhaar, 2011).
9. Rudolf and Emilie Mosse, *Unser gemeinschaftliches Testament*, 1920/29/01, Leo Baeck Institute, New York (hereafter LBI), Mosse Family Collection (MFC), AR 25184, Box 30, Folder 22.
10. For the first time, Jost Hermand has dealt with the Rudolf Mosse Collection. Hermand, "Zweierlei Moderne: Das Kunstverständnis Rudolf Mosses und Hans Lachmann-Mosses," in *Aufbruch in die Moderne*, ed. Anna-Dorothea Ludewig (Cologne: DuMont Buchverlag, 2012), 250–71; Landesarchiv Berlin (hereafter LAB), Bauakten A Rep. 010-02 Leipziger Platz 15.
11. Max Klein to Rudolf Mosse, 1894/08/11, LAB, NL Mosse E Rep. 061-16 1514-1517.
12. Michael A. Meyer, ed., *Deutsch-Jüdische Geschichte in der Neuzeit*, vol. 3, *Umstrittene Integration: 1871–1918* (Munich: C.H. Beck, 2000), 163.
13. Catalogs of the art collection of Rudolf Mosse from 1900, 1908, 1912, 1913, 1915, 1921, and 1929/32, MARI-Portal, 14 July 2020, https://www.mari-portal.de/page/sources.
14. Catalogs of the art collection of Rudolf Mosse from 1900, 1908, 1912, 1913, 1915, 1921, and 1929/32, MARI-Portal, 14 July 2020, https://www.mari-portal.de/page/sources.
15. Max Osborn, "Die Kunstsammlung Rudolf Mosse," *Kunstchronik*, 23, no. 18 (1 March 1912): column 282–83.
16. Horst Bredekamp, *Theorie des Bildakts* (Berlin: Suhrkamp, 2010).
17. Sven Kuhrau, *Der Kunstsammler im Kaiserreich: Kunst und Repräsentation in der Berliner Privatsammlerkultur* (Kiel: Ludwig, 2005).
18. Elisabeth Kraus, "Jüdisches Mäzenatentum im Kaiserreich: Befunde—Motive—Hypothesen," in *Bürgerkultur und Mäzenatentum im 19. Jahrhundert*, ed. Jürgen Kocka and Manuel Frey (Berlin: Fannei und Walz, 1998), 38–53.
19. Viktoria Gehricke, "Die Stifterportraits Rudolf und Emilie Mosses aus dem ehemaligen Mosse-Stift Berlin-Schmargendorf" (bachelor's thesis, Freie Universität Berlin, 2019).

20. Kraus, *Die Familie Mosse*, 187; Doctor honoris causa degree, 1918/1/12, LBI, MFC, AR 25184, Box 2, Folder 30.
21. Anette Thomas, "R. Mosse—Ein Medienzar im Kaiserreich," in *Berlin in Geschichte und Gegenwart*, Jahrbuch des Landesarchivs Berlin (Berlin: Gebrüder Mann, 2006), 51–72.
22. Kai Drewes, *Nobilitierungen von Juden im Europa des 19. Jahrhunderts* (Frankfurt am Main: Campus Verlag, 2013), 57–58.
23. Drewes, *Nobilitierungen von Juden*, 57–58.
24. Rudolf Mosse, *Haus der Sammlungen Rudolf Mosse* (Berlin: Mosse, 1932), 2.
25. Anton von Werner, "Skizze zu dem Wandbild [Ein Festmahl]," MARI-Portal, 13 July 2020, https://www.mari-portal.de/details/1474.
26. Willi Oswald Dressler, *Dresslers Kunstjahrbuch: Ein Nachschlagebuch für deutsche bildende und angewandte Kunst* (Berlin: Ernst Wasmuth, 1909), 452.
27. Paul Meyerheim to Rudolf Mosse, 1889–1913, LAB NL Mosse, E Rep. 061-016, 2027-2046.
28. George L. Mosse, *Confronting History: A Memoir* (Madison: University of Wisconsin Press, 2000).
29. *Besitz L.-M., Villa Maassenstrasse 28, Berlin W*, Auction Catalog, Auktions-Haus Union, Berlin, 1934/6-7/06.
30. Kammergericht Berlin, Decision 1954/11/12, cited after Bescheid über die Rückübertragung der Eigentumsrechte an einem Grundstück (Restitution) nach dem Gesetz zur Regelung offener Vermögensfragen in der Fassung des 2. VermRÄndG vom 14. Juli 1992 (BGBl. I Nr. 33 S. 1257)—VermG–, 1992/11/11, BVA File 26363, 4.
31. The Mosse Art Restitution Project (MARP), 13 July 2020, https://mosseartproject.com.
32. Thomas W. Gaehtgens, *Der Bürger als Mäzen* (Opladen: Westdeutscher Verlag, 1998); Sösemann, *Theodor Wolff*.
33. "Collection Catalogs," MARI-Portal, 13 July 2020, https://www.mari-portal.de/page/sources.
34. "Sammlungspräsentation im Mosse-Palais, Leipziger Platz," MARI-Portal, 13 July 2020, https://www.mari-portal.de/rooms.
35. LAB NL Mosse, E Rep. 061-016.
36. "Album Amicorum," MARI-Portal, 20 August 2020, https://www.mari-portal.de/album.
37. "Petrus Paulus Rubens, Werkstatt, *Die büßende Magdalena*," MARI-Portal, 13 July 2020, https://www.mari-portal.de/db/847.
38. "Karl Stauffer-Bern, *Selbstbildnis*," MARI-Portal, 13 July 2020, https://www.mari-portal.de/db/1055.
39. Museum Oskar Reinhart, *Fluchtgut II: Zwischen Fairness und Gerechtigkeit für Nachkommen und heutige Besitzer*, Museum Oskar Reinhart, Winterthur, 31 August 2015, https://www.lootedart.com/web_images/pdf2015/OR_FlyerA5_Fluchtgut2_RZ_V2_1.pdf.
40. "Anders Zorn, *Blondes Bauernmädchen am Fenster*," MARI-Portal, 13 July 2020, https://www.mari-portal.de/db/832.

41. Sara Angel, "Restitution About-Face: Max Stern, the Return of Nazi-Looted Art and Düsseldorf's Double Game," in *The Terezín Declaration—Ten Years Later. The Documentation, Identification and Restitution of the Cultural Assets of WWII Victims. Proceedings of an international academic conference held in Prague on 18–19 June 2019* (Prague: Documentation Centre for Property Transfers of Cultural Assets of WWII Victims, 2019), 88–97.

42. "Gari Melchers, *Schlittschuhläufer*," MARI-Portal, 13 July 2020, https://www.mari-portal.de/db/806.

43. "Hanns Fechner, *Theodor Fontane*," MARI-Portal, 13 July 2020, https://www.mari-portal.de/details/772.

44. Claudia Maewede-Dengg, "The Dispossession of the Lachmann-Mosse Family," MARI-Portal, 13 July 2020, https://www.mari-portal.de/page/the-dispossession-of-the-lachmann-mosse-family.

45. Peter de Mendelsohn, *Zeitungsstadt Berlin: Menschen und Mächte in der Geschichte der deutschen Presse* (Berlin: Ullstein, 1959), 335–38; Kraus, *Die Familie Mosse*, 506, 518–19.

46. Frank Bajohr, "Arisierung" in *Hamburg: Die Verdrängung der jüdischen Unternehmer 1933–1945* (Hamburg: Christians, 1997).

47. "Die Mosse Art Research Initiative (MARI)," MARI-Portal, 13 July 2020, https://www.mari-portal.de.

48. "Collection Catalogs," MARI-Portal, 13 July 2020, https://www.mari-portal.de/page/sources.

49. "Sammlungspräsentation im Mosse-Palais, Leipziger Platz," MARI-Portal, 13 July 2020, https://www.mari-portal.de/rooms.

17

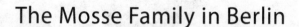

The Mosse Family in Berlin

Cultural Capital for Subsequent Generations

FRANK MECKLENBURG

Among the second-generation refugee historians, George Lachmann Mosse stands out with his productivity and originality. What enabled Mosse to produce that output? Was it that he figured as a witness to history in times of great changes? Was it that his background provided him with an unusual perspective? I want to look at the latter. The following biographical essay seeks to answer that question.

To begin, few of Mosse's fellow historians grew up in circumstances comparable to his own. Mosse's parents and grandparents were part of a small elite; the Mosse name remains a larger-than-life symbol of a short era between 1871 and 1933. The rapid economic and social ascendancy within only two generations was to be destroyed before George L. Mosse's generation came into its own. Mosse was a young teenager in Berlin in 1933. The city was then at the center of German history. Now, a century and a half later, the city has become a place that tries to remember an era that seems so unimaginable to us now. Mosse and his cousin, the economic historian Werner Mosse (henceforth Werner), eventually turned to the history of modern Germany. Library shelves have been filled with accounts of that history, not a small portion were added by the Mosse cousins. On these shelves we also find the one book by Elisabeth Kraus about the Mosse family story and a broader sense of the milieu the Mosse cousins grew up in, *Die Familie Mosse: Deutsch-jüdisches Bürgertum im 19. und 20. Jahrhundert*, published in 1999, the same year George L. Mosse died.[1] This monumental study of eight hundred densely printed pages is an amazing account. Kraus went through all imaginable archives and information sources to reconstruct a picture of the social and intellectual environment and the personal networks and connections

Figure 17.1. Mosse brothers: Albert, Salomon, Paul, Emil, Theodor, Rudolf, Max Mosse. (Image courtesy of Mosse Family Collection, Leo Baeck Institute Archives.)

Figure 17.2. Mosse sisters: Margrete Bloch, Anna Wetzlar, Clara Alexander, Elise Hartog, Leonore Cohn, Therese Litthauer. (Image courtesy of Mosse Family Collection, Leo Baeck Institute Archives.)

that give a very precise sense of the Mosse family milieu that informed his universe of ideas. In her chapter on Jewish identity and public involvement, "Jüdisches Selbstverständnis und Engagement," Kraus provides a detailed picture of the Mosse family and all their connections to the older established Jewish families of Berlin and, more so, shows the civil and philanthropic participation of the prominent Jewish families in the emerging metropolis in the decades before World War I.[2] She details the engagement in Jewish community affairs as another parallel universe of organized life in a complex society, which did not necessarily mean religion. Family wealth and the work of a foundation, das Stiftungswesen, characterized civil engagement when large amounts of capital enabled private welfare for the poor and needy. Most of these activities were destroyed first by the inflation after World War I and finally by the Nazi takeover.[3] It is at that moment when George was cast out from his milieu. But he was left with these impressions and experiences that took several decades to come to the surface in the form of a rich historiography.

Late in life, George wrote his memoirs, reflecting, among many other things, on his family history and how he emerged from this constellation. To a German reader, the title of the German edition, *Aus großem Hause*, would make reference to the nobility status of the Mosse family.[4] His grandfather, Rudolf Mosse, had made a tongue-in-cheek pun with a commissioned painting by Anton von Werner situating a family gathering in a Renaissance setting. But instead, "The House of Mosse" refers to the business empire of the Mosse company, which was essentially a family business. Mosse's cousin Werner used the phrase "the House of Mosse" in his 1959 essay on Rudolf Mosse and the company.[5] And rather than the family, it was the story of the Mosse company that shaped the legacy of the name and the reasons why that name virtually disappeared for many years from the history books—or, if mentioned, it appeared in ways that cast a light on personal failures and shortcomings. Owned by the Mosse family, the famous newspaper the *Berliner Tageblatt* was one of the leading liberal opposition voices to the rise of the Nazis and therefore one of the first targets in 1933. The chief editor was Theodor Wolff, a cousin (and nephew of Rudolf Mosse's mother Ulrike, née Wolff). Rudolf Mosse's younger brother Emil had entered the company as an apprentice in 1870 and ran the business side of all domestic and foreign branches until his death in 1911. "But without the involvement of Emil Mosse, the company would not have seen the expansion of the business. While Rudolf mainly dealt with the publishing company and the editorial side of his papers, Emil's task was the business side of the company. He controlled in an outstanding way all domestic and foreign branches of the advertisement business.... They called him the Napoleon of ads."[6]

Figure 17.3. Anton von Werner, *Das Gastmahl der Familie Mosse* (1899).

Figure 17.4. Emil Mosse. (*Fest-Schrift zur Feier des fünfzigjährigen Bestehens der Annoncen=Expedition Rudolf Mosse. Zum 1. Januar 1917 gewidmet von den Geschäftsführern* [Berlin, 1917].)

The writer of these lines, Alfred Schwabacher, was not a family member. He had worked for the company starting in 1901 as a very talented young man of twenty-one and stayed with the firm until 1939.[7] Schwabacher won Rudolf Mosse's trust in the early days of his employment and was dispatched to Zurich in 1903. Already before 1933, when the Nazi machine destroyed the company, he saved what could be saved with the Zurich branch. In 1933 he was called back from Zurich to Berlin—at that point he was the chief executive of the Mosse company (in the meantime he had become a Swiss citizen and was therefore less vulnerable to Nazi arrest)—to "negotiate" the "transfer" from the owners to the Nazi takeover. Hans Lachmann-Mosse, Mosse's father and part-owner after Rudolf's death in 1920, had to flee the country to avoid the fate of Rudolf S. Mosse, son of the elder Rudolf's brother Emil Mosse who died in April 1933 in Nazi custody. Schwabacher managed not only the Swiss branch but all the foreign offices of the company. It is remarkable that the two major postwar publications about the Mosse newspaper enterprise, Peter de Mendelssohn's *Zeitungsstadt Berlin* (1959) and Margret Boveri's *Wir lügen alle* (1965), do not mention Schwabacher at all. Boveri worked at the *Berliner Tageblatt* after it had been taken over by the Nazis and wants to make the reader believe that there was a continuity into the Third Reich. In both books, all blame for an apparent capitulation goes to Hans Lachmann-Mosse.[8] It is only in Elisabeth Kraus's book that Schwabacher returns to the story.[9] But the myth of the personal failure endured, and the details of the demise of the admittedly complex company remains a subject of future research. It is against this confusing backdrop and partial family history that George L. Mosse, and also Werner, came of age and received the impetus to start their scholarship on the roots and pursuits of Nazi Germany.

Rudolf and Emil's grandsons, George L. and Werner E. Mosse, investigated the era of the Great House of Mosse, that is from the late nineteenth century until the Hitler era, around the same time in the late 1950s. George pursued the story from a cultural point of view, while Werner analyzed the economic side. George wrote to his cousin after reading his article on their grandfather in the *Leo Baeck Institute Year Book* of 1959, "I am delighted to read for the first time an account of Rudolf Mosse that makes sense."[10] In the introductory paragraph, Werner wrote:

> The striking commercial and industrial development of Germany in the second half of the nineteenth century opened for many of the recently emancipated German Jews unrivaled opportunities for economic advancement. Among those who were enabled by the rapid economic expansion to acquire wealth and distinction, Rudolf Mosse occupies a prominent place. The father of large-scale

advertising in Germany, he was able during a business career extending over fifty-three years to build up a firm which acquired a world-wide reputation. His activities as a publisher gained for him a prominent position in German public life. He also became a millionaire.... Rudolf Mosse was not only a remarkable individual but also a typical representative of a generation and an age. His career, therefore, illustrates some aspects of German-Jewish relations.[11]

The article provided in-depth analysis of the emergence of the Mosse company, which started out as an advertisement agency, including the success and failures along the way, and also made clear that the move into the newspaper business, which greatly contributed to Rudolf's public prominence, was initially an afterthought. Werner Mosse demonstrated that these early complexities of the Mosse enterprise continued throughout the development of the company, growing into a conglomerate of diverse companies. Sixty years after the Nazi movement destroyed the enterprise, it was this complexity that became the focal point of criticism. The economic crisis of the late 1920s together with the end of the Weimar Republic made it almost impossible to continue, but then the attacks of the Nazis gave it the last push into the grave. Margret Boveri's account of the *Berliner Tageblatt* under the direction of Nazi journalists may have suggested a continuity, but that was not the case.[12] Werner Mosse's conclusion was: "The first great war destroyed his [Rudolf's] world and that of his generation. The generation which followed—Jewish and Gentile alike—was left to contend with sterner conditions and harsher ideologies in an impoverished and embittered world."[13]

George L. Mosse was born in 1918, the same year as his cousin Werner E. Mosse. Both became historians, and both changed the emphasis of their research over the course of their careers. George started out in early modern English history, Werner in Russian history. Both later moved on to topics related to the milieu of their families, George in cultural and intellectual history, Werner in economic history. In 1958 they were in contact about planned conferences and their mutual interest in the historical period of which the family history was part. Despite their shared interest and correspondence, however, George mentions his cousin Werner in his memoirs only once.[14]

We do not know much about Werner Mosse's upbringing. He was named after his father's younger brother who died early in World War I. Werner's father, Rudolf S. Mosse, named after his grandfather Rudolf, owned a country estate and supported youth emigration to Palestine. He was murdered in the early Nazi terror in 1933. We know much more about George's upbringing. Walter Laqueur, his longtime friend and collaborator, wrote in the introduction to George's memoir:

> Why did he prefer in later years the study of fascism to pursuing his studies in the history of the Reformation in England? He probably reached the conclusion that so much work had been done in the field of sixteenth-century history that there was not much room for any significant contributions on his part. On the other hand, the field of fascism was not yet systematically studied in the later 1950s and early 1960s.... There was, no doubt, also a psychological reason. George had lived, after all, through the period of Nazism and Italian Fascism; this was not, as far as he was concerned, an abstract subject but one which had had an enormous impact on his own life.... George presumably thought, that he had an instinctive understanding of the spirit of the epoch, simply because he had been exposed to it.[15]

Laqueur's insight could probably be applied as well to Werner, who worked in Russian and economic history.[16] Werner wrote:

> In his [Rudolf Mosse's] day, the legal status of the Jew in Germany was secure, the economic prospects seemed boundless. It was this which helped to shape the outlook of the German-Jewish liberal bourgeoisie. Their philosophy, like that of their grandfather Rudolf, depended on certain assumptions, none of them unreasonable at the time. In the first place, it was taken for granted that the emancipation of the Jews in Germany would never be revoked. It was also assumed that Germany would remain a *Rechtsstaat*, guaranteeing to all her citizens equality before the law, religious freedom, and personal security. Finally, it was taken for granted that German culture contained important human values. None of these assumptions were falsified in Rudolf Mosse's lifetime.[17]

And although "peace and security, severely and repeatedly shaken since 1905, ended in 1914," it was the shadow of that legacy that remained and informed the notion of what it was that was going to be destroyed.[18] Werner Mosse had perfectly described the environment in which the family and the milieu existed.

Mosse family members shared a commitment to philanthropic engagement in civil society beyond Berlin, and especially in the Jewish community. After Rudolf's death, his widow Emilie received a letter from Heidelberg, wherein the director of the Anatomical Institute asked for a picture that could be placed on the premises to commemorate the generous donation Mosse had made to

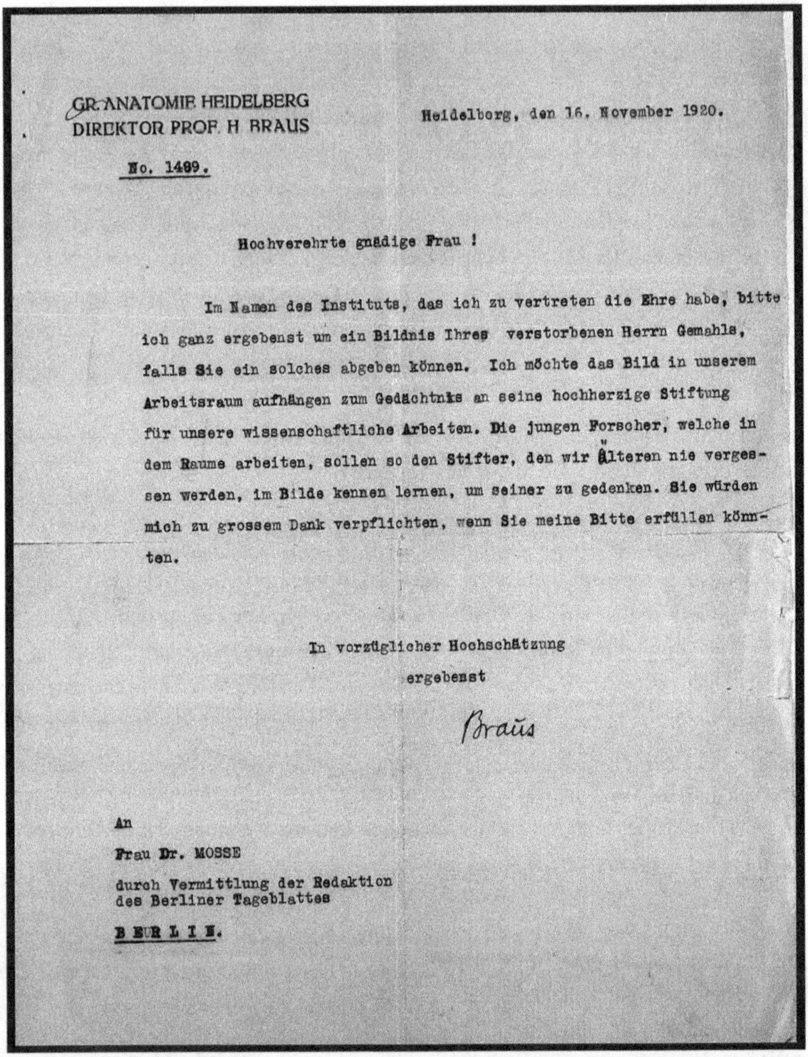

```
GR. ANATOMIE HEIDELBERG         Heidelberg, den 16. November 1920.
DIREKTOR PROF. H. BRAUS

No. 1499.


                    Hochverehrte gnädige Frau !

            Im Namen des Instituts, das ich zu vertreten die Ehre habe, bitte
    ich ganz ergebenst um ein Bildnis Ihres verstorbenen Herrn Gemahls,
    falls Sie ein solches abgeben können. Ich möchte das Bild in unserem
    Arbeitsraum aufhängen zum Gedächtnis an seine hochherzige Stiftung
    für unsere wissenschaftliche Arbeiten. Die jungen Forscher, welche in
    dem Raume arbeiten, sollen so den Stifter, den wir Älteren nie verges-
    sen werden, im Bilde kennen lernen, um seiner zu gedenken. Sie würden
    mich zu grossem Dank verpflichten, wenn Sie meine Bitte erfüllen könn-
    ten.



                    In vorzüglicher Hochschätzung
                            ergebenst

                                    Braus



    An

    Frau Dr. MOSSE
    durch Vermittlung der Redaktion
    des Berliner Tageblattes
    B E R L I N.
```

Figure 17.5. Letter from Professor H. Braus, director of the Anatomical Institute of the University of Heidelberg, to Emilie Mosse, 16 November 1920. (Image courtesy of Mosse Family Collection, Leo Baeck Institute Archives.)

support their work and studies. And as one of the major supporters of the Jewish Reform community, a memorial for "Herrn Dr.h.c. Rudolf Mosse" was held on 17 October 1920, with a eulogy given by Rabbi Dr. Julius Jelski.[19]

This tradition and commitment was, of course, maintained by the next generation. For instance, Hans Lachmann-Mosse was the chair of the Liturgy Committee of the Reform Community, and under his guidance and support a recording of the music was commissioned and completed within two years in 1930. In 1998 a collection from the original recordings was released by Beth Hatefutsoth, *The Musical Tradition of the Jewish Reform Congregation in Berlin*, as a set of CDs, supported by George. He wrote in the introduction to the new edition:

This beautiful music and these great and unique performances [legendary tenor Joseph Schmidt was one of the singers] are being made available once more, so long after the cruel end of the Jewish Reform Congregation in Berlin for which they were intended. The new liturgy was first conceived by the commission on liturgy of the Jewish Reform Community in which my father, Hans Lachmann-Mosse, its chairman, was the driving force. He was a businessman and publisher who had the interest and the means to finance the new liturgy, as well as to take an active part in its production. Certainly, it is a matter of great satisfaction to see his most important legacy come alive again.... He provided important support for the Berlin Philharmonic,... and until 1933 almost every New Year was spent by my family in the company of its conductor, Wilhelm Furtwängler. Though he was the proprietor, among other publications, of one of Germany's most important liberal newspapers, the *Berliner Tageblatt*, the talk at home around the dining table, as I remember it, was almost exclusively of music and art.[20]

But, as George pointed out in this introduction, concerning the liturgy edition, "There was one other subject under constant scrutiny: the Jewish Reform Congregation of Berlin. Rudolf Mosse had already played a prominent role in this, ... and my father followed in his footsteps. The Reform Congregation became an important part of the family's life."[21] And George mentioned a side of the liturgy project that went along in the same innovative spirit that the Mosse company had engaged in:

However, his interest in the newest technology was equally pronounced, and it is there that he got the idea which gave the new liturgy its special characteristic. Why not use the gramophone to bring good music and first-rate musicians into the synagogues which otherwise were unable to afford them? None of the often small new Reform congregations, old age homes and hospitals in need of religious services could have engaged famous singers to lead their service supported by a chorus of sixty to a hundred voices.... My father sat Sunday after Sunday [the Reform Shabbat day] at the main, or at a branch synagogue of the Berlin Jewish Reform Community above the *Bimah*, hidden by a curtain, cranking up the gramophone and changing the records.[22]

By these remarks, George also gave testimony to what it meant to the family to be part of the Jewish Reform community, including a strong commitment to Jewish traditions and yet the spirit of heartfelt reform and renewal. Such expressions of belonging and of faith in German-Jewish identity are often misunderstood, especially in post-Holocaust Germany.

Figure 17.6. Albert Mosse. (Image courtesy of Mosse Family Collection, Leo Baeck Institute Archives.)

Figure 17.7. Medal of the Imperial Japanese Order of the Rising Sun, awarded to Albert Mosse. (Image courtesy of Mosse Family Collection, Leo Baeck Institute Archives.)

Figure 17.8. Albert Mosse, seated, 1870 (person standing is unknown); he served in the Prussian Army during the Franco-Prussian War. (Image courtesy of Mosse Family Collection, Leo Baeck Institute Archives.)

Rudolf Mosse's next younger brother Albert Mosse was not in the family business; instead, he became the first high-ranking judge in Prussia without converting to Protestantism, after he had worked in Japan in the early 1890s to consult on the new Japanese constitution. Among his children were Dora, who married the art historian Erwin Panofsky, Martha Mosse, the first female lawyer at the Berlin police headquarters, and son Hans, also a lawyer, who died in 1916 in World War I. Albert Mosse had insisted on serving the fatherland in the Franco-Prussian War in 1870 despite his bad eyesight.

But it was the milieu around the turn of the century in Berlin and thereafter that was formative for shaping the public life of the Mosse family. The Mosses were newcomers who married into older Berlin Jewish families; for instance, Albert Mosse and Emil Mosse married sisters from the Siegmund Meyer family, wealthy silk and textile manufacturers, who had given rise to another family of unimaginable accomplishment. Similarly, Rudolf's daughter Felicia married Hans Lachmann, George's father, who took the name Mosse, Hans Lachmann-Mosse. The Lachmanns were entrepreneurs and philanthropists, supporting both the Berlin Jewish community and founding charities for the poor. The Panofskys came originally from the liquor business in Silesia, and Erwin Panofsky's uncle Eugen was a major banker in Berlin.[23]

In *Confronting History*, George L. Mosse writes about the "long shadow" cast by his grandfather and his Berlin-based milieu: "I discovered this tradition [i.e., that his great-grandfather Marcus Mosse was a Polish hero of 1848] relatively late in life... because the accomplishments of my grandfather, Rudolf Mosse, and his legacy, obscured all that went before and cast a long shadow."[24] However, the history of this milieu is by and large forgotten, and only historians are aware of the significance and impact. The history of the Mosse family reminds us of the richness and vibrancy of a community that was destroyed and buried after 1933. And yet, as Elisabeth Wagner has shown, some monuments remain, including the Mosse-Stift in Berlin-Wilmersdorf, a nondenominational orphanage established in 1895, Schloss Schenkendorf in the town of Mittenwalde near Berlin, the company building in Jerusalemer Straße, Mendelssohn's Woga complex on the Kurfürstendamm commissioned by Hans Lachmann-Mosse. They still dot the city of Berlin; however, several are located in what used to be East Berlin and resurfaced only later or disappeared from the memory landscape altogether, such as the Lachmann-Mosse villa on Maaßenstraße, or the Mosse Palais on Leipziger Platz. To be sure, the Nazi movement tried to erase the Mosse name. George and Werner helped undo the Nazi damage.

It helped that the memory was rich, and there are a number of landmarks that survived the bombings of the Second World War. The "Great House of Mosse" was celebrated in two *Festschriften*, long before George's birth, first in 1892 for the twenty-fifth anniversary of the company, and then in 1917 with a volume that not only hailed the three main protagonists, Rudolf, Emilie, and Hans Lachmann-Mosse, but also listed the central office of the advertisement agency Zentral–Bureau with over 250 branches in Germany and abroad as the main business, with an additional, seemingly endless number of newspapers, magazines, and specialized journals in medicine, technology, agriculture, and the law. The fact that his enormous enterprise was built within one generation and rose to such prominence and innovation, catapulting Rudolf into the top rank of Berlin families, indicates that the Mosses, like the Rathenaus, were industrial leaders of the Kaiserreich. The fact that the Nazi movement was eager to eliminate those voices, foremost the flagship newspaper, the *Berliner Tageblatt*, is a further testament of the political sway of the Mosse company as an outright voice of liberal Germany.[25]

In the 1980s George donated a collection of ninety-four company histories to the Leo Baeck Institute (LBI), mostly written before World War I. These books were given to Rudolf on the occasion of the fiftieth anniversary of the company

Figure 17.9. Rudolf Mosse. (*Fest-Schrift zur Feier des fünfzigjährigen Bestehens der Annoncen=Expedition Rudolf Mosse. Zum 1. Januar 1917 gewidmet von den Geschäftsführern* [Berlin, 1917].)

Figure 17.10. Hans Lachmann-Mosse.
(*Fest-Schrift zur Feier des fünfzigjährigen Bestehens der Annoncen=Expedition Rudolf Mosse. Zum 1. Januar 1917 gewidmet von den Geschäftsführern* [Berlin, 1917].)

wie dies in nachstehender Tabelle geschieht.

Zahl der Beamten:	insgesamt	davon im Berliner Stammhause	in den auswärtigen Filialen
Im Jahre 1870	20	20	—
Nach 25jährigem Bestehen der Firma . .	247	120	127
" 50 " " " " . .	1375	863	512

Das Zentral=Bureau

Die oberste Leitung der Annoncen=Expedition mit ihren 18 selbständigen Zweigniederlassungen und 260 Agenturen im In= und Ausland wird durch das Zentral=Bureau ausgeübt. Hier laufen alle Fäden des im übrigen stark dezentralisierten Unternehmens zusammen. Vom Zentral=Bureau gehen die erforderlichen Anregungen und Instruktionen an Filialen und Agenturen aus. Hier wird über die wichtigsten Geschäftsvorgänge, insoweit sie über die Kompetenzen der Geschäftsleitung einer Filiale hinausgehen, endgültig entschieden. Hier wird die Kontrolle über die Geschäftshandhabung der Filialen ausgeübt, hier werden die Bilanzen geprüft und endgültig abgeschlossen. Das Zentral=Bureau bearbeitet die Personalangelegenheiten und stellt die höheren Beamten an, deren Heranbildung im traditionellen Geiste der Firma es sich angelegen sein läßt. Zu seinen Obliegenheiten gehört auch der Abschluß aller Verträge und die Ueberwachung ihrer Ausführung. Insbesondere fallen hierunter die Verträge über die in den folgenden Abschnitten behandelten Geschäfte: „Die Verwaltung der Anzeigenteile von Zeitungen und Zeitschriften" und die „Uebernahme des Verlags und Vertriebs von Ausstellungs=Katalogen" u. dgl.

Figure 17.11. Statistics and narrative about the expansion of the Mosse company, from the beginning, after twenty-five years, and after fifty years. (*Fest-Schrift zur Feier des fünfzigjährigen Bestehens der Annoncen=Expedition Rudolf Mosse. Zum 1. Januar 1917 gewidmet von den Geschäftsführern* [Berlin, 1917].)

in 1917 along with the second *Festschrift*. The whole collection was published by the LBI and microfiched with great enthusiasm by University Publications of America in 1988, but it found few takers.[26] Professor Peter Hayes, at Northwestern University, who had just published the major book on IG Farben during the Nazi era, was the editor of the microfiche edition. He remarked in his introductory essay: "It is striking how understudied the history of business in Germany remains."[27] Hayes continued, "The German Empire was, on the eve of the First World War, not only 'the economic powerhouse of Europe,' but also the quintessential land of 'big industry, big agriculture, big unions, big banks, and big government,'" and that "the comparatively high incidence of Jews also have become famously contested explanations." "Scholarly examination of individual German enterprises or industries ... continue to occupy comparatively little space on library shelves. ... No single collection of sources can remedy this deficiency, but the one presented here will surely help."[28] Hayes's identified lack of research has since been remedied with numerous company histories and a general assessment of their roles during the Nazi period and before. George's cousin Werner had pioneered in that field and provided valuable studies for the history of Jews in German economic and public life starting in 1958 with *The European Powers and the German Question 1848–71* and in 1959 with the essay on Rudolf in the *Leo Baeck Institute Year Book*, followed by more articles and a number of books in economic history and the position of Jews in Imperial Germany and the Weimar Republic.[29] Werner Mosse was the author of several monographs and also coeditor, with LBI London director Arnold Paucker and several other members of the London LBI, for a number of volumes, several of them published in the *Schriftenreihe wissenschaftlicher Abhandlungen des Leo Baeck Instituts* between 1965 and 1999, that were directly concerned with German and German-Jewish history in the nineteenth and twentieth centuries.[30]

Real innovation of the field, however, came with George's approach when he began to look into the other side of the story, so to speak. In his memoirs, he quotes the conservative German historian Hans Rothfels's warning in a conversation in 1962 (that is, after he had published *The Culture of Western Europe* a year earlier), when he was about to publish an article about the occult origins of the Nazi movement: "Lassen Sie die Hände davon" (Stay away from that stuff).[31] German translations of George's books only started in the 1970s.[32] As a witness to the time he was beginning to investigate, and the prospective as the intellectual heir to a short-lived dynasty, George had an uncanny sense of the underlying social and cultural forces at the time of National Socialism's rise. The contributions of this book provide great detail about the enduring influence of George's pioneering research.

But the "shadow" of Rudolf also obscured the larger picture of his family and his generation. Perhaps using the word "shadow" is giving in to hindsight. The rise of a business empire within only two generations, and all that being suddenly lost in 1933, was a shining light that George followed as he came to understand what it was that had been destroyed. But George also understood that the family held a much larger influence than just the business, and he knew that the family was part of a much larger social network that extended into the philanthropic world and into the Jewish community, which in turn was much larger than religious observance. George recalled the shared family worldview at his sister Hilde's memorial in 1982: "Commitment, work, accomplishment, words which come easily to mind this afternoon. But also optimism about people, if not governments. Always faith in those given up by society, leading them back into productive life."[33] Hilde Lachmann-Mosse, the oldest of the Lachmann-Mosse children, had already been active in adolescent organizations in Berlin, the Jewish Reform community's Jugendgemeinschaft der Jüdischen Reformgemeinde, which was traditionally supported by her family. She studied medicine, received her medical degree in 1938 in Switzerland (as George pointed out in his memorial speech, "learning Swiss-German in order to broadcast from Basel in the anti-fascist struggle"), and came to the United States, where she was the cofounder of the Lafargue Mental Hygiene Clinic, the first free mental health clinic in Harlem, New York City. After Hilde's death, a foundation with substantial means was set up in her name, and George was the president. The purpose of the foundation was quite specific and pioneering: "To promote and encourage the use of the phonetic method of learning how to read, particularly in order to aid children to overcome their learning disabilities. It is the intention within this framework to help Black children, particularly in the New York Black community, to maximize their learning potential."[34] The Leo Baeck Institute Archives hold her diaries, which stretch from the end of 1928 until the summer of 1933.[35]

There are several archival collections in the LBI Archives of other family members and protagonists from the Berlin milieu, even if that gives us only a fragmentary impression. The Mosse Family Collection contains materials about a number of family members, going back to Rudolf Mosse's father, Marcus, and his generation. This includes a large body of correspondence of Rudolf's mother, Ulrike, née Wolff, and Rudolf's siblings. As already discussed, LBI holds extensive business files of the Mosse Company, including the complicated structure at the end of the company. For instance, LBI houses the Eric and Marianne Mosse Family Collection. Eric was one of Albert Mosse's children. Both Eric and his wife, Marianne, née Schoenfeld, were writers; he published under the pseudonym Peter Flamm, she had the pseudonyms Maria Boerner and Maria Kamp.[36]

Being part of the Mosse family, they had to flee Germany in 1933 and arrived in the United States as refugees. Of the same Mosse generation, LBI holds the memoirs of Martha Mosse, the oldest of Albert Mosse's children, who wrote about her childhood in a well-to-do Berlin Jewish family, including recollections of her father Albert as well as the deportations of Jews from Berlin and her imprisonment in Theresienstadt. Eva Noack-Mosse, one generation younger, the granddaughter of Theodor Mosse, one of the brothers of the Rudolf Mosse generation, wrote a diary about her time in Theresienstadt, where she was deported in February 1945. The diary was recently published as *Last Days of Theresienstadt* by the University of Wisconsin Press in the George L. Mosse Series in the History of European Culture, Sexuality, and Ideas.[37]

And as an example of the far-flung connections of the Mosse family network, the LBI Archives include the papers of the Guensburg/Ginsberg/Gilbert family, originally from Guenzburg near Ulm in Bavaria, who fled to Poland in 1617, one year prior to the start of the Thirty Years' War when the local ruler expelled all Jews from Guenzburg. The Ginsbergs were connected by marriage to the Lachmann and Liebermann families. Herbert Ginsberg was married to Olga Lachmann, who was the younger sister of Hans Lachmann-Mosse. Salomon Lachmann, Olga's grandfather, born in 1823, had his home where the Japanese Embassy in Berlin is now. Olga pointed out in her "Course of Life" document of 1941 that "since my sixteenth year I worked in hospitals and in 'Kinderhorte' [daycares] taking care of poor children."[38] Herbert Ginsberg was a partner of the Gebrüder Ginsberg Bank and Insurance Company (founded in 1866) as well as a member of the board of directors of the family-owned textile factory Zawiercie in western Poland, but these factories were lost at the end of World War I due to Russian banks being taken over in the Russian Revolution. He was a major collector of East Asian art and a member of the expert commission of the

Figure 17.12. One of the Medici tapestries from Rudolf Mosse's art collection, later displayed in George L. Mosse's home in Madison, Wisconsin. (Image courtesy of Mosse Family Collection, Leo Baeck Institute Archives.)

Eastern Art of the State Museum, Berlin (1924–38), as well as a cofounder and member of the board of directors of the "Gesellschaft für Ostasiatische Kunst" in Berlin. The Ginsbergs had come to Berlin around the same time as the Mosses, and before World War I lived in Tiergarten, not far from the Lachmann-Mosse home. There is a typical studio portrait of the older Lachmann-Mosse children Hilde and Rudolf (Jr.) together with Herbert Ginsberg's daughter Marianne taken in 1916 attesting to the close connection of the families.[39] And a letter from Fritz Rathenau of 1935 suggests that there was yet another family connection via the

Figure 17.13. Studio portrait of Hilde Mosse, Marianne Ginsberg (Gilbert), and Rudolf Mosse sitting on a sled. (Image courtesy of Herbert Ginsberg Collection, Leo Baeck Institute Archives, Leo Baeck Institute Photos, F 6191.)

Liebermann family.[40] Materials pertaining to Rudolf Mosse's mother, Ulrike, née Wolff, can be found in the Jacobi Family Collection,[41] as well as in the Witkowski Family Collection.[42] Hedwig Witkowski, née Mosse, was the daughter of Emil Mosse.

The detailed story of the Berlin milieu is available in Elisabeth Kraus's book in chapter 3 across 350 pages.[43] That story gives a glimpse of the shoulders George stood on. The LBI also holds an original fifteenth-century tapestry that was hanging in George's study above the bookshelves in Madison, Wisconsin, where he lived in a very unassuming house of innovative pre-fab design. George was familiar with the Rudolf Mosse *Kunstsammlung*, art collection, in the Mosse Palais that was auctioned in 1934. Since 2017 MARI, the Mosse Art Research Initiative at the Freie Universität in Berlin, has investigated the fate of Rudolf's and Emilie's art holdings: "For the first time, German institutions are cooperating with descendants of Nazi persecution in a public-private partnership," together with the Kulturstiftung der Länder and the Stiftung Preußischer Kulturbesitz as well as numerous museums and institutions.[44] And as George remarked in his memoirs:

> Life seemed to have come full circle.... The gulf which divided me from my own past was created by assimilation into a new world, but almost in equal measure by the new way I looked at the world and my place in it, by my immersion in the study of history. This change is difficult to put into words—briefly, it meant seeing everything in perspective, ordering all phenomena according to their past and present effects. This manner of thought does make a difference; it gives the mind a certain stability, and it determined the nature of my confrontation with the present according to the experiences of the past.[45]

Unfortunately, we do not know whether Werner Mosse saw his life in full circle: he did not write a memoir, but I surmise that he would have agreed with his cousin.

Notes

1. Elisabeth Kraus, *Die Familie Mosse: Deutsch-jüdisches Bürgertum im 19. und 20. Jahrhundert* (Munich: C.H. Beck, 1999).

2. Kraus, *Die Familie Mosse*, 327–99.

3. However, what exactly happened when the company went under has remained a mystery when reading Kraus or the older literature. See more on that topic in Meike Hoffmann's chapter in this volume.

4. George L. Mosse, *Aus großem Hause: Erinnerungen eines deutsch-jüdischen Historikers* (Munich: Ullstein, 2003).

5. Werner E. Mosse, "Rudolf Mosse and the House of Mosse, 1867–1920," *Leo Baeck Institute Year Book* 4, no. 1 (1959): 237–59.

6. "Aber ohne die Mitarbeit von Emil Mosse hätte der Betrieb nicht die Ausdehnung erfahren. Während sich Rudolf in der Hauptsache des Verlages und der Redaktion seiner Blätter annahm, lagen Emils Aufgaben in dem geschäftlichen Teil des Betriebs. In überragender Weise kontrollierte er alle in- und ausländischen Filialen der Annoncen-Expedition ... man nannte ihn den Napoleon des Annoncen-Wesens." Letter of Alfred Schwabacher, "Rudolf Mosse und Emil Mosse," *Leo Baeck Institute Year Book* 5 (1960): 396.

7. "1901–1926. Zur Erinnerung an das Geschäftsjubiläum unseres Herrn Alfred Schwabacher und die Feier im Zunfthaus zur Waag in Zürich am 20. März 1926. Zürich und Basel: Die Angestellten des Hauses Rudolf Mosse," Mosse Family Collection (MFC), Leo Baeck Institute Archives (hereafter LBI), AR 25184, Box 7, Folder 37, Subgroup II, Series 3; Alfred Schwabacher, "To my grandchildren: John Paul and Jacqueline Diane," Memoirs Collection, LBI, ME 585.

8. Peter de Mendelssohn, *Zeitungsstadt Berlin: Menschen und Mächte in der Geschichte der deutschen Presse* (Berlin: Ullstein, 1959); Margret Boveri, *Wir lügen alle: Eine Hauptstadtzeitung unter Hitler* (Olten und Freiburg im Breisgau: Walter Verlag, 1965).

9. See the correspondence about the setup and operation of the Swiss company in MFC, LBI, AR 25184, Subgroup II, Rudolf Mosse Firm, Series 3: Zurich. More about the complexities of the business situation of the company at the time in Meike Hoffmann's chapter.

10. Letter from George L. Mosse to Werner Mosse, 1 January 1960, George L. Mosse Collection (GLMC), LBI, AR 25137, Series III, Subseries 3, B.

11. Werner E. Mosse, "Rudolf Mosse," 237.

12. Boveri, *Wir lügen alle*.

13. Werner E. Mosse, "Rudolf Mosse," 255.

14. George L. Mosse, *Confronting History: A Memoir* (Madison: University of Wisconsin Press, 2000), 99.

15. Mosse, *Confronting History*, xii.

16. Werner apparently had witnessed his father's assassination, which haunted him for the rest of his life.

17. Werner E. Mosse, "Rudolf Mosse," 255.

18. Werner E. Mosse, "Rudolf Mosse," 255.

19. MFC, LBI, AR 25184, Box 2, Folder 32 (Mixed Materials).

20. George L. Mosse, "Personal Recollections," in *The Musical Tradition of the Jewish Reform Congregation in Berlin* [*Die Musiktradition der jüdischen Reformgemeinde zu Berlin*] (Beth Hatefutsoth, n.d. [1998]), 6.

21. Mosse, "Personal Recollections," 6.

22. Mosse, "Personal Recollections," 7.

23. On the interconnections of the Mosse family and established German-Jewish families, see Kraus, *Die Familie Mosse*, 143–491.

24. Mosse, *Confronting History*, 22.

25. And again, the false claim of Boveri that the paper continued to exist, but it was in name only. See note 8.

26. Peter Hayes, ed., *Germany's Business Leaders: The Rudolf Mosse Collection of Business Histories and Biographies* (microform) (Frederick, MD: UPA Academic Editions, 1988), ninety-four sets of fiches.

27. Hayes, "Introduction: Germany's Business Leaders, 1400–1917," in *Germany's Business Leaders*, x.

28. Hayes, *Germany's Business Leaders*, ix, x.

29. Werner E. Mosse, *The European Powers and the German Question, 1848–71* (Cambridge: Cambridge University Press, 1958); Werner E. Mosse, *Jews in the German Economy: The German-Jewish Economic Elite, 1820–1935* (Oxford: Clarendon Press, 1987).

30. To quote just a few, *Entscheidungsjahr 1932: zur Judenfrage in der Endphase der Weimarer Republik* (Tübingen: Mohr Siebeck, 1965); *Juden im Wilhelminischen Deutschland 1890–1914* (Tübingen: Mohr Siebeck, 1976); *Two Nations: British and German Jews in Comparative Perspective*, ed. Michael Brenner and Werner E. Mosse (Tübingen: Mohr Siebeck, 1999).

31. George L. Mosse, *The Culture of Western Europe: The Nineteenth and Twentieth Centuries* (Madison: University of Wisconsin Press, 2023).

32. Mosse, *Confronting History*, 170.

33. Memorial Service Speech by George L. Mosse, 1982, GLMC, LBI, Series I: Personal, Subseries 2: Family, (C) Hilde Lachmann-Mosse.

34. Foundation—Establishment 1982–1986, GLMC, LBI, Series I: Personal, Subseries 1: George L. Mosse, 1927–2001, (D) Hilde L. Mosse Foundation.

35. Hilde Lachmann-Mosse, Diaries, 1928–33, LBI, ME 1211.

36. Eric and Marianne Mosse Family Collection, circa 1919–1947, LBI, AR 25235.

37. Eva Noack-Mosse, *Last Days of Theresienstadt*, trans. Skye Doney and Birutė Ciplijauskaitė. (Madison: University of Wisconsin Press, 2018).

38. Gilbert Family Collection, LBI, AR 1028, Box 2, Folder 8, also the following citations.

39. Gilbert Family Collection, Studio Portrait of Hilde Mosse, Marianne Ginsberg (Gilbert), and Rudolf Mosse sitting on a sled, LBI Photos, F 6191.

40. Gilbert Family Collection, LBI, Box 2, Folder 8.

41. Jacobi Family Collection, 1836–circa 1935, LBI, AR 116.

42. Witkowski Family Collection, 1834–1935, LBI, AR 470.

43. See note 2.

44. Mosse Art Restitution Project, accessed 26 May 2020, https://mosseartproject.com/resources.php.

45. Mosse, *Confronting History*, 215–16.

AFTERWORD

A Family Message

The Mosse Berlin Legacy

Roger Strauch

The following essay is based on Roger Strauch's presentation "The Mosse Art Restitution Project: A Personal Perspective" at the June 2019 conference "Mosse's Europe: New Perspectives in the History of German Judaism, Fascism, and Sexuality."

Do you remember the excited motor leg under the coffee or dining table?
   Do you remember the joyous giggle?
   The aroma of a smoking pipe?
   The charming accent of a man educated in German and British and American English?
   And how about the booming voice of a passionate teacher? In front of hundreds of Western Civ students.
   Of course, you recall the fierce focus on scholarship and the discipline to produce strikingly impressive and innovative work—new knowledge and insight.
   And what about the tough professor who was available to become a friend for life?
   I remember social warmth, inclusivity, and curiosity, albeit impatience for intellectual stimulation.
   I remember a slippery ride in George's jalopy through the hills of Jerusalem during a rare snowstorm in January of 1980.
   And while in the holy city, George's generous hosting—tasty meals and lively discussions with his eclectic group of close friends and colleagues, including politicians and military officers at the Hebrew University.

Figure A.1. Mosse Palais, 1888.

Figure A.2. Hans Strauch with redesigned Mosse Palais, 1998.

Afterword

And I also recall the collaboration in Berlin with my brother, Hans, at a formative stage in his career as an architect and also how the love and respect of a devoted uncle was ever present.

I am George L. Mosse's nephew, actually step-nephew. George's father and mother divorced in the 1930s. His father remarried my grandmother, Omi Carola. George and his sister Hilde were close with my grandmother and Dad, their step-brother, in the course of their exile from Germany and eventual settlement in the United States.

The original Mosse Palais was on Leipziger Platz in 1888. This is the other side of the Mosse Palais—the courtyard entrance to the building on Voßstraße (fig. A.1). Hitler built the Reich Chancellery directly opposite the Mosse Palais on the same street. This is my brother Hans in front of the new Mosse Palais, 1998, which he designed (fig. A.2). This was the first building built in the previous "no man's land" associated with the Berlin Wall. And here is the Mosse Palais in 2016 (fig. A.3).

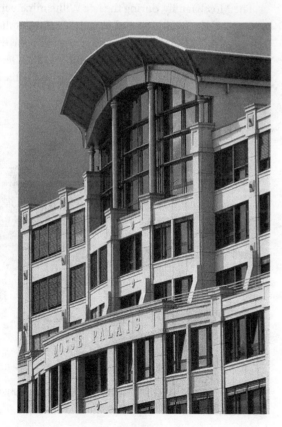

Figure A.3. Mosse Palais, 2016.

At the 2019 "Mosse's Europe" conference in Berlin, Hans and I were joined by my sons, Paul and Alex. Hans and I grew up with regular visits from George to our house in Lexington, Massachusetts. George, Dad, and Mom—two professors and a commercial artist. Lots of nice family dinners together. Conversations around the dining table included career and social updates on each of us.

The dynamics of the relationship between Karl (Dad) and Uncle George mellowed over the years from a couple of young and passionate academic peacocks to grateful, respectful, and brotherly aging professors. They were bound together by an especially close relationship with the other's natural parent. Dad with George's father, Hans. George with Dad's mother, Carola. There is only one surviving blood relative of George, his niece, Joy. Joy is the daughter of his elder brother, Rudolf, who died after emigrating to the United States.

This book is another special George L. Mosse occasion. Once again, we are in the midst of many accomplished and dedicated people who are friends, colleagues, and students inspired by Uncle George.

The Mosse family, during the late Wilhelmine period and Weimar Republic, was one of the wealthiest and most powerful families in Berlin. Rudolf Mosse was a self-made publishing and advertising magnate and a prolific philanthropist. He supported educational institutions, the German museum system, and many artists of his time and advocated for accessible healthcare services. Rudolf

Figure A.4. Rudolf Mosse's grandchildren in the 1930s. Hilde, George, and Rudolf Mosse. (Image courtesy of Mosse Family Collection, Leo Baeck Institute Archives.)

Mosse owned the *Berliner Tageblatt*, the "*New York Times*" of Weimer Germany, and the country's leading progressive voice. The paper spoke against the rise of German militarism, against the German entry into World War I, and attempted to counter the rise of the Nazis through editorials and satires. It is my understanding that Hitler, along with Goebbels, mentioned the Mosse family name more than twenty times in public speeches to demean and vilify Jewish businesspeople and politically progressive points of view.

In 1933, following Hitler's rise to power, the Mosse family lost control of their business and personal assets and were forced to leave the country. Goebbels, who only a few years earlier applied for and was declined a job at the newspaper, as well as Göring, were instrumental in orchestrating the looting and liquidating of the family's assets. The confiscation process was well documented and involved Nazi art-looting collaborators: Karl Haberstock, Hans Carl Kruger, and the Lepke and Union Auction Houses. They facilitated sales for the benefit of the Third Reich. The expropriation of the Mosse family assets, as well as those of the Wertheim family, were the first large expropriations undertaken by the Nazis, a template for a looting process that became a well-oiled machine.

In Elisabeth Kraus's eight-hundred-page biography of the Mosse family, she chronicles a several-hundred-year-old family legacy, including that of our step-great-grandfather, the successful German businessman and philanthropist Rudolf Mosse and my great-great-step-uncle Albert, who had a fundamental role in

Figure A.5. George and his nanny, Miss Squire, driving an electric vehicle on the grounds of their country summer castle (Rittergut), Schenkendorf. (Image courtesy of Mosse Family Collection, Leo Baeck Institute Archives.)

drafting the Japanese Meiji constitution. Rudolf, a business magnate, was Uncle George's grandfather—he died in 1920, a year after George was born.

It is still disorienting when I am reminded that George, Hilde, and my father, Karl, lived in the lap of luxury and privilege in Berlin—in palaces and mansions, with private chauffeurs and servants and frequent retreats to fancy European resorts.

George sold the restituted property in 1995 to an adopted son of Count Dracula's descendants, former owners of the property.

The lives of the Mosse family members were abruptly disrupted when they were exiled and forced to travel separate roads. They created new personal lives, became educated, and built professional careers, with only basic financial resources for food and lodging.

My father, Karl Strauch (1922–2000) (fig. A.6), became an experimental particle physicist, a Harvard professor for fifty years. He was for many years chairman of Harvard's physics department.

Hilde L. Mosse (1912–1982), my aunt (fig. A.7), became one of the first child psychiatrists to work in Harlem with children who had severe learning and reading disabilities. Her research was cited by Thurgood Marshall, then head of

Figure A.6. Karl Strauch (1922–2000).

the NAACP Legal and Educational Defense Fund, who thanked Hilde Mosse for her research, which the NAACP cited in the transformative Brown v. Board of Education Supreme Court case (1954). She was also passionate about the negative impact of violent graphic entertainment on adolescent psychology.

Uncle George's work and character as a historian and professor is here celebrated to commemorate his one hundredth birthday in a fashion that few academicians, including Nobel laureates, are remembered or honored, through all the ages.

All three Mosse children—Rudolf, Hilde, and George—lived modestly, cared little about personal wealth, were neither nostalgic nor bitter about their past, cared about and were proud of one another, and loved and were loved and appreciated by wide and deep social and academic networks of passionate and bright fellow life travelers. Real, not virtual networks! Actual human coffee table chats, not chat apps.

Because our family did not focus on the past, Hans and I knew little of our Mosse background until our late teens and early twenties when we had to write school essays that related to our family history. While in high school we learned of our parents' separate escapes from Europe in 1939. Hans Lachmann-Mosse saved our father's life in 1939 when he risked his own life by returning to Europe,

Figure A.7. Hilde Mosse (1912–1982).

specifically Paris, without proper visas to return to the United States to get Dad out following our father's school graduation.

Along the way, George would let us know of the *New York Times* reviews of his books. We took notice when Dad told us that he received some money from the sale of his stepfather's restituted properties in Berlin, a George project. Dad was going to save this money for a rainy day, which unfortunately came shortly thereafter, when Dad was diagnosed with Parkinson's disease, fifteen years ahead of his passing on New Year's Day 2000.

About twelve years ago, I became aware that George had abandoned efforts to recover valuable art expropriated by the Nazi regime from his grandfather's and father's collections. Uncle George had successfully restituted titles to many properties that had been illegally confiscated. After considerable time, effort, and costly international detective and legal investigations, I decided to reinvigorate Uncle George's restitution efforts. Today, we—The Mosse Art Restitution Project (MARP)—engage in what currently may be the world's most ambitious effort to restitute stolen Nazi artifacts.

This has been a personal journey, where my brother and I have learned more about our stepfamily's legacy as well as the character of our fellow world citizens as we attempt to locate, identify, authenticate, and recover Mosse artifacts. At a recent international Berlin conference, I met an art dealer and his daughter who flew from Zurich to meet me, just to express their objection to our restitution efforts on the basis that the art should remain with the current custodians (someone well-known to this particular man). His view: finders, keepers, losers, weepers! He flaunted that he knew where some of the Mosse art was located and had no intention of helping us find it. Commensurate with the development of our project has been the growing importance and influence of the German provenance research community who have the skills, integrity, and bravery to establish the legitimacy of claims like ours.

The Mosse Art Restitution Project includes over twelve hundred artifacts, listed on LostArt.de, not including many other art, antiquity, and antique objects yet to be identified. Through MARP (fig. A.8), I represent three heirs: the University of Wisconsin–Madison, Joy, and the Mosse Foundation.

The Mosse Foundation supports progressive educational, artistic, and economic development projects for economically disadvantaged people. The MARP is committed to returning property to the rightful heirs, as well as being sensitive to the inevitable awkwardness inherent in this process of restituting objects that have changed hands many times since the original expropriation. We endeavor to be collaborative and flexible in each restitution. We do not seek to cast blame.

Afterword

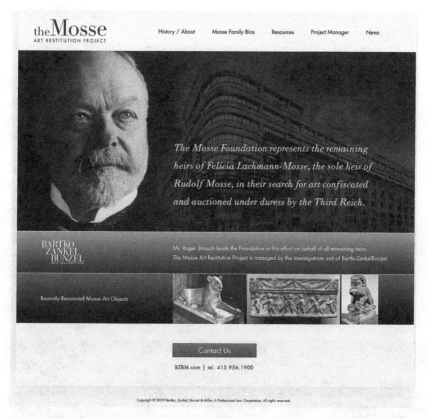

Figure A.8. The Mosse Art Restitution Project.

We are attempting to revive and restore the legacy of the prominent and progressive Mosse family, a German-Jewish family dedicated to philanthropy within the German state. The Mosse family deserves recognition for contributions to German society and culture, especially in Berlin, where their legacy still enriches this amazing and vibrant city.

To our knowledge, the objects listed on LostArt.de have been rendered unmarketable on legitimate world markets. We have located and restituted, in accordance with the Washington Principles, mostly paintings and sculptures from primarily, but not exclusively, public institutions in Germany. Other objects have been located and identified in Poland, Israel, Switzerland, Scandinavia, Austria, and the United States. Many of these objects have been sold back to the current custodians or sold at auction, raising sufficient capital to repay our considerable expenses, and to make distributions of financial recompense to the three heirs I represent.

Over the last seven years, we have developed strong relationships and cooperated with German provenance researchers, museums, institutional and government officials, international auction houses, and private collectors to restitute over twenty artifacts worth millions of dollars. These included Adolph von Menzel's 1850 pastel, *Emilie in a Red Blouse* (fig. A.9) (the restituted painting was sold at auction in Berlin in June 2016 for about $1 million); Karl Blechen's restituted painting *View of Santa Scholastica at Subiaco*, 1832 (fig. A.10) (the restituted painting was sold back to the custodian at the time, Staatliche Kunsthalle Karlsruhe, in 2016); and a Roman child's sarcophagus from the end of the second century AD (fig. A.11) (the restituted artifact was sold back to the custodian at the time, Berlin's national gallery, Stiftung Preußischer Kulturbesitz, in 2016).

We have eight more pieces in the process of restitution following our claim to the custodian. And there are many other specific objects under investigation in multiple countries. We offer collaboration and negotiation rather than entitlement, demands, and confrontation. We are one of the few family projects to partner with German public institutions to search for, identify, and authenticate

Figure A.9. Adolph von Menzel, *Emilie in a Red Blouse* (1850).

Figure A.10. Karl Blechen, *View of Santa Scholastica at Subiaco* (1832).

Figure A.11. Roman child's sarcophagus. (Photograph by Gisela Geng. Courtesy of Staatliche Museen zu Berlin, Antikensammlung)

looted art during the Third Reich. We are especially grateful for the financial support that is provided by the German government to research the provenance and whereabouts of the Mosse collection. We have employed experienced, talented, and highly reputable investigators, lawyers, and researchers to support our initiative.

Uncle George would get the biggest kick out of what we are doing with MARP and the progress we have made. He enjoyed this sort of adventure. And he would also appreciate all the characters with whom we have engaged in our journey.

Dr. Meike Hoffmann directs the Mosse Art Research Initiative (MARI). Dr. Hoffmann's analysis of some of the identified Mosse objects and the detective stories that have led to their discovery and authentication is included in this volume.

I think what defines us and those closely associated with the Mosse family are the following aspirations:

- to contribute to society, to create value—not necessarily financial value, but tangible value for our fellow human beings;
- to build and support friendships and relationships that are broad and deep, through time and distance, despite differences in culture and perspective;
- to experience, appreciate, and respect the complications of the human spirit;
- to invest our financial resources in communities or individuals with whom we relate or admire for their potential to make a positive difference in our global community.

Figure A.12. The Mosse Art Research Initiative (MARI).

As I mentioned, Uncle George was not distracted or impressed with personal finances. Uncle George led by example in so far as he put *his* money where his mouth was. He invested in people and institutions with whom he shared passion, devotion, and appreciation.

It is ironic and pertinent that today's recent news references to nationalism, fascism, socialism, and liberalism are so closely related to George's life work. Hopefully his insights and his students and disciples will help us navigate a peaceful path through a treacherous environment.

I would also like to acknowledge the friendship and partnership of Dr. Elisabeth Wagner and Dr. Klaus Scherpe of Humboldt University. Dr. Scherpe and George cofounded the Mosse Lecture Series at Humboldt University.

Thank you, Skye Doney, for leading the organization of this book and John Tortorice for your thirty years of friendship and guidance—and for the love and respect you shared with our uncle. Let's all savor and immerse ourselves in the Mosse spirit in the pursuit of excellence and professional accomplishment, and let's share the Mosse determination to make a difference in our communities that will positively impact the world as a whole.

Uncle George, charming and illuminating us for over a century and into the future . . .

July 2020: Or, as you have now read this volume, and enjoyed the preceding essays—a testament to the enduring legacy of Uncle George's scholarship.

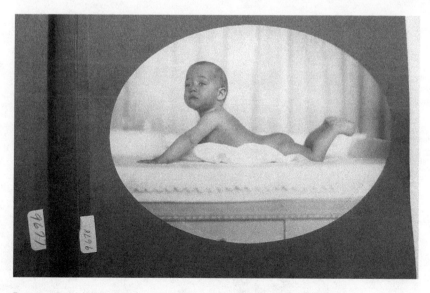

Figure A.13. George L. Mosse in Berlin, 1918. (Courtesy of Mosse Family Collection, LBI Archives.

BIBLIOGRAPHY

Archival Collections

Beit Hatfutsot: Museum of the Jewish People, Tel Aviv, Israel
Bundesarchiv Berlin Lichterfelde (BA), Berlin, Germany
Bundesarchiv-Militärarchiv Freiburg (BA-MA), Freiburg im Breisgau, Germany
Dokumentationsarchiv des österreichischen Widerstandes (DÖW), Vienna, Austria
Gerda Lerner, MC 769, Schlesinger Library on the History of Women in America, Radcliffe Institute for Advanced Study, Cambridge, MA
Hauptstaatsarchiv (HStA), Düsseldorf, Germany
Landesarchiv Berlin (LAB), Berlin, Germany
Leo Baeck Institute (LBI), New York, New York
   George L. Mosse Collection (GLMC), AR 25137
   Gilbert Family Collection, AR 1028
   Jacobi Family Collection, AR 116
   Joseph Lehmann Collection, AR 1596
   Leo Baeck Institute Memoir Collection, ME 1211
   Mosse Family Collection (MFC), AR 25184
   Weltverband für religiös-liberales Judentum Collection, AR 3499
   Witkowski Family Collection, 1834, 1935, AR 470
Museumsstiftung Post und Telekommunikation (MSPT), Frankfurt am Main, Germany
Public Record Office (PRO), War Office, London, England
United States Holocaust Memorial Museum Oral History Branch, Washington, DC

Published Sources

Adorno, Theodor W. *Aesthetic Theory.* New York: Continuum, 1997.
———. "The Meaning of Working through the Past." In *Critical Models: Interventions and Catchwords,* 89–104. New York: Columbia University Press, 2005.
———. *Minima Moralia: Reflections from Damaged Life.* New York: Verso, 2005.

Adorno, Theodor, et al. *The Authoritarian Personality*. New York: Verso, 2019.
Adorno, Theodor W., and Max Horkheimer. *Dialectic of Enlightenment*. Stanford, CA: Stanford University Press, 2002.
Adorno, Theodor W., and Siegfried Kracauer. *Briefwechsel 1923–1966*. Frankfurt am Main: Suhrkamp, 2008.
Akkerman, Tjitske. "Gender and the Radical Right in Western Europe: A Comparative Analysis of Policy Agendas." *Patterns of Prejudice* 49, nos. 1–2 (2015): 37–60.
Amesberger, Helga, and Brigitte Halbmayr. "Österreich." In Party program of the Freedom Party of Austria. https://www.fpoe.at/themen/parteiprogramm/parteiprogramm-englisch/.
———. *Rechtsextreme Parteien–eine mögliche Heimat für Frauen?* Wiesbaden: Leske und Budrich Verlag, 2002.
Angel, Sara. "Restitution About-Face: Max Stern, the Return of Nazi-Looted Art and Düsseldorf's Double Game." In *The Terezín Declaration—Ten Years Later: The Documentation, Identification, and Restitution of Cultural Assets of WWII Victims*, 88–97. Proceedings of an international academic conference held in Prague on 18–19 June 2019. Prague: Document Centre for Property Transfers of Cultural Assets of WWII Victims, 2019.
Aramini, Donatello. *George L. Mosse, l'Italia e gli storici*. Milan: FrancoAngeli, 2010.
Arzheimer, Kai. "Electoral Sociology—Who Votes for the Extreme Right and Why—and When?" In *The Populist Radical Right: A Reader*, edited by Cas Mudde, 277–89. New York: Routledge, 2016.
Aschheim, Steven E. *At the Edges of Liberalism: Junctions of European, German, and Jewish History*. New York: Palgrave Macmillan, 2012.
———. "George Mosse and Jewish History." *German Politics and Society* 18, no. 4 (Winter 2000): 46–57.
———. "George Mosse: Nationalism, Jewishness, Zionism and Israel." In "George L. Mosse, Nationalism, and the Crisis of Liberal Democracies," special issue, *Journal of Contemporary History* 56, no. 4 (October 2021): 854–63.
———. "German Jews beyond Bildung and Liberalism: The Radical Jewish Revival in the Weimar Republic." In *Culture and Catastrophe: German and Jewish Confrontations with National Socialism and Other Crises*, 31–44. New York: New York University Press, 1996.
———. "Max Nordau, Friedrich Nietzsche and Degeneration." *Journal of Contemporary History* 28, no. 4 (October 1993): 643–57.
Assmann, Aleida. "Das Zeitzeugengespräch als Quelle und Zugang zur Vergangenheit: Erinnerung, Geschichtsbewusstsein und Geschichtsvermittlung zwischen den Generationen." *heiEDUCATION Journal* 4 (2019): 29–49.
———. *Der europäische Traum: Vier Lehren aus der Geschichte*. Munich: Beck Verlag, 2018.
Assmann, Jan. "Collective Memory and Cultural Identity." *New German Critique* 65 (1995): 125–33.

———. *Religion and Cultural Memory: Ten Studies*. Translated by Rodney Livingstone. Stanford, CA: Stanford University Press, 2006.

Audoin-Rouzeau, Stéphane. "George L. Mosse: Réflections sur une méconnaissance française." *Annales: Histoire, Sciences sociales* 56, no. 1 (2001): 183–86.

Avineri, Shlomo. *The Making of Modern Zionism: Intellectual Origins of the Jewish State*. New York: Basic Books, 1981.

Avinoam, Reuven, ed. *Such Were Our Fighters: Anthology of Writings by Soldiers Who Died for Israel*. New York: Herzl Press, 1965.

Ayalon, Ella. "Who Is an Orphan? Orphan Care as a Touchstone for Changes in the Jewish Community in Mandatory Palestine and Israel, 1920–1960." PhD diss., Tel Aviv University, 2021.

Azaryahu, Maoz. "Mount Herzl: The Creation of Israel's National Cemetery." *Israel Studies* 1, no. 2 (1996): 46–74.

Baader, Benjamin M. *Gender, Judaism, and Bourgeois Culture in Germany, 1800–1870*. Bloomington: Indiana University Press, 2006.

Bach, Jonathan. *What Remains: Everyday Encounters with the Socialist Past*. New York: Columbia University Press, 2017.

Badley, Linda, R. Barton Palmer, and Steven Jay Schneider, eds. *Traditions in World Cinema*. Edinburgh: Edinburgh University Press, 2006.

Baedeker, Karl. *Das Generalgouvernement: Reisehandbuch von Karl Baedeker*. Leipzig: Baedeker, 1943.

Bajohr, Frank. *"Arisierung" in Hamburg: Die Verdrängung der jüdischen Unternehmer 1933–1945*. Hamburg: Christians, 1997.

Baldwin, James. "The White Man's Guilt." In *Collected Essays*, 723–27. New York: Literary Classics, 1998.

Baldwin, P. M. "Liberalism, Nationalism, and Degeneration: The Case of Max Nordau." *Central European History* 13, no. 2 (June 1980): 99–120.

Barnett, Victoria. *For the Soul of the People: Protestant Protest against Hitler*. Oxford: Oxford University Press, 1992.

Barr, Doron. *Ide'ologyah Ye-Nof Simli: Ḳevuratam Ba-Shenit Shel Anshe Shem Be-Admat Ereṣ Yiśra'el 1904–1967*. Jerusalem: Magnus Press, 2015.

Bartal, Israel. "The Image of Germany and German Jewry in East European Jewish Society during the 19th Century." In *Danzig, between East and West: Aspects of Modern Jewish History*, edited by Isadore Twersky, 3–17. Cambridge, MA: Harvard University Press, 1985.

Bartana, Ortsion. "The Image of the 'Living-Dead' in Nathan Alterman's Poetry: From Archetype to National Symbol." *Israel Affairs* 20, no. 2 (2014): 182–94.

Barthes, Roland. *Camera Lucida*. New York: Hill & Wang, 1981.

———. "La grande famille des hommes." In *Mythologies*, 173–76. Paris: Éditions du Seuil, 1957.

Bartov, Omer. *Hitler's Army: Soldiers, Nazis, and War in the Third Reich*. New York: Oxford University Press, 1991.

Batnitzky, Leora. *How Judaism Became a Religion: An Introduction to Modern Jewish Thought*. Princeton, NJ: Princeton University Press, 2011.

Battistella, Edwin. "The Art of the Public Apology." *Politico*, 7 May 2014. https://www.politico.com/magazine/story/2014/05/the-art-of-the-political-apology-106458.

Begin, Menachem. "Milhama Belit Breira—O Milhama 'Im Breira." *Ma'ariv*, 20 August 1982.

Benadusi, Lorenzo, and Giorgio Caravale, eds. *George L. Mosse's Italy: Interpretation, Reception, and Intellectual Heritage*. New York: Palgrave Macmillan, 2014.

Benjamin, Walter. *Berlin Childhood around 1900*. Cambridge, MA: Belknap Press of Harvard University Press, 2006.

———. *Das Kunstwerk im Zeitalter seiner technischen Reproduzierbarkeit*. 4th ed. Berlin: Suhrkamp Verlag, 2010.

———. "The Work of Art in the Age of Mechanical Reproduction." In *Illuminations: Essays and Reflections*, edited by Hannah Arendt, 217–51. New York: Schocken Books, 1968.

Bennhold, Katrin. "One Legacy of Merkel? Angry East German Men Fueling the Far Right." *New York Times*, 5 November 2018.

Beorn, Waitman. *Marching into Darkness: The Wehrmacht and the Holocaust in Belarus*. Cambridge, MA: Harvard University Press, 2014.

Berghahn, Klaus, ed. *The German-Jewish Dialogue Reconsidered: A Symposium in Honor of George L. Mosse*. New York: Peter Lang, 1996.

Bering, Dietz. "Jews and the German Language: The Concept of Kulturnation and Anti-Semitic Propaganda." In *Identity and Intolerance: Nationalism, Race, and Xenophobia in Germany and the United States*, edited by Norbert Finzsch and Dietmar Schirmer, 251–91. Cambridge: Cambridge University Press, 1998.

Berkowitz, Michael. *Zionist Culture and West European Jewry before the First World War*. New York: Cambridge University Press, 1993.

Bialas, Wolfgang. *Moralische Ordnungen des Nationalsozialismus*. Göttingen: Vandenhoeck & Ruprecht, 2014.

———. "Nationalsozialistische Ethik und Moral: Konzepte, Probleme, offene Fragen." In *Ideologie und Moral im Nationalsozialismus*, edited by Wolfgang Bialas and Lothar Fritze, 23–63. Göttingen: Vandenhoeck & Ruprecht, 2014.

Bialas, Wolfgang, and Lothar Fritze, eds. *Ideologie und Moral im Nationalsozialismus*. Göttingen: Vandenhoeck & Ruprecht, 2014.

Bloch, Ernst. *Heritage of Our Times*. Berkeley: University of California Press, 1990.

Blumenau, Emil. "Die Frau im Gotteshaus." *Jüdisch-liberale Zeitung*, 5 November 1926.

Bob, Clifford. *The Global Right Wing and the Clash of World Politics*. Cambridge: Cambridge University Press, 2012.

Bobbio, Norberto. *Ideological Profile of Twentieth-Century Italy*. Translated by Lydia Cochrane. Princeton, NJ: Princeton University Press, 1995.

Bock, Gisela. "Racism and Sexism in Nazi Germany: Motherhood, Compulsory Sterilization, and the State." *Signs: Journal of Women in Culture and Society* 8, no. 3 (1983): 400–421.

———. *Zwangssterilisation im Nationalsozialismus: Studien zur Rassenpolitik und Frauenpolitik*. Opladen: Westdeutscher Verlag, 1986.

Bomhoff, Hartmut. "'The Woman in the House of God' (1926) Revisited." In *Gender and Religious Leadership: Women Rabbis, Pastors, and Ministers*, edited by Hartmut Bomhoff et al., 71–88. Lanham, MD: Lexington Books, 2019.

Boveri, Margret. *Wir lügen alle: Eine Hauptstadtzeitung unter Hitler*. Olten and Freiburg im Breisgau: Walter Verlag, 1965.

Bracke, Sarah, and David Paternotte. "Unpacking the Sin of Gender." *Religion & Politics* 6, no. 2 (2016): 143–54.

Brecht, Bertolt. *Poems, 1913–1956*. Edited by John Willet and Ralph Manheim. London: Eyre Methuen, 1976.

Bredekamp, Horst. *Theorie des Bildakts*. Berlin: Suhrkamp, 2010.

Breitbart, Andrew. *Righteous Indignation: Excuse Me While I Save the World*. New York: Grand Central Publishing, 2011.

Breuer, Mordechai. "1873: Samson Raphael Hirsch Oversees the Secession of Jewish Orthodoxy in Nineteenth-Century Germany." In *Yale Companion to Jewish Writing and Thought in German Culture, 1096–1996*, edited by Sander L. Gilman and Jack Zipes, 205–11. New Haven, CT: Yale University Press, 1997.

Brinkmann, Tobias. *Migration und Transnationalität*. Paderborn: Verlag Ferdinand Schöningh, 2012.

Bronstein, Galit. "Kulam Hayu Baneino? Siach Shakulim Ve-Shikulei Ha-Shkhol." *Hamishpaṭ* 13 (2002): 54–65.

Brown, Wendy. *Undoing the Demos: Neoliberalism's Stealth Revolution*. New York: Zone Books, 2015.

Browning, Christopher. *Ordinary Men: Reserve Police Battalion 101 and the Final Solution in Poland*. New York: HarperCollins, 1992.

Bruttmann, Tal, Stefan Hördler, and Christoph Kreutzmüller. *Die fotografische Inszenierung des Verbrechens: Ein Album aus Auschwitz*. Darmstadt: WBG, 2019.

Buber-Neumann, Margarete. *Als Gefangene bei Stalin und Hitler: Eine Welt im Dunkel*. Berlin: Ullstein, 1997.

Buggeln, Marc. *Arbeit & Gewalt: Das Außenlagersystem des KZ Neuengamme*. Göttingen: Wallstein, 2009.

Burrin, Philippe. "Le champ magnétique des fascismes." In *Fascisme, nazisme, autoritarisme*, 211–46. Paris: Seuil, 2000.

———. "L'imaginaire politique du fascisme." In *Fascisme, nazisme, autoritarisme*, 49–72. Paris: Seuil, 2000.

Butler, Judith. *Parting Ways: Jewishness and the Critique of Zionism*. New York: Columbia University Press, 2013.

Cameron, David. "Speech at the Imperial War Museum on First World War Centenary Plans on 11 October 2012." https://www.gov.uk/government/speeches/speech-at-imperial-war-museum-on-first-world-war-centenary-plans.

Camus, Renaud. *You Will Not Replace Us!* Plieux: Chez l'auteur, 2018.

Caplan, Jane, and Nikolaus Wachsmann. *Concentration Camps in Nazi Germany: The New Histories*. London: Routledge, 2010.
Carol, Sarah, and Nadja Milewski. "Attitude toward Abortion among the Muslim Minority and Non-Muslim Majority in Cross-National Perspective: Can Religiosity Explain the Differences?" *Sociology of Religion* 78, no. 4 (Winter 2017): 456–91.
Carter, Elisabeth. "Party Ideology." In *The Populist Radical Right: A Reader*, edited by Cas Mudde, 29–58. New York: Routledge, 2016.
Casanova, Julián. *The Spanish Republic and Civil War*. New York: Cambridge University Press, 2010.
Case, Mary-Ann. "The Role of the Popes in the Invention of Complementarity and the Vatican's Anathematization of Gender." *Religion & Gender* 6, no. 2 (2016): 155–72.
Celan, Paul. *Selected Poems*. Middlesex: Penguin, 1972.
Chrisafis, Angelique. "'We Feel Very Close to Her': Can 'Fake Feminist' Marine Le Pen Win the Female Vote?" *Guardian*, 18 March 2017.
Churchill, Randolph S., ed. *The Sinews of Peace: Post-war Speeches by Winston S. Churchill*. London: Riverside Press, 1949.
Claus, Robert, Esther Lehnert, and Yves Müller, eds. *"Was ein rechter Mann ist . . .": Männlichkeit im Rechtsextremismus*. Berlin: Karl Dietz, 2010.
Coenen Snyder, Saskia. *Building a Public Judaism: Synagogues and Jewish Identity in Nineteenth-Century Europe*. Cambridge, MA: Harvard University Press, 2013.
Cohen, Uri S. *Ha'nosach Ha'bitchoni Ve'tarbut Hamilchama Ha'ivrit*. Jerusalem: The Bialik Institute, 2017.
Confino, Alon. "From Psychohistory to Memory Studies: Or, How Some Germans Became Jews and Some Jews Nazis." In *History Flows through Us*, edited by Roger Frie, 17–30. New York: Routledge, 2018.
Craig, Gordon A. *Germany, 1866–1945*. Oxford: Clarendon Press, 1978.
Dann, Carrie. "Almost 70 Percent of Americans OK with Gay Presidential Candidate, Poll Finds." NBC News, 2 April 2019.
Datta, Niel. *Restoring the Natural Order: The Religious Extremists' Vision to Mobilize European Societies against Human Rights on Sexuality and Reproduction*. Brussels: European Forum on Population and Development, 2018.
Daum, Andreas W., and Sherry L. Föhr. "George Lachmann Mosse." In *The Second Generation: Émigrés from Nazi Germany as Historians*, edited by Andreas W. Daum, Hartmut Lehmann, and James J. Sheehan, 414–16. New York: Berghahn, 2016.
de Grazia, Victoria. *How Fascism Ruled Women: Italy, 1922–1945*. Berkeley: University of California Press, 1993.
Dellamora, Richard. "Productive Decadence: 'The Queer Comradeship of Outlawed Thought': Vernon Lee, Max Nordau, and Oscar Wilde." In "Forms and/of Decadence," special issue, *New Literary History* 35, no. 4 (Autumn 2004): 529–46.
DePalma, Anthony. "Myths of the Enemy: Castro, Cuba and Herbert L. Matthew of the *New York Times*." Kellogg Institute for International Studies Working Papers, July 2004. https://kellogg.nd.edu/sites/default/files/old_files/documents/313_0.pdf.

Dickinson, Thorold, dir. *Hill 24 Doesn't Answer*. Teaneck, NJ: Ergo Media, 1955.
Dillon, Christopher. *Dachau and the SS: A Schooling in Violence*. Oxford: Oxford University Press, 2015.
Dobry, Michel. *Le mythe de l'allergie française au fascism*. Paris: Albin Michel, 2003.
Donner, Batia. *Natan Rapoport: Oman Yehudi*. Jerusalem: Yad Yitsḥaḳ Ben-Tsevi; Yad ya'ari, 2014.
Dormitzer, Else. "Die Frau im Gotteshaus." *Jüdisch-liberale Zeitung*, 5 November 1926.
Doron, Joachim. "Special Concepts Prevalent in German Zionism: 1883–1914." *Studies in Zionism* 5 (April 1982): 1–31.
Douglas, Mary. *Purity and Danger: An Analysis of Concepts of Pollution and Taboo*. London: Routledge, 2002.
Drescher, Seymour, David Sabean, and Allan Sharlin, eds. *Political Symbolism in Modern Europe: Essays in Honor of George L. Mosse*. New Brunswick, NJ: Transaction Books, 1982.
Dressler, Willi Oswald. *Dresslers Kunstjahrbuch: Ein Nachschlagebuch für deutsche bildende und angewandte Kunst*. Berlin: Ernst Wasmuth, 1909.
Drewes, Kai. *Nobilitierungen von Juden im Europa des 19. Jahrhunderts*. Frankfurt am Main: Campus Verlag, 2013.
Einhorn, Barbara. *Cinderella Goes to Market: Citizenship, Gender and Women's Movements in East Central Europe*. London: Verso, 1993.
Elyada, Aya. *A Goy Who Speaks Yiddish: Christians and the Jewish Language in Early Modern Germany*. Stanford, CA: Stanford University Press, 2012.
Even Shmuel, Judah. *Zikkaron Le-Shmuel*. Jerusalem: n.p., 1950.
———. *Zohara Levyatov: Ketavim Nivharim*. Jerusalem: n.p., 1952.
Farris, Sara R. "Femonationalism and the 'Regular' Army of Labor Called Migrant Women." *History of the Present* 2, no. 2 (Fall 2012): 184–99.
———. *In the Name of Women's Rights: The Rise of Femonationalism*. Durham, NC: Duke University Press, 2017.
Fassin, Éric. "Gender and the Problem of Universals: Catholic Mobilizations and Sexual Democracy in France." *Religion and Gender* 6, no. 2 (2016): 173–86.
Fechner, Eberhard. *Der Prozess: Eine Darstellung des Majdanek-Verfahrens in Düsseldorf*. Norddeutscher Rundfunk, 1984. 3 parts (video cassettes). 270 min.
Feldestein, Ariel. "Filming War: The 1948 War in 'Hill 24 Doesn't Answer' and 'Kedma.'" *Zmanim: A Historical Quarterly* 113 (2011): 58–67.
Feldman, Jackie. *Above the Death Pits, Beneath the Flag: Youth Voyages to Poland and the Performance of Israeli National Identity*. New York: Berghahn Books, 2010.
Félix, Anikó. "Hungary." In *Gender as Symbolic Glue: The Position and Role of Conservative and Far Right Parties in the Anti-Gender Movement in Europe*, edited by Eszter Kováts and Maari Põim, 62–82. Brussels: Foundation for European Progressive Studies, 2015.
Ferziger, Adam S. "Ashes to Outcasts: Cremation, Jewish Law, and Identity in Early Twentieth-Century Germany." *AJS Review* 36, no. 1 (2012): 71–102.

Fielitz, Maik, and Laura Lotte Laloire. "Introductory Remarks." In *Trouble on the Far Right: Contemporary Right-Wing Strategies and Practices in Europe*, edited by Mike Fielitz and Laura Lotte Laloire, 13–26. Bielefeld: Transcript Verlag, 2016.

Finchelstein, Federico. *From Fascism to Populism in History*. Berkeley: University of California Press, 2017.

———. *Transatlantic Fascism: Ideology, Violence, and the Sacred in Argentina and Italy, 1919–1945*. Durham, NC: Duke University Press, 2010.

Finder, Gabriel N. "Final Chapter: Portraying the Exhumation and Reburial of Polish Jewish Holocaust Victims in the Pages of Yizkor Books." In *Human Remains and Identification: Mass Violence, Genocide and the "Forensic Turn,"* edited by Jean-Marc Dreyfus and Élisabeth Gessat-Anstett, 34–58. Manchester: Manchester University Press, 2015.

Finke, Johannes, and Christian Unger. "Jung, weiblich, rechts." *Berliner Morgenpost*, 5 April 2018. https://www.morgenpost.de/politik/article213924617/Jung-weiblich-rechts.html.

Fitzpatrick, Sheila. "Revisionism in Retrospect: A Personal View." *Slavic Review* 67, no. 3 (2008): 682–704.

Freimark, Peter. "Language Behaviour and Assimilation: The Situation of the Jews in Northern Germany in the First Half of the Nineteenth Century." *Leo Baeck Institute Year Book* 24, no. 1 (January 1979): 157–78.

Freud, Sigmund. *The Standard Edition of the Complete Psychological Works of Sigmund Freud*. Vol. 4, *1900: The Interpretation of Dreams*. Vintage: London, 2001.

Frevert, Ute. *Die Politik der Demütigung: Schauplätze von Macht und Ohnmacht*. Frankfurt am Main: Fischer, 2017.

Fried, Erich. *Anfechtungen: Fünfzig Gedichte*. Berlin: Wagenbach, 1967.

Frum, David. "A Gangster in the White House." *The Atlantic*, 28 December 2019.

———. *Trumpocracy: The Corruption of the American Republic*. New York: HarperCollins, 2018.

Fukuyama, Francis. *Identity: Contemporary Identity Politics and the Struggle for Recognition*. London: Profile Books, 2018.

Funke, Hajo. *Von Wutbürgern und Brandstiftern: AfD-Pegida-Gewaltnetze*. Berlin: VBB, 2016.

Furet, François. *Interpreting the French Revolution*. New York: Cambridge University Press, 1981.

Fussell, Paul. *The Great War and Modern Memory*. Oxford: Oxford University Press, 2014.

Gaehtgens, Thomas W. *Der Bürger als Mäzen*. Opladen: Westdeutscher Verlag, 1998.

Galinsky, Karl, ed. *Memoria Romana: Memory in Rome and Rome in Memory*. Ann Arbor: University of Michigan Press, 2014.

Gebhardt, Miriam. *Als die Soldaten kamen: Die Vergewaltigung deutscher Frauen am Ende des Zweiten Weltkrieges*. Munich: DVA, 2015.

Gehricke, Viktoria. "Die Stifterportraits Rudolf und Emilie Mosses aus dem ehemaligen Mosse-Stift Berlin-Schmargendorf." Bachelor's thesis, Freie Universität Berlin, 2019.

Geissmar, Berta. *The Baton and the Jackboot*. London: Hamish Hamilton, 1944.

Gelber, Mark H. *Melancholy Pride: Nation, Race, and Gender in the German Literature of Cultural Zionism*. Tübingen: Niemeyer Verlag, 2000.

Gellately, Robert. *Hingeschaut und Weggesehen: Hitler und sein Volk*. Stuttgart and Munich: Deutsche Verlags-Anstalt, 2002.
Geller, Jay Howard. *The Scholems: A Story of the German-Jewish Bourgeoisie from Emancipation to Destruction*. Ithaca, NY: Cornell University Press, 2019.
Geller, Jay Howard, and Leslie Morris, eds. *Three-Way Street: Jews, Germans, and the Transnational*. Ann Arbor: University of Michigan Press, 2016.
Gentile, Emilio. *Il fascino del persecutore: George L. Mosse e la catastrofe dell'uomo moderno*. Rome: Carocci, 2007. Translated by John and Anne C. Tedeschi as *Fascination with the Persecutor: George L. Mosse and the Catastrophe of Modern Man* (Madison: University of Wisconsin Press, 2021).
——. *Politics as Religion*. Princeton, NJ: Princeton University Press, 2006.
——. *Renzo De Felice: Lo storico e il personaggio*. Rome: Laterza, 2003.
——. *The Sacralization of Politics in Fascist Italy*. Cambridge, MA: Harvard University Press, 1996.
Geva, Dorit. "Daughter, Mother, Captain: Marine Le Pen, Gender, and Populism in the French National Front." *Social Politics* 27, no. 1 (2020): 11–17.
Gidal, Nachum Tim. "Photography Is My Passion." In *Nachum Tim Gidal: Photographs, 1929–1991*, edited by The Open Museum, n.p. Migdal Tefen: Open Museum–Tefen Industrial Park, 1992.
Gidal, Sonia, and Tim Gidal. *My Village in India*. New York: Pantheon Books, 1956.
Gidal, Tim. *Deutschland: Beginn des modernen Photojournalismus*. Lucerne: Bucher, 1972.
——. "A Photo Reporter in Israel." *Ariel* 57 (1984): 106–22.
——. "What India Wants from England." Photograph of the article, Tim Gidal Collection, Israel Museum, publication unknown.
Gilman, Sander. *Jewish Self-Hatred: Anti-Semitism and the Hidden Language of the Jews*. Baltimore: Johns Hopkins University Press, 1986.
——. *The Jew's Body*. New York: Routledge, 1991.
Ginsburg, Shai. *Rhetoric and Nation: The Formation of Hebrew National Culture, 1880–1990*. Syracuse: Syracuse University Press, 2014.
Givens, Terri E. "The Radical Right Gender Gap." In *The Populist Radical Right: A Reader*, edited by Cas Mudde, 295–97. New York: Routledge, 2017.
Glover, Jonathan. *Humanity: A Moral History of the Twentieth Century*. New Haven, CT: Yale University Press, 2012.
Goethe, Wolfgang von. *Faust I & II*. Translated by Stuart Atkins. Princeton, NJ: Princeton University Press, 1994.
Gordon, Linda. *The Second Coming of the KKK: The Ku Klux Klan and the American Political Tradition*. New York: W. W. Norton, 2017.
Gordon, Peter E. "The Authoritarian Personality Revisited: Reading Adorno in the Age of Trump." *boundary 2*, 15 June 2016. https://www.boundary2.org/2016/06/peter-gordon-the-authoritarian-personality-revisited-reading-adorno-in-the-age-of-trump/.
Gotzmann, Andreas. "Reconsidering Judaism as a Religion—The Religious Emancipation Period." *Jewish Studies Quarterly* 7, no. 4 (2000): 352–66.
Gouri, Haim. *'Ad 'Alot Ha-Shahar*. Tel Aviv: ha-Kibuts ha-meuhad, 2000.

———. "Hineh Mutalot Gufoteinu." '*Itim: hadashot be-sifrut uve-amnut*, 19 March 1946, 1.
———. *Pirḥe-Esh: Shirim*. Merhavia: Sifriyat Po'alim, 1949.
Govrin, Nurit. "'Yalkut Hare'im': Metziut Shel Hemsheck Umitos Shel Hatchala." In *Keri' at Ha-Dorot: Sifrut 'Ivrit Be-Ma'aglehah*, 101–31. Tel Aviv: Gevanim, 2015.
Greenberg, Udi. "Christianity, Democracy, and Populism." *Boston Review*, 22 October 2019.
———. "The Myth of a New Nazism." *Spiked*, 10 August 2018. https://www.spiked-online.com/2018/08/10/the-myth-of-a-new-nazism/.
Grill, Tobias. *Der Westen im Osten: Deutsches Judentum und jüdische Bildungsreform in Osteuropa (1783–1939)*. Göttingen: Vandenhoeck & Ruprecht, 2013.
Gross, A. "Berlin im Zeichen des Terrors." *Weltspiegel*, Berlin, 19 January 1919.
Gross, Raphael. *Anständig geblieben: Nationalsozialistische Morale*. Frankfurt am Main: S. Fischer, 2010.
Gross, Raphael, and Werner Konitzer, eds. *Moralität des Bösen: Ethik und nationalsozialistische Verbrechen*. Frankfurt am Main: Campus-Verlag, 2009.
Grossman, Jeffrey A. *The Discourse on Yiddish in Germany: From the Enlightenment to the Second Empire*. Rochester, NY: Camden House, 2000.
Grossmann, Rebekka. "Image Transfer and Visual Friction: Stating Palestine in the National Socialist Spectacle." *Leo Baeck Institute Year Book* 64 (2019): 19–45.
Gruner, Wolf. "The Forgotten Mass Destruction of Jewish Homes during Kristallnacht." *The Conversation*, 8 November 2019. https://theconversation.com/the-forgotten-mass-destruction-of-jewish-homes-during-kristallnacht-123301.
Grzebalska, Weronika. "Poland." In *Gender as Symbolic Glue: The Position and Role of Conservative and Far Right Parties in the Anti-Gender Movement in Europe*, edited by Eszter Kováts and Maari Põim, 89–92. Brussels: Foundation for European Progressive Studies, 2015.
Guber, Rivka. *Eleh Toldot Kefar Ahim*. Tel Aviv: Hotsa'at Melo, 1974.
Gur, Batya. *Even Taḥat Even*. Jerusalem: Keter, 1998.
———. "Hachaver shenafal bakrav." *Ha'aretz, Tarbut v'sifrut*, 3 December 1993.
Guterman, Norbert, and Leo Löwenthal. *Prophets of Deceit: A Study of the Techniques of the American Agitator*. New York: Harper and Brothers, 1949.
Ha'am, Ahad. "Altneuland." *Hashiloach* 8, no. 60 (December 1902).
———. "Pirkei zikhronot." In *Kol kitve ahad ha-am*, 467–96. Jerusalem: Dvir, 1964.
Haam, Achad. "Zur Sprachenfrage an den jüdischen Schulen Palästinas." *Ost und West* 1 (January 1914): 19–26.
Haas, Peter. *Morality after Auschwitz: The Radical Challenge of the Nazi Ethic*. Philadelphia: Fortress Press, 1988.
Hahn, Kurt. "Address at the Founding Day Ceremony of the Athenian School." 21 November 1965.
———. "An Experiment in Education." *The Listener*, 16 November 1950.
———. *Frau Elses Verheißung*. Munich: Albert Langen, 1910.
Halen, Andreas, and Uwe Greve. *Vom Mosse-Verlag zum Mosse-Zentrum*. Berlin: DBM-Media-Verlag, 1995.

Halevy, Judah. *Sefer Ha-Kozari*. Translated by Yehuda (Judah) Even-Shemuel. Tel Aviv: Devir, 1973.
Halkin, Hillel. *Jabotinsky: A Life*. New Haven, CT: Yale University Press, 2014.
Halperin, Liora R. *Babel in Zion: Jews, Nationalism, and Language Diversity in Palestine, 1920–1948*. New Haven, CT: Yale University Press, 2014.
Hamburger, Richard. *Zeitungsverlag und Annoncen-Expedition Rudolf Mosse Berlin*. Berlin: Organisation Verlagsgesellschaft (Hirzel), 1928.
Hank, Sabine, and Paula-Irene Villa, eds. *Anti-Genderismus: Sexualität und Geschlecht als Schauplätze aktueller politischer Auseinandersetzung*. Bielefeld: Transcript Verlag, 2015.
Harcourt, Bernard E. *The Counterrevolution: How Our Government Went to War against Its Own Citizens*. New York: Basic Books, 2018.
Hardie, Philip R. *Rumour and Renown: Representations of* Fama *in Western Literature*. Cambridge: Cambridge University Press, 2012.
Hark, Sabina, and Paula-Irene Villa, eds. *Anti-Genderismus: Sexualität und Geschlecht als Schauplätze aktueller politischer Auseinandersetzungen*. Bielefeld: Transcript Verlag, 2015.
Harnik, Ra'yah. *Shirim Le-Guni*. Tel Aviv: Hakibbutz Hameuchad, 1983.
Harrison, Robert Pogue. *The Dominion of the Dead*. Chicago: University of Chicago Press, 2003.
Harrisville, David A. *The Virtuous Wehrmacht: Crafting the Myth of the German Soldier on the Eastern Front, 1941–1944*. Ithaca, NY: Cornell University Press, 2021.
Harteveld, Eelco, Wouter van der Brug, Stefan Dahlberg, and Andrej Kokkonen. "The Gender Gap in Populist Radical-Right Voting: Examining the Demand Side in Western and Eastern Europe." *Patterns of Prejudice* 49, nos. 1–2 (2015): 103–30.
Hartmann, Christian. *Wehrmacht im Ostkrieg: Front und militärisches Hinterland, 1941–42*. Munich: R. Oldenbourg Verlag, 2009.
Härtsch, Fritz. *Rudolf Mosse—ein Verleger revolutioniert das Werbegeschäft*. Zürich: Mosse, 1996.
Harvey, Elizabeth. *Women in the Nazi East: Agents and Witnesses of Germanization*. New Haven, CT: Yale University Press, 2003.
Haus, Andreas. "Photography at the Bauhaus: Discovery of a Medium." In *Photography at the Bauhaus*, edited by Jeannine Fiedler, 126–83. Cambridge, MA: MIT Press, 1990.
Hayes, Peter, ed. *Germany's Business Leaders: The Rudolf Mosse Collection of Business Histories and Biographies*. Frederick, MD: UPA Academic Editions, 1988.
Heer, Hannes, and Klaus Naumann, eds. *War of Extermination: The German Military in World War II, 1941–1944*. Translated by Roy Shelton. New York: Berghahn Books, 2000.
Heinrich Böll Stiftung. *Anti-Gender Movements on the Rise? Strategising for Gender Equality in Central and Eastern Europe*. Berlin: Heinrich Böll Stiftung, 2015.
Heller, Daniel Kupfert. *Jabotinsky's Children: Polish Jews and the Rise of Right-Wing Zionism*. Princeton, NJ: Princeton University Press, 2017.
Helmbold-Doyé, Jana, and Thomas Gertzen. "Mosse and Museum: The Support of Berlin Publisher Rudolf Mosse (1843–1920) for the Egyptian Museum Berlin, 2017." MARI-Portal, 14 July 2020. https://www.mari-portal.de/posts.

Hendel, Yehudit. *Har Ha-Toim*. Tel Aviv: Hakibbutz Hameuchad, 1991.
Herbert, Ulrich. *Hitler's Foreign Workers: Enforced Foreign Labor in Germany under the Third Reich*. New York: Cambridge University Press, 1997.
Herbert, Ulrich, Karin Orth, and Christoph Dieckmann. *Die nationalsozialistische Konzentrationslager: Entwicklung und Struktur*. Frankfurt am Main: Fischer Taschenbuch, 1998.
Herf, Jeffrey. *Reactionary Modernism: Technology, Culture, and Politics in Weimar and the Third Reich*. Cambridge: Cambridge University Press, 1984.
Hermand, Jost. "Fall of an Empire: The Fate of Rudolf Mosse's Art Collection." YouTube, 2 December 2010. https://www.youtube.com/watch?v=hgTWG-TuHNU.
———. "Zweierlei Moderne: Das Kunstverständnis Rudolf Mosses und Hans Lachmann-Mosses." In *Aufbruch in die Moderne*, edited by Anna-Dorothea Ludewig, 250–71. Cologne: DuMont Buchverlag, 2012.
Herzl, Theodor. *Der Judenstaat: Versuch einer modernen Lösung der Judenfrage*. Leipzig and Vienna: M. Breitenstein, 1896.
———. *The Jewish State: An Attempt at a Modern Solution of the Jewish Question*. Translated by Sylvie d'Avigdor and Israel Cohen. New York: Scopus, 1943.
———. *Zionistisches Tagebuch 1895–1899*. Edited by Johannes Wachten and Chaya Harel. Berlin: Ullstein, 1983.
Herzog, Dagmar. *Sex after Fascism: Memory and Morality in Twentieth-Century Germany*. Princeton, NJ: Princeton University Press, 2007.
Hesse, Klaus, and Philipp Springer, eds. *Vor aller Augen: Fotodokumente des nationalsozialistischen Terrors in der Provinz*. Essen: Klartext, 2002.
Hever, Hannan. *Suddenly, the Sight of War: Violence and Nationalism in Hebrew Poetry in the 1940s*. Stanford, CA: Stanford University Press, 2016.
Hillje, Johannes. *Return to the Politically Abandoned: Conversations in Right-Wing Populist Strongholds in Germany and France*. Berlin: Progressives Zentrum, 2018.
Hilmer, Richard, Bettina Kohlrausch, Rits Müller-Hilmer, and Jérmie Gagné. "Einstellung und soziale Lebenslage: Eine Spurensuche nach Gründen für rechtspopulistische Orientierung, auch unter Gewerkschaftsmitgliedern." *Working Paper Forschungsförderung* 44. Düsseldorf: Hans Böckler Stiftung, August 2017.
Hirsch, Rabbi Samson Raphael. "Religion Allied to Progress." In *Judaism Eternal: Selected Essays from the Writings of Rabbi Samson Raphael Hirsch*, vol. 2, translated and annotated by Dr. I. Grunfeld, 224–44. London: Soncino Press, 1960–66.
Hirschfeld, Ariel. *Rishumim Shel Hitgalut*. Tel Aviv: 'Am 'Oved, 2006.
Hollander, Philip. *From Schlemiel to Sabra: Zionist Masculinity and Palestinian Hebrew Literature*. Bloomington: Indiana University Press, 2019.
Hördler, Stefan. *Ordnung und Inferno: Das KZ-System im letzten Kriegsjahr*. Göttingen: Wallstein, 2013.
Horkheimer, Max. "The End of Reason." In *The Essential Frankfurt School Reader*, edited by Andrew Arato and Eike Gebhardt, 26–48. New York: Urizen Books, 1978.
Horkheimer, Max, and Theodor Adorno. *Dialectic of Enlightenment*. Stanford, CA: Stanford University Press, 2002.

Horvilleur, Delphine. *Refléxions sur la question antisémite*. Paris: Grasset, 2019.
Hughes, Everett. "Good People and Dirty Work." *Social Problems* 10, no. 1 (1962): 3–11.
Huyssen, Andreas. "Behemoth Rises Again. Not an Analogy!" *N+1*, 29 July 2019. https://www.nplusonemag.com/online-only/online-only/behemoth-rises-again/.
———. "Breitbart News und die Frankfurter Schule." *Merkur*, 71 Jahrgang, July 2017, 85–90. http://www.publicseminar.org/2017/09/breitbart-bannon-trump-and-the-frankfurt-school/.
Invictus, Augustus. "Physical Removal: More than a Meme." In *A Fair Hearing: The Alt-Right in the Words of Its Members and Leaders*, edited by George T. Shaw, 208–14. Middletown, DE: Arktos Media Ltd., 2018.
"Izkor: The Commemoration Site of Fallen Defense and Security Forces of Israel." State of Israel, Ministry of Defense, 2022. https://www.izkor.gov.il.
Jabotinsky, Ze'ev. *Avtobiografia*. Jerusalem: Eri Jabotinsky, 1946.
———. "Max Nordau." In *Memories of a Son of My Generation*, 227–35. Tel Aviv: Amichai Publishing, 1957.
Jaeger, Roland. "Die Länder der Erde im Bild: Die Reihe Orbis Terrarum im Verlag Ernst Wasmuth, Berlin, und im Atlantis-Verlag, Berlin/Zürich." In *Autopsie: Deutschsprachige Fotobücher 1918 bis 1945*, edited by Manfred Heiting and Roland Jaeger, 98–131. Göttingen: Steidl, 2012.
Jaffe, Leib. *Bishelihut am: Mikhtavim uteudot*. Jerusalem: Ha-sifria ha-tsiyonit, 1968.
JanMohamed, Abdul R. "Sexuality on/of the Racial Border: Foucault, Wright, and the Articulation of 'Racialized Sexuality.'" In *Discourses of Sexuality: From Aristotle to AIDS*, edited by Donna C. Stanton, 94–116. Ann Arbor: University of Michigan Press, 1992.
Jay, Martin. "Dialectic of Counter-Enlightenment: The Frankfurt School as Scapegoat of the Lunatic Fringe." *Salmagundi* 168/69 (Fall 2010/Winter 2011). Also available at http://canisa.org/blog/dialectic-of-counter-enlightenment-the-frankfurt-school-as-scapegoat-of-the-lunatic-fringe.
———. "Dialectic of Counter-Enlightenment: The Frankfurt School as Scapegoat of the Lunatic Fringe" (updated and expanded version). In *Splinters in Your Eye*, 151–72. New York: Verso, 2020.
———. "Trump, Scorsese, and the Frankfurt School's Theory of Racket Society." *Los Angeles Review of Books*, 5 April 2020. https://lareviewofbooks.org/article/trump-scorsese-and-the-frankfurt-schools-theory-of-racket-society/.
Jelavich, Peter. "Popular Entertainment and Mass Media: The Central Arenas of German-Jewish Cultural Engagement." In *The German Jewish Experience Revisited*, edited by Steven E. Aschheim and Vivian Liska, 103–16. Berlin: De Gruyter, 2015.
Jensen, Uffa, and Stefanie Schüler-Springorum. "Einführung: Gefühle gegen Juden: Die Emotionsgeschichte des modernen Antisemitismus." *Geschichte und Gesellschaft* 39, no. 4 (2013): 413–42.
Judaken, Jonathan. "Introduction." *American Historical Review* 123, no. 4 (2018): 1122–38.
Judd, Robin. *Contested Rituals: Circumcision, Kosher Butchering, and Jewish Political Life in Germany, 1843–1933*. Ithaca, NY: Cornell University Press, 2011.

Judis, John B. *The Populist Explosion: How the Great Recession Transformed American and European Politics.* New York: Columbia Global Reports, 2016.

Jüdisch-Liberale Zeitung. "Die Konferenz-Beratungen des Sonntags." *Jüdisch-Liberale Zeitung* 8, no. 34 (24 August 1928): 5–7.

Juhász, Borbála. "Forwards or Backwards? Strategies to Overcome Gender Backlash in Hungary." In *Anti-Gender Movements on the Rise? Strategising for Gender Equality in Central and Eastern Europe,* 28–32. Berlin: Heinrich Böll Stiftung, 2015.

Jünger, Ernst. *The Worker: Domination and Form.* Edited by Laurence P. Hemming. Evanston, IL: Northwestern University Press, 2017.

Kałczewiak, Marusz. "Anticolonial Orientalism: Perets Hirshbeyn's Indian Travelogue." *In Geveb: A Journal of Yiddish Studies* (July 2019): 1–20.

Kaplan, Danny. *The Men We Loved: Male Friendship and Nationalism in Israeli Culture.* New York: Berghahn Books, 2006.

Kaplan, Marion A. *Between Dignity and Despair: Jewish Life in Nazi Germany.* Oxford: Oxford University Press, 1999.

———. "Redefining Judaism in Imperial Germany: Practices, Mentalities, and Communities." *Jewish Social Studies* 9, no. 1 (2002): 1–33.

———. "Religious Practices, Mentalities, and Community." In *Jewish Daily Life in Germany, 1618–1945,* edited by Marion A. Kaplan, 235–51. Oxford: Oxford University Press, 2005.

Kasztelan, Marta, Marta Soszynska, Agnieszka Liggett, Mustafa Khalili, Charlie Phillips, and Juliet Riddell. "Pretty Radical: A Young Woman's Journey into the Heart of Poland's Far Right." *Guardian,* 19 January 2015.

Katz, Albert. "Nachruf auf Rudolf Mosse." *Allgemeine Zeitung des Judentums* 84, no. 32 (17 September 1920).

Kaufman, Shmuel. *Imrot Ve-Hagigim.* Jerusalem: n.p., 1956.

———. *Mivhar Ketavim.* Jerusalem: Derfus Ronald, 1959.

———. *Mivḥar Ketavim Huv'u Le-Defus Be-Yede Aviv.* Edited by Judah Even Shmuel. Jerusalem: Defus Hashiloach, 1949.

Kay, Alex J., Jeff Rutherford, and David Stahel, eds. *Nazi Policy on the Eastern Front, 1941: Total War, Genocide, and Radicalization.* Rochester, NY: University of Rochester Press, 2012.

Kemper, Andreas. *Keimzelle der Nation? Familien- und geschlechterpolitische Positionen der AfD–eine Expertise.* Friedrich Ebert Stiftung, 2014. http://library.fes.de/pdf-files/dialog/10641-20140414.pdf.

Kerl, Kristoff. *Männlichkeit und moderner Antisemitismus: Eine Genealogie des Leo-Frank-Case, 1860er bis 1920er Jahre.* Cologne: Böhlau, 2017.

Khan, Yasmin. *India at War: The Subcontinent and the Second World War.* Oxford: Oxford University Press, 2015.

Klapheck, Elisa. *Fräulein Rabbiner Jonas: Kann die Frau das rabbinische Amt bekleiden?* Teetz: Hentrich & Hentrich, 1999.

Klemperer, Victor. *I Shall Bear Witness: The Diaries, 1942–1945.* London: Weidenfeld & Nicolson, 1999.

Knebel, Irith Dublon. "'Erinnern kann ich mich nur an eine Frau Danz ...' die Aufseherin Luise Danz in der Erinnerung ihrer Opfer." In *Genozid und Geschlecht: Jüdische Frauen im nationalsozialistischen Lagersystem*, edited by Gisela Bock, 66–84. Frankfurt am Main: Campus, 2005.

Koestler, Arthur. *Menschenopfer unerhört: Ein Schwarzbuch über Spanien*. Paris: Éditions du Carrefour, 1938.

Kohut, Thomas. *A German Generation: An Experiential History of the Twentieth Century*. New Haven, CT: Yale University Press, 2012.

Kolitz, Zvi. *Mussolini: Ishiyuto Ve-torato*. Tel Aviv: Tevel, 1936.

———. *Yosl Rakover Talks to God*. Translated and edited by Carol Brown Janeway. New York: Pantheon Books, 1999.

König, Martin. "Die 'deutsche Frau und Mutter': Ideologie und Wirklichkeit." In *Ulm im Zweiten Weltkrieg*, edited by Hans Eugen Specker, 99–127. Stuttgart: Kohlhammer, 1996.

Koonz, Claudia. "Eugenics, Gender, and Ethics in Nazi Germany: The Debate about Involuntary Sterilization, 1933–1936." In *Reevaluating the Third Reich*, edited by Thomas Childers and Jane Caplan, 66–85. New York: Homes & Meier, 1992.

———. *The Nazi Conscience*. Cambridge, MA: Harvard University Press, 2003.

———. *Women, Family and Nazi Politics*. New York: St. Martin's, 1988.

Kornberg, Jacques, ed. *At the Crossroads: Essays on Ahad Ha'am*. Albany: State University of New York Press, 1983.

Korolczuk, Elżbieta, and Agnieszka Graff. "Gender as 'Ebola from Brussels': The Anticolonial Frame and the Rise of Illiberal Populism." *Signs: Journal of Women in Culture and Society* 43, no. 4 (2018).

Köttig, Michaela, Renate Bitzan, and Andrea Petö, eds. *Gender and Far Right Politics in Europe*. London: Palgrave Macmillan, 2017.

Kováts, Eszter, and Maari Põim, eds. *Gender as Symbolic Glue: The Position and Role of Conservative and Far Right Parties in the Anti-Fender Movement in Europe*. Brussels: Foundation for European Progressive Studies, 2015.

Kraus, Elisabeth. *Die Familie Mosse: Deutsch-jüdisches Bürgertum im 19. und 20. Jahrhundert*. Munich: C.H. Beck, 1999.

———. "Jüdisches Mäzenatentum im Kaiserreich: Befunde—Motive—Hypothesen." In *Bürgerkultur und Mäzenatentum im 19. Jahrhundert*, edited by Jürgen Kocka and Manuel Frey, 38–53. Berlin: Fannei und Walz, 1998.

Krogh, Steffen. "'Doz iz eyne vahre geshikhte ...': On the Germanization of Eastern Yiddish in the Nineteenth Century." In *Jews and Germans in Eastern Europe*, edited by Tobias Grill, 88–114. Berlin: De Gruyter, 2018.

Kuby, Gabriele. *The Global Sexual Revolution: Destruction of Freedom in the Name of Freedom*. Kettering, OH: Angelico Press, 2015.

Kuhrau, Sven. *Der Kunstsammler im Kaiserreich: Kunst und Repräsentation in der Berliner Privatsammlerkultur*. Kiel: Ludwig, 2005.

Kundrus, Birthe. "'Die Unmoral deutscher Soldatenfrauen': Diskurs, Alltagsverhalten und Ahndungspraxis 1939–1945." In *Zwischen Karriere und Verfolgung: Handlungsräume von Frauen im nationalsozialistischen Deutschland*, edited by Kirsten Heinsohn, Barbara Vogel, and Ulrike Weckel, 96–110. Frankfurt am Main: Campus, 1997.

———. "'Verbotener Umgang': Liebesbeziehungen zwischen Ausländern und Deutschen 1939–1945." In *Nationalsozialismus und Zwangsarbeit in der Region Oldenburg*, edited by Katharina Hoffman and Andreas Lambeck, 149–70. Oldenburg: Universität Oldenburg, 1999.

LaCapra, Dominick. *Writing History, Writing Trauma*. Baltimore: Johns Hopkins University Press, 2001.

Lafleur, William, and Susumu Shimazono, eds. *Dark Medicine: Rationalizing Unethical Medical Research*. Bloomington: Indiana University Press, 2008.

Laqueur, Thomas Walter. *The Work of the Dead: A Cultural History of Mortal Remains*. Princeton, NJ: Princeton University Press, 2015.

Laskov, Shulamit. *Ahad Ha-Am: Mikhtavim be'inyanei erets yisrael (1891–1926)*. Jerusalem: Yad Ben Zvi, 2000.

Lässig, Simone. *Jüdische Wege ins Bürgertum: Kulturelles Kapital und sozialer Aufstieg im 19. Jahrhundert*. Göttingen: Vandenhoeck & Ruprecht, 2004.

Lässig, Simone, and Swen Steinberg. "Knowledge on the Move: New Approaches toward a History of Migrant Knowledge." *Geschichte und Gesellschaft* 43, no. 3 (2017): 313–46.

Lebel, Udi. "'Beyond the Pantheon': Bereavement, Memory and the Strategy of Delegitimization against Herut." *Israel Studies* 10, no. 3 (2005): 104–26.

———. *Ha-Derekh El Ha-Panten: Etsel, Lehi U-Gevulot Ha-Zikaron Ha-Israeli*. Jerusalem: Sapir, 2007.

Lederhendler, Eli. *Jewish Responses to Modernity: New Voices in America and Eastern Europe*. New York: New York University Press, 1994.

Lepsius, Sabine. *Ein Berliner Künstlerleben*. Munich: G. Müller, 1972.

Levinsohn, Isaac-Bär. *Teuda Be-Israel*. Vilnius: R.M. Romma, 1855.

Levy, Yagil. *Israel's Death Hierarchy: Casualty Aversion in a Militarized Democracy*. New York: New York University Press, 2016.

Levyatov, Zohara, and Shmuel Even Shemu'el [Kaufman]. *Ule-Hathil Mi-Bereshit: Mikhtavim*. Edited by Meir Edelstein. Jerusalem: Y. Markus, 1982.

Lewinsky, E. L. "A bisele kongres-loshen." *Der Yud*, 16 January 1902.

Libeskind, Daniel. "Between the Lines." In *Extension of the Berlin Museum with Jewish Museum Department*, edited by Kristin Feireiss, 57–125. Berlin: Ernst & Sohn, 1992.

———. Mosse Lecture at Humboldt University, Berlin, 6 June 1997.

Lieblich, Amia. *Yalde Kefar 'etsyon*. Jerusalem: Keter, 2007.

Lifton, Robert Jay. *The Nazi Doctors: Medical Killing and the Psychology of Genocide*. New York: Basic Books, 1986.

Lind, William S. "The Origins of Political Correctness." *Accuracy in Academia*, 5 February 2000. https://www.academia.org/the-origins-of-political-correctness/.

———. *Victoria: A Novel of 4th General War*. Kouvola, Finland: Castalia House, 2014.

Litvin, Rina. "Hatekst hasamui shel hakhayim hashakulim." *'Iton 77: Journal of Literature and Culture* 144–45 (1992): 44–45.

Loeffler, James. *Rooted Cosmopolitans: Jews and Human Rights in the Twentieth Century.* New Haven, CT: Yale University Press, 2018.
Loewe, Heinrich. *Die Sprachen der Juden.* Cologne: Jüdischer Verlag, 1911.
Lombroso, Cesare. *Criminal Man—According to the Classification of Cesare Lombroso.* New York: Knickerbocker Press, 1911.
Loomis, Barbara, and William N. Bonds, eds. "Sexuality and German Fascism." Special issue, *Journal of the History of Sexuality* 11, nos. 1/2 (January–April 2002).
Löwith, Karl. *From Hegel to Nietzsche: The Revolution in Nineteenth-Century Thought.* New York: Holt, 1964.
Lüdtke, Alf. "People Working: Everyday Life and German Fascism." *History Workshop Journal* 50, no. 1 (2000): 74–92.
———. "Soldiering and Working: Almost the Same? Reviewing Practices in Industry and the Military in Twentieth-Century Contexts." In *Work in a Modern Society: The German Historical Experience in Comparative Perspective*, edited by Jürgen Kocka, 109–30. New York: Berghahn Books, 2010.
———. "War as Work: Aspects of Soldering in the Twentieth-Century Wars." In *No Man's Land of Violence: Extreme Wars in the 20th Century*, edited by Alf Lüdtke and Bernd Weisbrod, 127–51. Göttingen: Wallstein, 2006.
———. "Working the Passage: East German Border Checkpoints, 1961–90: The Case of GÜSt Bahnhof Friedrichstraße, Berlin." *Journal of Contemporary History* 50, no. 3 (2015): 600–705.
Lukács, Georg. *The Destruction of Reason.* Atlantic Highlands, NJ: Humanities Press, 1981.
Luria, Yosef. "Be-shulei ma'halakho shel ha-kongress." *Sefer ha-kongres.*
Machtan, Lothar. *Prinz Max von Baden: Eine Biographie.* Berlin: Suhrkamp, 2013.
Maewede-Dengg, Claudia. "The Dispossession of the Lachmann-Mosse Family." MARI-Portal, 13 July 2020. https://www.mari-portal.de/page/the-dispossession-of-the-lachmann-mosse-family.
Magilow, Daniel. *The Photography of Crisis: The Photo Essays of Weimar Germany.* University Park: Pennsylvania State University Press, 2012.
Maik, Linda L. "Nordau's Degeneration: The American Controversy." *Journal of the History of Ideas* 50, no. 4 (Oct.–Dec. 1989): 607–23.
Mailänder, Elissa. *Female SS Guards and Workaday Violence: The Majdanek Concentration Camp, 1942–1944.* Translated by Patricia Szobar. Lansing: Michigan State University Press, 2015.
———. "'Going East': Colonial Experiences and Practices of Violence of the Female and Male Camp Guards in Majdanek (1941–1944)." *Journal of Genocide Research* 10, no. 4 (2008): 563–82.
———. "Meshes of Power: The Concentration Camp as Pulp or Art House in Liliana Cavani's *The Night Porter.*" In *Nazisploitation! The Nazi Image in Low-Brow Cinema and Culture*, edited by Daniel H. Magilow, Elizabeth Bridges, and Kristin T. Vander Lugt, 175–95. New York: Continuum, 2012.
———. "A Specialist: The Daily Work of Erich Muhsfeldt, Chief of the Crematorium at Majdanek Concentration and Extermination Camp, 1942–44." In *Destruction and*

Human Remains: Disposal and Concealment in Genocide and Mass Violence, edited by Elisabeth Anstett and Jean-Marc Dreyfus, 46–68. Manchester: Manchester University Press, 2014.

Mann, Barbara. *A Place in History: Modernism, Tel Aviv, and the Creation of Jewish Urban Space*. Stanford, CA: Stanford University Press, 2005.

Mann, Golo. "Der Pädagoge als Politiker: Kurt Hahn (1965)." In *Zwölf Versuche*, 61–104. Frankfurt: Suhrkamp, 1973.

———. *Reminiscences and Reflections: A Youth In Germany*. Translated by Krishna Windsont. New York: Norton, 1990.

Mann, Klaus. "Homosexualität und Faschismus (1934/35)." In *Heute und Morgen: Schriften zur Zeit*, 130–37. Munich: Nymphenburger, 1969.

Mann, Nir. "Zohara Levyatov: Giboret Mofet O Mitos?" *Cathedra: For the History of Eretz Israel and Its Yishuv* 118 (2006): 145–76.

Manojlovic, Katharina. "Strolling through India: The Austrian Photographer and Journalist Alice Schalek." *Austrian Studies* 20 (2012): 193–205.

Mansfield, Harvey G. *Manliness*. New Haven, CT: Yale University Press, 2006.

Marcuse, Herbert. "The New German Mentality (1942)." In *Technology, War and Fascism: Collected Papers of Herbert Marcuse*, edited by Douglas Kellner, 139–90. London: Routledge, 1998.

Mark, Yudl. "Problemen baym normiren di yidishe klal-shprakh." *Yidishe shprakh* 18, no. 2 (September 1958): 33–50.

Mason, Timothy. "Women in Nazi Germany." *History Workshop* 1 (Spring 1976): 74–113.

———. "Women in Nazi Germany." *History Workshop* 2 (Autumn 1976): 5–32.

Matthäus, Jürgen. "Holocaust als angewandter Antisemitismus? Potential und Grenzen eines Erklärungsfaktors." In *Der Holocaust: Ergebnisse und neue Fragen der Forschung*, edited by Frank Bajohr and Andrea Löw, 102–23. Frankfurt am Main: Fischer, 2015.

Matthes, Olaf. *James Simon: Die Kunst des sinnvollen Gebens*. Berlin: Bostelmann & Siebenhaar, 2011.

Matthews, Herbert L. "Saint or Charlatan?" *New York Times*, 28 March 1943.

Matyus, Stephan. "Auszeit vom KZ Alltag: Das Bretstein-Album." In *Täter: Österreichische Akteure im Nationalsozialismus*, edited by Dokumentationsarchiv des österreichischen Widerstandes, 107–33. Vienna: Jahrbuch, 2014.

Mayer, Hans. *Outsiders: A Study in Life and Letters*. Cambridge, MA: MIT Press, 1982.

Mayer, Nonna, and Mariette Sineau. "France: The Front National." In *Rechtsextreme Parteien*, edited by Helga Asperger and Brigitte Halbmayr, 61–112. Leverkusen: Leske & Budrich, 2002.

McPherson, Tara. "Platforming Hate: The Right in the Digital Age." Lecture, Anniversary Celebration of the Center for Twenty-First Century Studies, University of Wisconsin-Milwaukee, Fall 2018.

Meier, Christian. *Das Gebot zu Vergessen und die Unabweisbarkeit des Erinnerns: Vom öffentlichen Umgang mit schlimmer Vergangenheit*. Munich: Siedler Verlag, 2010.

Mendelssohn, Peter de. *Zeitungsstadt Berlin: Menschen und Mächte in der Geschichte der deutschen Presse*. Berlin: Ullstein, 1959.

Menusi, Didi (lyrics), and Yohana Zarai (music). "Mi She'khalam." Performed by the Armored Corps Military Band, 1967.
Meret, Susi. "Charismatic Female Leadership and Gender: Pia Kjærsgaard and the Danish People's Party." *Patterns of Prejudice* 49, nos. 1–2 (2015): 92–94.
Messerschmidt, Manfred. *Die Wehrmacht im NS-Staat: Zeit der Indoktrination*. Hamburg: R.v. Deckers Verlag, 1969.
Meybohm, Ivonne. *David Wolffsohn: Aufsteiger, Grenzgänger, Mediator*. Göttingen: Vandenhoeck & Ruprecht, 2013.
Meyer, Michael A., ed. *Deutsch-Jüdische Geschichte in der Neuzeit*. Vol. 3, *Umstrittene Integration, 1871–1918*. Munich: C.H. Beck, 2000.
———. "*Gemeinschaft* within *Gemeinde*: Religious Ferment in Weimar Liberal Judaism." In *In Search of Jewish Community: Jewish Identities in Germany and Austria, 1918–1933*, edited by Michael Brenner and Derek J. Penslar, 15–35. Bloomington: Indiana University Press, 1998.
———. "'How Awesome Is This Place!' The Reconceptualization of the Synagogue in Nineteenth-Century Germany." *Leo Baeck Institute Year Book* 41 (1996): 51–63.
———. "Liberal Judaism in Nazi Germany." In *On Germans and Jews under the Nazi Regime: Essays by Three Generations of Historians*, edited by Moshe Zimmermann, 281–95. Jerusalem: Magnes, 2006.
———. *Response to Modernity: A History of the Reform Movement in Judaism*. New York: Oxford University Press, 1988.
———. "Women in the Thought and Practice of the European Jewish Reform Movement." In *Gender and Jewish History*, edited by Marion A. Kaplan and Deborah Dash Moore, 139–57. Bloomington: Indiana University Press, 2010.
Mineau, André. *Operation Barbarossa: Ideology and Ethics against Human Dignity*. Amsterdam: Rodopi, 2004.
Miron, Dan. *Mul Ha'ah Hashoteq: 'Iyyunim Beshirat Milhemet Ha'atsma'ut*. Tel Aviv: Keter, 1992.
Mishra, Pankaj. "The Crisis in Modern Masculinity." *Guardian*, 17 March 2018.
Missalla, Heinrich. *Wie der Krieg zur Schule Gottes wurde: Hitlers Feldbischof Rarkowski: Eine notwendige Erinnerung*. Oberursel: Publik-Forum, 1997.
Moenninghoff, Burkhard. "Baum." In *Metzler Lexikon literarischer Symbole*, edited by Günter Butzer and Joachim Jacob, 36-7. Stuttgart: Metzler, 2008.
Moholy-Nagy, László. "Production-Reproduction." In *Photography in the Modern Era: European Documents and Critical Writings, 1913–1940*, edited by Christopher Phillips, 79–82. New York: Metropolitan Museum of Art/Aperture, 1989.
Moldenhauser, Wilhelm. *Im Funkwagen der Wehrmacht durch Europa: Balkan, Ukraine, Stalingrad: Feldpostbriefe des Gefreiten Wilhelm Moldenhauser 1940–1943*. Edited by Jens Ebert. Berlin: Trafo, 2008.
Monod, Jacques. *Chance and Necessity: An Essay on the Natural Philosophy of Modern Biology*. New York: Alfred A. Knopf, 1971.
Morris, Benny. "The New Historiography: Israel Confronts Its Past." *Tikkun* 3, no. 6 (1988): 19–23, 99–102.

Mosse, George L. *Aus großem Haus: Erinnerungen eines deutsch-jüdischen Historikers*. Munich: Ullstein, 2003.

———. *Can Nationalism Be Saved? About Zionism, Rightful and Unjust Nationalism*. Rehovot: Yad Chaim Weizmann, 1995.

———. *Confronting History: A Memoir*. Madison: University of Wisconsin Press, 2000.

———. *The Crisis of German Ideology: Intellectual Origins of the Third Reich*. Madison: University of Wisconsin Press, 2021.

———. *The Culture of Western Europe: The Nineteenth and Twentieth Centuries*. Madison: University of Wisconsin Press, 2023.

———. *Fallen Soldiers: Reshaping the Memory of the World Wars*. New York: Oxford University Press, 1990.

———. *The Fascist Revolution: Toward a General Theory of Fascism*. Madison: University of Wisconsin Press, 2021.

———. "Friendship and Nationhood: About the Promise and Failure of German Nationalism." *Journal of Contemporary History* 17, no. 2 (1982): 351–67.

———. *George Mosse on the Occasion of His Retirement: 17.6.85*. Jerusalem: Hebrew University, 1986.

———. *German Jews beyond Judaism*. Cincinnati: Hebrew Union College Press, 1985.

———. *Hanoflim Bakrav* [Hebrew edition of *Fallen Soldiers*]. Tel-Aviv: 'Am 'Oved, 1990.

———. "The Image of the Jew in Popular Literature: Felix Dahn and Gustav Freytag." *Leo Baeck Institute Year Book* 2 (1957): 218–27.

———. *The Image of Man: The Creation of Modern Masculinity*. New York: Oxford University Press, 1996.

———. Interview with David Strassler. In "Antisemitism," *Jerusalem Post*, 17 September 1991.

———. Interview with Michael Ledeen. In *Nazism: A Historical and Comparative Analysis of National Socialism*. New Brunswick, NJ: Transaction Books, 1978.

———. "Jewish Emancipation: Between *Bildung* and Respectability." In *Confronting the Nation: Jewish and Western Nationalism*, 131–45. Waltham, MA: Brandeis University Press, 1993.

———. *Jüdische Intellektuelle in Deutschland: Zwischen Religion und Nationalismus*. Frankfurt am Main: Campus Verlag, 1992.

———. "Max Nordau, Liberalism and the New Jew." *Journal of Contemporary History* 27, no. 4 (1992): 565–81.

———. "Mosse: Federation Is Best Hope." *Capital Times*, 27 August 1979.

———. *Nationalism and Sexuality: Middle-Class Morality and Sexual Norms in Modern Europe*. Madison: University of Wisconsin Press, 2020.

———. *The Nationalization of the Masses: Political Symbolism and Mass Movements in Germany from the Napoleonic Wars through the Third Reich*. Madison: University of Wisconsin Press, 2023.

———. *Der nationalsozialistische Alltag: So lebte man unter Hitler*. Königstein im Taurus: Athenäum, 1979.

———. *Nazi Culture: Intellectual, Cultural, and Social Life in the Third Reich.* Madison: University of Wisconsin Press, 2003.
———. "Personal Recollections." In *Die Musiktradition der jüdischen Reformgemeinde zu Berlin.* Beth Hatefutsoth, 1998.
———. "Political Style and Political Theory: Totalitarian Democracy Revisited." In *Totalitarian Democracy and After: International Colloquium in Memory of Jacob L. Talmon. Jerusalem, 21–24 June 1982,* 167–76. Jerusalem: Israel Academy of Sciences and Humanities / Magnes Press / Hebrew University, 1984.
———. "Renzo De Felice e il revisionismo storico." *Nuova Antologia* 133, no. 2206 (1998): 177–86.
———. "School for Germany Opposed." *New York Times,* 24 January 1950.
———. *Toward the Final Solution: A History of European Racism.* Madison: University of Wisconsin Press, 2020.
———. "Two World Wars and the Myth of the War Experience." *Journal of Contemporary History* 21, no. 4 (1986): 491–513.
Mosse, Rudolf. *Haus der Sammlungen Rudolf Mosse.* Berlin: Mosse, 1932.
Mosse, Werner E. *Entscheidungsjahr 1932: Zur Judenfrage in der Endphase der Weimarer Republik.* Tübingen: Mohr Siebeck, 1965.
———. *The European Powers and the German Question, 1848–71.* Cambridge: Cambridge University Press, 1958.
———. *Jews in the German Economy: The German-Jewish Economic Elite, 1820–1935.* Oxford: Clarendon Press, 1987.
———. *Juden im Wilhelminischen Deutschland 1890–1914.* Tübingen: Mohr Siebeck, 1976.
———. "Rudolf Mosse and the House of Mosse 1867–1920." *Leo Baeck Institute Year Book* 4 (1959): 237–59.
Mosse, Werner E., and Michael Brenner, eds. *Two Nations: British and German Jews in Comparative Perspective.* Tübingen: Mohr Siebeck, 1999.
Mosse, Werner E., and Arnold Paucker, eds. *Entscheidungsjahr 1932: Zur Judenfrage in der Endphase der Weimarer Republik.* Tübingen: Mohr Siebeck, 1965.
Mudde, Cas. "Introduction." In *The Populist Radical Right: A Reader,* edited by Cas Mudde, 1–10. New York: Routledge, 2017.
———. *Populist Radical Right Parties in Europe.* Cambridge: Cambridge University Press, 2007.
Mudde, Cas, and Cristóbal Rovira Kaltwasser. "*Vox populi* or *vox masculini*? Populism and Gender in Northern Europe and South America." *Patterns of Prejudice* 49, nos. 1–2 (2015): 16–36.
Müller, Jan-Werner. *What Is Populism?* Philadelphia: University of Pennsylvania Press, 2016.
Murdoch, Iris. "Against Dryness: A Polemical Sketch." *Encounter* 16 (January 1961): 16–20.
Museum Oskar Reinhart. *Fluchtgut II: Zwischen Fairness und Gerechtigkeit für Nachkommen und heutige Besitzer.* Museum Oskar Reinhart, Winterthur, 31 August 2015.
Nathan, Paul. *Palästina und palästinensischer Zionismus.* Berlin: H. S. Hermann, 1914.

Netanyahu, Benzion. "In Remembrance of Nordau." *Doar Ha-Yom*, 3 February 1931.

———. "Max Nordau." In *Max Nordau to His People*, 18–19. Tel Aviv: Hozaa Medinit, 1936, 18–19.

Neumann, Franz. *Behemoth: The Structure and Practice of National Socialism, 1933–1944*. New York: Harper & Row, 1966.

Nieden, Susanne zur. "'Erotic Fraternization': The Legend of German Women's Quick Surrender." In *Home/Front: The Military, War and Gender in Twentieth-Century Germany*, edited by Karen Hagemann and Stefanie Schüler-Springorum, 297–310. Oxford: Berg, 2002.

Niewyk, Donald L. *The Jews in Weimar Germany*. New Brunswick, NJ: Transaction Books, 2001.

Nini, Yehuda. *He-Hayit O Halamti Halom: Teimanei Kinneret, Parashat Hityashvutam Ve-'akiiratam, 5672–5690*. Tel Aviv: 'Am 'Oved, 1996.

Noack-Mosse, Eva. *Last Days of Theresienstadt*. Translated by Skye Doney and Birutė Ciplijauskaitė. Madison: University of Wisconsin Press, 2018.

Nora, Pierre. *Rethinking France: Les Lieux de Mémoire*. 4 vols. Translated by Richard C. Holbrook et al. Chicago: University of Chicago Press, 2001.

Nordau, Anna, and Max Nordau. *Max Nordau: A Biography*. New York: Nordau Committee, 1943.

Nordau, Max. "Ahad Ha'am über Altneuland." *Die Welt*, 13 March 1903.

———. "The Arabs and Us (1918)." In *Zionist Writings*, 4:49–55. Jerusalem: Zionist Library, 1954.

———. *Max Nordau to His People: A Summons and a Challenge*. New York: Scopus, 1941.

———. "Speech at the Eighth Zionist Congress (1907)." In *Zionist Writings*, 3:43–51. Jerusalem: Zionist Library, 1954.

Norddeutscher Rundfunk. *Der Prozess: Eine Darstellung des Majdanek-Verfahrens in Düsseldorf*. Video cassettes, 270 min., 1984.

Olmert, Dana. *Ke-Homah 'Amodnah: Imahot Le-Lohamim Ba-Sifrut Ha-'Ivrit*. Bene Brak: Hakibbutz Hameuchad, 2018.

'Omer, Devorah. *Le-ehov 'ad Mavet*. Tel Aviv: Y. Sreberk, 1980.

Osborn, Max. "Die Kunstsammlung Rudolf Mosse." *Kunstchronik* 23, no. 18 (1 March 1912): column 282–83.

Patai, Raphael. *Tents of Jacob: The Diaspora, Yesterday and Today*. Englewood Cliffs, NJ: Prentice-Hall, 1971.

Payne, Stanley G. *The Collapse of the Spanish Republic, 1933–1936: Origins of the Civil War*. New Haven, CT: Yale University Press, 2006.

———. "George L. Mosse and Walter Laqueur on the History of Fascism." *Journal of Contemporary History* 50, no. 4 (2015): 750–67.

Payne, Stanley G., David Sorkin, and John S. Tortorice, eds. *What History Tells: George L. Mosse and the Culture of Modern Europe*. Madison: University of Wisconsin Press, 2004.

Peltz, Rakmiel. "The Undoing of Language Planning from the Vantage of Culture History: Two Twentieth Century Examples." In *Undoing and Redoing Corpus Planning*, edited by Michael Clyne, 327–56. Berlin: De Gruyter, 1997.
Penslar, Derek J. *Jews and the Military: A History.* Princeton, NJ: Princeton University Press, 2013.
Piltsch, Yehuda. "Der goldener tseylem." *Daily Jewish Courier*, 7 September 1933.
Pinsker, Leon. *Autoemancipation! Mahnruf auf seine Stammesgenossen von einem russischen Juden.* Berlin: Commissions-Verlag von W. Issleib, 1882.
Plessini, Karel. *The Perils of Normalcy: George L. Mosse and the Remaking of Cultural History.* Madison: University of Wisconsin Press, 2014.
Plessner, Helmuth. *Conditio Humana.* Gesammelte Schriften VIII., 1. Auflage. Frankfurt am Main: Suhrkamp Taschenbuch Wissenschaft, 2003.
Presner, Todd Samuel. *Muscular Judaism: The Jewish Body and the Politics of Regeneration.* London: Routledge, 2010.
Przyrembel, Alexandra. "Ambivalente Gefühle: Sexualität und Antisemitismus während des Nationalsozialismus." *Geschichte und Gesellschaft* 39, no. 4 (2013): 527–54.
———. *"Rassenschande": Reinheitsmythos und Vernichtungslegitimation im Nationalsozialismus.* Göttingen: Vandenhoeck & Ruprecht, 2003.
Quadrifoglio, Matteo. "Statism and Italophilia: Risorgimento and the Italian State in the Zionist-Revisionist Imagination, 1922–1940." MA thesis, University of Haifa, 2018.
Rabinbach, Anson. "'The Abyss That Opened before Us': Thinking about Auschwitz and Modernity." In *Catastrophe and Meaning: The Holocaust and the Twentieth Century*, edited by Moishe Postone and Eric Santner, 51–66. Chicago: University of Chicago Press, 2003.
———. "Ernst Bloch's *Heritage of Our Times* and the Theory of Fascism." *New German Critique* 11 (Spring 1977): 5–21.
———. "George Mosse and the Culture of Antifascism." *German Politics and Society* 18, no. 4 (2000): 30–45.
———. "George L. Mosse 1919–1999: An Appreciation." *Central European History* 32, no. 3 (1999): 331–36.
Rapoport-Albert, Ada. "From Woman as Hasid to Woman as 'Tsadik' in the Teachings of the Last Two Lubavitcher Rebbes." *Jewish History* 27, nos. 2/4 (2013): 435–73.
Redden, Elizabeth. "Hungary Officially Ends Gender Studies Programs." *Inside Higher Ed*, 17 October 2018. https://www.insidehighered.com/quicktakes/2018/10/17/hungary-officially-ends-gender-studies-programs.
Reibert, W. *Der Dienstunterricht im Heer: Ausgabe für den Kanonier der bespannten Batterie.* Berlin: E.S. Mittler & Sohn, 1940.
Reimann, Brigitte. *Die Frau am Pranger.* Berlin: Neues Leben, 1956.
Riba, Na'ama. "165 Monuments: How the Golan Heights Became the Most Commemorated Place." *Ha'aretz*, 20 September 2015. https://www.haaretz.co.il/gallery/architecture/1.2735063.
Riesser, Gabriel. *Gesammelte Schriften.* Vol. 2. Hildesheim: Georg Olms, 2001.
Rietz, Hedwig. "Die Frau im Gotteshaus." *Jüdisch-liberale Zeitung*, 5 November 1926.

Robcis, Camille. "Catholics, the 'Theory of Gender,' and the Turn to the Human in France: A New Dreyfus Affairs?" *Journal of Modern History* 87 (December 2015): 892–923.

Robinson, Ira. "A Life to Remember: Yehuda Even Shmuel's Memorialization of His Son, Shmuel Asher Kaufman, and the Crisis of His Zionist Vision." *Contemporary Review of the Middle East* 6, nos. 3–4 (2019): 280–92.

Röder, Antje. "Immigrants' Attitudes toward Homosexuality: Socialization, Religion, and Acculturation in European Host Societies." *International Migration Review* 49, no. 4 (2015): 1042–70.

———. "Religious Differences in Immigrants' Gender Role Attitudes: The Changing Impact of Origin Country and Individual Religiosity." *Ethnic and Racial Studies* 37, no. 14 (2014): 2615–35.

Roland, Joan G. *The Jewish Communities of India: Identity in a Colonial Era*. New Brunswick, NJ: Transaction Books, 1998.

Rothberg, Michael. *Multidirectional Memory: Remembering the Holocaust in the Age of Decolonization*. Stanford, CA: Stanford University Press, 2009.

Rozental, Rubik. *Ha-Im Ha-Shekhol Met?* Jerusalem: Keter, 2001.

Rubinstein, Arthur. *My Young Years*. New York: Knopf, 1999.

Rühe, Peter. *Gandhi: A Photo Biography*. New York: Phaidon Press, 2001.

Runge, Irene, and Uwe Stelbrink. *"Ich bleibe Emigrant": Gespräche mit George L. Mosse*. Berlin: Dietz, 1991.

Rürup, Reinhard. "Vorwort." In *Vor aller Augen: Fotodokumente des nationalsozialistischen Terrors in der Provinz*, edited by Klaus Hesse and Philipp Springer, 7–9. Essen: Klartext, 2002.

Rutherford, Jeff. *Combat and Genocide on the Eastern Front: The German Infantry's War, 1941–1944*. Cambridge: Cambridge University Press, 2014.

Sachse, Carola. *Siemens, der Nationalsozialismus und die moderne Familie: Eine Untersuchung zur sozialen Rationalisierung in Deutschland im 20. Jahrhundert*. Bremen: Rasch und Röhring, 1990.

Sadeh, Shuki. "Who's behind Anti-LGBT, Anti-Reform Signs in Cities?" *Ha'aretz*, 10 April 2019, 6.

Said, Edward. *Orientalism*. New York: Pantheon Books, 1978.

Sait, Bryce. *The Indoctrination of the Wehrmacht: Nazi Ideology and the War Crimes of the German Military*. New York: Berghahn Books, 2019.

Salvini, Matteo. "The European Dream Is Being Buried by the Bureaucrats, the Buonistas, and the Bankers Who Are Governing Europe for Too Much Time." *New York Times*, 15 April 2019.

Sandbank, Shimon. *Avot Ve-Bahim: Memuar*. Tel Aviv: Hostaat ha-kubts ha-meuhad, 2004.

———. *Ha-Shir Ha-Nachon*. Tel Aviv: Sifriat Po'alim, 1982.

Santomassimo, Gianpasquale. "Il ruolo di Renzo De Felice." In *Fascismo e antifascismo: Rimozioni, revisioni, negazioni*, edited by Enzo Collotti, 415–29. Rome: Laterza, 2000.

Saure, Gabriele. "Eine neue Künstlergilde? Serielle Bildformen in der illustrierten Presse 1925 bis 1944." In *Photo-Sequenzen: Reportage, Bildgeschichten, Serien aus dem Ullstein*

Bilderdienst von 1925 bis 1944, edited by Gabriele Saure, 19–38. Berlin: Haus am Waldsee, 1993.

Schechtman, Joseph B. *The Life and Times of Vladimir Jabotinsky: Rebel and Statesman*. Silver Springs, MD: Eshel Books, 1986.

Schepple, Kim. "Worst Practices and Transnational Legal Order (or How to Build a Constitutional 'Democratorship' in Plain Sight)." http://lawsdocbox.com/Politics/78000 703-Worst-practices-and-the-transnational-legal-order-or-how-to-build-a-constitutional-democratorship-in-plain-sight-kim-lane-scheppele.html.

Scherpe, Klaus R. "Im Geist des Hauses." In *Mosse Almanach 2017*, edited by Elisabeth Wagner, 23–27. Berlin: Vorwerk 8 Verlag, 2017.

Schilling, Britta. "Crossing Boundaries: German Women in Africa, 1919–33." In *German Colonialism and National Identity*, edited by Michael Perraudin and Juergen Zimmerer, 150–69. New York: Routledge, 2010.

Schmincke, Imke. "Das Kind als Chiffre politischer Auseinandersetzung am Beispiel neuer konservativer Protestbewegungen in Frankreich und Deutschland." In *Anti-Genderismus: Sexualität und Geschlecht als Schauplätze aktueller politischer Auseinandersetzung*, edited by Sabine Hark and Paula-Irene Villa, 93–107. Bielefeld: Transcript Verlag, 2015.

Schroer, Timothy L. "Civilization, Barbarism, and the Ethos of Self-Control among the Perpetrators." *German Studies Review* 35, no. 1 (February 2012): 33–54.

Schüler-Springorum, Stefanie. *Die jüdische Minderheit in Königsberg, 1871–1945*. Göttingen: Vandenhoeck & Ruprecht, 1996.

———. "Gender and the Politics of Anti-Semitism." *American Historical Review* 123, no. 4 (2018): 1210–22.

———. "Geschlecht und Gewalt: Zur Emotionsgeschichte des Antisemitismus." In *Emotionen und Antisemitismus: Geschichte—Literatur—Theorie*, edited by Stefanie Schüler-Springorum and Jan Süselbeck, 212–32. Göttingen: Wallstein, 2021.

———. "Gewalt gegen Tote: Zur Ikonographie des Spanischen Bürgerkriegs." In *Bilder kollektiver Gewalt—Kollektive Gewalt im Bild: Annäherungen an eine Ikonographie der Gewalt*, edited by Michael Kohlstruck, Stefanie Schüler-Springorum, and Ulrich Wyrwa, 137–45. Berlin: Metropol, 2015.

Schwartz, Johannes. *"Weibliche Angelegenheiten": Handlungsräume von KZ-Aufseherinnen in Ravensbrück und Neubrandenburg*. Hamburg: Hamburger Edition, 2018.

Schwarz, Minna. "Die Frau im Gotteshaus." *Jüdisch-liberale Zeitung*, 5 November 1926.

Scrinzi, Francesca. "Gender and Women in the Front National Discourse and Policy: From 'Mothers of the Nation' to 'Working Mothers'?" *New Formations* 91 (2017): 87–101.

———. "A 'New' National Front? Gender, Religion, Secularism and the French Populist Radical Right." In *Gender and Far Right Politics in Europe*, edited by Michaela Köttig, Renate Bitzan, and Andrea Pető, 127–39. Cham, Switzerland: Palgrave Macmillan, 2016.

Segev, Tom. "Ma 'Osot Ha-Andarteot Baleylot: Dokh Mas'a." *Ha'aretz*, 27 April 1990.

———. *The Seventh Million: The Israelis and the Holocaust*. Translated by Haim Watzman. New York: Hill and Wang, 1993.

Seidel, Esther. "Women Students at the Berlin Hochschule für die Wissenschaft des Judentums." In *Gender and Religious Leadership: Women Rabbis, Pastors, and Ministers*, edited by Hartmut Bomhoff et al., 53–70. Lanham, MD: Lexington Books, 2019.

Sekula, Allan. *Photography against the Grain: Essays and Photo Works, 1973–1983*. London: Mack, 2016.

———. "The Traffic in Photographs." *Art Journal* 41, no. 1 (Spring 1981): 15–25.

Semprún, Jorge. *What a Beautiful Sunday*. London: Abacus, 1982.

Serwer, Adam. "White Nationalism's Deep American Roots." *The Atlantic*, April 2019.

Shafak, Elif. "From Spain to Turkey, the Rise of the Far Right Is a Clash of Cultures Not Civilisations," *Guardian*, 6 May 2019.

Shapira, Anita. "Kola Shel 'Mahleket Ha-Har Ha-Ilemet.'" *Ha'aretz*, 10 May 2011. https://www.haaretz.co.il/1.1173528.

———. *Land and Power: The Zionist Resort to Force, 1881–1948*. New York: Oxford University Press, 1992.

Shapira, Miriam, Slava Danziger-Caspi, and Yehudit Chernaki. "Yad Labanim." *Davar*, 28 December 1948, 2.

Shaviṭ, Ya'aḳov. *Jabotinsky and the Revisionist Movement, 1925–1948*. London: F. Cass, 1988.

Shaw, George T., ed. *A Fair Hearing: The Alt-Right in the Words of Its Members and Leaders*. Middletown, DE: Arktos Media Ltd., 2018.

Shimoni, Gideon. *The Zionist Ideology*. Waltham, MA: Brandeis University Press, 1995.

Shmeruk, Khone. *Yiddish Literature: Aspects of Its History*. Tel Aviv: Mif'alim universita'iyim le'hotsa'ah le'or, 1978.

Shoham, Reuven. "From the Naive to the Nostalgic in the Poetry of Haim Gouri." *Prooftexts* 18, no. 1 (1998): 19–43.

Shumsky, Dmitry. *Beyond the Nation-State: The Zionist Political Imagination from Pinsker to Ben-Gurion*. New Haven, CT: Yale University Press, 2018.

Sica, Alan, ed. *The Anthem Companion to Max Weber*. London: Anthem, 2016.

Sider, Gerald. "Anthropology, History, and the Problem of Everyday Life." In *Alltag, Erfahrung, Eigensinn: Historisch-Anthropologische Erkundungen*, edited by Belinda Davis, Thomas Lindenberger, and Michael Wildt, 121–32. Frankfurt am Main: Campus, 2008.

Silber, Michael K. "The Historical Experience of German Jewry and Its Impact on Haskalah and Reform in Hungary." In *Toward Modernity: The European Jewish Model*, edited by Jacob Katz, 107–57. New Brunswick, NJ: Transaction Books, 1987.

———. "Josephinian Reforms." In *The YIVO Encyclopedia of Jews in Eastern Europe*, edited by Gershon David Hundert, 1:831–34. New Haven, CT: Yale University Press, 2008.

Sivan, Emmanuel. *Dor Tashach: Mitos, Deyoḳan Ve-Zikaron*. Tel Aviv: Ma'archot, 1991.

Slobodian, Quinn. "Neoliberalism's Populist Bastards: A New Political Divide between National Economies." *Public Seminar*, 15 February 2018. http://www.publicseminar.org/2018/02/neoliberalisms-populist-bastards/.

[Smolenskin, Perets.] "Yedi'at sfarim." *Ha-Shahar* 3 (1883).

Snyder, Timothy. *The Road to Unfreedom: Russia, Europe and America*. New York: Tim Duggan Books, 2018.

Sofsky, Wolfgang. *The Order of Terror: The Concentration Camp.* Princeton, NJ: Princeton University Press, 1999.

Sofsky, Wolfgang. *Traktat über die Gewalt.* Frankfurt am Main and Vienna: Büchergilde Gutenberg, 1997.

Sösemann, Bernd. *Theodor Wolff: Ein Leben mit der Zeitung.* Stuttgart: Franz Steiner Verlag, 2013.

Spierings, Niels, and Andrej Zaslove. "Gendering the Vote for Populist Radical Right Parties." *Patterns of Prejudice* 49, nos. 1–2 (2015): 135–38.

Spierings, Niels, Andrej Zaslove, Liza M. Mügge, and Sarah L. de Lange. "Gender and Populist Radical-Right Parties: An Introduction." *Patterns of Prejudice* 49, nos. 1–2 (2015): 3–15.

Springer, Philipp. "Auf Straßen und Plätzen: Zur Fotogeschichte des nationalsozialistischen Deutschland." In *Vor aller Augen*, edited by Klaus Hesse and Philipp Springer, 11–33. Essen: Klartext, 2002.

Stanislawski, Michael. *Zionism and the Fin de Siècle: Cosmopolitanism and Nationalism from Nordau to Jabotinsky.* Berkeley: University of California Press, 2001.

Stanley, Jason. *How Fascism Works: The Politics of Us and Them.* New York: Random House, 2018.

Stargardt, Nicholas. *Der deutsche Krieg: Zwischen Angst, Zweifel und Durchhaltewillen—wie die Menschen den Zweiten Weltkrieg erlebten. 1913–1945.* Frankfurt: Fischer, 2017.

Steinberg, Michael P. "The Narcissism of Major Differences: Richard Wagner and the Peculiarities of German Antisemitism." *Social Research* 89, no. 1 (Spring 2022): 21–46.

Steinorth, Karl, ed. *Internationale Ausstellung des Deutschen Werkbundes, Film und Foto: Stuttgart, 1929.* Stuttgart: Deutsche Verlags-Anstalt GmbH, 1979.

Stelzel, Philipp. *History after Hitler: A Transatlantic Enterprise.* Philadelphia: University of Philadelphia Press, 2019.

Stenographisches Protokoll der Verhandlungen des II. Zionisten-Congresses gehalten zu Basel vom 28. Bis 31. August 1898. Vienna: Verlag des Vereines "Eretz Israel," 1898.

Stenographisches Protokoll der Verhandlungen des V. Zionisten-Congresses in Basel, 26., 27., 28., 29. Und 30. December 1901. Vienna: Verlag des Vereines "Eretz Israel," 1901.

Stenographisches Protokoll der Verhandlungen des VII. Zionisten-Kongresses in Haag vom 14. Bis 21. August 1907. Cologne: Juedischer Verlag, 1907.

Stenographisches Protokoll der Verhandlungen des X. Zionisten-Kongresses in Basel vom 9. Bis 15. August 1911. Berlin and Leipzig: Kommission beim Juedischen Verlag, 1911.

Stenographisches Protokoll der Verhandlungen des XI. Zionisten-Kongresses in Basel vom 2. Bis 9. September 1913. Berlin and Leipzig: Kommission beim Juedischen Verlag, 1914.

Stenographisches Protokoll der Verhandlungen des XII. Zionisten-Kongresses in Karlsbad vom 1. Bis 14. September 1921. Berlin: Jüdischer Verlag, 1922.

Stenographisches Protokoll der Verhandlungen des XVIII. Zionistenkongresses und der dritten Tagung des Council der Jewish Agency für Palästina, Prag, 21. August bis 4. September 1933. Vienna: Fiba Verlag, 1934.

Sternhall, Ze'ev. *La Droite révolutionnaire: Les origines françaises du fascisme*. Paris: Gallimard, 1997.
———. *Neither Right nor Left: The Fascist Ideology in France*. Berkeley: University of California Press, 1986.
Strauss, William, and Neil Howe. *The Fourth Turning: An American Prophecy*. New York: Broadway Books, 1997.
Stübig, Heinz. "Kurt Hahn und seine Erlebnistherapie." In *Abenteuer, Erlebnisse und die Pädagogik*, edited by Peter Becker, Karl-Heinz Braun, and Jochem Schirp, 99–114. Leverkusen: Barbara Budrich, 2007.
Süsskind, Natan. "Printsipn baym forshn yidishe leshoynes." *Yidishe shprakh* 25, no. 1 (June 1965): 1–17.
Swet, Gershon. "Russian Jews in Zionism and the Building of Palestine." In *Russian Jewry*, vol. 1, edited by Jacobin Frumkin, Gregor Aronson, and Alexis Goldenweiser, 172–208. New York: Thomas Yoseloff, 1966.
Talmon, Jacob L. *The Origins of Totalitarian Democracy*. London: Secker & Warburg, 1952.
Tamir, Dan. *Hebrew Fascism in Palestine, 1922–1942*. New York: Palgrave Macmillan, 2018.
Tholander, Christa. *Fremdarbeiter 1939 bis 1945: Ausländische Arbeitskräfte in der Zeppelin-Stadt Friedrichshafen*. Essen: Klartext, 2001.
Thomas, Anette. "R. Mosse—Ein Medienzar im Kaiserreich." In *Berlin in Geschichte und Gegenwart*, 51–72. Jahrbuch des Landesarchivs Berlin. Berlin: Gebrüder Mann, 2006.
Tooze, Adam. "Framing Crashed (10): 'A New Bretton Woods' and the Problem of 'Economic Order'—Also a Reply to Adler and Varoufakis." Blog, 9 February 2019. https://adamtooze.com/2019/02/09/framing-crashed-10-a-new-bretton-woods-and-the-problem-of-economic-order-also-a-reply-to-adler-and-varoufakis/.
Toury, Jacob. "Die Sprache als Problem der jüdischen Einordnung im deutschen Kulturraum." *Jahrbuch des Instituts für deutsche Geschichte* 4 (1982): 75–96.
Travereso, Enzo. *The New Faces of Fascism*. New York: Verso, 2019.
Troebst, Stefan, and Nicole Dittmer. "Verstoß für neues NS-Dokumentationszentrum." *Deutschlandfunk Kultur*, 22 May 2020. https://www.deutschlandfunkkultur.de/historiker-initiative-vorstoss-fuer-neues-ns.1008.de.html?dram:article_id=477208.
Tsur, Muky. *Le-Hofe Yarden Ve-Kineret: Be-'Ikvot Shire Rahel, Bet Ha-Kevarot Shel Kineret*. Jerusalem: Ariel, 1998.
Turner, Fred. "The Family of Man and the Politics of Attention in Cold War America." *Public Culture* 24, no. 1 (66) (2012): 55–84.
Ueberschär, Gerd R., and Wolfram Wette, eds. *"Unternehmen Barbarossa": Der deutsche Überfall auf die Sowjetunion 1941*. Paderborn: Schöningh, 1984.
Umansky, Ellen M. "The Origins of Liberal Judaism in England: The Contribution of Lily H. Montagu." *Hebrew Union College Annual* 55 (1984): 320–21.
Ungerfeld, M. "Ha-kongres ha-hamisha asar, mikhtavim me'ha-kongres." *Ha-Tsfira*, 6 September 1927.

Usborne, Cornelie. "Female Sexual Desire and Male Honor: German Women's Illicit Love Affairs with Prisoners of War during the Second World War." *Journal of the History of Sexuality* 26, no. 3 (2017): 454–88.
Usher, Tom. "Want a Larger Penis? Then Your Problems May Be Upstairs, not Downstairs." *Guardian*, 16 April 2019.
van Oord, Lodewijk. "Kurt Hahn's Moral Equivalent of War." *Oxford Review of Education* 36, no. 3 (June 2010): 253–65.
Verona Declaration. XIII World Congress of Families, 31 March 1919. https://profam.org/verona-declaration-adopted-at-wcf-xiii-on-31-march-2019/.
"Der vierte Zionistencongress." *Krakauer jüdische Zeitung* 1, no. 23 (July 1900).
Vogelstein, Rabbi Dr. Hermann. "Die Frau im Gotteshaus." *Jüdisch-liberale Zeitung*, 5 November 1926.
Vogt, Stefan. *Subalterne Positionierungen: Der deutsche Zionismus im Feld des Nationalismus in Deutschland, 1890–1933*. Göttingen: Wallstein Verlag, 2016.
Volkov, Shulamit. "The Ambivalence of *Bildung*." In *Germans, Jews, and Antisemites: Trials in Emancipation*, 248–55. Cambridge: Cambridge University Press, 2006.
———. "Sprache als Ort der Auseinandersetzung mit Juden und Judentum in Deutschland, 1780–1933." In *Jüdische Intellektuelle und die Philologen in Deutschland, 1871–1933*, edited by Wilfried Barner and Christoph König, 223–38. Göttingen: Wallstein, 2001.
Volovici, Marc. *German as a Jewish Problem: The Language Politics of Jewish Nationalism*. Stanford, CA: Stanford University Press, 2020.
———. "Leon Pinsker's *Autoemancipation!* And the Emergence of German as a Language of Jewish Nationalism." *Central European History* 50, no. 1 (March 2017): 34–58.
von Braun, Christina. "Zur Bedeutung der Sexualbilder im rassistischen Antisemitismus." *Feministische Studien* 33, no. 2 (2015): 293–307.
Vowinckel, Annette. "German (Jewish) Photojournalists in Exile: A Story of Networks and Success." *German History* 31, no. 4 (2013): 473–96.
VOX. *Asuntos sociales*. Chapters 2 and 3, "Familia, Democracia y Natalidad." 2015. https://www.voxespana.es/wp-content/uploads/2015/05/2.3.FAMILIA-150518-1.pdf
Wachsmann, Nikolaus. *KL: A History of the Nazi Concentration Camps*. New York: Farrar, Straus and Giroux, 2015.
Wagner, Elisabeth, ed. *Mosse Almanach 2017: Zum zwanzigjährigen Jubiläum der Mosse-Lectures an der Humboldt Universität*. Berlin: Vorwerk 8, 2017.
Wagner, Richard. "Judaism in Music." In *Richard Wagner: Stories and Essays*, edited by Charles Osborne, 23–39. London: Peter Owen, 1973.
Walter, Richard D. "What Became of the Degenerate? A Brief History of a Concept." *Journal of the History of Medicine and Allied Sciences* 11, no. 4 (October 1956): 422–29.
Wassermann, Jakob. *Mein Weg als Deutscher und Jude*. Berlin: S. Fischer, 1921.
Wehner, Markus. "AfD-Adventskalender: Luther, Brecht und andere weiße Männer." *Frankfurter Allgemeine*, 6 December 2018. https://www.faz.net/aktuell/politik/inland/afd-adventskalender-hinter-jeden-tuerchen-ein-weisser-mann-15928357.html.
Weigel, Moira. "The Authoritarian Personality 2.0." *Polity* 54, no. 1 (2022): 146–80.

Weikart, Richard. *Hitler's Ethic: The Nazi Pursuit of Evolutionary Progress*. New York: Palgrave Macmillan, 2009.

Weisgal, Meyer Wolfe. *Meyer Weisgal . . . So Far: An Autobiography*. New York: Random House, 1972.

Weiss, Volker. *Die autoritäre Revolte: Die neue Rechte und der Untergang des Abendlandes*. Stuttgart: Klett-Cotta, 2017.

Weiss, Yfaat. "Central European Ethnonationalism and Zionist Binationalism." *Jewish Social Studies* 11, no. 1 (Fall 2004): 93–117.

Weitz, Yechiam, and Ofira Gravis-Kowalski. "The Reburial of Ze'ev Jabotinsky in the Discussions of Israel's Cabinet." *Cathedra* 155 (2014): 161–94.

Weizman, Chaim. "Fifty Years of Zionism." In *The Jubilee of the First Zionist Congress, 1897–1947*, 9–24. Jerusalem: The Executive of the Zionist Organization, 1947.

Wertham, Frederic. *Seduction of the Innocent*. Port Washington, NY: Kennikat, 1953.

Wieviorka, Annette. *The Era of the Witness*. Translated by Jared Stark. Ithaca, NY: Cornell University Press, 2006.

Wildenthal, Lora. *German Women for Empire, 1884–1945*. Durham, NC: Duke University Press, 2001.

Wildt, Michael. *An Uncompromising Generation: The Nazi Leadership of the Reich Security Main Office*. Madison: University of Wisconsin Press, 2009.

——. *Volksgemeinschaft als Selbstermächtigung: Gewalt gegen Juden in der deutschen Provinz 1919 bis 1939*. Hamburg: Hamburger Edition, 2007.

Winkler, Dörte. *Frauenarbeit im "Dritten Reich."* Hamburg: Hoffmann und Campe, 1975.

Winter, J. M. *Sites of Memory, Sites of Mourning: The Great War in European Cultural History*. Cambridge: Cambridge University Press, 1995.

——. *War beyond Words: Languages of Remembrance from the Great War to the Present*. Cambridge: Cambridge University Press, 2017.

Winter, J. M., and Emmanuel Sivan, eds. *War and Remembrance in the Twentieth Century*. Cambridge: Cambridge University Press, 1999.

Wobick-Segev, Sarah. "'The Religion We Plant in Their Hearts': A Critical Exploration of the Religiosity of a German-Jewish Family at the Beginning of the Twentieth Century." *Jewish History* 28, no. 2 (2014): 159–85.

Woolsey, Gamel. *Death's Other Kingdom*. London: Longman, 1939.

Wohl, Robert. "French Fascism, Both Right and Left: Reflections on the Sternhell Controversy." *Journal of Modern History* 63, no. 1 (1991): 91–98.

Wolfram, Lavern. "KZ-Aufseherinnen—Parteigängerinnen der NSDAP?" In *Im Gefolge der SS: Aufseherinnen des Frauen-KZ Ravensbrück: Begleitband zur Ausstellung*, edited by Simone Erpel, 39–47. Berlin: Metropol, 2007.

Yablonka, Hanna. "Holocaust Consciousness as an Identity-Shaping Factor." In *He-'Asor Ha-Sheni: 718–728*, edited by Tsevi Tsameret and Hanna Yablonka, 363–78. Jerusalem: Yad Yitshak Ben-Tsevi, 2000.

——. *Survivors of the Holocaust: Israel after the War*. Translated by Ora Cummings. New York: New York University Press, 1999.

Yeivin, Yehushua. "Max Nordau." *Beitar* 2 (1933): 179–84.

Yerushalmi, Yosef Hayim. *Zakhor: Jewish History and Jewish Memory*. Edited by Harold Bloom. Seattle: University of Washington Press, 1996.

Young, James E. "The Biography of a Memorial Icon: Nathan Rapoport's Warsaw Ghetto Monument." *Representations* 26 (1989): 69–106.

Zelizer, Barbie. "Covering Atrocity in Image." In *Remembering to Forget: Holocaust Memory through the Camera's Eye*, 86–140. Chicago: University of Chicago Press, 1998.

Zervigón, Andrés Mario. *John Heartfield and the Agitated Image: Photography, Persuasion, and the Rise of Avant-Garde Photomontage*. Chicago: University of Chicago Press, 2012.

Zionistische Vereinigung für Deutschland. *Zionistisches A-B-C Buch*. Berlin: Zionistisches Zentralbureau, 1908.

Zipperstein, Steven J. *Elusive Prophet: Ahad Ha'am and the Origins of Zionism*. Berkeley: University of California Press, 1993.

Zuckermann, Moshe. *Haroshet Ha-Yisreeliyut: Mitosim Ve-Ideologyah Be-Hevrah Mesukhsekhet*. Tel Aviv: Resling, 2001.

Zúquete, José Pedro. *The Identitarians: The Movement against Globalism and Islam in Europe*. Notre Dame: University of Notre Dame Press, 2018.

Zweig, Ronald W. *German Reparations and the Jewish World: A History of the Claims Conference*. Hoboken, NJ: Taylor and Francis, 2014.

CONTRIBUTORS

ADI ARMON is the editor of *Haaretz's* book review and the author of *Leo Strauss between Weimar and America* (2019). From 2017 to 2019, Armon was a visiting assistant professor with the George L. Mosse Program in History at the University of Wisconsin–Madison. He is currently working on the first in-depth study of historian and neoconservative thinker Benzion Netanyahu, father of Benjamin Netanyahu, the former prime minister of Israel.

STEVEN E. ASCHHEIM is an emeritus professor of history at the Hebrew University in Jerusalem, where he taught Cultural and Intellectual History in the Department of History since 1982 and held the Vigevani Chair of European Studies. He also acted as the director of the Franz Rosenzweig Research Centre for German Literature and Cultural History. Apart from academic journals, he has written for the *Times Literary Supplement*, the *New York Times*, the *Los Angeles Review of Books*, the *Jewish Review of Books*, and *Haaretz*. He is the author of *Brothers and Strangers: The East European Jew in German and German-Jewish Consciousness, 1800–1923* (1982); *The Nietzsche Legacy in Germany, 1890–1990* (1992), which has been translated into German and Hebrew; *Culture and Catastrophe: German and Jewish Confrontations with National Socialism and Other Crises* (1996); *In Times of Crisis: Essays on European Culture, Germans and Jews* (2001); *Scholem, Arendt, Klemperer: Intimate Chronicles in Turbulent Times* (2001), which has also appeared in Italian; and *Beyond the Border: The German-Jewish Legacy Abroad* (2007). Aschheim is the editor of the conference volume *Hannah Arendt in Jerusalem* (2001), also translated into Hebrew. His *At the Edges of Liberalism: Junctions of European, German and Jewish History* was published in 2012. A volume coedited with Vivian Liska, entitled *The German-Jewish Experience*

Revisited, appeared in 2015, and his volume *Fragile Spaces: Forays into Jewish Memory, European History and Complex Identities* appeared in 2018.

ALEIDA ASSMANN studied English literature and Egyptology at the universities of Heidelberg and Tübingen. From 1993 to 2014, Assmann held the chair of English Literature and Literary Theory at the University of Konstanz, Germany, and has been a guest professor at a number of universities, including Rice University, Princeton University, Yale University, the University of Chicago, and the University of Vienna. Her main research foci are the history of media, the history and theory of reading, and cultural memory, with special emphasis on the Holocaust and trauma. The Max Planck Research Award allowed her to establish a research group on memory and history (2009–2015). Together with her husband, Jan Assmann, she received the Peace Prize of the German Book Trade in 2018. Currently she is directing a research group at the University of Konstanz on civic strength. Her recent English-language publications include *Memory in a Global Age: Discourses, Practices and Trajectories* (edited with Sebastian Conrad, 2010), *Cultural Memory and Western Civilization: Functions, Media, Archives* (2012), *Memory and Political Change* (edited with Linda Shortt, 2012), *Introduction to Cultural Studies: Topics, Concepts, Issues* (2012), *Shadows of Trauma: Memory and the Politics of Postwar Identity* (2016) and *Is Time Out of Joint? On the Rise and Fall of the Modern Time Regime* (2020).

DARCY BUERKLE is a professor of history at Smith College and has taught at the Humboldt University of Berlin as the Walter Benjamin Chair in German Jewish History and Culture. She is the author of numerous essays on Jewish visual and cinematic cultures and the history of emotion. Her first book, *Nothing Happened: Charlotte Salomon and an Archive of Suicide*, was published in 2014, and her manuscript "Incomplete Departures" on Fred Zinnemann's cinema is presently under review. Buerkle's next project concerns neglected and gendered imaginaries of democracy in early post–World War II Germany and, in particular, a rethinking of a well-established and gendered history of guilt and complicity after 1945.

SKYE DONEY is the director of the George L. Mosse Program in History at the University of Wisconsin–Madison and at the Hebrew University of Jerusalem. He is a Series Advisor to the George L. Mosse Series in the History of European Culture, Sexuality, and Ideas and the editor of the Collected Works of George L. Mosse. He most recently published *The Persistence of the Sacred: German Catholic Pilgrimage, 1832–1937* (2022) as well as translated, edited, and annotated Eva

Noack-Mosse's Holocaust memoir, *Last Days of Theresienstadt* (2018). His articles have appeared in the *Journal of Contemporary History*, the *Catholic Historical Review*, and *Environment, Space, Place*.

ARIE M. DUBNOV is an associate professor of history who holds the Max Ticktin Chair of Israel Studies at George Washington University. His publications include the intellectual biography *Isaiah Berlin: The Journey of a Jewish Liberal* (2012) and three edited volumes, *Zionism—A View from the Outside* (2010 [in Hebrew]); *Partitions: A Transnational History of Twentieth-Century Territorial Separatism* (edited with Laura Robson, 2019); and *Amos Oz's Two Pens: Between Literature and Politics* (forthcoming).

REBEKKA GROSSMANN is a postdoctoral fellow at the Jacob Robinson Institute for the History of Individual and Collective Rights at the Hebrew University. Her research focuses on the intersections of international Jewish politics, global visual culture, and migratory mobility. Before joining the Jacob Robinson Institute, she was a postdoctoral fellow at the Franz Rosenzweig Minerva Research Center for German-Jewish Literature and Cultural History at the Hebrew University and the Pacific Regional Office of the German Historical Institute at the University of California, Berkeley. Her work has also been supported by the George L. Mosse Program in History, the Jack, Joseph and Morton Mandel School for Advanced Studies in the Humanities at the Hebrew University, and the Leo Baeck Fellowship Program. Aspects of her research have been published in *Jewish Social Studies*, the *Leo Baeck Institute Year Book*, and *Israel Studies*.

DAVID HARRISVILLE is an independent scholar specializing in the history of modern Germany, the Third Reich, and the Second World War. He received his PhD in history in 2017 from the University of Wisconsin–Madison, where he also held several academic posts. He has been awarded numerous fellowships, including at the Hebrew University of Jerusalem and the Free University of Berlin. He served as a visiting assistant professor of history at Furman University from 2018 to 2019 and currently works as a learning designer at Brown University. His book, *The Virtuous Wehrmacht: Crafting the Myth of the German Soldier on the Eastern Front, 1941–1944*, was published in 2021.

MEIKE HOFFMANN received her PhD from the Free University of Berlin, where she teaches in the Department of Art History on Nazi art policy and provenance research. Closely involved in her teaching are the projects she directs there, including the "Degenerate Art" Research Center as well as the Abraham

Adelsberger Art Research Project and the Mosse Art Research Initiative, in which, for the first time, descendants of victims of National Socialist persecution are cooperating with public institutions in Germany. Hoffmann was an accredited member of the Schwabing Art Trove Taskforce set up by the German government to examine the Gurlitt Collection, found in a private apartment in Munich in 2013, for Nazi-looted art. Since then, her provenance research projects at the Free University have been funded by both the federal and state governments. Hoffmann is the author of numerous publications on her field in German and English, most recently *Hitlers Kunsthändler: Hildebrand Gurlitt, Die Biographie* (2016), *Escape into Art? The Brücke Painters in the Nazi Period* (edited with Aya Soika, 2019), and *Unmastered Past? Modernism in Nazi Germany: Art, Art Trade, Curatorial Practice* (edited with Dieter Scholz, 2020).

ANDREAS HUYSSEN is the Villard Professor Emeritus of German and Comparative Literature at Columbia University in New York and is founding editor of *New German Critique* and founding director of Columbia's Institute for Comparative Literature and Society. His books include *After the Great Divide: Modernism, Mass Culture, Postmodernism* (1986), *Postmoderne: Zeichen eines kulturellen Wandels* (edited with Klaus Scherpe, 1986), *Twilight Memories: Marking Time in a Culture of Amnesia* (1995), *Present Pasts: Urban Palimpsests and the Politics of Memory* (2003), the edited volume *Other Cities, Other Worlds: Urban Imaginaries in a Globalizing World* (2008), *William Kentridge and Nalini Malani: The Shadowplay as Medium of Memory* (2013), *Miniature Metropolis: Literature in an Age of Photography and Film* (2015), and *Memory Art in the Contemporary World: Confronting Violence in the Global South* (2022).

ELISSA MAILÄNDER is an associate professor of contemporary history at Sciences Po, Center for History (CHSP), Paris, France. She is a historian of gender and everyday life, specializing in the history of Nazism. In her monograph *Female SS Guards and Workaday Violence: The Majdanek Concentration Camp, 1942–1944* (2015, originally published in German in 2009) and other articles, Mailänder focuses on perpetrator history and the structures, mechanisms, and dynamics of violence in Nazi concentration and extermination camps. Her recently published book *Amour, mariage, sexualité: Une histoire intime du nazisme, 1930–1950* (2021) examines friendship, intimacy, and heterosexual relationships in Nazi Germany, highlighting the importance of mass participation and practices of everyday conformity to dictatorship. Her new collaborative project "Trophy Photographs in WWII: An Interdisciplinary Transnational Debate" explores performative transgressions of soldiers in private photography through the lens of gender, sexuality, and cultural self-assertion.

FRANK MECKLENBURG received his PhD in 1981 in modern German history from the Technische Universität Berlin. In 1984 Mecklenburg became an archivist at the Leo Baeck Institute in New York, eventually becoming the director of research and chief archivist in 1995. He played a leading role in the establishment of the Leo Baeck Institute Archives branch at the Jewish Museum Berlin and the digitization of the Leo Baeck Institute Archives, DigiBaeck. Mecklenburg has published on emigration history and German-Jewish life before the Holocaust.

MARY NOLAN is a professor of history emerita at New York University. She works on twentieth-century European-American relations, German history, and most recently social and economic human rights in the age of neoliberalism and the gender politics of right radical populist movements. She is the author of *Social Democracy and Society: Working-Class Radicalism in Düsseldorf, 1890–1920* (1981), *Visions of Modernity: American Business and the Modernization of Germany* (1995), and *The Transatlantic Century: Europe and America, 1890–2010* (2012). Nolan is the coeditor of *Crimes of War: Guilt and Denial in the Twentieth Century* (2002) and *The Routledge Handbook of the Global Sixties* (2018).

STEFANIE SCHÜLER-SPRINGORUM is a historian who served as the director of the Institute for German Jewish History in Hamburg from 2001 to 2011. Since 2011 she has been the director of the Center for Research on Antisemitism and since 2012, the codirector of the Selma Stern Center for Jewish Studies, both in Berlin. In 2020 Schüler-Springorum also became the director of the Berlin branch of the Center for Research on Social Cohesion. Her fields of research include Jewish, German, and Spanish history as well as gender history. Her recent publications include *Hans Litten—Anwalt gegen Hitler* (edited with Knut Bergbauer and Sabine Fröhlich, 2022), *Football and Discrimination: Antisemitism and Beyond* (edited with Pavel Brunssen, 2021), *Emotionen und Antisemitismus: Geschichte—Literatur—Theorie* (edited with Jan Süselbeck, 2021), *Four Years After: Ethnonationalism, Antisemitism, and Racism in Trump's America* (edited with Noam Zadoff, Mirijam Zadoff, and Heike Paul, 2020), "Gender and the Politics of Anti-Semitism," *American Historical Review* 123 (2018), and *La guerra como aventura: La Legión Cóndor en la Guerra Civil española 1936–1939* (2014).

ROGER STRAUCH is George L. Mosse's nephew, technically step-nephew (George's father, Hans Lachmann-Mosse, married Strauch's grandmother, Carola, in the 1930s). Strauch and his younger brother, Hans, enjoyed generous attention from Uncle George and his sister, Hilde. Strauch and his wife, Dr. Julie Kulhanjian, a retired pediatric infectious disease physician, have three adult children. They divide their time between homes in Piedmont, California, and Martha's Vineyard.

Strauch is the leader of the Mosse Art Restitution Project (MARP), a more than ten-year effort to recover title to numerous valuable artifacts expropriated from the Mosse family following Hitler's assumption of power in 1933. While Strauch is not personally a beneficiary of this effort, the nonprofit Mosse Foundation for which he and his brother are responsible, the University of Wisconsin–Madison, and a private individual are the heirs to the Mosse estate. This project relies on legal, investigative, research, and governmental resources on three continents, including the Mosse Art Restitution Initiative in Berlin, led by Dr. Meike Hoffmann, as well as the law firms Bartko Zankel Bunzel & Miller (John and Eric Barkto) in San Francisco and Raue (Jan Hegemann) in Berlin. Strauch is an electrical engineer, entrepreneur, venture capitalist, and philanthropist with an undergraduate degree from Cornell University and a graduate degree from Stanford University, both in electrical engineering. As chair of The Roda Group, Strauch currently focuses on the development of several enterprises whose products and services will mitigate the negative impact of industry on global climate change and human health. He currently serves on the boards of Chart Industries, the Mathematical Sciences Research Institute, the Berkeley Repertory Theater, Northside Center (a mental health service agency in Harlem in New York City), and the University of California, Berkeley's College of Engineering. Strauch has coauthored several technical papers and patents in the field of electrical signal processing. He earned a bachelor's degree with honors from Cornell University and a master's degree from Stanford University, both in electrical engineering.

ENZO TRAVERSO was born in Italy, studied history at the University of Genoa, and received his PhD from the École des hautes études en sciences sociales (EHESS) of Paris in 1989. He taught political theory in France for twenty years and was a visiting professor in several European and Latin American countries. Since 2013, he has been the Susan and Barton Winokur Professor in the Humanities at Cornell University. His work deals with modern intellectual history in Europe. His books, translated into a dozen languages, include *Singular Pasts: The "I" in Historiography* (2022), *Revolutions: An Intellectual History* (2021), *The*

Jewish Question: A Marxist Debate (2018), *Left-Wing Melancholia: Marxism, History and Memory* (2017), *Fire and Blood: The European Civil War, 1914–1945* (2016) and *The End of Jewish Modernity: A Conservative Turn* (2015).

MARC VOLOVICI is an Alfred Landecker Lecturer in the University of Haifa's Department of Jewish History. He is the author of *German as a Jewish Problem: The Language Politics of Jewish Nationalism* (2020) and the coeditor, with David Feldman, of *Antisemitism, Islamophobia and the Politics of Definition* (forthcoming). Volovici served as an academic advisor and coedited the catalog for the exhibition *Jews, Money, Myth*, which was staged at the Jewish Museum London in 2019. He holds a PhD from Princeton University's Department of History, and he served as a Leverhulme Early Career Fellow at the Birkbeck Institute for the Study of Antisemitism and the Department of History at Birkbeck, University of London.

ELISABETH WAGNER is a research assistant at the Humboldt University of Berlin in the Department of German Culture and Literature. Currently, Wagner is working on a research project titled "The Women of the Mosse Family," drawing on her time as the managing director of the Mosse Lectures at Humboldt University from 1997 to 2019. She is the coeditor of *VerWertungen von Vergangenheit* (2009) *Staatsbürgerschaft-Citizenship* (2013), "Europa in anderen Kulturen" (2015) *Konversionen* (2017), *Mosse-Almanach* (2017) and *Non-Finito* (2019).

SARAH WOBICK-SEGEV is a research associate at the Universität Hamburg. She completed her PhD in modern European Jewish history at the University of Wisconsin–Madison in 2010. In addition to numerous articles and book chapters, she is the author of *Homes Away from Home: Jewish Belonging in Twentieth-Century Paris, Berlin, and St. Petersburg* (2018) and the coeditor of *The Economy in Jewish History: New Perspectives on the Interrelationship between Ethnicity and Economic Life* (with Gideon Reuveni, 2010) and of *Spiritual Homelands: The Cultural Experience of Exile, Place and Displacement among Jews and Others* (with Richard I. Cohen and Asher Biemann, 2019). She is now working on a book-length project that explores the contributions of Jewish women in Western Europe in the public-religious sphere during the nineteenth and twentieth centuries.

ROBERT ZWARG held the Guest Professorship for Critical Social Theory at Justus Liebig University Giessen in 2021 and 2022. He studied philosophy, cultural studies, and translation at Leipzig University, the University of California,

Davis, and the National Autonomous University of Mexico, Mexico City. His research interests include the intellectual history of the twentieth century, especially Western Marxism and the Frankfurt School, the philosophy of culture, and modern Jewish thought. He wrote his dissertation on the reception of the Frankfurt School in the United States, which was published in 2017 as *Kritische Theorie in Amerika: Die Verwandlung einer Tradition*. Zwarg recently published "Aus unsicherer Distant: Über Silvia Bovenschen," *WestEnd: Neue Zeitschrift für Sozialforschung* 19, no. 1 (2022): 155–66.

INDEX

Adorno, Theodor, 73, 100–101, 106–9, 274–81
aesthetics, 6, 65. See also beauty
Aesthetic Theory (Adorno), 277–79
All Quiet on the Western Front (Remarque), 28
Alltag. See everyday life
Alternative for Germany (AfD, Alternative für Deutschland), 82–91
Altneuland (Herzl), 216, 253–54
alt-right (American), 100–105, 108–10. See also populist radical right (PRR) parties
Anielewicz, Mordechai, 187–88
antifascism, 62, 102. See also fascism
anti-genderism, 89–92. See also gender
antisemitism, xvii, 6, 11, 25, 42, 73, 80, 118–28, 131, 132n4. See also anti-types
anti-types, 6, 27, 73–74. See also antisemitism; stereotypes
Arendt, Hannah, 12, 73, 249
Aschheim, Steven E., 66
Assmann, Aleida, 23, 235
Assmann, Jan, 180
Aus großem Hause (Mosse, George L.), 337
The Authoritarian Personality (Adorno), 107

Autoemancipation! (Pinsker), 221, 254
Avinoam, Reuven, 180, 183

Baldwin, James, 31
Bannon, Steve, 101, 105–6
Barthes, Roland, 29, 270. See also studium
Bauhaus, 236
beauty, 6–7, 277–78. See also aesthetics
Begin, Menachem, 182, 186
Behemoth, 100, 111. See also Leviathan
Behemoth (Neumann), 111
Ben-Gurion, David, 184–85
Benjamin, Walter, 73, 187, 269
Berlin, Germany, xviii, xxiii, 33, 287, 335, 354
Berliner Tageblatt, 54, 303, 306, 312, 337–40, 348, 361. See also Mosse, Rudolf; Mosse family
Bernstein, Nina, 285, 293
Biden, Joe, 37n5, 105
Bildung, 8–12, 75, 201–3, 212n5, 299
biological determinism, 90, 93
Bloch, Ernst, 102–4
Bloom, Harold, 24
Bock, Gisela, 80, 147
Bolshevism, 66, 69, 103, 123–24
Bolsonaro, Jair, 13, 79
Bosshard, Walter, 237, 239, 338

bourgeoisie, 6–7, 26–27, 74, 259
Boveri, Margaret, 339–40
Brecht, Bertolt, 277–79
Breitbart, Andrew, 100–101, 105–6
Breslau, Germany, 128–31
Brown, Wendy, 101
Brown v. Board, 363
Butler, Judith, 90

Cameron, David, 34
capitalism, xix, 64, 88, 111
Castro, Fidel, 252n21
Catholicism, 71, 90
Celan, Paul, 278
centenary commemoration of WWII, 33–34
Central Holocaust monument (Eisenman), 33
Chance and Necessity (Monod), 268
Charlottesville, VA, 102, 109
Churchill, Winston, 31
Cohen, Michael, 109
colonialism, xix, 72–75, 234–45, 248–49
commemoration, 173–86, 190–91, 193n9, 194n10, 194n13. See also memory studies
communism, 65, 68–71
concentration camps, xx, 280
Confronting History (Mosse, George L.), xix, 40–54, 347
The Conventional Lies of Our Civilization (Nordau), 253
countertypes. See anti-types
The Crisis of German Ideology (Mosse, George L.), 5–6, 10, 40, 43, 63, 69, 76n26, 258
critical theory, 105–6. See also Frankfurt School
Cuba, 252n21
Cultural Marxism, 105–7. See also Marxism
The Culture of Western Europe (Mosse, George L.), 350

Dachau, Germany, 137
Danish People's Party (DF), 82, 87
Das Gastmahl der Familie Mosse (von Werner), 338
Declaration of Human Rights (UN, 1948), 248
De Felice, Renzo, 61–62, 70
Degeneration (Nordau), xxii, 253–62, 263n4
democracy, 5, 65, 68
Der Judenstaat (Herzl), 216
Der Stürmer (Streicher), 121–22
Der Winkel von Hahrdt (Hölderlin), 277–78
Deutsche Freisinnige Partei (DFP), 314–15
Dialectic of Enlightenment (Horkheimer & Adorno), 106, 276
Die Familie Mosse (Kraus), 335, 339, 354
Dormitzer, Else, 207–8
Douglas, Mary, 145–46
Dutch Party for Freedom (PVV, Partij voor de Vrijheid), 87, 99n82

Elias, Norbert, 36, 51
Eliot, T. S., 192
Emilie in a Red Blouse (Menzel), 366
empathy, 62–63, 67
Enlightenment, 66–71, 119, 299
Errell, Lotte, 237, 251n8
Ethiopia, 70–72
The European Powers and the German Question 1848–71 (Mosse, Werner), 314–15, 350
European Union, 34–36
Even-Shmuel, Judah, 181–82
everyday life, 137, 148, 274–81, 283n3

Facebook, 108. See also social media; Zuckerberg, Mark
A Fair Hearing (Shaw), 103, 110
Fallen Soldiers (Mosse, George L.), xxi, 6, 27, 74, 173
Fama (cult of), 174

family, 26, 81, 85–88, 91
Family of Man (Steichen), 248
Fanon, Frantz, 73
fascism, xviii–xx, 5, 61–75, 77n37, 79–92, 100–104, 109, 137. See also antifascism; Italian Fascism
"Fascism and the French Revolution" (Mosse, George L.), 66
fascist agitator, 19, 100, 107–8
The Fascist Revolution (Mosse, George L.), 66, 72, 104
Faust (Goethe), 275
female SS guards, xx, 139–45, 148–49. See also gender; women
feminism, 13, 92
Fichte, Johann Gottlieb, 220
fin de siècle, 253–55, 258, 261–62
Forest of Martyrs, 183
The Fourth Turning (Strauss and Howe), 105
France, 71–72
Franco, Francisco, 35, 70–72
Frankfurt School, 100, 105–7, 111. See also critical theory
Freedom Party of Austria (FPÖ, Freiheitliche Partei Österreichs), 84–88, 91
French Nationalists (FN, Front National), 84
French Revolution, 6, 65–67
Furet, François, 65–66
Futurism (Italian), 69, 71

Gandhi, Mahatma, 237–41
Gaul, August, 290, 331
gender, xvii–xviii, 51, 80–82, 85, 89–92, 95n7, 98n63, 119, 203. See also antigenderism; female SS guards
Generation X, 106
Generation Zero (Bannon), 105–6
Gentile, Emilio, 62–63, 75n5
German (language), 216–29, 230n4. See also High German

German Jews beyond Judaism (Mosse, George L.), 5, 8, 23, 201–3, 211, 213n24
Germanophone movement, 222–23
Germany: nationalism in, 65, 122, 137, 147, 158, 259; outsiders in, 37, 127, 131; and war, 30–31
Gidal, Tim, xxii, 234–45, 248–50, 251n15
Ginsberg, Herbert, 352–53
Ginsberg, Marianne, 353
Gobineau, Arthur de, 65
Goebbels, Joseph, 69, 131, 159, 361. See also propaganda
Goethe, Johann Wolfgang von, 275
Gouri, Haim, 177–82, 190, 195n21
Gramsci, Antonio, 106
Great House of Mosse, 348
Great War. See World War I
Gross, Raphael, 158–59
Guber, Rivka, 182–83
Guevara, Che, 252n21
Gur, Batya, 174
Guterman, Norbert, 106–7

Ha'am, Ahad, 253, 262n1
Habermas, Jürgen, 110
Hahn, Charlotte, 45, 57n46
Hahn, Kurt, 43–48
Hebrew (language), 223–28
Hegel, Georg Wilhelm Friedrich, 66
Heidegger, Martin, 71
Herbert, Ulrich, 126–27
Herder, Johann Gottfried, 220–21
Heritage of Our Time (Bloch), 102
Herzl, Theodor, 183, 216, 222, 225, 228, 253–58, 262n1
Herzog, Dagmar, 80, 121–22, 129
High German, 217–18. See also German (language)
Hill 24 Doesn't Answer (Kolitz), 188–90
Himmler, Heinrich, 127, 146
Hirsch, Samson Raphael, 205, 213n28, 218
Hitler, Adolf, 11, 30, 63–66, 71–72, 102, 127, 160, 280, 299, 361

Hoffman, Harald, 158–59
Holocaust, 4, 32, 74–75, 117, 186–87, 190, 201, 274
homophobia, xvii, 50–51, 120
Horkheimer, Max, 73, 106, 109, 276

The Image of Man (Mosse, George L.), 6–7, 10–12, 47–49
Im ha-Banim (Guber), 183
immersive racism, 110. *See also* racism
immigration, 14, 92–94
India, 238–45, 249
International Holocaust Remembrance Alliance (IHRA), 33
Interpreting the French Revolution (Furet), 65
Islam, 92–94
Israel, xxi, 11, 173–78, 181, 186–87, 190, 193n9
Israeli exceptionalism, 176
Israeli Ministry of Defense, 178
Italian Fascism, xix, 67, 70–71, 74. *See also* fascism

Jabotinsky, Vladimir (Ze'ev), 185, 225–27, 254–55, 260, 263n2
Jacobinism, 65–69
James, William, 43
January 6, 2021 insurrection, 101–2, 105, 109
Jewish Reform Congregation of Berlin, 290, 343. *See also* Reform Congregations
Jews: and antisemitism, 74, 121; Eastern European, 124, 229; as exiles, xxiii, 229, 236–38, 248–50, 252n27; German, xviii–xxiii, 4–9, 201–3, 211, 218–19, 229, 238, 250, 291, 339–44; history of, 4, 235; identity of, xviii, 202, 236, 337, 344; intellectual, 24–25; and nationalism, 11, 15, 222; and public life, 350–51; Russian, 219–22, 225; stereotypes of, 5, 9–11, 73, 82, 124, 259; victimization of, 5–6, 11, 25, 127–28, 274; women, xxi–xxii,
53, 119–20, 206–11, 214n31, 214n35, 214n38; Zionist, 11, 253
The Jew's Body (Gilman), 120
Jonas, Regina, 206, 210
Judaism, xxi, 202–7, 210, 216
Jünger, Ernst, 70

Kant, Immanuel, 277–78
Kaplan, Marion, 80, 202
Kibbutz Yad Mordechai, 187
Kinneret Cemetery, 184–85, 197n39
Kjærsgaard, Pia, 82–83
Klausner, Joseph, 185, 256
Kleine Reise zu schwarzen Menschen (Errell), 237
Kongressdeutsch, 227–28. *See also* Zionist Congress
Koonz, Claudia, 80, 158–59
Kraus, Elizabeth, 41, 335–39, 354, 361
Kristallnacht, 126, 128, 291
Ku Klux Klan, 122

LaCapra, Dominick, 63
Lachmann-Mosse, Felicia, 209, 317, 347
Lachmann-Mosse, Hans, 204, 209, 291, 307, 317, 321, 339, 343, 349–51
Laqueur, Walter, 5, 9, 340–41
Last Days of Theresienstadt (Noack-Mosse, Eva), 352
Lazare, Bernard, 224
A leaf, treeless (Celan), 278
Lebanon War (Israeli), 174–75, 193n5
Lehmann, Joseph, 204–5, 291
Leipziger Platz, 287–88, 317, 359
Le Pen, Jean-Marie, 82–83, 88
Le Pen, Marine, 82, 86–88
lesbianism, 52–54, 82. *See also* sexuality
Leviathan, 100. *See also* Behemoth
LGBTQ+, 12, 89, 92–93
liberalism, 12, 49, 54, 68, 260
"The Liberal Legacy and the Public of National Socialism" (Mosse, George L.), 298

Libeskind, Daniel, 285–87
Lind, William S., 106, 109
Löwenthal, Leo, 106–7
Löwith, Karl, 66–67, 73
Lublin, Germany, 141
Lüdtke, Alf, 137–38, 146–49
Lukács, György, 66–67, 106

MAGA (Make America Great Again), 104–5
Majdanek, xx, 136–42, 145–47
manliness. *See* masculinity
Mann, Klaus, 49, 52
The Man of Genius (Lombroso), 256
Marcuse, Herbert, 70, 73, 106
Marinetti, Filippo Tommaso, 70
Marx, Karl, 148
Marxism, 101–3, 253. *See also* Cultural Marxism
masculinity, 7–13, 18n38, 42–47, 73–74, 80–86, 177, 188, 259
Mass, Rubin, 178–79, 183
mass movements, 64–65
mass politics, xviii, 11
Matthäus, Jürgen, 117–18
Matthews, Herbert L., 239–40, 251n21
Max of Baden, Prince, 43–44
Meineket Rivkah (Tikiner), 208
Mein Kampf (Hitler), 121
memory studies, 27–28, 31–36. *See also* commemoration
Merkel, Angela, 83
millennials, 106
Minima Moralia (Adorno), 274–79
Ministry of Propaganda, 131. *See also* Goebbels, Joseph; propaganda
misogyny, 120, 124–28, 131
Moeller van den Bruck, Arthur, 258
Montagu, Lily H., 209–10
Montagu, Samuel, 209
monuments, 173–76, 187, 194n10
morality, 6–7, 158–60, 163–68
Mosse, Albert, 336, 344–47

Mosse, Emil, 336–38
Mosse, Emilie, 285, 295, 313, 324
Mosse, Felicia, 51–54, 295
Mosse, George L.: and antisemitism, xvii–xviii; at Berlin-Weißensee, 286; and fascism, 61–75, 100, 111, 137, 274–80, 341; as historian, xix, xxii–xxiii, 3–4, 8–14, 23–24, 40, 235, 335–40, 350; and Jewish identity, 4–6, 15, 47, 201–5, 262, 291; and memory studies, 27–28, 33–34, 173–77, 183, 190–92; and nationalism, 36, 104, 158; on Nordau, 258–62; and outsiderdom, 37, 42, 48; and respectability, 27, 146, 159, 254; and sexuality, xvii, 4, 10, 13, 26, 40–44, 47–48, 52–53, 120, 262; and the subjunctive, 43–50, 54; and war, 29–31, 149; and women, 51–53, 80, 211. *See also* Myth of the War Experience (MWE)
Mosse, Hilde, 51–52, 58n71, 295, 353, 363
Mosse, Rudolf, xxiii–xxiv, 53, 204, 285–93, 302–24, 336–43, 348–53, 360–62. *See also Berliner Tageblatt*
Mosse, Werner, xxiii, 335, 339–41, 350
Mosse Art Research Initiative (MARI), 301–2, 317–21, 324–30, 354, 365, 368
Mosse Art Restitution Project (MARP), 357, 364, 368
Mosse family, xxi–xxv, 24–26, 41–51, 203–13, 269, 283–85, 298–99, 351–71. See also *Berliner Tageblatt*
The Mosse Family Banquet (von Werner), 314–15
Mosse Foundation, 298, 317
Mosse Palais, 287–90, 309–11, 315–17, 359
Mosse Publishing House, 298, 303, 307–8, 317
Mount Herzl, 175, 183–86, 190
Munich Illustrated (Bosshard), 237
Mussolini, Benito, 35, 62–66, 71–72, 102
Myth of the War Experience (MWE), 28–31, 34–36. *See also* Mosse, George L.
My Village in India (Gidal), 245–49

National Association for the Advancement of Colored People (NAACP), 363
National Democratic Party of Germany (NPD, Nationaldemokratische Partei Deutschlands), 86
nationalism, xviii, 6–15, 26, 36, 42, 65–72, 80, 100–104, 158, 259–61
Nationalism and Sexuality (Mosse, George L.), 6–10, 40, 54, 80
The Nationalization of the Masses (Mosse, George L.), 5, 11, 62–63, 277
National Socialism, 29, 47–52, 62, 69–74, 80, 100, 111, 121, 147, 274–80
Nazi Culture (Mosse, George L.), 274, 279
Nazism, xvii–xviii, xix–xx, 5–7, 66–71, 80–82, 103–4, 121–22, 158–67, 214n31, 258–59. See also Third Reich
necrochronology, 176, 186, 190
necrogeography, 176–78, 183–90
necrography, 176–78, 190
necropoesis, 177–83, 190
Netanyahu, Benzion, xxii, 254–58, 261–62
Neumann, Franz, 73, 111
1948 War, 177–80, 186–87
Nordau, Max, xxii, 177, 222, 226, 253–62
Nuremberg Laws, 74, 120–22, 125, 318

Oath Keepers, 102
Obama, Barack, 37n5
one-drop rule, 120
Orbán, Viktor, 79, 86
The Order of Terror (Sofsky), 138
Orientalism (Said), 73
The Origins of Totalitarianism (Arendt), 73
outsiderdom, 4–10, 14, 24–27, 36–37, 47–48, 52–54, 74

Palestine, xxii, 177–86, 216–27, 234, 238, 254–57
Paradoxes (Nordau), 253

The Passing of the Great Race (Grant), 102
Peasant Girl at the Window (Zorn), 326
Peterson, Jordan B., 13
photography, 236–37, 251n10, 252n21
photojournalism, 238, 252n21
Pinsker, Leon, 221–22, 254, 258
The Politics of Cultural Despair (Stern), 258
populist radical right (PRR) parties, 79–94, 98n63. See also alt-right (American)
postcolonialism, 61, 73, 248
propaganda, 127, 131. See also Goebbels, Joseph; Ministry of Propaganda
Prophets of Deceit (Löwenthal and Guterman), 106
Proud Boys, 102
Przyrembel, Alexandra, 122, 128
Putin, Vladimir, 13

QAnon, 101

Rabinbach, Anson, 69–70
race defilement, 117, 120–30
racism, 6, 25, 73, 80–82, 90, 110, 120–21, 124–31, 147, 165–67. See also immersive racism
racketeering, 108–11
Rapoport, Nathan, 187–88
Ravensbrück (concentration camp), 139–40
realism (German), 312, 328
Reclining Lion (Gaul), 290, 309, 331
Reform Congregations, 205, 290–92, 344. See also Jewish Reform Congregation of Berlin
Reformgemeinde, 204
Reform Synagogue, 290–93
refugees, 24–25, 148, 238, 251n17
Repentant Magdalene (Rubens), 324–25
respectability, 7–10, 26, 49, 53–54, 74, 146, 158, 259

Revisionist Zionism, 185, 254–61, 263n4.
  See also Zionism
Righteous Indignation (Breitbart), 105
Röder, Hans, 287, 297
Rousseau, Jean-Jacques, 68

The Sacralization of Politics in Fascist
  Italy (Gentile), 75n5
Sartre, Jean-Paul, 73
Schenkendorf, 292–95, 300n3, 317
Schloss Salem, 43–47
Schmitt, Carl, 29, 69–71
Scholem, Gershom, 14
Semprún, Jorge, 278–79
sexuality, xviii, 4, 10–13, 26, 40–53, 80–82,
  88–89, 120–24, 130, 259–62. See also
  lesbianism
Shaping National Memory (Assmann,
  Aleida), 23
Shaw, George T., 103, 110
Shoah Visual History Foundation, 32
Simon, James, 309, 313
The Sin Against the Blood (Dinter), 120
Sittlichkeit, 7, 75
Skater (Melchers), 327
Smolenskin, Peretz (Piotr), 185, 220–22
Social Darwinism, 158, 256
Socialist Zionism, 255. See also Zionism
social media, 108–11. See also Facebook
Sokolow, Nahum, 220, 226–28
Sontag, Susan, 63
Spanish Civil War, 69–71
Speer, Albert, 62–63
Spielberg, Steven, 32
Springer, Philipp, 124, 131
stereotypes, xvii, 5–6, 9, 74, 124, 249, 259.
  See also anti-types
Stern, Fritz, 258–59
Sternhell, Ze'ev, 67, 72
Strauch, Roger, 298, 357
studium, 270. See also Barthes, Roland
the subjunctive, 42–50, 54
symbols, 23–24, 29

Talk about Trees (Fried), 278
Thatcher, Margaret, 83
Theodor Fontane (Fechner), 328
Third Reich, xviii, xix, 30, 158–59, 168. See
  also Nazism
Tikiner, Rebekka, 208, 214n38
To Those Born Later (Brecht), 277–78
Toward the Final Solution (Mosse, George
  L.), 6, 73, 158
Triumph of the Will (Riefenstahl), 65
Trump, Donald, xix, 13, 79, 100–111
Trumpism, xix, 111

Uncompromising Generation (Wildt), 117,
  131
Undoing the Demos (Brown), 101
Ungleichzeitigkeit (nonsynchronicity),
  100–104
United Nations, 248

Vichy France, 72
View of Santa Scholastica at Subiaco
  (Blechen), 366–67
violence, xvii, xx, 6, 117–19, 122–25, 128–29,
  138, 143–46. See also workaday violence
völkisch ideology, 5, 124, 259
Volksgeist, 221
Volksgemeinschaft, 299
VOX party, 85

Wagner, Elizabeth, 347, 369
Wagner, Richard, 218
Wehrmacht, xxi, 138, 158–65, 168, 169n4,
  170n14–15
Weimar Republic, xviii, 29, 41–42, 51–54,
  121, 248
Weizmann, Chaim, 184, 228
Weltanschauung, 5, 213n24
Werner, Anton von, 314–15, 337–38
What a Beautiful Sunday (Semprún),
  278
Wildt, Michael, 124–25, 128–31
Wilhelm II, Emperor, 315

Wings of Desire (Wender), 287
Wir lügen alle (Boveri), 339
Wolff, Theodor, 303, 337
Wolffsohn, David, 184, 226
The Woman on the Pillory (Reinmann), 130
women: bodies of, 123, 130; German, 127, 131, 205–6, 211; Jewish, xxi, xxii, 119 20, 206–11, 214n31, 214n35, 214n38; Mosse on, 51–53, 80, 211; radical right, 80–90, 93, 95n7, 147; violence against, 117, 129. *See also* female SS guards
work, 138, 143–48
workaday violence, 143–44, 149. *See also* violence
The Worker (Jünger), 70
World War I, 28–30, 64, 75
World War II, 30–35, 71

Yad Labanim, 178–81, 195n19
Yerushalmi, Yosef Hayim, 174
Yiddish (language), 217–23, 227–29
yizkor books, 180–81
Yom Ha-Shoah, 186

Zangwill, Israel, 254–58
Zeitungsstadt Berlin (de Mendelssohn), 339
Zionism, xxii, 11–12, 15, 185, 216–17, 222–29, 248, 253–62, 262n1. *See also* Revisionist Zionism; Socialist Zionism
Zionist A-B-C Book (Zionist Federation of Germany), 216–17
Zionist Congress, xxii, 184, 216–17, 224–27. *See also* Kongressdeutsch
Zionist Federation of Germany, 216
Zuckerberg, Mark, 101. *See also* Facebook

George L. Mosse Series in the History of
European Culture, Sexuality, and Ideas

STEVEN E. ASCHHEIM, SKYE DONEY,
MARY LOUISE ROBERTS, AND DAVID J. SORKIN

Series Editors

Of God and Gods: Egypt, Israel, and the Rise of Monotheism
JAN ASSMANN

Messengers of Disaster: Raphael Lemkin, Jan Karski, and Twentieth-Century Genocides
ANNETTE BECKER; translated by KÄTHE ROTH

Respectability and Violence: Military Values, Masculine Honor, and Italy's Road to Mass Death
LORENZO BENADUSI; translated by ZAKIYA HANAFI

The Enemy of the New Man: Homosexuality in Fascist Italy
LORENZO BENADUSI; translated by
SUZANNE DINGEE and JENNIFER PUDNEY

The Holocaust and the West German Historians: Historical Interpretation and Autobiographical Memory
NICOLAS BERG; translated and edited by JOEL GOLB

Collected Memories: Holocaust History and Postwar Testimony
CHRISTOPHER R. BROWNING

Contemporary Europe in the Historical Imagination
Edited by DARCY BUERKLE and SKYE DONEY

Cataclysms: A History of the Twentieth Century from Europe's Edge
DAN DINER; translated by WILLIAM TEMPLER with JOEL GOLB

Fascination with the Persecutor: George L. Mosse and the Catastrophe of Modern Man
EMILIO GENTILE; translated by JOHN and ANNE C. TEDESCHI

La Grande Italia: The Myth of the Nation in the Twentieth Century
EMILIO GENTILE; translated by SUZANNE DINGEE and
JENNIFER PUDNEY

The Invisible Jewish Budapest: Metropolitan Culture at the Fin de Siècle
MARY GLUCK

Carl Schmitt and the Jews: The "Jewish Question," the Holocaust, and German Legal Theory
RAPHAEL GROSS; translated by JOEL GOLB

Unlearning Eugenics: Sexuality, Reproduction, and Disability in Post-Nazi Europe
DAGMAR HERZOG

Reason after Its Eclipse: On Late Critical Theory
MARTIN JAY

Some Measure of Justice: The Holocaust Era Restitution Campaign of the 1990s
MICHAEL R. MARRUS

The Best Weapon for Peace: Maria Montessori, Education, and Children's Rights
ERICA MORETTI

Confronting History: A Memoir
GEORGE L. MOSSE

Nazi Culture: Intellectual, Cultural, and Social Life in the Third Reich
GEORGE L. MOSSE

Last Days of Theresienstadt
EVA NOACK-MOSSE; translated by SKYE DONEY and
BIRUTĖ CIPLIJAUSKAITĖ

What History Tells: George L. Mosse and the Culture of Modern Europe
Edited by STANLEY G. PAYNE, DAVID J. SORKIN, and
JOHN S. TORTORICE

The Perils of Normalcy: George L. Mosse and the Remaking of Cultural History
KAREL PLESSINI

Shaping the New Man: Youth Training Regimes in Fascist Italy and Nazi Germany
ALESSIO PONZIO

The Jews in Mussolini's Italy: From Equality to Persecution
MICHELE SARFATTI; translated by JOHN and ANNE C. TEDESCHI

A History of Italian Fascist Culture, 1922–1943
ALESSANDRA TARQUINI; translated by MARISSA GEMMA

Jews and Other Germans: Civil Society, Religious Diversity, and Urban Politics in Breslau, 1860–1925
TILL VAN RAHDEN; translated by MARCUS BRAINARD

An Uncompromising Generation: The Nazi Leadership of the Reich Security Main Office
MICHAEL WILDT; translated by TOM LAMPERT